ORIGI

THE PREDICAMENT OF MAN

Phillip Day

Origins III – The Predicament of Man

ISBN 1-904015-32-8

Manufactured in Great Britain and Australia.
Distributed globally by:

Credence Publications Ltd
PO Box 3
TONBRIDGE
Kent TN12 9ZY UK
www.credence.org

1st ed.

TABLE OF CONTENTS

AUTHOR'S NOTE **7**

INTRODUCTION **9**

Extraterrestrial contact 11
Unique, transcendent 15
Hebrew 20
Point of departure 22

MOSES – SETTING THE SCENE **24**

Moses/Exodus - an overview 25
Are Moses and the Exodus historical? 27
The 'Shepherd Kings' 33
The pharaoh who knew Joseph not 37
Why don't we know the pharaohs' names? 39
Placing Moses in history 43

MOSES – THE EARLY YEARS **46**

The genocidal pharaoh 50
The river saga 53
The child is named 57
Moses - from boy to man 59
The reign of the male queen 64

MOSES – THE MIDIAN YEARS **71**

The cuckoo in the nest 72
The pharaoh of the oppression 74
An Egyptian killing - 1486 BC 78
Midian, the sanctuary 80
A wife and family 82
Mt Sinai/Horeb and the burning bush 86
Trouble at the inn or seminary? 95

THE BATTLE OF THE GODS **105**

The pharaoh of the Exodus 105
Snakes alive! 113
The first plague: water turned to blood 116
The second plague: frogs 120
The third plague: lice 121
The fourth plague: flies 122

The fifth plague: livestock diseased 125
The sixth plague: boils and sores 126
The seventh plague: hail 127
The eighth plague: locusts 130
The ninth plague: darkness 134
The tenth plague: death of the firstborn 137
Pharaoh's fateful firstborn 142
Plague summary 147
The release 148

THE EXODUS 150

The route 153
Bridge over troubled waters 168
The punitive campaign 171
Marah – the waters made sweet 177
"What is it?" 185
Rephidim - The first incident with the rock 193

FROM SINAI TO THE JORDAN 197

God's holy mountain 197
Israel at Sinai 203
The Ten Commandments 207
Broken stones 219
The blessings and cursings 234
The Tabernacle 235
God leads the Exodus generation 257
The order of the camp 257
The move to Kadesh 259
The twelve spies 262
Kadesh Barnea 266
Moses blows it 270
The brazen serpent 273
Confronting Sihon the giant 274
The end of Og 280

THE CANAAN HOLOCAUST 283

The new commander 284
Genocide 288
The sin of Canaan 293
Repent or perish 296
The two spies go in 298

Forewarned and foreskinned 305
The foolishness of God 307
Ground Zero Jericho 310
The lesson of Ai 313
The enemy gets wisdom 317
The sun stands still 321
The end of conquest 331
Inheritance, refuge and warning 334

A LOVE STORY 338

Affliction brings opportunity 338
What are the chances? 341
An immediate bond 345
Shoes in the gate 349
Ruth - the surprising summary 352
The Bride prefigured – that's you... 353
Kinsman-Redeemer for the Creation 356

THE JUDGES 359

The cycle of sin 361
Othniel 362
Ehud 365
Shamgar 367
Deborah 367
Lessons for nations 375
Hyperspaces and the 'metacosm' 377
The Flats 382
The coming of the desert scourge 383
Gideon - a farmer is called 385
The strangest battle ever 391
Trouble called Abimelech 397
A good case of worms 400
Jephthah – hard man with a heart 404
Jephthah's daughter 409
War with Ephraim 414
The coming of the wild Nazirite 416
Party animal 424
Outfoxed 426
Gates away 430
Betrayed by beauty 431
The wildest party 435

Samson in summary 437

SAMUEL, LAST OF THE JUDGES 441

The birth of Israel's last Judge 443
Robbing God and the consequences 444
Trouble with the Ark 448
A painful lesson in hubris 453
Israel punished 457
"Make us a king!" 459

SAUL AND THE BIRTH OF THE MONARCHY 464

The siege of Jabesh 470
The end of the Judges 471
Saul blows it 473
Jonathan's two-man army 475
Further kingly disobedience 480

DAVID, THE SHEPHERD BOY 485

David and Goliath 486
David at court 492
A bloody showdown 496
Hounded from pillar to post 499
The fool and the prize 503
Saul and David – the end game 508
A nasty surprise 514
The Battle of Gilboa and aftermath 517
David gets the news 519
Saul eternal 520

KING DAVID, THE LORD'S ANOINTED 525

A problem called Abner 526
Bloodfeud 529
King over all Israel 532
Yerushalayim – capital seat of holiness 534
The Ark comes to Jerusalem 537
The everlasting house 542
Genesis 38 codes 544
David's mighty men 547
David establishes his empire 549

POSTSCRIPT 556

Running amok 556

The remedy 562
INDEX 564
ABOUT THE AUTHOR 573

AUTHOR'S NOTE

The book you are about to read is a compendium of research material compiled on a complex but enthralling series of subjects. During the course of my travels and teachings over the past 30 years, I resolved to do some leg-work and gather some principal sources, drawing together the raw data, differing opinions, research and commentaries, and present them to you in some sort of cohesive form. Now you can sit back in your armchair with more than a few facts at your fingertips: the hard slog is done. And if you want to investigate a particular point further, plenty of sources and recommendations are provided in the text and footnotes.

Often, seemingly meaningless information takes on a new significance when placed in context with other pieces of the overall jigsaw. This is the excitement of working the information puzzle. For instance, putting together different events in history known to have occurred at the same time gives a greater clue as to why historical characters acted the way they did, and why the world is as we find it today. Many personalities have spoken out and commented on one or more of the subjects covered in the following pages. It has been my aim to quote them as accurately as I can, and scour book and article releases to reflect the most up-to-date positions on these issues for your consideration.

I have included sources that do not necessarily reflect my own views, but enhance the subject matter, and quoted much source material verbatim with references. Where newspapers are cited, those selected are typically publications representing the wider readerships. Biblical commentaries are from a wide spectrum of denominational camps, and quotes are from the Authorised King James Version (KJV) unless otherwise indicated. Forgive me for underlining sections of quotes to draw the reader's attention to something specific. You will notice in places that I have labelled quotes from 'John's gospel' as 'Fourth Gospel' (FG). The later attribution of the fourth gospel to John Zebedee of Galilee is purely ex-Biblical tradition, and, I believe, in error. This in no way detracts from the inspired nature of the book, and we will discover that the anonymity of the gospel and its uniqueness from the Synoptics was eminently intentioned and necessary. So please bear with this labelling in *Origins I, II & III,* and I will present the full case and evidence for this intriguing enigma, together with the most surprising candidate for its authorship, in *Origins IV – Tetelestai.*

Lastly, scientific and medical data are indexed where appropriate and intended for educational purposes only. Specialists in certain of the subjects covered are quoted and their opinions discussed. Places covered in the text are referenced, where possible, with Google Earth co-ordinates, which can be typed into Google Earth as given to reveal science's best guess for these locations.

The reader must, of course, appreciate that no source is 100% accurate or unbiased, not even this one. However, neither should a particular source be discounted because the position held is contentious. As always, it is up to you, the reader, to do your own research and come to your own conclusions. Happy hunting!

Phillip Day

INTRODUCTION

For the invisible things of Him from the Creation of the world are clearly seen, being understood by the things that are made, even His eternal power and Godhead; so that they are without excuse.
(Rom 1:20)

"The sun shines and warms and lights us, and we have no curiosity to know why this is so; but we ask the reason of all evil, of pain, and hunger, and mosquitoes and silly people." – **Ralph Waldo Emerson**

Welcome to *Origins III – The Predicament of Man.*

So, here we all are on Planet Earth. But are we here by blind, random chance, or are we an unwitting part of a far larger plan being rolled out? Is there a God who created the universe and all within it, or did the universe make itself? Or perhaps we were seeded here by some extraterrestrial progenitors – a popular view today known as panspermia. Is life essentially meaningless, or can we attach any ultimate significance to our existence? And if so, on what grounds? Has the Universal Mind (God) ever made contact? If so, how would we know?

These are some of the fascinating questions we have been examining in the first two books of the *Origins* series. Is the ultimate choice we have to make really between God and science? Actually, no. There are tens of thousands of scientists who believe in a Creator, and I am happy to report that not all of them are deluded cranks. What these men and women have done is to remain faithful to their scientific calling and continued asking the questions, in spite of where the evidence leads.

"I woke up this morning."

"Good for you, Jack. So what?"

"I wasn't stuck to the ceiling, and I want to know why not."

"Er, gravity?"

"Yes. What is that? How does it work? Put some in a bottle and paint it green while you are at it."

In *Origins I – The Greatest Scientific Discovery*, I presented the irrefutable evidence that the world we inhabit is very different from what we have been taught as reality in the classroom. The fact that there is evidence of design *everywhere* is contemptuously ignored by our scientific peers, which takes a bit of doing when you come to examine DNA and the cell. Dig deeper, and the Oprah moment comes upon you when you realise that arguments about human origins are not really about science at all, but *belief*. Richard Lewontin, Professor of Zoology and Biology at Harvard University, paints the scandal this way:

"Our willingness to accept scientific claims that are against common sense is the key to an understanding of the real struggle between science and the supernatural. We take the side of science in spite of the patent absurdity of some of its constructs, in spite of its failure to fulfill many of its extravagant promises of health and life, in spite of the tolerance of the scientific community for unsubstantiated just-so stories, because we have a prior commitment, a commitment to materialism. It is not that the methods and institutions of science somehow compel us to accept a material explanation of the phenomenal world, but, on the contrary, that we are forced by our *a priori* adherence to material causes to create an apparatus of investigation and a set of concepts that produce material explanations, no matter how counter-intuitive, no matter how mystifying to the uninitiated. Moreover, that materialism is absolute, for we cannot allow a Divine Foot in the door."[1]

In other words, many scientists know that evolution is nonsense, but believe in it anyway, because a) it produces a pay-cheque, and b) under no circumstances can God ever be permitted to crash the party.

Of course, the truth of our origins bears extraordinary implications for us as individuals, and not least society, for if life is ultimately meaningless and there is no big plan, then you and I are living without any ultimate hope or a future. So why not do what we want, free of any eventual responsibility or reckoning? Why bother working when the do-gooders can pay our benefits? Who cares if we rape, murder, lie, cheat and steal our way to the top of the evolutionary pile, if there is no ultimate accountability? After all, it's survival of the fittest on the Serengeti, according to David Attenborough. Aren't human animals just the same?

And if there is no design, no Creator, no accountability, the universe doesn't have us in mind, and Earth made itself, then why not start genetically modifying everything with our newfound

[1] **Lewontin R C** "Billions and Billions of Demons", *New York Review*, 9th January 1997. A review of **Sagan, Carl** *The Demon-Haunted World: Science as a Candle in the Dark*, Paw Prints, 2008

brilliance to improve our environment, even ourselves, if, in the end, nothing really matters?

And what about religion - man's attempt to cover himself before an ultimate Creator? Is religion a dangerous fake, or is there something to it? If so, which religion is valid, and which is fake? They can't all be right. Indeed, why do any need to be right? Why do we have to take some book's word for it? How can we know for sure?

I named the first book in this series *Origins I - The Greatest Scientific Discovery.* That discovery is that humans are provably taking part in an intricate, spacetime, digital simulation on a multi-dimensional/galactic scale, wherein we are meant to discover the deeper truths to our existence and ultimate destiny. In other words, huge effort has been spent crafting the Creation and everything in it *for our discovery and benefit,* so it must have been done for a reason. What is that purpose? Can we ever know? What is our role in that purpose? Where do we turn for guidance? *What is the authenticated source material?*

Extraterrestrial contact

Perhaps atheist Professor Richard Dawkins is right in the eyes of many. Maybe mankind could have been seeded on Earth by an alien race, [2] which periodically pops by the planet to ensure that we haven't yet detonated ourselves to kingdom come. These questions, many may be surprised to learn, are being taken seriously by governments, the Vatican and other organisations around the world, and there is an expectation among many that a disclosure-type event of some kind regarding the existence of ETs is in our near future.

One of the most popular fields of entertainment these days is alien science fiction. Into this you can toss the whole smorgasbord of werewolves, zombies, vampires, trolls, sylphs, fairies, monsters, giants and miscellaneous demonic ne'er-do-wells, which have traditionally dominated cinema theatres since the 1950s, and lately iTunes, Lovefilm and Netflix. This genre has softened up the world to the idea that Earth has been, and is being regularly visited by aliens - a concept that has been hinted at by three US presidents, leading Vatican spokesmen, and numerous NASA astronaut and air force personnel.[3] Today, a sizeable chunk of the population now believes

---

[2] *Expelled - No Intelligence Allowed,* DVD documentary, Premise Media Corporation, 2008, www.credence.org

[3] **Horn T and Putnam C** *Exo-Vaticana,* Defender Pub, Crane, MO, USA, 2013

that we came from the star people, and religion was a control mechanism given to us by our space brethren to keep us in line. It's a comfortable position for many: no ultimate accountability; the excitement of knowing that one day we will meet our star-brothers. Millions these days are up for just about any alien as our progenitor, even a Sigourney Weaver one, just so long as it's not the God Alien.

In any event, as we'll discover in *Origins VI – Parousia,* serious preparations are being made by religions and governments for just such a deceptive announcement. Science programmes like SETI (The Search for Extraterrestrial Intelligence) spend fortunes scanning space for some signal or message from beyond, though millions are convinced that contact has long since been made with extraterrestrial intelligence, and our governments are keeping quiet because of the chaos and panic disclosure might cause. Consider what the global impact on existing religious belief systems might be if such an announcement were made. Consider also that any message received from 'out there' would have to give unequivocal proof of its authenticity as an intelligent source.

The movie *Contact,* which was written by atheist Carl Sagan and starred Jodie Foster and Matthew McConaughey, explores this very theme. The plot goes that one day, just before her SETI funding runs out, Jodie Foster's astrophysicist character, Dr Ellie Arroway, comes upon a powerful signal emitting an unmistakable sequence of prime numbers from the distant star Vega. Notice that she receives what she interprets as *information,* which means *an intelligent source,* which means *a mind,* which means *a person.*

Author Dr Chuck Missler believes that we are solidly in the realm of the information sciences here, specifically teleology (the study of purpose or design), epistemology (the study of knowledge, its scopes and limits), and hermeneutics (the theory of information interpretation). Dr Missler reasons that any genuine Creator wishing to authenticate His message to Earth would need to do so in such a way as to demonstrate an unequivocally transcendent/extra-dimensional intelligence, in contradistinction to human authorship, which is characteristically flawed. In other words, in the rap, neon and jet exhaust of the 21st century, we seem too smart these days to fall for scrolls written by old men in caves, passed off on the world as 'God's Word'. "Where is the *scientific proof!*" the boffins clamour. Very well. Several methods could be used to get our attention in such a message, *each revealing an attribute only the Designer possesses.*

- He could place improbably intricate design patterns in the words and letters passed to us in the message system (code).
- He could tell us things that have not happened yet to demonstrate that He exists outside of the time dimension (transcendence).
- He might reveal advanced knowledge unknown in ancient times, only to be discerned in the future (prophecy).
- And, of course, if He wished, there is nothing stopping the Creator of the universe from very publicly announcing His existence, even to atheists, by starting each new day with the following words etched across our skies: "I AM GOD AND THERE IS NONE LIKE ME!" (revelation). That He has so far failed to do so actually does tell us a lot, as we will discover.

If 'contact' has in fact been made, we might reasonably expect a celestial message replete with design; after all, the Designer appears to be a mathematical prodigy.[4] In the movie *Contact,* the message Dr Arroway receives comprises 60,000 pages of technical specifications. Dr Missler is not the first to examine whether quantum design can be detected, for example, in any of the Earth's great religious books; he has written and lectured extensively on the subject.[5] Professor M Montiero-Williams, former Boden professor of Sanskrit, spent forty-two years studying the religious books of the East to determine whether anything *provably* transcendent was contained within. Montiero-Williams arrived at the same conclusion as Dr Missler and thousands of others. In summing up the wealth of his findings, Montiero-Williams stated:

"Pile them [the Eastern books], if you will, on the left side of your study table; but place your own Holy Bible on the right side - all by itself, all alone - and with a wide gap between them. For... there is a gulf between it and the so-called sacred books of the East which severs one from the other utterly, hopelessly and forever.... a veritable gulf which cannot be bridged over by any science of religious thought."6

---

[4] **Day, Phillip** *Origins I – The Greatest Scientific Discovery,* Credence, 2015, www.credence.org

[5] www.khouse.org

[6] **Collett, Sidney** *All About the Bible,* Old Tappan: Revell, pp.314-315

What did he and the others find? And what bigotry to insist that the Creator is the God of the Bible! Why not Allah of the Koran, the god of the Mormons, aliens from a distant galaxy, the Flying Spaghetti Monster, or even someone we don't know about yet? Why can't God be all things to all people? Strewth, *why not a She?* How can we know? Why couldn't the Bible have been faked for nefarious gain, to con people into thinking it was God's book when it wasn't? The simple answer is, none of the other great religious books on Earth hang themselves on the hook with such extensive *prophetic* writings for self-verification. Dr Missler explains:

"The Bible is the only book on Planet Earth that will stake its credibility on its track record in prophecy. You will not find that true of the Koran of Islam, or the Vedas of the Hindus, or the Bhagavad Gita of India, or the Book of Mormon or [even] Nostradamus's *Centuries*… [which has] many known failures. Occultic mediums, channelers and New Age spirit guides may make claims of this sort of thing, but they will not stand up under investigation, certainly not with a 20/20 unbroken track record."[7]

One third of the Bible is prophecy in the form of the *pre-written history* of the twelve tribes of Israel - God's 'chosen' people. Most of this prophecy has been discharged, giving us a unique view of how well the Judaeo-Christian God has done. The remaining prophecies cover key events of worldwide significance in the 'last days' before Jesus Christ's return sometime in the future. In total, the Bible contains over 8,000 predictive verses, with 1,817 specific prophecies on over 700 matters, dwarfing the attempts of Michel de Nostradame, Edgar Cayce and Gordon Michael Scallion to peek behind the veil and get it right, ten out of ten. This should get the attention of any serious, unbiased researcher. It got mine.

After thirty years of study, my conclusion is that an extraterrestrial intelligence has long since made contact with us - the Creator, in fact - and this can be proved beyond any doubt *scientifically*.[8] We are in possession of His (note the gender[9]) extensive, transcendent, self-authenticating Message System, which clears up any queries one might have on who we are, where we came from,

---

[7] **Missler, Chuck** *Macrocodes: 'Past'*, www.khouse.org

[8] *Origins I – The Greatest Scientific Discovery*, op. cit.

[9] "Is God a woman? To ask the question is to miss the point", *The Guardian*, 1st June 2015

what we're doing here, and what will happen to us when this life is over. *It also tells us what we are not.* Mankind's reaction? Modern, right-on, politically correct, atheist, lip-quivering, hand-wringing, 21st century society doesn't like the Creator's tone, and we don't like what He has to tell us either. Worse: if the Message System is what it purports to be, then many of us are going to be in serious trouble five seconds after our hearts stop beating.

In *Origins II – Holy War,* I summarise how this Message System, known as 'the Bible', can be scientifically authenticated *beyond doubt,* using a number of different methods. Then I begin tracing what information the Author of this Message System has to tell us from the very first line: **In the beginning God created the Heaven and the Earth.** (Gen 1:1) I find it noteworthy that God throws down the credibility gauntlet right from the start. Do you believe that God made everything, or don't you? I asked that question to one American pastor. This was his reply: "Well, it's not really that simple...."

Yikes. *A Christian minister doesn't believe that God made the Heaven and the Earth?*

He is by no means on his own.

There is another intriguing angle to this. The Bible comprises 66 books written by 40 authors over 1,500 years, which agree in the smallest part across dozens of controversial subjects with no errors or contradictions. The science, history, detailed genealogies, prophecy and supernatural acrostics contained in this work pale before the astonishing whole, which has been spread across the entire transmission/bandwidth of the publication, **precept upon precept, line upon line, here a little, there a little** (Isa 28:10,13). This has been done in such a way, so that if one part of the message is lost, the key message survives. Dr Missler, who has a background in cryptography and the US defence industry, believes that the Bible is a classic example of a message system carefully compiled to anticipate hostile jamming. For instance, there is no one chapter on baptism, nor one on salvation. Each theme has been spread throughout the whole, using a remarkable patterning format we will examine as we go.

Unique, transcendent

So the God Alien has made contact, but we don't like what He has to tell us. Then again, we've known the cure for cancer for eighty years (it's the immune system), and we don't like that either, since the answer doesn't make Porsche payments. Thus modern man finds himself in a bit of a pickle; the protagonist in a slow-motion car-crash, unfolding in glorious Panavision. Blinded by scientific hubris into believing he is now God - putting fish genes into tomatoes, and scorpion juice into cabbages - this preposterous, self-deified techno-bully crashes around his Internet jungle, ruthlessly suppressing any notion of a Supreme Being not preening back at him in the mirror. While the atheist has few kind words to say about religion and its propensity for control and slaughter of unbelievers, his own desire for sovereign control over the belief of others is manic; insane even. An atheist defends his own religion like a pitbull, cowering others into submission with the elephant-gun mantra: "We have science on our side!" when really they don't. What they do have is a form of collective, social insanity I cover in *Origins I,* that has come to be known as the double mind: A mind profoundly at war with itself, and ignorant even of that fact (Jam 1:8).[10]

I'll tell you something else. In my view, the Bible stands alone as the most terrifying book ever written. Firmly hung on the hook of its hyperdimensional pedigree, it must either self-authenticate its otherworldly authorship, or be exposed as a fraud. It's a book of action, which describes the Holy War between good and evil. The players in this conflict may surprise you. They are not God versus Satan, nor Muslim versus Jew, nor even Republican versus Democrat. In a nutshell, God is good and *we are evil,* so God is going to put the Bad Lads' Army through boot camp to see if He can make something of us. We will be confronted with evil in all its forms, and we're supposed to overcome it. Most won't.

What is the Bible about? In one word: redemption. In another word: Yeshua. Jesus Christ. The Name that is above every name. God's book has been given to man to show us how to get back to God via His Son, the long-awaited *Mashiach* (Messiah). You and I have been created to participate in what I term 'the Earth Programme'. The Bible is our instruction manual, and contains everything we need to know to succeed; to overcome; to finish well; to come out on the winning side.

Many have remarked that life sometimes seems like an intricate dream. I would not disagree. You are I are participating in a highly elaborate, on-the-job training programme under live-fire conditions to assess our suitability for the Eternal Kingdom. Will I be for or

---

[10] **Hoffman Michael** *Secret Societies and Psychological Warfare,* Wiswell Ruffin House, 1992, p.90

against my Creator? Will I learn His ways, or will I follow Frank Sinatra and do it *My Way?* The Bible gives us the overview; about paradise lost and paradise regained. One researcher describes the Bible as a love story written in blood on a wooden cross 2,000 years ago in Judea.[11] The Bible claims the Creator made everything. It claims the Creator went to the extremes of despatching his Son to Earth in human form to suffer death, so that sinful man could be reconciled with a perfect Creator after the Holy War was won.

You have to admit, the Bible is the ultimate script. There's love, betrayal, sex, battles, sacrifice, incest, royal court life, palace plots, stunning beauties, ordinary heroes, drugs, drunkenness, gruesome executions, fantastic penances, miracles, plot-twists, deception, giants, demons, aliens, an arch villain, natural disasters, celestial catastrophes, extreme weather, thunders and lightnings, space wars and superhuman champions. In fact, about the only the thing the Bible doesn't feature is football. And through it all, the leading personality, the protagonist, God, aka YHWH[12] ('Yahweh'), aka Yeshua aka Jesus Christ, aka the LORD God Almighty, Father of Creation walks with you through every page of the greatest story ever told. Your Maker. The entire panoply of history - His Story – is rolled out, and we are its witness. Turn to the back of the book and you can see who wins. We are told that each of us needs to be on that winning side before we die, because the implications either way are eternal. Right now, most of us are not on the winning side; hence the need for an *authenticated* Message System.

The Bible, then: the most extraordinary, bestselling book of all time, provoking extraordinary reactions. Indeed, we are told it can only be unlocked and understood under the light of God's Holy Spirit, which God gives to whom He will. That does not mean that Joe in the street cannot pick up the scriptures and have a thumb-through – he is more than welcome to – but he won't unless God prompts him (Rom 8:7; 1 Cor 2:12-14). To people like Joe, the Bible has no form or comeliness that he should desire it, until it is illuminated with God's Spirit, after which it will make the most blazing sense in the world. I know. I've been on both sides of the fence.

A sampling of comments on the Bible by atheists is revealing:

---

[11] www.khouse.org

[12] God's name in Hebrew. God's holy name 'Yahweh' is represented by the Tetragrammaton 'YHWH'. It is sometimes extrapolated as 'JeHoVaH'.

"Nobody questions that the Bible possibly contains some elements of historical fact. It is the concept of the existence of a supernatural deity that many people have problems with." - grayle, London, United Kingdom

"The holy bible has already been proven wrong multiple times. Just read Genesis. The universe and the earth were not created in 6 days around 6000 years ago and we can prove it, end of debate, easy...."

And:

"I'm not saying that what the bible teaches doesn't have some value, only that it is not a literal historically accurate document, and shouldn't be used as fact. If taken metaphorically, some of it teaches some decent lessons about morality (although it also teaches some pretty horrible stuff as well). The point is, it is a book of fables and should be treated as such." - milesp, wigan, United Kingdom

"If the bible was ever 'accurate like a newspaper', then isn't that enough to tell us it's complete rubbish?! I like the one where Moses definitely parted the sea - pretty sure that happened." - John Dough, London, United Kingdom

"My favorite is the talking snake, why take the apple? I would have grabbed the snake and said to Adam check out this talking snake. The first Dr Doolittle moment recorded. Or how about 20 million varieties of wildlife on the Ark – that's another good one. Trouble is there are so many comedy events it's hard to just pick one." - Roger, Guildford, United Kingdom

"How do you know [the Bible is] true? Before you answer that - go away and think about it for a minute and ask yourself HONESTLY how you actually know it's true? Like most historical documents, it is likely to be based on a mixture of truth, mis-remembered content and downright untruths, generally recorded for political expediency. But how do we know which is true and which isn't? You think it's all true because you have convinced yourself that some deity inspired its writing, but you have not grounded that belief on any solid evidence. You believe it because you choose to believe it." - Stu, Laholm, Sweden

"Some day in the distant future ... I foresee some being picking up a copy of Harry Potter and realising that thousands of years ago the ancient people travelled by brooms." - just me, pluto

Atheists suppose that exposure of the Bible as fake, self-contradicting 'scripture' has long been accomplished. *It hasn't.* They pour scorn on a young Earth, claiming this too has been exposed by science as a ridiculous falsehood. *It hasn't.* In claiming that the Bible has been discredited thousands of times as error-ridden non-history, they do so, not *à propos* of their own study, which they have not undertaken, but on the hearsay of others. Many also state - like Stu above - that a believer's faith is not based on any solid evidence. This too is a myth trotted out by those who were never motivated to do the research because, to date, they have not been - ah - *called.*[13]

On the other hand, when 'smart' people reject God and His Word, just sit back and watch what nonsense they start believing instead. Why? Because man is programmed to believe in *something*, even if it's believing that there's nothing to believe in, and that life is essentially hopeless. Many reject the Bible because of a deep spiritual antagonism they can neither rationalise nor identify. In fact, not only is atheism a belief, it is actually the classic definition of Satanism, defined here by none other than American occultist Anton LaVey, who founded the worldwide Church of Satan in San Francisco:

> "And he must, as a Satanist, knowing this, realising what his human potential is, eventually, and here is one of the essential points of Satanism, attaining his own godhood in accordance with his own potential. Therefore, each man, each woman, is a god or goddess in Satanism."[14]

Peter Gilmore, who took over as 'high priest' after LaVey's death in 1997, elaborates:

> "Satanists do not believe in the supernatural, in neither God nor the Devil. To the Satanist, he is his own God. Satan is a symbol of Man living as his prideful, carnal nature dictates. The reality behind Satan is simply the dark evolutionary force of entropy that permeates all of nature and provides the drive for survival and propagation inherent in all living things. Satan is not a conscious entity to be worshipped, rather a reservoir of power inside each human to be tapped at will. Thus any concept of sacrifice is rejected as a Christian aberration—in Satanism there's no deity to which one can sacrifice."[15]

As opposed to *theistic* Satanism, which is worshipping the Devil as God, involving the practice of magic(k), arcane ritual and sometimes animal and child sacrifice.

---

[13] Isa 49:1,5; Jer 1:5; FG 6:44; 6:64; Acts 13:48; Rom 1:7; Eph 1:4-5; 2 Tim 2:19; 2 Thess 2:13; Gal 1:15

[14] **Holmberg, Eric** *The Allure of Rock* DVD, American Portrait Films, 1999

[15] www.churchofsatan.com/Pages/Feared.html

Atheistic Satanism then, according to LaVey and Gilmore, who should know, is not worshipping the Devil at all. It is egotism (pride), acknowledging no higher power above you, not even Satan. It's spirit-led; the serpent's hiss in the Garden; the Devil's desire to **'be like the Most High'**; man liberated to become his own god; to be who he wants to be and do what he wants to do with no singeing of the conscience. Aleister Crowley's *"Do what thou wilt shall be the whole of the law"* is the endgame, along with *"Life is the great indulgence. Death is the great abstinence. Therefore make the most of life here and now."* (Book of Satan 1:4).

In other word, there is only one law: do what you want. Sound familiar?

Hebrew

Then there is the language angle to the scriptures. Ninety percent of the Bible was originally written in Hebrew. Most think that the New Testament writings came to us from an original Greek version, but this is not true. John Klein and Adam Spears explain:

"What most scholars now call the Mattityahu Document (i.e. the Matthew Document), containing Matthew, Mark, Luke and Acts 1:1-15:35, was originally written on one scroll, in Hebrew. Later on, these were broken out into separate scrolls. It's difficult to be as certain about the other New Testament books, but many signs also indicate that the original text of Revelation, if not written in Hebrew, might have been recorded first in Aramaic, an ancient dialect of Hebrew. Beyond all that, "Revelation's 404 verses contain as many as 278 quotes, or allusions to the Old Testament (Tanakh), especially Psalms, Isaiah, Ezekiel, Daniel and Zechariah".[16] In other words, 68.2 percent of Revelation either is or contains Hebrew Scripture, and the rest probably is or does the same!"[17]

Researchers David Bivin and Roy Blizzard write:

"We tend to forget that the Old Testament comprises approximately 78% of the biblical text, and the New Testament only 22 percent. When we add the highly Hebraic portions of the New Testament (Matthew, Mark, Luke and Acts 1:1-15:35, approximately 43 percent of the New Testament) to the Old Testament, the percentage of the biblical material originally written in Hebrew rises to 88 percent (or 87% if we omit the

---

[16] www.baonline.com, click on 'Study the Books of the Bible', select rev.pdf

[17] **Klein, J & A Spears** *Devils, Demons and the Return of the Nephilim,* Xulon Press, 2005, p.14

portions of Ezra and Daniel – less than 1 percent of the Old Testament – composed in Aramaic). Not more than 12 percent of the entire Bible was originally written in Greek. When we subtract from that 12 percent the 176 quotations from the Old Testament... the percentage of the Bible originally composed in Hebrew rises to over 90 percent." [18]

Why is this important? Because to process the astonishing world we are about to visit, we need to have some understanding of the cultural context into which the Message System was originally sent. The language itself is a good start.

Hebrew is a remarkable, other-worldly tongue, whose strange characters convey not only words and meaning like any language, but also *numbers* and *concepts*. Hebrew is phonetic, numeric and pictographic - each letter having a range of meanings of its own. Hebrew contains no vowels, and is therefore an extremely 'dense' language, which makes maximum use of available bandwidth for transmission.[19] Hebrew is also remarkable for the unique attribute of having been the only language to have passed into history, only to be resurrected for use by an entire nation in the modern age. What a tremendous metaphor for the journey we are about to take.

Hebrew is such a remarkable communications medium, it is deserving of our further study for these reasons alone. That Earth's most popular, bestselling book of all time, which self-verifies with buckets of prophecy and purports to have come from God, was almost entirely compiled in this language, should make even the hardened sceptic sit up and take note. Even on a superficial level, we have something weird going on. With letters which can be replaced with numbers and concepts, the multi-dimensional properties of Hebrew are matched only by the most extraordinary concepts it describes in the Message System. The whole work quickly leaves the superficial and soars to unfathomable heights when you start delving deeper. The ancients knew it, and today an increasing number of scientists are loosening up to the evidence that the black book in our hands might be far more extraordinary than just a collection of quaint tales of moral rectitude that used to amuse or scare our children at bedtime. The Old and New Testament writings, in their original, linguistic form, *appear to be an integrated message system delivered from*

---

[18] **Bivin, David and Roy Blizzard** *Understanding the Difficult Words of Jesus: New Insights From a Hebraic Perspective,* Destiny Image, 1995, pp.4-5

[19] In other words, fewer letters and words are required to convey the same meaning; a little like text-speak.

outside spacetime, having been given to the authors to write down, with every letter, word, phrase, number and name there by supernatural design.

Point of departure

The purpose of *Origins III – The Predicament of Man* is not only to examine some of these incredible claims in more detail, and see how they stack up against science, history and logic, but to discover whether these ancient writings are valid to use as source material for shedding light on mankind's origins, history and ultimate destiny. What does the Designer expect of us? Many make this intensely personal quest through faith alone, and yet intriguingly, the God of the Bible encourages us **to prove that these things are so** and to **study to show ourselves approved** so we won't be deceived.[20]

That the existence of God is a mathematical certainty will come as a shock to many, though probably not to UK bookmakers Paddy Power, who slashed the odds on proof being found of God's existence to just 4-1.[21] For you the reader, however, you should steel yourself for what follows, or shut this book now. In the movie *The Matrix,* the lead character Neo is offered a red pill or a blue pill. The red pill will cause Neo to witness the unveiling of the true reality – like hitting the Reveal Codes button on a word-processing programme. Once Neo swallows the red pill, however, he has assumed a responsibility *to know,* and will never be able to *unlearn,* nor revert to the way he was. On the other hand, swallowing the blue pill will leave Neo in blissful ignorance the way he is, none the wiser.

It's a sobering revelation that mankind prefers a reassuring lie over an inconvenient truth. After my thirty years of research in this area, I am still intrigued by mankind's propensity for gobbling down blue pills and believing the sanitised untruths fed to them daily by the media. The reason? Laziness, dependency and apathy; and above all, fear. Fear of what the red pill might mean for them; that if they don't like what they find, there is no turning back.

The *Origins* series will invite you to rethink and restructure your priorities for a glorious future – your future. Over time, you will see the scenarios described in this book unfolding in the newspapers and on TV. In fact, you are already aware of some, but perhaps have not yet come to the point where you can connect all the dots. What I will

---

[20] Rom 12:2; 1 Thess 5:21; 1 John 4:1; Acts 17:11. But NB Deut 6:16.

[21] *Daily Telegraph,* 3rd November 2008

reveal in the coming chapters is going to affect you personally and profoundly – I make no apologies for it. I will bring you to *The Matrix's* red pill, blue pill moment. Forget Dan Brown's *The Da Vinci Code* or *Angels and Demons*, while the journey you are about to take may well cause your hair to stand on end, it will also provide an astounding, heart-warming perspective on an incredible hope: Who you are; where you fit in; why what you do matters; why you are alive at this point in Earth's history; what the Creator has in store for you personally in the months and years ahead; and the proof behind all of it. *Nothing has happened to you by accident, however wonderful or awful,* and you will see this played out in the astonishing panorama we are about to examine.

Origins II – Holy War covered the period from the Creation up to the death of Joseph in Egypt. Let us now reprise the story centuries later in the year 1526 BC, when the birth of a squalling babe in a foreign country is set to change the world forever.

Buckle up for this ride.

MOSES – SETTING THE SCENE

There is probably no more important human character in the Old Testament than Moses, son of the Levite Amram. For those who have little knowledge of matters Biblical, most have an inkling of the dividing of the Red Sea and the Ten Plagues of Egypt, as well as that stentorian clamour, "Let my people go!"

Moses has featured in countless books, songs, and several mammoth-budget Hollywood epics. Two films were directed by Cecil B. DeMille on the subject: one, a 1923 silent film starring Theodore Roberts in the lead role, and the more famous colour outing in 1956 VistaVision, *The Ten Commandments,* starring Charlton Heston as Moses, Yul Brynner as Pharaoh, and not forgetting that mind-boggling cast of thousands scattered across the desert. More recently, Christian Bale has taken up the staff and sandals in the elaborate, CGI-no-holds-barred *Exodus - God and Kings* film (2014), directed by Ridley *'Gladiator'* Scott. While long on drama and awe-inspiring set-pieces, the astonishing, deeper revelations of both the Biblical Moses and his Exodus are predictably missing in these productions, as any serious student of God's Word knew they would be.

Let's review the original source material. On one level, the Biblical account of the Exodus can be easily viewed as a historical record - and, by the way, is intended by the Author as such. This is, of course, contested at every level by today's Big Atheism, which mocks any notion of historicity for the period. As usual, most of these detractors, never having studied this incredible era themselves (of course), mouth only what they heard pontificated by their equally godless peers, who also never carried out the legwork. In the following chapters we will do that legwork. Prepared to be amazed, even bewildered.

Not for nothing does the Hebrew text of Exodus 1:1 commence with the word 'and';[22] it is intended as a direct continuation of the narrative of Genesis before it. Exodus, like Genesis, reads compellingly as 'surface' text, but there are all sorts of hidden gems ripe for discovery, as we'll see. Warren Wiersbe writes:

---

[22] 'And', 'Now'.

"The theme of Exodus is *deliverance*, and you can't have a deliverance without a deliverer. That's where Moses comes in, the great liberator, legislator, and mediator." [23]

We are going to examine Moses and his era, not just from this important, plain-text aspect, nor just from the historical perspective, but also from the prophetic standpoint, where huge insights can be gained. Once again, if the Bible truly is the Extraterrestrial Message System given to us by our Creator, then it can be authenticated as such on a number of different levels. We have already examined this phenomenon in our studies in *Origins II - Holy War,* and this is precisely what we find in the Moses/Exodus saga - if anything on a more transcendent scale. But you have to dig for these nuggets. It is God's intention that you dig for them, for in so doing you are committing to Him that most precious and irreplaceable of your own resources: your time in His presence.

It is the glory of God to conceal a thing: but the honour of kings is to search out a matter (Prov 25:2).

I rejoice at Thy word, as one that findeth great spoil (Psa 119:162).

For whatsoever things were written aforetime were written for our learning, that we through patience and comfort of the scriptures might have hope (Rom 15:4).

Moses/Exodus - an overview

The Exodus story on a prophetic level is just extraordinary. When you consider that the author, Moses,[24] is writing this account 1,500 years before Christ, the transcendent element of what we will discover becomes starkly apparent. The Bible focuses on one supreme personage throughout: God Himself as YHWH in the Old Testament, and in the person of Yeshua *ha-Mashiach,* Jesus Christ the Saviour, in the New (Psa 40:7; FG 5:39). Same God, same Creator, same character.

---

[23] **Wiersbe, Warren** *The Wiersbe Bible Commentary,* David C Cook, Colorado Springs, USA, p.148

[24] Mark 7:10. A lot has been made of the 'Documentary (Wellhausen) Hypothesis', which seeks to undermine the validity of the Torah (first five books of the Bible) by attributing its authorship to various scribes, whose writings were eventually combined into their current form by a variety of later scribes/editors. Not only is this theory done to nought by the Torah's textual integrity, which we will study, Jesus Christ Himself quoted from each book of the Torah during His ministry, separately attributing the authorship of each to Moses.

Information given centuries before Christ prefigures the coming of God to Earth in human form in every detail. We will experience the presence of Jesus in the Ten Plagues, the Passover, manna in the desert, a tree thrown into a bog, the smitten rock, the brazen serpent on a pole, and the most striking Messianic model of all - the Tabernacle. Idioms and types are stitched into the narratives on a micro as well as macro scale; so too are puns, placed there by the Holy Spirit not just for fun, but also for our further instruction.

Moses becomes a type of Christ in the Exodus story, delivering His chosen people from spiritual and physical bondage. Egypt is portrayed consistently by the Holy Spirit throughout the Bible as a model of the unregenerate, carnal world. Pharaoh plays the role of Satan resisting all attempts by Moses to secure physical and spiritual liberty for God's people from a sinful world. Finally, after unblemished lambs and goats are slaughtered and their innocent blood daubed in a cross-like configuration on the doorposts of God's chosen, the death angel passes over God's elect without judgment (the Passover), while killing all the firstborn of those not under the blood. After this, Pharaoh (Satan) holds no further power over the elect, and Moses is able to lead God's people out of Egypt heaped in rewards (spoil). They pass through the baptism of the divided waters (dividing God's Word - Eph 5:26; 2 Tim 2:15), which proves to be life for the believer and death for the unbeliever hounding them (Pharaoh/Satan's pursuing hordes). The chosen people (the elect) head off into the Wilderness of Sin - a time of spiritual uncertainty, testing and discovery for the new believer - where battles are fought, lost and won. The Law/Word is given to the believer at Mt Horeb ('Sinai'), then we have more wanderings and adventures, culminating in the final crossing of the Jordan to claim the elects' rightful inheritance in the Promised Land. The whole saga is a model for the predicament of man: the path he has been given to redemption and salvation. This is the central theme of the entire Bible.

Wikipedia packages the Moses story thus:

"According to the book of Exodus [Exo 6:20], Moses was born to a Hebrew mother, Jochebed, who hid him when the Pharaoh ordered all newborn Hebrew boys to be killed, and he ended up being adopted into the Egyptian royal family. After killing an Egyptian slave-master, Moses fled and became a shepherd, and was later commanded by God to deliver the Hebrews from slavery. After the Ten Plagues were unleashed on Egypt, he led the Hebrew slaves out of Egypt, through the Red Sea, where they wandered in the desert for 40 years, during which time, according to the Bible, Moses received the Ten Commandments. Despite living to 120, Moses died before reaching the Land of Israel. According to the Torah, Moses was denied entrance to that destination because he himself disobeyed God's instructions about how to release water from a rock."[25]

Alas, a blander summary of the life of Moses one could not wish to read, but such is Jimmy Wales and his Wikipedia, which goes on to label the Exodus as:

"...the founding myth of Israel.... The archeological evidence does not support the Book of Exodus and most archaeologists have abandoned the investigation of Moses and the Exodus as 'a fruitless pursuit'." [26]

Really? No, not really. The Exodus saga continues to fascinate people today even as in ages past. Let's find out what actually happened, and we will pick up the archaeology and other scientific details so conveniently overlooked as we go.

Are Moses and the Exodus historical?

A fabulous question, which provokes a spectrum of angry and awed responses. The general consensus in the secular world is that Moses, if he ever existed at all, is a figure conflated from multiple accounts. Mostly, though, he is just portrayed as myth. This puts detractors, even Christians and Jews, in the unenviable position of calling God a liar, since the Torah expects to be read as actual history, and Jesus, as well as His form as the Old Testament God YHWH, *viewed the Torah as historical truth,* not legend or allegory.

Not a great start. Another problem is that if you wish to place Moses and the Exodus in real history, then you are dealing with Egyptian pharaonic history, and the first thing you learn about pharaonic history is that even the experts are hard put to agree on even some of the basic details of which pharaoh reigned when. The dating of the various dynasties by regular historians is well known to be a mess. There are sometimes dozens, even hundreds of years of variance. There is significant dissention even among Christian and Jewish scholars in deciding the identity of the Joseph- or Moses-era

---

[25] www.wikipedia.org, 'Moses'

[26] http://en.wikipedia.org/wiki/The_Exodus

Pharaoh. In fact, the more you get into reconciling the chronologies of Egypt and their corresponding Hebrew protagonists according to the current wisdom, the bigger the pickle you find yourself in. This has caused some scholars to re-think the whole approach, while others on the secular side have cast up their hands and denied Jacob and his sons ever went to Egypt in the first place, and that the figure we know as Moses probably did not exist at all.

This capitulation cannot be maintained in view of the evidence. For instance, those who deny Israel spent any time in Egypt need to explain why there are a significant number of Egyptian names in the genealogies of the Levites. Examples are Moses, Assir, Pashhur, Hophni, Phenehas, and Merari. Moreover, details of life and customs in Egypt cited in the Bible appear genuine and consistent with a protracted Israelite sojourn in Egypt. We'll examine examples as we proceed. But I'm interested in the re-thinkers. When faced with a mess, stand back and look at the whole era to see if you've missed something obvious.

In view of the broad spectrum of scholarly controversy surrounding the historicity of Moses and the Exodus, I will not engage in a protracted explanation of the various positions, since that will derail our narrative. Instead, allow me to propose the following approach: The stories of Joseph, Moses, the Exodus and the Canaan invasion would be so extraordinary in their historical impact that, if they happened at all, some imprint of these events on discovered, secular history and the archaeological record would surely be knowable. Even though Egyptology is a quagmire, there has been a huge amount of study and archaeology carried out on this part of human history, so we know the broad-strokes and many of the details. So let's look at what established historical sources have to say on the Egyptian periods in question, and let us see if they throw up anything intriguing. Watch carefully!

THE FIRST INTERMEDIATE PERIOD (2181 - 2055 BC)

Discovering Egypt writes:

"About this time the Old Kingdom state collapsed. Egypt simultaneously suffered political failure and environmental disaster. There was famine, civil disorder and a rise in the death rate. With the climate of Northeast Africa becoming dryer, combined with low inundations of the Nile and the cemeteries rapidly filling, this was not a good time for the Egyptians....

"The years following the death of Pepy II are most obscure. The only person from this era to have left an impression on posterity is a woman called Nitokris who appears to have acted as king.....

"For a time, petty warlords ruled the provinces. Then from the city of Herakleopolis there emerged a ruling family led by one Khety who for a time held sway over the whole country. However, this was short-lived and the country split into North, ruled from Herakleopolis and South, ruled from Thebes. Whereas the Theban dynasty was stable, kings succeeded one another rapidly at Herakleopolis. There was continual conflict between the two lands which was resolved in the 11th dynasty."[27]

And just to check our facts, the British Museum has this to say on the First Intermediate Period:

"Following the death of King Pepy II, Egypt was controlled by a number of rulers (Seventh to Eighth Dynasties) with very brief reigns. Power in Egypt became fragmented: the north of Egypt was ruled by kings from Heracleopolis, while rulers at Thebes had dominion over the south. Literary works that looked back on the period were influenced by concerns about the fragility of the state and the position of the individual within it.

"There are relatively few lavish monuments from this period. However, the decoration of the rock cut tombs of provincial governors shows that artistic traditions continued. The richness of these burials suggests that the provinces flourished during this time of political disunity. Tomb inscriptions stress the independence of the individual, sometimes referring to local conflict. The use of funerary symbols and concepts previously reserved for the king shows that members of the élite could hope to reach the afterlife.

"Control of the south eventually passed to the Theban king Nebhepetre Mentuhotep II (about 2055 - 2004 BC), who became king of a united Egypt. Little evidence is available as to the progress of his conquest of northern Egypt. The greatest surviving monument from the First Intermediate Period is the mortuary temple of Nebhepetre Mentuhotep II at Deir el-Bahri, close to Thebes."[28]

Summary: So, due to political and environmental factors, there is a period of instability in early Egypt, but eventually the kingdom gets it together under a centralised government, and we enter...

---

[27] http://discoveringegypt.com/

[28] www.britishmuseum.org: First Intermediate Period summary

THE MIDDLE KINGDOM (2055 - 1700 BC)

Historyworld.net writes:

"When stability returns, it is under the rule of a family deriving their power from middle Egypt. Mentuhotep II (also known by his throne name, Nebhepetre) wins control of the whole country in about 2000 BC. His base is Thebes, which now begins its central role in the story of ancient Egypt - though relatively little survives of Mentuhotep's own monuments in the region.

"The Middle Kingdom, spanning the 11th and 12th dynasties, is notable for the first serious effort to colonize Nubia [approx. modern-day southern Egypt, northern Sudan]. This region now becomes of great importance to Egypt's trade in luxuries. Nubia's mines are the chief source of Egyptian gold. Rare commodities such as ivory and ebony, the skins of leopards and the plumes of ostriches, now travel down the upper Nile to be traded for Egyptian goods.

"The market place is at the second cataract (today submerged under Lake Nasser). Here the Nubians exchange their commodities - and their slaves, always an important element in the trade of this region - for the manufactured goods and the weapons of the more developed economy."[29]

Let's check that with the British Museum's summary:

"Following the reunification of Egypt by the Theban king Nebhepetre Mentuhotep II (about 2055-2004 BC), the first king of the Twelfth Dynasty, Amenemhat I, founded a new capital south of Memphis, called Itjtawy. He also annexed Lower Nubia, primarily in order to control the gold resources of the area. The Twelfth Dynasty was made up of a series of mostly strong rulers, all except the last named Amenemhat or Senwosret, who expanded and maintained Egyptian control to the south and even, to a limited extent, in the Near East." [30]

Wikipedia adds:

"The brilliant Egyptian twelfth dynasty came to an end at the end of the 19th century BC with the death of Queen Sobekneferu (1806–1802 BC). Apparently, she had no heirs, causing the twelfth dynasty to come to a sudden end, and, with it, the Golden Age of the Middle Kingdom; it was succeeded by the much weaker thirteenth dynasty of Egypt.... The thirteenth dynasty is notable for the accession of the first formally

---

[29] www.historyworld.net/wrldhis/PlainTextHistories.asp?historyid=aa28

[30] www.britishmuseum.org: The Middle Kingdom summary

recognised Semitic king, Khendjer. The thirteenth dynasty proved unable to hold onto the entire territory of Egypt, however, and a provincial ruling family of Canaanite descent in Avaris, located in the marshes of the eastern delta, broke away from the central authority to form the fourteenth dynasty."[31]

Summary: During the Middle Kingdom period (2055 - 1700 BC), Egypt pushes its influence south into Nubia. Trade and wealth increase. Migrant populations become interested in coming to Egypt to enrich themselves, most notably a coalition of Semitic and Mesopotamian tribes, later dubbed the Hyksos, who migrate to Egypt from the north-eastern Levant.[32] They settle in the eastern Delta of Lower Egypt and begin increasing their populations. Political instability causes an eventual collapse of the Egyptian state and the Hyksos foreigners take over. We now enter...

THE SECOND INTERMEDIATE PERIOD (1700 - 1550 BC)

Peeters Publishers writes:

"In the eastern Nile Delta, a community of Asiatic origin proclaimed its own rulers, known later as the Hyksos, who ultimately controlled the entire northern half of Egypt. Kings at Thebes [to the south] maintained a fragile independence, then went to war and defeated the Hyksos, restoring national unity." [33]

British Museum concurs:

"The Second Intermediate Period is dominated by the first foreign rulers of Egypt, the Hyksos. This group came from the Levant [Middle-eastern land-bridge: Canaan, Syria, etc.], and ruled as the Fifteenth and Sixteenth Dynasties of Manetho from their capital at Avaris in the Nile Delta.

"The Hyksos controlled most of the northern part of Egypt, and also traded with the Levant and the Aegean, as well as with the kingdom of Kush. Power in the Delta was, however, somewhat fragmented.

"The last rulers of the Theban Seventeenth Dynasty openly campaigned against the Hyksos kings and King Seqenenre Tao was

---

[31] http://en.wikipedia.org/wiki/Second_Intermediate_Period_of_Egypt

[32] The Levant is a geopolitical term used to describe the Middle-East land-bridge between Europe, Asia and Africa. The area encompasses the modern-day nations of Syria, Lebanon, Jordan and Israel.

[33] www.peeters-leuven.be/boekoverz.asp?nr=8651

probably killed during a battle against them. The Hyksos were eventually defeated by Kamose and his successor, Ahmose."[34]

THE NEW KINGDOM (1550 - 1070 BC)

Knowing the Bible writes:

"Ahmose I, the brother of Kamose, led a successful revolt against the Hyksos and drove them completely out of Egypt. Thus Ahmose I was the first ruler of the 18th dynasty and established the New Kingdom as a military empire. With the expulsion of the Hyksos at the end of the Second Intermediate Period, the Theban Prince Ahmose I now reigned supreme. The Egyptian army pushed beyond the traditional frontiers of Egypt into Syria-Palestine and brought Nubia (Kush) under control. The Theban conquerors had thus established the 18th dynasty, creating a great empire under a succession of powerful rulers. The New Kingdom that Ahmose inaugurated was the period of greatest imperial might in Egypt's long history." [35]

The British Museum concurs:

"The New Kingdom is composed of the Eighteenth to the Twentieth Dynasties, following the expulsion of the Hyksos and the reunification of the country by Ahmose. The New Kingdom was a time of great prosperity in Egypt. The massive building projects at Thebes, the religious centre and sometime capital of the period, demonstrate the power and wealth of the kings of the New Kingdom. The Temple of Amun at Karnak, the Luxor Temple and the many mortuary temples on the west bank of the Nile record great battles and other royal exploits. Several kings of the Eighteenth Dynasty led campaigns into Palestine, parts of which were brought under Egyptian control."[36]

OK, let's hit the pause button and see what we have so far:

THE FIRST INTERMEDIATE PERIOD (2181 - 2055 BC)

The stable Old (First) Kingdom collapses and Egypt undergoes a period of instability.

THE MIDDLE KINGDOM (2055 - 1700 BC)

Stability is regained and we're back to the Egypt we know. Wealth is built through trade, and Egypt experiences an expansion of

---

[34] www.britishmuseum.org: Second Internediate Period summary

[35] www.knowingthebible.net/the-pharaohs-of-the-exodus

[36] www.britishmuseum.org: New Kingdom summary

military and cultural influence. During this period, a coalition of Semitic and Mesopotamian peoples, later known as the Hyksos, begin emigrating to Lower (northern) Egypt to partake in the empire's wealth. As their numbers increase, so does their influence and power.

THE SECOND INTERMEDIATE PERIOD (1700 - 1550 BC)

The Middle Kingdom runs into trouble with a succession problem, which terminates the 12th Dynasty. Political instability follows, and the Asiatic Hyksos seize control of Lower Egypt, forming a state of their own. The Egyptian princes move south to Thebes and rule a rival state, plotting revenge on the foreign Hyksos usurpers over two centuries. So Egypt is now two lands: Upper (Theban) Egypt ruled by the previous pharaonic line, and Lower (Delta) Egypt ruled by the Asiatic Hyksos.

THE NEW KINGDOM (1550 - 1070 BC)

The Egyptians ruling Upper (southern) Egypt finally manage to invade and drive out the Hyksos. Egypt unifies once more, this time as a military state under the very capable 18th Dynasty. Egypt enters its golden age with huge building projects and unparalleled wealth and influence.

The 'Shepherd Kings'

Did you spot the glaring non-sequitur of the Second Intermediate Period? In his book, *Act of God,* Graham Phillips recounts that a few decades before Joseph (around 1800 BC) and a thousand kilometres to the north-east, another drama has been playing out in the archaeological record. The Babylonians attack and sack a Mesopotamian city named Mari (modern-day Tell Hariri, Syria). The tribes of the Mari and their vassal states flee the Chaldean invaders and migrate south-west into Canaan. During their exodus, the Mari co-mingle with the Semite peoples of Canaan, and soon a powerful alliance is formed with considerable military muscle. The Mari exodus eventually ends up on the fertile plains of northern Egypt. These nomadic peoples bring with them mobile resources as yet unknown to the Egyptians, such as the war-horse, which make these *Hikau khasut,* or 'rulers of the desert highlands', a formidable enemy. Abraham, Isaac and Jacob would have been very familiar with them among the Canaanite peoples. The Hyksos, or 'Shepherd Kings', as they have mistakenly come to be known,[37] are also skilled in advanced fortification techniques, greatly improved battle-axes, the deadly compound bow, and the latest in moving platforms from which to fire it - the sleek and manoeuvrable war-chariot.[38]

The Hyksos must have been a worrying development for the Egyptians. We know of their existence only from the writings of the 4th century BC Graeco-Egyptian historian, Manetho. Almost none of Manetho's works are still extant, but his non-surviving works are quoted at some length by the 1st century AD Jewish chronicler, Flavius Josephus, and we have most of his. Some historians have taken Josephus at Manetho's word that there is a bloody Hyksos invasion of northern Egypt, in which the weakened pharaonic dynasty is routed and sent packing south to Thebes. However, the archaeological evidence appears to indicate that the Hyksos tribes gradually settle in the region of the Nile Delta and build up a rival population base, which finally gains control of Lower Egypt.

Phillips' research reveals a text currently displayed in the Brooklyn Museum dating from the reign of Sobekhotep III (13th Dynasty), which depicts 79 household servants for the pharaoh, of which 45 appear to be Hyksos, identifiable through their tell-tale Semite appearance and dress. This factor seems to indicate a protracted assimilation of the Hyksos rather than outright confrontation, though there must have been 'incidents'.[39] Obviously, Hyksos would not be in the majority serving in the king's household if they were an invading force. What is clear from the recovered history of Lower (northern) Egypt during the Hyksos period (15th Dynasty), Phillips maintains, is that these new foreign leaders viewed and styled themselves as pharaohs when they eventually seized power, and were viewed by their own as such. Traditional Egyptian pharaohs were to be admired and worshipped, and the Hyksos rulers were well up for adoration and worship. The true Egyptian faction was banished south to Thebes, where they muttered and plotted revenge on the Hyksos for the next two centuries.

In *Origins II – Holy War,* you may remember reading that when Joseph is sold into slavery by his brothers, he finds himself in Egypt

---

[37] Flavius Josephus famously mistranslated the Greek word as 'shepherd kings'. Egyptians named them *hega-khase*: 'rulers of foreign lands', and did their best to expunge all memory of them after driving them out of Lower Egypt centuries later.

[38] **Phillips, Graham** *Act of God,* Pan, 1998, pp.190-193

[39] Ibid, p.192

in the house of a royal official named Potiphar, head of Pharaoh's guard. The scriptural evidence indicates that Potiphar himself is an Egyptian, or maybe Hyksos settled long enough to be termed 'an Egyptian'. Notice that the Holy Spirit sees fit *twice* to repeat that Potiphar is an Egyptian (Gen 39:1-3). As we know by now, God never does anything for no reason. It's a *remez,* an invitation to dig deeper. One is tempted to ask, "Why bother mentioning that detail? Potiphar's obviously an Egyptian because he's in Egypt, and he's been given a position of great authority by Pharaoh himself, so obviously Potiphar's an Egyptian!" Then you ask, "OK, we're told twice that Potiphar is an Egyptian... *as opposed to what?"*

We also read that Potiphar is familiar in some way with the Hebrew God: **"And Joseph was brought down to Egypt; and Potiphar, an officer of Pharaoh, captain of the guard, an Egyptian, bought him of the hands of the Ishmeelites, which had brought him down thither. And the LORD was with Joseph and he was a prosperous man; and he was in the house of his master the Egyptian. And his master** [i.e. Potiphar] **saw that the LORD was with him and that the LORD made all that he did to prosper in his hand."** (Gen 39:1-3)

Phillips wonders whether Potiphar is a naturalised Hyksos. As scripture does not record a migration of Hebrews to Egypt prior to Joseph, it is unlikely that Potiphar, a native in Egypt, would have had any prior knowledge of the Hebrew Deity - or even care, and yet he appears to be familiar with Him. After Joseph interprets Pharaoh's dreams, the king releases him from prison and makes him vizier over Egypt. Genesis 41:38-40 reads: **And Pharaoh said unto his servants, "Can we find such a one as this, a man in whom the Spirit of God is?" And Pharaoh said unto Joseph, "Forasmuch as God hath shewed thee all this, there is none so discreet and wise as thou art: Thou shalt be over my house, and according unto thy word shall all my people be ruled: only in the throne will I be greater than thou."** (Gen 41:38-40)

It's an extraordinary, revealing detail. Here Pharaoh, in addition to Potiphar, recognises the Holy Spirit at work in Joseph's life! This is not the language of a pagan, polytheistic king ruling over a culture worshipping hundreds of gods. Notice Pharaoh does not say 'your God', just 'God'. If Pharaoh is Hyksos, Phillips contends, he would have first-hand knowledge of the Hebrew Deity (the Hyksos were part-Canaanite), and would have no qualms about promoting a Hebrew (even a recent jailbird) to an exalted post, so the theory is at least feasible. On the other hand, if Pharaoh is an Egyptian who has been worshipping Re and the Egyptian pantheon with no prior knowledge of YHWH, he has just committed an act of unprecedented insanity in the eyes of his people. He has promoted a foreign criminal to prime minister on the basis of a fanciful interpretation of a royal dream yet to be realised.[40]

Joseph's pharaoh is also so friendly to Joseph's family that he invites his new Hebrew vizier to find suitable herdsmen from among his own family, who are actually shepherds (despised by the Egyptians - Gen 46:34) to tend the royal herds! (Gen 47:6) To Phillips this is a problem. Even a cursory examination of pharaonic religion will reveal that bulls and calves were sacred to the king, often regarded as divine incarnations. How credible is it that an Egyptian monarch would have done such a thing? What is more remarkable, if this pharaoh is a true Egyptian, is that his people apparently have no problem with 'an alien criminal' being promoted over their heads and receiving orders to bow down before him (Gen 41:43). In other words, *we are told the 'Egyptian' people go along with it all.* None of this is explainable if the pharaoh in question is an Egyptian, says Phillips. All of it is if he is Hyksos. One of the last 16th Dynasty pharaohs is named Yakob-aam. Not very Egyptian-sounding.[41]

The curtain closed on *Origins II - Holy War* with Joseph's extraordinary story. Egypt is saved from famine and prospers mightily. In fact, the measures Joseph enforces to ride out the famine enable Pharaoh to end up *owning* most of Egypt (Gen 47:20). Jacob and the family emigrate from Canaan to Egypt for an emotional reunion. Can we identify this beneficent pharaoh? There are next to no decent records of the period due to the Hyksos being expunged from history by their subsequent New Kingdom Egyptian conquerors. Ancient history scholar George Rawlinson reckons a good candidate is Apophis (Apepi), one of the last of the 15th Dynasty Hyksos kings.

"There was an ancient tradition, that the king who made Joseph his prime minister, and committed into his hands the entire administration of Egypt, was Apepi. George the Syncellus says that the synchronism was accepted by all. It is clear that Joseph's arrival did not fall, like Abraham's, into the period of the Old Empire, since under Joseph, horses and

---

40 Phillips, Graham, *Act of God,* op. cit., "The Children of Israel", p.194

41 **Clayton, P A** *Chronicle of the Pharaohs,* London, 1994

chariots are in use, as well as wagons or carts, all of which were unknown till after the Hyksos invasion. It is also more natural that Joseph, a foreigner, should have been advanced by a foreign king than by a native one, and the favour shown to his brethren, who were shepherds (Gen. xlvi. 32), is consonant at any rate with the tradition that it was a 'Shepherd King' who held the throne at the time of their arrival. A priest of Heliopolis, moreover, would scarcely have given Joseph his daughter in marriage unless at a time when the priesthood was in a state of depression. Add to this that the pharaoh of Joseph is evidently resident in Lower Egypt, not at Thebes, which was the seat of government for many hundred years both before and after the Hyksos rule.

"If, however, we are to place Joseph under one of the 'Shepherd Kings', there can be no reason why we should not accept the tradition which connects him with Apepi. Apepi was dominant over the whole of Egypt, as Joseph's pharaoh seems to have been. He acknowledged a single god, as did that monarch (Gen. 41:38-39). He was a thoroughly Egyptianized king. He had a council of learned scribes, a magnificent court, and a peaceful reign until towards its close. His residence was in the Delta, either at Tanis or Auaris [Avaris]. He was a prince of a strong will, firm and determined; one who did not shrink from initiating great changes, and who carried out his resolves in a somewhat arbitrary way. The arguments in favour of his identity with Joseph's master are, perhaps, not wholly conclusive; but they raise a presumption, which may well incline us, with most modern historians of Egypt, to assign the touching story of Joseph to the reign of the last of the Shepherds." [42]

The pharaoh who knew Joseph not

And Joseph died, and all his brethren, and all that generation. And the children of Israel were fruitful, and increased abundantly, and multiplied, and waxed exceeding mighty; and the land was filled with them.

Now there arose up a new king over Egypt, which knew not Joseph. And he said unto his people:

"Behold, the people of the children of Israel are more and mightier than we. Come on, let us deal wisely with them, lest they multiply, and it come to pass, that, when there falleth out any war, they join also unto our enemies, and fight against us, and so get them up out of the land."

---

[42] **Rawlinson, G** *Ancient Egypt,* http://en.wikisource.org/wiki/Ancient_Egypt_(Rawlinson)/The_Great_Invasion

Therefore they did set over them taskmasters to afflict them with their burdens. And they built for Pharaoh treasure cities, Pithom and Raamses. But the more they afflicted them, the more they multiplied and grew. And they were grieved because of the children of Israel (Exo 1:6-12).

Something has happened to change the Hebrews' rosy existence. A new pharaoh has come to power. In the New Testament (NT), Stephen tellingly describes this event: **"Till another king arose, which knew not Joseph"** (Acts 7:18). Some time has evidently passed since Joseph's spectacular saga, and a change of dynasty is the most rational explanation for why the new king knows neither of Joseph, nor what he did to save Egypt. In Greek, there are two words for 'another' that can be used in this context: *allos* and *heteros.* Ancient Greek's extraordinary specificity as a language gives us a clue as to what occurred. *Allos* is used to mean another of the same kind. *Heteros* is used to describe another of a different kind. *Heteros* is used here by Stephen before numerous Jewish scholars in the Sanhedrin, who do not correct him, implying that it is common knowledge among the Jews of the 1st century that this new pharaoh was a completely different ball of wax, i.e. a change of dynasty. So what happened?

The true Egyptian princes to the south at Thebes have not been idle during their expulsion from Lower Egypt. They breed horses and copy the Hyksos compound bow and chariot before embarking on a series of campaigns to re-take the north.[43] Seqenenre II is the first 17th Dynasty Theban king to revolt against the north, probably, according to the following inscription, due to punitive Hyksos taxation. His attack fails and Seqenenre is evidently hacked to death. His mummified body was discovered in 1881 displaying sword-wounds to the head and neck.[44] Egyptologist and weapons expert Gary Shaw concludes, after a close study of the king's wounds:

"…that the most likely cause of Seqenenre's death is ceremonial execution at the hands of an enemy commander, following a Theban defeat on the battlefield." [45]

---

[43] Phillips, Graham, *Act of God,* op. cit., p.196; **Yadin, Y** *The Art of Warfare in Biblical Lands in the Light of Archaeological Discovery,* London: 1963

[44] **Wilson, Ian** *The Exodus Enigma,* London, 1985, p.73. See also documentary at www.museumsecrets.tv/dossier.php?o=80

[45] **Shaw, Garry J** "The Death of King Seqenenre Tao", *Journal of the American Research Center in Egypt,* 2009, p.45

His son and successor Pharaoh Kamose launches a full-on, furious assault against the northern 'Asiatics' who just murdered his father. Kamose's frustration as a true Egyptian is evident in an inscription on the Carnarvon Tablet I:

"Let me understand what this strength of mine is for! [One] prince is in Avaris [the Hyksos capital in the Nile Delta], another is in Ethiopia,[46] and [here] I sit associated with an Asiatic [Hyksos] and a Negro! Each man has his slice of this Egypt, dividing up the land with me.... No man can settle down when despoiled by the taxes of the Asiatics. I will grapple with him, that I may rip open his belly! My wish is to save Egypt and to smite the Asiatic!"

Kamose holds his own against his enemy's superior strength and finally Ahmose overcomes the Hyksos dynasty, unites Egypt once more, and becomes the first 18th Dynasty pharaoh to rule over a unified Egypt (c. 1570 BC). After reunification, we see successive Egyptian pharaohs doing all possible to expunge the memory of the 15th Dynasty Hyksos pharaohs in what was evidently regarded as a shameful period in Egyptian history. The Hyksos kings do not appear in any surviving kings' lists. We only know of them through the Egyptian priest and chronicler, Manetho, via the Jewish writer, Josephus, and through fragments of extant *stelae* and inscriptions on tombs.

Why don't we know the pharaohs' names?

Some researchers maintain that this retaking of the north by the Theban princes to re-establish the true Egyptian line may also account for two important details of the Biblical sojourn of Israel in Egypt: firstly, why we don't know the identity of the Joseph-era pharaoh ('he was excised from the record by his successors'), and secondly, why there later arose a pharaoh 'who knew Joseph not', who began the oppression of the Israelites, the name of whom has not come down to us either.

It is a bothersome detail seized upon by those who maintain not only that Moses could not have authored the Torah for this reason alone, but that he didn't even exist, and the whole Joseph-Moses-

---

[46] Egypt's Nubian (Ethiopian) province to the south takes full advantage of the Hyksos usurping the north to revolt and crush the Theben princes in between. However, after Ahmose I sacks Avaris, he sails southward to Khenti-hen-nefer to destroy the Nubian nomads.

Exodus saga is complete fiction. You can see their point: Moses knew the Exodus pharaoh *personally;* would have known the previous oppression pharaoh *personally;* would have known his stepmother, 'Pharaoh's daughter', *personally;* would have known the name of the genocidal pharaoh who ordered the killing of the Hebrew babies, and lived long enough to know him *personally;* and there's no reason to suspect that Moses would have been ignorant of the benevolent pharaoh of Joseph's era centuries before, faithfully passed down the Hebrew tribal generations to Moses' own time. So the question remains: If Moses wrote the Torah, and he did,[47] why didn't he include the pharaohs' praenomens (i.e. Sesostris, Tuthmosis, Amenhotep, etc.)?

Some apologetics ministries dismiss the matter by declaring that the pharaohs went unnamed by Moses for theological reasons in order to humble them; to register disapproval for their actions, especially in the matter of the Exodus king denying YHWH's existence in Exo 5:2. Yet this doesn't wash with Joseph's beneficent pharaoh, who should have been accorded all Biblical honours by reciprocal reasoning. Besides, in later historical books, Pharaoh Shishak is mentioned seven times[48] (and never merely as 'Pharaoh'), and Pharaoh Necho gets his named plugged nine times.[49]

Bible scholar Doug Petrovich solves the mystery:

"If Moses did not omit Pharaoh's personal name for theological reasons, then why did he omit it? The answer is found in the historical development of monarchial terms. The dynastic title 'pharaoh' derives from the word that literally means 'great house'. During Egypt's Old Kingdom (ca. 2715–2170 BC), the word was used of the royal palace. Not until sometime during the middle of the 18th Dynasty, slightly before the reign of Thutmose III (ca. 1506–1452 BC), the father of Amenhotep II, was it used as an epithet for the Egyptian monarch. However, the standard practice of Thutmose III's time was to leave enemy kings unnamed on official records [emphasis mine]. The campaign of Thutmose III against a rebellious coalition at Megiddo, instigated by the Empire of Mitanni, was fomented by the King of

[47] Exo 17:14; 24:4,7; 34:27; Josh 8:32; 23:6; 1 Kings 2:3; 2 Kings 14:6. Jesus also authenticated Moses, not only as the scribe who took down the Law, but also the wider authorship of the Pentateuch: Matt 8:4; 19:7,8; 23:2; Mark 1:44; 7:10; 10:3–5; 12:26; Luke 5:14; 16:29–31; 20:37; 24:27, 44; FG 3:14; 5:39,45-47; 6:32; 7:19, 22,23

[48] 1 Kings 11:40, 14:25; 2 Chr 12:2, 5 (x2), 7,9

[49] 2 Kings 23:29, 33, 34, 35; 2 Chr 35:20, 21, 22; 36:4; and Jer 46:2

Kadesh (on the Orontes River), who—in The Annals of Thutmose III—merely was called, "that wretched enemy of Kadesh." Moreover, when Egyptian scribes listed the booty that was confiscated after the Battle of Megiddo, they did not name the opposing king whose possessions the Egyptians plundered, referring to him only as "the prince," or "the Prince of Megiddo."

The Amada Stele of Amenhotep II, which boasts of the king's successful battles against seven Syrian tribes of Takhsi, identifies these foreign rulers only as "seven chieftains," whose names are all left unrecorded. In the Memphis Stele of Amenhotep II, reference is made to his campaigns in Edom, Canaan, and Syria. All of the foreign kings whom he defeated, deposed, or killed also went unnamed in this victory stele. Mention was even made of the chieftains of Naharin (the land to the east of the Euphrates River), Khatti (the Hittites), and Babylon. Despite the prominence of these kings, they nonetheless remain anonymous as well….

Therefore, the exodus-pharaoh's name was neither omitted for theological reasons, nor to discourage the curiosity of modern historians who desire to identify him. Instead, the exodus-pharaoh's throne-name is absent for one reason alone: a skilled writer named Moses, born in Egypt and trained as a prince in all of the ways of the royal court of Egypt (Acts 7:22), followed the standard practice of his day by leaving unnamed the foreign monarch who assumed the role of a dreaded enemy of his own nation, in this case Israel."[50]

There's another pharaoh mentioned in scripture who has attracted wide debate among scholars; namely, the pharaoh who commenced the oppression of the Israelites after Joseph's golden era.

Isaiah 52:4 reads: **For thus saith the Lord GOD, "My people went down aforetime into Egypt to sojourn there; and the Assyrian oppressed them without cause."**

This is an interesting verse for several reasons. It has been interpreted by many expositors to mean that an Assyrian was the pharaoh of the Exodus, but that is not what the verse says. A Hyksos pharaoh for the Exodus would not accord with the most popular date for Moses' famous grandstand performance (1446 BC), not least due to the chronology implied by 1 Kings 6:1. Egyptologist Doug Petrovich also favours this date for another reason:

---

[50] www.biblearchaeology.org/post/2010/02/04/Amenhotep-II-and-the-Historicity-of-the-Exodus-Pharaoh.aspx#Article

"A compelling argument for choosing 1446 BC [for the Exodus] is that the Jubilee cycles agree with this date exactly, yet are completely independent of the 479+ years of 1 Kings 6:1. The Jubilee dates are precise only if the priests began counting years when they entered the land in 1406 BC (cf. Lev. 25:2–10)." [51]

We can infer several things from the above Isaiah passage:

- An Assyrian pharaoh commenced the oppression of the Hebrews
- God is indignant that this Assyrian had no valid reason for oppressing His people. The Egyptians certainly would have had good reason, having been expelled from Lower Egypt

God's vexation only makes sense if this Assyrian pharaoh indeed oppressed the Hebrews without cause. This strongly suggests that an Assyrian pharaoh from the Hyksos period develops a gripe with the Hebrews, who have dominated the political scene since Joseph's exemplary salvation of the nation. The Assyrian and his faction gain power over the Hebrews and begin oppressing them. From Biblical dating, this appears to occur quite soon after the Joseph/pharaoh saga, making the Assyrian's victimisation of the Hebrews even more reprehensible in God's eyes.

While the implication in Stephen's passage in Acts 7:18 (*allos/heteros*) is that the king who initiates the lengthy oppression of the Hebrews is not of the royal caste with which Joseph was familiar, he could still be an Assyrian Hyksos pharaoh (14th - 16th Dynasty)[52] antagonistic towards the Hebrews. If the Jews had been the most powerful contingent within the coalition following Joseph's rule (and it seems reasonable to assume so), an Assyrian Hyksos pharaoh may well have commenced the Hebrew oppression after gaining power over them. The Hebrews suffer for many years before the Exodus, so simple deduction would conclude that an Assyrian pharaoh, while mentioned by God in Isaiah as the one who commences the Hebrew oppression, *is not the famous Egyptian pharaoh of the Exodus!* We can also deduce this because few pharaohs survived longer than forty

[51] Ibid.

[52] Experts are divided as to whether the obscure 16th Dynasty pharaohs described by the Egyptian historian Manetho were Hyksos, vassals of the Hyksos, or Theban (Egyptian). The fact that the Second Intermediate Period is so poorly attested in archaeology would indicate that later Egyptian expungement of the evidence was carried out: implying, for instance, that the 13th, 14th, 15th and even 16th Dynasties were all Hyksos or Hyksos-influenced.

years on the throne, and the Israelites were not oppressed for a mere forty years; their troubles continued for centuries. Moreover, following the eventual defeat and expulsion of the Hyksos from Lower Egypt by Ahmose I, all Egypt is unified, the 'true' pharaohs are back, the New Kingdom commences, and the 18th Dynasty pharaohs are more than happy to continue the oppression of the Israelites who fall into their hands: a ready slave-force to build the dream that will become Egypt's glorious New Kingdom.

Placing Moses in history

So if we can reasonably place Joseph in the Hyksos era, what about Moses? Everyone has their pet Exodus pharaoh, and I am no exception, but let us see if history and science can help out, along with some intriguing giveaways in the Bible by Moses himself. Let's examine the following four verses:

And He [God] **said unto Abram, "Know of a surety that thy seed shall be a stranger in <u>a land</u>** [singular] **that is not theirs, and shall serve them; and they shall afflict them four hundred years. And also <u>that nation</u>** [i.e. a singular, specific and unified nation]**, whom they shall serve, will I judge: and afterward shall they come out with great substance** (Gen 15:13-14).

And it came to pass at the end of the four hundred and thirty years, even the selfsame day it came to pass, that all the hosts of the LORD went out from the land of Egypt (Exo 12:41).

And it came to pass in the four hundred and eightieth year after the children of Israel were come out of the land of Egypt, in the fourth year of Solomon's reign over Israel, in the month Zif, which is the second month, that he began to build the house of the LORD (1 Kings 6:1)

I wish to spare the more zealous readers days, if not weeks, of laborious Exodus research by summarising the above passages. Scholars put themselves through strictures in an attempt to bend dates to suit pet theories, favourite pharaohs, and sympathetic archaeological dating. Biases come into play in a major way. Inconvenient truths are omitted from otherwise scholarly works. On the one hand, religious scholars attempt to get everything to fit the Biblical timeframe, and are accused of doing violence to 'established history' and secular archaeological interpretations (a movable feast in Egyptology). On the other hand, secular or atheist commentators write reams on how the Bible is clearly in error as God cannot make up His mind whether Israel is in bondage for 400 or 430 years. What a mess. And a mess generally caused by people who do not read the text.

- Read the first passage again. It is obvious from Gen 15:13-14 that God Himself is predicting that Abram's people will serve a single nation,[53] and that this nation later turns out to be Egypt, for the Hebrews do indeed quit the land of the pharaohs loaded with loot (Exo 12:35-36). And God indeed judges Pharaoh and his gods in a mighty way with the plagues.
- In the second passage, it's hard to get around the fact that the Bible teaches a highly specific period for Israel's sojourn in Egypt (**even the selfsame day,** i.e. *to the very day*), and that this sojourn period refers to Egypt only and is not split fifty/fifty with Canaan, as some scholar argue.
- In the third passage, the Holy Spirit is again overly specific in describing the period between the Exodus and the commencement of the First Temple construction under King Solomon. The period given is 480 years, and we're supposed to take it at face value. Many scholars either ignore or allegorise this period because it does to death Ramesses II as their pet Exodus pharaoh (Ridley Scott take note). The date for Solomon's reign is more or less agreed as 970–931 BC, the fourth year being 967-976 BC. That gives us the 1446 BC date for the Exodus.

Interestingly, that also gives us Amenhotep II for the Exodus pharaoh, and he certainly does some interesting things. There could be an intriguing confirmation of this pharaoh's participation in two passages of Exodus 2:23 and 4:19:

And it came to pass in process of time, that the king of Egypt died: and the children of Israel sighed by reason of the bondage, and they cried, and their cry came up unto God by reason of the bondage. (Exo 2:23)

And the LORD said unto Moses in Midian, "Go, return into Egypt: for all the men are dead which sought thy life." (Exo 4:19)

---

[53] i.e. Egypt, not Canaan too! Some scholars state that the 430 years can be broken down as 215 years served in Canaan and 215 served in Egypt. The Bible also makes clear that Canaan was never a unified nation until it became known as 'Israel' under King Saul.

Q: How long has Moses been on the run in Midian from a hostile pharaoh?

A: 40 years (*cf.* Exo 7:7; Acts 7:23,30).

Q: Why does Moses flee?

A: He murders an Egyptian, so Pharaoh seeks to kill Moses (Exo 2:15).

The context of the first passage in Exo 2:23 implies that this is the same king of Egypt who sought to kill Moses eight verses earlier in Exo 2:15. I am therefore intrigued whether the 40 years in Midian were required for Moses to outlive this pharaoh. If so, there are only two pharaohs within three hundred years of our period who live longer than 40 years: Tuthmosis III and Ramesses II. Ramesses II is far too late to be Biblically viable. Tuthmosis III, on the other hand, *dies in 1452 BC, six years before the putative date for the Exodus.*

The late-date Exodus pharaoh, Ramesses II (1279-1213 BC), is popular with scholars as Moses' nemesis, not least because Exodus 1:11 states that the Jewish workforce built supply cities named Pithom and Raamses, and no trace of the name Raamses or Ramesses is found prior to that. This is flimsy supposition, contested by many, since the name Ramesses simply means 'son of Ra', and was a common cognomen for pharaohs dating from the 5th Dynasty. 'Raamses' may well have started out as a geographical location; it is referred to as such in Gen 47:11 and Num 33:3-5. The time of Ramesses II does not accord with 1 Kings 6:1, nor accounts for the period of the Judges (Judg 11:26). Tuthmosis III is therefore suitable as candidate for the 'oppression pharaoh' immediately prior to the Exodus, and he has every reason to persecute Moses, as we will see. Tuthmosis III's death makes Moses' return to Egypt from Midian possible in order to free his people. And when he gets back to Egypt, a young, arrogant Amenhotep II has ascended the throne in his father's place to wear the Two Crowns of a united Egypt. The Exodus commences when Moses is 80 years of age, placing the prophet's birth around 1526 BC. It is therefore here that our search for the historical Moses should begin.

MOSES – THE EARLY YEARS
(1526-1486 BC)

Without preamble, the book of Exodus throws us into the Moses narrative:

Now these are the names of the children of Israel, which came into Egypt; every man and his household came with Jacob. Reuben, Simeon, Levi, and Judah, Issachar, Zebulun, and Benjamin, Dan, and Naphtali, Gad, and Asher. And all the souls that came out of the loins of Jacob were seventy souls: for Joseph was in Egypt already. And Joseph died, and all his brethren, and all that generation. And the children of Israel were fruitful, and increased abundantly, and multiplied, and waxed exceeding mighty; and the land was filled with them.

Now there arose up a new king over Egypt, which knew not Joseph. And he said unto his people, "Behold, the people of the children of Israel are more and mightier than we: Come on, let us deal wisely with them; lest they multiply, and it come to pass, that, when there falleth out any war, they join also unto our enemies, and fight against us, and so get them up out of the land."

Therefore they did set over them taskmasters to afflict them with their burdens. And they [the Israelites] **built for Pharaoh treasure cities, Pithom and Raamses. But the more they afflicted them, the more they multiplied and grew. And they** [the Egyptians] **were grieved because of the children of Israel.** (Exo 1:1-12)

This new king does not know who Joseph was. It is reasonable to suspect that not only has a significant period of time passed since Joseph's life (to build up the Hebrew population for the pharaoh's comment to make sense), but also that, as covered in the previous chapter, the new pharaoh's dynasty is completely different from the one familiar with Joseph's appointment to vizier.[54] At the time of Joseph, this new pharaoh's forebears would have been located to the south around Thebes, and would not know, remember or care how Joseph saved the north from famine, especially if this event was several centuries in the past. Among the Hyksos though, Joseph's deeds would still be remembered through oral tradition.

---

[54] This 'oppression' pharaoh is different from the Assyrian pharaoh God mentions in Isa 52:4, who, centuries before, initiated hostilities against the Hebrews after Joseph's golden period.

Graham Phillips makes an interesting observation. This new pharaoh declares that it is **the people of the children of Israel** who are becoming mightier than them. He is implying that the children of Israel are part of a *larger people,* but that the former are a controlling part of this alliance. **The people of the children of Israel** is a perfect phrase to describe the Hyksos, within which the Hebrew faction seems sufficiently powerful to field a Hyksos pharaoh of their own at one point with the Semitic name of Yakob-aam. One may reasonably suppose that the Hebrews originally became powerful within the Hyksos alliance because of Joseph's actions in saving Egypt from the famine.

This new oppression pharaoh's concern in Exo 1:10 above is that, in the event of war, the multitude of Hebrews will join his enemies and fight against him. Phillips points out that the word for 'also' in the passage above has been translated from the Hebrew *gam* (Strongs 1571), which often means 'again'. So this verse may equally read, **"...let us deal wisely with them; lest they multiply, and it come to pass that, when there falleth out any war, they join <u>again</u> unto our enemies, and fight against us...."** In other words, this pharaoh may well be voicing his concern that the Hyksos could come against the Egyptians again, *as they did before,* and that he that fears the children of Israel will play a key part in the Egyptians' defeat, *as they did before.* As mentioned, the original defeat and expulsion of the Egyptians by the Hyksos came about through the latter's superior weapons and numbers. Since then, the Egyptians have solved the technology problem and regained control over Lower Egypt, but are still intimidated by the numbers.

As for Pharaoh's '**let us deal wisely with them** [the Israelites]', beware the wisdom of men! Chuck Missler points out that before the first chapter of Exodus is even over, 'wise' Pharaoh will have provided luxurious board, lodging, and a first-class education for the very person who will later ravage his nation, its gods and military![55] The apostle Paul remarks:

For the wisdom of this world is foolishness with God. For it is written, <u>He taketh the wise in their own craftiness</u>. (1 Cor 3:19)

For it is written, I will destroy the wisdom of the wise, and will bring to nothing the understanding of the prudent. (1 Cor 1:19)

Now we learn of Pharaoh's 'wise' population control strategy:

---

[55] **Missler, Chuck,** *The Exodus Notes,* www.khouse.org, p.10

And the king of Egypt spake to the Hebrew midwives, <u>of which the name of the one was Shiphrah ['glisten'], and the name of the other Puah ['glitter']</u>: And he said, "When ye do the office of a midwife to the Hebrew women, and see them upon the stools; if it be a son, then ye shall kill him: but if it be a daughter, then she shall live."

But the midwives feared God, and did not as the king of Egypt commanded them, but saved the men children alive. And the king of Egypt called for the midwives, and said unto them, "Why have ye done this thing, and have saved the men children alive?"

And the midwives said unto Pharaoh, "Because the Hebrew women are not as the Egyptian women; for they are lively, and are delivered ere [before] **the midwives come in unto them."**

Therefore God dealt well with the midwives: and the people multiplied, and waxed very mighty. (Exo 1:15-20)

A couple of points here:

A number of times during Jewish history, *ha-Satan* attempts to wipe out the Jewish race to thwart the promise of the Seed of the Woman, by whom the serpent (*nachash*) shall be judged (Gen 3:15). God employs two canny midwives to head off this particular genocide, though not without infant casualties. Warren Wiersbe comments:

> "This is the first instance in Scripture of what today we call 'civil disobedience', refusing to obey an evil law because of a higher good. Scriptures like Matthew 20:21-25, Romans 13 and 1 Peter 2:13 admonish Christians to obey human authorities, but Romans 13:5 reminds us that our obedience must not violate our conscience. When the laws of God are contrary to the laws of man, then 'we ought to obey God rather than men' (Acts 5:29)."[56]

The fact that Pharaoh or Pharaoh's messengers are able to summon and converse with the Goshen-based Hebrew midwives without difficulty indicates that this pharaoh is based at Memphis, not a two- to three-week journey south at the traditional capital of Thebes. This is more supporting evidence that Tuthmosis I is the pharaoh in question, not only because of the firmed-up chronology, but also because Tuth I is famous for having moved the Egyptian court from Thebes to Memphis and constructed an elaborate palace there. Until the time of Pharaoh Akhenaten, pharaohs, their regents,

---

[56] Wiersbe, Warren, *The Wiersbe Bible Commentary,* op. cit., p.149

and the entire military headquarters of Egypt will work out of Memphis and launch numerous expeditions from this Lower Egypt centre of military operations. This accords with the logistics we will examine later when another pharaoh rides out with his army after the departing Israelites, and why this king is relatively local to Goshen so Moses can later drop in for a chat.[57]

Notice that two of the Hebrew midwives are singled out by name. Why would the Holy Spirit register this obscure detail? Of course, to honour their risking death to save the Hebrew children and thus the Jewish race from obscurity. But also: two is the number of witness and will be used under Hebrew law to determine guilt or innocence. Notice the proviso God later gives to Moses:

At the mouth of two witnesses, or three witnesses, shall he that is worthy of death be put to death; but at the mouth of one witness he shall not be put to death. (Deut 17:6)

And:

One witness shall not rise up against a man for any iniquity, or for any sin, in any sin that he sinneth: at the mouth of two witnesses, or at the mouth of three witnesses, shall the matter be established. (Deut 19:15)

Notice that this principle is even established twice! God always provides two witnesses for what will follow, in the same way that Moses and his elder brother Aaron will be used before Pharaoh to witness the latter's speech, actions and guilt. Two witnesses will be around in the end times (Rev 11) to witness the depravities of the Antichrist, False Prophet and their 'earth dwellers' in the lead-up to Christ's judgment of Planet Earth. Two witnesses - Moses and Elijah - are at 'the holy mount' to witness the astonishing sight of Christ's transfiguration, as well as Peter, James and John.[58] Paul confirms the witness theme in 2 Cor 13:1: **"In the mouth of two or three witnesses shall every word be established"**, which is always applied to Biblical hermeneutics. The Bible is thus self-interpreting. For instance, a difficult theme, doctrine or passage will be explained and clarified elsewhere in the Bible to inform and educate, as well as refute heresies and 'one-verse theology'.

This new oppression pharaoh instructs the Hebrew midwives to kill any male Israelite children they deliver. This is an odd population

---

[57] **Grimal, N** *A History of Ancient Egypt,* translated by Ian Shaw, Oxford, UK, Blackwell, 1992, p.220

[58] Matt 17:1–9; Mark 9:2-8; Luke 9:28–36; 2 Pet 1:16–18

strategy. It would make more sense to kill the girls, since it was their fertility that gave rise to the population explosion that was spooking Pharaoh. Michal Hunt gives an intriguing answer:

"Since the time of Joseph, all Egyptian land belonged to the ruling Pharaoh except the land controlled by the Egyptian priests and the land owned by the Israelites [Gen 47:20-27]. If there were no men for Israelite girls to marry, they would marry Egyptians and without male heirs, the Egyptians would inherit the property owned by the Israelite families, thus effectively forcing the Israelites to be assimilated into Egyptian society, and at the same time ending Israelite control over the fertile Delta region of Goshen."[59]

The Hebrew women disobey Pharaoh, and intriguingly in Exo 1:19 draw a parallel between Hebrew birthing methods and those of the Egyptians. This is further evidence that the pharaoh they are addressing is not a Semite/Hyksos but a true Egyptian, confirming once more that by Exodus 1, the Hyksos have already been removed from power by a new Egyptian dynasty, which views the Israelites as having been the author of its woes for the past two centuries. This is a powerful incentive for the Egyptian 18th Dynasty to keep the Hebrews in bondage and further afflict them, and this is precisely what we see this pharaoh doing (Exo 1:11-14).

The genocidal pharaoh

Can we identify this oppression king? Permit me to save you a lot of research time by summarising what I have found: no-one knows for certain who this pharaoh is, no matter what they tell you, due to the aforementioned issues with dating methods, interpreting archaeological finds, personal biases, and so on. There is, however, an excellent candidate who fits the parameters. If we take the Exodus date of 1446 BC (derived from 1 Kings 6:1 in the previous chapter); acknowledge that the Bible says that Moses was 80 (Exo 7:7) when he returned from Midian to confront the new pharaoh after the previous one dies (Exo 2:23); the most likely pharaoh for the slaying of the Hebrew male children is a very paranoid Tuthmosis I (1529–1516 BC), who has an interesting daughter with a name that sounds like a sneeze. *Knowing the Bible* writes:

---

[59] www.agapebiblestudy.com/exodus/Exodus_Lesson_1.htm

"The pharaoh in Ex.1:22 responsible for the genocide of the Hebrew baby boys is most likely Tuthmosis I, which matches what we know of his character from Egyptian records. Pharaoh's daughter in Ex. 2:5-10 was most likely Hatshepsut, who would later become Pharaoh herself. Her power and influence would explain why Moses had a reasonable amount of security among those of the ruling Egyptian dynasty despite being a Hebrew."[60]

Egyptologist and Biblical scholar Doug Petrovich agrees:

"All of the evidence points to Hatshepsut as the most likely candidate for Moses' stepmother, for several reasons: (1) Hatshepsut's blood-sister, Princess Akhbetneferu [Nefrubity], was the only other daughter whom Queen Ahmose is known to have borne, but her death in infancy eliminates her candidacy. (2) Lady Mutnofret bore several sons to Thutmose I before she died, but there is no indication that she ever bore him any daughters. (3) The text of Exo 2:10 states that after "the child [Moses] grew, she [his mother] brought him to Pharaoh's daughter, and he became her son." Therefore, Moses' Egyptian stepmother obviously lived a considerable length of time *after* she retrieved him from the Nile, increasing the likelihood that an account of this 'Daughter of Pharaoh' (Exod 2:5) would be documented and preserved somewhere in the Egyptians' detailed records, a qualification true of Hatshepsut alone."[61]

Let's back up for a moment and frame the beginning of Moses' life to get our bearings. The 18th Dynasty commences with the expulsion of the hated Hyksos from Lower Egypt. Scholars dub the period that follows 'The New Kingdom'. Recently unified Egypt is back with a vengeance, characterised by strong kings, national discipline, hard work, painstaking organisation, mammoth building projects, unity and military triumphs. Ahmose I (1570–1546 BC), conqueror of the Hyksos, founds the 18th Dynasty which will propel Egypt into her unique golden age of military, cultural and economic glory. His son and successor is Amenhotep I (1546-1529 BC), who twice quells an uprising by the Libyans to the west, thwarting their attempts to invade the Delta. During his 17-year reign, Amenhotep I is also responsible for elaborate complexes at the Karnak Temple in Thebes. But Amenhotep I dies without an heir, so his commander-in-

[60] www.knowingthebible.net/the-pharaohs-of-the-exodus

[61] www.biblearchaeology.org/post/2010/02/04/Amenhotep-II-and-the-Historicity-of-the-Exodus-Pharaoh.aspx#Article

chief, Djehutymes, who is married to the pharaoh's sister, comes to power as Tuthmosis I in 1526 BC.

Tuthmosis I is a true warrior in every sense of the word. He is sensitive to the shameful period his nation endured for two centuries due to the over-population of Asiatic opportunists. Raised a professional soldier from common stock,[62] Tuthmosis wastes little time deploying his military prowess without restraint. He marches his army south beyond the Third Cataract into Nubia and slays the Nubian king in hand-to-hand combat, returning with the chief's body stuck on the prow of his ship.

Not content with his conquest of Nubia, Tuthmosis I turns his attention to the continued destruction of the Hyksos princes, by this time hanging out with the remnants of their armies among the Baal-worshipers of Carchemish, northern Syria. Tuthmosis I continually brings them to battle, slaughtering their armies and pushing the Egyptian military machine all the way to the Euphrates, which he claims as his empire's eastern border. The *Encyclopaedia Britannica* is impressed:

"In his second year Tuthmosis led a river-borne expedition deep into Nubia, beyond his predecessor's frontier. As shown by inscriptions carved along the way, he thrust past the Fourth Nile Cataract and set up a new boundary at Kurgus. The venture is attested by the biographies of two Upper Egyptians who were among the forces that made up the campaign. One reason for the deep thrust into Nubia was the land's rich gold deposits, which were intensely exploited during the 18th dynasty (1539–1292 BC). Another motivation was the fact that a hostile Kushite kingdom, centred near the Third Cataract, had seriously menaced Egypt during the 17th dynasty (c. 1630–1540 BCE)." [63]

Tuthmosis I is a don't-mess-with-me king; a ruthless hard-man; a blue-knuckled backstreet brawler; a military-trained, professional, "you talkin' to me?" flogged-up-the-ranks, xenophobic skullcracking commoner. If you were pharaoh and had a problem, you called this one, and Amenhotep I did so repeatedly, and felt the Two Kingdoms would be safe in those gashed and gnarled hands after his own passing. In the course of time, Djehutymes becomes king and personal representative of the gods, ruler of the known world with the Two Crowns of a united Egypt on his furrowed brow. As Pharaoh

---

[62] His mother's name comes down to us as Senseneb.

[63] www.britannica.com/EBchecked/topic/594485/Tuthmosis-I

Tuthmosis I, Djehutymes has no intention of letting things slip on his watch.

On the family side, Tuthmosis has two wives: the aforementioned Queen Ahmose, whom he married while her brother, Pharaoh Amenhotep I, was still alive, and a secondary wife, Mutnofret. Both wives are recognised as royals, but scholars are divided as to Mutnofret's origins; she could even have been Queen Ahmose's younger sister.[64]

The children are interesting: Pharaoh Tuthmosis I's firstborn heir by Queen Ahmose is Amenmose, who is trained up as a military commander just like Dad, who accords Amenmose the awesome title of 'Great Overseer of Soldiers', and bases him at the new military operations centre at Memphis (12 miles south of modern-day Cairo). Alas, Crown Prince Amenmose predeceases his father - we're not told how. Tuthmosis has three other children by Queen Ahmose: a second son, Wadjmose, and two daughters, Hatshepsut ('Foremost of Noblewomen') and Nefrubity. Wadjmose also dies before his father, and Nefrubity dies as a toddler, leaving Hatshepsut the sole surviving heir by Queen Ahmose. One other child is produced by the secondary wife, Mutnofret, and this son later becomes Tuthmosis II. Sensing there will be trouble between stepson and a very wilful daughter after his death, Pharaoh Tuthmosis I marries Tuthmosis to Hatshepsut, and appoints Tuthmosis II as his heir to the throne of Two Lands.[65]

The river saga

I believe Tuthmosis I to be the pharaoh paranoid enough to issue an edict that all male newborns among the Hebrews be cast into the Nile to regulate the burgeoning population of slaves. The date of Tuth I's accession fits and also explains why Aaron, Moses' elder brother, was not victimised in the subsequent genocide: Aaron was three years older than Moses (Exo 7:7) and the kill order was given after he was born. The uncompromising slaughter edict certainly fits what we know of how this tough, uncompromising commander got things done. Tuthmosis has every reason to fear a resurgence of immigrants taking over the realm, just as they did before:

---

[64] Not much is known of her, though it is evident that Mutnofret was of royal blood, as an inscription at Karnak calls her 'the King's Daughter'.

[65] **Hayes, William C** *Egypt: Internal Affairs from Tuthmosis I to the Death of Amenophis III*, Part 1, Cambridge University Press, London, 1962, pp.5-8

And Pharaoh charged all his people, saying, "Every son that is born ye shall cast into the river, and every daughter ye shall save alive."

And there went a man of the house of Levi, and took to wife a daughter of Levi. And the woman conceived, and bare a son: and when she saw him that he was a goodly child, she hid him three months.

And when she could not longer hide him, she [Moses's mother, Jochebed] **took for him an ark of bulrushes, and daubed it with slime and with pitch, and put the child therein; and she laid it in the flags by the river's brink. And his** [Moses's] **sister** [Miriam?] **stood afar off to witness what would be done to him. And the daughter of Pharaoh** [note definite article, only one daughter] **came down to wash herself at the river; and her maidens walked along by the river's side; and when she saw the ark among the flags, she sent her maid to fetch it. And when she had opened it, she saw the child: and, behold, the babe wept. And she had compassion on him, and said, "This is one of the Hebrews' children."** (Exo 1:22-2:6).

Pharaoh makes every Egyptian citizen an agent of the state. Everyone is to be on the lookout for male Hebrew children. When found, they are to be thrown into the Nile. The daughters are to be saved. We are not told the names of Moses' parents until Exodus 6:20, but courageous they certainly are:

And Amram took him Jochebed his father's sister to wife; and she bare him Aaron and Moses: and the years of the life of Amram were an hundred and thirty and seven years.[66]

The Moses-in-the-bulrushes story has unmissable overtones of Noah's deliverance and new beginning. I am curious as to whether the discovery of Moses' little ark by the princess also occurred on the Feast of Firstfruits: the very date, not only of Noah's Ark coming to rest on the mountains of Ararat (Gen 8:4), but of the Resurrection of Jesus Christ (the first day after the Sabbath following Passover). Some may be surprised to learn that the tale of a baby being found in a little ark in a river is not unique to Jewish literature. Broadcaster Magnus Magnusson tells of a Mesopotamian myth dating back to 2400 BC, in which Sargon I declares:

---

[66] Notice that lifespans in some by Moses's day still exceed what they are today. Lifespans have been steadily reducing since the Flood in response to genetic load and changed terrestrial conditions. Within a few hundred years of the Exodus, the average will settle around 'threescore years and ten' (70), approximating today's longevity. (See *Origins I – The Greatest Scientific Discovery*)

"My changeling mother conceived me, in secret she bore me. She set me in a basket of rushes, with bitumen she sealed my lid. She cast me into the river [probably the Euphrates] which rose not over me.... Akki, the drawer of water, took me as his son and reared me." [67]

The two stories are too similar to be coincidental:

- The baby is abandoned in a river
- He is put into an ark
- The ark is made of bulrushes
- The ark is sealed with pitch
- The baby survives
- The baby is recovered by someone drawing him out of the water.

There are some interesting twists in the Moses story. Jochebed hides her baby in the very river Pharaoh intends to use to drown the unwanted Hebrew children. In other words, when you're under God's protection, safety is often found in the very jaws of trouble.[68] Remarkably, Moses' mother actually complies with Pharaoh's command to put her baby in the water; Pharaoh said nothing about pulling the baby out again. God softens a princess's heart, yet later hardens a pharaoh's heart. Evidently Pharaoh drowns a number of Israelite boys in this evil quest. *Later God will drown another pharaoh's entire northern army.*

Also worth noting, the Sargon myth hails from Mesopotamia, the same place where the Hyksos originated. So, what of the story of Moses in the Nile? We have some choices.

- Deceitful Biblical scribes indulged in some fanciful, mythological plagiarism to explain the origins of Moses and his placement in Pharaoh's household
- The Sargon myth was later copied from the Moses story and 'pre-dated' [69]

---

[67] **Magnusson, Magnus** *BC: The Archaeology of the Bible Lands,* London: 1977

[68] Gen 7:1-5; Exo 13:17-14:29; 2 Kings 6:15-17; Dan 3:16-26; 6:16-24; Mark 4:35-41, etc.

[69] This is a more common phenomenon in historical research than most people imagine. For instance, it is fashionable for liberal theologians and atheists to assert that Christianity's beliefs about Jesus cannot be trusted, since they were allegories of, or even plagiarised from far earlier pagan religions featuring virgin births, resurrections, and so on. This transpires archaeologically and literally not only *not* to be true, but that these so-called 'earlier' pagan religions and belief systems were plagiarised in the 2nd and 3rd centuries AD specifically from OT and NT writings! Lee Strobel gives a scholarly summary of this issue in his *The Case for the Real Jesus,* Zondervan, 2007, pp.157-188.

- We have a situation where what worked once with King Sargon was felt to be worth trying again by a desperate mother almost 1,000 years later.
- God told Jochebed, the mother, what to do (Heb 11:23).

The point is, if the Sargon story were a genuine Mesopotamian myth, the Hyksos would certainly have been familiar with it, originating as they did from Mesopotamia. After all, abandoned babies in rivers being rescued and surviving to become kings is the stuff of riveting children's stories. The tale was obviously passed from one generation to the next through oral tradition, and in the case of the Hyksos would have circulated among the Hebrews. If Pharaoh really did implement the casting of Hebrew babies into the Nile, is it beyond possible that a desperate Hyksos mother would not think of copying the measures taken by another desperate mother centuries earlier? If you are a mother, what *wouldn't* you do to save your child?

Notice God's initial weapon in the war against the Egyptian empire: a baby's tears, which melt the heart of an Egyptian princess! (Exo 2:6) The Bible states that Moses has an elder sister who stakes out the little bobbing ark to see what becomes of her three-month-old baby brother (Exo 2:4; Acts 7:20). She witnesses the rescue by Pharaoh's daughter. At the risk of bashing home the point, notice once again that the text does not say, 'one of Pharaoh's daughters' but **Pharaoh's daughter**. If this is an allusion to Pharaoh's only daughter, then this ties in with Hatshepsut, the only surviving daughter of Tuthmosis I. Hatshepsut rescuing a Hebrew baby who later becomes an adopted prince of Egypt may also explain the strange, unsettling treatment both Hatshepsut and Moses receive from the state later in their lives. More about this later.

Moses' sister (Miriam - Exo 15:20) sees Pharaoh's daughter rescue her baby brother and manoeuvres herself into the royal presence to offer help in the matter of providing a nurse for the child. There is no evidence from the Biblical narrative that Pharaoh's daughter is aware that the young Hebrew girl is the baby's sister. The princess merely instructs the Hebrew girl to go and find a nurse to raise the child. Moses' sister runs off and brings back... Moses' mother, Jochebed! The mother is doubtless stunned not only to learn of the survival of her baby, but also that he has earned royal protection, that she will be the one to raise him, and that she will actually be paid for nursing her own infant! (Exo 2:9) This is more of God making fools of the wise (1 Cor 1:19; 3:19). Pharaoh's daughter is almost certainly ignorant of the irony being played out before her eyes.

The child is named

And the child grew, and she [Moses' true Hebrew mother, Jochebed] **brought him unto Pharaoh's daughter, and he became her son. And she called his name Moses: and said, "Because I drew him out of the water."** (Exo 2:10)

A couple of points here. Firstly, Moses grows under the nursing and guidance of his biological mother, Jochebed. The child would have been named by his Levite parents (Exo 2:1), as it appears the toddler is around three by the time his mother finishes breastfeeding and surrenders him to the princess.[70] The Bible does not tell us the original Hebrew name Moses was given, but we can be sure that he received one. You don't raise a child for a couple of years without calling him something.

We do know from scripture that, upon taking possession of the child, the princess names him 'Moses' and adopts him as her son. This means – and this is an important point – that Moses becomes the legal son of the daughter of the king of Egypt. In the context of Tuthmosis I's family, if the princess Hatshepsut is the eldest surviving progeny of Pharaoh Tuthmosis I, this potentially lines her up for the throne ahead of any future brothers, and Hatshepsut does in fact become Pharaoh two decades later. That she even adopts a Hebrew child suggests to some scholars that there were suspicions in the royal household even at this time that the princess may have been barren.[71]

---

[70] www.greenprophet.com/2008/12/breastfeeding-judaism/

[71] There is a Hebrew Midrash tradition that this daughter of Pharaoh is later punished for bringing Moses into the royal household as her adopted son. Hatshepsut is, in fact, severely punished later by the state 'for no apparent reason', according to the available archaeology. A 'daughter of Pharaoh' does intriguingly show up in 1 Chron 4:18 under the Jewish name of Bithiah (lit. 'daughter of Yah'), married to Mered the Judahite. No more information is given in scripture as to who this person is or where she came from. Due to age constraints (Moses was eighty at the time of the Exodus), it is likely that Bithiah was a daughter of the Exodus pharaoh rather than an extremely ancient crone hailing from the royal house of Moses' infancy. This Bithiah, whom God sees fit to record in scripture, is taken to wife by Mered, indicating that she was of child-bearing age. If the pharaoh of the Exodus is indeed Amenhotep II, then the following paragraph from Wiki may be of interest:
"After becoming pharaoh, Amenhotep married a woman of uncertain parentage named Tiaa. As many as ten sons and one daughter have been attributed to him. Amenhotep's most important son was Tuthmosis IV, who succeeded him; however, there is significant evidence

In fact, Hatshepsut will end up having a daughter, Neferure, who dies around sixteen years of age.

The Bible states in Exo 2:10 that he was named Moses by the Egyptian princess because 'she drew him out of the water'. Almost all Bible commentaries tell the reader that the word 'Moses' comes from the Hebrew root *mosheh,* meaning 'to draw out'. While I am not rejecting this out of hand, there would have been difficulties. How credible is it that the royal daughter would call her illicit son a Hebrew name (lit: *Moshe*) in front of her father, the skullcracking Tuthmosis I, who has a standing extermination order for all male Hebrew children to be drowned in the Nile? Or further: imagine even a wilful princess of Hatshepsut's calibre coming clean to her dad: "I called his name 'Moses'. It's a Hebrew name, Father, because *I defied your express orders* and pulled one of the Hebrew children out of the river!"

Is it not more plausible that she called the lad an Egyptian name to hide his true origins, which, if discovered, would have acutely embarrassed the king before his people, and no doubt assured the child's immediate destruction in the croc-infested river? There are two viable options here. Firstly, the 1st century Hebrew chronicler, Flavius Josephus, writes:

> "Hereupon it was that Thermuthis[72] imposed this name *Mouses* upon him, from what had happened when he was put into the river; for the Egyptians call water by the name of *Mo,* and such as are saved out of it, by the name of *Uses:* so by putting these two words together, they imposed this name upon him."[73]

Another possibility for how Moses gains his name is that the princess states that the child is to be her son, so she may well have given him a name with the suffix 'Mosis', the Egyptian method of denoting 'son'. Just as, in English, we have WilliamSON, JacobSON, ThompSON, in ancient Egypt we have KaMOSIS, TuthMOSIS and AhMOSIS. It is with this suffix in mind that the search for the historical Moses can begin.

---

for him having many more children. Princes Amenhotep, Webensenu, Amenemopet, and Nedjem are all clearly attested, and Amenemhat, Khaemwaset, and Aakheperure as well as a daughter, Iaret, are also possible children." (Wikipedia: Amenhotep II).

[72] The name Josephus gives for Pharaoh's daughter.

[73] **Josephus, F** *Antiquities of the Jews,* 2:9:6

Moses - from boy to man

What was Moses really like as a person? Can we know? His physical appearance, even as a child, was apparently striking. The Christian evangelist Stephen remarked in 32 AD:

"...In which time Moses was born, and was exceeding fair, and nourished up in his father's house three months: And when he was cast out, Pharaoh's daughter took him up, and nourished him for her own son. And Moses was learned in all the wisdom of the Egyptians, and was mighty in words and in deeds." (Acts 7:20-22).

On this occasion, Stephen is giving evidence while on trial for his life before the Jewish ruling council, the Sanhedrin. This august body is replete with historical scholars, none of whom contradict Stephen on his observations, at least concerning this part of his testimony.

Upcoming events in the Exodus saga will also reveal that Moses is both physically strong and courageous: someone you would definitely notice if they passed you. Educated by the very best tutors in Egypt, Moses becomes well versed in all the wisdom and science of the most advanced nation on Earth, so intellectually he is no slouch. All the more curious, then, to discover later that Moses himself admits that he is slow of speech and definitely no public speaker. He may even have had a speech impediment (Exo 4:10)

The Biblical life of Moses is segmented into three periods of 40 years each (40 - the Biblical number of testing/judgment). Some view this as symbolic because the precision is an embarrassment to them. I believe these periods are accurate and literal because God wants them that way. The first 40-year period (*c.* 1526–1486 BC) covers Moses' upbringing, firstly as the adopted grandson of the current pharaoh, Tuthmosis I, then almost certainly the stepson and nephew of Pharaoh's successor, Tuthmosis II, the step-brother of Moses' Egyptian stepmother. The next 40 years (1486-1446 BC) are spent in the desert wilderness of Midian after Moses flees following his murder of the Egyptian. Once the pharaoh and his faction who sought his life are dead, Moses returns to Egypt aged 80 for the epic showdown of the plagues and Exodus with the new pharaoh. The final 40-year period (1446 - 1406 BC) runs from the Exodus to Moses' eventual death, with the Hebrew armies under Joshua poised to invade Canaan.

Now let's examine the first of our 18th Dynasty pharaohs to see how the Egyptology squares up with the Biblical account:

Ahmose I (1570-1546 BC); 1st Pharaoh of 18th Dynasty. Expels the Hyksos, unifies Egypt and re-establishes native Egyptian rule. Fathers....

Amenhotep I (1546-1529 BC): Military campaigns are Kush, Nubia and possibly Libya. Dies without issue. Is succeeded by his commander-in-chief, the tough guy....

Tuthmosis I (1529-1516 BC): Born from non-royal stock, Tuthmosis I proves a ruthless but militarily successful pharaoh. He is my candidate for carrying out the genocide on the male Hebrew babies (Exod. 1:15-22). He is father of two sons and two daughters by his Great Royal Wife, Ahmose. Alas, Crown Prince Amenmose, Wadjmose and Nefrubity predecease their father, leaving a sole child - a daughter - by this marriage, the enigmatic Hatshepsut. She is 'Pharaoh's daughter' who draws Moses out of the Nile. Tuthmosis I has a further son by a secondary wife, who succeeds him to the throne instead of the wilful Hatshepsut....

Tuthmosis II (1516-1504 BC) marries his half-sister Hatshepsut to strengthen his claim to the throne.

The skullcracking Tuthmosis I dies around 1516 BC when Moses is aged 9. My research indicates that the king's successor, Tuthmosis II, is the monarch in whose royal household Moses is raised from age 9 to 22 and given his education in all the wisdom of the most advanced nation on Earth. Moses doubtless endures the usual spiritual upheavals and mood-swings of the teenage years, made all the more awkward by the Egyptian context of his Hebrew heritage. The new pharaoh is now both Moses' stepfather and step-uncle, but more significant is the fact that the power behind Tuthmosis II's throne is Queen Hatshepsut - 'Pharaoh's daughter' who drew Moses out of the Nile; now fiercely protective of her blossoming, comely eight-year-old Hebrew prince. It will take Hatshepsut's regal power to keep Moses safe from the surviving political hawks of her father's administration, who doubtless disapprove of this Hebrew foundling insinuated into the royal midst. That Moses is not only able to survive but thrive in an Egypt still smarting from the Hyksos shame would be incomprehensible without Hatshepsut's protection.

Tuthmosis II comes across as weak and vacillating. Archaeological and medical evidence provided by the discovery of Tuthmosis II's body reveals that the new pharaoh lacks the vigour of his common-born, conqueror father. He is slight and weak in appearance. French Egyptologist Gaston Maspero, who discovered the tomb of Tuthmosis II in 1881, unwrapped the king's body five years later:

"He resembles Thutmosis I, but his features are not so marked, and are characterised by greater gentleness. He had scarcely reached the age of thirty when he fell a victim to a disease, of which the process of embalming could not remove the traces. The skin is scabrous in patches and covered with scars, while the upper part of the skull is bald; the body is thin and somewhat shrunken, and appears to have lacked vigour and muscular power." [74]

Historians largely agree that Tuthmosis II's reign has Hatshepsut stamped all over it, not least since the foreign policies enacted during the reign are almost identical to those prosecuted under Hatshepsut's subsequent own rule as pharaoh. Nubia's customary revolt occurs at the changing of the pharaohs to test the mettle of the new king now the skullcracking Tuth I is gone. According to the *Encyclopaedia Britannica,* an Egyptian force is despatched south by Tuthmosis II and Hatshepsut with orders to - wait for it - conquer the Nubian rebels *and execute all the males.*[75]

Moses comes to manhood during this time. Numbers 12 records an event I find captivating. Decades later during the Exodus, Moses will have a brief mutiny on his hands with his elder siblings Aaron and Miriam, which God Himself aggressively quells. The bust-up centres on Moses marrying an unnamed 'Ethiopian' (i.e. black Nubian) woman. The Jewish historian Flavius Josephus makes a big thing out of Moses, the successful military commander in Nubia, claiming a royal Ethiopian bride during a campaign.[76] Is there any evidence that Moses was ever in Nubia in command of troops during the first forty years of his life? No other mention of this 'Ethiopian' wife of Moses is made in scripture, indicating irrelevance or disapproval, but the fact that she crops up as an issue of contention *at all* during the Exodus indicates that the Holy Spirit wants us to know about her. A whole chapter of the Bible (Num 12) is devoted to the incident.

---

[74] **Maspero, Gaston** *History of Egypt, Chaldaea, Syria, Babylonia, and Assyria,* Volume 4 (of 12), Project Gutenberg EBook, 16th December 2005: www.gutenberg.org/files/17324/17324-h/17324-h.htm

[75] www.britannica.com/EBchecked/topic/594490/Thutmose-II

[76] Josephus, *Antiquities*, op. cit., 2:10

In fact, it is Zipporah who is later mentioned as Moses' wife and father to his two children, Gershom and Eliezer. Moses will marry this Kenite daughter of a priest during the second 40-year period of his life - the exile in Midian (Exo 2:21). Zipporah appears to be an unbeliever who either leaves Moses or is sent away by him after a strange, apparently near-deadly incident at an inn (Exo 4:24-26). Some scholars solve 'the wives of Moses' problem by stating that the Ethiopian woman and Zipporah are the same person, and that Aaron and Miriam are expressing their contempt for Zipporah by calling her 'an Ethiopian'. The problem is, that is not the context in which the term is used. Here is the scripture:

And Miriam and Aaron spake against Moses because of the Ethiopian woman whom he had married: for he had married an Ethiopian woman (Num 12:1).

Why would the Holy Spirit see fit to repeat *twice* that Moses married an Ethiopian woman if he didn't? The fact that the woman is an Ethiopian is not attested to by Aaron or Miriam in speech, but by the expositor/author of the piece, widely accepted to be Moses under guidance of the Holy Spirit![77] So if you believe the Bible is the inspired Word of God, the wife in Num 12:1 is going to be Ethiopian and mentioned for a reason. If you don't believe the Bible is the inspired Word of God, you may have bigger problems than the nationality of Moses' first missus. The only other time we hear about the second wife, Zipporah, is when she is brought out by her father Jethro to Moses at the 'holy mount' during the Exodus, accompanied by the two sons Zipporah bore him. The meeting is apparently cordial, but Zipporah thereafter vanishes from the record without further comment, as does the Ethiopian bride.

As a young Egyptian prince during the reign of Tuthmosis II (covering Moses from age 9 to 22), Moses would have been trained in all the arts of war from before puberty, and it is inconceivable as an Egyptian prince that he would still be unmarried by his fortieth year. So this leads me to surmise that he would have had a wife prior to his exile in Midian. Did Moses accompany one of Hatshepsut's Nubian expeditions during the rule of Tuthmosis II by way of earning his spurs as a military commander? We'll track down the enigma of this

---

[77] Exo 17:14; 24:4,7; 34:27; Josh 8:32; 23:6; 1 Kings 2:3; 2 Kings 14:6. Jesus also authenticated Moses not only as the scribe who took down the Law, but also the wider authorship of the Pentateuch: Matt 8:4; 19:7,8; 23:2; Mark 1:44; 7:10; 10:3–5; 12:26; Luke 5:14; 16:29–31; 20:37; 24:27, 44; FG 3:14; 5:39,45-47; 6:32; 7:19, 22,23

Ethiopian beauty a little later using archaeology and extra-Biblical sources. There is no other mention of Moses in connection with Ethiopia anywhere else in scripture, but of interest in *Encyclopaedia Britannica* is the following passage relating to this Egyptian period:

"One of the [Nubian] chief's sons was taken captive to Egypt, probably to be Egyptianized and returned to his country as a client ruler. Some time later, as shown by the biography of one of the soldiers who had accompanied his father, Thutmose II sent forces against some Bedouins in southern Palestine."[78]

In rounding up some Nubian royals on the expeditions, could a comely Ethiopian princess have been among those brought back to Egypt for 're-education'? Empires do this a lot. An effective method for dealing with a troublesome province is to take the troublemakers' sons (and daughters), and rather than execute them (which only produces resistance movements), bring them back to the mother country and thoroughly Egyptianise them, even marry them into the noble or common stock, then return them to their own land to spread the cultural benefits of the empire. Did this happen with Moses and the Ethiopian? The Romans had such a programme centuries later with, for example, the Judaean royal family of Herod the Great, and this would be British foreign policy across the vast reach of her empire during the 18th and 19th centuries, especially in India.

A further, fascinating question occurs to me: Is a royal, Egyptianised Moses part of Hatshepsut's strategy to keep the Hebrew sub-culture in line? Egypt needs a compliant slave-force for the mammoth building projects of the 18th Dynasty to be possible. In times of acute hardship, perhaps a struggling, despondent Hebrew slave might turn his eyes to behold a regal Moses afar off, reasoning that if one of their own could attain the royal household as Pharaoh's 'son', there might be far worse fates to which a people could be cursed. There is resentment over Moses' privileged status, to be sure, as witnessed when Moses steps in to break up a fight between two Hebrew workers, one of whom retorts:

"Who made thee a prince and a judge over us?" (Exo 2:14)

The answer to that would be Hatshepsut and a co-operative Tuthmosis II, and behind them, the sovereign will of the LORD who controls the affairs of *all nations* (even today!) to bring about His

---

[78] www.britannica.com/EBchecked/topic/594490/Thutmose-II

purpose.[79] Against this background, Moses grows to manhood, educated by the finest minds of Egypt, trained in the arts of war, basking in the newfound glories of the nation's rising fortunes, and fêted with positions of privilege in the service of the Crown of Two Lands. Equally, during this time of rebuilding, it is the Hyksos peoples, along with their Hebrews (in surviving inscriptions: *Habiru/Apiru*), enslaved before and after reunification, afflicted with tribulations and onerous duties, who form the backbone of the colossal work force that makes this golden age possible.

The reign of the male queen

Tuthmosis II and Hatshepsut have a daughter, Neferure, but she does not survive beyond age 16. *Moses is therefore still sole child and heir of the royal family.* Then Tuthmosis has a son by a concubine named Isis. Around 1506 BC, Tuthmosis II dies of heart disease, weakened by a scabrous illness. Hatshepsut becomes regent for the child her husband nominated as his successor, and this infant becomes Tuthmosis III. Seven years into Tuthmosis III's reign, however, scholars largely agree that Hatshepsut assumes the full titles and powers of Pharaoh and rules the Two Lands successfully until her death in 1484 BC. French Egyptologist Gaston Maspero, discoverer of Tuthmosis II in 1881, writes:

"By his marriage with his sister, Thutmosis left daughters only, but he had one son, also a Thutmosis, by a woman of low birth, perhaps merely a slave, whose name was Isis.[80] Hatshopsitu proclaimed this child her successor, for his youth and humble parentage could not excite her jealousy. She betrothed him to her one surviving daughter, Hatshopsitu II [Neferure], and having thus settled the succession in the male line, she continued to rule alone in the name of her nephew who was still a minor, as she had done formerly in the case of her half-brother."[81]

Discovering Egypt gives us the following details:

---

[79] Exo 9:29; Dan 4:17,25,32; Psa 75:6-7; FG 19:11; Eph 1:11

[80] Maspero notes: "The name of the mother of Thûtmosis III. was revealed to us on the wrappings found with the mummy of this king in the hiding-place of Deîr el-Baharî; the absence of princely titles, while it shows the humble extraction of the lady Isis, explains at the same time the somewhat obscure relations between Hâtshopsîtû [Hatshepsut] and her nephew."

[81] **Maspero, Gaston** *History of Egypt, Chaldaea, Syria, Babylonia, and Assyria,* Volume 4 (of 12), Project Gutenberg EBook, December 16, 2005: www.gutenberg.org/files/17324/17324-h/17324-h.htm

"To support her cause [in seizing the throne], Hatshepsut claimed that the god Amun had taken the form of her father and visited her mother, and she herself was the result of this divine union. As the self-proclaimed daughter of God, she further justified her right to the throne by declaring that the god Amun-Ra had spoken to her, saying, 'Welcome my sweet daughter, my favorite, the king of Upper and Lower Egypt, Maatkare, Hatshepsut. Thou art the king, taking possession of the Two Lands.'

"Hatshepsut dressed as a king, even affecting a false beard, but it was never her intention to pass herself off as a man; rather, she referred to herself as the 'female falcon'. Her success was due, at least in part, to the respect of the people for her father's memory [Tuth I, the skullcracker] and the loyal support of influential officials who controlled all the key positions of government." [82]

National Geographic writes:

"At first, Hatshepsut acted on her stepson's behalf, careful to respect the conventions under which previous queens had handled political affairs while juvenile offspring learned the ropes. But before long, signs emerged that Hatshepsut's regency would be different. Early reliefs show her performing kingly functions such as making offerings to the gods and ordering up obelisks from red granite quarries at Aswan. After just a few years she had assumed the role of 'king' of Egypt, supreme power in the land. Her stepson—who by then may have been fully capable of assuming the throne—was relegated to second-in-command. Hatshepsut proceeded to rule for a total of 21 years.

"What induced Hatshepsut to break so radically with the traditional role of queen regent? A social or military crisis? Dynastic politics? Divine injunctions from Amun? A thirst for power? 'There was something impelling Hatshepsut to change the way she portrayed herself on public monuments, but we don't know what it is,' says Peter Dorman, a noted Egyptologist and president of the American University of Beirut. 'One of the hardest things to guess is her motive.' " [83]

Motive? Try this on for size. There is another prince in the royal household not mentioned in surviving inscriptions, having been later excised - the Hebrew Moses. Tuthmosis II dies when Moses is around 22 years old. The king has previously nominated the infant Tuthmosis III as his successor since Hatshepsut has no sons of her own, save the

[82] http://discoveringegypt.com/ancient-egyptian-kings-queens/hatshepsut/

[83] http://ngm.nationalgeographic.com/2009/04/hatshepsut/brown-text/3

adopted Hebrew Moses, *her only son and heir.* Tuthmosis II discounts Moses due to his Hebrew/Hyksos heritage. Fierce to protect her position, one can only guess at the high plans Hatshepsut harbours for her comely Hebrew prince. It would certainly have rankled the ambitious First Wife that her husband's son of a mere concubine (Isis) was taking the Two Crowns in precedence over a) Hatshepsut and b) her by-now thoroughly Egyptianised, adopted, eldest son and heir, Moses. Worse, as Tuthmosis III grows and becomes aware of his destiny and the Hebrew cuckoo in the nest, it is not hard to imagine the resentment and anger the young prince feels towards the political faction denying him the throne's full power. This faction would include his stepmother, Hatshepsut, Moses, and a sizable chunk of ministers of past and present administrations, over which Hatshepsut retains power and patronage.

Our kings list now looks like this:

Ahmose I (1570-1546 BC); 1st Pharaoh of 18th Dynasty. Expels the Hyksos, unifies Egypt and re-establishes native Egyptian rule. Fathers….

Amenhotep I (1546-1529 BC): Military campaigns are Kush, Nubia and possibly Libya. Dies without issue. Is succeeded by his commander-in-chief, the tough guy….

Tuthmosis I (1529-1516 BC): Born from non-royal stock, Tuthmosis I proves a ruthless but militarily successful pharaoh. He is my candidate for carrying out the genocide on the male Hebrew babies (Exod. 1:15-22). He is father of two sons and two daughters by his Great Royal Wife, Ahmose. Alas, Crown Prince Amenmose, Wadjmose and Nefrubity predecease their father, leaving a sole child – a daughter – by this marriage, the enigmatic Hatshepsut. She is 'Pharaoh's daughter', who draws Moses out of the Nile (Exo 2:5-6). Tuthmosis I has a further son by a secondary wife, who succeeds him to the throne instead of the wilful Hatshepsut….

Tuthmosis II (1516-1504 BC) marries his half-sister Hatshepsut to strengthen his claim to the throne. Archaeological and medical evidence provided by the discovery of Tuthmosis II's body reveals that the new pharaoh lacks the vigour of his common-born, conqueror father, being slight and weak in appearance. Scholars are generally in agreement that Hatshepsut is the power behind this reign.

Hatshepsut (1504-1498-1484 BC): Upon the death of Tuthmosis II, the appointed heir, Tuthmosis III, takes the crown, the son of the concubine, Isis. Since Tuthmosis III is an infant, his stepmother Queen Hatshepsut rules as regent, finally adopting full royal titulary as Pharaoh 7 years into the first 22 years of Tuthmosis III's 54-year rule. She is in her early 30s at this point. In technical terms, since Tuthmosis III is never deposed throughout Hatshepsut's rule but maintains his position as co-ruler, it cannot be argued that Hatshepsut usurps the throne. But the move is contentious by Egyptian standards, and Hatshepsut moves immediately to strengthen her position as Pharaoh.

Hatshepsut is one of only three women ever to rule as pharaoh in Egypt's 3,000-year ancient history, and the first to exercise full power. Only Cleopatra, the last of the pharaohs, will rule in a similar fashion centuries later. According to *Encyclopaedia Britannica,* Hatshepsut quickly sets about consolidating her reputation as a stable, highly capable ruler:

"Hatshepsut never explained why she took the throne or how she persuaded Egypt's élite to accept her new position. However, an essential element of her success was a group of loyal officials, many handpicked, who controlled all the key positions in her government. Most prominent amongst these was Senenmut, overseer of all royal works and tutor to Neferure....

"Traditionally, Egyptian kings defended their land against the enemies who lurked at Egypt's borders. Hatshepsut's reign was essentially a peaceful one, and her foreign policy was based on trade rather than war. But scenes on the walls of her Deir al-Bahri temple, in western Thebes, suggest that she began with a short, successful military campaign in Nubia. More complete scenes show Hatshepsut's seaborne trading expedition to Punt,[84] a trading centre (since vanished) on the East African coast beyond the southernmost end of the Red Sea. Gold, ebony, animal skins, baboons, processed myrrh, and living myrrh trees were brought back to Egypt, and the trees were planted in the gardens of Deir al-Bahri."[85]

And this from *Biography*:

"[Hatshepsut] began having herself depicted in the traditional king's kilt and crown, along with a fake beard and male body. This was not an attempt to trick people into thinking she was male; rather, since there

[84] Thought to be modern-day Somalia.
[85] www.britannica.com/EBchecked/topic/256896/Hatshepsut

were no words or images to portray a woman with this status, it was a way of asserting her authority.

"Hatshepsut's successful transition from queen to pharaoh was, in part, due to her ability to recruit influential supporters, and many of the men she chose had been favored officials of her father, Thutmose I. One of her most important advisors was Senenmut. He had been among the queen's servants and rose with her in power, and some speculate he was her lover as well."[86]

And this from *History.com*:

"As pharaoh, Hatshepsut undertook ambitious building projects, particularly in the area around Thebes. Her greatest achievement was the enormous memorial temple at Deir el-Bahri, considered one of the architectural wonders of ancient Egypt. Another great achievement of her reign was a trading expedition she authorized that brought back vast riches – including ivory, ebony, gold, leopard skins and incense – to Egypt from a distant land known as Punt (possibly modern-day Eritrea)."[87]

There we have the standard story of Hatshepsut. Of particular note:

- Hatshepsut is apparently the model consort during the early part of the Tuthmosis III regency. Images show her depicted 'in her rightful place' behind Tuthmosis III during this time
- Seven years into Tuthmosis III's reign, however, Hatshepsut commits the unprecedented act of taking sole power in defiance of the will of Tuthmosis II, who had nominated his son by a concubine as his successor
- *There is no reason for Hatshepsut to have done this* in order to carry out a common enough role in ancient Egypt: that of royal regent to an infant pharaoh. *Some extraordinary circumstances have compelled Hatshepsut to act in this way*
- There is no evidence to suggest that the young Tuthmosis III resented his stepmother's rule, had anything to fear from her, or that she organised threats against the young pharaoh's life. On the contrary, Hatshepsut ensures Tuthmosis's education as a scribe and priest, trains him as a soldier, and by the time she dies in 1484 BC, Tuthmosis III has successfully conducted a short military campaign in the Levant. He is elevated to

[86] www.biography.com/people/hatshepsut-9331094#ascent-to-power
[87] www.history.com/topics/ancient-history/hatshepsut

commander-in-chief of the Egyptian armed forces and is fully prepared for the throne. Tuthmosis III will not disappoint. He will become, in the eyes of most scholars, the most successful warrior king in Egyptian history, ruling in his own right for a further 32 years.

BBC History reports what happened next:

"Tuthmosis took his throne in unsettled times. His eastern vassals, for so long quiet, were starting to challenge Egypt's dominance. A series of glorious campaigns, including the dramatic capture of Megiddo (Biblical Armageddon), saw Egypt restored to her position of power. Egypt now controlled an empire which stretched from beyond the third cataract in Nubian to the banks of the River Euphrates in Syria. The rewards of empire – plunder, tribute, taxes and gifts from those eager to be friends – made Tuthmosis the richest man in the world.

"Using his hard-won wealth, Tuthmosis attempted to out-build Hatshepsut. Once again the Nile Valley echoed to the sound of hammer and chisel. But now there was destruction alongside the construction. The royal masons had been charged with the task of removing all traces of the female pharaoh. By the time of his death, some thirty-three years after his solo accession, Tuthmosis was confident that Hatshepsut's unorthodox reign would soon be forgotten."[88]

British Egyptologist Joyce Tyldesley scotches popular rumours of foul play in Hatshepsut's demise:

"While there have been rumours that perhaps Thutmose III or other enemies might have had Hatshepsut murdered, Hatshepsut actually died due to an abscessed tooth. She was perhaps in her late forties or early fifties when she died. Historians have long believed that Thutmose III, in an act of revenge after her death, removed Hatshepsut's name from the historical record. However, due to new evidence, it appears that her name wasn't removed until the end of Thutmose III's reign, when he was co-regent with his son and heir Amenhotep II. Not only did Thutmose III remove images of Hatshepsut, he also claimed many of her accomplishments for his son. This was done probably in an attempt to have the record read that the throne had come down to Amenhotep II in a strictly patrilineal line. Images of Hatshepsut as Queen however were kept." [89]

---

[88] www.bbc.co.uk/history/ancient/egyptians/hatshepsut_01.shtml

[89] **Tyldesley, Joyce** *The Female Pharaoh,* Penguin, 1996

Live Science reports:

"In 2007, researchers announced that Hatshepsut's mummy had been identified in tomb KV 60 in the Valley of the Kings. A 'CT scan of a single tooth in a box with Hatshepsut's name on it perfectly matched a tooth socket in the mummy's jaw,' writes Cornell University anthropologist Meredith Small in a *LiveScience* article. She notes that she was around 50 when she died, balding, suffering from diabetes and wearing black and red nail polish. She also had a desire for perfume.

"Small writes that despite her health problems, and the post-mortem destruction of some of her images, history still remembers her as a successful ancient Egyptian ruler. 'Hatshepsut's image couldn't be erased because even with the weight, the beard, and the nail polish, she was a ruler, and a grand one,' she writes. 'In ancient Egypt, just like today, you simply can't keep a good woman down.' "[90]

---

[90] www.livescience.com/28510-hatshepsut-first-female-pharaoh.html

MOSES – THE MIDIAN YEARS
(1486-1446 BC)

Let us now turn to the Biblical record to see if there is any serious, unequivocal correlation between what Egyptologists have discovered of the 18th Dynasty and what happens in scripture to Moses.

Although raised and educated in all the wisdom and science of Egypt (Acts 7:22), and still in his adoptive land upon his fortieth year, Moses is a troubled man with inner conflicts at this point. It seems likely that he has been in constant contact with his Hebrew birth parents, Amram and Jochebed, his elder brother Aaron, his sister Miriam and the wider family, all the while living his *alter persona* as nephew of the current pharaoh. How do we know that he is aware of his roots and still has contact with his kin? There are a couple of pointers. Firstly, we read in the Biblical record:

And it came to pass in those days, when Moses was grown, that he went out unto his brethren, and looked on their burdens.... (Exo 2:11).

So Moses knows who his brethren are. As an 'Egyptian' prince, why would Moses care what happened to the Hebrews if he was not aware he was one of them? One can infer from this that the princess Hatshepsut, who became his stepmother, either never concealed his ethnic roots from Moses, or made him aware of them as he matured. Remember that Moses was, tops, three years old when Jochebed was obliged (after weaning) to surrender him to the royal household. Henceforth, Moses would have entered the rarefied world of the royal court with little or no contact with the *hoi polloi*. Probably the only way Moses could ever have known of his origins was if the young Hatshepsut told him, and in this regard the princess seems to have been unabashed. Which suggests that Hatshepsut enjoyed a special position of privilege with her skullcracking pharaoh father, who ordered the slaying of the male Hebrew babies. Note once again that the princess is referred to in Exo 2:5 as the daughter of Pharaoh (singular), not a daughter of Pharaoh (one of many). Most pharaohs had a flock of children and more than one wife. A pharaoh with a single daughter causes our antennae to twitch. A single daughter gets what she wants from her Dad - I know, I have one and she tries it on all the time. That Tuthmosis I had four children by the First Wife, then loses all but one, provides further motivation for the king to concentrate his favour on his sole, surviving daughter by Ahmose. I don't think Hatshepsut wanted for anything, growing up. On the face of it, the pharaoh fits. The timeline fits. Let's dig deeper.

The cuckoo in the nest

Moses goes out and gazes upon the afflictions and burdens of his people, the children of Israel, as they labour in harrowing conditions. The book of Hebrews also records the change in Moses' spiritual outlook: **By faith Moses, when he was come to years, refused to be called the son of Pharaoh's daughter; choosing rather to suffer affliction with the people of God, than to enjoy the pleasures of sin for a season; esteeming the reproach of Christ greater riches than the treasures in Egypt: for he had respect unto the recompence of the reward....** (Heb 11:24-26)

Scholars have hotly debated the phrase **when he was come to years** to determine precisely when Moses refuses to be called the son of Pharaoh's daughter: the point at which he publicly renounces his Egyptian royal heritage. The book of Hebrews' statement with regard to Christ seems to indicate that Moses has been undergoing a spiritual awakening as he approaches forty, causing him to start turning his back on fleshly Egypt ('the world') and identify more closely with his oppressed people. It is a metamorphosis which will have serious, unintended consequences for all concerned. The mystics among us will also read into the above Hebrews passage that Moses apparently receives an epiphany of his Messiah *(Mashiach)* in the role of the smitten, suffering servant (Isa 53). This will be an intriguing theme throughout the Exodus, cropping up in the unlikeliest of places.

On our timeline, we are now at 1486 BC, forty years on from Moses' birth in 1526 BC, which occurred three years into the reign of the skullcracking Tuthmosis I.[91] In review, Hatshepsut, this pharaoh's sole surviving daughter, is my candidate for the princess who drew Moses out of the Nile and adopted him. When her father dies, Hatshepsut becomes the wife of her stepbrother Tuthmosis II, a son of the skullcracker by a second royal wife, Mutnofret. Together, Hatshepsut and Tuth II have only one child, a daughter, Neferure, who dies around sixteen. Tuth II has a son by a concubine, Isis, whom

[91] By way of revision, Moses is 80 years of age when he leads his people out of Egypt in the Exodus (Exo 7:7). The Biblical date of the Exodus is 1446 BC, derived from adding 480 years (1 Kings 6:1) to the generally agreed 4th year of Solomon's reign: 967-966 BC – the year construction of the First Temple commences.

Tuth II appoints as his heir. This lad will become the famous Tuth III, today known as the 'Napoleon of Ancient Egypt'. This infant, Tuth III, is therefore Hatshepsut's stepson.

Upon her husband Tuth II's death, Hatshepsut becomes regent for the first seven years of the infant Tuthmosis III's reign, then makes herself fully pharaoh for the remainder of her life, dying in 1484 BC. Carefully note that Hatshepsut *never deposes Tuthmosis III during the regency*, which she could easily have done. Instead, she remains loyal to the wishes of husband Tuthmosis II by carefully supervising the young royal's education, training and political metamorphosis into the formidable ruler Tuthmosis III will become. This tells you something about Hatshepsut. Whatever is said about her, she's a straight-shooter. There is no evidence to the contrary, other than the fact that she took the unusual and not uncontroversial step of assuming the full powers of a pharaoh. Scholars struggle to give good reason why she did this, since a regular regency arrangement had served adequately for child pharaohs in the past. Put Moses into the household, however, and Hatshepsut's actions become clear.

One would be surprised if the queen had not at some point harboured ambitions of putting Moses on the throne as her sole surviving, legal heir, yet no evidence of this has come down to us. And if ever she had thought thus, such plans would have been scotched the moment Moses began turning his back on his Egyptian heritage, which would have included rejecting Hatshepsut as his 'mother'. The impression one gets is that this change of heart appears to have been a process:

Now when he was full forty years old, it came into [Moses'] **heart to visit his brethren, the children of Israel....** (Acts 7:23)

Hebrews 11:24-27 gives us further insight into tensions that would have arisen in the royal household when Moses makes it clear that he has no intention of continuing life either as Hatshepsut's son and heir, or even as an Egyptian:

By faith Moses, when he was come to years, refused to be called the son of Pharaoh's daughter; choosing rather to suffer affliction with the people of God, than to enjoy the pleasures of sin for a season; esteeming the reproach of Christ greater riches than the treasures in Egypt: for he had respect unto the recompence of the reward. By faith he forsook Egypt, not fearing the wrath of the king: for he endured, as seeing Him who is invisible.

By 1486 BC, Hatshepsut's only other progeny, her daughter Neferure, is dead. Time has marched on and Hatshepsut is now in her mid-fifties. She is bald, overweight and suffering from diabetes. She is also beset by a debilitating psoriasis condition, for which she takes copious tar creams, which will eventually kill her via metastatic bone cancer. Her own adopted son, Moses, has increasingly estranged himself. The ageing queen has started noticing the inevitable, subtle jockeying of position among her ministers in an attempt to ally themselves closer to her rising young buck of a successor, Tuthmosis III. The year 1486 BC could well be when Hatshepsut loses her most loyal and powerful advisor, Senenmut, as documentation on him ceases a few years before Hatshepsut's own death in 1484 BC. Though some researchers have speculated whether Tuthmosis III does away with Senenmut, and even murders Hatshepsut, there is simply no evidence of this.

Tuthmosis III has been showing early signs of the steely resolve that will characterise his astonishing reign, earning him the aforementioned 'Napoleon of Ancient Egypt' accolade. The writing is on the wall with Hatshepsut nearing her end. Moses knows that the moment his stepmum is gone, Tuthmosis III won't want a Hebrew cuckoo in the nest. This motivates Moses to take stock of his own future, one with his own people. He has no right to the throne of Egypt, and an attempted *coup* would surely meet with failure and his own ignominious demise. Tuthmosis III is the rightful heir, and Moses has a humble side (Num 12:3). Tuth III is in his early 20s by this time, and Moses is pushing 40. I'm comfortable with Moses seeing sense and backing off from any confrontation with the forthright young pharaoh. The key to understanding what happens next, I believe, lies in determining what we know about the character of this young monarch, and why his relationship with Moses so rapidly deteriorates.

The pharaoh of the oppression

In 1486 BC, two years before Pharaoh Hatshepsut dies, Moses murders an Egyptian, and scripture states *that a male pharaoh* reacts by wanting Moses killed (Exo 2:15). Though Hatshepsut is still in charge in 1486 BC, power is now transferring steadily into the hands of Tuthmosis III, as Egypt comes to the realisation that the queen is not long for this world.

We know a lot about Tuthmosis III's military exploits because his royal scribe Thanuny (also a military commander), kept detailed accounts. Tuthmosis III conducts seventeen barnstorming campaigns during his life, which are described in detail across the inner wall of the great chamber at the Karnak Temple of Amun. Pharaoh Tuth III triumphs in all to which he turns his hand. He never loses a battle. To his soldiers he is a hero. To Egypt he is a god. By the close of Tuthmosis III's reign just prior to the Exodus, Egypt will control the largest empire the world will have witnessed to that time, stretching from the boundaries of northern Syria out to the Euphrates, down through Canaan, and as far south into Africa as the Nile's Fourth Cataract. Tuthmosis III is magnanimous with his enemies, often sparing and 're-educating' them in the benefits of Egyptian culture. The archaeological record depicts him as fair, civilised, thoughtful and mature, but then it would. Inscriptions always conceal the flaws and defeats of its kings. *Discovering Egypt* describes the rising new monarch thus:

"Thutmose III is often compared to Napoleon, but unlike Napoleon he never lost a battle. He conducted sixteen campaigns in Palestine, Syria and Nubia and his treatment of the conquered was always humane. He established a sort of *Pax Egyptica* over his empire. Syria and Palestine were obliged to keep the peace and the region as a whole experienced an unprecedented degree of prosperity.

"His impact upon Egyptian culture was profound. He was a national hero, revered long after his time. Indeed, his name was held in awe even to the last days of ancient Egyptian history. His military achievements brought fabulous wealth and his family presided over a golden age that was never surpassed.

"He was also a cultured man who demonstrated a curiosity about the lands he conquered; many of his building works at Karnak are covered with carvings of the plants and flowers he saw on his campaigns. He also set up a number of obelisks in Egypt, one of which, erroneously called Cleopatra's Needle, now stands on the Embankment in London. Its twin is in Central Park in New York. Another is near the Lateran, in Rome, and yet another stands in Istanbul. In this way, Thutmose III maintains a presence in some of the most powerful nations of the last two thousand years."[92]

At some point after Hatshepsut's death, a determined effort is made to erase all memory of the queen from the architectural record. In ancient Egypt, this is akin to sentencing someone to eternal,

---

[92] http://discoveringegypt.com/ancient-egyptian-kings-queens/thutmose-iii-the-napoleon-of-ancient-egypt/

spiritual obliteration. The majority of scholars blame Tuthmosis III for this, reasoning that he resented his stepmother's regency, and wished to portray himself to posterity as having reigned the full 54 years without having to split it 'with a woman'. Biblical scholar and Egyptologist Doug Petrovich demurs:

"According to most Egyptologists, this massive effort to destroy all record of Hatshepsut's existence was launched by Thutmose III, with a predictable motive: out of sexist pride, he attempted to eliminate every trace of this dreaded female pharaoh's rule, intending to rewrite Egyptian history to portray a smooth succession of male rulers from Thutmose I to himself. 'Wounded male pride may also have played a part in his decision to act; the mighty warrior king may have balked at being recorded for posterity as the man who ruled for 20 years under the thumb of a mere woman.'[93] But was Thutmose III actually the perpetrator? Did he seethe with hatred and resentment toward his former co-ruler before viciously attacking all remnants of her? Are cavalier accusations of sexism justifiable?" [94]

That Tuthmosis III is guilty of an attempt to obliterate Hatshepsut from history is nonsensical given the evidence of what we know of him. For example, Petrovich points out that Tuthmosis actually venerated his stepmother's memory by enhancing her building projects:

"A scene on the dismantled Chapelle Rouge at Djeser-Djeseru portrays Hatshepsut and identifies her as 'The Good God, Lady of the Two Lands, Daughter of Ra, Hatshepsut.'[95] Thutmose III, who is pictured as steering his barque toward Deir al-Bahri, actually completed the Chapelle Rouge, added the topmost register of decorations in his own name, then claimed the shrine as his own." [96]

If Tuthmosis III were the culprit, how likely is it that *he waited 20 years* before whimsically desecrating his stepmother's image?

"He could not have accomplished the feat before his 42nd regnal year, a full 20 years after Hatshepsut left office. Thutmose III's construction

---

[93] **Tyldesley, Joyce** *Hatchepsut: The Female Pharaoh,* Viking, 1996, p.225

[94] www.biblearchaeology.org/post/2010/02/04/Amenhotep-II-and-the-Historicity-of-the-Exodus-Pharaoh.aspx#Article

[95] Tyldesley, Joyce, *Hatchepsut: The Female Pharaoh,* op. cit., p.219

[96] www.biblearchaeology.org/post/2010/02/04/Amenhotep-II-and-the-Historicity-of-the-Exodus-Pharaoh.aspx#Article

projects at Karnak – which include the Hall of Annals, whose texts were written no earlier than Year 42 – inadvertently concealed a few inscriptions and illustrations related to Hatshepsut. The scenes were in place by Year 42, yet show no signs whatsoever of any desecration. Conversely, those parts of the scenes that were unprotected by his post-Year-42 construction were defaced during the anti-Hatshepsut campaign. It seems impossible that he would wait until over 20 years after she had left office to initiate a campaign of anti-feminism out of personal hatred. 'While it is possible to imagine and even empathize with Thutmose III indulging in a sudden whim of hatred against his stepmother immediately after her death, it is far harder to imagine him overcome by such a whim some 20 years later.'[97] Moreover, this whim would have been a schizophrenic one, given Thutmose III's recent positive disposition toward Hatshepsut, as displayed by his completion of her projects at Djeser-Djeseru and Armant."[98]

Petrovich further argues that Tuthmosis III would need a serious reason for carrying out such a landmark desecration: an action which would have posthumous implications for his own reputation and wordfame:

"According to Egyptian religion, removing the name or image of a deceased person was a direct assault on his/her spirit. For him to live forever in the Field of Reeds, his body, image, or name must survive on Earth. If all memory of him were lost or destroyed, the spirit too would perish, initiating the much-dreaded 'second death': a total obliteration from which there could be no return. This act against Hatshepsut was an attempt to condemn her to oblivion – a fate worse than death for an Egyptian.[99] Thus the extermination of Hatshepsut's image from the Earth was indeed a drastic step: the removal of her spirit from its perpetual existence in the afterlife. Such reprisal seems far too severe to fit the motive of mere sexism."[100]

Tuthmosis III cannot reasonably be indicted for the attempted obliteration of Hatshepsut's memory based on existing evidence. There is every indication from the archaeological and inscription

---

[97] Tyldesley, Joyce, *Hatchepsut: The Female Pharaoh,* op. cit., pp.224-225
[98] www.biblearchaeology.org/post/2010/02/04/Amenhotep-II-and-the-Historicity-of-the-Exodus-Pharaoh.aspx#Article
[99] Grimal, Nicolas, *A History of Ancient Egypt,* op. cit., p.216
[100] www.biblearchaeology.org/post/2010/02/04/Amenhotep-II-and-the-Historicity-of-the-Exodus-Pharaoh.aspx#Article

record, however, that Tuthmosis III's angry younger son and successor, Amenhotep II, had every reason to consign his step-grandmother to the eternal dark. We will examine our Exodus pharaoh later in context with those momentous events. Does the evidence, both secular and Biblical, stack up?

An Egyptian killing – 1486 BC

It cannot have been easy for Tuthmosis III growing up in the royal household with Moses. By 1486 BC, Tuthmosis is in his early 20s while Moses is 40. Both men are superbly bright and courageous. Moses, in turn, will have recognised no shrinking violet in the emerging powerhouse monarch, flexing young muscles not just against any threat from Moses to his divine destiny, but against his formidable stepmother and all who follow her. By 1486 BC, Tuthmosis III is now the highly capable commander-in-chief of Egypt's military, fully trained in the arts of war and state, and doubtless beginning to chafe under his stepmother's rule, desiring the reins of power for himself. For his part, Tuthmosis III, by now with an iron grip on the military as its commander, could quite easily have carried out a *coup d'état* on his stepmother's administration and even had her murdered. *He does not.* But there is the longstanding problem of the Hebrew cuckoo in the nest: his adopted step-brother Moses.

For his part, Moses knows his life will be in danger the moment Hatshepsut is gone. No Egyptian pharaoh tolerates a rival for very long, especially a Hyksos pretending to be an Egyptian in the royal household. This state of affairs is doubtless the reason Hatshepsut holds the Two Crowns until her death, not just to protect her own position, but to protect Moses, the son she saved from her father's genocide, and who now has spurned her. Tuthmosis III sees his future as supreme leader of the known world – a world without Hatshepsut or Moses. His stepmother is not long for the tomb. As for the other problem, Tuthmosis needs a legitimate excuse to get Moses out of the way for good – one that will wash with his stepmother. He soon gets his chance.

In 1486 BC, Moses commits murder. It's a telling incident which shapes the future, not only of Moses and Tuthmosis III, but of Egypt and the entire planet:

And it came to pass in those days, when Moses was grown, that he went out unto his brethren, and looked on their burdens: and he spied an Egyptian smiting an Hebrew, one of his brethren. And

[Moses] **looked this way and that way, and when he saw that there was no man, he slew the Egyptian, and hid him in the sand** (Exo 2:11-12).

The Hebrew word used here for 'smiting' can also infer that the Egyptian was beating the Hebrew to death. The scriptures don't provide details of any weapon Moses may have used to despatch the assailant, so it's possible that he either gave the Egyptian a dose of his own medicine and beat the fellow to death or, since he was out alone without a bodyguard, it was probably his custom to go tooled up with a dagger or sword.

Word of the heinous deed spreads quickly, especially word concerning a Hebrew playing at being an Egyptian prince who kills an Egyptian in front of a Hebrew. There is a popular view that the slain Egyptian is one of Pharaoh's cruel taskmasters (*cf.* Exo 1:11; 5:6-9 etc.). Though the text does not give this detail, beatings were certainly dished out by the Egyptian overseers to wailing recalcitrants (Exo 5:14).

The day following the murder, Moses comes upon two Hebrews slugging it out. He breaks up the fight. "Why are you hitting your companion?" he snaps at the aggressor. Judging by the arrogant reply and the circumstances of the previous day's killing, we can infer five things from this incident. Firstly, the Hebrew thug's amazing reply: **"Who made you a prince and a judge over us? Do you intend to kill me as you killed the Egyptian?"** (Exo 2:14, NKJV)

We can surmise the following:

- Moses is not frightened of physically confronting bullies, be they Egyptian or Hebrew. That tells us something of Moses' physical stature and courage
- Moses is busted. Everyone knows what he did to the Egyptian the previous day
- It is evident that the scrapping Hebrew doesn't think much of one of his own number going native (Moses looks and dresses like an Egyptian - Exo 2:19). The Hebrew thug would hardly have responded in such a manner if Moses was regarded as a *bona fide* member of Egyptian royalty. Slaves risked execution or having their tongues torn out for such impertinence
- The Hebrew recognises that Moses holds no real power. His reply would be suicidal in any other context. If Moses had been a true prince with princely duties, would a lowly slave, even a thuggish one, have said, **"Who made you a prince and judge over us?"**?

- ➢ The Hebrew worker thinks he can get away with being insolent because he knows what Moses did to the Egyptian the previous day
- ➢ In possibly saving the life of the Hebrew worker due to his slaughterous intervention the previous day, Moses's motives are misconstrued and he is rejected by one of his own. Notice the level of stress among the Hebrew workers, who cannot even get along with each other.

Realising that word of the murder is out, Moses panics. Exo 2:15 states that when Pharaoh gets to hear about it, he seeks to kill Moses. On the face of it, this is an odd reaction for a head of state to have. Would a trial not be in order first? Egyptian pharaohs pride themselves on the Rule of Ma'at, one of the defining characteristics of Egyptian culture. Though often personified as a goddess, Ma'at is better viewed as a concept symbolising 'that which is straight', 'truth', 'order' and 'balance'; doing the right thing in the eyes of many. Moses knows there will be no Ma'at applied in his case, no trial. He is guilty as sin; there is even a witness to the nefarious deed - the Hebrew he saved - who can be thrashed for as long as it takes to get Tuthmosis III the evidence he needs to present to Hatshepsut.

If good relations existed between Moses and the regency at this point, it would seem reasonable for Moses to have thrown himself on the mercy of his family to obtain an acquittal based on his royal station. But in the matter of murder, not even the cancer-ridden Hatshepsut will be able to save him, even supposing she ever wished to after Moses turned his back on her. Moses knows there will be no mercy. His first reaction is to leave town as quickly as possible, and put as much shoe-leather between himself and a king who now wants him dead and dusted for murder.

Midian, the sanctuary

Moses flees to Midian and enters the second, 40-year period of his life: an idyllic phase, during which he settles down to a simple, nomadic existence as a shepherd and family man. Researchers tend to gloss over Moses' flight from Egypt in their haste to get to the Burning Bush. They don't pause for a moment to consider what a disorientating, all-encompassing wrench this must have been for the Hebrew. All Moses has ever known hitherto has been Egypt, wealth and privilege. Now, the teaming military metropolis of humid Memphis with its fragrance of spices and noisy yipping of the river riggers has been abruptly replaced by the hot, dry air of the desert. Gone from Moses are the people who ever meant anything to him: his stepmother Hatshepsut, her trusted advisor, Senenmut, and whatever true friends he may have had at court. Gone too from his life now are his true parents, Amram and Jochebed, and his siblings Aaron and Miriam, whom he probably met on occasion when visiting the supply city of Avaris in Goshen, slipping out of the palace for a stroll, ostensibly to take the evening air, shadowed afar off by Hatshepsut's agents. It is likely at this point that Moses has also been forced to abandon his first wife, perhaps the Ethiopian woman who later becomes a source of upset in Num 12:1. From what we know of this period, it seems unlikely that Moses, an Egyptian prince, would still be unmarried at forty. No children at this stage are mentioned.

Moses ends up in Midian. The precise location of this area is important for us to establish, not just because this is where Moses finds sanctuary, but because Midian is, according to some, the region where the famous Mount Sinai is located, which will play such a pivotal role in the story we are examining.

There are two schools of thought on the location of Mount Sinai/Mount Horeb (the names are mostly used interchangeably). One camp puts it in the Sinai peninsula, the 'V'-shaped bit between Egypt and Canaan, and the other in north-western Arabia. Most Bible maps place 'Mount Sinai' in the southern Sinai peninsula, yet the apostle Paul clearly tells us in Galatians 4:25 that the Mount Sinai of the covenant is located in 'Arabia', and that this is the land of Hagar's children, which Paul himself visited for a period (Gal 1:17).

Bible researcher Dr Chuck Missler writes:

"Traditionally, 'Horeb' is regarded as the range, Mount Sinai as the specific peak within that range (Ex 24:12,13). Recent discoveries, however, place the mount in Arabia (Gal 4:25). This same location is used with Elijah (1 Kgs 19:4-11), and a tradition exists among many scholars that it was at Mount Sinai where Paul was given the gospel. Paul was schooled separately (Gal 1:17; 4:25). Some scholars infer that he may have been in exile himself and received revelation in that area."[101]

Which naturally begs the question: Can we know for sure the precise location of Mt Sinai/Horeb? Are we expected to look for it? Is there any extra-Biblical evidence or archaeology whatsoever to support such a candidate? We will embark on our own quest a little

---

[101] **Missler, C** *Exodus notes,* www.khouse.org, p.16

later when we find ourselves in the shadow of this fearsome place. Meanwhile, back to the story:

A wife and family

Now when Pharaoh heard this thing [heard about the murder], **he sought to slay Moses. But Moses fled from the face of Pharaoh, and dwelt in the land of Midian: and he sat down by a well.**

Now the priest of Midian had seven daughters: and they came and drew water, and filled the troughs to water their father's flock. And the shepherds came and drove them away: but Moses stood up and helped them, and watered their flock.

And when they came to Reuel their father, he said, "How is it that ye are come so soon today?"

And they said, "An Egyptian delivered us out of the hand of the shepherds, and also drew water enough for us, and watered the flock."

And he said unto his daughters, "And where is he? Why is it that ye have left the man? Call him, that he may eat bread."

And Moses was content to dwell with the man: and he gave Moses Zipporah his daughter. And she bare him a son, and he called his name Gershom: for he said, "I have been a stranger in a strange land." (Exo 2:15-22)

A few points on this passage:

- Some scholars see Reuel as synonymous with Jethro, the Midian priest who becomes Moses' father-in-law. This is not necessarily the case[102]

[102] Some are puzzled over the apparent diverse names given to Moses' father-in-law. He is referred to as Jethro in a number of passages in Exodus, Jether in some translations of Exo 4:18, Reuel in Exo 2:18, Raguel in Num 10:29, and there is mention of Hobab being Moses' father-in-law in Judg 4:11. The resolution to this lies in a) the word translated as 'father-in-law' means 'to contract affinity by marriage': (*chathan,* Strongs 2859), which can be used to describe a range of marital affiliations (*cf.* Gen 19:14; Exo 4:18,26; Deut 7:3; 27:23; Isa 62:5; Ezra 9:14; 1 Kings 3:1). Hobab, who is asked by Moses to act as a wilderness guide in Num 10:29-32, is clearly young and vigorous, and not an old father of seven daughters! The most likely explanation from the various passages in scripture is that Reuel was the father of Jethro, and thus the patriarch of the family of Zipporah. Jethro was the father of Zipporah, and thus the father-in-law of Moses. Hobab was the grandson of Reuel, the son of Jethro, and thus the brother-in-law of Moses. Jethro can be a title meaning 'His Excellence" (*yithrow*: Strongs 3503); and Jether is a familiar version of Jethro. www.3amthoughts.com/article/people-and-places/moses-relatives

- Moses' style, clothing and physical appearance make it apparent to the locals that he is an Egyptian, Moses seems unconcerned that he is perceived as such – another clue that he is now outside territory controlled by Egypt and therefore safe
- Once again we see the Hebrew's physical prowess. Moses strong-arms a gang of shepherds. Don't mess with Moses
- Have you noticed how many Biblical characters have life-changing encounters by a well? Wells are a source of water, and water is life. Wells/water in the Bible speak typologically of the Holy Spirit, the Word and are used consistently as a type of Christ - idiomatic of eternal life [103]
- A father with seven daughters will always be keen to learn of any rich, male stranger in the neighbourhood
- There's that number seven again - the number of God/completion
- We read of Jethro's seven daughters, one of which, Zipporah, is given to Moses as a Gentile bride, foreshadowing for the mystics among us the seven Gentile brides of the OT;[104] the seven churches of Revelation 2-3; the mystery of the bride of Christ (which some see and some don't - Eph 5:32; 2 Cor 11:2; Rev 19:7-8); Jesus taking a Gentile bride, echoed as a type in the story of Boaz (the kinsman redeemer) and Ruth; Israel as the first bride who commits spiritual fornication, so God divorces her under the Law but restores her through grace – a model for Christ Himself (Hos 1; 5:15; Jer 3:8; Rom 11:1-5)
- Moses names his eldest son Gershom ('a sojourner there'), and states **"I have been a stranger in a strange land"**, which can ambiguously apply to his sojourning in Egypt and/or Midian. Either way, Midian is once again referred to as a strange land, implying Moses is not currently located in some far-flung province of Egypt

---

[103] Hagar: Gen 21:15-19; Abraham: Gen 21:25; Eliezer: Gen 24:13-14; Isaac: Gen 24: 62-65; Jacob: 29:8-10; Joseph: Gen 49:22; *cf*: FG 4:7-15;

[104] Eve (from Eden), Rebekah (Haran), Asenath (Egypt), Zipporah (Midian), Rahab (Jericho), The Shulamite, Ruth (Moab).

So Moses weds Zipporah, the daughter of a non-covenant Midianite priest named Jethro.[105] Jethro is a sympathetic, wise cove who takes Moses under his wing and allows him to tend the flocks. During the years that follow, Zipporah bears Moses another son, Eliezer ('comforter' - Exo 4:20; 18:4). While all's well for now in the world of Midian, hundreds of miles away to the west, Hatshepsut succumbs to bone cancer two years later in 1484 BC.

The History Channel reports:

"The Egyptian queen Hatshepsut might have accidentally poisoned herself with skin lotion, according to a new study. Researchers have detected a highly carcinogenic substance in the dried contents of a cosmetic vial found among the female pharaoh's possessions. One of ancient Egypt's most powerful rulers, Hatshepsut is thought to have died of bone cancer....

"A flask of lotion believed to have belonged to the female pharaoh Hatshepsut contains a carcinogenic substance that might ultimately have killed the Egyptian queen, German researchers said today. Part of the permanent collection at the University of Bonn's Egyptian Museum, the vessel was thought to have held perfume until a two-year study uncovered traces of what appears to be an ancient treatment for eczema or psoriasis. Its ingredients include palm and nutmeg oil, fatty acids that can relieve certain skin conditions and a type of cancer-causing tar residue, which is also found in cigarette smoke....

"A CT scan revealed that she had died in her 50s of bone cancer and also suffered from diabetes and arthritis.... Did Hatshepsut inadvertently poison herself while trying to soothe her itchy, irritated skin? 'There is a lot that speaks for this hypothesis,' said Helmut Wiedenfeld of the University of Bonn's pharmaceutical institute. 'If you imagine that the queen had a chronic skin disease and that she found short-term improvement from the salve, she may have exposed herself to a great risk over the years.' " [106]

Tuthmosis III finally becomes sole ruler of Egypt. Fed up with what he perceives as his stepmother's weak foreign policy reliant on trade, Tuthmosis III sets about doing what Tuthmosis III does best. American Egyptologist William C Hayes explains:

---

[105] We understand that Jethro is not under the covenant because of the extreme reaction displayed by his daughter Zipporah to the rite of circumcision in Exo 4:25-26.

[106] *History in the Headlines,* "Did Skin Cream Kill Egypt's Queen Hatshepsut?" 19th August 2011

"During the thirty-two years of his independent reign... Tuthmosis III proved himself to be, incontestably, the greatest pharaoh ever to occupy the throne of Egypt.... We shall have occasion to follow his expansion and consolidation of Egyptian control over Nubia and the northern Sudan, his vigorous exploitation of the resources of the empire, his very considerable augmentation of the national wealth of Egypt, his efficient organization of the internal administration of the country, his vast programme of building, and the notable advances in Egyptian art and culture achieved under his sponsorship. Thus we may gain some insight into the many-sidedness, the diverse abilities and talents of this Napoleonic little man, who appears to have excelled not only as a general, a statesman, and an administrator, but also as one of the most accomplished horsemen, archers, and all-round athletes of his time."[107]

Under Tuth III, Egypt truly enters its golden age of wealth, expansionism, art and opulence, and it will be this very Egypt which Moses will shortly plunder for the LORD's benefit. Some researchers have pegged Tuthmosis III as the proud, expansionist Exodus pharaoh whom God humbles with the plagues. There are a couple of problems with this: Tuthmosis III does not come across in the archaeological record as paranoid and proud. More decisively, you have to account for the following scriptural development:

And it came to pass <u>in process of time</u> that the king of Egypt died: and the children of Israel sighed by reason of the bondage, and they cried, and their cry came up unto God by reason of the bondage. And God heard their groaning, and God remembered his covenant with Abraham, with Isaac, and with Jacob. And God looked upon the children of Israel, and God had respect unto them. (Exo 2:23-25)

As previously covered, the Exodus can be Biblically dated to 1446 BC, during the reign of Amenhotep II. That Tuthmosis III is the 'oppression' pharaoh and not the one confronting Moses prior to the Exodus is down to one finding an Egyptian king occupying the throne *for at least the forty-year period* of Moses' exile in Midian (*cf.* Acts 7:23; Exo 7:7). As previously mentioned, there are only two contenders: Tuthmosis III and Rameses II, the latter of whom can be discounted as occupying a different historical timeframe. Moreover, if you read Exo 2:15-23 in one go, it is hard not to come to the conclusion that the king of Exo 2:15 who sought Moses' death because of the Egyptian's

---

[107] **Hayes, W C** *Egypt: Internal Affairs from Tuthmosis I to the Death of Amenophis III,* part I, Cambridge University Press, 1962, p.9

murder is the same one who dies **in the process of time** (a quaint phrase for 'after quite a while') forty years later in Exo 2:23. And just so that we get the point, God tells Moses in Exo 4:19: **"Go, return into Egypt: for all the men are dead which sought thy life"**, which presumably includes the oppression pharaoh of Exo 2:15.

Mt Sinai/Horeb and the burning bush

So, after forty years of sheep/goats, Moses is wrenched out of his comfort zone one day as he leads his (actually Jethro's) flock beside a strange mountain called Horeb. Scholars, researchers and adventurers alike have written reams and argue heatedly to this day on where this mountain is located. See **Chart A** for the leading contenders. Does it really matter? Not theologically. Does God intend for us to look? One way of answering that might depend on whether enough geographical clues have been left in the scriptures inviting us to dig, *and there are.* If God has taken the trouble to lay out the breadcrumbs for us, we should roll up our sleeves and have a look – I mean, if we really care. The clues are tantalising, so only the dogged need apply. Another, similar treasure hunt we'll engage in later is the location of the Israelites' Red Sea crossing where Pharaoh's army meets its Waterloo. We'll find the same tantalising breadcrumb trail; the same invitation to dig.

Mt Sinai is not only the site of the burning bush incident we'll examine in a minute, it's the location to which Moses returns with over 2 million Israelites and a mixed multitude (Gentile 'hangers-on') for one of the most epic events of the Old Testament: the giving of the Law to Israel by God personally, including those Ten Commandments. The Law-giving at Mt Sinai is a defining event in Judaism and Christianity, and is a major turn in the central theme of the Bible itself: the redemption of man by his Creator.

You'll see from **Chart A** that the traditional site is Jebel Musa (*lit.* 'Moses' mountain') in the southern Sinai. This site is Bedouin tradition, but it was formalised by the Emperor Constantine's Christian convert mother Helena ('St Helen' - early 4th century AD), who was tasked by Constantine to track down relics of the Judeo-Christian religion. A monastery, St Catherines, stands there to this day, reputedly built on her orders. Alas, Jebel Musa can be discounted for a number of reasons we'll examine later, not least because it does not host a plain before it capable of supporting up to 2 million displaced Israelite and miscellaneous personages for a period of weeks. It is also not on the direct route from Midian to Egypt, which would be Moses's requirement to meet up with Aaron (coming up in a minute). It's also not a friendly goat-herding distance from Midian – a further qualification.

Another crowd believes that Mt Sinai is located at Jebel Al-Lawz in Saudi Arabia, and that the Red Sea crossing was at the Strait of Tiran at the mouth of the Gulf of Aqaba. They make the understandable error of assuming that when Moses visits 'Mt Sinai' for the first time grazing Jethro's flocks, he is still in Midian, located in modern-day, north-western Arabia. This is not the case. For starters, Bedouin practices even to this day allow for a 60–70 km wander with your beasts – even further in times of drought. Those researchers claiming the Israelites crossed the Red Sea at Sharm el-Sheikh ('the Tiran Crossing') to get to a Mt Sinai in Midian (Jebel al-Lawz) point to Acts 7:29, which states that Moses fled to Midian (I agree), and Gal 4:25, which states that Mt Sinai is in Arabia (I agree). *Ha! So Mt Sinai must be in Saudi Arabia!* Not so fast. Hold your goats a moment. Perhaps you should ask what a 1st century AD, highly educated scholar like Paul would understand when he used the geographical term 'Arabia' (Gal 4:25)? The House of Saud did not put its name to the present-day territory until 1932.

Gordon Franz has made a detailed study of the 'Mount Sinai is in Midian' claim and refutes it as follows:

"One can easily argue that the Apostle Paul used the First Century AD Roman concept of Arabia in this passage. In the first century AD, based on the prior use by Herodotus, Pliny and Strabo, Arabia extended from the Persian Gulf to the Nile Delta, thus including the Sinai peninsula in Arabia. Paul would be perfectly correct in placing Mt. Sinai in the Sinai peninsula because the Sinai peninsula was part of Arabia of his day."

And:

"Two Biblical passages clearly place Mt. Sinai outside the Land of Midian. In Exodus 18, Moses and the Israelites are camped at 'the Mountain of God' (Mt. Sinai) when Jethro, Moses' father-in-law, visits them. Verse 27 says, "Then Moses let his father-in-law depart [from Mt. Sinai], and he went his way to his own land [Midian]." Jethro departs from Mt. Sinai to return to the Land of Midian. According to *Mandelkern Biblical Concordance*, the phrase 'his own land' (third person singular possessive) is used 30 times in the Hebrew Scriptures (Ex. 18:27; Num.

21:24,26,34,35; Deut. 2:24,31; 3:2; 4:47; 11:3; 29:1 [29:2 Eng.]; 33:13; 34:11; Josh. 8:1; I Kings 22:36; II Kings 18:33; Isa. 2:7,8; 13:14; 18:2,7; 36:18; 37:7; Jer. 2:15; 27:7; 50:18; Prov. 8:31; Dan. 11:19,28; Neh. 9:10; Mandelkern 1896:153). In the Pentateuch the phrase is use 13 times. Each time it is used of a specific geo-political entity, a kingdom, nation or tribal area. It is used of the Kingdom of the Amorites (Num. 21:24,26; Deut. 2:24,31; 4:47), with the borders clearly delineated as going from the Arnon to the Jabbok (Num. 21:24). The Kingdom of Bashan (Num. 21:34,35; Deut. 3:2; 4:47), which is implied as going from the Jabbok to Mt. Hermon (Deut. 4:48). The nation of Egypt (Deut. 11:3; 29:1 [29:2 Eng.]; 34:11) as well as the tribal territory of Joseph (Deut. 33:13). Joshua gives the delineation of the tribal territory of Ephraim and Manasseh which make up the tribes of Joseph (Deut. 33:17; Josh. 13:29-33; 16:1-10; 17:1-18). If Moses is consistent with his use of the word, and I think he is, the context suggests Jethro returned to the country of Midian, not to a plot of ground that he controlled as the proponents of Jebel al-Lawz [i.e. Mt Sinai in Midian] contend."[108]

See what I mean? You can almost hear them gnashing their teeth down at the Goatherders Association. We'll unravel this mystery as we go because the clues are given as the story progresses. For now, let's see what happens when Moses passes by this strange mountain and something catches his eye on the slope....

Now Moses kept the flock of Jethro his father-in-law, the priest of Midian: and he led the flock to the backside of the desert, and came to the mountain of God, even to Horeb. And the Angel of the LORD appeared unto him in a flame of fire out of the midst of a bush: and he looked, and, behold, the bush burned with fire, and the bush was not consumed. And Moses said, "I will now turn aside and see this great sight, why the bush is not burnt." (Exo 3:1-3)

The backside of the desert is an unusual expression. Pastors have used it allegorically for sermons: for example, what to do when you find yourself spiritually in **the backside of the desert**; in the deep wilderness. I believe at this stage in his life, Moses has had plenty of time to think, constantly churning over in his mind his bizarre life's path thus far; what it all means if anything; what will become of him; the nature of his calling. His Creator is about to address these questions in the most personal way, leading Moses **to the backside of the desert**, perhaps at the point of Moses' deepest loneliness and doubt.

[108] http://ldolphin.org/franz-ellawz.html

Geographically, **the backside of the desert** could be giving us an interesting clue from an eyewitness to the actual location of Mount Horeb, which we will examine later. In other words, there must be a frontside to the desert too! The point to note for now is that the location of the burning bush incident is on the same mountain Moses will return to with the Israelites after they leave Egypt in the Exodus. In fact, God promises this very thing (Exo 3:12).

A bush burning in the desert will have been a common sight to Moses as a shepherd; bushes catch fire all the time in the hot season. What's different about this burning bush is that it is not being consumed. As he approaches it, the bush speaks! The Angel of the LORD heralds Moses from out of the fire.

Unlike other angels, the Angel of the LORD has some unusual characteristics. He is identified with YHWH and speaks in the first person of God,[109] yet at other times He is distinct from the LORD.[110] Since no-one has seen or heard the Father at any time,[111] scholars speculate that the Angel of the LORD is a pre-incarnate theophany of Yeshua (Jesus). The clue to this is that the Angel of the LORD introduces Himself to Moses as YHWH, the pre-existent 'I AM': the same name Jesus will accord Himself centuries later in FG 8:58, inviting the Sanhedrin's death penalty for blasphemy. This connection between the Old and New Testament God is not lost on Bible expert Dr Chuck Missler, and neither are some other intriguing aspects to the event:

"The burning bush has some very interesting symbolism. Fire is always symbolic of judgment (in the Scripture); brass was always used in the Tabernacle for vessels which needed to hold fire, so brass speaks of fire and thus judgment. (*cf.* Num 21:5-20 and the brazen serpent; Heb 12:29 "our God is a consuming fire"; Heb 1:13 notes that He cannot even look upon evil). So, with fire speaking of judgment, what is being judged here? The bush. The Hebrew for this bush is *seneh*, which actually comes from the word 'to prick' and it thus means a bramble or thorn bush (sometimes called an acacia bush); the thorn bush of the desert.

The symbol for sin is a thorn (Gen 3:18). When we see Christ crucified, we find the Roman soldiers made a crown of thorns and placed it upon Christ's head. Christ was made sin for us (Gal 3:13), He bore our sins on His brow. Here with the burning bush, we have sin being judged

---

[109] Gen 16:13; 22:11-12; 31:11,13; 48:16; Judg 6:11,16,22; 13:22-23; Zech 3:1-2

[110] 2 Sam 24:16; Zech 1:12

[111] Exo 33:20; FG 1:18; 5:37; 6:46; 1 Tim 6:15-16

by God's consuming fire! The thorn bush is not consumed; sin in the Hands of the Living God, not being destroyed, is a model of mercy.... Also, it is interesting that here we see thorns and not fruit."[112]

This is the first time God actually gives His name to a human, in the form of the tetragrammaton YHWH - sometimes transposed for pronunciation as YaHWeH or YeHoWaH (Jehovah). It means 'I AM', 'I CAUSE TO BE'. Later, when Moses is experiencing setbacks in confronting Pharaoh, God tells him:

I am the LORD [YHWH]. **And I appeared unto Abraham, unto Isaac, and unto Jacob, by the name of God Almighty** [*lit.* El Shaddai - 'The One Who Suffices'], **but by My name YHWH** [Yahweh, Jehovah] **was I not known to them.** (Exo 6:2-3)

Let's examine this astonishing person-to-person meeting between Moses and the Creator of the universe. Here is the first part:

Now Moses kept the flock of Jethro his father-in-law, the priest of Midian: and he led the flock to the backside of the desert, and came to the mountain of God, even to Horeb. And the angel of the LORD appeared unto him in a flame of fire out of the midst of a bush: and [Moses] **looked, and, behold, the bush burned with fire, and the bush was not consumed.**

And Moses said, "I will now turn aside, and see this great sight, why the bush is not burnt."

And when the LORD saw that he turned aside to see, God called unto him out of the midst of the bush, and said, "Moses, Moses." And Moses said, "Here am I."

And He said, "Draw not nigh hither: put off thy shoes from off thy feet, for the place whereon thou standest is holy ground."

And the LORD said, "I have surely seen the affliction of My people which are in Egypt, and have heard their cry by reason of their taskmasters; for I know their sorrows. And I am come down to deliver them out of the hand of the Egyptians, and to bring them up out of that land unto a good land and a large, unto a land flowing with milk and honey; unto the place of the Canaanites, and the Hittites, and the Amorites, and the Perizzites, and the Hivites, and the Jebusites.

"Now therefore, behold, the cry of the children of Israel is come unto Me: and I have also seen the oppression wherewith the Egyptians oppress them. Come now therefore, and I will send thee

---

[112] Missler, C, *Exodus notes,* op. cit., p.17-18

unto Pharaoh, that thou mayest bring forth My people, the children of Israel, out of Egypt."

And Moses said unto God, "Who am I, that I should go unto Pharaoh, and that I should bring forth the children of Israel out of Egypt?"

And [YHWH] **said, "Certainly I will be with thee; and this shall be a token unto thee, that I have sent thee: When thou hast brought forth the people out of Egypt, ye shall serve God upon this mountain."**

And Moses said unto God, "Behold, when I come unto the children of Israel, and shall say unto them, The God of your fathers hath sent me unto you; and they shall say to me, 'What is His name?' what shall I say unto them?"

And God said unto Moses, "I AM THAT I AM." and He said, "Thus shalt thou say unto the children of Israel, 'I AM hath sent me unto you.' " (Exo 3:1-14)

Some highlights here:

- God has Moses remove his shoes, for the place where the Hebrew is standing is 'holy ground'. Shoes are used consistently throughout the Bible as a model for a person's spiritual walk or personal authority. God wants the shoes off because His own sovereignty takes precedence. Holiness is a property God possesses: a metacosmic link to the consummate perfection and overall character of the Creator
- The Hebrew word for 'God' used throughout the passage is *Elohim* (plural), implying the triune godhead [113]
- God identifies Himself as the God of Abraham, Isaac and Jacob: the God of the Abrahamic covenant. The God of the Land Promise
- He comments on the plight of His people. He has *seen* their affliction, *heard* their cries, *knows* their sorrows, will *deliver* them out of the hands of the Egyptians, and *bring* them to a new land flowing with milk and honey. In other words, God

[113] Answering criticism that the Bible does not teach a Trinitarian Deity, Daniel B Wallace Ph.D, Professor of New Testament Studies at Dallas Theological Seminary, and one of the world's great experts on textual criticism and Biblical exegesis, comments: *"The Bible clearly contains these four truths: the Father is God, Jesus is God, the Holy Spirit is God, and there is only one God… And that's the Trinity."* - **Strobel, Lee** *The Case for the Real Jesus*, Zondervan, 2007, p.94

has total sensory experience of his people's suffering. The land in question already has residents living there, and God lists them

- Canaan at this time is apparently extremely lush and fertile
- God is going to send Moses to Pharaoh to arrange the release of the Israelites from Egyptian servitude

It's all too much for the eighty-year-old. Forty years of sheep and goats have definitely blunted the old edge. God reassures Moses that not only will he succeed in leading the Israelites out of Egypt with God's help, he will bring the lot to this very mountain to serve the LORD.

Moses baulks. "But, but, but ..." **"Behold, when I come unto the children of Israel, and shall say unto them, The God of your fathers hath sent me unto you; and they shall say to me, 'What is His name?' what shall I say unto them?"**

And God said unto Moses, "I AM THAT I AM." and He said, "Thus shalt thou say unto the children of Israel, 'I AM hath sent me unto you.' " (Exo 3:13-14)

Nothing but problems crowd themselves onto Moses' lips. God forestalls him. Moses, you're to present yourself to the elders of the afflicted Hebrew tribes and deliver the word of the LORD: God has seen the afflictions of His people and has come with you to free and lead them to the Promised Land of Canaan. And what is the name of The One who has sent you? I AM THAT I AM.

Oh, great. And they're going to believe me? "But, but, but ..."

Moses, you and these Hebrew elders will then proceed to Pharaoh and request permission for the Israelites to go three days into the wilderness to sacrifice to God. I will harden Pharaoh's heart and the king will not release the Hebrews. Because of this, I will stretch out My hand and strike Egypt with a series of plagues.

All this out of a burning bush.

God also tells Moses that while He is chastising Egypt with fearsome wonders, the Israelites will amazingly find favour with the Egyptian public, who will willingly hand over gold, silver, clothing and other treasures to the Hebrews as they leave! In fact, God predicted this unlikely detail to Abraham centuries before (Gen 15:13-14). It will also be an interesting replay of what occurred with Abram's dealings with the pharaoh of his time over the latter's infatuation with Sarai (Gen 12:14ff.). God often uses the most bizarre means to accomplish His will. Why? *Because only God can,* and no human will be able to claim the credit, especially since God prophesied the event beforetime.

Moses is extremely reluctant to play saviour. He makes excuses. *The Hebrews won't listen to me. They won't believe me. They'll think I'm making it all up. I failed with them once before when I killed the Egyptian.*

God gives Moses some exotic demonstrations of His power, including an intriguing preview of Christ healing the lepers in the New Testament. YHWH turns Moses' hand leprous and then heals it. Not even this convinces Moses, who whines that he is not a good speaker and will fail at the task. Moses is demonstrating human nature with which we are all too familiar. He has become comfortable with, and reconciled to his humdrum existence in Midian. He's married, he's looked after, he's multiply-whelped, and he's not looking forward to appearing insane when he tells the burning bush story over family dinner the following evening.

And Moses answered and said, "But, behold, they will not believe me, nor hearken unto my voice: for they will say, 'The LORD hath not appeared unto thee.' "

And the LORD said unto him, "What is that in thine hand?"

And [Moses] **said, "A rod."**

And [God] **said, "Cast it on the ground." And he cast it on the ground, and it became a serpent; and Moses fled from before it.**

And the LORD said unto Moses, "Put forth thine hand, and take it by the tail." And he put forth his hand, and caught it, and it became a rod in his hand. "That they may believe that the LORD God of their fathers, the God of Abraham, the God of Isaac, and the God of Jacob, hath appeared unto thee." (Exo 4:1-5)

"But I'm no public speaker!"

After losing patience, God finally wins Moses to the cause by explaining that Aaron will use his communication skills to do the talking to the Hebrew people while God talks to Moses. So the transmission of command will be: God to Moses to Aaron to the Hebrews.

And then in Exo 4:19 the LORD gives us a valuable piece of intelligence: **Now the LORD said to Moses in Midian, "Go, return to Egypt for <u>ALL THE MEN</u> who sought your life are dead."** (NKJV) If you couple up this verse with Exo 2:23: **And it came to pass in process of time, that the king of Egypt died,** this undoes any notion that the Exodus pharaoh will be Tuthmosis III, because it is clear from the context of Exo 2:15 - 2:23, that this is the same king of the oppression, who is now dead after 40 years. Once again, just to hammer it home, the only other pharaoh who reigns for that length of time is centuries ahead - Rameses II - and he doesn't fit with the timescale of 1 Kings 6:1.

ALL THE MEN who sought your life are dead? Sounds like a sizeable faction in addition to Tuthmosis III. *All over the murder of an Egyptian?* There's something more going on here, which dovetails precisely with what we now know of this period of Egyptian history.

It seems from scripture that this faction had some other axe to grind with Pharaoh's ex-nephew and God's new prophet. Let's put ourselves in the Napoleonic Tuthmosis III's shoes. When Moses fled Egypt after killing the Egyptian, it was two years before the ailing Queen Hatshepsut's death. Tuthmosis III now had the reins of power firmly in his grasp - the regency was over in all but name. Moses was branded an enemy of the state; Hatshepsut could not defend a murderer. Not only did Tuthmosis III want Hatshepsut's 'son' out of the way as a potential rival to the throne, it cannot have escaped Tuthmosis' notice that Moses was reacquainting himself with his Hebrew roots. Such a troublemaker with royal connections causing ructions among the huge Hyksos slave-force of Egypt was a scenario which could only alarm the ruling élite. Tuthmosis was fully aware that Moses had the potential either to trigger a rebellion among the empire's valuable slave-force or, more lethally, execute a re-run of the historic Hyksos disaster when the princes of Thebes lost control of their entire nation for two centuries. You will recall that this not unreasonable fear drove the skullcracking Tuthmosis I to move the empire's centre of military operations all the way from Thebes in the south up to Memphis in the Delta: to keep a close eye on the volatile north; to dwell among the potential troublemakers.

Behind the scenes in the metacosm, *ha-Satan* has been moving to have Moses and the Hebrews exterminated at all costs, for within their number resides the Scarlet Thread through which the Messiah will come to judge the Devil and his fallen realm, and reclaim title to the Earth (Rev 5), which was lost at the Fall (Gen 3). Jesus the Messiah will be God's firstborn and only begotten Son, yet now, fascinatingly, God refers to Israel as His firstborn, directly linking Israel to the Messiah:

And the LORD said unto Moses in Midian, "Go, return into Egypt: for all the men are dead which sought thy life."

And Moses took his wife and his sons, and set them upon an ass, and he returned to the land of Egypt: and Moses took the rod of God in his hand.

And the LORD said unto Moses, "When thou goest to return into Egypt, see that thou do all those wonders before Pharaoh, which I have put in thine hand: but I will harden his heart, that he shall not let the people go. And thou shalt say unto Pharaoh, 'Thus saith the LORD, Israel is My son, even My firstborn: And I say unto thee, Let My son go, that he may serve Me: and if thou refuse to let him go, behold, I will slay thy son, even thy firstborn.' " (Exo 4:19-23)

- Once again, there is a significant period of 40 years, then a pharaoh's death. The pharaoh seeking to kill Moses in Exo 2:15 is obviously the same pharaoh who is reported dead in Exo 2:23. There is a gap of 40 years between Exo 2:15 and Exo 2:23 (Acts 7:29-30). Only one pharaoh qualifies for this **process of time**: Tuthmosis III
- Where did God speak to Moses? At the burning bush, also stated as the location of God's holy mountain (Exo 3:12)
- The pharaoh Moses will confront will be stubborn to the 'nth' degree. The pharaoh following the now dead Tuthmosis III in the Egyptian record is Amenhotep II. If you look up the word 'insecure' in any dictionary, you'll find a picture of Amenhotep II next to it
- God equates the Hebrew twelve tribes in Egyptian bondage as 'Israel' and names them His firstborn son (heir)
- God gets personal. If Pharaoh won't let His firstborn son go, God will slay Pharaoh's own firstborn son. This will happen during the tenth plague, and if this calamity is in fact an actual event, there should be ample evidence of it in the secular Egyptian record relating to Amenhotep II's firstborn. There is!

Trouble at the inn or seminary?

So Moses takes Zipporah, his wife, and two sons Gershom and Eliezer, famously saddles that ass, and heads for Egypt after securing permission from Jethro as his adoptive son (by marriage). Where do they set out from? Jethro's estate in Midian, east of the Gulf of Aqaba. Where are they headed? Egypt. It is reasonable to suppose that Moses will take the most direct route, which will lead from Jethro's place up to the northern tip of the Gulf of Aqaba (modern-day Eilat), then directly across central Sinai using a famous and ancient trade route known as The King's Highway – part of which today is known as the Trans-Sinai Highway. More about this later. What Moses won't be doing is heading hundreds of miles out of his way into southern Sinai over terrible terrain to pass Jebel Musa on the way back to Egypt!

Then we get to three of the most troublesome verses in the Old Testament, which have spawned reams of scholarly conjecture and public outrage.

At a lodging place on the way, the LORD met Moses and was about to kill him. But Zipporah took a flint knife, cut off her son's foreskin and touched Moses' feet with it. "Surely you are a bridegroom of blood to me," she said. So the LORD let him alone. (At that time she said "bridegroom of blood", referring to circumcision.) (Exo 4:24-26, NIV)

Strewth, what just happened? Has God suddenly swung into homicidal mode straight after promising Moses a shining destiny?

It is widely taught in Jewish and Christian circles that just after spending two chapters (Exo 3 and 4) explaining to Moses that the latter will free the Hebrews from captivity with God's help and lead them off to a promised land flowing with milk and honey, the Creator of the universe then has a schizophrenic episode and seeks to kill Moses when the family stops at an inn. Moses has failed to circumcise his son according to God's covenant arrangement (Gen 17). To save her husband's life, therefore, a bitter Zipporah takes a blade and does the deed, flinging (we assume the firstborn) Gershom's foreskin at her husband's feet, manifestly outraged that Moses belongs to such a primitive, bloodthirsty religion.

Let Us Reason Ministries puts forth this view:

"God could not have Moses be the deliverer of the Hebrew people while he was being disobedient to the Abrahamic covenant, something required of every Hebrew male. To dishonor that sign and seal of the covenant was sinful to a Hebrew, Gen 17:10: **This is My covenant which you shall keep, between Me and you and your descendants after you: Every male child among you shall be circumcised.** Gen 21:4: **Then Abraham circumcised his son Isaac when he was <u>eight days old</u>, as God had commanded him.**"[114]

Alden Bass PhD of *Apologetics Press* writes:

"This story is particularly difficult to understand because of its brevity, and the unusual wording of verse 24: "<u>The Lord sought to kill Moses</u>." Though the phrasing of the verse may elicit dark images of God slinking about the encampment, waiting to ambush Moses, the fact that God would kill someone is not unusual in other contexts. The wicked

---

[114] www.letusreason.org/Biblexp81.htm

were slain by God in the Great Flood because of their violent and ungodly actions (Genesis 6:1-7). The Lord killed Er and Onan, two of Judah's sons, because of their overt rebellion (Genesis 38:7,10). In Moses' later years, God would legislate the death penalty for those guilty of disobeying certain laws (Leviticus 20). In these instances and many more, God 'killed' a person or persons, albeit indirectly. In Exodus 4, we can be assured that Moses was afflicted because he was guilty of some sin." [emphasis mine] [115]

The problem is, Exo 4:24 in the Hebrew Torah doesn't say that 'the LORD sought to kill Moses'! People have got the wrong end of the stick with these three verses *because they are reading corrupted translations and confusing the context.* Let's back up.

Bible *aficionados* will have noticed by now that I quote the scriptures almost always using the King James Authorised Version (KJV). I do this because, although the language is archaic and a tad chewy, the KJV is the least faulty English translation from the original, inspired Hebrew, Aramaic and Greek texts comprising the Bible, and these three dramatic verses are a classic example of why I choose the KJV. So let's look at those three verses again side by side, firstly from the previously quoted, popular New International Version, and then from the King James. Firstly, the NIV:

At a lodging place on the way, the LORD met Moses and was about to kill him. But Zipporah took a flint knife, cut off her son's foreskin and touched Moses' feet with it. "Surely you are a bridegroom of blood to me," she said. So the LORD let him alone. (At that time she said "bridegroom of blood", referring to circumcision.) (Exo 4:24-26, NIV)

Now the literal, accurate King James translation, which raises some questions:

And it came to pass by the way in the inn, that the LORD met him, and sought to kill him [met whom, and sought to kill whom?]**. Then Zipporah took a sharp stone, and cut off the foreskin of her son, and cast it at his feet, and said, "Surely a bloody husband art thou to me." So he** [who?] **let him** [who?] **go: then she said, "A bloody husband thou art, because of the circumcision."** (Exo 4:24-26, KJV)

The difference? The NIV translators have inserted the three names I've underlined in their translation. They have done this in an honest, albeit misguided effort to help the reader identify who is

[115] www.apologeticspress.org/apcontent.aspx?category=11&article=1279

doing and saying what. You've noticed that I sometimes pop square brackets into a Bible quote myself to clarify the narrative in similar manner. The King James translators, by contrast, have remained faithful to the original Hebrew text and haven't done that, and neither have a number of other translations with this piece.[116] Which raises the all-important question: who is the LORD seeking to kill here?

To answer that, we have to go back a few verses to get the overall context of the passage. We must also appreciate that the original scriptures were written on continuous scrolls without breaks or chapter and verse markings. The latter were added by Archbishop Stephen Langdon and others in the 13-14th centuries AD, and while they are often helpful in giving us great reference points, they can mess up the context in spectacular fashion by dividing passages which were intended to flow together.

Let's examine the passage in context, but this time be sensitive grammatically to the pronouns used, which refer to the nearest antecedent character being discussed:

21 **And the LORD said unto Moses, "When thou goest to return into Egypt, see that thou do all those wonders before Pharaoh, which I have put in thine hand: but I will harden his heart, that he shall not let the people go.**

22 **"And thou shalt say unto Pharaoh, 'Thus saith the LORD, Israel is My son, even My firstborn:**

23 **And I say unto thee, Let My son go, that he may serve Me: and if thou refuse to let him** [God's 'firstborn' Israel] **go, behold, I will slay thy son, even thy firstborn** [i.e. Pharaoh's firstborn son]**.' "**

24 **And it came to pass by the way in the inn, that the LORD met him** [Pharaoh's firstborn]**, and sought to kill him** [nearest antecedent: Pharaoh's firstborn son]**.**

<PAUSE>

25 **Then Zipporah took a sharp stone, and cut off the foreskin of her son, and cast it at his** [nearest antecedent: her son's] **feet, and said, "Surely a bloody husband art thou to me."**

26 **So he** [nearest antecedent: 'bloody husband', Moses] **let him go** [released his son]**: then she said, "A bloody husband thou art, because of the circumcision."** (Exo 4:21-26)

KJV Today explains:

"In verse 23, God makes it clear that he will slay Pharaoh's firstborn son if Pharaoh refuses to let go of Israel. Now, in verse 24, the underlined

---

[116] NKJV, ESV, NASB, ERV, Jubilee, etc.

'him', refers not to Moses but to Pharaoh's firstborn son. This interpretation makes sense grammatically because the nearest antecedent is 'firstborn' in verse 23. This interpretation also makes sense narratologically because the previous verse speaks of God promising to kill Pharaoh's firstborn son. Thus verse 24 belongs together in the same episode as that of verse 23. Many translations (even some KJV editions) begin a new section after verse 23 (often with a new section heading), obscuring the fact that 'him' in verse 24 refers to Pharaoh's firstborn son mentioned in verse 23. Having a break between verse 23 and 24 is not necessarily wrong because there seems to be a *chronological* break between the two verses (e.g. "**And it came to pass....**" (verse 24)), but there is no *thematic* break.

"Verse 24 says that the LORD met Pharaoh's firstborn son in an inn and determined ('sought') to kill him. God had the foreknowledge of Pharaoh's refusal to let Israel go, so God was already prepared to seek the death of the firstborn son. This sentence also serves to foreshadow the future narrative." [117]

Now let's look at the circumcision incident described in verses 25-26. It's usual for readers to assume that this impromptu circumcision was performed on a baby or young boy. Not true. If Moses married Zipporah months after fleeing Egypt as a murderer and coming to Midian (which the text implies), then Moses was around 40 years old at his wedding (Acts 7:23). If Moses and Zipporah had the first of their sons within a few years of that marriage, which seems reasonable, then Gershom, the eldest son, would by now be a grown man in his late thirties (*cf.* Acts 7:23,30) That's a painful age to have a circumcision procedure carried out on you with a flint knife. You may recall in *Origins II – Holy War* that the pagan men of Shechem agreed to be circumcised to avoid a war over Dinah's defiling, and the procedure put them out of action as fighting men for a number of days, enabling Jacob's sons, Simeon and Levi, to enter the city and slaughter the lot (Gen 34). Concerning Gershom's circumcision, *KJV Today* explains:

"A new section begins from verse 25. The narrative begins with a picture of Zipporah circumcising her son. The immediate question is, "Why is Moses not performing the circumcision?" The answer is that Moses had to hold on to the son so that the son would stay still. Imagine the situation. Here is a grown boy who had to be circumcised. A typical child would not stay still for a scary procedure such as

[117] www.kjvtoday.com/home/is-the-kjv-confusing-in-exodus-424-26

circumcision. Some parents who have taken their children to the dentist or vaccination will understand. Zipporah, being a woman, probably did not have enough strength to completely keep still a grown boy. So Moses had to keep the boy still. Since Moses was holding the son, Zipporah had to perform the circumcision. That is why when the circumcision was over, verse 26 says, "he let him go." This "he" is Moses because the nearest male antecedent is "bloody husband." This phrase is not about God letting Moses go, but about Moses letting his son go after the circumcision was over.

"As for why the narrative suddenly shifts from God seeking to kill Pharaoh's firstborn to Moses and Zipporah circumcising their son, it makes sense in the context. In verse 23 God had pronounced a judgment upon Pharaoh's son, but it may have been obvious to Moses that God's judgment affects not only the king of Egypt but all the Egyptians. Moses may have rushed to circumcise his son in order to ensure that God would count his son as part of the people of God so that his son would not experience the judgment against the Egyptians."[118]

So the endless seminary wranglings which attempt to rationalise the supposed actions of a 'murderous' Deity hunting Moses down to kill him for failing to circumcise his son are rather redundant. God does not need us to defend Him, unlike the gods of other religions. Secondly, failure to circumcise your son was not a capital offence. It excluded you from the Abrahamic covenant relationship which God laid down in Genesis 17. Moreover, any punishment for not being circumcised fell upon the child, not the father (Gen 17:14). As Moses makes his way back along the King's Highway to confront Pharaoh in Egypt, God's promise to kill Pharaoh's firstborn if the Israelites aren't released absolutely plays on Moses' mind, causing him to rue not circumcising his own firstborn, Gershom, eight days after his birth, which was the norm (Lev 12:3). And the only reason Moses, as a Levite, would not have carried out his son's circumcision thus far would reasonably have been because of Zipporah's refusal to have her beloved son undergo what she saw as a bloodthirsty ritual. This tells us that her family, whatever their beliefs, were not under the covenant relationship with YHWH, or they would have had little problem complying with circumcision at any age.[119] Some scholars even suggest that Moses had his son circumcised to avoid God killing him for the murder of the Egyptian, which is even more ridiculous

---

[118] Ibid.

[119] Witness also Jethro's startled realisation about YHWH in Exo 18:10-11.

since there is nothing about circumcision which atones for sin. Only the shedding of innocent blood by sacrifice can atone for sin.

So what have we got here? Well, picture the scene if you dare. Fresh from that heady encounter with God on the mountain, and now on his way back to an uncertain future confronting the king of the known world in an Egypt he hasn't set eyes on for forty years, Moses abruptly decides to override Zipporah's longstanding refusal over the matter of Gershom's circumcision. Perhaps the scene even occurs at a wayside inn or wilderness encampment along the King's Highway trade route. A family argument ensues. Moses – still mighty and vital at 80 – grabs Gershom from behind in a body lock, then shouts at Zipporah to get the deed done. Gershom is probably 37-39 years old at this point, so he's not going to be as compliant as an eight-day-old baby.

The sequence of events in Exodus 4 has occasioned raised eyebrows among sceptics and atheists of "Contradiction! Biblical Errancy!" so let's get this out of the way. A straightforward chronological reading of Exodus 4 lays out the following sequence:

In the burning bush incident, Moses is conversing with the Creator on God's mountain (Mt Sinai/Horeb), raising every kind of objection with the Creator over having to go back to Egypt to confront Pharaoh.

God patiently overcomes his every obstacle, both real and imagined. He gives Moses a few demonstrations of His power, including enduing Moses' walking staff with the power to transform itself into a snake. This will serve as proof to others that God is with Moses.

God finally loses patience with Moses' continued reluctance to comply with the Egypt mission. God explains that his elder brother Aaron is even now on his way out from Egypt to the mountain for a joyful reunion, after which he will accompany Moses back to Egypt and serve as his spokesman. This gives us another valuable clue as to Mt Sinai's location. It's literally on the way from Midian back to Egypt, using the most direct route along the King's Highway.

The prospect of seeing his big brother once more *after 40 years* sways it for Moses, who then travels from Mt Sinai/Horeb back home to Jethro's place. He returns the goats to their pens and asks his father-in-law's permission to go back to Egypt. Moses is, after all, in charge of Jethro's flocks, so it's the right thing to do.

Notice in Exo 4:18 that Moses neglects to inform Jethro (and presumably Zipporah) of the true reason for his return to Egypt, which is to confront Pharaoh himself over the release of Egypt's entire Hebrew slave infrastructure - on the face of it a kamikaze mission. Instead, Moses tells his father-in-law that he wants to find out if his brethren are still alive. This obviously refers to his immediate kin, as Moses would be quite certain that 600,000[120] Hebrew male slaves and their families have not perished in the intervening 40 years he's spent in exile.

Note: Why does Moses not come clean to Jethro about the meeting with God on the mountain and his true mission? Would you tell your father-in-law the dangerous truth that you were about to take one of his daughters and two of his grandkids on such a lethal quest? (If it were me, I would have thrown the rod down at my father-in-law's feet just to see him jump at the snake! *Hisssssss!!*) Moses does not. He decides on the path of least resistance.

Next, Moses saddles that ass and leaves Jethro's estate with his wife, his two sons, some provisions, and that trusty rod of God. In departing Midian (modern-day northwestern Saudi Arabia), the geography of the north end of the Gulf of Aqaba means that Moses must round that point at Ezion Geber (modern-day Eilat) to avail himself of the most direct route back to Egypt - west along the King's Highway. Mount Sinai is evidently along this road. God waits until they have committed to the first leg of the journey out to Horeb, then has another word with Moses:

"When thou goest to return into Egypt, see that thou do all those wonders before Pharaoh, which I have put in thine hand: but I will harden his heart, that he shall not let the people go. And thou shalt say unto Pharaoh, 'Thus saith the LORD, Israel is My son, even My firstborn: And I say unto thee, Let My son go, that he may serve Me: and if thou refuse to let him go, behold, I will slay thy son, even thy firstborn.' " (Exo 4:21-23)

Robert Roe winces:

"Two things He tells Moses. 'Go back to Egypt and do all these wonders, and they aren't going to work. Secondly, tell Pharaoh to his face that God has said, "These people are special to Me. They are My firstborn. You won't let them go. You have killed their male children, so I am going to kill your firstborn." '

---

[120] The rounded number of males, 20 years of age or older, given in Exo 12:37. The precise figure given in Exo 38:26 is 603,550.

"Mind you, this is to be spoken in Egypt to someone who is god. Pharaoh is not just king. He is viewed as a direct descendent of god. He is known as deity. He is worshipped as deity. He is a child directly born of the sun, their highest god, Ra. He is called the perfect god on their monuments. He is called the great god on their monuments, not a son of the great god, THE great god. They don't worship Pharaoh as a representation of god. They worship Pharaoh as being deity, god. So Moses is told to go back into Egypt, perform all these wonders, and, 'I've got news for you, Moses, not one of them is going to work. Then when nothing works, you are to tell Pharaoh, "My God said, 'I'm going to kill your firstborn." ' " [121]

As I said - a kamikaze mission. Intercut a scene here where God looks down on an eighteen-year-old pharaoh, recently crowned, with his beautiful wife and child overnighting at an encampment. The child is Amenhotep II's firstborn and heir, whom God has lined up for the tenth plague. More about this tragic *historical* figure later.

Moses blenches. God is dead serious about the firstborn, while Moses has been slack in circumcising his own sons, doubtless due to Zipporah's unbelief and opposition. So Moses gets the deed done but has to hold Gershom in an iron grip while an outraged Zipporah is forced to cut the foreskin off her squirming son. She casts it down in disgust: "Surely you are a husband of blood to me!" Gershom is going to be raw and sore for a week or two.

Moses and the family then arrive at Mt Horeb to find a grinning Aaron awaiting them. The heavy mood lifts as Moses is reunited with his long-lost brother. He introduces a sulking Zipporah and his baffled sons to their uncle. Over the campfire that night, after Zipporah and the sons have retired to their tent, Moses updates his brother on everything God has said and done. Aaron nods sagely, having had a similar briefing himself. He is unprepared, however, when Moses takes his rod and casts it down at Aaron's feet.

Hisssssss!!!

Aaron recoils, startled. Moses grabs the serpent by the tail and regains control of his rod. "So that's it," he sniffs.

Aaron sighs. The elders and tribal fathers are going to love that one. Robert Roe comments:

"Moses is going back to Egypt as God's devastator of the most powerful kingdom in that part of the globe at that time. He has been gone 40 years. The people who want his life are dead. They have even

---

[121] www.pbc.org/system/message_files/14744/14743_moses06.html

taken his poster down off the post office wall. He is a nothing. His peer group is 80 years old, a little senile and are thinking, 'Whatever happened to old what's his name?' So 'old what's his name', a nothing, a forgotten person goes back to destroy Egypt and takes with him 'What's that in your hand?' Old 'what's his name' goes back with old 'what's that in your hand', and the two of them are going to devastate Egypt."[122]

It appears that Moses, after talking with Aaron, decides that the mission is simply too hazardous for his wife and sons, and sends them back to Jethro in Midian (Exo 18:2). We can infer this because the next and last time we meet Zipporah (Exo 18), she is brought by Jethro to Mt Sinai to visit Moses when the children of Israel are brought there months later in the Exodus. Once again, this implies that Mt Sinai is no great distance from Jethro's place with all this toing and froing. Moses may even have come clean to his family at this point with Aaron about the nature of the mission awaiting them in Egypt. At any rate, it is perhaps at this point that Moses bids farewell to his two beloved sons and wife, and packs them off along the King's Highway back to Midian and Jethro. Then, tossing the saddle over that ass, Moses bids his brother ride alongside for the journey back to the Hebrew enclave at Goshen in the Nile Delta. The journey to Pi-Ramesses from Mt Sinai is around 200 miles and takes them two weeks. Once back in Egypt, the brothers waste little time convening a meeting with the elders of the children of Israel:

And Aaron spake all the words which the LORD had spoken unto Moses, and did the signs in the sight of the people [*Hisssssss!!!*]**. And the people believed: and when they heard that the LORD had visited the children of Israel, and that He had looked upon their affliction, then they bowed their heads and worshipped.** (Exo 4:30-31)

---

[122] www.pbc.org/system/message_files/14744/14743_moses06.html

THE BATTLE OF THE GODS
(1446 BC)

After 40 years in barren Midian, Moses is back, immersing himself once more in the heady smells, noise, intrigue and bustling commerce of Egypt's sophisticated culture. It must have been an amazing, if daunting experience for the eighty-year-old ex-prince to be back in the land of his birth. Who was this new pharaoh he and Aaron were about to confront? When Moses fled Egypt four decades before, a young, powerful, no-nonsense Tuthmosis III was about to take the full reins of power from Moses' terminally ill stepmother, Queen Hatshepsut. Moses has been out of the loop for decades, save any intelligence gleaned over the years from travellers and traders passing along the King's Highway on their way north into the Levant.

And word was that Tuthmosis III had been a spectacular pharaoh, pushing the boundaries of the empire the furthest they had ever been. Moses did not doubt it. Conquests in Syria, Canaan, Nubia, and subjugation of the Mitanni state all went hand-in-hand with what the Hebrew recalled of the over-achieving, enemy-slaying, elephant-hunting, temple-building, literary-artisan-priest-soldier god. Moses heard that Pharaoh's eldest son and heir, the Crown Prince Amenemhat, had sadly died as a young man and so had his mother, Satiah. Tuthmosis III had to marry again, this time to a non-royal woman, Merytre-Hatshepsut. Their first son was declared heir to the throne at his birth and became co-regent with Tuthmosis towards the end of the great king's reign when the lad attained fifteen. His birthname was Amenhotep II.

The pharaoh of the Exodus

In the process of time, Tuthmosis III dies in his mid-fifties on the thirtieth day of the third month of Peret in 1452 BC (*cf.* Exo 2:23). His body is prepared, embalmed, taken aboard the royal funerary barge, then sailed the 384 miles south down the Nile to Waset/Thebes/Luxor, flanked and followed by hundreds of lesser craft. With great procession, Tuthmosis III is feted with honours by his son and heir, the eighteen-year-old 'new Horus' Amenhotep II, and buried in the lavishly prepared, cliff-cut tomb in the Valley of the Kings. The 18th Dynasty kings from Amenhotep I onwards had designated this spectacular sun-drenched valley in the Theban Hills outside Luxor as the site of their new necropolis. Dominated by a pyramid-like outcrop known as *ta dehent* ('the Peak'), the valley was isolated, enjoyed restricted access, and was easily guarded by the Pharaoh's *Medjay*, or tomb police.

The new pharaoh is Tuthmosis III's second son, Amenhotep II, crowned in his eighteenth year in 1452 BC after a three-year regency under his father. The new king is young, arrogant, immature, possessed of an ego to match his father's monuments, trained up in the arts of war and state, *über*-competitive and keen to surpass his father's word-fame. He is soon put to the test when the Syrian coastal cities rebel upon hearing of Tuthmosis III's death, deciding to test the mettle of the new pharaoh. Barely is his father sealed into his 'mansion of eternity' than Amenhotep is back in Memphis gathering troops and equipment for the first campaign of his reign. Noted for his athletic prowess, the young king has already made a name for himself with his ability to shoot an arrow through a palm-thick copper target from a moving chariot with the reins tied about his waist:

"This deed was recorded in numerous inscriptions, including a stele at Giza and depictions at Thebes. So famous was the act that it was also miniaturized on scarabs that have been found in the Levant. Sara Morris, a classical art historian, has even suggested that his target-shooting success formed the basis hundreds of years later for the episode in the Iliad when Achilles is said to have shot arrows through a series of targets set up in a trench. He was also recorded as having wielded an oar of some 30 ft in length, rowing six times as fast as other crew members, though this may certainly be an exaggeration."[123]

Seven years later in 1446 BC, Amenhotep II has become accustomed to the total power of a ruling god. At 25 he is undisputed master of the largest empire Egypt will ever see. All the extensive organs of military, state and religion, refined by his father, are his to command. Doug Petrovich reminds us:

"A compelling argument for choosing 1446 BC [for the Exodus] is that the Jubilee cycles agree with this date exactly, yet are completely independent of the 479+ years of 1 Kings 6:1. The Jubilee dates are precise only if the priests began counting years when they entered the land in 1406 BC (cf. Lev 25:2–10). The Talmud (*'Arakin* 12b) lists 17 cycles from Israel's entry into Canaan until the last Jubilee in 574 BC,

---

[123] www.touregypt.net/featurestories/amenhotep2.htm

which is 14 years after Jerusalem's destruction by using the Tishri calendar, a statement also found in chap. 11 of *The Seder 'Olam*, which predates the Talmud.[124] Consequently, 1446 BC is preferred over 1445 BC."[125]

Another provocative qualification for Amenhotep II as Exodus pharaoh is that a king with a 40-plus year rule dies a few years prior to 1446 BC, enabling Moses to return to Egypt to confront that pharaoh's successor. A further confirming qualification that Amenhotep II is the pharaoh of the Exodus is that he isn't the firstborn of his father. In scripture, 'Pharaoh' survives the tenth plague, wherein all the firstborn are killed by the Death Angel, from Pharaoh's eldest on down to the least in the kingdom, even extending to the beasts of the field (Exo 11:1–12:36). If Pharaoh had been the firstborn of his father, he too would have been killed on Passover night, yet a few verses after the Passover is covered in Exodus, we find him riding out with great anger at the head of the Egyptian northern army to deal with the escaping Israelites in the famous parting of the Red Sea episode (*cf.* Exo 14:5).

Which leads to yet another qualification for Amenhotep II: namely, that the pharaoh of the Exodus must have a firstborn son who mysteriously disappears from the official record for no apparent reason when he's killed in the tenth plague. Pharaohs do not record their setbacks, tragedies or failures, so there should be an indication of an anomaly in the archaeological inscription record concerning his heir. *There are several*. Amenhotep II is around 25 years old at the time of the plagues. Assuming he married his wife Tiaa in his early to mid teens, any firstborn from the marriage would be, tops, 11 years old by the time the Death Angel comes for him (Exo 12:29), and in all likelihood a few years younger. Too young, even, to be awarded recordable positions of power or even titles. More on this later.

Another qualification for Amenhotep II as pharaoh of the Exodus lies in the economic ramifications for the empire when Moses pulls the entire Hebrew slave infrastructure out of Egypt. We are told in

---

[124] Young, "When Did Solomon Die?" pp.599–603. Advocates of a 13th-century-BC Exodus have not only to ride roughshod over 1 Kings 6:1, but also explain the remarkable coincidence of the Jubilee cycles, which align perfectly with an Exodus date of 1446 BC.

[125] www.biblearchaeology.org/post/2010/02/04/amenhotep-ii-and-the-historicity-of-the-exodus-pharaoh.aspx#Article

scripture that the Israelites loot the Egyptian population with great spoil as they depart. Reasonably, therefore, we might expect to find in the Egyptian historical records some evidence for:

- socio-economic upheavals due to slaves deserting the empire
- the loss of the entire Egyptian northern army in the Red Sea
- the destruction of some 600 chariots

We do. We would also *not* expect the catastrophe itself to be recorded by a seething pharaoh, but indirectly and unequivocally inferred by evidence of the 'butterfly' effect on an Egypt losing in excess of 1.5 million slaves and millions in wealth in a single shot. *We do.*

The above dovetails with another qualification for Amenhotep II as pharaoh of the Exodus: namely, that in spite of his boastful martial accomplishments in the teenage years of his regency, and the fact that he inherits colossal armies, a well-blooded military infrastructure and the fruits of his Napoleonic father's successful *seventeen* campaigns, *Amenhotep only completes two campaigns as pharaoh across a reign of 35 years.*[126] This certainly doesn't add up. A sudden lack of soldiers perhaps?

Out of these two campaigns, Amenhotep's first is to squash the aforementioned predictable Syrian rebellion which occurs to test the new pharaoh's resolve upon the death of the mighty Tuthmosis III. The second campaign is launched in year 9 of Amenhotep II's reign, placing it in late 1446 BC. The target is Palestine, but the expedition only travels as far north as the Sea of Galilee. The reason for this second and last military foray of Amenhotep's is a mystery to researchers, since it is launched in a rainy, cold November in marked contrast to the custom of military campaigns in the ancient world commencing in the spring (*cf.* 1 Chron 20:1). No-one launches an expensive military campaign in November unless they are desperate, so obviously some emergency has occurred in Egypt which needs addressing without delay. We'll find out later that the archaeological record unequivocally attests to Amenhotep II attempting, with some success, to redress critical losses in this last campaign of his reign, replacing chariots, slaves, weapons and booty lost earlier that year due to the Hebrew Exodus.

Amazingly, for the rest of Amenhotep II's reign, not only is there no further military action, the pharaoh goes out of his way to sign

---

[126] Some scholars argue for three campaigns, yet a close examination of the evidence yields only two.

peace treaties with that old Egyptian enemy, Mitanni, and shore up alliances against the emerging might of the new Hittite empire. Scholars cannot explain this, but are generally in agreement that Egypt goes into marked decline during Amenhotep II's reign:

"It seems possible to consider this reign as unsuccessful, a time of decline: a few exploits abroad, a few preserved memorials, an almost complete absence of sources after the ninth year of the reign,"[127]

Yet, as Doug Petrovich points out:

"....the intervening years featured neither Egypt's engagement/loss in war nor a significant change in the political climate." [128]

Two other research authors remark:

"Already in the days of Amenhotep II, the son of Thutmose III, cracks began to appear in the structure of the Egyptian Empire." [129]

The showdown begins

Six years into Amenhotep II's reign, with no hint of the disasters to come, two old Hebrews are led into the royal court and compelled to kneel before the mighty Horus seated on the Throne of the Two Lands. The matter concerns some apparent reluctance among Goshen's Hebrew slaves to perform their usual construction duties.

And afterward Moses and Aaron went in, and told Pharaoh, "Thus saith the LORD God of Israel, Let my people go, that they may hold a feast unto Me in the wilderness."

And Pharaoh said, "Who is the LORD, that I should obey his voice to let Israel go? I know not the LORD, neither will I let Israel go."

And they said, "The God of the Hebrews hath met with us: let us go, we pray thee, three days' journey into the desert, and sacrifice unto the LORD our God; lest He fall upon us with pestilence, or with the sword."

And the king of Egypt said unto them, "Wherefore do ye, Moses and Aaron, let the people from their works? Get you unto your

---

[127] **Vandersleyen, Claude** *L'Egypte et la Vallée du Nil,* Presses Universitaires de France, 1995, vol.2, p.341

[128] www.biblearchaeology.org/post/2010/02/04/amenhotep-ii-and-the-historicity-of-the-exodus-pharaoh.aspx#Article

[129] **Aharoni, Yohanan and Michael Avi-Yonah** *The Macmillan Bible Atlas,* New York: Macmillan, 1977), p.34

burdens." And Pharaoh said, "Behold, the people of the land now are many, and ye make them rest from their burdens." [130]

And Pharaoh commanded the same day the taskmasters of the people, and their officers, saying, "Ye shall no more give the people straw to make brick, as heretofore: let them go and gather straw for themselves. And the tale [quota] **of the bricks, which they did make heretofore, ye shall lay upon them; ye shall not diminish ought thereof: for they be idle; therefore they cry, saying, 'Let us go and sacrifice to our God.' Let there more work be laid upon the men, that they may labour therein; and let them not regard vain words."** (Exo 5:1-9)

These are not the words of a mature ruler like Tuthmosis III, but those of an insecure, petulant, Game-of-Thrones-type teenage King Joffrey. Movies like *The Ten Commandments* and *Exodus: Gods and Kings* have conditioned the public to view the Exodus pharaoh as some daunting Yul Brunner/Joel Edgerton macho figure. The evidence repeatedly suggests otherwise. Amenhotep II in his inscriptions behaves as consistently adolescent as the pharaoh of the Exodus, and here we have the first example. Imagine you are Pharaoh in this situation. Your slaves are not working. If the idea is to get the brick-building business going again, and Moses and Aaron are the culprits hindering this effort **with vain words**, the logical action for you to take as a feudal ruler is to make a public example of the troublemakers - a flogging or hanging - then get the people back to work as quickly as possible. Amenhotep doesn't do that. Instead, *he hinders the building further* by ordering the puerile measure of withholding the straw just to show these bearded weirdos who is boss. I'll submit to you that God sees Pharaoh's immaturity too, which is why I believe the LORD doesn't kill Amenhotep II when He has ample occasion to do so over the coming months. God's anger

---

[130] There are expositors who hold that two million Israelites leaving Egypt to wander the desert lands for forty years is simply preposterous, given the enormity of logistics involved in keeping them alive in such a hostile environment. The refuge of these historians lies in the 'mistranslation' of the Hebrew *eleph,* which can mean 'clan' as well as 'thousand'. Thus, these scholars maintain, perhaps ten to twenty thousand in total left Egypt. This revisionist view is done to death in a number of places, not least here, where Pharaoh baldly states that the people of the land are many. Eighty years before, the oppression pharaoh worried in Exo 1:9: **"Behold, the people of the children of Israel are more and mightier than we..."** The population of Egypt at the time of the Exodus is largely agreed on as being around 4-5 million. Ten to twenty thousand Israelites causing Pharaoh a problem simply doesn't cut it. More on this interesting problem later!

will be less directed towards Satan's hapless human pawn-king than against the gods (demons) behind the scenes manipulating Egypt's destiny, upon whom the LORD will execute judgment (Exo 12:12; 18:11). The Creator of the universe is stern but fair. His goal with the coming showdown will be:

1) to demonstrate to Israel that He is their God (Exo 6:7)
2) to punish Egypt for its long-running abuse of the Israelites (Exo 6:6)
3) to demonstrate to Egypt that He is the Name that is above every name and judge their demon gods (Exo 7:5; 12:12; Num 33:4; Phil 2:9-11;)
4) to manifest His great power to the planet in a literal manner and have His name declared throughout the nations and talked about for centuries to come (Exo 9:14,16; Josh 2:9-11; 9:9).

Pharaoh is having none of it. "**Who is the LORD, that I should obey his voice to let Israel go?**" Over the next chapters, this preening coxcomb is going to find out exactly who the LORD is, and he will be given some compelling reasons to let Israel go before God is through with him.

Though this is the first time Moses and Amenhotep meet, it seems reasonable to assume that Amenhotep would have received a detailed briefing by state minsters on who Moses is. While on some hunting expedition, surely his father had told him family stories: how slaves can be dangerous, especially when mobilised *en masse*; the shameful Hyksos episode and Egypt's desire not to repeat the experience; how Moses came to be part of the royal family; Grandmother Hatshepsut's traitorous role in raising a Hebrew rebel as son of Pharaoh's daughter rather than consigning him to crocodile chow in the Nile. The murder committed by Moses; the exile; how your past always has a habit of catching up with you; keep them divided, son. If any troublemongers arise among the slave-force, the best tactic is to turn their own people against them.

Then the officers of the children of Israel came and cried out to Pharaoh, saying, "Why are you dealing thus with your servants? There is no straw given to your servants, and they say to us, 'Make brick!' And indeed your servants are beaten; but the fault is in your own people."

But [Pharaoh] **said, "You are idle! Idle! Therefore you say, 'Let us go and sacrifice to the LORD.' Therefore go now and work; for**

no straw shall be given you, yet you shall deliver the quota of bricks."

And the officers of the children of Israel saw that they were in trouble after it was said, "You shall not reduce any bricks from your daily quota."

Then as they came out from Pharaoh, they met Moses and Aaron who stood there to meet them. And [the elders] **said to them, "Let the LORD look on you and judge, because you have made us abhorrent in the sight of Pharaoh and in the sight of his servants, to put a sword in their hands to kill us."** (Exo 5:15-21, NKJV)

Moses predictably goes before God with a site report:

"LORD, why have You brought trouble upon this people? Why is it You have sent me? For since I came to Pharaoh to speak in Your name, he has done evil to this people; neither have You delivered Your people at all." (Exo 5:22-23, NKJV)

Moses failed once before with his people when he killed the Egyptian. Now he's failing again. "God! You didn't do what You said You would do!" It's a common cry even today, but God has the big picture and we do not, and Moses seems already to have forgotten that YHWH told him He would harden Pharaoh's heart to rack up the tension (Exo 4:21). This is not just going to be a showdown, it's going to be THE SHOWDOWN the world will never forget. And it hasn't to this day. Even atheists are still making movies about it. [131]

God patiently explains to Moses how things will play out by giving him the following message to take back to the people. God rubberstamps the entire address, front and back, with the words "I am the LORD." In other words, Moses, they can take this to the bank.

And God spake unto Moses, and said unto him, "I am the LORD: And I appeared unto Abraham, unto Isaac, and unto Jacob, by the name of God Almighty [El Shaddai], **but by My name JEHOVAH** [YHWH] **was I not known to them. And I have also established My covenant with them, to give them the land of Canaan, the land of their pilgrimage, wherein they were strangers.**

"And I have also heard the groaning of the children of Israel, whom the Egyptians keep in bondage; and I have remembered My covenant.

"Wherefore say unto the children of Israel, 'I am the LORD, and I will bring you out from under the burdens of the Egyptians, and

---

[131] http://rockingodshouse.com/movie-exodus-gods-and-kings-moses-movie-christian-review/

I will rid you out of their bondage, and I will redeem you with a stretched-out arm, and with great judgments: And I will take you to Me for a people, and I will be to you a God: and ye shall know that I am the LORD your God, which bringeth you out from under the burdens of the Egyptians. And I will bring you in unto the land, concerning the which I did swear to give it to Abraham, to Isaac, and to Jacob; and I will give it you for an heritage: I am the LORD.'" (Exo 6:2-8)

So Moses goes and gives God's message to the children of Israel, but they are so upset with the situation they ignore Moses. So God tells Moses to present himself before Pharaoh once more. Moses is growing weary of the impasse.

And the LORD said unto Moses, "See, I have made thee a god to Pharaoh: and Aaron thy brother shall be thy prophet. Thou shalt speak all that I command thee: and Aaron thy brother shall speak unto Pharaoh, that he send the children of Israel out of his land.

"And I will harden Pharaoh's heart, and multiply My signs and My wonders in the land of Egypt. But Pharaoh shall not hearken unto you, that I may lay My hand upon Egypt, and bring forth Mine armies, and My people the children of Israel, out of the land of Egypt by great judgments. And the Egyptians shall know that I am the LORD, when I stretch forth Mine hand upon Egypt, and bring out the children of Israel from among them."

And Moses and Aaron did as the LORD commanded them, so did they. And Moses was fourscore years old [80 years old]**, and Aaron fourscore and three years old** [83 years old]**, when they spake unto Pharaoh.** (Exo 7:1-7)

Snakes alive!

God tells Moses what to do:

"When Pharaoh shall speak unto you, saying, 'Shew a miracle for you': then thou shalt say unto Aaron, 'Take thy rod, and cast it before Pharaoh, and it shall become a serpent.' "

And Moses and Aaron went in unto Pharaoh, and they did so as the LORD had commanded: and Aaron cast down his rod before Pharaoh, and before his servants, and it became a serpent.

Then Pharaoh also called the wise men and the sorcerers: now the magicians of Egypt, they also did in like manner with their enchantments. For they cast down every man his rod, and they became serpents: but Aaron's rod swallowed up their rods. (Exo 7:9-12)

Hissssssss!!

The temptation is to exclaim "Strewth!" over such a bizarre incident and move on, but let's hit that pause button for a moment. The incident is fraught with meaning.

Instant replay: Aaron casts down his rod before Pharaoh and his court and it turns into a serpent. Unimpressed, Amenhotep II calls for his wise men and sorcerers and instructs them to do likewise. Two of these magicians, probably the chiefs among the wizards present, have been recorded for posterity. Their names are Jannes and Jambres (2 Tim 3:8). The sorcerers all cast down their rods, which promptly turn into serpents. Then Aaron's serpent swallows up the counterfeit serpents. We know from God's previous demonstration of the rod with Moses that Aaron's serpent then turns back into a rod, indicating that Aaron has been given control over the power.

As covered earlier, the coming showdown between Moses and Pharaoh will primarily not be a contest between men, but between God and his fallen realm (the 'gods of Egypt'), whom the LORD intends publicly to judge for man's instruction. Rods in the Bible are a type or model of authority, be they representative of man's own authority, or that given to man by God or Satan.[132] The concept of two witnesses represents 'truth being established'.[133] This rod/serpent contest is therefore about Satan challenging God's authority: Moses and Aaron are the two witnesses endued with the authority (rod) of the God of the Universe, which authority is challenged by Satan, the god of this world, represented by Pharaoh of Egypt ('the world'), and his two witnesses, Jannes and Jambres, wielding their own rods (Satan's authority). God's rod becoming a serpent is God's authority being made into the appearance of sin: an image of Jesus Christ, who was made sin for the world, and who in the last days will judge the sin/authority/'rods' of the world, represented by the god of this world, Satan, and his two witnesses, the Antichrist and False Prophet. Interestingly, there is compelling evidence that one of the witnesses for God in the last days will be Moses himself. Jesus will then rule the nations in the 1,000-year Millennial Kingdom with a 'rod of iron' (strong, unequivocal authority). (Rev 2:27; 12:5; 19:15; 20:4,6)

---

[132] The rod as a symbol of authority is bound up with the model of legal or royal authority chastising the wicked to bring them to heel: 2 Sam 7:14; Prov 13:24; 22:15; 29:15; Psa 74:2; 125:3; Jer 10:16; Job 9:34; 21:9; Isa 9:4; 14:29; etc. For more information on the rods/authority connection, see http://joanneaz_2.tripod.com/positivedisciplineresourcecenter/id4.html

[133] Num 35:30; Deut 19:15; Matt 18:16; FG 8:17; 1 Tim 5:19; 2 Cor 13:1; Heb 10:28.

Round 1: God.

And [God] **hardened Pharaoh's heart, that he hearkened not unto them, as the LORD had said.** (Exo 7:13; *cf.* 7:3)

Two things bother people about this episode. Firstly, that God can skew the game by hardening Pharaoh's heart, and secondly, that Satan can do miracles. By hardening Pharaoh's heart ('searing his conscience'),[134] God is not overriding the king's free will, but reinforcing Pharaoh's own refusal to yield to God's command (*cf.* Exo 8:15; 32; 9:34; 1 Sam 6:6). God will do that to anyone. He'll give you a piece of Truth or a beneficial break to see what you do with it. If you recognise the treasure you've been given, give God the glory for it and put it to good use, then God will give you more. The parable of the talents Yeshua gives during His ministry illustrates this concept (Matt 25: 14-30). It's about forming a relationship with the One who made you. However, if you count the Truth you have been given a common thing and scorn it, God will take away not only the Truth He gave you, but also harden your heart against future revelations if you persist in refusing to yield. Yeshua states that giving Truth to the uncalled or profane can even be dangerous:

"Give not that which is holy unto the dogs, neither cast ye your pearls before swine, lest they trample them under their feet, and turn again and rend you." (Matt 7:6)

Some commentators are uncomfortable with the idea that these sorcerers in the royal court appear to be 'doing magic', so they explain away the phenomenon as 'parlour games' or illusions. The Bible makes it quite clear that the rebellious cherub is quite capable of miracles that will astound – *ha-Satan* is hardly powerless in this area. He is the great deceiver of the whole world (Rev 12:9), and uses a particular deceptive strategy to maximum effect: He is the counterfeiter of God and all His ways, desiring to be like the most High (Isa 14:14). Many of his imitations are so close to the real thing that the deception of the world, and even the elect, will occur (Mark 13:22; 2 Cor 11:3-4). Yet any power *ha-Satan* possesses is allowed him

---

[134] *gotquestions.org* comments: "The seared conscience is referred to in 1 Timothy 4:2, where Paul talks about those whose consciences—their moral consciousness—have been literally 'cauterized' or rendered insensitive in the same way the hide of an animal scarred with a branding iron becomes numb to further pain. For human beings, having one's conscience seared is a result of continual, unrepentant sinning. Eventually, sin dulls the sense of moral right or wrong, and the unrepentant sinner becomes numb to the warnings of the conscience that God has placed within each of us to guide us (Romans 2:15)." - www.gotquestions.org/seared-conscience.html

by God specifically to accomplish God's aims, though Satan's pride fools him into thinking the power is his alone to exercise (Luke 4:6). There will be miracles performed during the coming 'Crazy Days' reign of Satan's Antichrist that will utterly astonish even God's chosen;[135] wonders that will convince the world that they are in the presence of God (2 Tim 2:3-4), *yet none of the glory for these will be given to Jesus Christ.* This is the acid test for whether a miracle is of God or Satan. Satan is in the counterfeiting business, so the Earth will be duped into believing in the counterfeit trinity of *ha-Satan* the father, the human Antichrist as the son, and the False Prophet, a most unholy spirit (Rev 13). This 'trinity pattern' is common in false religions too. Notice Pharaoh – in his role as a type of Satan as the god of this world - has two witnesses (Jannes and Jambres), and so does God (Moses and Aaron). The 'two witnesses' pattern will also be prominent throughout the Bible, playing a special role in the end times with the reappearance of Moses and Elijah to astonish the world on CNN and Sky in Revelation 11:3-13. Yes, really.[136]

The first plague: water turned to blood

So, without further ado, let us leap into the Ten Plagues to get the full flavour of the action, for the pace and content of what follows grants some special insights you won't get from a more surgical study.

At the burning bush, Moses was originally told by God that he would be unsuccessful initially in getting Pharaoh to release the

---

[135] Dan 8:23-25; Rev 13:13-14

[136] Two mysterious witnesses for God appear in Revelation 11 to harass the wicked during the last days of man's rule on Earth under the Antichrist. These witnesses are given power and a prophetic ministry by God for 42 months. If anyone attempts to harm them, they are summarily killed. The likelihood is that these two enigmatic figures will be Moses and Elijah, two prominent prophets whose ancient fates were an enigma. Why Moses and Elijah? The two witnesses are given four powers: 1) the power to shut heaven so no rain will fall; 2) the power to turn water into blood; 3) the power to devour enemies with fire called down from Heaven, and 4) the power to strike the Earth with plagues. Two of these powers are reminiscent of those given by God to the prophet Elijah (1 Kin 17:1; 2 Kin 1:10), and the other two are powers given by God to Moses (Exo 7-12). These two witnesses are then killed by the Antichrist's forces in Jerusalem and their bodies left in the street. We are told *the whole world* gazes upon this spectacle with glee (Rev 11:.9-10) – a feat not possible without satellite TV. After three and a half days of celebration, these dead prophets are resurrected by God before their stupefied global audience and taken up in a cloud to Heaven. Hollywood has certainly missed making a movie of that story so far.

Israelites (Exo 3:19-20). The purpose of this will be to 'ramp up the ante' to achieve a better result. God will show Himself strong, and what a show it's going to be. Not only **all the Egyptians shall know that I am the LORD,** but what occurs in the following chapters resonates throughout the world's nations to this day in ways few Jews and Christians even comprehend. More about this as we proceed. There will also be far more behind the following judgments spiritually than just God rousting Amenhotep II to shake loose the Israelites from Egypt. The Exodus narrative and subsequent Canaan conquest will be extraordinarily echoed and amplified in the apocalyptic showdown between good and evil due to occur in the hi-tech last days of the head-chopping regime of the Antichrist.[137]

We are also about to witness a very different Moses in the coming contest. Gone the apologetic, excuse-making, tongue-tied bumbler of Midian: Moses in Egypt, filled to the brim with God's Spirit, will be transformed into Egypt's terrifying nemesis, empowered with a bowel-loosening, nature-warping, cosmic power that will turn the golden Egypt of Tuthmosis III into a corpse-strewn wasteland of wailing and ash.

And the LORD said unto Moses, "Pharaoh's heart is hardened, he refuseth to let the people go. Get thee unto Pharaoh in the morning; lo, he goeth out unto the water; and thou shalt stand by the river's brink against he come [i.e. to meet him]**; and the rod which was turned to a serpent shalt thou take in thine hand. And thou shalt say unto him, 'The LORD God of the Hebrews hath sent me unto thee, saying, "Let My people go, that they may serve Me in the wilderness": and, behold, hitherto thou wouldest not hear. Thus saith the LORD, In this thou shalt know that I am the LORD: behold, I will smite with the rod that is in Mine hand upon the waters which are in the river, and they shall be turned to blood. And the fish that** [are] **in the river shall die, and the river shall stink; and the Egyptians shall lothe to drink of the water of the river.' "**

And the LORD spake unto Moses, "Say unto Aaron, 'Take thy rod, and stretch out thine hand upon the waters of Egypt, upon their streams, upon their rivers, and upon their ponds, and upon all their pools of water, that they may become blood; and that there may be blood throughout all the land of Egypt, both in vessels of wood, and in vessels of stone.' "

---

[137] Who beheads today? Rev 6:9-11 and 20:4 lead many expositors to surmise that the Antichrist system may have an Islamic component.

And Moses and Aaron did so, as the LORD commanded; and he lifted up the rod, and smote the waters that were in the river, in the sight of Pharaoh, and in the sight of his servants; and all the waters that were in the river were turned to blood. And the fish that [were] **in the river died; and the river stank, and the Egyptians could not drink of the water of the river; and there was blood throughout all the land of Egypt.**

And the magicians of Egypt did so with their enchantments: and Pharaoh's heart was hardened, neither did he hearken unto them; as the LORD had said.

And Pharaoh turned and went into his house, neither did he set his heart to this also. And all the Egyptians digged round about the river for water to drink; for they could not drink of the water of the river. And seven days were fulfilled, after that the LORD had smitten the river. (Exo 7:14-25)

Water turned to blood - points to note:

- Scholars assume that Pharaoh is participating in some religious ritual at the Nile at the time this first miracle occurs. This would make the judgment even more poignant
- The Nile is the key to Egypt's commercial and agricultural success. Water in the Bible is used as a type or model of the Holy Spirit, the Word, or the Word made flesh – Yeshua, the living water from which we drink, and in whom we wash to make ourselves clean (symbolic of baptism).[138] The Egyptians worship the Nile and wash in their false Word, *which God judges first*
- The Nile is the source of life to the Egyptians. God turns it to blood, a symbol of death
- Pharaoh's magicians are able to replicate this miracle, yet since this event is a cause of some anguish to the people of Egypt, the sorcerers do not possess the power to *undo* the baleful effects, *only increase the suffering*
- Many books over the years have attempted to ascribe natural causes to the Ten Plagues. I've read a few of the more popular, and their explanations are contrived, to say the least. The need to naturalise the plagues is, in itself, a 'no-blame' phenomenon, the significance of which most people miss. Man, whose fallen nature is ever at enmity with God, will go

[138] *cf.* Jer 2:13; Isa 11:9; Hab 2:14; Mark 16:15; FG 4:10-14; 7:37; 15:3; Eph 5:25; 1 Cor 6:11; 10:4

out of his way to duck any notion of an ultimate accountability for how he lives his life, so great efforts are undertaken to excise God's role in the story and ascribe the plagues to natural causes

- One of the most popular of these, which we will examine in more detail later, is that the plagues are a result of the Thera super-eruption, known to have occurred in the Mediterranean hundreds of miles to the north at the location of the modern-day island of Santorini during the Bronze Age. So, the story goes, this first plague is not really *blood* in the Nile but the fallen red-oxide residue from the Thera explosion. Exponents of this theory have a tough time reconciling the much earlier, known dating of Thera with the Exodus period, much less explaining how the red oxide from the volcanic aerosol managed to contaminate water contained **both in vessels of wood and vessels of stone** – in other words, *sealed jars.*[139] I find it interesting that the Holy Spirit actually includes this detail in the account, almost for no reason other than specifically to refute this latter-day attempt to deny God's role in the event. The uncomfortable truth? We're seeing God being God, and many of us don't like the idea
- If the Bible says it's blood, then it's blood, in the same way that if Jesus turned the water into wine at the wedding at Cana, it was wine and not grape juice! [140]
- The contamination of the water apparently abates after seven days
- God used water once before to judge man's sin. There was a seven-day period associated with this event also (Gen 7:10)
- Seas and rivers will also be turned into blood during the final brief rule of Antichrist and his global followers: **"For they have shed the blood of saints and prophets, and Thou hast given them blood to drink; for they are worthy."** (*cf.* Rev 8:8; 16:3-6)

---

[139] Water jars would have been covered or sealed to prevent contamination from, for example, dust or inquisitive insects, the same as today.

[140] www.reclaimingthemind.org/blog/2012/11/did-jesus-turn-water-into-fermented-wine/

The second plague: frogs

And the LORD spake unto Moses, "Go unto Pharaoh, and say unto him, 'Thus saith the LORD, Let My people go, that they may serve Me. And if thou refuse to let them go, behold, I will smite all thy borders with frogs. And the river shall bring forth frogs abundantly, which shall go up and come into thine house, and into thy bedchamber, and upon thy bed, and into the house of thy servants, and upon thy people, and into thine ovens, and into thy kneading-troughs: And the frogs shall come up both on thee, and upon thy people, and upon all thy servants.' "

And the LORD spake unto Moses, "Say unto Aaron, 'Stretch forth thine hand with thy rod over the streams, over the rivers, and over the ponds, and cause frogs to come up upon the land of Egypt.'"

And Aaron stretched out his hand over the waters of Egypt; and the frogs came up, and covered the land of Egypt. And the magicians did so with their enchantments, and brought up frogs upon the land of Egypt.

Then Pharaoh called for Moses and Aaron, and said, "Entreat the LORD, that he may take away the frogs from me, and from my people; and I will let the people go, that they may do sacrifice unto the LORD."

And Moses said unto Pharaoh, "Glory over me: when shall I entreat for thee, and for thy servants, and for thy people, to destroy the frogs from thee and thy houses, that they may remain in the river only?" [Moses is nailing Pharaoh down to a time for the Hebrews' release]

And [Pharaoh] **said, "Tomorrow."**

And [Moses] **said, "Be it according to thy word: that thou mayest know that there is none like unto the LORD our God. And the frogs shall depart from thee, and from thy houses, and from thy servants, and from thy people; they shall remain in the river only."**

And Moses and Aaron went out from Pharaoh: and Moses cried unto the LORD because of the frogs which He had brought against Pharaoh. And the LORD did according to the word of Moses; and the frogs died out of the houses, out of the villages, and out of the fields. And they gathered them together upon heaps: and the land stank. But when Pharaoh saw that there was respite, he hardened his heart, and hearkened not unto them; as the LORD had said. (Exo 8:1-15)

Frogs - points to note:

- Heqet, an Egyptian goddess of fertility and childbirth, is represented by the frog and worshipped. So God gives the Egyptians an overdose of Heqet
- As before, the sorcerers can only increase Egypt's experience of the loathsome frogs, not make them vanish
- When Amenhotep II complains about the frogs to Moses, the prophet tries to get the king to commit to giving in. Pharaoh breaks his word
- Once again, there is a spiritual tie-in with the frog-like demonic spirits in Revelation which emerge out of the mouths of each member of the blasphemous trinity and lead the world into war against God in the last days (Rev 16:13-14)

The third plague: lice

And the LORD said unto Moses, "Say unto Aaron, 'Stretch out thy rod, and smite the dust of the land, that it may become lice throughout all the land of Egypt.' "

And they did so; for Aaron stretched out his hand with his rod, and smote the dust of the earth, and it became lice in man, and in beast; all the dust of the land became lice throughout all the land of Egypt. And the magicians did so with their enchantments to bring forth lice, but they could not: so there were lice upon man, and upon beast.

Then the magicians said unto Pharaoh, "This is the finger of God." And Pharaoh's heart was hardened, and he hearkened not unto them; as the LORD had said. (Exo 8:16-19)

Lice - points to note:

- Notice that there is no warning given by Moses to Pharaoh before this plague
- The magicians try to replicate this miracle – again attempting only to increase the scourge, not remove it – but they fail. Bible commentator Chuck Missler observes:

> "There was something about lice that freaked them out; the serpents, the water to blood and the frogs they could deal with. When we get to the lice, not only can they not do it, they go to Pharaoh and tell him that it is 'the finger of God.' What is so unique about lice? Herodotus gives us a clue: the priests of the Egyptian system had a big thing about cleanliness, they wore special linen garments, and they shaved their head every third day. In order for them to worship according to their system, they

had to be totally clean. The infestation of the lice made it impossible for them to worship. The priests themselves could not officiate in accordance with the system they were following. The bringing of the lice against them made them recognize that God was dealing with them. They went to Pharaoh to point out that this was 'the finger of God.' "[141]

The fourth plague: flies

And the LORD said unto Moses, "Rise up early in the morning, and stand before Pharaoh; lo, he cometh forth to the water; and say unto him, 'Thus saith the LORD, Let My people go, that they may serve Me. Else, if thou wilt not let My people go, behold, I will send swarms [of flies] **upon thee, and upon thy servants, and upon thy people, and into thy houses: and the houses of the Egyptians shall be full of swarms** [of flies]**, and also the ground whereon they are. And I will sever in that day the land of Goshen, in which My people dwell, that no swarms** [of flies] **shall be there; to the end thou mayest know that I am the LORD in the midst of the Earth. And I will put a division between My people and thy people: tomorrow shall this sign be.' "**

And the LORD did so; and there came a grievous swarm [of flies] **into the house of Pharaoh, and into his servants' houses, and into all the land of Egypt: the land was corrupted by reason of the swarm** [of flies]**.**

And Pharaoh called for Moses and for Aaron, and said, "Go ye, sacrifice to your God in the land."

And Moses said, "It is not meet so to do; for we shall sacrifice the abomination of the Egyptians to the LORD our God: lo, shall we sacrifice the abomination of the Egyptians before their eyes, and will they not stone us? We will go three days' journey into the wilderness, and sacrifice to the LORD our God, as He shall command us."

And Pharaoh said, "I will let you go, that ye may sacrifice to the LORD your God in the wilderness; only ye shall not go very far away: entreat for me."

And Moses said, "Behold, I go out from thee, and I will entreat the LORD that the swarms [of flies] **may depart from Pharaoh, from his servants, and from his people, tomorrow: but let not Pharaoh deal deceitfully any more in not letting the people go to sacrifice to the LORD."**

---

[141] Missler, Chuck, *Exodus notes,* pp.41-42

And Moses went out from Pharaoh, and entreated the LORD. And the LORD did according to the word of Moses; and He removed the swarms [of flies] **from Pharaoh, from his servants, and from his people; there remained not one. And Pharaoh hardened his heart at this time also, neither would he let the people go.** (Exo 8:20-32)

Flies – points to note:

- Moses is instructed by God to meet Pharaoh once again at the water. Scholars assume that the king undergoes some sort of daily purification rite at the Nile at dawn. He's going to need cleansing with what's coming up in a minute
- Once again, the warnings are back. God lays out to Amenhotep what's going to happen if he doesn't comply and let His people go. One might imagine that Pharaoh should be getting the message by now, but pride and anger blind the best and the worst of us
- Flies are common enough in the marshy reaches of the Nile Delta region, and special measures such as screens and mosquito nets are used these days to make life bearable. Otherwise it's insects in your mouth, in your eyes, ears, and up your nose. Back in ancient Egypt, similar, practical measures were employed, but none that would have any efficacy against the forthcoming, frightful scourge about to descend
- I've square-bracketed 'flies' in the Biblical text. Although the word occurs in the King James and other translations, 'fly' is not mentioned in the original Hebrew. The word that is mentioned seven times is ברעה (Strongs H6157- *arob*), denoting a mixture or swarm of insects descending on the land
- This won't be your average house-fly buzzing around the fruitbowl, but a noisome *potpourri* of ghastly creatures inflicting stings and bites, including devouring beetles crawling over you with strong jaws, and all other manner of creepy-crawlies exacting horrifying retribution in the most personal manner. The mix would doubtless include the scarab or dung-beetle (*Scarabaeus sacer*), the famous faeces-gobbler, deemed sacred to Egypt and a manifestation of Shu, the son of Ra. Imagine waking up and seeing a handful of those perched on your chest, horny legs waving a semaphore
- In the 'fly' plague, God judges a variety of Egyptian 'gods' (demons). Scholars are divided as to whether Beelzebub (*lit.*

'Lord of the Flies') was just another name for *ha-Satan* or a title of one of his senior henchmen. Arthur W Pink writes:

- "The fourth plague was designed to destroy the trust of the people in Beelzebub, or the Fly-god, who was reverenced as their protector from visitation of swarms of ravenous flies, which infested the land generally about the time of the dog-days, and removed only as they supposed at the will of their idol. The miracle now wrought by Moses evinced the impotence of Beelzebub and caused the people to look elsewhere for relief from the fearful visitation under which they were suffering."[142]
- God promised **"I will send swarms upon thee..."** So Pharaoh is affected *personally* by these critters in his own household. A picture comes to mind of Amenhotep II, the sacred incarnation of Ra, hopping around the palace with his wife Tiaa and the kids, desperately smacking their robes to free themselves of the nibbling scourge. That's got to damage your pride, especially if you are a god
- *This is the first time that a providential separation is made between Israel and Egypt.* God commences the process of cleaving Israel ('the chosen') from Egypt ('the world'). Goshen, where the Hebrews dwell, is not afflicted by the swarms. Once it dawns on Amenhotep and his ministers that the Hebrews have been spared the curse by some supernatural act of election right down to the individual insect, the realisation must have been chilling
- God is now moving to prove His claim that He is the God of the Earth, that He can manipulate nature at will, and that the Israelites have been set aside as His special people. You mess with Israel at your peril – a *caveat* that remains in force today but is forgotten as usual by the legions of demonically driven anti-Semites in our own age who, like Amenhotep, are on schedule for their own disturbing wake-up call
- Shaken, Amenhotep calls for Moses and Aaron and begs them to **"go sacrifice to your God in the land"** – i.e. sacrifice but remain in Egypt. But that would mean sacrificing cows and sheep (sacred to the Egyptians) in a place fresh from the squiggly abominations brought upon the Egyptians. There

---

[142] **Pink, Arthur W** "The Plagues Upon Egypt," www.scripturestudies.com/vol11/k5/ot.html

would be a riot. Even now, Pharaoh cannot bring himself to submit to God and allow the Israelites their three-day journey into the wilderness to honour God.[143] In so doing, Amenhotep II apes the very Devil upon whom he is modelled. So, alas, it's time for....

The fifth plague: livestock diseased

Then the LORD said unto Moses, "Go in unto Pharaoh, and tell him, 'Thus saith the LORD God of the Hebrews, Let My people go, that they may serve Me. For if thou refuse to let them go, and wilt hold them still, Behold, the hand of the LORD is upon thy cattle which is in the field, upon the horses, upon the asses, upon the camels, upon the oxen, and upon the sheep: there shall be a very grievous murrain [pestilence]**. And the LORD shall sever between the cattle of Israel and the cattle of Egypt: and there shall nothing die of all that is the children's of Israel.' "**

And the LORD appointed a set time, saying, "Tomorrow the LORD shall do this thing in the land."

And the LORD did that thing on the morrow, and all the cattle of Egypt died: but of the cattle of the children of Israel died not one. And Pharaoh sent, and, behold, there was not one of the cattle of the Israelites dead. <u>And the heart of Pharaoh was hardened</u>, and he did not let the people go. (Exo 9:1-7)

Cattle disease – points to note:

- Another warning, then disaster strikes
- Next on the judgment slate is Hathor, another Egyptian goddess (fecundity, female, joy). Represented by a cow and worshipped
- This judgment also strikes the sacred herds of Pharaoh, prized beyond measure (*cf.* Gen 47:6). *CLC* writes:

  "This plague demonstrates that Yahweh has power over the livestock of Egypt. He is able to strike the animals with disease and death, thus delivering a blow to the economic as well as religious life of the land. By the former plagues many of the Egyptian religious ceremonies would have been interrupted and

---

[143] This is another indirect confirmation that Egypt's eastern border was demarked by the Canal of the Pharaohs (modern-day Suez Canal) down to the northern edge of the Gulf of Suez. The Sinai peninsula was treated by the pharaohs as a military buffer zone, and Egypt did host garrison forts there, especially along the King's Highway, as we will discover.

objects of veneration defiled or destroyed. Now some of the important deities will be attacked.

"In Goshen, where the cattle are merely cattle, no disease hits; but in Egypt it is a different matter. Osiris, the savior, cannot even save the brute in which his own soul is supposed to dwell. Apis and Mnevis, the ram of Ammon, the sheep of Sais, and the goat of Mendes, perish together. Hence, Moses reminds Israel afterwards, "Upon their gods also Yahweh executed judgments" (Num. 33:4). And Jethro, when he heard of all these events, said, "Now I know that Yahweh is greater than all gods;[144] for in the thing wherein they dealt proudly, He was above them (Exo 18:11)." [145]

- Pharaoh is so spooked, he sends for proof that no Israelite cattle have perished. The worst is confirmed, so now it's personal. Amenhotep's heart is hardened. He cannot be seen by his people to cave in to a foreign god. Thus it becomes a contest of wills. God is more than willing to make the next plague a bit personal too....

The sixth plague: boils and sores

And the LORD said unto Moses and unto Aaron, "Take to you handfuls of ashes of the furnace, and let Moses sprinkle it toward the heaven in the sight of Pharaoh. And it shall become small dust in all the land of Egypt, and shall be a boil breaking forth with blains [sores] **upon man, and upon beast, throughout all the land of Egypt."**

And they took ashes of the furnace, and stood before Pharaoh; and Moses sprinkled it up toward heaven; and it became a boil breaking forth with [sores] **upon man, and upon beast.**

And the magicians could not stand before Moses because of the boils; for the boil was upon the magicians, and upon all the Egyptians.

And the LORD hardened the heart of Pharaoh, and he hearkened not unto them; as the LORD had spoken unto Moses. (Exo 9:8-12)

Boils and sores – points to note:

---

[144] i.e. Jethro didn't know this before, illustrating that this priest of Midian was outside the covenant relationship peculiar to the Jews, as also witnessed by Zipporah's repugnance of the circumcision ritual in Exo 4:25-26.

[145] www.christianleadershipcenter.org/exod.15.pdf

- There is no warning given for this one
- God now begins to touch human life. The magicians not only cannot replicate this scourge, they cannot even heal themselves from it. In the abysmal pharmacopeia of Egyptian cures, ash and soot were not the cause but the *cures* for boils, overseen by the god Thoth. God inverts the process to judge the spiritual world and assert His sovereignty
- There is speculation among researchers that this plague is anthrax, since the disease is a bacterial problem spread by spores which hide in the dust. Anthrax mostly strikes herbivores and occasionally humans who come in contact with the spores, which then multiply the bacteria. The disease cannot be spread directly from one human to another as in classic contagion, only by spores. The disease typically presents on the skin with large, angry zones of inflammation and boils which form ulcers with a black centre (cutaneous anthrax). The more lethal pulmonary (lung) and gastrointestinal varieties had a mortality rate in the ancient world of around 85%
- So, a nasty scourge that would have wrought havoc on Egypt's economy, food chain, and killed thousands of the population, not to mention decimating the royal herds
- The wise men of Egypt (magicians) **could not stand before Moses** because of God's judgment

The seventh plague: hail

And the LORD said unto Moses, "Rise up early in the morning, and stand before Pharaoh, and say unto him, 'Thus saith the LORD God of the Hebrews, Let My people go, that they may serve me. For I will at this time send all My plagues upon thine heart, and upon thy servants, and upon thy people; that thou mayest know that there is none like Me in all the Earth.

"For now I will stretch out My hand, that I may smite thee and thy people with pestilence; and thou shalt be cut off from the Earth. And in very deed for this cause have I raised thee up, for to shew in thee My power; and that My name may be declared throughout all the Earth. As yet exaltest thou thyself against My people, that thou wilt not let them go?

"Behold, tomorrow about this time I will cause it to rain a very grievous hail, such as hath not been in Egypt since the foundation thereof even until now. Send therefore now, and gather thy cattle,

and all that thou hast in the field; for upon every man and beast which shall be found in the field, and shall not be brought home, the hail shall come down upon them, and they shall die.' "

He that feared the word of the LORD among the servants of Pharaoh made his servants and his cattle flee into the houses: And he that regarded not the word of the LORD left his servants and his cattle in the field.

And the LORD said unto Moses, "Stretch forth thine hand toward heaven, that there may be hail in all the land of Egypt, upon man, and upon beast, and upon every herb of the field, throughout the land of Egypt."

And Moses stretched forth his rod toward heaven: and the LORD sent thunder and hail, and the fire ran along upon the ground; and the LORD rained hail upon the land of Egypt. So there was hail, and fire mingled with the hail, very grievous, such as there was none like it in all the land of Egypt since it became a nation. And the hail smote throughout all the land of Egypt all that was in the field, both man and beast; and the hail smote every herb of the field, and brake every tree of the field. Only in the land of Goshen, where the children of Israel were, was there no hail.

And Pharaoh sent, and called for Moses and Aaron, and said unto them, "I have sinned this time: the LORD is righteous, and I and my people are wicked. Entreat the LORD (for it is enough) that there be no more mighty thunderings and hail; and I will let you go, and ye shall stay no longer."

And Moses said unto him, "As soon as I am gone out of the city, I will spread abroad my hands unto the LORD; and the thunder shall cease, neither shall there be any more hail; that thou mayest know how that the Earth is the LORD'S. But as for thee and thy servants, I know that ye will not yet fear the LORD God."

And the flax and the barley was smitten: for the barley was in the ear, and the flax was bolled [in bud]. But the wheat and the rie were not smitten: for they were not grown up.

And Moses went out of the city from Pharaoh, and spread abroad his hands unto the LORD: and the thunders and hail ceased, and the rain was not poured upon the earth. And when Pharaoh saw that the rain and the hail and the thunders were ceased, he sinned yet more, and hardened his heart, he and his servants. And the heart of Pharaoh was hardened, neither would he let the children of Israel go; as the LORD had spoken by Moses. (Exo 9:13-35)

Hail – points to note:

- A warning is given, wherein God declares the purpose of the judgments: to show that there is none like the LORD in the whole Earth (Isa 44:6); that Amenhotep will eventually be cut off from the Earth; that God in fact raised Amenhotep II to the throne *for this very purpose:* to show Himself strong to the world in His power. This ties in with the constant hardening of Amenhotep's heart
- The hail is the first plague in which God extends grace and a chance for the victims to avoid what's coming. He makes known beforehand what the Egyptians must do to avoid the judgment. Those who listen and take action will be spared. Those who don't will perish
- Notice how God declares His absolute sovereignty over all the affairs of men. As the saying goes, 'He's either the God of everything or He isn't', which, as previously covered, raises the issue of predestination versus free will. Does Pharaoh actually have a choice in how he behaves, or is God pulling the strings of a marionette? The paradox is resolved when one understands that God is operating both inside and outside the time dimension, so knows the end from the beginning.[146] God has always been and always will be (Isa 48:12; Heb 7:3). He inhabits eternity, which is defined not by long periods of time, but by the *complete absence* of time - the ultimate in hyperdimensionality.[147] That God knows what Pharaoh is going to do does not absolve Amenhotep from the responsibility of what he chooses to do. The prophet Daniel will understand the same concept when he gives thanks to the LORD 900 years later after being given the interpretation of a king's dream. God is in control of absolutely EVERYTHING (Ecc 3:11):

  "Blessed be the name of God for ever and ever: for wisdom and might are His: And He changeth the times and the seasons: He removeth kings, and setteth up kings: He giveth wisdom unto the wise, and knowledge to them that know understanding. He revealeth the deep and secret things: He knoweth what is in the darkness, and the light dwelleth with Him." (Dan 2:20-22)

---

146 Isa 46:9-10; Rev 1:8,17; 2:8; 21:6; 22:13;

147 Isa 57:15; Psa 90:2,4; 93:2; 102:12, 24-27;

Proverbs 16:4 states: **The LORD hath made all things for Himself: yea, even the wicked for the day of evil.**

In the New Testament, Paul paints the same picture of the Creator: **For the scripture saith unto Pharaoh, "Even for this same purpose have I raised thee up, that I might shew My power in thee, and that My name might be declared throughout all the Earth." Therefore hath He mercy on whom He will have mercy, and whom He will He hardeneth.** (Rom 9:17-18)[148]

- Fire and hail don't mix, so this plague demonstrates God's supremacy over the Egyptian god of the sky and weather, Nut, and Hephaistos the fire god. This plague smashes men, beasts, orchards and crops but miraculously spares Goshen, the Hebrew region. God once again spookily demarks victim and survivor. This must be making an impression on Amenhotep by this time, and it does....
- For the first time Pharaoh appears to *repent*. He asks Moses to halt the scourge and promises the Israelites their trip into the desert, saying, **"I have sinned this time** [*'this time'?*]. **The LORD is righteous and I and my people are wicked** [a little learning is taking place]. **Intreat the LORD (for it is enough) that there be no more mighty thunderings and hail; and I will let you go, and ye shall stay no longer."** (Exo 9:27-28) But he doesn't, so roll up your royal sleeves, Amenhotep, for they're coming....

The eighth plague: locusts

And the LORD said unto Moses, "Go in unto Pharaoh: for I have hardened his heart, and the heart of his servants, that I might shew these My signs before him: And that thou mayest tell in the ears of thy son, and of thy son's son, what things I have wrought in Egypt, and My signs which I have done among them; that ye may know how that I am the LORD."

And Moses and Aaron came in unto Pharaoh, and said unto him, "Thus saith the LORD God of the Hebrews, How long wilt thou refuse to humble thyself before Me? Let my people go, that they may serve Me. Else, if thou refuse to let My people go, behold, tomorrow will I bring the locusts into thy coast: And they shall cover the face of the earth, that one cannot be able to see the earth:

---

[148] See also 1 Pet 2:8-10

and they shall eat the residue of that which is escaped, which remaineth unto you from the hail, and shall eat every tree which groweth for you out of the field.

"And they shall fill thy houses, and the houses of all thy servants, and the houses of all the Egyptians; which neither thy fathers, nor thy fathers' fathers have seen, since the day that they were upon the earth unto this day. "

And he turned himself, and went out from Pharaoh. And Pharaoh's servants said unto him, "How long shall this man be a snare unto us? Let the men go, that they may serve the LORD their God. Knowest thou not yet that Egypt is destroyed?"

And Moses and Aaron were brought again unto Pharaoh: and he said unto them, "Go, serve the LORD your God. But who are they that shall go?"

And Moses said, "We will go with our young and with our old, with our sons and with our daughters, with our flocks and with our herds will we go; for we must hold a feast unto the LORD."

And [Pharaoh] **said unto them, "Let the LORD be so with you, as I will let you go, and your little ones: look to it; for evil is before you.** [i.e. "The LORD will certainly need to be with you if I let you take your little ones! I can see through your evil plan!"] **Not so: go now ye that are men** [i.e. just the men go]**, and serve the LORD; for that ye did desire." And they were driven out from Pharaoh's presence.**

And the LORD said unto Moses, "Stretch out thine hand over the land of Egypt for the locusts, that they may come up upon the land of Egypt, and eat every herb of the land, even all that the hail hath left.

And Moses stretched forth his rod over the land of Egypt, and the LORD brought an east wind upon the land all that day and all that night; and when it was morning, the east wind brought the locusts.

And the locusts went up over all the land of Egypt, and rested in all the coasts [territories] **of Egypt: very grievous were they; before them there were no such locusts as they, neither after them shall be such. For they covered the face of the whole earth, so that the land was darkened; and they did eat every herb of the land, and all the fruit of the trees which the hail had left: and there remained not any green thing in the trees, or in the herbs of the field, through all the land of Egypt.**

Then Pharaoh called for Moses and Aaron in haste; and he said, "I have sinned against the LORD your God, and against you. Now

therefore forgive, I pray thee, my sin only this once, and intreat the LORD your God, that he may take away from me this death only."

And [Moses] **went out from Pharaoh and intreated the LORD. And the LORD turned a mighty strong west wind, which took away the locusts, and cast them into the Red Sea; there remained not one locust in all the** [territories] **of Egypt.**

But the LORD hardened Pharaoh's heart, so that he would not let the children of Israel go. (Exo 10:1-20)

Locusts – points to note:

- In his address to Moses, God declares that He is setting up these miracles in Israel's collective memory so they will be passed from generation to generation, testifying that He is the LORD of all. In effect, God is laying the foundations for their faith. It will astonish us how quickly these and other miracles will be forgotten a few chapters hence when the Israelites are bemoaning their lot in the desert as free men. "Would that we had died in Egypt!" (Exo 14:12; 16:3)
- Another god of Egypt is rendered useless now when swarms of locusts descend in such a way that the whole land is darkened. These pestilential insects devour what the hail does not destroy. Egypt's citizens, the worshippers of Nepri, the god of grain and Ermutet, the goddess of childbirth and crops, can only gawp at the devastation, ensuring no locusts fly into their mouths. Not one of their deities comes to the rescue
- This plague almost certainly collapses the Egyptian economy to such an extent that even Pharaoh's ministers are emboldened to address Amenhotep's stubbornness to his face. *The land has been all but wrecked by the hail and previous curses! Now locusts? Ye gods! Let them go worship their god! What's the worst that can happen?*
- Pharaoh doesn't. He calls back Moses and Aaron and proceeds to *negotiate. Only the men shall go into the desert.* Wrong answer, Amenhotep –
- *Buzzzzzzzzzz!*
- Locust pie, locust pizza, locusts in your bath, up your nose, kids screaming; even the royal kids screaming. The last of Egypt is crunched up in insect jaws and masticated into green goo
- This plague also mirrors the locusts that come upon the Earth in the last days of Revelation. These emerge out of the

bottomless pit, unleashed by God onto the planet's surface to wreak havoc and agony:

- **And there came out of the smoke locusts upon the earth: and unto them was given power, as the scorpions of the earth have power. And it was commanded them that they should not hurt the grass of the earth, neither any green thing, neither any tree; but only those men which have not the seal of God in their foreheads.**

  And to them it was given that they should not kill them, but that they should be tormented five months: and their torment was as the torment of a scorpion, when he striketh a man. And in those days shall men seek death, and shall not find it; and shall desire to die, and death shall flee from them. (Rev 9:3-6)
- Curiously, the Holy Spirit via the apostle John sees fit to *describe* the locusts in the Revelation passage, as if we don't know what locusts look like already. Which means that the following verses are a *remez* – a hint of something deeper. The Revelation locusts in the following description are certainly not your average cornerstore bugs. Some researchers have wondered whether John, who is being given a series of mindboggling visions throughout Revelation of events leading up to Armageddon and the Second Coming, could even be employing first-century language to describe modern-day weapons technology – even helicopter gunships deploying a type of non-lethal weaponry. I wouldn't be dogmatic about this, though the phenomenon of modern-technology descriptions appears to occur elsewhere in the Bible, as covered in *Origins I*.
- **And the shapes of the locusts were like unto horses prepared unto battle** [armoured?]**; and on their heads were as it were crowns like gold** [the rotorblade effect?]**, and their faces were as the faces of men** [men can be seen in the cockpit?]**. And they had hair as the hair of women, and their teeth were as the teeth of lions. And they had breastplates, as it were breastplates of iron** [more armour?]**; and the sound of their wings** [rotors?] **was as the sound of chariots of many horses running to battle** [a pounding din? Thump, thump, thump?]**. And they had tails like unto scorpions, and there were stings in their tails: and their power was to hurt men five months. And they had a king over them, which is the**

angel of the bottomless pit, whose name in the Hebrew tongue is Abaddon, but in the Greek tongue hath his name Apollyon. (Rev 9:7-11)

- Whatever these beasts/aliens/machines are, we are told they are demonically guided (though permitted by God) and used to punish the wicked of the Earth. *CLC* writes:

- "The plague is brought on them (10:12-15), and then the expected confrontation ensues (Exo 10:16-20). Here too the king confesses that he has sinned, but adds a request for forgiveness for this sin this time. He wants them to take away this death (metonymy for the locusts' effect). The result is that the destructive insects are swept into their death in the Red Sea. Pharaoh's confession does not quite match genuine confession. He still refers to the LORD as "your" God. The fact that he humbles himself before Moses is not sufficient for forgiveness. He will eventually humble himself before God. Since his heart was not yet submissive, his confession was vain.

  "It is interesting to note here that God can raise up the destroyers (locusts) so that they do his bidding in the land of Egypt, and then drive them to their death in the Red Sea. He will have the same power with Egypt, for he raised up this powerful empire and will drown them in the Sea. Israel would hereby receive another powerful demonstration of the LORD's sovereignty. Nations and kings would be forced to recognize that their God was Lord of all the earth. God will humble those who persistently refuse to submit to his will. That humbling will inevitably lead to death."[149]

- Amenhotep appears to repent once again, but these are crocodile tears. He does not release the Israelites after this one either. *Oh, Amenhotep…*

The ninth plague: darkness

And the LORD said unto Moses, "Stretch out thine hand toward heaven, that there may be darkness over the land of Egypt, even darkness which may be felt."

And Moses stretched forth his hand toward heaven; and there was a thick darkness in all the land of Egypt <u>three days</u>: They saw

---

[149] www.christianleadershipcenter.org/exod.18.pdf

not one another, neither rose any from his place for three days: but all the children of Israel had light in their dwellings.

And Pharaoh called unto Moses, and said, "Go ye, serve the LORD; only let your flocks and your herds be stayed: let your little ones also go with you."

And Moses said, "Thou must give us also sacrifices and burnt offerings, that we may sacrifice unto the LORD our God. Our cattle also shall go with us; there shall not an hoof be left behind; for thereof must we take to serve the LORD our God; and we know not with what we must serve the LORD, until we come thither."

But the LORD hardened Pharaoh's heart, and he would not let them go. And Pharaoh said unto him, "Get thee from me, take heed to thyself, see my face no more; for in that day thou seest my face thou shalt die."

And Moses said, "Thou hast spoken well, I will see thy face again no more." (Exo 10:21-29)

Darkness – points to note:

- No warning again for this plague
- Having machined His way through the Egyptian pantheon (Exo 12:12), the LORD now fixes His attention upon Amun-Ra, the sun god, the shining one (*ha-Satan*), Egypt's supreme deity, of which PhaRAoh is considered the living incarnation and divine authority
- The sun is blotted out for three days in a darkness so deep it can be 'felt'. That's dark. It also implies a spiritual darkness descending on the Crown of Two Lands, yet in the land of Goshen the Israelites have light. Some scholars believe this to be the special light emanating from God Himself - the Shekinah
- Three days of darkness, during which you can do nothing, see nothing, and socialise with no-one, brings Egypt to a shuddering halt. Even if He hadn't before, God has everyone's attention now
- The darkness lasts for the enigmatic 'three days' period, symbolically used in the Bible to point toward *"an act of divine intervention which impacts salvation history."*[150] Three days is a long time for a man to ponder his sinful predicament before a

[150] *cf.* 'The Symbolic Significance of the Third Day in Scripture': www.agapebiblestudy.com/documents/The%20Symbolic%20Significance%20of%20the%20third%20day.htm

perfect Creator. By now the beleaguered peoples of Egypt – even Pharaoh himself – must be wondering whether the end of days is upon them. But worse is to come....

- Egypt, a land perpetually bathed in bright sun, is plunged into a darkness *that can be felt.* Darkness in the Bible is used as a model for sin and blindness, both literal and spiritual [151]
- That which is darkness to Egypt ('the world') is light to God's people ('the elect/chosen'). This is spiritually true (FG 3:19), **"For the preaching of the cross is to them that perish foolishness; but unto us which are saved it is the power of God."** (1 Cor 1:18)
- The darkness model also holds for the 'pillar' that will lead the Israelites out of Egypt. A juxtapositioning of salvation and condemnation – the elect and the damned. To the Egyptians, God appears as a dark cloud; to the Israelites bright light (Exo 14:20)
- The same Creator visiting darkness on Egypt will later state as Yeshua/Jesus in the NT: **"I AM the light of the world: he that followeth Me shall not walk in darkness, but shall have the light of life."** (FG 8:12). This is one of seven 'burning bush' I AM statements Jesus makes which serve as a theme for the Fourth Gospel. Also: **"I am come a light into the world, that whosoever believeth on Me should not abide in darkness."** (FG12:46)
- A three-hour darkness comes over Jerusalem immediately prior to Jesus being 'judged' in our place on the cross (Matt 27:45; 2 Cor 5:21). God cannot look upon sin (Hab 1:13), which is why Jesus cries from the cross: **"My God, My God, why hast thou forsaken Me?"** (Matt 27:46).[152] This is the only time Jesus does not call Him 'Father' because He is in our shoes
- With the darkness plague, we once again note a parallel with the end times judgments described in Revelation, when a deep darkness is predicted to fall upon the world in the fifth bowl judgment (Joel 2:2; Zeph 1:15; Acts 2:20; Rev 16:10).
- Amenhotep calls in Moses and Aaron and still negotiates. Can you beat it? *OK, you can take your families into the desert, even*

---

[151] Gen 15:12; 19:11; Deut 28:27-29; 2 Kings 6:18; Matt 6:23; FG 3:19; Rom 11:25; Eph 4:18

[152] These words were predicted by King David a thousand years before the crucifixion (Psa 22:1)

your little ones now, to sacrifice to your God, but leave your livestock possessions behind so you come back! Moses refuses: *So what are we to sacrifice with, eh? We're taking the lot, Amenhotep! Every hoof!* Which will also include a hefty slice of Egyptian booty. Israel is going to CASH IN Egypt

- Pharaoh refuses to let them go and even issues a physical threat: **"Get thee from me, take heed to thyself** [i.e. watch out!], **see my face no more; for in that day thou seest my face thou shalt die."**
- **And Moses said, "Thou hast spoken well, I will see thy face again no more."** In other words, "Amenhotep, we're done, son."

The tenth plague: death of the firstborn

The LORD pulls Moses aside:

"Yet will I bring one plague more upon Pharaoh, and upon Egypt; afterwards he will let you go hence: when he shall let you go, he shall surely thrust you out hence altogether. Speak now in the ears of the people, and let every man borrow [*lit.* request with no intention of returning] **of his neighbour, and every woman of her neighbour, jewels of silver, and jewels of gold."**

And the LORD gave the people favour in the sight of the Egyptians. Moreover the man Moses was very great in the land of Egypt, in the sight of Pharaoh's servants, and in the sight of the people. (Exo 11:1-3)

In great anger, Moses prophesies a tenth plague upon Egypt, pronouncing:

"Thus saith the LORD, About midnight will I go out into the midst of Egypt, and all the firstborn in the land of Egypt shall die, from the firstborn of Pharaoh that sitteth upon his throne, even unto the firstborn of the maidservant that is behind the mill, and all the firstborn of beasts. And there shall be a great cry throughout all the land of Egypt, such as there was none like it, nor shall be like it any more. But against any of the children of Israel shall not a dog move his tongue, against man or beast, that ye may know how that the LORD doth put a difference between the Egyptians and Israel. And all these thy servants shall come down unto me and bow down themselves unto me, saying, 'Get thee out, and all the people that follow thee.' And after that I will go out." And he [Moses] **went out from Pharaoh in a great anger.** (Exo 11:4-8)

Just pause for a moment and imagine what this final plague entails. Imagine waking up in your town or village to find death everywhere, *but specific death, even in your own household. Even extending to the firstborn of your animals.* It's unequivocal. Inarguable. Supernatural. Horrific. Up to now, God's judgment against Egypt has been corporate. Now it turns personal. Individual families will be afflicted with a special kind of grief, from the Pharaoh's royal household on down; the same grief the Father Himself has already experienced outside of time concerning His own Firstborn's sacrifice and death in the metacosm. God is certainly going **put a difference** between His chosen and the rest, and it will be ever so. Moses passes God's instructions on to the Israelites on how to protect themselves. Notice how specific the details are:

Speak ye unto all the congregation of Israel, saying, "In the tenth day of this month they shall take to them every man a lamb, according to the house of their fathers, a lamb for an house.... Your lamb shall be without blemish, a male of the first year: ye shall take it out from the sheep or from the goats. And ye shall keep it up until the fourteenth day of the same month, and the whole assembly of the congregation of Israel shall kill it in the evening [*lit.* 'between the evenings'].

And they shall take of the blood, and strike it on the two side posts and on the upper door post of the houses, wherein they shall eat it. And they shall eat the flesh in that night, roast with fire, and unleavened bread; and with bitter herbs they shall eat it. Eat not of it raw, nor sodden at all with water, but roast with fire; his head with his legs, and with the purtenance thereof. And ye shall let nothing of it remain until the morning; and that which remaineth of it until the morning ye shall burn with fire.

And thus shall ye eat it; with your loins girded, your shoes on your feet, and your staff in your hand, and ye shall eat it in haste: it is the LORD'S passover. For I will pass through the land of Egypt this night and will smite all the firstborn in the land of Egypt, both man and beast; and against all the gods of Egypt I will execute judgment: I am the LORD. And the blood shall be to you for a token upon the houses where ye are, and when I see the blood, I will pass over you, and the plague shall not be upon you to destroy you, when I smite the land of Egypt. And this day shall be unto you for a memorial and ye shall keep it a feast to the LORD throughout your generations; ye shall keep it a feast by an ordinance forever." (Exo 12:3…14)

Death of the firstborn – points to note:

- The tenth plague will institute that most famous of holy feasts, the Passover, with its attendant celebrations of the Feast of Unleavened Bread and the Feast of Firstfruits
- First of all, *how bizarre is all this?* Why not just level Egypt with a visitation of bolides and earthquakes? Why go to all the trouble with the lamb and the blood and the doorposts and the detailed instructions? Obviously God's up to something. It gives you chills when you realise that YHWH is actually pre-enacting His own death for the remission of sins and an end to the Holy War with this astonishing procedure. Later, during the Exodus, YHWH will codify the Passover ritual with the following features:
- The lamb must be selected by a household on the 10th Nisan, 4 days before Passover. **The Lamb of God, which taketh away the sin of the world** (FG 1:29), is later presented to the world almost fifteen centuries later with Jesus riding the donkey into Jerusalem on 'Palm Sunday', the 10th of Nisan
- The lamb must be unblemished, symbolising sinlessness, for only by the shedding of innocent blood may sins be covered. Yeshua fulfils this requirement, as evidenced by the Resurrection - the empty tomb - signifying that God has accepted the ultimate substitutionary sacrifice
- Not a bone of the lamb's body is to be broken (Exo 12:46; Psa 34:20). Not a bone of Jesus' body is broken by Roman soldiers during the crucifixion (FG 19:32-36)
- The lamb shall be kept until the 14th Nisan (Passover), at which time the household will kill it 'between the evenings'. Yeshua is crucified over precisely this period
- The blood of the lamb shall be taken and used to daub the jambs and lintel of the door of the house, wherein the lamb shall be eaten
- You must burn what you cannot eat
- You shall eat the lamb in haste, with yourself dressed, shoes on and ready to go!
- The lamb is always referred to in the singular, and the language switches from 'a' lamb to 'the' lamb. i.e. *Your* personal lamb for the covering of *your* sin
- God won't be looking at the house, He'll be looking for the blood

- Passover is obviously a detailed prefiguring of the coming sacrifice of Yeshua *ha-Mashiach,* the Seed of the woman (Gen 3:15). God will institute Passover as a memorial feast forever to teach the Jews, as well as wider mankind, that by the shedding of innocent blood their sins will be covered and salvation assured
- Notice that the faithful will not be saved by literal lamb's blood, which is a token for their benefit (Exo 12:13), *but by their faithful obedience in carrying out God's command under frightening circumstances*
- Passover differs from the Levitical feasts in that the offering is not sacrificed by the priests but by the individual households, who consume it personally
- Notice that substitutionary atonement was instituted back in Eden when God clothed Adam and Eve with animal skins to cover their 'nakedness' (sin)
- The same model is also witnessed when Abel observes the 'bloodworthiness' of his offering while Cain offers the fruit of his own labour (Gen 4:1-8)
- How about God's instruction to Abraham to offer his son Isaac on Mount Moriah? When Isaac asks where the lamb will come from to use in the sacrifice, Abraham responds with the enigmatic, **"God will provide Himself a lamb."** (Gen 22:8) Abraham knows he is acting out prophecy when he names the place YHWH Yireh: **'in the mount of the LORD it shall be seen'.** (Gen 22:14). The site where Abraham and Isaac enact this strange event? Mount Moriah/Golgotha
- The lamb symbolises sinless (unblemished) innocence to be sacrificed for sin (indeed made sin), *whose blood will cover that portion of sinful humanity who claim it, so judgment won't fall.* John the Baptist introduces Yeshua thus: **"Behold the Lamb of God which taketh away the sin of the world."** (FG 1:29)
- The Feast of Unleavened Bread becomes a type of the LORD's Communion: **"This is My body which is given for you: this do in remembrance of Me"** (Luke 22:19).
- Fire symbolises judgment throughout the Bible, so God's insistence on the lamb being roasted and then eaten is symbolic of the sinless one being judged in place of the sinner. We see the same enactment insisted on by Jesus at the Last Supper when He introduces the concept (type) of bread and wine at the Communion and the 'consummation' of His body

and blood, so misunderstood by the Catholics as 'transubstantiation', or literal cannibalism (Luke 22:19)

- Another surprising observation is that if you daub lamb's blood across the jambs and lintel of a door the way Moses instructs, you've drawn *a cross of blood:*

  Then Moses called for all the elders of Israel, and said unto them, "Draw out and take you a lamb according to your families, and kill the passover. And ye shall take a bunch of hyssop [symbol of purging/humiliation]**, and dip it in the blood that is in the basin, <u>and strike the lintel and the two side posts</u> with the blood that is in the basin; and none of you shall go out at the door of his house until the morning."** (Exo 12:21-22)

Any Hebrew carrying out this task in Egypt to save himself from God's wrath would, of course, have no idea of the significance of the lamb, the blood or the cross in the atonement of man's sins. (We shall see the cross and atonement types repeated later during the Exodus in some surprising ways.)

Another point here is, did the Creator of the universe really need the lamb's blood on the door to tell him where the Israelites were living so He could spare them? Of course not. God actually states in Exo 12:13 that the slain lamb routine *is a token,* or type, for the benefit of the lamb's benefactors

So you are tempted to ask: What if a Hebrew *didn't* daub his door with the lamb's blood? Answer: God judged the house and slew the Hebrew's firstborn. A tough lesson which poses a further question: What if a 'good' person doesn't avail themselves of Christ's sacrifice before they die? Here is Jesus's answer: **"I said therefore unto you, that ye shall die in your sins: for if ye believe not that I am He, ye shall die in your sins."** (FG 8:24)

Heavy stuff.

And it came to pass, that at midnight the LORD smote all the firstborn in the land of Egypt, from the firstborn of Pharaoh that sat on his throne unto the firstborn of the captive that was in the dungeon; and all the firstborn of cattle.

And Pharaoh rose up in the night, he, and all his servants, and all the Egyptians; and there was a great cry in Egypt; for there was not a house where there was not one dead. (Exo 12:29-30)

Can we be sure no Egyptians found out about the lamb/blood routine and carried out the instructions to save themselves, even though they weren't Israelites? After all, the scriptures say that the

Egyptians were in absolute awe of Moses, and the Hebrews found favour in their sight (Exo 11:3). The penny was dropping around Egypt that the Israelite God was not just another god, he *was* GOD. We are not specifically told whether any Egyptian families heard about Moses' instructions and tried the lamb's blood for themselves, but if they did, *God spared them.* This hints at an astonishing truth to come: that God has in mind for salvation *every creature* He created, whether Jew or Gentile:

The Lord is not slack concerning His promise, as some count slackness, but is longsuffering toward us, not willing that any should perish but that all should come to repentance (2 Pet 3:9, NKJV).

For God so loved the world, that He gave His only begotten Son, that <u>whosoever</u> believeth in Him should not perish, but have everlasting life. For God sent not His Son into the world to condemn the world; but that the world through Him might be saved.

He that believeth on Him is not condemned: but he that believeth not is condemned already, because he hath not believed in the name of the only begotten Son of God.

And this is the condemnation, that light is come into the world, and men loved darkness rather than light, because their deeds were evil. For every one that doeth evil hateth the light, neither cometh to the light, lest his deeds should be reproved. But he that doeth truth cometh to the light, that his deeds may be made manifest, that they are wrought in God. (FG 3:16-21)

Justice is getting what we deserve.
Grace is getting what we do not deserve.
Mercy is not getting what we deserve.
You want the last two, not the first one.

Pharaoh's fateful firstborn

If Amenhotep II is indeed the Exodus pharaoh, there should be evidence that he had a firstborn son who died early. As previously mentioned, Amenhotep is 18 when his father Tuthmosis III dies, and is around 25 years of age by the year of the Exodus: 1446 BC. So even assuming an early/young marriage to his consort Tiaa, customary for a crown prince and regent, Amenhotep's firstborn would not be older than 8 to 11 years by the time he is struck down by the tenth plague. Is there any secular evidence of this?

Firstly, though Pharaoh himself is included in the tenth plague curse, he clearly participates in the Red Sea episode, which means that Amenhotep II was not himself the eldest son of his father, Tuthmosis III. This is well attested to, says Egyptian expert Doug Petrovich:

"Toward the middle of Thutmose III's reign, in Year 24, the heir to the throne was not Amenhotep II, but Amenemhet, who was called 'the king's eldest son'. There is little doubt that he was the older half-brother of Amenhotep II who died before he could assume the throne. In an inscription from the Karnak Festival Hall that dates to Year 24, Amenemhet was being appointed to an administrative position in the temple of Amun: '…appointing the king's eldest son [Amen]emhet as overseer of cattle.'[153] Since Amenemhet probably was no longer a child when the inscription was composed, he would have been born fairly early in the coregency of Thutmose III and Hatshepsut. Therefore, Amenhotep II would not have died during the tenth plague, as the record bears out that he was not the firstborn son of Thutmose III." [154]

So what of Amenhotep II's eldest who perished at the Death Angel's hand in the tenth plague? Who was he? Is there any secular evidence for his existence?

We know that Amenhotep II reigned until his death in 1418 BC, a further 28 years after the Exodus. This means that if Amenhotep II is the Exodus pharaoh, he did not drown in the Red Sea episode, and contrary to popular belief, there is *no scriptural evidence* that Pharaoh followed his army into the waters and drowned. We will examine this later. We also have Pharaoh Amenhotep II's corpse too, and he wasn't drowned. So far, so good.

So what do we know of Amenhotep II's children? Peter Der Manuelian, Philip J King Professor of Egyptology at Harvard University, has researched and written extensively on Amenhotep II's reign. Der Manuelian reveals that Papyrus B.M. 10056, which dates to sometime after Amenhotep II's tenth year, refers to a king's son and *setem* (chief) priest, Amenhotep.[155] Wiki comments:

"This Amenhotep might also be attested in a stele from Amenhotep II's temple at Giza, however the stele's name has been defaced so that

---

[153] **Der Manuelian, Peter** *Studies in the Reign of Amenophis II,* Hildesheimer Ägyptologische Beiträge 26, Gerstenbeg Verlag, Hildesheim, 1987, p.19

[154] www.biblearchaeology.org/post/2010/02/04/Amenhotep-II-and-the-Historicity-of-the-Exodus-Pharaoh.aspx#Article

[155] Der Manuelian, Peter, *Studies in the Reign of Amenophis II,* op. cit., p.174

positive identification is impossible. Stele B may belong to another son, Webensenu. Webensenu's name is otherwise attested on a statue of Amenhotep's chief architect, Minmose, and his canopic jars and a funerary statue have been found in Amenhotep II's tomb. Another Giza stele, stele C, records the name of a Prince Amenemopet, whose name is otherwise unattested. The same statue with the name Webensenu on it is also inscribed with the name of prince Nedjem, who is otherwise unattested.

"There are other references to king's sons from this period who may or may not be sons of Amenhotep II. Two graffiti from Sahel mention a king's son and stable master named Khaemwaset, but specifically which king is his father is unknown. A figure with the name Amenemhet is recorded behind a prince Amenhotep in Theban tomb 64, and assuming this Amenhotep is indeed the king's son from [papyrus] B.M. 10056, Amenemhat would also be Amenhotep II's son. Additionally, a prince Aakheperure is mentioned in a Konosso graffito alongside a prince Amenhotep, and if one again assumes that this Amenhotep was the same person as the one in B.M. 10056, Aakheperure would also have been Amenhotep II's son. However, in both these cases the figure identified as Amenhotep has been identified by some as possible references to the later King Amenhotep III, which would make these two princes sons of Thutmose IV. In addition to sons, Amenhotep II may have had a daughter named Iaret, but she could have also been the daughter of Thutmose IV."[156]

So the inscription and papyrus record reveals that Amenhotep II probably had the following princes by his consort Tiaa: Amenhotep (who pre-deceases his father), Tuthmosis IV (who succeeds his father), Webensenu, Amenemopet, Nedjem, Amenemhat, Khaemwaset and Aakheperure. A daughter also: Iaret. More about this lady later.

Inevitably, Exodus researchers become excited about this son named Amenhotep, yet there is an anomaly, says Doug Petrovich:

"Amenhotep undoubtedly was an important figure, as he was called "the one who enters before his father without being announced, providing protection for the King of Upper and Lower Egypt," and "commander of the horses." Since his name was enclosed in a cartouche, he was the heir apparent [to Amenhotep II] when the stele was carved, meaning that he stood in line for the throne ahead of Thutmose IV, who

[156] http://en.wikipedia.org/wiki/Amenhotep_II

obviously was his younger brother. Therefore, some conclusions about this prince may be drawn: (1) he was the royal son of Amenhotep II; (2) he was never called "the king's eldest son"; (3) he served as the sm-priest and lived in the royal palace at Memphis; (4) he was once the heir to the throne; (5) he lived approximately until Year 30 or 35 of his father's reign; and (6) he never ascended to the throne. If Amenhotep was the heir to the throne without being the firstborn son of Amenhotep II, then who was the eldest son of this noted pharaoh?"[157] [emphasis mine]

The plot thickens. So if this mysterious son of Amenhotep II (also called Amenhotep, just to confuse you) was *not* originally the firstborn ('the king's eldest son'), *who was?*

Canadian Egyptologist and archaeologist Donald B Redford is Professor of Classics and Ancient Mediterranean Studies at Pennsylvania State University. He considers the Bible's Exodus account to be mythical, yet makes an intriguing observation:

"The fact that he [Amenhotep II's son Amenhotep] was named Amenhotep like his father might be taken to indicate that he was not the firstborn; that an older son named Thutmose had been born to Amenhotep II. It would be necessary to assume, however, that this Thutmose had passed away in childhood without leaving a trace."[158]

Doug Petrovich has another piece of the archaeological puzzle, which bears out Redford's reflection on the custom of 18th Dynasty pharaoh-designates to be alternately birthnamed 'Amenhotep' and 'Tuthmosis'. Here we find evidence of a missing Tuthmosis, the original firstborn of Amenhotep II:

"In Tomb 64 of the Theban necropolis is an important wall painting that displays two royal tutors: Hekreshu and his son, Hekerneheh, who are in the company of their princely charges: Thutmose and Amenhotep [sons of Pharaoh Amenhotep II]. Hekreshu is seated, facing right, with the young heir apparent, Thutmose, on his lap. Standing before him is Hekerneheh and a small Prince Amenhotep, who is carrying a bouquet. Hekreshu is specifically stated to be a "tutor of the king's eldest bodily son, Thutmose," whose nomen is represented in a cartouche [indicating royal heir]. Hekerneheh's title is "tutor of the king's son, Amenhotep." Behind Hekerneheh appear six other princes, originally all named, but

---

157 www.biblearchaeology.org/post/2010/02/04/Amenhotep-II-and-the-Historicity-of-the-Exodus-Pharaoh.aspx

158 **Redford, Donald B** "The Coregency of Tuthmosis III and Amenophis II," *JEA* 51, December 1965, p.114

the hieroglyphs are now almost completely destroyed. One name alone can be made out, that of a certain Amenemhet….

"Redford suggests that the practice of these pharaohs was not to name their firstborn sons after themselves, but to use an alternative birth-name. If Prince Amenhotep was not the eldest son of Amenhotep II, who by custom may have named his first son 'Thutmose', then the Thutmose sitting on the lap of the royal tutor Hekreshu in a wall painting at Thebes may be 'the eldest son' of the king. Therefore, if Amenhotep II was the Exodus pharaoh, perhaps his eldest son was Thutmose, who died in the plague without leaving a trace, thus satisfying both the Egyptological and Biblical records (Exo 12:29)."[159]

After a troubled reign of 34 years, Amenhotep II is eventually succeeded by Tuthmosis IV in 1418 BC, some 28 years after the Exodus. Further inscriptional and papyrus evidence also confirms that Thutmose IV was not the eldest son of Amenhotep II. For example, Tuthmosis IV commissions a monument known as 'the Dream Stele', located on a block of red granite between the paws of the Great Sphinx, *which tells us that he was not the original heir to the throne.*[160] The stele records a prophecy that Tuthmosis IV would one day be pharaoh, which, as Merrill F Unger points out, would be a fatuous observation if Tuth IV was in fact Amenhotep II's eldest son and destined for the throne. Of course he would succeed! The law of primogeniture was in force in Egypt at that time.[161]

Wiki summarises the situation thus:

"Thutmose IV was born to Amenhotep II and Tiaa but was not actually the crown prince and Amenhotep II's chosen successor to the throne. Some scholars speculate that Thutmose ousted his older brother [Amenhotep] in order to usurp power and then commissioned the *Dream Stele* in order to justify his unexpected kingship. Thutmose's most celebrated accomplishment was the restoration of the Sphinx at Giza and subsequent commission of the *Dream Stele.* According to Thutmose's account on the *Dream Stele*, while the young prince was out on a hunting trip, he stopped to rest under the head of the Sphinx, which was buried up to the neck in sand. He soon fell asleep and had a dream in which the Sphinx told him that if he cleared away the sand and restored it he would

---

[159] www.biblearchaeology.org/post/2010/02/04/Amenhotep-II-and-the-Historicity-of-the-Exodus-Pharaoh.aspx

[160] Der Manuelian, Peter, *Studies in the Reign of Amenophis II,* op. cit., p.40

[161] **Unger, Merrill F** *The New Unger's Bible Dictionary,* "The Date of the Exodus", Moody Publishers, 2009

become the next Pharaoh. After completing the restoration of the Sphinx, he placed a carved stone tablet, now known as the *Dream Stele*, between the two paws of the Sphinx. The restoration of the Sphinx and the text of the *Dream Stele* would then be a piece of propaganda on Thutmose's part, meant to bestow legitimacy upon his unexpected kingship."[162]

Amenhotep II's heirs:

The original Prince Tuthmosis: age 8-11. Too young to be given a state position and memorialised. Dies in the tenth plague, 1446 BC

Prince Amenhotep: Becomes heir after his sibling's death. Dies sometime in year 30-34 of his father's reign and does not come to the throne

The new Prince Tuthmosis: Succeeds his sibling, Amenhotep, as crown prince and becomes Tuthmosis IV upon his father's death. Commissions the Dream Stele to strengthen his unexpected elevation to the Crown of Two Lands

Plague summary

There is a structural grouping to the plagues:

1. Water turned to blood (Exo 7:14-25) – 1st warning
2. Frogs on land and into the homes (Exo 8:1-15) – 2nd warning
3. Infestation of lice (Exo 8:16-19) – *no warning*
4. Plague of flies (Exo 8:20-24) – 3rd warning
5. Plague on cattle (Exo 9:1-7) – 4th warning
6. Boils and sores on man and beast (Exo 9:8-12) – *no warning*
7. Thunder and hail (Exo 9:18-35) – 5th warning
8. Plague of locusts (Exo 10:1-20) – 6th warning
9. Darkness for three days (Exo 10:21-29) – *no warning*
10. Death of the firstborn (man/beast) (Exo 11,12) – 7th warning

Chuck Missler writes:

"What is missing in [the] third plague? Compared to the first two: a warning. In the previous cases, Moses went to Pharaoh and warned him. In this third one, there is no warning, Moses just does it. We will discover that of the nine plagues (the 10th being set aside as a special case), they are divided in groups of three, they are clustered by a variety of strange

[162] http://en.wikipedia.org/wiki/Thutmose_IV

structural techniques. One of these techniques is that there is a warning, a warning and then no warning. This same sort of thing is done in the 7 letters for 7 churches [expounded in Revelation 2 & 3]....

"Something else that is interesting is that the first three plagues, Aaron's rod is specifically the instrumentality. In the middle three plagues, it is not mentioned. In the last three plagues, Moses himself is the agency, not Aaron, and in the ninth itself the rod is not mentioned, it is Moses' hands.

"There is also a progression of these plagues, the first three really attack simply the comfort of the Egyptians. The next three plagues attack their possessions, and the last three plagues actually result in death and destruction. There is a definite progressive effect. Aaron is the agency early, and Moses later. Also, it is interesting to see the magicians testify to the power of God. The magicians make the declaration that this is "the finger of God," and they leave the stage not to be seen again (Actually they are mentioned once more in Ex 9:11). Where did the lice come from? The dust (see John 8 with Jesus and the woman caught in adultery, when her accusers approach Christ bends down and writes in the dust, the finger of God)....

"In this conflict between God and Egypt, we will see the conflict between good and evil in far broader terms than simply the relief of an oppressive administration in North Africa thousands of years ago. There is far more at stake here than simply the issue of slavery and freedom. Here is a foreshadowing of the fundamental conflict between good and evil; the model of the world is what Egypt really represents. Pharaoh represents Satan, whose heart is hardened (contrast with the origin of Lucifer, Isa 14; Ezek 28; Rev 12). We will see in this narrative the absolute triumph of God; nothing conditional or marginal. We will see Him redeem His people and we will see the utter overthrow of the enemy."[163]

The release

Nothing but disaster befalls Amenhotep II after his run-in with Moses, Aaron and the Creator of the universe. After the Death Angel destroys Egypt's firstborn that fateful night of 14 Nisan, 1446 BC, the screams throughout the palace are echoed across the entirety of the nation. Amenhotep concedes defeat.

And [Pharaoh] **called for Moses and Aaron by night, and said, "Rise up, and get you forth from among my people, both ye and the children of Israel; and go, serve the LORD, as ye have said. Also**

[163] **Missler Chuck** *Exodus notes*, pp.36,42, www.khouse.org

take your flocks and your herds, as ye have said, and be gone; and bless me also."

And the Egyptians were urgent upon the people, that they might send them out of the land in haste; for they said, "We be all dead men."

And the people took their dough before it was leavened, their kneadingtroughs being bound up in their clothes upon their shoulders. And the children of Israel did according to the word of Moses; and they borrowed of the Egyptians jewels of silver, and jewels of gold, and raiment: And the LORD gave the people favour in the sight of the Egyptians, so that they lent unto them such things as they required. And they spoiled [plundered] **the Egyptians.** (Exo 12:31-36)

It is estimated that almost two million souls take part in the Exodus. The Israelites are so keen to be gone, they don't even wait for their bread to rise. Thus is born the significance of the unleavened bread **because they were thrust out of Egypt.** God is compelling His people to thrust themselves out of the world's system – another type or model. We will discover later that leaven (yeast or sourdough culture) is an interesting idiom for sin and pride, for it corrupts by puffing up.[164] Unleavened bread to the Jew is a model for living new lives henceforth untainted by the old leaven. They have been redeemed, not by their own doing, but because of the lamb's blood shed for the Passover. The apostle Paul sums this up:

Purge out therefore the old leaven, that ye may be a new lump, as ye are unleavened. For even Christ our passover is sacrificed for us. Therefore let us keep the feast, not with old leaven, neither with the leaven of malice and wickedness; but with the unleavened bread of sincerity and truth (1 Cor 5:7-8).

The Egyptian public appears to act in perfect accord as a nation now: suddenly there's a new and powerful reason to be nice to the Hebrews who, a few days prior, had been despised slaves under the yoke. What but a series of epic catastrophes could account for such a sudden change in behaviour? Deep-seated memories of God's judgment of the Flood arise, along with the threat of further hostilities from this transcendent Deity, who holds in His hands the fate of us all.

---

[164] *cf.* Matt 13:33; 16:6; Mark 8:15, etc.

THE EXODUS
(1446 BC) [165]

And so, to the Exodus.

There are important consecrations occurring as the Israelites leave the land of their bondage. In our haste to get to the meat of the Exodus action, we often overlook these important details:

And Moses said unto the people, "Remember this day, in which ye came out from Egypt, out of the house of bondage; for by strength of hand the LORD brought you out from this place: there shall no leavened bread be eaten. This day came ye out in the month Abib [=Nisan]**. And it shall be when the LORD shall bring thee into the land of the Canaanites, and the Hittites, and the Amorites, and the Hivites, and the Jebusites, which He sware unto thy fathers to give thee, a land flowing with milk and honey, that thou shalt keep this service in this month.**

"Seven days thou shalt eat unleavened bread, and in the seventh day shall be a feast to the LORD. Unleavened bread shall be eaten seven days; and there shall no leavened bread be seen with thee, neither shall there be leaven seen with thee in all thy quarters.

"And thou shalt shew thy son in that day, saying, 'This is done because of that which the LORD did unto me when I came forth out of Egypt.' And it shall be for a sign unto thee upon thine hand, and for a memorial between thine eyes, that the LORD'S law may be in thy mouth: for with a strong hand hath the LORD brought thee out of Egypt. Thou shalt therefore keep this ordinance in his season from year to year." (Exo 13:3-10)

How strange is this? To this day, small leather boxes known as phylacteries (*tefillin*) are worn by orthodox, observant Jews during weekday morning prayers. They are strapped on the arm (the *shel-yad*) and above the forehead (the *shel rosh*) (Ex 13:9,16; Deut 6:8; 11:18). The boxes contain verses of the Torah. The LORD intends this as a

---

[165] 1 Kings 6:1 states: **And it came to pass in the four hundred and eightieth year after the children of Israel were come out of the land of Egypt, in the fourth year of Solomon's reign over Israel, in the month Zif, which is the second month, that he began to build the house of the LORD.** Scholars are generally settled that Solomon's reign commences on or around 970-971 BC, giving us 1446 BC as a suggested date for the Exodus. While this does not align with all scholars' datings, leading Egyptian scholar Prof. JH Breasted concurs, placing the 18th Dynasty between 1580 – 1350 BC.

memorial to Passover as well as a token of obedience, and phylacteries are regarded as such by devout Jews. But notice that *ha-Satan*, the great counterfeiter of all God's ways, will even copy this ritual in the last days of the Antichrist and his 'False Prophet':

And he [the False Prophet] **causeth all, both small and great, rich and poor, free and bond, to receive a mark in their right hand, or in their foreheads: And that no man might buy or sell, save he that had the mark, or the name of the beast, or the number of his name** (Rev 13:16-17)

The infamous 'Mark of the Beast' will be as much an economic requirement to survive in this brutal age as a one-way swearing of allegiance to the Antichrist (*lit:* pseudo-Christ). Without it, citizens will not only not be able to eat or function without this currency during the 42-month reign of Satan's ruler, they will be murdered out of hand. Yet taking the mark of the Antichrist will guarantee eternal damnation before God in the final judgment (Rev 14:9-11). The way out of this Gordian Knot? Ensure that you are evacuated before this gruesome time commences.[166]

As they leave Egypt, God also institutes the law of the firstborn:

"And it shall be when the LORD shall bring thee into the land of the Canaanites, as he sware unto thee and to thy fathers, and shall give it thee, that thou shalt set apart unto the LORD all that openeth the matrix [womb]**, and every firstling that cometh of a beast which thou hast; the males shall be the LORD'S.**

"And every firstling of an ass thou shalt redeem with a lamb; and if thou wilt not redeem it, then thou shalt break his neck: and all the firstborn of man among thy children shalt thou redeem.

"And it shall be when thy son asketh thee in time to come, saying, 'What is this?' that thou shalt say unto him, 'By strength of hand the LORD brought us out from Egypt, from the house of bondage: and it came to pass, when Pharaoh would hardly let us go, that the LORD slew all the firstborn in the land of Egypt, both the firstborn of man, and the firstborn of beast: therefore I sacrifice to the LORD all that openeth the matrix, being males; but all the firstborn of my children I redeem.'

And it shall be for a token upon thine hand, and for frontlets between thine eyes: for by strength of hand the LORD brought us forth out of Egypt." (Exo 13:11-16)

---

[166] A full examination of the *harpazo* ('Rapture') will be highlighted later in *Origins VI - Parousia.*

God has not taken his killing of the Egyptian firstborn lightly. He intends the occasion to be remembered *forever*. Some students of the above passage are startled that God apparently intends OT Hebrews to sacrifice the firstborn, not only of their children but also their animals. *He does.* But the children are to be redeemed for a small payment of silver, a material used throughout the Bible as a model for the blood of redemption (Exo 30:15-16; Num 18:15-17; Mark 10:45).

The redemption price is the same for rich or poor, reflecting Christ's future sacrifice for the remission of sins. When God later instructs Moses to construct the Tabernacle to serve as a portable temple and sanctuary for the Holy Spirit, 9,600 lbs of solid silver, looted from Egypt, will be used to form the foundation sockets upon which the whole structure stands: literally resting on the blood of redemption. Both Jesus and Joseph were sold for silver. Judas was paid off in silver for his betrayal of Yeshua, which coins he later cast into the Temple, declaring to the chief priests, **"I have sinned in that I have betrayed the innocent blood."** (Matt 27:3-8)[167] Notice that there is no mention of silver in heaven anywhere in the Bible. The sinner has already been redeemed.

There is also another intriguing model which the Holy Spirit employs to consistent effect throughout the scriptures. Chuck Missler explains:

"The ass is a type of unclean animal, the 'natural man' (Job 11:12). Ishmael in contrast to Isaac was born of the flesh, a type of natural man, described as a 'wild ass' (Gen 16:12; Gal 4:30). In Gen 22:3, the ass was saddled and was not among them going up the hill [for the 'sacrifice' of Isaac] (Gen 22:5). In Gen 49:10, he is always seen as a beast of burden. In Deut 22:10, he is shut out of service, in a priestly sense. In 1 Sam 9:3, he was symbolic of those who were lost (*cf.* Jer 22:19)." [168]

When Yeshua presents Himself to the world in Jerusalem on 'Palm Sunday', the multitude view Him as the long-awaited Messiah, in the role of the King of the Jews. However, this King is not riding a

[167] **And the chief priests took the silver pieces, and said, "It is not lawful for to put them into the treasury, because it is the price of blood." And they took counsel, and bought with them the potter's field, to bury strangers in** (Matt 27:6-7). Translation: The holiest men in Judaism apparently have no problem hiring an assassin to do their 'wet work', yet struggle over the implications of immoral accounting!

[168] Missler, Chuck, *Exodus notes*, ch.13-15, op. cit.

white horse but a donkey, fulfilling Zechariah 9:9.[169] The significance is lost on many. Jesus is presenting Himself for inspection as the Passover lamb without blemish on the appointed day (10th Nisan), and will be sacrificed 4 days later between the evenings on Passover (14th Nisan) for the collective sins of the 'natural man', represented by the ass (Matt 21:1-11). And it will be the 'natural man', the 'lost', even some of the most august men in Jewry, who will take Him to His death.

The route

The literature is veritably busting at the seams with different routes the children of Israel take on their trek out of bondage. You will find a dozen diverse crossing points argued for that monumental scene at the Red Sea, not to mention a dozen disparate mountains spread across hundreds of miles proposed for God's holy mountain, Sinai/Horeb.

So the questions start: Is there any scientific evidence whatsoever for this most momentous of epics? Would close on two million souls trekking around the desert for 40 years leave anything detectable three and a half millennia later? Secular archaeology screams a resounding 'No!" but they should hold their horses for a moment. These are the same ninnies who stare at mountains with fossils and seashells in them and can't come up with a Flood. Let's do some sleuthing and see what we find.

The first question that needs to be asked is, does it really matter what route the Israelites took, where they crossed, and where God's holy mountain actually is? In his book *Exodus,* R Alan Cole remarks:

"The exact place of Israel's crossing of the Red Sea has no direct theological importance."[170]

I would certainly agree, and so would Joel McQuitty, but with a caveat in his unpublished 1986 Capital Bible Seminary thesis *The Location and Nature of the Red Sea Crossing*:

"In the form of the statement Mr. Cole is correct, geography normally impinges very little upon theology. However, *how* one

---

[169] **"Rejoice greatly, O daughter of Zion; shout, O daughter of Jerusalem: behold, thy King cometh unto thee: he is just, and having salvation; lowly, and riding upon an ass, and upon a colt the foal of an ass."**

[170] **Cole R A** *Exodus,* IVP Academic, 2008, p.44

determines the geography of the Bible may speak volumes concerning one's theology."

Does God intend for us to look? The answer to that may lie in what clues He has provided for us in His Word. Is there enough information given that makes any geographical quest of the Exodus relevant or even feasible? The answer is, yes. Also, we are expected by the Author to take the astonishing Exodus account as plain, historical fact, so why wouldn't God want us to search, especially when He has given us more than enough clues? Remember Prov 25:2? **It is the glory of God to conceal a thing: but the honour of kings is to search out a matter.** The central theme of the Bible hangs completely on what happened at Mt Sinai, so I would say that we need to examine this subject fully. And believe me when I say that you enter a whole new territory in research acrimony when you open up the Exodus/Red Sea/Mt Sinai saga.

Before examining the bizarre crossing of the Red Sea by Moses and the Israelites, so memorably played out by Charlton Heston and Christian Bale, let us consider the beginning of their trek out of Egypt and search for clues.

And it came to pass, when Pharaoh had let the people go, that God led them not through the way of the land of the Philistines, although that was near; for God said, "Lest peradventure the people repent when they see war, and they return to Egypt." But God led the people about, through the way of the wilderness of the Red Sea: and the children of Israel went up harnessed out of the land of Egypt.

And Moses took the bones of Joseph with him: for he [Joseph] **had straitly sworn the children of Israel, saying, "God will surely visit you; and ye shall carry up my bones away hence with you."**

And they took their journey from Succoth, and encamped in Etham, in the edge of the wilderness. And the LORD went before them by day in a pillar of a cloud, to lead them the way; and by night in a pillar of fire, to give them light; to go by day and night: He took not away the pillar of the cloud by day, nor the pillar of fire by night, from before the people. (Exo 13:17-22)

The Bible tells us:

- The Exodus begins at the Nile Delta city of Pi-Ramesses in Goshen (Exo 12:37)
- The Israelites take the bones of their patriarch Joseph with them (Gen 50:24-26; Exo 13:19)

- The Israelite numbers exceed 600,000 men before you count the women and children (Exo 12:37; 603,550 is the precise figure given in Exo 38:26). The total number leaving has been estimated at as many as *2 million*. That's going to impose space limitations on our search criteria, which works for us. There are just so many places you can put a population the size of Houston, Texas
- Some scholars argue that the Hebrew word *eleph* (אלף - Strongs #H505) really means 'clan/family' and not 'thousand', seeking to lower the Hebrew numbers leaving Egypt. While it is true that both meanings can be attributed to *eleph*, the context is all-important. The *eleph* meaning of 'thousand' is used for the results of a census.[171] Elsewhere, for instance, when the men of Beth Shemesh interfere with the Ark of the Covenant in 1 Sam 6:19, we are told 50 *eleph* were killed by the LORD. The meaning here is widely taken as 50 clans not 50,000 men slaughtered [172]
- Some of this number appear to comprise Egyptian or other foreign Gentiles – the troublesome 'mixed multitude' we'll encounter later (Exo 12:38)
- Did Pharaoh's daughter go with them at this time? A 'pharaoh's daughter' is mentioned in 1 Chron 4:18 as being wed to Mered of the tribe of Judah. She is known by a Hebrew name Bithiah (*lit.* 'daughter of Yah'). Was this Iaret, Amenhotep II's only known daughter? Nothing more is mentioned of her. Jewish tradition holds that 'Pharaoh's daughter' was exiled from Egypt for bringing the renegade Moses into the royal household as a baby. This is quaint anachronism, considering that 'Pharaoh's daughter' (Hatshepsut) was approximately 15 around the time of the bulrushes episode and would hardly be in a position to bear Mered children 80 years later at the age of 95, though stranger things have happened! (Gen 17:17)
- The Israelites have been in the land of Egypt 430 years *to the day* (Exo 12:41). How about that for precision? They came down as a family with Jacob and will leave as a nation of armies under Moses and Aaron (Exo 6:26; 7:4; 12:17; 12:51)

---

[171] Exo 12:37; Num 1:45-46; 11:21; 26:51

[172] www.bible.ca/archeology/bible-archeology-exodus-route-population-of-jews-hebrews.htm

Moses is instructed by God not to lead his people up the faster, coastal route towards Canaan, known as the Horus Way (aka 'The Way of the Sea'), but out of the land of Egypt towards the wilderness (Exo 13:17-18). The reason given is that the Philistines are apparently in a state of bellicose mobilisation at this time (Exo 13:17). Notice that shortly after they leave the supply/market city of Pi-Ramesses, *they depart the geographical nation of Egypt* (Exo 13:18). This is an important point for those who maintain that the Sinai peninsula is under direct rule of Egypt at this time, and actually part of Egypt. We'll look at this later.

The Israelites are led in a more south-easterly direction up to the threshold of the Sinai. As they depart, the Hebrews believe they are leaving with Pharaoh's full consent, especially since they have been given wagon-loads of valuables by a willing Egyptian citizenry. We can also infer that 600,000 Israelites plus women children, hangers-on (up to 2 million souls), plus animals and booty won't be doing better than 7-10 miles per day tops. Yohanan Aharoni was an Israeli archaeologist and historical expert on geography in Tel-Aviv University until his death in 1976. In his book *The Land of the Bible,* he describes the march by Tuthmosis III and his army outbound on their first campaign to Megiddo as having covered the 150 miles from the Egyptian frontier post of Sile to Gaza *"in nine or ten days, a very rapid pace"*.[173] That's 15-16 miles per day. Realistically, a huge mass of people such as the Israelites will not be doing better than 7-10 miles a day. Notice they travel by day and night during the opening stretch (Exo 13:21). Sure enough, we learn from scripture that the Israelites' first proper camp is pitched at a place called Succoth, 23 miles from Pi-Ramesses.[174] What do we know about this location?

Gary Byers writes:

"Succoth (Ex 12:37; Nm 33:5–6) was the first stop (the second place mentioned in the Exodus itinerary). The Hebrew name (meaning 'temporary shelters', 'tents' or 'booths') probably corresponds to the Egyptian name tkw (Tjeku), a site known in Egyptian texts and preserved in the modern Arabic name of the village located at the ancient site, Tell el-Maskhuta. Linguistically, the hieroglyphic name is probably borrowed from Hebrew (Hoffmeier 2005: 65). Both names probably reflect a site

---

173 **Ahroni, Y** *The Land of the Bible – A Historical Geography,* Westminster Press, 1979, p.153

174 Succoth is identified with Tell el-Maskhuta - Google Earth: 30°33'9.96"N 32° 5'55.01"E

where, from early times, Semitic-speaking people, desert clans and merchant traders camped along the Wadi Tumilat. It may not have been a permanent city, but a site of camp-style dwellings—probably structures constructed from bundles of plant stalks and branches as can still be seen in the delta region today. Such a meaning makes sense, as the Israelites would not have wanted to have to deal with an occupied Egyptian town as they were departing the country (Shea 1990: 105–106; Kitchen 2003: 257–58; Hoffmeier 1997: 179)." [175]

Wadi Tumilat describes a river valley running west-east in the eastern Delta region to Lake Timsah (see **Chart C**). In Moses's day, Succoth in Wadi Tumilat appears to have been a tent or booth 'city' near Egypt's eastern border, the first port of call for immigrants coming in from the Levant. A number of attempts were made to construct a canal along the wadi to link the Pelusiac branch of the Nile to the Gulf of Suez via Lake Timsah and the Great Bitter Lake. This would provide a Suez Canal-type strategic waterway from the Mediterranean to the Gulf, with which to facilitate trade and military movement. According to Aristotle, Strabo and Pliny the Elder, the work on this 'Canal of the Pharaohs' was initiated by Pharaoh Sesostris of the 12th Dynasty, but abandoned due to the engineering challenges of the water level.[176] Several further attempts were made centuries later by Darius I and Necho II, but these efforts were also forsaken for the same reasons. Success was finally achieved by Ptolemy II when a lock was fitted, regulating water height. The canal enjoyed some use during the early Islamic era before being closed in 767 AD. Napoleon found the remains of the canal during his Egyptian expedition in 1799.

After Succoth, the children of Israel camp at Etham on the edge of the wilderness (Exo 13:20).

And the LORD went before them by day in a pillar of cloud to lead the way, and by night in a pillar of fire to give them light, so as to go by day and night [i.e. they are constantly on the move]**. He did not take away the pillar of cloud by day or the pillar of fire by night from before the people.** (Exo 13:21-22, NKJV)

Theories abound by those who seek naturalistic explanations for everything that the Israelites are in fact looking at the Thera volcanic

---

[175] www.biblearchaeology.org/post/2008/08/23/New-Evidence-from-Egypt-on-the-Location-of-the-Exodus-Sea-Crossing-Part-II.aspx#Article

[176] Aristotle: *Meteorology* 1:15; Strabo: XVII 1, 25 C 804. 805; Pliny the Elder: Plin. n. h. VI 165f

plume that would have risen over 100 kilometres into the atmosphere. Although well over the horizon at the modern-day island site of Santorini in the eastern Mediterranean, they argue that the erupting super-volcano would indeed have made an impressive pillar of cloud by day and perhaps an apocalyptic column of fire by night. The problem is, Thera's ejecta cloud would need to exceed 100 km in height to be visible from Egypt due to the Earth's curvature. And there is an issue with getting the direction of the Israelite march from Succoth to Etham to line up with Thera. Also, this pillar of cloud later comes between the camp of the Egyptians and the camp of Israel (Exo 14:19-20), so there's a limit to how far you can push natural, volcanic explanations at this time!

My take on this? We are told the pillar and cloud are a miracle wrought by God and evidence of His presence. The notion that poor, bumbling old Moses was woefully misguided into mistaking the mother of all volcanic eruptions across the sea for 'the bearded man in the sky' is simply atheist condescension. It does not even accord with the known dating of the Thera eruption (100-150 years earlier), let alone the practical problems of getting the action to line up with any Thera plume.

Exo 14:5 tells us: **Now it was told the king of Egypt that the people fled....** Amenhotep is not at Pi-Ramesses in Goshen at the time the Israelites pull out, or he could just have looked out of the window with a snarl to watch them tromping by. It is more likely from the following passage that Pharaoh has hastened 80 miles southwest back to military HQ at Memphis to round up the army for what will follow. We are told that Pharaoh has once again hardened his heart against the Hebrews: **"Why have we done this, that we have let Israel go from serving us?" So he made ready his chariot and took his people with him. Also he took six hundred choice chariots, and all the chariots of Egypt with captains over every one of them.** (Exo 14:5–7, NKJV)

Of course, Amenhotep is out for revenge for the death of his son, the humiliation of his nation and people, and he wants his loot back. He leads out what is probably the entire northern Egyptian army to confront the Hebrews wherever he catches up with them (Exo 14:9). Put yourself in Amenhotep's position. You have looked on as your nation has been repeatedly laid waste by the most appalling of scourges. The hated Hyksos Hebrews have struck Egypt once more. Moses, a known murderer, has humiliated you in front of your court, your people, your army, your family and gods with his 'One God'.

The meddlesome prophet is personally responsible for invoking pestilence and calamities which have decimated thousands, including the heir to the Egyptian throne, *your own beloved firstborn prince, Tuthmosis*. Your religious advisors at Heliopolis had hastily revised their analysis in view of the plagues, advocating appeasement of YHWH by allowing the Israelites to leave with gold and treasure from the citizenry. Now you receive word that a significant chunk of your slave population just walked out of the side door, which will likely paralyse what's left of the economy for years to come.

Further intelligence reports come in during the week it takes to prepare and provision the army. The wretched two-million-plus Israelites are wandering aimlessly around, too afraid to go into the wilderness, too afraid to surrender and return to their homes in Goshen. Enough is enough. You ride out at the head of the mightiest army on Earth. There's going to be blood. You know it, your army knows it, and the cowardly Israelites beholding the might of your approaching cohorts will know it.

Where do they cross?

This is a great question that has fuelled libraries of books, all sorts of expeditions and speculations, and the subject is hotly debated even today among theologians, archaeologists and the public. Many claims have been made. To date, alas, no chariot wheels have been uncovered anywhere, nor rusted weaponry or skeletons.[177] Let's do some sleuthing to see if we can figure out the crossing point. Gordon Franz outlines the main contenders:

---

[177] We're back to the colourful claims of our friend, Ron Wyatt, the amateur Bible archaeologist who claimed to have found Noah's Ark, Sodom and Gomorrah, the Tower of Babel, and the original stones of the Ten Commandments. www.truthorfiction.com reports: "Wyatt's focus on Nuweiba, and his claims of finding chariot remains on the floor of the sea, have brought other adventurers to the site, but even Wyatt's supporters urge caution about their enthusiastic findings. Richard Rives, the president of Wyatt Archeological Research in Tennessee, told journalist Joe Kovacs, 'All kinds of people are finding coral and calling it chariot parts.' Wyatt's wife, Mary Nell, told Kovacs the same. She went diving with Wyatt at the Red Sea site and said that at first she thought everything was a chariot wheel. The bottom line is that at this point, all that seems to exist to support the claims of chariot parts on the bottom of the Red Sea are pictures, most of which are of coral formations. No documented artefacts have been retrieved and preserved from the site, and now the Egyptian government prohibits bringing any findings to the surface, so the questions may remain for a long time to come." - www.truthorfiction.com/rumors/c/chariot-wheels.htm

"In the literature, I have been able to discern five general areas that have been proposed for the Red Sea Crossing. Within each area there are several variations….

The Mediterranean Sea sites. Usually the crossing is placed at Lake Sirbonis. This identification is based on placing Baal-Zephon with a sanctuary of Zeus Casios nearby. The leading proponents of this view are O. Eissfeldt, M. Noth, H. Cazelles, Y. Aharoni and M. Avi-Yonah.

The northern sites. Several lakes north of the Bitter Lakes have been proposed. They are Lake Timsah, Lake Balah or the southern extension of Lake Menzaleh. The proponents of this area are E. Naville, M. F. Unger, K. A. Kitchen and J. Hoffmeier.

The central site. The proponents of this view place the crossing at the Bitter Lakes. Some would suggest that the Gulf of Suez actually came up to the Bitter Lakes in antiquity. The proponents of this view are J. Simons, C. Condor, U. Cassuto, John J. David.

The southern sites. The proponents place the crossing at the northern end of the Gulf of Suez. Within this view there are two areas. One view places it just offshore from the modern-day Suez City. The other places it at a land bridge 4 miles south of Suez City between Ras el-Adabiya and Birket Misallat. The proponents of this view are E. Robinson, A. Smith, E. H. Palmer, Keil and Delitzsch, James Murphy, John Rea, J. McQuitty and G. Franz.

The south-eastern site. This view places the crossing in the Gulf of Akaba/Eilat. Within the gulf there are two proposed crossings. One crossing, proposed by R. Wyatt and L. Moller, is a land bridge to the east of Nuweiba. The second crossing that was proposed is at a land bridge at the Strait of Tiran. R. Knuteson, J. Irwin, B. Cornuke and L. Williams hold this view."[178]

Let's examine the Biblical text to see what we can logically deduce. **Chart C** will be helpful, as will Google Earth. We are initially told:

And it came to pass, when Pharaoh had let the people go, that God led them not through the way of the land of the Philistines, although that was near; for God said, "Lest peradventure the people repent when they see war, and they return to Egypt." But God led the people about, through the way of the wilderness of the Red Sea: and the children of Israel went up harnessed [Strongs H2571: *'chamush'*, staunch, disciplined, armed, able-bodied] **out of the land of Egypt.**

---

[178] http://ldolphin.org/franz-ellawz.html

And Moses took the bones of Joseph with him: for he had straitly sworn the children of Israel, saying, "God will surely visit you; and ye shall carry up my bones away hence with you."

And they took their journey from Succoth, and encamped in Etham, in the edge of the wilderness. And the LORD went before them by day in a pillar of a cloud, to lead them the way; and by night in a pillar of fire, to give them light; to go by day and night. He took not away the pillar of the cloud by day, nor the pillar of fire by night, from before the people. (Exo 13:17-22)

We can infer the following from the text:

- God did not lead them out east and north-east along the Mediterranean coast route up into Canaan (the Horus Road/'Way of the Sea'). This was the quickest way to the Promised Land but Philistia was apparently in a state of war at the time
- So God heads them out of Egypt in a different direction, specifically given as **the way of the wilderness of the Red Sea**. Interesting phrase. According to the Bible, wherever this wilderness begins, you're out of Egypt, you go into wilderness, and at the end of the wilderness, you will be crossing the Red Sea. Again, here's the important bit: they are *leaving Egypt* (*cf.* Exo 14:11), which means that we can discount any speculative 'Red Sea crossing-points' along the Mediterranean coast at Lakes Manzalah, Balah, Bardawil and the Serbonian Bog, as well as those further south at Lake Timsah and the Great Bitter Lake. The reason? There is no wilderness to traverse before you arrive at these locations
- Take a look at **Chart C** and find Pi-Ramesses in Goshen.[179] Discount the northern coastal route up into Gaza and Canaan. The only logical route you are left with for **the wilderness of the Red Sea** is the trek which heads south-east, down the west side of the Great Bitter Lake to the northern tip of the Red Sea (Gulf of Suez). This is classic wilderness country, but the plain is constant and well able to support the transit of up to 2 million-plus people in addition to animals
- The second stop is at Etham, described as **in the edge of the wilderness.** This means that Etham is where the green gives way to the brown

[179] Google Earth 30°47'56"N 31°50'9"E at the modern-day town of Quantir.

- Notice in the text that some time passes once they leave Etham. Blink and you miss it. Exo 13:21-22 states: **And the LORD went before them by day in a pillar of a cloud, to lead them the way; and by night in a pillar of fire, to give them light; to go by day and night: He took not away the pillar of the cloud by day, nor the pillar of fire by night, from before the people.** Pedantic phrasing, isn't it? It's hard not to get the impression that once Etham is behind them, the Israelites settle into the routine of a journey, a common enough undertaking in those days. This would discount the localised crossings and accord with a brisk (Exo 12:33) and more lengthy trip down to the Gulf of Suez (78 miles), which could interestingly take the six days of the Feast of Unleavened Bread with a day off for *Shabbat* (Sabbath) (*cf.* Lev 23:42-43; Deut 16:3)
- As if to reinforce 'time passing', there is an obvious chronological gap between Exo 13:22 and 14:1, which inspired medieval scribes to insert a chapter break
- The Israelites are no fleeing rabble as some imagine. They come out of Egypt in orderly ranks (Exo 13:18) and will soon be armed, for they fight a battle in a few weeks

Notice that when the Israelites see the great Egyptian northern army preparing to attack them 'on the shore' (Exo 14:9) immediately prior to the Red Sea crossing, they lament to Moses and we get some good intel: **"Because there were no graves in Egypt, hast thou taken us away to die in the wilderness?** [i.e. they're in the wilderness, not Egypt!] **Wherefore hast thou dealt thus with us, to carry us forth out of Egypt?** [i.e. wherever they are, they are now *out of Egypt,* again discounting the northern crossing points!] **Is not this the word that we did tell thee in Egypt** [i.e. they're not in Egypt now!]**, saying, 'Let us alone, that we may serve the Egyptians?' For it had been better for us to serve the Egyptians, than that we should die in the wilderness."** (Exo 14:11-12)

Let's carry out an elimination exercise: One of the requirements for the location of the Red Sea crossing is that the children of Israel need to be encamped on the shore by the Red Sea. I think when God calls it the Red Sea, I think he means the Red Sea, which will include its bifurcated northern sections: the Gulfs of Suez and Aqaba. 'The Red Sea' won't be the Serbonian Bog up on the Mediterranean coast because a) it's not the Red Sea, and b) Moses was told not to go that way. In spite of some scholars' best efforts to equate Red Sea with 'Sea of Reeds' or 'Weeds', the children of Israel won't have crossed any of the reedy lakes such as Timsah, Balah, Manzalah with water piled high on either side(!), since these lakes are but a few feet deep. Neither will the momentous event take place at the Great Bitter Lake because a) it is not the Red Sea and b) not even God has in mind to drown the entire Egyptian army in three feet of water. Gordon Franz settles the reed/weed issue thus:

"Within the debate on the location of the Red Sea crossing there is a sub-debate on the meaning of the name *Yam Suph*. The common interpretation of these words today is 'Reed Sea'. The first to suggest *Yam Suph* means 'reedy swamp' appears to be Rabbi Shelomoh Yetzhaki (Rashi) in the 11th century AD. Personally I am not comfortable with that etymology. I will leave that discussion for another paper. I think the meaning of *Yam Suph* is Red Sea....

"In the Hebrew Scriptures, the *Yam Suph* refers to either the Gulf of Suez or the Gulf of Akaba/Eilat. The context determines the location. For example, Exodus 10:19 says, **And the LORD turned a very strong west wind, which took the locusts away and blew them into the Red Sea. There remained not one locust in all the territory of Egypt.** As J. Rea points out, the 'strong west wind' should be translated 'sea wind'. In Egypt, the sea winds are from north-northwest to the south (1975:1:572). Since the locusts covered **the face of the whole earth** [land of Egypt] (Exo 10:15), there would need to be a large body of water to destroy the locusts. The Gulf of Suez is what is in view. Exodus 13:18 and 15:4,22; Num. 33:10 refer to the Gulf of Suez. On the other hand, I Kings 9:26 says **King Solomon also built a fleet of ships at Ezion Geber, which is near Elath on the shore of the Red Sea, in the land of Edom.** This is clearly referring to the Gulf of Akaba/Eilat. Judges 11:16 and Jer. 49:20,21 are most likely referring to this gulf as well."[180] [emphasis mine]

Out of the proposed 'proper' Red Sea crossings, we can discount two further putative sites - the ones south in the Gulf of Aqaba at Nuweiba and the Tiran Strait - for no other reason than because there are no realistic sub-sea 'land bridges' at these locations, despite the claims. At Nuweiba, there is not only no seashore plain where you can gather 2 million Israelites plus hangers-on, there's an immediate catastrophe once you attempt walking upon the sea-bed: the gradient plunges sharply down 2,575 feet *within one mile*. That's some gradient.

---

[180] www.ldolphin.org/franz-ellawz.html

When you get to the Midian side, you've got an even more Herculean task before you. The seabed rises *2,500 feet in 0.6 mile* – enough at any rate to have the cattle and goats, not to mention hundreds of thousands of sandal-shod humans rolling down unassailable gradients (see **Chart E**).

The Tiran Strait crossing is featured in the Ridley Scott movie, *Exodus: Gods and Kings* at 44 mins 32 secs on Moses's outbound exile to Midian. The panoramic scene gives the viewer the impression that there is a shallow land-bridge across the straits, with little islands forming a rocky necklace across the billows. Sure enough, a few seconds later we watch Christian Bale gamely negotiating his horse through two feet of water between the rocks as he traverses the strait. The Tiran Strait reality is, alas, a little different (see **Chart D**). There are two shipping channels marked on maritime charts: the Enterprise and Grafton Passages. Proponents of the Red Sea Crossing at Tiran have not done their homework with naval soundings. In their book, *In Search of the Mountain of God – The Discovery of the Real Mt. Sinai,* Robert Cornuke and David Halbrook write:

> "Due north sat an oddity of *Ripley's Believe it or Not*: a five-hundred-yard-wide coral reef, invisible on the surface yet spanning the entire straits like a stealth aircraft carrier.... The coral reef we inspected is sturdy and broad enough and situated in water shallow enough to meet this 'dry land' criteria. Two million Israelites, columns of cattle, flocks, fleets of carts and wagons, even Egyptian troops and chariots, would have been able to pass quickly over the tightly compacted coral without getting their feet wet.... the distance shore to shore at the Strait of Tiran is no more than two miles, by far the narrowest channel on both sides of the gulf" [181]

The authors boast a two-mile land-bridge like it's a walk in the park, but it's *twelve miles in total across.* What's more, the first part of this heavenly jaunt sees a drop of over 660 feet – that's over two and a half times the height of London's Big Ben – *in the first one-third of a mile.* This is the Enterprise Passage. Then the seabed climbs back up to 164 feet below sea-level across coral that would rasp the skin off those sore feet, then back down again for the Grafton Passage. At ages 80 and 83 respectively, that workout won't be a cup of tea for Moses and Aaron if ever they try to bring two million plus people through that watery bottleneck. Gordon Franz is similarly unimpressed:

---

[181] **Cornuke, R & D Halbrook, D** *In Search of the Mountain of God. The Discovery of the Real Mt. Sinai*, Broadman and Holman, Nashville USA, 2000, pp.200,214-215

"The British Admiralty map 801 and the American NOAA map 62222 show that [the authors'] statements are not accurate. The shallow reefs do not go all the way across and the land bridge is not flat. In the midst of the Strait of Tiran is the Enterprise Passage.... This is an underwater passage/channel that goes north south through the Strait. It is approximately 3/4 of a mile wide with a depth of 700 feet. The eastern side has a slope with at least a 60% incline. To put this incline number in perspective, in Bergen County, NJ, where I live, roads cannot have an incline of more than 10%. The 60% would be an extremely difficult, if not impossible, obstacle for travel. One of the proponents acknowledges this depth, but does not seem to grasp the significance of the problem. It would be a near impossible process for 2 million people to go down and up these slopes, along with their carts and wagons. It would be next to impossible for the Egyptian chariots to go down and up unless they were SUV chariots with traction tires! Also, if any of them stumbled going down the slopes they would be cut very badly on the coral. This passage would be next to impossible, if not an impossible obstacle, because it would slow the pace of the Israelites down considerably or even stop it, as well as cause serious problems for the Egyptian chariots."[182]

So the only candidates left are the two crossing points in the northern tip of the Gulf of Suez; and of the two, one stands out. Around seven days into the Exodus, the LORD proposes a tactical ruse for Moses:

"Speak unto the children of Israel, that they turn and encamp before Pi-Hahiroth, between Migdol and the sea, over against Baal Zephon: before it shall ye encamp <u>by the sea</u>. <u>For Pharaoh will say of the children of Israel, 'They are entangled in the land, the wilderness hath shut them in</u>.' And I will harden Pharaoh's heart, that he shall follow after them; and I will be honoured upon Pharaoh, and upon all his host; that the Egyptians may know that I am the LORD." And they did so. (Exo 14:1-4)

A number of geographical clues are given here; firstly the names:

- Pi-Hahiroth ('mouth of the canal')
- Migdol ('fortress', 'watchtower')
- Baal Zephon ('lord of the north')
- There are inter-relational details given for these locations
- There's enough room for two million people to encamp on the huge plain stretching from the Suez Canal in the east to an

[182] www.ldolphin.org/franz-ellawz.html

impressive ridge of mountains to the west, known as Jebel Ataqa. Today's Suez City covers the eastern portion of this plain by the Red Sea (see **Chart F**). Pi-Hahiroth ('mouth of the canal') is therefore identified with Suez City to the west of the mouth of the Canal of the Pharaohs where the modern-day Suez Canal commences at the Port of Suez. Such is the topography of this location that Amenhotep will believe that the Israelites have boxed themselves between the sea, the wilderness and the mountain Jebel Ataqa with no way out

- Pharaoh will be taken in by the ruse and attempt to herd the children of Israel to their doom. (He won't kill them all, he wants his slaves back)
- Numbers 33:7 (NKJV) tells us that Pi-Hahiroth is east of Baal Zephon, and that the children of Israel camped near Migdol. Migdol was a common term in this period of Egyptian history to describe a fortress or watchtower guarding an important location, such as the beginning of the Canal of the Pharaohs. The canal demarks Egypt's border, after all, so a fortress is expected here
- Baal Zephon ('lord of the north') is identified as a pagan god of sailors, says Franz:

"Dr. Hoffmeier has pointed out that the 'expression literally means 'lord of the north' and is a deity in the Ugaritic pantheon associated with Mount Casius just north of Ugarit' (1997:190). Eissfeldt suggested it was located at Ras Qasrun based on the account of Herodotus (*Persian Wars* 2:6, *LCL* 1:281; 3:5, *LCL* 2:9). Baal-Zephon was worshiped at Memphis and Tell Defeneh and a cylinder seal depicting Baal-Zephon as the 'protector of sailors' was found at Tell el-Dab'a (Hoffmeier 1997:190). W. F. Albright states that, 'Baal-saphon was the marine storm-god *par excellence*, like Greek Poseidon. As such, he was also the protector of mariners against storms. In his honour temples were built and ports were named along the Mediterranean litoral as far as Egypt, where we find Baal-zephon worshiped at Tahpanhes (Daphne) and Memphis' (1968:127.128). Quite possibly there would have been a temple on Jebel Ataqa overlooking the northern end of the Gulf of Suez. The sailors could petition him on their way out to sea for a safe trip and thank him when they arrive safely to port."[183]

---

[183] Ibid.

The geography of this area is interesting, in that a bottleneck is formed if the Israelites are forced south into the funnel of the plain where they become trapped between Jebel Ataqa and the Red Sea (**Chart F**). This seems to be the scenario God has in mind to force Pharaoh's hand. There is a land-bridge four miles south of Suez City which runs across the Gulf of Suez between Ras el-Adabiya and Birket Misallat (see **Chart F**). Shore to shore, the crossing is 5.84 miles long. The land-bridge is 1 mile across and averages a depth of 20 feet. The drop-off either side goes down 70 feet in depth. Today, the Suez Canal runs right through the land-bridge, so the channel used by shipping has been considerably deepened to avoid ocean-going vessels running aground. The channel is extensively buoyed and regularly dredged.

And it was told the king of Egypt that the people fled: and the heart of Pharaoh and of his servants was turned against the people, and they said, "Why have we done this, that we have let Israel go from serving us?" And he made ready his chariot, and took his people with him: And he took six hundred chosen chariots, and all the chariots of Egypt, and captains over every one of them.

And the LORD hardened the heart of Pharaoh king of Egypt, and he pursued after the children of Israel: and the children of Israel went out with an high hand. (Exo 14:5-8)

Pharaoh will be coming in from Memphis to the west towards the northern tip of the Gulf of Suez. Pharaoh's scouts now report back that the Israelites are boxed in by the mountain and shoreline. They are ripe for the taking. They're just sitting there at Pi-Hahiroth.

The road is good. Pharaoh will round Jebel Ataqa and take the Israelite hordes completely by surprise. Sure enough, the abrupt appearance of Pharaoh's well-tooled northern army has an electrifying effect upon the Israelites:

[So] **the Egyptians pursued after them, all the horses and chariots of Pharaoh, and his horsemen, and his army, and overtook them encamping by the sea, beside Pi-Hahiroth, before Baal Zephon.**

And when Pharaoh drew nigh, the children of Israel lifted up their eyes, and, behold, the Egyptians marched after them; and they were sore afraid: and the children of Israel cried out unto the LORD.

And they said unto Moses, "Because there were no graves in Egypt, hast thou taken us away to die in the wilderness? Wherefore hast thou dealt thus with us, to carry us forth out of Egypt? Is not this the word that we did tell thee in Egypt, saying, 'Let us alone,

that we may serve the Egyptians?' For it had been better for us to serve the Egyptians, than that we should die in the wilderness."

And Moses said unto the people, "Fear ye not, stand still, and see the salvation of the LORD, which He will shew to you today. For the Egyptians whom ye have seen today, ye shall see them again no more forever. The LORD shall fight for you, and ye shall hold your peace." (Exo 14:9-14)

The answer Moses gives to the querulous? Fear not, stand still and watch what God's going to do for you now. How many of us need to do just that when we're facing an insurmountable, implacable enemy?

Bridge over troubled waters

It is dusk.

And the LORD said unto Moses, "Wherefore criest thou unto Me? Speak unto the children of Israel, that they go forward: But lift thou up thy rod, and stretch out thine hand over the sea, and divide it: and the children of Israel shall go on dry ground through the midst of the sea. And I, behold, I will harden the hearts of the Egyptians, and they shall follow them: and I will get Me honour upon Pharaoh, and upon all his host, upon his chariots, and upon his horsemen. And the Egyptians shall know that I am the LORD, when I have gotten Me honour upon Pharaoh, upon his chariots, and upon his horsemen."

And the angel of God, which went before the camp of Israel, removed and went behind them; and the pillar of the cloud went from before their face, and stood behind them:

And it came between the camp of the Egyptians and the camp of Israel; and it was a cloud and darkness to them [the Egyptians], **but it gave light by night to these** [to the Israelites]**: so that the one came not near the other all the night.**

And Moses stretched out his hand over the sea; and the LORD caused the sea to go back by a strong east wind all that night, and made the sea dry land, and the waters were divided.

And the children of Israel went into the midst of the sea upon the dry ground: and the waters were a wall unto them on their right hand, and on their left. And the Egyptians pursued, and went in after them to the midst of the sea, even all Pharaoh's horses, his chariots, and his horsemen. (Exo 14:15-23)

Note that the crossing of the Red Sea occurs at night - in fact, it takes all night (Exo 14:21,27). To gain a sense of the scale of this endeavour, consider that London's world-famous Wembley Stadium holds a capacity crowd of 90,000. Imagine evacuating *twenty times that number* in men, women, old folks, children, donkeys, sheep, cattle and all the loot. It's going to take all night.

The most powerful nation on Earth at this time is about to lose its entire northern army - horses, chariots, trained professionals and all the kit:

And it came to pass, that in the morning watch [4 am – 8 am] **the LORD looked unto the host of the Egyptians through the pillar of fire and of the cloud, and troubled the host of the Egyptians, and took off their chariot wheels, that they drave them heavily: so that the Egyptians said, "Let us flee from the face of Israel; for the LORD fighteth for them against the Egyptians."**

And the LORD said unto Moses, "Stretch out thine hand over the sea, that the waters may come again upon the Egyptians, upon their chariots, and upon their horsemen." And Moses stretched forth his hand over the sea, and the sea returned to his strength when the morning appeared; and the Egyptians fled against it; and the LORD overthrew the Egyptians in the midst of the sea. And the waters returned and covered the chariots and the horsemen and all the host of Pharaoh that came into the sea after them. There remained not so much as one of them.

But the children of Israel walked upon dry land in the midst of the sea; and the waters were a wall unto them on their right hand, and on their left.

Thus the LORD saved Israel that day out of the hand of the Egyptians; and Israel saw the Egyptians dead upon the sea shore [not a lake!]. **And Israel saw that great work which the LORD did upon the Egyptians: and the people feared the LORD, and believed the LORD, and his servant Moses.** (Exo 14:24-31)

The above passage tells us the following:

- The Egyptians are getting bogged down and decide to call off the attack
- While they are desperately attempting to extricate themselves from the trench, the waters return to engulf them
- The wording appears to indicate that only that portion of the army which enters the trench in pursuit of the Israelites is destroyed. If the entire army perished, there would be no need to qualify the description with **that came into the sea after them.** The last phrase, **There remained not so much as one of**

them seems to refer to those who entered the trench. Nevertheless this is the major portion of the Egyptian force

- There is no mention of Pharaoh perishing in the catastrophe, only his chosen captains (Exo 15:4). If the king had died, this would certainly have been mentioned in the Songs of Moses and Miriam (Exo 15)
- Amenhotep, having already witnessed the plagues visited upon his nation at the hand of YHWH, wisely sits this one out on the shoreline. No quick death for Amenhotep but the ignominy of 28 years of further rule
- Most who study this particular part of the Exodus often pass over the significance of what just happened; what the economic ramifications for Egypt might be. Three monumental observations may be inferred here:
- At the zenith of her empire, 1) Lower Egypt loses a significant portion of her slave infrastructure. 2) She has just ceased to be a military power. 3) Pharaoh *survives*

The passing through the Red Sea is seen by many as a model of death to life, of baptism for the Israelites, who have the body of Joseph accompanying them through the experience – a type of Christ. The Red Sea symbolises the boundary of Satan's/Amenhotep's authority (Egypt – 'the world'), and God triumphs unequivocally over the world's temporal power, making an open spectacle of it (Col 2:15). The sea is always idiomatic in the Bible of the Gentile nations, and the raging seas symbolise the Gentile world in turmoil (Psa 65:7; Isa 55; Dan 7:2; Rev 17:15.)

Which brings me to another question not often asked. Why did Pharaoh even bother sending his army into the trench after the Israelites? After his harrowing experience with YHWH and the plagues over the previous months, it must have been sinking into even Amenhotep's amorphous curds that water piled high on either side spelled more supernatural trouble for himself and Egypt. Notice that God once again hardens Egyptian hearts (Exo 14:17), forcing Pharaoh into an unwinnable quandary. He either has to act to redeem the shame of Egypt; allow his beloved warriors to revenge themselves after the death of their firstborn and the unspeakable grief and horror suffered in their own households; or he has travelled all the way across to the Gulf of Suez *to do nothing*. I believe, staring at the astonishing water spectacle before him, with the Israelites trekking down the modest incline into the trench, Pharaoh knows YHWH wants the Egyptian army too. It is, after all, the only thing in Egypt apart from himself that God has not yet destroyed. I believe at this point, even had Amenhotep attempted to restrain his cohorts from so obvious a trap, the troops were so mad with bloodlust, grief and revenge that they would have gone in anyway. What else could Pharaoh do? What other action could have been taken? *Nothing?*

The Egyptian army is gone. Sunk without a bubble. It's been a bad night for heavy armour and bronze chariots, washed off the shallow land-bridge by raging waters and now entombed under 50 - 70 feet of Red Sea. Of the nature of the Red Sea crossing, Gordon Franz bravely concludes:

> "There is no naturalistic explanation for this occurrence; it is a first-class miracle." [184]

I agree. The impact of this dramatic saga gains its everlasting power from being *completely unexplainable and in defiance of the natural laws.* God's miracle.

The punitive campaign

Some scholars are still divided as to whether Pharaoh actually perished in the catastrophe. Those who believe he did point to Psa 106:11, which reads: **And the waters covered their enemies: there was not one of them left**, and Psa 136:15: **But overthrew Pharaoh and his host in the Red Sea...**

The problem in secular Egyptology is that no pharaoh deaths are recorded for the year 1446 BC, leading some dogmatic researchers such as William Shea to punt the tortuous proposal that Amenhotep II did in fact die in the Red Sea episode chasing his slaves, but royal officials covered up the shameful death and installed a changeling pharaoh. Yes, one ingloriously titled Amenhotep IIB, who ruled until his death around 1418 BC. I won't get into the immense problems this presents to those Egyptians and foreign rulers who would have known Amenhotep II personally and busted the ruse. There is a far easier explanation, and one which accords with the record.

In the above verse from Psa 136:15, the verb translated 'overthrew' is Strongs H5287, *naw-ar*, רענו, which is translated elsewhere as 'shook off' (Psa 109:23). The point being made in Psa 136:15 is about God's unequalled might shaking off the most powerful army in the world like a fly; the LORD redeeming His

---

[184] Ibid.

people as a result of His intervention. Notwithstanding that no pharaoh within the Exodus period is known to have died violently (we do have their bodies, including Amenhotep II's), the Bible tellingly does not state anywhere that Pharaoh actually perished. Why would it NOT if he had? If I were a Hebrew of the period, that would be the first subject covered in *my* Song of Victory. *"Pharaoh, you're dead!"* I'd chant it until I fell over. Pharaoh to me would have been the personification of all that was cruel, harsh, vindictive, unjust and unfair in my life to date. The wretched Amenhotep has become the veritable embodiment of Satanic oppression and death to his slaves. With God's most obvious *imprimatur* on the king's immolation, why wouldn't I dance and sing to celebrate the wicked king's death until I drop? I mean, *if Pharaoh really died?* The Bible is unabashed at recording other monarchs' deaths in unflinching detail: How about Ahab and Jezebel (dogs and pigs licked their blood), King Saul (run through by an Amalekite), King Ishbosheth (murdered and decapitated by two of his officers) and King Herod the Great (died horribly, consumed with worms). Why not this bad fellow? Why not "Amenhotep II: Gone to sleep with the fishes!" as his epitaph? Doug Petrovich writes:

"Another argument against the view that Ps 136:15 signals the death of pharaoh is that this verse is probably taken from Exod 14:27, which uses the same verb, 'to shake off', but (purposefully?) omits pharaoh from the list of those whom the LORD shook off from the Israelites' garments. Instead, the text clearly states, 'I [God] will be honored through pharaoh and all his army, and the Egyptians will know that I am the LORD' (Exod 14:4; *cf.* 14:17). God was honored through pharaoh in the mass destruction of his army, but pharaoh did not have to die for this to occur….

"Shea disagrees: 'Yahweh says that he will get glory over pharaoh. While some of that glory could be maintained by his loss of troops in the [Red Sea], if he escaped with his own life, some of that glory could have been diminished' (Shea, *Amenhotep II as Pharaoh,* 46). This statement, though well intended, is not true whatsoever. God displayed his glory by decimating Sennacherib's army when the Assyrians marched against Judah (2 Kgs 19:35), but his glory was not diminished when Sennacherib returned to Assyria unscathed. A far greater shame for a defeated monarch is to be left in humiliation to rule over a shell of his former empire after being defeated by God, depleted of his army, and—in the case of the exodus pharaoh—stripped of his servantile workforce….

"In Ps 136:15, the psalm writer was not rejoicing over the death of anyone, but that almighty God shook off the Egyptians from Israel's garments by freeing them from their enemy's clutches."[185]

So Amenhotep II survives and, boy, is he upset! A king is no pharaoh at all, and certainly no god, who is careless enough to lose his army and slaves in a single night. Now Egypt's king must return home to explain to his gawping council how, in the space of not even a single year, the nation has been utterly ruined as an economic and military power. Amenhotep's own father, the Napoleon of Egypt, the mighty Tuthmosis III, must be spinning like a lathe in his 'mansion of eternity' grave at Luxor as the son now wends his woeful way back to Memphis HQ with the few aides he restrained when their army galloped into the trench. I imagine few words were spoken on the way home. Amenhotep II, son of the greatest pharaoh who ever lived, cuts a dejected figure navigating his way back along the desert plain swept clean by four million feet, picking over the chariot-crash of his own reign in his mind's eye. Army gone. Heir gone. Nation gone. Each hour of the trek back, Memphis and his disgrace grow closer. Amenhotep II does not feel like a god now.

If the king had considered suicide at this time, I would not have been surprised. Perhaps the remembrance of Tiaa and his remaining children kept Amenhotep from committing the unthinkable. Certainly, from what follows afterwards, his pride smouldered still. Award-winning American archaeologist James B Pritchard writes:

"Amenhotep II gloried in his reputation for personal strength and prowess. His records, therefore, contrast with those of his predecessor and father, Thutmose III, in emphasizing individual achievement."[186]

In fact, the father conducted 17 blistering campaigns throughout the Levant, brought the hated Mitanni to heal, and built the greatest empire the world had ever seen. By contrast, the son, up to 1446 BC, has conducted just one campaign: a foray into Canaan to quell the serious revolt which occurred upon the passing of his illustrious father; a rebellion to test the mettle of the kid; who just lost an army; who just lost his slaves.

---

[185] www.biblearchaeology.org/post/2010/02/04/Amenhotep-II-and-the-Historicity-of-the-Exodus-Pharaoh.aspx#Article

[186] **Pritchard, James** *Ancient Near-Eastern Texts (ANET),* Princeton, NJ: Princeton University Press, 1950, p.245

The Exodus pharaoh disappears from the Biblical record after the Red Sea episode, but the secular evidence to support an Egyptian king and empire in disarray at this time is compelling. According to the Memphis Stele,[187] Amenhotep II does something very strange later in 1446 BC. He launches a military expedition into the Levant in November - an unheard-of action unless some emergency has occurred. Monarchs in the ancient world customarily never campaigned in the winter months due to the foul weather. They would conduct domestic politics during this time as well as plan the forthcoming military season, which commenced in the spring - **the time that kings go out to battle** (1 Chron 20:1). Claude Vandersleyen perceptively notes the unusual timing for Amenhotep's new venture:

"The second Asiatic campaign began on the 25th day of the 3rd month (*akhet*) [*c.* 16th November] of the 9th year, during an unusual season for military campaigns. It was probably induced by the necessity of urgent intervention."[188]

Yet scholars are at a loss to understand the nature of this necessity. Egypt was not under attack, and there is nothing in the recovered *official* Egyptian records of this time that gives any clue to another threat. *Or is there?* Unusually, Amenhotep's second campaign, which he personally leads, seems focussed on a particular region of Philistia/Canaan, not the far wider and distant military scope of his own first campaign and his father's illustrious forays. Not even the Mitanni are harassed.

The lack of inscription and papyrus evidence is the dealbreaker for historians who refuse to accept the Exodus as a historical event. Doug Petrovich enlightens:

"According to Num 1:45–46, the Israelites' post-exodus male population over 20 years old totalled 603,550, which does not include the 22,000 Levite males of Num 3:39. When women and children are added, they well would have exceeded 2,000,000 people. A populace of this magnitude must have provided the backbone of the Egyptian slave-force, given both their vast numbers and rigorous labors (Exod 1:11–14). To most Egyptology students, however, the Exodus narrative is considered

---

[187] This famous stele, which begins with Amenhotep's full titulary, describes his two campaigns in the Levant and the booty derived therefrom. The second campaign, launched in Year 9, only goes as far as the Sea of Galilee. The haul proves a surprise.

[188] **Vandersleyen, Claude** *L'Egypte et la Vallée du Nil,* vol. 2, Presses Universitaires de France, Paris, 1995, p.321

little more than a fanciful folktale designed to impress Jewish children with grand illusions of a glorious, ethnic past. The virtual absence of historical and archaeological evidence to verify the Israelite occupation and mass exodus from Egypt serves only to bolster this skepticism."[189]

Celebrated Canadian Egyptologist and Exodus sceptic Donald B Redford explains his reticence:

"...to the historian, [the Exodus] remains the most elusive of all the salient events of Israelite history. The event is supposed to have taken place in Egypt, yet Egyptian sources know it not.... The effect on Egypt must have been cataclysmic – loss of a servile population, pillaging of gold and silver (Exod. 3:21–22, 12:31–36), destruction of an army – yet at no point in the history of the country during the New Kingdom is there the slightest hint of the traumatic impact such an event would have had on economics or society." [190]

Redford is being disingenuous. An Egyptologist, especially of Donald's renown, knows all too well that pharaohs do not record their defeats; they are gods, what would the common rabble say? Barbara Mertz writes:

"The Egyptians suffered from a sort of official amnesia with regard to the unpleasant facts; one has the feeling that the conquest (by the Hyksos) would never have been mentioned at all if there had been a reasonable way of glorifying a king for liberating his country without referring to what he was liberating it from."[191]

And would we not expect a preening coxcomb of Amenhotep II's pre-eminence to go well out of his way to avoid any hint of disaster recorded in stone or papyrus to prejudice his wordfame for eternity? In fact, Amenhotep becomes extremely keen to prejudice someone else's wordfame for eternity: He initiates a campaign to smash up any monuments and inscriptions dedicated to Hatshepsut, the aunt and stepmother of his father, Tuthmosis III. Experts are hard put to explain such vandalous inclinations which, by best estimates, mysteriously occur *forty years after the queen's death,* when any

---

[189] www.biblearchaeology.org/post/2010/02/04/Amenhotep-II-and-the-Historicity-of-the-Exodus-Pharaoh.aspx#Article

[190] **Redford, Donald B** *Egypt, Canaan, and Israel in Ancient Times,* Princeton University Press, USA, 1992, p.408

[191] **Mertz, B** *Temples, Tombs and Hieroglyphs: The Story of Egyptology,* William Morrow, 2009, p. 150.

expected rancour would have long since cooled. What abruptly triggers such an emotional blitzkrieg? Scholars wag their heads and throw up their hands; but put Moses and the Exodus catastrophe in the middle, and all is made clear.

A prideful, sore loser wishes to settle scores, damning Hatshepsut to a bleak oblivion for the crime of having insinuated the renegade Moses into the royal household. Yet Amenhotep fails even in this plot of woeful destruction. Enough inscriptions have survived for archaeologists to piece together Hatshepsut's successful reign, merely serving to highlight Amenhotep's own craven role in the attempted desecration of his venerable grandmother.

The real surprise is what happens next. Amenhotep's mid-November campaign, launched seven months after the Exodus, is the clincher for Egyptologist Doug Petrovich. The pharaoh leads this expedition personally, and he's not after conquest or subjugation. He heads his army up into Abraham's historic territory of Canaan to grab as many slaves, chariots, gold, silver, cattle and miscellaneous booty he can lay hands on to repair the losses of the Red Sea disaster. It takes Amenhotep a full seven months to call up troops from the southern regiments of Upper Egypt and bring them to Memphis HQ, where they are rested, provisioned, then marched out up the Horus Road and into Philistine and Amorite territory. Doug Petrovich records the outcome:

"[Donald B] Redford declares that "at no point in the history of the country during the New Kingdom is there the slightest hint of the traumatic impact [that] such an event" as the "loss of a servile population" must have had upon Egypt. This bold declaration must be strongly contested. At the conclusion of both campaign narratives recorded on the Memphis Stele, the scribe meticulously listed the spoils, with their quantities, that were taken as plunder.

"By comparing the booty lists recorded after the conquests of Amenhotep II and Thutmose III, it will be seen whether A2 [i.e. Amenhotep II's second winter campaign] is distinguished among these campaigns, and if it might attest to the Exodus or the post-Exodus events. The focus of [the second campaign] was upon the spoils that Amenhotep II reaped. 'A record of the plunder that his majesty carried off: 127 princes of Retenu; 179 brothers of princes; 3,600 Apiru [Hebrews];[192] 15,200 Shasu; 36,300 Kharu; 15,070 Nagasuites/Neges;

[192] These *Apiru* or Hebrews would have been indigenous descendants of Abraham, who never went to Egypt in the Jacob emigration.

30,652 of their family members; total: 89,600 people, and their endless property likewise; all their cattle and endless herds; 60 chariots of silver and gold; 1,032 painted chariots of wood; 13,500 weapons for warfare.'

"Regarding the '89,600' total prisoners, the sum is actually 101,128 when the numbers are added. The error may be a mere mistake in addition, as the individual numbers are probably more reliable than the recorded sum. Therefore, a final tally of 101,128 is preferred over 89,600 for the total number of prisoners. Before contrasting A2 with other contemporary campaigns, it should be noted that the Egyptians confiscated 1,082 chariots, which, along with the 13,500 weapons, would be critical for replacing the '600 select chariots and all the other chariots of Egypt' that were lost in the Red Sea (Exod 14:7)."[193]

The surprising number of captives/slaves taken in this winter campaign is in marked contrast to those taken during the campaigns of Amenhotep's father Tuthmosis III in the Levant, and even the tally taken on Amenhotep's first campaign. Petrovich lists those campaigns where the slave tally is known:

Tuthmosis III's 1st campaign (T1) = 5,903 captives
T6 = 217 captives
T7 = 494 captives
Amenhotep II's 1st campaign = 2,214 captives
and **A2 = 101,128 captives**

Suddenly the king of Egypt needs an awful lot of slaves and chariots; so much so that he is prepared to break ancient custom and campaign in wintertime in order to procure them. There is another point missed by scholars: namely, that Amenhotep may have expected to fall upon the Exodus Israelites in his second campaign, believing them already back in Canaan at this point. Yet God has His people still in the wilderness, protecting them from any revenge attack.

Marah – the waters made sweet

Back to the Exodus! No sooner have the Israelites finished celebrating God's dunking of the Egyptians than Moses gets the Israelites going again:

So Moses brought Israel from the Red Sea, and they went out into the wilderness of Shur; and they went three days in the

[193] www.biblearchaeology.org/post/2010/02/04/Amenhotep-II-and-the-Historicity-of-the-Exodus-Pharaoh.aspx#Article

wilderness, and found no water. And when they came to Marah, they could not drink of the waters of Marah, for they were bitter: therefore the name of it was called Marah [*lit.* 'bitter'. *cf.* Ruth 1:20].

And the people murmured against Moses, saying, "What shall we drink?"

And he cried unto the LORD; and the LORD shewed him a tree, which when he had cast into the waters, the waters were made sweet. There He made for them a statute and an ordinance, and there He proved them. And said, "If thou wilt diligently hearken to the voice of the LORD thy God, and wilt do that which is right in His sight, and wilt give ear to His commandments, and keep all His statutes, I will put none of these diseases upon thee, which I have brought upon the Egyptians, for I am the LORD that healeth thee." (Exo 15:22-26)

More fascinating insights can be gleaned from this odd episode. Predictably, *Christian Tips* wonders:

"What was this tree? Are there really trees that can turn bad water into clean drinking water — trees that will purify water quickly to make it drinkable? One of the most remarkably useful trees is one being cultivated heavily for use in the Sudan. The Food and Agriculture Organization of the United Nations said that village women had successfully used the tree *Moringa oleifera* to cleanse the highly turbid water of the River Nile. After trying other *moringa* species in Egypt, Namibia, Somalia, and Kenya, they too have shown properties that clarify water quickly.

"When moringa seeds are crushed and poured into a pot or bottle of dirty water, the water turns transparent within seconds. The seeds' anti-bacterial properties can turn low, medium, and high turbidity waters into tap-water quality in an hour or two. Studies on the effectiveness of moringa seeds for treating water have been done since the 1970s, and have consistently shown that moringa is especially effective in removing suspended particles from water with medium to high levels of turbidity (muddiness or dirtiness). In water with high turbidity, a litre of water needs only one of the horseradish-smelling seeds for effective treatment. In low turbidity, one seed may do 4 litres. When the water is boiled, this increases its nutritional effectiveness by making inactive a nutrition-inhibiting protein (lectin)." [194]

---

[194] www.creationtips.com/bitter_sweet_water.html

'What was this tree?' really should not be our first question. Celebrations over, Moses leads the people away from the Red Sea into a new wilderness (*fig.* a time of testing), known as the Wilderness of Shur. Notice an oddity remarked upon by few expositors: In Num 33:8 this wilderness is also described as the Wilderness of Etham, which implies that it has some relevance with the previous camp at Etham; that Etham was located on the edge of the Wilderness of Etham *before they crossed.* This tells you something of the Red Sea crossing geography; for instance, in the case of the Tiran crossing, how could Etham be one side of the Gulf of Aqaba, and the Wilderness of Etham the other?

Soon there is a water problem and the people begin to murmur. I've lived in the desert. Three days without water in such an environment is lethal. Israel has just got through watching God convert the world's mightiest military power into shark biscuit *with too much water,* and now they are panicking *because they can't find any.* Perhaps we roll our eyes at Israel's lack of faith, but my tongue's not glued to the roof of my mouth with thirst whilst writing this. Let's start asking the real questions.

Who has led the Israelites into the wilderness where there is no water? *God has, using the pillar of cloud by day and pillar of fire by night.* Has God gone to all the trouble of extricating them from Egypt only to kill them with dehydration in the desert? *Of course not.* At Marah, God is going to teach them something. Again we have the enigmatic 'three days' period (repeated contextually in Num 33:8). Throughout the Bible, 'three days' symbolises a period of divine intervention foreshadowing the deliverance of God's chosen.[195] Notice that the people complain to Moses instead of entreating God, so Moses (a type of Christ) intercedes and God shows him a tree (probably a desiccated branch), and the prophet tosses it into the bitter pool. Now picture it: Moses, a type of Christ, staggering up to the water with a branch across his shoulders. The waters are miraculously healed or sweetened when he throws it in. God positively *delights* in showing us strange stuff so we'll remember it!

Immediately afterwards, the Almighty makes a statute and an ordinance for the people: that if they are obedient and heed His commandments and walk in righteousness, He will not visit upon

---

[195] *cf.* 'The Symbolic Significance of the Third Day in Scripture': www.agapebiblestudy.com/documents/The%20Symbolic%20Significance%20of%20the%20third%20day.htm

them the diseases which He has brought upon the Egyptians. After that, the narrative moves on without any explanation for this bizarre Marah episode. Which by now you know is an invitation to hit the Pause button.

Water in the Bible symbolises the Holy Spirit, cleansing, renewal, and the Word,[196] though this water is bitter. Jesus also symbolises the Word (FG 1:14), and His lot is bitter in Gethsemane (Matt 26:36-46) prior to being arrested, scourged, tortured, then led through the streets with a weighty crossbeam across His shoulders, before being crucified for the remission/healing of the world's sins. The tree symbolises the Law/statutes given by God. *How does a tree heal?* The fulfilment of the Law is Jesus Christ.... **who His own self bare our sins in His own body on the tree, that we, being dead to sins, should live unto righteousness: by whose stripes ye were healed** (1 Pet 2:24).

And in the final chapter of the Bible, the apostle John is given a vision of Heaven:

And he [the angel] **shewed me a pure river of water of life, clear as crystal, proceeding out of the throne of God and of the Lamb. In the midst of the street of it, and on either side of the river, was there the tree of life, which bare twelve manner of fruits, and yielded her fruit every month: and the leaves of the tree were for the healing of the nations. And there shall be no more curse: but the throne of God and of the Lamb shall be in it; and his servants shall serve Him...** (Rev 22:1-3)

Psalm 1 reads: **Blessed is the man that walketh not in the counsel of the ungodly, nor standeth in the way of sinners, nor sitteth in the seat of the scornful. But his delight is in the law of the LORD; and in His law doth he meditate day and night. And he shall be like a tree planted by the rivers of water, that bringeth forth his fruit in his season; his leaf also shall not wither; and whatsoever he doeth shall prosper.** (Psa 1:1-3)

So in Marah we have the concept of bitterness and 'the curse'. Adam and Eve were cursed through consuming the fruit of one tree (falling foul of God's Law), while all mankind can be healed by another tree, which is the fulfilment of the Law and its statutes embodied in Jesus Christ, who maintains His role as the living water

---

[196] Jer 2:13; Isa 11:9; Hab 2:14; Mark 16:15-16; FG 4:10-14; 7:37; 15:3; Eph 5:25-27; 1 Cor 6:11; 10:4

in the New Testament; who through His sacrifice, provides the only way for flawed mankind to be reconciled with a perfect Designer:

In the last day, that great day of the feast, Jesus stood and cried, saying, "If any man thirst, let him come unto Me and drink. He that believeth on Me, as the scripture hath said, out of his belly shall flow rivers of living water." (FG 7:37-38)

In the Old Testament, while desperate and exiled in the wilderness of Judaea, David writes: **"O God, thou art my God; early will I seek Thee: my soul thirsteth for Thee, my flesh longeth for Thee in a dry and thirsty land, where no water is..."**(Psa 63:1)

Arthur W Pink writes:

"It is only after we are saved that we become aware that this world can be a barren and desolate desert to us. To the natural man and woman there is much to be desired in this world. However the eye of faith sees nothing but death written across the entire scene. So far as the spiritual life is concerned, the world is simply a desert. It is a place for travelers. But believers understand this is not their home; they are looking forward to the New Jerusalem, the city with foundations, whose architect and builder is God (Heb 11:10). Consequently, they are aliens and strangers on the Earth (Heb 11:13). It is in this sense that believers live in a desert."[197]

Trees, water, God's Law and His statutes are all themes running overtly throughout the Bible, as well as encoded in their respective types or models. Notice that this event has less to do with the sweetening of Marah's bitter waters than it does the sweetening of the non-YHWH-centred, grumbling, bitter hearts of the Israelites - a process that will take 40 years, even as it does in most of us. Marah speaks to us of another central theme of the Bible: the dual nature of man once God has redeemed us. The celebrations of crossing the Red Sea and being delivered from Egypt ('the world') are quickly over. Reality sets in for the converts. Israel was Egypt-centred for four centuries; now God wants them YHWH-centred. Man will never completely lose the old nature until death, but God's new nature implanted in us by the Holy Spirit grants us power over the old. Some are more effective at using God's power to suppress the old nature than others, depending on how Christ-centred they become. Notice it takes around 40 hours to get Israel out of Egypt. Yet it will take *40 years* to get Egypt out of Israel. Chuck Missler notices something else:

---

[197] **Pink, AW** *Gleanings in Exodus,* Moody Press, Chicago, IL, 1981, p.119

"There were no statutes in Egypt. The statutes did not apply until they were delivered. They weren't delivered from Egypt because they kept statutes.... They applied the blood, they were delivered from Egypt, they passed through the Red Sea... now He gives them a statute...." [198]

In other words, what did it cost the Israelites to be delivered from the bondage of Egypt? *Nothing*. What did the Israelites have to do to be delivered from the bondage of Egypt ('the world's system')? *Simply apply the blood*. What precisely did the Israelites have to do to be delivered from certain death at the hands of Pharaoh and his forces? *Nothing*. Well, actually 'Fear not, stand still, and watch the salvation of the LORD.' What did the tree cost to sweeten the water? *Nothing*. It was a gift. Marah points to the gift of salvation through Jesus Christ (FG 5:39), which costs nothing, but you have to choose it. If you do choose to end your unHoly War against God and are delivered, your life changes and now there are rules/statutes so you can fellowship with your Creator *directly*. And there will be wars to fight too between your two natures. The old, worldly nature will ambush and snipe at you when least expected; constantly; and often where you think you are strongest. How comforting that the central message of the whole Bible is summarised in a verse in the Song of Moses the Israelites sing by the shores of the Red Sea: **Thou in Thy mercy hast led forth the people which Thou hast redeemed: Thou hast guided them in Thy strength unto Thy holy habitation** (Exo 15:13).

Geographically, can we find Marah? The Bible quotes a number of 'stations' (waypoints) the children of Israel visit throughout the Exodus - Marah being one of them. A number of these are lost to us today, but I will cite popular candidates and theories as we go. The Moses Wells at Ain Musa on the Mousa Coast ('Moses Coast') are a popular, traditional tourist destination for Marah, but they are not three days into any wilderness from the crossing point previously cited. Some identify Ain Musa with Elim with the 12 wells and 70 palms (see the photos on Google Earth).[199]

The waypoints on the Exodus after the crossing are given in Numbers 33 as Marah, Elim, the Red Sea Camp, the Wilderness of Sin, Dophkah, Alush, Rephidim and then Mount Sinai/Horeb. Placing these stops depends heavily on where you place Mt Sinai/Horeb.

---

[198] Missler, Chuck, *Exodus notes,* ch. 13-15, www.khouse.org

[199] Google Earth, 29°52'21.47"N 32°39'0.98"E

Some unique geography hints can help us here. Midian is the land to the east of the Gulf of Aqaba (see **Chart A**). To get from Egypt to Midian and vice versa, the most direct and only route because of the Gulf of Aqaba's geography is across what is today the Trans-Sinai Highway, but in ancient times was known as the King's Highway, an important trade route. Wiki writes:

"The [King's] Highway began in Heliopolis, Egypt and from there went eastward to Clysma (modern Suez), through the Mitla Pass and the Egyptian forts of Nekhl and Themed in the Sinai desert to Eilat and Aqaba. From there the Highway turned northward through the Arabah [Jordan Rift Valley], past Petra and Ma'an to Udruh, Sela, and Shaubak. It passed through Kerak and the land of Moab to Madaba, Rabbah Ammon/Philadelphia (modern Amman), Gerasa, Bosra, Damascus, and Tadmor, ending at Resafa on the upper Euphrates."[200]

Ancient World History concurs:

"There were two main highways in ancient times between Mesopotamia, Egypt, and the lower Arabian Peninsula: the King's Highway and the Way of the Sea. The King's Highway largely skirted the desert and served desert peoples. It ran from Damascus to the Gulf of Aqabah, and from there it forked into a route that crossed the Sinai to Egypt and a route that ran the eastern coast of the Red Sea into the Hejaz, or western Arabic coastal region. While the term appears often in historical records, it may have originally meant simply 'royal road' or 'principal highway', with no connection to a particular king or kingdom.

The King's Highway has always been an important road for pilgrims, traders, and conquerors. The Bible records it as the route that Moses and the 'children of Israel' might well have taken after they fled from ancient Egypt. Most likely it was the path that Abraham used to pursue the desert kings who had taken his nephew Lot as hostage."[201]

We'll examine the various candidates for Mt Sinai/Horeb in more detail when we get to the fabulous 'mountain scene'. For now, the children of Israel leave the Red Sea after the crossing, go three days to Marah, then to Elim, then back to the Red Sea before heading out to the mountain. Some researchers state that they crossed at Lake

---

[200] http://en.wikipedia.org/wiki/King's_Highway_(ancient)

[201] http://earlyworldhistory.blogspot.co.uk/2012/03/kings-highway-and-way-of-sea.html

Timsah, and that Marah ('bitter') is in fact the Great Bitter Lake. This fails on three accounts:

- Timsah and the Great Bitter Lake are only 10 miles apart
- The journey follows the path of the Canal of the Pharaohs (hardly '**three days in the wilderness**')
- And would God really bother drowning Egypt's northern army in the *three feet of water* that is Lake Timsah?

With the Gulf of Suez crossing, however, you emerge the other side at Birket Misallat,[202] and what's facing you is, well, wilderness (see **Chart F** and Google Earth). The larger wilderness to the north abuts my choice for Etham, so this can reasonably be described as the 'Wilderness of Etham'. Notice that we are tied into the constraint that these camps must cater for 2 million souls and all the beasts and kit. This limits our geographical choices. The Israelites go three days into the wilderness, which, at approximately 7-10 miles per day, will be 30 miles, tops. Moses knows from the previous promise God made at the burning bush (Exo 3:12) that He will be leading them back to Mount Sinai/Horeb. The prophet is familiar with this territory, having fled Egypt 40 years before out to Midian, then returning with Aaron to Egypt from Mount Sinai months previously, not unreasonably employing the same direct route. Today this same journey can be taken using the Trans-Sinai Highway, which is the most direct route from Suez City out to Eilat at the northern tip of the Gulf of Aqaba.

After Marah, Moses leads the people onward, and things start to look up: **And they came to Elim, where were twelve wells of water, and threescore and ten palm trees: and they encamped there by the waters** (Exo 15:27). Why would the Holy Spirit put in these odd details? It's a straightforward reference to the discipleship which Jesus will organise in the New Testament. First, twelve disciples go out, then the seventy (Luke 10:1-24), to act as a witness to Yeshua/Jesus and baptise with water (the wells) and spread the message of righteousness (the trees/palms). And that is what God has intended both geographical and spiritual Israel to be from the beginning: a living witness to Him throughout all the Earth (Gen 17:7-8; Deut 7:6; Isa 43:10; 44:8). God is asking the world: "Are you going to live My ways or not?" (Zech 3:7) To this day, predictably, the world system blasphemes God to His face, uses His name as a swear-word at every opportunity, hates those He has chosen, loathes His ways, and can't stand His statutes either.

---

[202] Google Earth: 29°54'10.93"N 32°35'50.22"E.

Steve Rodeheaver comments:

"This story is about the journey from Marah to Elim, from bitter water to twelve springs and seventy palm trees. The journey takes place externally and internally.... It is another revelation of the power and trustworthiness of Yahweh. The message for us is clear: Whatever the bitter obstacles that we encounter in life's journey, we can count on God to transform them, to use/redeem them for good, as God leads us to Elim. When we cry our Marahs out to God, God is able to 'sweeten' them, that is, to make them drinkable, to turn them into a resource for the next leg of the journey. God is big enough to deal with, redeem, and even transform whatever external problems we might face." [203]

Of course, a happy ending to the journey of life awaits those who are called. You have nothing to lose and everything to gain by having the God of the universe on your side. Why not stay the course? Why not endure life's trials and experience God walking with you in the wilderness? Take those blows with a cheerful disposition, because nothing happens to you without God's sanction. Learn. You are undergoing the Earth programme. You are experiencing on-the-job training under live-fire conditions during your 70 – 80 years on Earth, so God can toughen you up to administer His Eternal Kingdom. Smile! Celebrate! It's all been for YOU! Visit the Oasis! Have a slurp!

"What is it?"

From Elim, God leads the Israelites back to the Red Sea shore where they briefly camp (Num 33:10). The estimated two million souls, including the non-Hebrew 'mixed multitude' (Exo 12:38; Num 11:4), not to mention the huge herds, flocks and miscellaneous quadrupeds, quickly become predatory to the local ecosystem, not least in a desert. For Moses, the question of food and water is never far from his mind. To survive with this number in such an unforgiving environment seems impossible, yet, so far as God is concerned, this is the whole point: circumstances will compel reliability on Him. Moaning breaks out constantly:

And they took their journey from Elim, and all the congregation of the children of Israel came unto <u>the wilderness of Sin</u>, which is

[203] www.crivoice.org/biblestudy/exodus/bbex21.html

between Elim and Sinai, on the fifteenth day of the second month after their departing out of the land of Egypt.[204]

And the whole congregation of the children of Israel murmured against Moses and Aaron in the wilderness [get used to this sentence!]. **And the children of Israel said unto them, "Would to God we had died by the hand of the LORD in the land of Egypt, when we sat by the flesh pots and when we did eat bread to the full;** [sounds like a fanciful remembrance of their slavery – see Num 11:5-6] **for ye have brought us forth into this wilderness, to kill this whole assembly with hunger."**

Then said the LORD unto Moses, "Behold, I will rain bread from heaven for you, and the people shall go out and gather a certain rate every day, that I may prove them, whether they will walk in My law, or no. And it shall come to pass that on the sixth day they shall prepare that which they bring in, and it shall be twice as much as they gather daily." (Exo 16:1-5)

A month after the Israelites leave Egypt, we are presented with another compelling model of Yeshua in the OT. God will provide the bread of life to the Israelites in the desert when all other hope of sustenance is forfeit. Notice God openly admits that the method of the gathering will be a test to find out whether the people will be obedient to Him. Welcome to a continuation of the Holy War of flesh versus the Spirit. Welcome to the moany, whiny, crabby Israelites – a terrific model for the rest of us.

And Moses and Aaron said unto all the children of Israel, "At even[ing]**, then ye shall know that the LORD hath brought you out from the land of Egypt: And in the morning, then ye shall see the glory of the LORD; for that He heareth your murmurings against the LORD: and what are we, that ye murmur against us?"**

And Moses said, "This shall be, when the LORD shall give you in the evening flesh to eat, and in the morning bread to the full; for that the LORD heareth your murmurings which ye murmur against Him: and what are we? Your murmurings are not against us, but against the LORD." (Exo 16:6-8)

The non-believer will ascribe adverse events or circumstances to 'bad luck', but a believer should know better. How many times do we bemoan our lot and blame God for it? The hardest skill for believers

---

204 The Israelites leave Egypt on the fifteenth day of Nisan, the first month of the new calendar year, the day after the death of the firstborn at Passover (Num 33:3).

to acquire is to understand that *all things happen by God's permission.*[205] His omnipotence is otherwise an illusion and meaningless. Thus *any adverse event or disaster befalling us,* however harsh, becomes a test or conditioning exercise God desires us to pass through. Someone close to us has a terrible accident and dies. We don't have the whole picture. Atheists decry God's existence by proclaiming that a real God would not allow bad things to happen to 'good people', but 'good' by whose standards? The truth from God's perfect perspective is that there are no 'good people' (Rom 3:10-18), hence the need for the greatest work God has accomplished within His Creation: the redemption of man for eternity. The question atheists should be asking is, 'If God exists, why would He ever allow *good* things to happen to *bad* people?' Some of us so hate the idea that we're bad, we'll not only convince ourselves that we're good by our own fungible yardstick, we'll talk ourselves out of the only eternal reprieve available, which costs us nothing, offered freely by the only One who is good. In fact, we will disdain it to God's face. This was one of the lessons we picked up in *Origins II – Holy War* in studying the origins of evil. Evil is the absence of good; a choice we make; no-one else's fault but our own. The enemy is close. Very close. It's us! Flesh will always be at enmity with the Spirit until the Earth Programme is over for each of us.

For there is not a just man upon Earth, that doeth good, and sinneth not. (Ecc 7:20)

For all have sinned, and come short of the glory of God.... (Rom 3:23)

If we say that we have no sin, we deceive ourselves, and the truth is not in us. (1 John 1:8)

So, the contumacious multitude moan at Moses and Aaron: "...**for ye have brought us forth into this wilderness, to kill this whole assembly with hunger."** (Exo 16:3) But who in reality has brought them out of Egypt for them to endure the Wilderness of Sin? (I love those Holy Spirit puns!). And does the Israelite honestly believe that the God who wielded such incredible power recently before his very eyes would have gone to all the bother of extricating him from those terrible 'fleshpots of Egypt' (*Ha! What happened to the oppression and the whips?*) only to slaughter him in the desert? *Of course not.* At the very least, it would reflect badly on God's good Name.

[205] Isa 45:7; Amos 3:6; Lam 3:38

And the one thing we are learning is that God cares deeply about His Name.

And Moses spake unto Aaron, "Say unto all the congregation of the children of Israel, 'Come near before the LORD: for He hath heard your murmurings.' "

And it came to pass, as Aaron spake unto the whole congregation of the children of Israel, that they looked toward the wilderness, and, behold, the glory of the LORD appeared in the cloud.

And the LORD spake unto Moses, saying, "I have heard the murmurings of the children of Israel. Speak unto them, saying, 'At even[ing] **ye shall eat flesh, and in the morning ye shall be filled with bread, and ye shall know that I am the LORD your God'."**

And it came to pass, that at even[ing] **the quails came up and covered the camp, and in the morning the dew lay round about the host. And when the dew that lay was gone up, behold, upon the face of the wilderness there lay a small round thing, as small as the hoar frost on the ground. And when the children of Israel saw it, they said one to another, "It is manna"** [*lit.* 'What is it?'], **for they wist not what it was. And Moses said unto them, "This is the bread which the LORD hath given you to eat."** (Exo 16:9-15)

The name 'manna' – literally 'what is it?' – is a derogatory term.[206] Though scientists have, as usual, attempted natural and quite bizarre explanations for its existence over the years, manna matches nothing thus far found. I imagine God crafted the unique properties especially to flummox the whimsical guesses of natural man. Moses tells the people what to do with the stuff:

"This is the thing which the LORD hath commanded, 'Gather of it every man according to his eating, an omer for every man, according to the number of your persons; take ye every man for them which are in his tents.' "

And the children of Israel did so, and gathered, <u>some more, some less</u>. And when they did mete it with an omer, <u>he that gathered much had nothing over, and he that gathered little had no lack; they gathered every man according to his eating</u>.

And Moses said, "Let no man leave of it till the morning."

Notwithstanding they hearkened not unto Moses; but some of them left of it until the morning, and it bred worms, and stank: and Moses was wroth with them. And they gathered it every morning,

---

206 Whenever God refers to this substance, He calls it 'bread'. The Israelites disdainfully refer to it as 'manna'.

every man according to his eating: and when the sun waxed hot, it melted.

And it came to pass, that on the sixth day they gathered twice as much bread, two omers for one man: and all the rulers of the congregation came and told Moses.

And he said unto them, "This is that which the LORD hath said, 'Tomorrow is the rest of the holy Sabbath unto the LORD: bake that which ye will bake today, and seethe [boil] that ye will seethe [boil]; and that which remaineth over lay up for you to be kept until the morning.'"

And they laid it up till the morning, as Moses bade: and it did not stink, neither was there any worm therein.

And Moses said, "Eat that today; for today is a Sabbath unto the LORD: today ye shall not find it in the field. Six days ye shall gather it; but on the seventh day, which is the Sabbath, in it there shall be none."

And it came to pass, that there went out some of the people on the seventh day for to gather, and they found none.

And the LORD said unto Moses, "How long refuse ye to keep My commandments and My laws? See, for that the LORD hath given you the Sabbath, therefore He giveth you on the sixth day the bread of two days; abide ye every man in his place, let no man go out of his place on the seventh day."

So the people rested on the seventh day. And the house of Israel called the name thereof Manna: and it was like coriander seed, white; and the taste of it was like wafers made with honey.

And Moses said, "This is the thing which the LORD commandeth, 'Fill an omer of it to be kept for your generations; that they may see the bread wherewith I have fed you in the wilderness, when I brought you forth from the land of Egypt.' "

And Moses said unto Aaron, "Take a pot, and put an omer full of manna therein, and lay it up before the LORD, to be kept for your generations."

As the LORD commanded Moses, so Aaron laid it up before the Testimony, to be kept. And the children of Israel did eat manna forty years, until they came to a land inhabited; they did eat manna, until they came unto the borders of the land of Canaan.

Now an omer is the tenth part of an ephah. (Exo 16:16-36)

God establishes His work-ethic:

And the manna was as coriander seed, and the colour thereof as the colour of bdellium [light pearl]. And the people went about and gathered it, and ground it in mills or beat it in a mortar, and baked

it in pans, and made cakes of it: and the taste of it was as the taste of fresh oil. (Num 11:7-8)

So what's manna really all about?

As the food they had plundered from Egypt (representing 'the world') runs out, so the Israelites must rely on God's provision of the quail (flesh) and manna (tastes like oil - 'the Spirit'). They will eat manna for the entire time they are in the wilderness. "What is it?" is the classic question asked today of God's will for those who do not quail. What is God's will? The Exodus will teach the twelve tribes that God's will is to do as God says, learn God's ways, practise God's righteousness, and keep doing it until thy need for oxygen ceaseth. You're engaged in on-the-job training for eternity and the purpose is to learn to stay the course and overcome.[207] As with the Israelites during the Exodus, you're either going to overcome the obstacles put in your path with God's help or you won't. Remember when Satan tempts Yeshua in the desert in Matthew 4?

And when the tempter came to Him, he said, "If thou be the Son of God, command that these stones be made bread."

But [Jesus] **answered and said, "It is written, 'Man shall not live by bread alone, but by every word that proceedeth out of the mouth of God.' "** (Matt 4:3-4)

How about these passages:

And Jesus said unto them, "I am the bread of life: he that cometh to Me shall never hunger; and he that believeth on Me shall never thirst." (FG 6:35)

And:

"I am that bread of life. Your fathers did eat manna in the wilderness, and are dead. This is the bread which cometh down from Heaven, that a man may eat thereof and not die. I am the living bread which came down from Heaven. If any man eat of this bread, he shall live forever, and the bread that I will give is My flesh, which I will give for the life of the world." (FG 6:48-51)

We have just explored the thirst issue at Marah, now we are dealing with the bread. Yeshua links Himself to manna in the NT, proclaiming Himself the bread of life. He will be hated by His own (FG 1:10-11). The bread of life provided by God in the desert will also be loathed by His people. Your flesh will always be at enmity with God's Spirit within you up until the day you die. Just as the 1st century

---

[207] Gen 4:7; Psa 34:14; Psa 37:27; Dan 4:27; Matt 3:8-10; Luke 13:3,5; Acts 26:20; Rom 12:21; Gal 5:24; Eph 5:1; Titus 1:16; 1 Pet 3:10; 2 Pet 3:9; Rev 2:26

Jewish religious council, the Sanhedrin, will desire to hurl rocks at their Creator, the Israelites will repeatedly seek to stone Moses and Aaron for their own failures in faith. The spirit at work here is not holy, it's the spirit of the prince of this world, *ha-Satan*. If you are prone to a moan, a daily diet of manna pizza, manna fritters, manna pancakes, panacotta à la manna, manna burgers and Kentucky Fried Manna will wear thin in short order. But God is not running the manna programme to wind His people up. The lesson being taught here is obedience and trust to His will and timing, not our own. The manna model is superb. As a testimony to the future, a jar of manna will even be gathered by the Israelites and laid up in the future Ark of the Covenant along with the Ten Commandments tablets and Aaron's rod that buds (Exo 16:32-34, Heb 9:4). Even this action has significance. We assume the manna placed in the Ark will not spoil.

So manna is the bread from Heaven, a model for Jesus and the Word. God wants us to feed on His Son and His Word. Let's see how the manna model stacks up:

- Manna is free. So is God's Son
- Manna is a supernatural gift. So is God's Son
- For those chomping at the bit to provide a natural explanation for manna based on some subtle, weird freak of nature happening to obscure shrubbery in this part of the world, you'll have a problem, reckons Chuck Missler. An omer is 6 pints, so across 2 million people, you're looking at finding 9 million lbs or 4,500 tons of this stuff each day, or 1.6 million tons per year for 40 years, "*very remarkably scheduled*" [208]
- Manna falls six days from Heaven but not on the seventh. On the sixth day, a remarkable thing will occur. You'll awaken to find twice as much lying around to see you through the Sabbath, so you don't have to work on your rest day to gather it
- Manna only falls on God's chosen, the Israelites, wherever they are. It is not given to Egypt or Canaan, symbols of the unregenerate world (*cf.* Matt 7:6). Jesus Himself states: **"Give not that which is holy unto the dogs, neither cast ye your pearls before swine, lest they trample them under their feet, and turn again and rend you."** (Matt 7:6) The apostle Paul writes: "**For the preaching of the cross is to them that perish**

---

[208] Missler, Chuck, *Exodus notes*, p.75, www.khouse.org

foolishness; but unto us which are saved it is the power of God" (1 Cor 1:18)

- Manna comes to where the people are. So does God's Son
- Manna is required *daily*, in the morning (**'Give us this day our daily bread'** – Matt 6:11). So is God's Son
- You have to work at gathering it, promoting daily discipline
- Manna is white, symbolising purity and righteousness
- It is sweet to the tongue (*cf.* Song 2:3; Psa 104:34; Jer 15:16; Rev 10:1-11)
- In the process of harvesting manna, you either have to gather it or trample it underfoot. The same with God's Son
- In Num 11:9, we read: **And when the dew fell upon the camp in the night, the manna fell upon it.** In other words, manna rests on the dew (i.e. water = Holy Spirit) not on the dust ('natural man'). So does God's Son
- The Israelites come to despise manna, and so does the 'mixed multitude' (i.e. non-Hebrews, symbolising 'the natural man'). Jesus even today is despised by his own (the Jews), as well as the unregenerate world at large
- Gathering six pints of this material each day is a non-trivial task better accomplished on your knees. Either that, or you'll break your back
- You can't gather it for anyone else, you have to gather your own. The same with God's Son
- Some gather more, some less, but each according to their appetites
- It won't do you any good unless you eat it. There's no point in someone telling you about it, you have to eat it *yourself* for nourishment. The same with God's Son
- If you don't eat it, you'll wither away and die. Jesus said: **"I said therefore unto you, that ye shall die in your sins: for if ye believe not that I am *He*, ye shall die in your sins"** (FG 8:24)
- Manna must be used, not stored. If the manna is not consumed but left until the following morning, it breeds worms and stinks, yet this does not occur on the Sabbath
- The stuff is tiny and needs careful and humble gathering. It melts in the sun so its gathering and preparation must be carried out in early morning – no oversleeping!
- God requires every family to gather according to their own need, so no exploitation of the poor to fetch manna for the

wealthy: no slavery, no socialism. *Each person must provide for himself*

- Manna will cease when the Israelites enter Canaan (the Promised Land), so the only manna left will be in the pot laid up in the Ark of the Covenant (symbolising God's throne in Heaven). This is physically hidden from the world at present (Rev 2:17), even as Christ for now is physically hidden.

Rephidim - The first incident with the rock

And all the congregation of the children of Israel journeyed from the wilderness of Sin, after their journeys, according to the commandment of the LORD, and pitched in Rephidim: and there was no water for the people to drink.

Wherefore the people did chide with Moses, and said, "Give us water that we may drink." And Moses said unto them, "Why chide ye with me? Wherefore do ye tempt the LORD?"

And the people thirsted there for water; and the people murmured against Moses, and said, "Wherefore is this that thou hast brought us up out of Egypt, to kill us and our children and our cattle with thirst?"

And Moses cried unto the LORD, saying, "What shall I do unto this people? They be almost ready to stone me."

And the LORD said unto Moses, "Go on before the people, and take with thee of the elders of Israel; and thy rod, wherewith thou smotest the river, take in thine hand, and go. Behold, I will stand before thee there upon the rock in Horeb; and thou shalt smite the rock, and there shall come water out of it, that the people may drink."

And Moses did so in the sight of the elders of Israel. And he called the name of the place Massah, and Meribah, because of the chiding of the children of Israel, and because they tempted the LORD, saying, "Is the LORD among us, or not?" (Exo 17:1-7)

These are seven verses many people read, raise one eyebrow, then move on. When the Israelites get to the next stage of their journey, Rephidim, in the region of Mt Horeb/Sinai, there is once again no water to drink. The multitude becomes grouchy and threatens Moses once more. Moses laments to God that he is about to be stoned. YHWH instructs him to strike the rock upon which He will stand and water will gush forth. Moses obeys, strikes the rock with his staff, water gushes out, the people's thirst is quenched, and violence averted. Aside from the Author intending this to be understood as a real, physical event, it's once again a type or a model illustrating the underlying theme of the Exodus, which is the path each of us must take to redemption and salvation. After being baptised by passing through the Red Sea, the Israelites enter the wilderness of Sin where there is no water.

- Who led them to where there is no water? God.
- Their sin (lack of water) is provided for by the water and the rock
- Notice that in each of these tests we are examining, God is repeatedly conditioning his chosen to trust Him. The sinful nature of man (flesh) is intrinsically at enmity with trusting God (Spirit)
- Notice the Israelites are not happy in their sin (lack of water)
- There is no way on a human level that their thirst can be quenched. They are in the desert. Only a supernatural gift of God can save them
- Who is the rock? God gives us a clue: He stands on the rock! The rock is Jesus Christ the Messiah[209]
- What does water symbolise? The Holy Spirit, the Word, gushing forth from the smitten rock
- With what is the rock smitten? The rod, symbolising God's authority, Law and judgment.[210] Isaiah 53 deals with this prophecy of Christ's crucifixion, especially verses 4 - 5

The apostle Paul covers this period of the Exodus in the NT:

Moreover, brethren, I would not that ye should be ignorant, how that all our fathers were under the cloud, and all passed through the sea; and were all baptized unto Moses in the cloud and in the sea; and did all eat the same spiritual meat; and did all drink the same spiritual drink: for they drank of that spiritual Rock that followed them: and that Rock was Christ.

But with many of them God was not well pleased: for they were overthrown in the wilderness. Now these things were our examples, to the intent we should not lust after evil things, as they also lusted. (1 Cor 10:1-6)

---

[209] Deut 32:15, 2 Sam 22:2, Psa 95:1;118:22; Dan 2:34, 45; Isa 32:2; Matt 16:18; 21:42-44; Acts 4:11

[210] The rod as a symbol of authority is bound up with the model of legal or royal authority chastising the wicked to bring them to heel: 2 Sam 7:14; Prov 13:24; 22:15; 29:15; Psa 74:2; 125:3; Jer 10:16; Job 9:34; 21:9; Isa 9:4; 14:29; etc. For more information on the rods/authority connection, see http://joanneaz_2.tripod.com/positivedisciplineresourcecenter/id4.html

During the Exodus, there are two telling incidents involving moaning, thirsty Israelites, Moses, a rock, and water gushing forth. In the first incident at Rephidim, Yeshua will be the rock smitten, from which the living water shall flow (Matt 16:18; FG 7:37-39), "... **and whosoever drinketh of the water that I shall give him shall never thirst."** (FG 4:14) Notice that the water (Holy Spirit) doesn't flow for the people until after the rock (Christ) is smitten (crucified), analogous to the day of Pentecost, 50 days (the Jubilee) after the Resurrection, when the Holy Spirit falls upon the believers (Acts 2).

The second time a rock is smitten is during the Exodus years later at Meribah-Kadesh in the Wilderness of Zin (more Sin!). On this occasion there will be major trouble for Moses, as we will see. For now, at Rephidim, disaster is averted, but Rephidim has a nasty surprise in store for the Israelites before they leave to continue on their journey to the mountain. They experience their first encounter with the notorious desert nomads, the Amalekites.

This is Israel's first fight. Notice it occurs immediately after they get the water from the smitten rock! Once you come around to God's way of thinking, the flesh really starts objecting to the Spirit, you become an enemy of the unregenerate world, and the sparks begin to fly. This startles many new Christians. Amalek was a grandson of Esau and fathered a nomadic tribe which became a byword for violence, ruthlessness and cunning. The Amalekites will be one of the most implacable enemies of the Jews throughout the coming centuries, perpetuating the ongoing Holy War between the seeds of Jacob and Esau - the seeds of the Spirit and the flesh. Thus Amalek becomes a model of the dual nature of man. Isn't it interesting that God intends to blot out all remembrance of Amalek from under Heaven (Exo 17:14; Deut 25:19), as He will also do with our sinful nature. Do we have any Amalekites alive today? Not that I've been able to find.

Then came Amalek and fought with Israel in Rephidim. And Moses said unto Joshua, "Choose us out men and go out and fight with Amalek. Tomorrow I will stand on the top of the hill with the rod of God in mine hand."

So Joshua did as Moses had said to him and fought with Amalek. And Moses, Aaron and Hur went up to the top of the hill. And it came to pass, when Moses held up his hand, that Israel prevailed: and when he let down his hand, Amalek prevailed. But Moses' hands were heavy; and they took a stone, and put it under him, and he sat thereon. And Aaron and Hur stayed up his hands,

the one on the one side, and the other on the other side; and his hands were steady until the going down of the sun.

And Joshua discomfited Amalek and his people with the edge of the sword. And the LORD said unto Moses, "Write this for a memorial in a book and rehearse it in the ears of Joshua, for I will utterly put out the remembrance of Amalek from under heaven." (Exo 17:8-14)

God pronounces a sentence of annihilation over the Amalekites for their sneaky hit-and-run tactics. The fact that the Jews don't carry out God's order later and utterly destroy Amalek will create serious problems for Israel all the way through the Judges era and into the monarchy under Saul and David centuries later. For now, at the Battle of Rephidim, we are introduced to a young, valorous commander of Moses' developing mega-army: Joshua, son of Nun. Joshua will be a mainstay for the Israelites and one day inherit the mantle of Moses as leader. Significantly, Joshua and another stalwart - Caleb - *will be the only original Jews over age 20 to make it from Egypt to Canaan*. Not even Moses and Aaron will make it. At Rephidim we once more get a glimpse of the bizarre methods God uses to fight and win His battles, **that no flesh may glory in His presence** (1 Cor 1:29).

FROM SINAI TO THE JORDAN

God's holy mountain

Two months after leaving Egypt, God brings the Hebrews to the foot of the famous Mount Sinai/Horeb. The inevitable question is posed. Where is Mt Sinai? It obviously still exists. Can we know for sure where it is? Is it even a mountain, some ask. Could all that fire, roaring and rumbling simply mean that Moses brought the children of Israel *to a volcano?* God has certainly made a mystery out of Mt Sinai, *which means that He intends it that way*. Does He wish for us to search? To answer that, the same criteria applies as to the Red Sea Crossing conundrum: Knowing physically where Mt Sinai is has little impact on us theologically; it's all about what happens there. But if God has provided enough detailed information for a geographical search, why not have a look-see?

There is enough scriptural information given to us about Mt Sinai/Horeb's physical location that makes the hunt for God's mountain not an entirely fruitless exercise, but one in which, perhaps, only the dedicated student might wish to indulge. I'm all up for the search, so I'll save you hours of frustration by outlining the contenders and giving you my reasons for my selection. As always, it's up to you, the reader, to do your own research and come to your own conclusions. There are some benefits to looking:

1) Searching for the Biblical Mt Sinai requires a closer examination of the Biblical text – never a bad thing
2) The search may help us to confirm the Red Sea crossing point
3) In searching, one gains an appreciation of the uniformity and congruence of information given in the Bible
4) One also gains a reinforcement of the view that a single Author masterminded the entire text, which 40 authors were inspired to write down
5) And let's not forget that the underpinnings of Judaism and Christianity heavily depend on what happens at Mt Sinai/Horeb. If God's mountain is fanciful myth, what about the events that are supposed to have happened there?

Firstly, let's get the search for Mt Sinai out of the way so we can proceed to the meaty stuff. Predictably there are a number of rocky candidates, some of them impressive. In the interests of keeping up the pace of the narrative, I'll list the main contestants and indulge in some elimination based on the information supplied by the Bible, archaeology and logic. We should certainly be able to narrow down the area, if not the actual rock. So what do we know about Mt Sinai that can be useful? Consider the following:

- Moses flees to Midian after killing the Egyptian (Exo 2:15)
- Scholars are in agreement that Biblical Midian occupies the land to the east of the Gulf of Aqaba and ranges north as far as the Jordanian Wadi Rum
- The action in Egypt centres around Lower Egypt, and specifically Goshen in the eastern Nile Delta, the enclave where the Israelites dwell
- When Moses flees Egypt for Midian, he will reasonably choose the most direct route, which is the ancient King's Highway trade route eastward across the Sinai peninsula to the northern tip of the Gulf of Aqaba - modern-day Eilat. There are some forts and watering points along the way, which sustain travellers on such a journey. Once Moses has reached the tip of the Gulf, he can then head into Midian
- Notice that the Gulf's unique geography forces Moses to head for the tip. The only other option would be for him to head south and cross the Straits of Tiran into Midian, which we've already discounted. No serious scholar believes Moses fled that way because of the insurmountable undersea issues linked with that crossing
- Mt Sinai needs to be within walking/grazing range of Jethro's home in Midian (Exo 3:1)
- The scriptures imply that while Mt Sinai is reasonably close to Midian, it's not actually in Midian. How do we know this? After visiting Moses at Mt Sinai, we are told that **Moses let his father-in-law depart; and he went his way <u>into his own land</u>** (Exo 18:27). This implies that Jethro was not in Midian when he was at Mt Sinai
- The successful candidate *must be climbable*. During Israel's sojourn at the mountain, Moses is repeatedly toing and froing from the summit relaying God's instructions, not to mention carrying two sets of stone tablets. He's 80 years old at this point and doesn't require climbing ropes, crampons, carabiners and pitons to make the ascent. The 'walkable ascent' requirement alone eliminates a number of prospective mountains put forward by scholars over the years. On one occasion, Moses, Aaron and a small crowd of elders actually

make the ascent to the summit for a spot of fellowship and a meal with the LORD in Exo 24:9-11. No Tom Cruise swinging from a sheer rock face dangling on a rope in *Mission Impossible* here

- The successful candidate must have *a backside to the desert* mentioned in Exo 3:1, where 2 million souls can dwell before the proposed mountain (Exo 3:12). A backside implies that there is something about the topography of the mountain which suggests there is a 'frontside' – perhaps identified by a nearby road such as the King's Highway
- In Exo 4:27, God summons Aaron to go out from Egypt to meet Moses at Mt Sinai as the latter comes from Midian towards Egypt. This means that Mt Sinai is reasonably located along or near to the direct route one takes from the northern tip of the Gulf of Aqaba across the Sinai peninsula: in this case the aforementioned King's Highway
- The mountain will have to be towards the eastern (Eilat) end of the King's Highway to make the aforementioned goat-herding distance from Midian practical
- Deut 1:2 states that it is an 11-day journey from Mt Sinai to Kadesh Barnea by way of Mt Seir. Since 1905, Kadesh Barnea has generally been viewed by scholars to be located at Ain el-Qudeirat in the Wadi el-Ain of northern Sinai. Is this correct? We'll find out later (see **Chart H**)

Now let's bring up the candidates and see how they check out.

JEBEL MUSA (*lit.* MOSES' MOUNTAIN): Located in southern Sinai, this is the traditional site marked in all the Bible maps. Most serious archaeologists and Bible expositors reject its candidacy for the following reasons:

- Jebel Musa is nowhere near Midian, so Moses would not have happened upon it with a flock of goats or sheep!
- There is no suitable plain nearby for two million souls to gather. No backside to the desert either
- You can't walk up it to the summit. This rock is completely user-unfriendly. That's why the St Catherine's Monastery is at the bottom in the mouth of the gorge, not at the top
- It's far out of the way on the direct route between Midian and Egypt, which means Moses would not have passed it on his way back to Egypt. Jebel Musa also makes no sense as a

rendezvous point for Aaron, coming out from Goshen, to meet up with Moses, coming from Midian

- Local legend attributes the naming of Jebel Musa as the Biblical Mt Sinai/Horeb to Helena, the Christian mother of the Roman Emperor Constantine, around 330 AD
- Kadesh Barnea is not an 11-day march from Jebel Musa

MT SERBAL: Western Sinai. Fifth highest peak in Egypt. This is the candidate for the earliest Christian traditions, and a monastery was built at its base, the remains of which, along with numerous early AD anchorite dwellings, can be seen to this day. Mt Serbal fails my test for the Biblical Mt Sinai, however, for most of the Jebel Musa reasons above, though it does have a front plain but no backside to the desert. Mt Serbal fell out of favour too with the early Christians, and the monastery was abandoned when the following candidate was proposed.

MT CATHERINE: Southern Sinai, close to Jebel Musa. This became popular after Josephus announced, based on tradition, that the true Mt Sinai was the highest peak in the area. St Catherine's monastery was thus built, and remains to this day the oldest, working monastery on Earth. I reject this site also for the Jebel Musa reasons above.

JEBEL AL-LAWZ: The highest peak in Midian, located in today's north-western Saudi Arabia, proposed by our old friend, Ron Wyatt. Jebel al-Lawz became popular when the volcanic theory of Mt Sinai was punted. Its candidacy was highlighted by adventurers Howard Blum and Robert Cornuke in various publications, and many Christian groups today endorse the site. Here are the chief Biblical problems I have with Jebel al-Lawz as Mt Sinai:

- It depends on the Israelites using the Tiran Strait crossing, which is way too steep and deep to work. And there's no land-bridge (see previous chapter)
- The Bible (especially Gal 4:25) does not say that Mt Sinai was in Saudi Arabia, only Arabia, whose 1st century definition markedly differs from what we know as modern 'Saudi Arabia', which can include the Sinai peninsula [211]
- Jebel Al-Lawz is nowhere near the direct route between Midian and Egypt, so Moses would not have passed it heading out from Jethro's place on his way back to Egypt

---

[211] https://againstjebelallawz.wordpress.com/jebel-al-lawz/

- And poor old Aaron would be facing a serious hike out from Egypt, across the Sinai peninsula (King's Highway), around the northern tip of the Gulf of Aqaba, then 60 miles down the east side of the Gulf in order to rendezvous with Moses at Jebel al-Lawz. *Quelle inconvenience!*
- Moses' father-in-law stated that he was going to leave Moses at Mt Sinai and return to his own land (Midian), therefore Mt Sinai cannot be in Midian (Exo 18:27; Num 10:29-32)
- Kadesh Barnea is not an 11-day march from Jebel al-Lawz
- It's also further than a 60-day haul out from Goshen (actually, further than 52 days' march excluding the Sabbaths)
- Gordon Franz gives a more in-depth study of why Jebel al-Lawz cannot be the Biblical Mt Sinai at the following footnote[212]

MT YERHORAM: Located in the northern Negev, southwest of the Dead Sea. Proposed by Gerald E. Aardsma. Rejected on the grounds that it is inside the Promised Land.[213] It's also far too close to Kadesh Barnea to be an 11-day journey

HAR KARKOM: A 2,700-foot ridge located in the southern Negev. Popularised by Emmanuel Anati. Rejected because it is already in the Promised Land,[214] nowhere close to the road between Midian and Egypt, and too close to Kadesh Barnea to be an 11-day journey

JEBEL UM ADAAMI: Jordan. Rejected for being out of the way from a direct route from Midian to Egypt

JEBEL AL-MADHBAH: Located in the area of Petra. Rejected for the same reasons

JEBEL KHASHM EL-TARIF: Located 21 miles north-northwest of Eilat. While I'm not dogmatic about this site, if not my precise choice for the Biblical Mt Sinai, the general area certainly meets all the Biblical requirements for God's holy mountain: [215]

- Jebel Khashm el-Tarif is on the main route (King's Highway) between Midian and Egypt
- It's within goat-herding distance of Midian

---

[212] www.ldolphin.org/franz-ellawz.html

[213] www.biblicalchronologist.org/answers/sinai_location.php

[214] www.biblicalarchaeology.org/daily/biblical-topics/exodus/searching-for-biblical-mt-sinai/

[215] Google Earth: 29°40'9.25"N 34°38'1.29"E. See also: http://en.wikipedia.org/wiki/Hashem_el-Tarif; www.biblearchaeology.org/post/2008/04/In-Search-of-Mt-Sinai.aspx

- Yet it's not in Midian
- It's in the desert wilderness and has a backside. It also has a huge, natural, semi-circular amphitheatre which a speaker can address from an elevated cleft in the rock
- The surrounding plain can well support the required numbers
- There are many ancient stone shrines (open-air sanctuaries) at this site, as well as graves near the summit, suggesting that from ancient times this mountain was regarded as 'holy'
- Jebel Khashm el-Tarif is an 11-day journey to Kadesh Barnea

It's also the right distance (300 miles) from Goshen relating to the time of travel given (Exo 19:1: around 52 days, excluding Sabbaths)

Bryant Wood has been to see the site:

"'The mountain of God' is the name used for Mt. Sinai in the burning bush account (Ex 3:1), the meeting place of Moses and Aaron (Ex 4:27), the location where Jethro visited Moses (Ex 18:5) and Elijah's hiding place (1 Kgs 19:8). The fact that the burning bush theophany occurred at Mt. Sinai indicates that it was within grazing distance of Midian, since Moses was 'pasturing the flock of Jethro' when he met God at 'Horeb, the mountain of God' (Ex 3:1). Midian was located east of the eastern arm of the Red Sea, the modern Gulf of Aqaba or Gulf of Elat. The reference to the meeting place of Moses and Aaron following Moses' call is very important for locating Mt. Sinai.

"When Moses set out from Midian to return to Egypt, he would have taken the most direct route, the Trans-Sinai Highway [King's Highway], which traversed central Sinai from the northern end of the Gulf of Aqaba/Elat to the northern end of the western arm of the Red Sea, the Gulf of Suez. Aaron, whom God had told to meet Moses in the wilderness (Ex 4:27), would have taken the same direct route in travelling from Egypt toward Midian. Therefore, their meeting place, The Mountain of God, must have been located somewhere along this road. Furthermore, in order to be within grazing distance of Midian, it must have been near the eastern end of the road. Jebel Khashm el-Tarif, the mountain visited by an ABR team [Associates for Bible Research] in 2007, is located in precisely this area, on the Trans-Sinai Highway ca. 22 mi west-northwest of the northern end of the Gulf of Aqaba/Elat (Wood 2007)."[216]

---

[216] www.biblearchaeology.org/post/2008/11/What-Do-Mt-Horeb2c-The-Mountain-of-God2c-Mt-Paran-and-Mt-Seir-Have-to-Do-with-Mt-Sinai.aspx

Israel at Sinai

In the third month, when the children of Israel were gone forth out of the land of Egypt, the same day[217] came they into the wilderness of Sinai. For they were departed from Rephidim, and were come to the desert of Sinai, and had pitched in the wilderness; and there Israel camped before the mount.

And Moses went up unto God, and the LORD called unto him out of the mountain, saying, "Thus shalt thou say to the house of Jacob, and tell the children of Israel;

'Ye have seen what I did unto the Egyptians, and how I bare you on eagles' wings, and brought you unto myself. Now therefore, if ye will obey My voice indeed, and keep My covenant, then ye shall be a peculiar treasure unto Me above all people: for all the Earth is Mine: And ye shall be unto Me a kingdom of priests, and an holy nation.' These are the words which thou shalt speak unto the children of Israel."

And Moses came and called for the elders of the people, and laid before their faces all these words which the LORD commanded him.

And all the people answered together, and said, "All that the LORD hath spoken we will do." And Moses returned the words of the people unto the LORD (Exo 19-1-8).

Why does God bring them to a mountain? Because the mountain is Christ, the rock of God's salvation (Deut 32:15; Matt 16:18; 21:42-44; Acts 4:11). We have previously seen water gushing from the smitten rock at Rephidim, a model for Christ's first coming. God is described as being mankind's rock, our fortress and Deliverer in 2 Sam 22:2. In Dan 2, Daniel volunteers to interpret Babylonian King Nebuchadnezzar's strange 'golden idol' dream (on pain of execution if he can't!). The idol represents a succession of pagan kingdoms which will rule before the whole is struck by a stone made without hands: **and the stone that smote the image became a great mountain, and filled the whole Earth** (Dan 2:34-35). This again is Christ.

And the LORD said unto Moses, "Lo, I come unto thee in a thick cloud, that the people may hear when I speak with thee, and believe thee forever." And Moses told the words of the people unto the LORD.

---

[217] The children of Israel have been out of Goshen now for precisely 60 days, or 52 travelling days excluding Sabbaths.

And the LORD said unto Moses, "Go unto the people, and sanctify them today and tomorrow, and let them wash their clothes, and be ready against the third day. For the third day the LORD will come down in the sight of all the people upon Mount Sinai.[218] **And thou shalt set bounds unto the people round about, saying, 'Take heed to yourselves, that ye go not up into the mount, or touch the border of it: whosoever toucheth the mount shall be surely put to death. There shall not an hand touch it, but he shall surely be stoned, or shot through; whether it be beast or man, it shall not live: when the trumpet soundeth long, they shall come up to the mount.'"**

And Moses went down from the mount unto the people, and sanctified the people; and they washed their clothes. And he said unto the people, "Be ready against the third day: come not at your wives." (Exo 19:9-15)

We feel the classic build-up of tension to something momentous that will happen on the third day. But while we're waiting in anticipation on the amphitheatre-shaped plain below the mountain on the backside of the desert from the main King's Highway, it's worth once again revisiting an old conundrum: The Bible states categorically that *no-one has ever heard or seen God at any time,*[219] and this is declared so by none other than Yeshua Himself: "**And the Father himself, which hath sent Me, hath borne witness of Me. Ye have neither heard His voice at any time, nor seen His shape.**" (FG 5:37) The LORD Himself will later tell Moses: **"Thou canst not see My face, for there shall no man see Me and live.** (Exo 33:20) The problem is, a number of other verses clearly state that God *has* appeared to mankind, and they *have* heard His voice:

And when Abram was ninety years old and nine, the LORD appeared to Abram and said unto him, "I am the Almighty God. Walk before Me and be thou perfect." (Gen 17:1)

And the LORD appeared unto him in the plains of Mamre: and he sat in the tent door in the heat of the day.... (Gen 18:1)

And God spake unto Moses [at the burning bush], **and said unto him, "I am the LORD. And I appeared unto Abraham, unto Isaac, and unto Jacob, by the name of God Almighty, but by My name YHWH was I not known to them.** (Exo 6:2-3)

---

[218] Once again, we have the enigmatic 'third day', which in the Bible consistently points to an event or events which will impact the witnesses' salvation prospects.

[219] Exo 33:20; FG 1:18; 5:37; 6:46; 1 Tim 6:15-16

Then went up Moses, and Aaron, Nadab, and Abihu, and seventy of the elders of Israel. And they saw the God of Israel, and there was under His feet, as it were, a paved work of a sapphire stone, and, as it were, the body of Heaven in His clearness. And upon the nobles of the children of Israel He laid not His hand: also they saw God, and did eat and drink. (Exo 24:9-11)

And He said, "Hear now My words: If there be a prophet among you, I the LORD will make myself known unto him in a vision, and will speak unto him in a dream. My servant Moses is not so, who is faithful in all mine house. With him will I speak mouth to mouth, even apparently, and not in dark speeches; and the similitude of the LORD shall he behold: wherefore then were ye not afraid to speak against My servant Moses? (Num 12:6-8)

And he [Stephen] **said, "'Men, brethren, and fathers, hearken; The God of glory appeared unto our father Abraham, when he was in Mesopotamia, before he dwelt in Charran** [Haran]**, and said unto him, "Get thee out of thy country, and from thy kindred, and come into the land which I shall shew thee."** (Acts 7:2)

As usual, the atheists pop their champagne corks in celebration at another brazen mistake in the scriptures. "Honestly, how can God be so careless? And don't be getting God off the hook by saying that these appearances were just dreams, visions, hallucinations or apparitions people had. Your book says they *saw/heard* God!"

The answer to the conundrum is that these OT patriarchs indeed saw and heard God, but in the form of the 'Angel of the LORD', never the Father (FG 1:18). This *remez* reveals that any human sensory perception of the LORD God of Israel is accomplished via this enigmatic 'Angel of the LORD', who appears to have been granted the special distinction of speaking personally in God's name in the first person. A number of scholars wrestle over whether this is a pre-incarnate theophany of Jesus Christ at various points throughout the OT, or, when the Son is present and a voice speaks from Heaven, such as at Yeshua's baptism scene in Bethabara in the NT (Mark 1:9-11), the Holy Spirit.[220] Still others cite a number of scriptures to posit that the Law was given to Moses and mankind on Mt Sinai via a 'super Angel' – the Angel of the LORD – and that this could not have been Jesus Christ, since Yeshua was **made so much better than the angels**

[220] Compare FG 5:37 with Mark 1:11; FG 12:28; Luke 9:35. The 'Us' of Gen 1:26, Gen 11:7 and Psa 2 prefigure the triune God as Father, Son and Holy Spirit.

(Heb 1:4-5), was therefore not an angel, but was far higher in station and authority (Heb 1:13-14).[221]

My research concludes that this Angel of the LORD is a pre-incarnate Yeshua, who is the One giving the Law to Moses and the people on Mount Sinai, and who speaks in the name of, and with the power of God. The clincher is Exo 23:20-23, where we are told that this Angel/Messenger will be sent before the Israelites to lead them into the Promised Land; that He must be obeyed, do not provoke Him, for He has the power over forgiveness of sins, and will fight on behalf of Israel if they are obedient. The Bible is clear about the Trinity, much to the chagrin of those who have been erroneously taught that the triune nature of God is false. Daniel B Wallace Ph.D, a professor of New Testament Studies at Dallas Theological Seminary and one of the world's great experts on textual criticism and Biblical exegesis, puts the record straight this way:

> "The Bible clearly contains these four truths: the Father is God, Jesus is God, the Holy Spirit is God, and there is only one God… And that's the Trinity." [222]

The second member of the Trinity is given a classic introduction at the start of the Fourth Gospel: **In the beginning was the Word, and the Word was with God, and the Word was God. The same was in the beginning with God. All things were made by Him** [Yeshua], **and without Him was not anything made that was made. In Him was life, and the life was the light of men.... And the Word was made flesh and dwelt among us, (and we beheld His glory, the glory as of the only begotten of the Father,) full of grace and truth.** (FG 1:1-4, 14)

So who is this addressing Moses on the mountain? Jesus Christ in His pre-incarnate form, who has been taking an active role in the Exodus (1 Cor 10:1-4). The writer of the Fourth Gospel (FG) makes this very point in the NT: **No man hath seen God at any time; the only begotten Son, which is in the bosom of the Father, He hath declared Him** (FG 1:18). Jesus Himself even states later in the same Gospel: **"Search the scriptures** [which, in Yeshua's time would have been the collective books of the OT]**; for in them ye think ye have eternal life: and they are they which testify of Me."** (FG 5:39; *cf:* Psa 40:7)

---

[221] http://askelm.com/essentials/ess003a.htm#_ftn6

[222] **Strobel, Lee** *The Case for the Real Jesus*, Zondervan, 2007, p.94

Next, we are also picking up on further intriguing dynamics of the Creator's extraordinary property of 'holiness', where shoes have to be removed, comprehensive washing and purification procedures observed, abstention from sex before going into the LORD's presence, physical boundaries set, and one deafening trumpet!

The Ten Commandments

On the third day after Israel's arrival at Mt Sinai/Horeb, the people on the plain stir from their sleep early in anticipation. They do not have long to wait.

And it came to pass on the third day in the morning, that there were thunders and lightnings, and a thick cloud upon the mount, and the voice of the trumpet exceeding loud; so that all the people that was in the camp trembled. And Moses brought forth the people out of the camp to meet with God; and they stood at the nether [lower] **part of the mount.**

And Mount Sinai was altogether on a smoke, because the LORD descended upon it in fire: and the smoke thereof ascended as the smoke of a furnace, and the whole mount quaked greatly. And when the voice of the trumpet sounded long, and waxed louder and louder, Moses spake, and God answered him by a voice.

And the LORD came down upon Mount Sinai, on the top of the mount: and the LORD called Moses up to the top of the mount; and Moses went up.

And the LORD said unto Moses, "Go down, charge the people, lest they break through unto the LORD to gaze, and many of them perish. And let the priests also, which come near to the LORD, sanctify themselves, lest the LORD break forth upon them."

And Moses said unto the LORD, "The people cannot come up to Mount Sinai: for Thou chargedst us, saying, 'Set bounds about the mount, and sanctify it.' "

And the LORD said unto him, "Away, get thee down, and thou shalt come up, thou, and Aaron with thee: but let not the priests and the people break through to come up unto the LORD, lest He break forth upon them."

So Moses went down unto the people, and spake unto them. (Exo 19:16-25)

Though there are flashings and thunderings and quakings and smoke everywhere, not to mention the deafening trumpet blasts growing ever louder, the Bible is quite clear that this is no volcanic eruption! There are no lava flows, no raining pumice, no devastating pyroclastic clouds. The humanist brigade absolutely loathe the slightest notion that this could be God Himself putting on the ultimate *son et lumière* event for His chosen people to be remembered forever. Well, here we are 3,500 years later, reading all about it. Jewish Torah scholar Dr Baruch J. Schwartz writes:

"At God's summons, Moses ascends the mountain, where he is instructed to offer a covenant to the Israelite people. In light of all he has done for them, God invites the Israelites to be his treasured people forever more, as long as they agree to obey his commands. The Israelites immediately accept the offer, though they have not yet heard the terms (Exo 19:1–8). Before presenting these, however, God informs Moses that he plans to hold a special audience with Moses, during which the people will be asked to 'listen in' to ensure their belief in Moses' prophecy. After some preparation, a sound-and-light presentation takes place. From the cloud-covered mountain, amidst thunder and lightning, the people overhear the voice of God saying the 'Ten Words', or Decalogue ['Ten Commandments'], to Moses [Exo 19:9]. The Ten Words are not the laws themselves, but rather a sampling of divine pronouncements, offered so that the people may hear the divine voice speak to a prophet."[223]

And God [Heb: *Elohim,* plural] **spake all these words, saying, "I am the LORD** [YHWH] **thy God** [Heb: *Elohim*, plural],[224] **which have brought thee out of the land of Egypt, out of the house of bondage.**

YHWH formally introduces Himself to the multitude on the plain so everyone knows precisely who is addressing them.

[COMMANDMENT 1]: **Thou shalt have no other gods before Me.**

Simple enough. Not only should you not hold any other deities (Fallen Angels/demons) before your Creator, you should not hold any material possessions dearer than your LORD. That would be the Porsche, Rolex, house, business, YOURSELF, and other temporal concepts or possessions.

[COMMANDMENT 2]: **Thou shalt not make unto thee any graven image, or any likeness of any thing that is in Heaven above, or that is in the Earth beneath, or that is in the water under the Earth. Thou shalt not bow down thyself to them, nor serve them: for I the**

---

223 http://thetorah.com/what-happened-at-mount-sinai/

224 Notice the proper name YHWH is identified within the context of the Trinity (*Elohim*).

LORD thy God am a jealous God, visiting the iniquity of the fathers upon the children unto the third and fourth generation of them that hate Me; And shewing mercy unto thousands of them that love Me, and keep My commandments.

Elaborating on Commandment 1: No worshipping of demons, talismans, pictures of the Virgin Mary, the gods of ANY other religions, and so on. (This commandment is curiously missing from Catholic literature).[225] The way we tell God we love Him is *by keeping His commandments.* This also has the benefit of allowing others to know us by our fruits, good or bad. This introduces the idea of ambassadorship covered in the next commandment. Our good works do not 'save us', but are an expression of our love for, and our belonging to the Creator.[226] In return, the LORD will show us mercy.

[COMMANDMENT 3]: **Thou shalt not take the name of the LORD thy God in vain; for the LORD will not hold him guiltless that taketh His name in vain.**

If you take the name of the LORD and intend to represent Him, God takes this commitment of yours seriously, so do not fail to be a good witness. This commandment has less to do with foul language/swearing than it does ambassadorship, though it is noteworthy that no-one uses the names Buddha, Mohammed, Allah, Nostradamus, Shiva or Joseph Smith as a profanity - only Jesus Christ. This tells us all we need to know about the real nature of the enmity the world has for its Creator. We're back to the Holy War: the flesh versus the Spirit.

[COMMANDMENT 4]: **Remember the Sabbath day, to keep it holy. Six days shalt thou labour, and do all thy work: But the seventh day is the Sabbath of the LORD thy God: in it thou shalt not do any work, thou, nor thy son, nor thy daughter, thy manservant, nor thy maidservant, nor thy cattle, nor thy stranger that is within thy gates: For in six days the LORD made heaven and earth, the sea, and all that in them is, and rested the seventh day: wherefore the LORD blessed the Sabbath day, and hallowed it.**

The Sabbath was ordained in Genesis (Gen 2:2-3). Notice that nowhere in the Bible does it state that the seventh day is Saturday or Sunday! There are three other points often missed concerning the Sabbath:

---

[225] www.beginningcatholic.com/catholic-ten-commandments.html; www.catholicbible101.com/thetencommandments.htm

[226] Matt 5:16; 6:1,14-15; 7:16-20; 21-23; Luke 6:46-49; FG 3:19-21; 5:28-29; 10:27; 2 Thess 1:8-9; 2 Cor 7:1; Eph 5:6; Titus 1:16

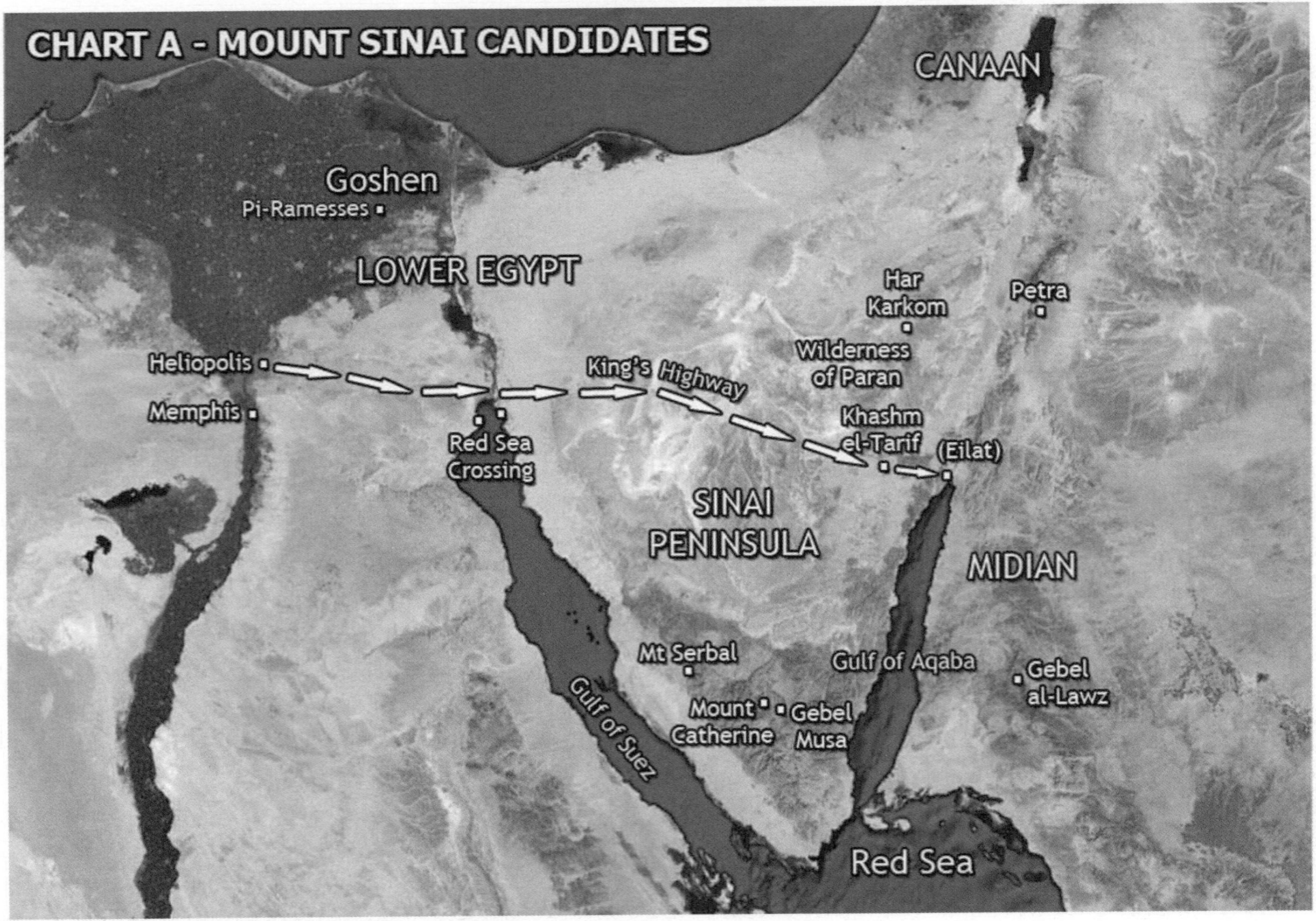
CHART A - MOUNT SINAI CANDIDATES
CANAAN
Goshen
Pi-Ramesses
LOWER EGYPT
Har Karkom
Petra
Heliopolis
Memphis
King's Highway
Wilderness of Paran
Khashm el-Tarif
(Eilat)
Red Sea Crossing
SINAI PENINSULA
MIDIAN
Mt Serbal
Gulf of Aqaba
Gebel al-Lawz
Gulf of Suez
Mount Catherine
Gebel Musa
Red Sea

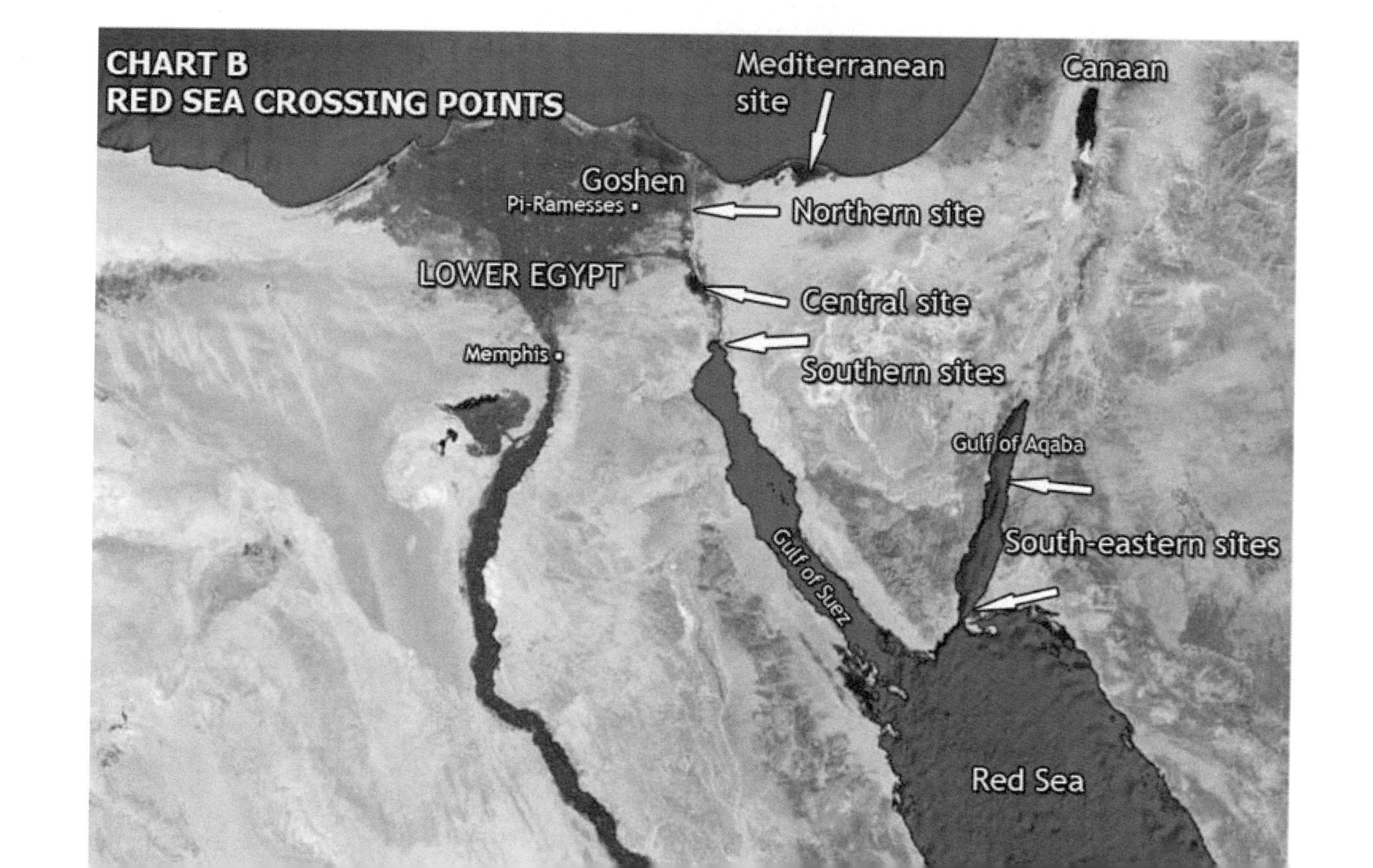
CHART B
RED SEA CROSSING POINTS
Mediterranean site
Canaan
Goshen
Pi-Ramesses
Northern site
LOWER EGYPT
Central site
Memphis
Southern sites
Gulf of Aqaba
South-eastern sites
Gulf of Suez
Red Sea

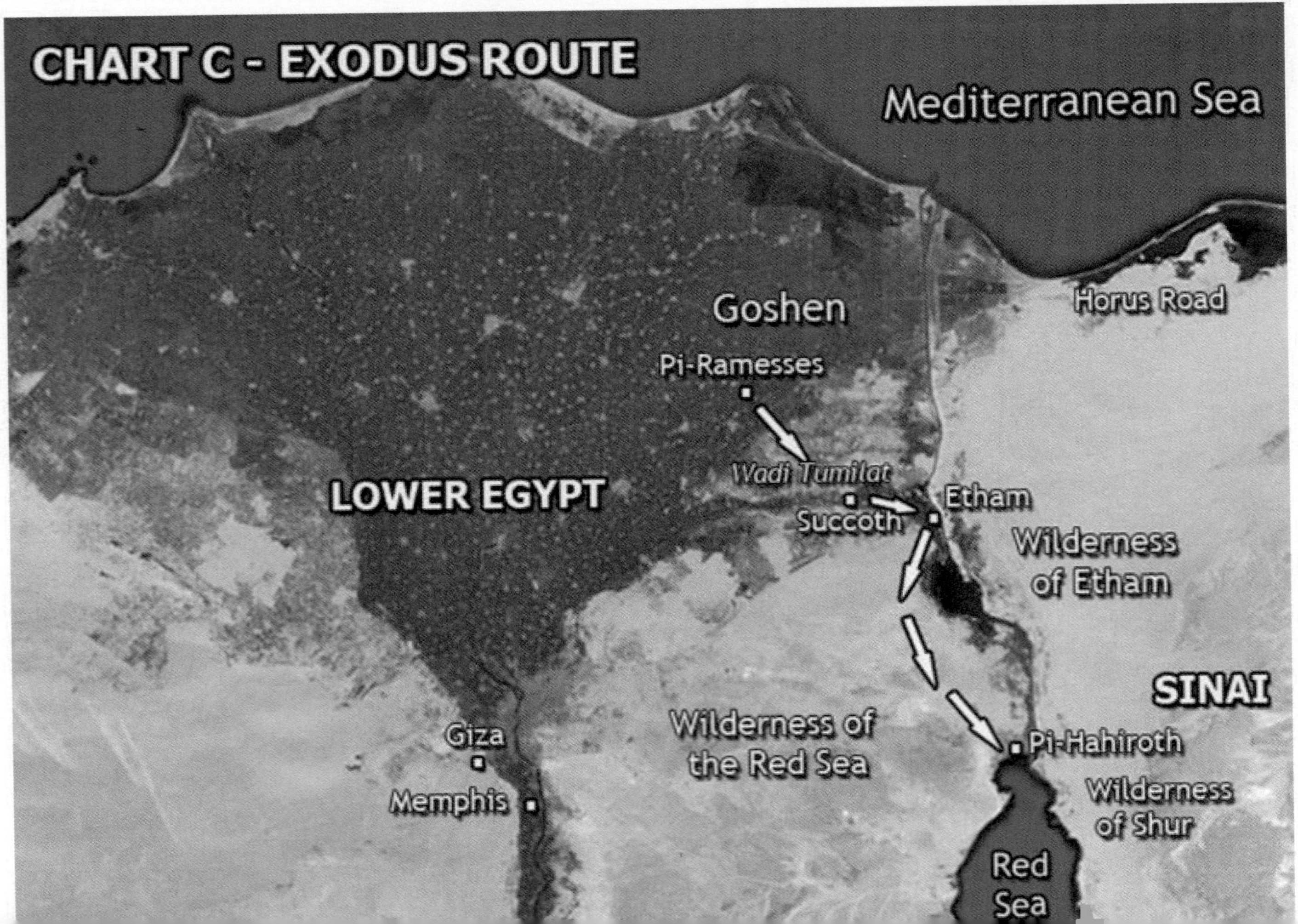
CHART C - EXODUS ROUTE
Mediterranean Sea
Horus Road
Goshen
Pi-Ramesses
Wadi Tumilat
Succoth
Etham
Wilderness of Etham
LOWER EGYPT
SINAI
Giza
Memphis
Wilderness of the Red Sea
Pi-Hahiroth
Wilderness of Shur
Red Sea

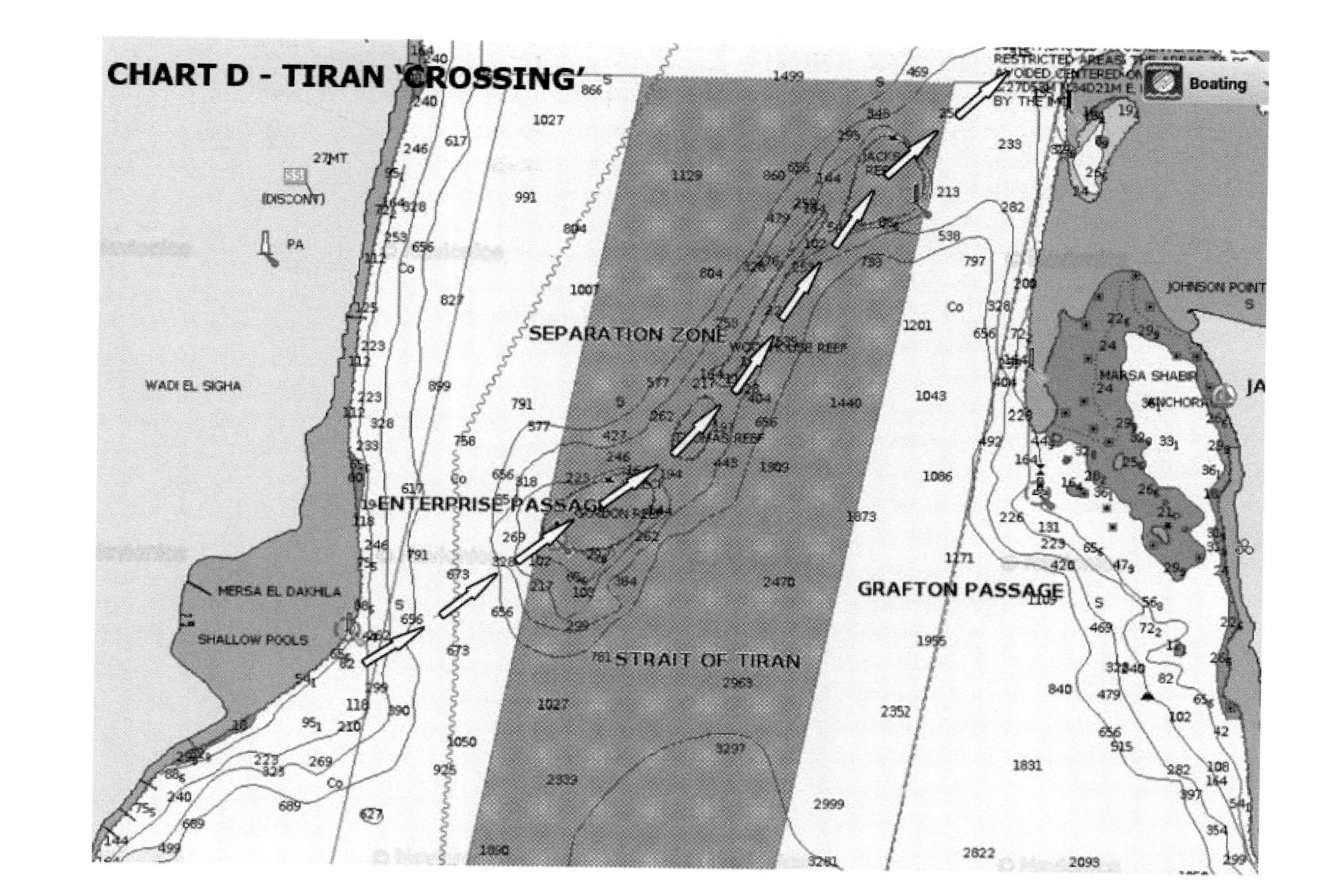
CHART D - TIRAN 'CROSSING'
SEPARATION ZONE
ENTERPRISE PASSAGE
STRAIT OF TIRAN
GRAFTON PASSAGE
WADI EL SIGHA
MERSA EL DAKHILA
SHALLOW POOLS
(DISCONT)
PA
27MT
JACKSON REEF
WOODHOUSE REEF
THOMAS REEF
GORDON REEF
MARSA SHABIR
ANCHORAGE
JOHNSON POINT
RESTRICTED AREAS
AVOIDED CENTERED ON
BY THE IMT
Boating

CHART E - NUWEIBA 'CROSSING'

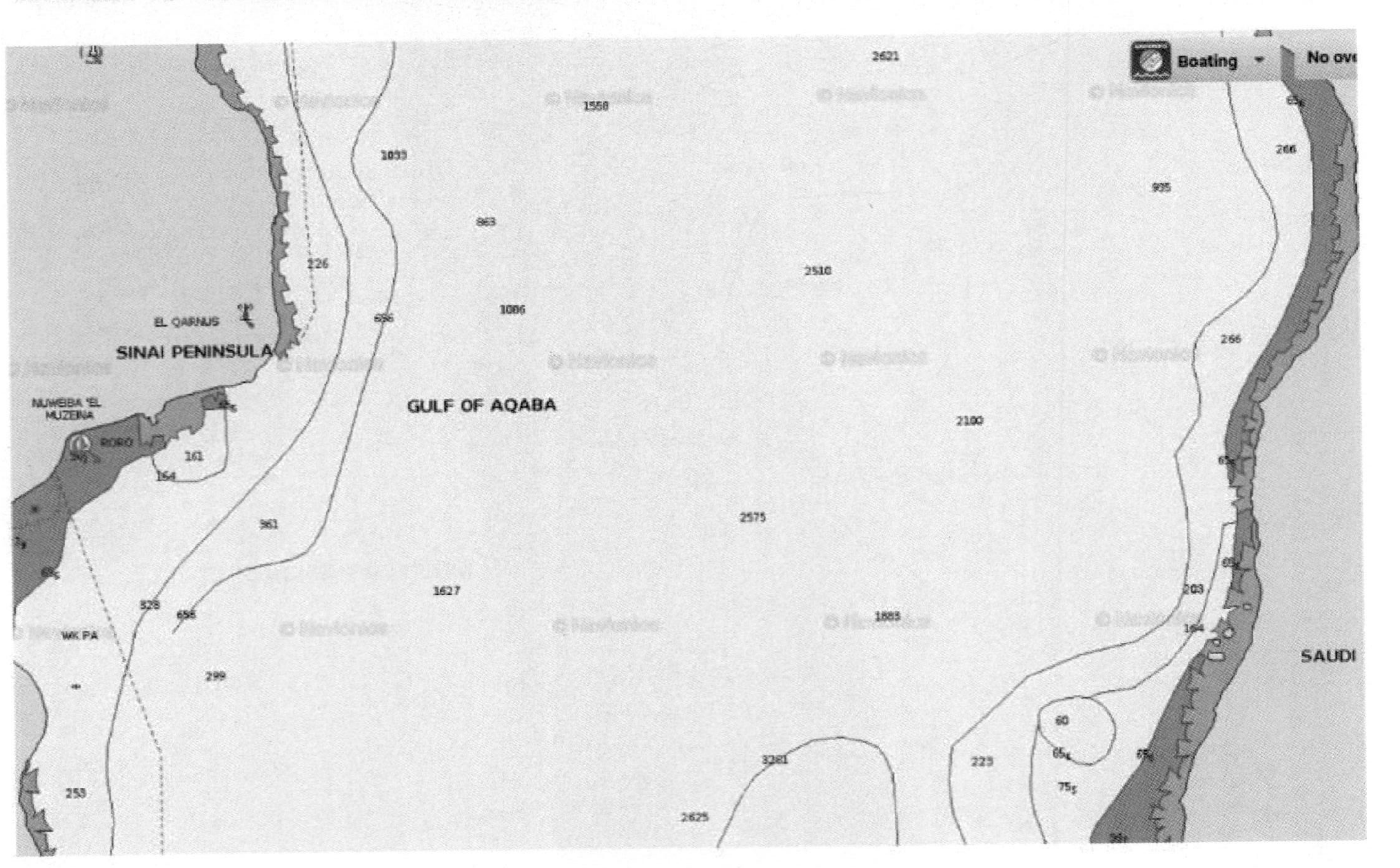

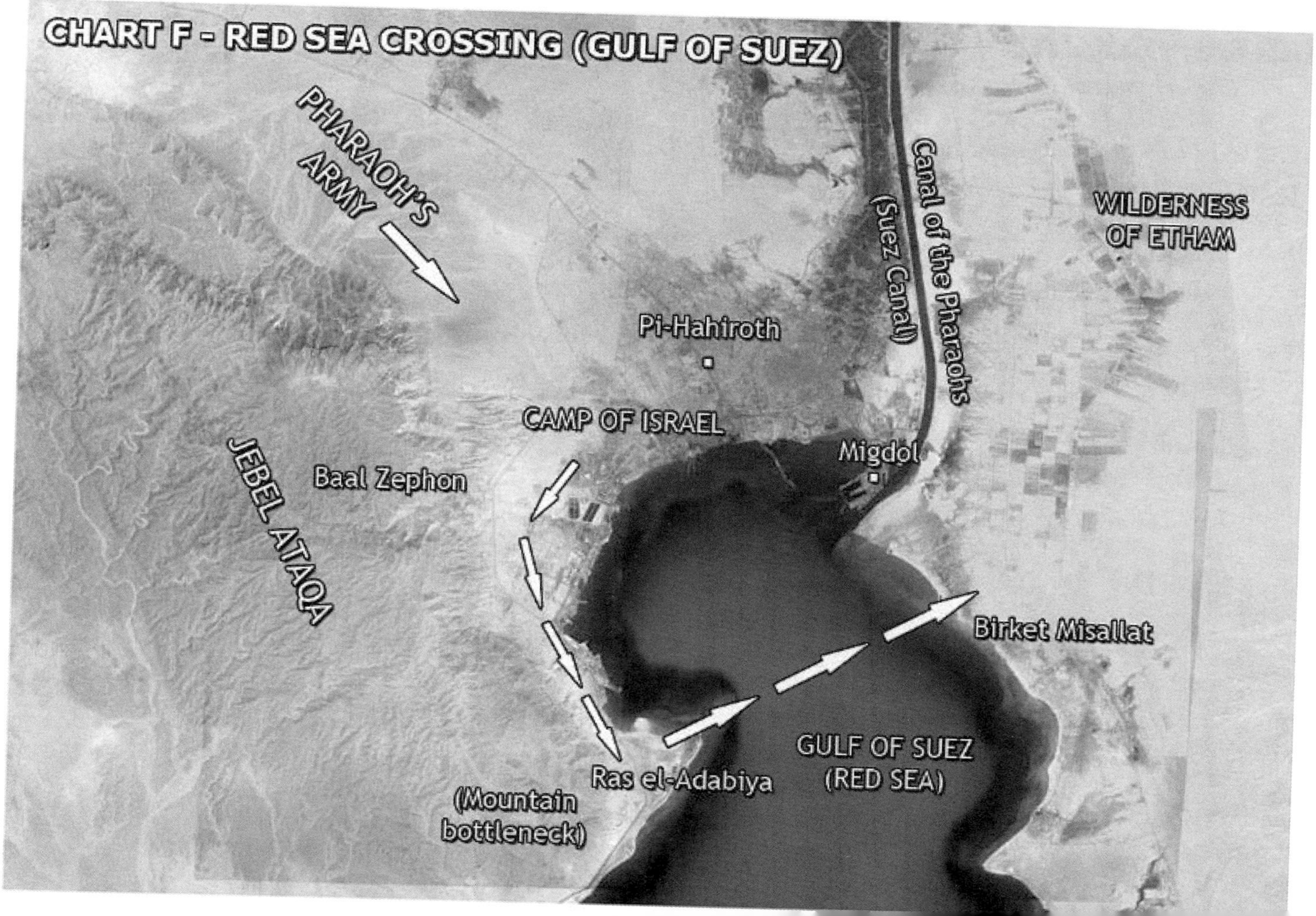
CHART F - RED SEA CROSSING (GULF OF SUEZ)
PHARAOH'S ARMY
Pi-Hahiroth
Canal of the Pharaohs
(Suez Canal)
WILDERNESS OF ETHAM
CAMP OF ISRAEL
Baal Zephon
JEBEL ATAQA
Migdol
Birket Misallat
GULF OF SUEZ (RED SEA)
Ras el-Adabiya
(Mountain bottleneck)

CHART G - SUEZ CROSSING

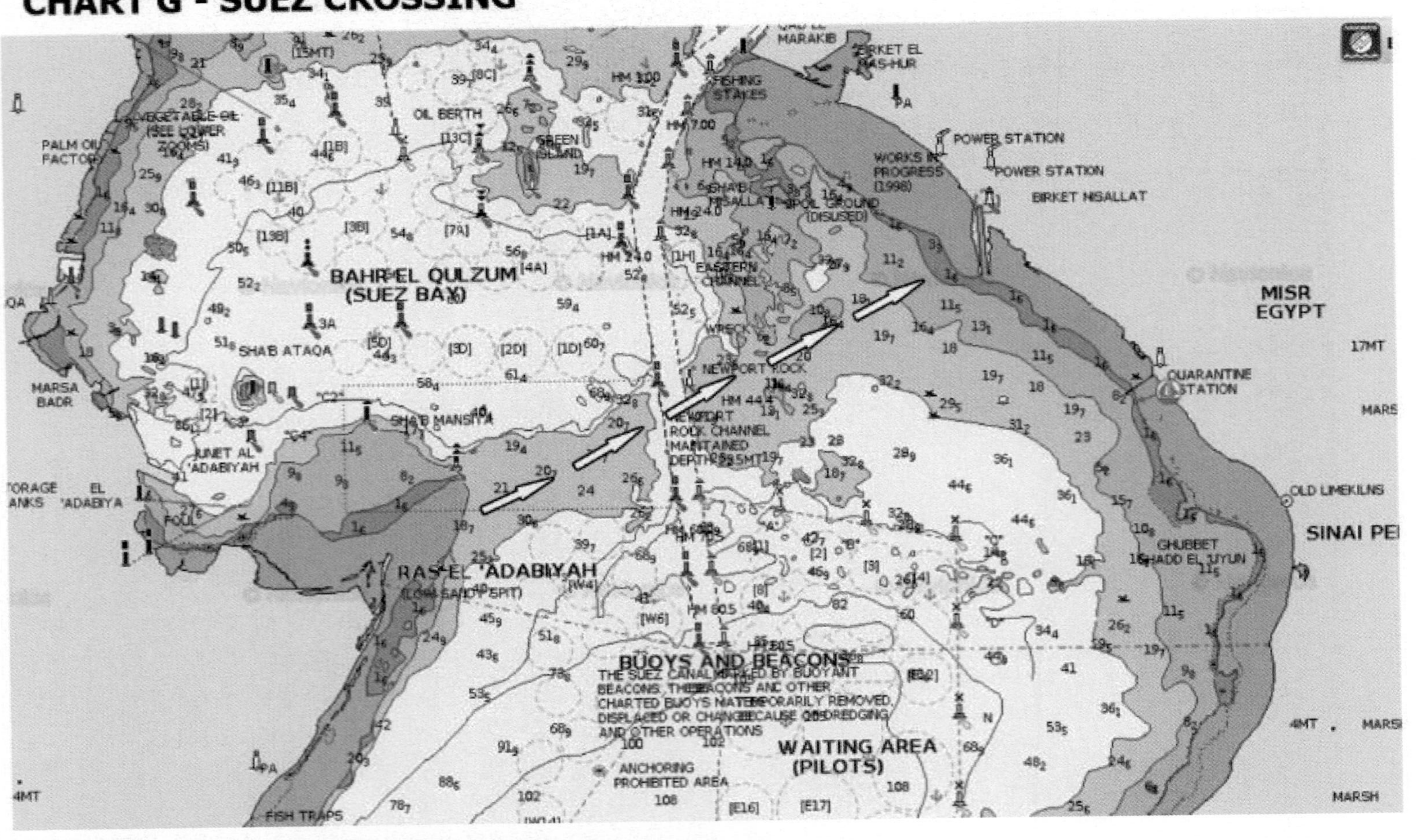

CHART H - EXODUS AND INVASION

- It was made for man and not for God (Mk 2:27; Heb 4:9)
- Sabbath-keeping is *not* a salvation/works issue. It certainly was not deemed so by the Jerusalem Council in Acts 15:1-29, attended by both Paul and Peter. Don't let others judge you in this matter (Col 2:16)
- It's not just that you should have one day off for your own benefit and that of your family, *but that you should work the other six!* (Exo 16:26)

[COMMANDMENT 5]: **Honour thy father and thy mother: that thy days may be long upon the land which the LORD thy God giveth thee.**

Honour Mum and Dad, especially if you don't agree with them or even like them. Your longevity may depend upon it. Any problems you have with your parent(s) should be taken in prayer before the LORD. Why? Because you did not choose your parents, *God did!* Your parents are on the hook with the LORD for how they treat you, so that's between them and the LORD. Meanwhile, don't you be a parent-hater, for God is dead serious about checking you out early.

[COMMANDMENT 6]: **Thou shalt not murder.**

All life is sacred because it is God-given. No life comes about by accident (i.e. evolutionary 'biogenesis').[227] It is the LORD who determines every aspect of what happens to you, right down to the day, hour, minute and second of your death, as well as the way you will die.[228] The LORD instituted the death penalty for murder in Gen 9:5-6 *and has never repealed it*. This also includes the murdering of babies in the womb and euthanasia of the elderly. Notice the difference between capital punishment for murder implemented by the state as a result of appropriate judicial processes (ordained in the Torah), and the wilful murder of one person by another, which is a capital offence.[229] You are also forbidden from murdering yourself (suicide). S Michael Houdmann writes:

> "The Bible mentions six people who committed suicide (Judges 9:54; 1 Samuel 31:4-6; 2 Samuel 17:23; 1 Kings 16:18; Matthew 27:5). None of them were righteous, to say the least. The Bible nowhere explicitly states "it is a sin to commit suicide," but the Bible does condemn murder (Exodus 20:13). Suicide is 'self-murder', therefore suicide is a sin since

---

[227] *Origins I – The Greatest Scientific Discovery,* "The great debate"

[228] Job 14:5; Ecc 3:1-8; Psa 139:1-16; Jam 4:13-15

[229] There is also the intriguing question of the 'Cities of Refuge', which God ordains. We will examine this later.

murder is a sin. Aside from the "do not commit murder" command, suicide is also sin for the following two reasons, one theological and one practical: (1) it is God and God alone who has the right to determine life and death,[230] and (2) suicide reveals a belief that God is not powerful enough to help you solve your problems." [231]

[COMMANDMENT 7]: **Thou shalt not commit adultery.**

And thou shalt not even *think* about it either, or look it up on thy favourite porn site (Matt 5:27-28). More on Yeshua's shocking interpretations of the commandments in a moment.

[COMMANDMENT 8]: **Thou shalt not steal.**

Today this includes theft, robbery, embezzlement, copyright theft, fiddling thy parliamentary expenses, short-changing, not paying a worker, and miscellaneous fiscal chicanery. God sees everything, even if the Tax Office doesn't. Notice in this commandment that God *is endorsing private ownership of property,* the complete antithesis of atheistic Communism and Socialism.

[COMMANDMENT 9]: **Thou shalt not bear false witness against thy neighbour.**

Many people are confused about this one. Dr Chuck Missler clarifies:

"Have you ever passed on a story about someone without checking it out? Hearsay evidence? Gossip causes much pain and suffering. Note that this commandment is not dealing with lying, but with false witness. This includes if you stand by while another is being slandered. Are you being a true witness or a false witness?" [232]

[COMMANDMENT 10]: **Thou shalt not covet** [be jealous of, desire] **thy neighbour's house, thou shalt not covet thy neighbour's wife, nor his manservant, nor his maidservant, nor his ox, nor his ass, nor any thing that is thy neighbour's."** (Exo 20:1-17)

Add to that thy neighbour's Porsche, black BMW 4 x 4 with the tinted windows, their clothing brands, fake teeth, Rolex, Jimmy Choos and foreign holidays.

Phew!

It's a measure of just how confused mankind has become over the Ten Commandments in general, and the notion of 'being good' in

---

[230] Gen 4:1; 9:6; Deut 32:39; 1 Sam 1:20,27; 2:6; Psa 31:15; 104:29

[231] www.blogos.org/gotquestions/suicide-Bible.html

[232] Missler, Chuck, *Exodus notes*, p.91

particular, that even atheists are struggling. Alain de Botton writes in *The Telegraph*:

"Even for a lifelong atheist, there is something interesting about these [religious] efforts. What might we learn from them? The standard answer is that we can't learn anything, because religious morality comes from God, which by definition atheists have no time for. Yet the origins of religious ethics couldn't, of course (as far as an atheist is concerned), have come from God, they lay in the pragmatic need of our earliest communities to control their members' tendencies towards violence, and to foster in them contrary habits of harmony and forgiveness.

"Religious codes began as cautionary precepts, which were projected into the sky and reflected back to earth in disembodied and majestic forms. Injunctions to be sympathetic or patient stemmed from an awareness that these were the qualities that could draw societies back from fragmentation and self-destruction. So vital were these rules to our survival that for thousands of years we did not dare to admit that we had formulated them, lest this expose them to critical scrutiny and irreverent handling. We had to pretend that morality came from the heavens in order to insulate it from our own laziness and disregard." [233]

Oh, Alain, Alain! Not willing to be outdone by your mythical Almighty, you go on to list your own Ten Commandments – for atheists. Naturally, you must forget the terrible, fun-wrecking 'Thou shalt nots' (way too judgmental), and substitute the following ten character traits, which I must say are right-on for your average, self-improving humanist: *Resilience, empathy, patience, sacrifice, politeness, humour, self-awareness, forgiveness, hope, confidence.*

Isn't it interesting that even atheists recognise that human nature's default position is towards violence, fragmentation and self-destruction? Why should that even be the case? In fact, if you believe in evolution, why not murder, rape, cheat, steal and kidnap thy neighbour's wife to survive and reproduce if it helps you scrape your way to the top of that evolutionary ladder? Animals do it all the time on David Attenborough's programmes.

Then there's that thorny question of 'being good'. Consider that one day, Alain de Botton and his God-denying cohorts will arrive at their final death scene, wondering what's next. Sensing the Reaper approaching, some might even mouth in their morphine haze: "But

---

[233] www.telegraph.co.uk/culture/9843244/Alain-de-Bottons-10-Commandments-for-Atheists.html

I'm a good person! I led a good life! I don't break commandments, not even my own!" An agnostic wobbler might even quiver (just to be on the safe side): "I've been GOOD! Why would God punish *me?*"

That depends on what yardstick you're using for 'good'. On a human level, you may not have been Reinhard Heydrich's favourite henchman, nor a Boko Haram or ISIS mass-murderer of defenceless villagers, neither slave-trader nor medieval Crusader vying with your mates to see how many Jewish babies you could get on your sword. But did I ever tell a lie? Yes, hundreds, probably thousands. Then I'm a liar. Did I ever take anything that wasn't mine? Of course. Many times. Then I'm a thief. Did I ever lust after a woman who was not my wife? Blimey, do I *have* to answer that? Then I'm a fornicating adulterer. Did I ever think angry thoughts and wished anyone dead? Coots, *I wrote the book on it!* Then I'm a murderer. Did I ever disrespect my parents? Of course. Then I'm a parent-hater. Did I ever do anything inappropriate on the seventh day (whenever that is)? *Strewth, every week!* Then I'm a Sabbath-breaker. Did I ever take God's name in vain? Well, I had several dogs who thought their names were Jesus Christ. In that case, I'm a blasphemer. Did I ever love any material thing more than God? Yes, I once had a Mitsubishi 3000GT sports roadster. Then I'm an idolater.

So here's Phillip Day. I'm a lying, thieving, adulterous, parent-hating, fornicating killer who blasphemes God on a regular basis - every seventh day, in fact (whenever that is). What does God have to say to that?

Know ye not that the unrighteous shall not inherit the kingdom of God? Be not deceived: neither fornicators, nor idolaters, nor adulterers, nor effeminate, nor abusers of themselves with mankind, nor thieves, nor covetous, nor drunkards, nor revilers, nor extortioners, shall inherit the kingdom of God. (1 Cor 6:9-10)

This from the book that's never been wrong. Forget Alain de Botton, I'M FINISHED.

Gulp.

"But I've been a good person!"

Alain's first and obvious mistake is denying the existence of God. Of course, as a philosopher, he knows better. *It is a philosophical impossibility to prove the absolute or universal non-existence of something.* You would have to possess omniscience, omnipresence and omnipotence (properties usually attributed to the God Alain doesn't believe in) to be everywhere at once just to check that the LORD isn't skulking behind some rock as you pass by (you know God). Alain's second mistake is in assuming that the lights just wink out after he dies; that there is nothing beyond death; just an inky blackness; a restful oblivion; no ultimate accountability or judgment for how you've lived your life. And *definitely* no Lake of Fire. Life is merely pointless; a complete waste of your time.

Alain de Botton and all atheists make the above erroneous assumptions based on zero evidence and a whole lot of wishful thinking. Alain seems pretty smart, so here's a concept for him to mull over. I term it 'belief anthropics'. Notice how man's total experience of life appears to have been fine-tuned in such a way that death remains to this day entirely unknowable until you pass through the veil. We acknowledge this without demur since, even in an age of burgeoning scientific endeavour in which we've cracked the atom, gene-spliced fish genes into tomatoes, and can even stand Sam Smith's wailing music eleven times a day on the radio, death still remains the ultimate enigma. Notice how Jesus Christ the Creator is unknowable to millions until they seek Him with all their heart, after which they will die for Him. Are we mad? Knowing that all things work together for good for those who love God (Rom 8-28-29) is utter insanity to the atheist, yet stands as the fundamental axiom of truth for the committed Christian. In other words, the preaching of the cross is to them that perish foolishness, yet to those *who already have eternal life*, it is the power of God (1 Cor 1:18).

This fine-tuning of belief is entirely deliberate. You can't believe in God until He calls you![234] There is a selection process underway and you are both the pawn and the prize. God actually has two claims on you: 1) as your Creator, and 2) as the Purchaser of your redemption at great price. The Creation only cost God six days. Your redemption cost God His only Son. God wants you to make peace with Him through His Son, but He will never force Himself upon you. He will never violate the sovereignty of your free will, make a puppet out of you, nor appear at the end of your bed at 2 am for a jolly good talking to. What He will do is set up daily situations in which you can make the first move towards making peace with Him, but you have to choose it (Jam 4:8). Take your time. God has given you have your whole life to think it over, right up until the moment that steam puffs out of your mouth for the final time. But since you never know for

[234] Isa 49:1,5; Jer 1:5; FG 6:44; 6:64; Acts 13:48; Rom 1:7; Eph 1:4-5; 2 Tim 2:19; 2 Thess 2:13; Gal 1:15

sure which day that will be (Jam 4:13-15), your toes are hanging over the edge of eternity in the fullest sense, so getting right with your Creator today would be better than a week next Tuesday. The same Creator addressing Moses and Israel out of the smoke at Sinai will be the One who says the following as a human fifteen centuries later:

"For God so loved the world, that He gave His only begotten Son, that whosoever believeth in Him should not perish, but have everlasting life. For God sent not His Son into the world to condemn the world; but that the world through Him might be saved. He that believeth on Him is not condemned: but he that believeth not is condemned already, because he hath not believed in the name of the only begotten Son of God." (Fourth Gospel (FG) 3:16-18)

"Ye are from beneath; I am from above: ye are of this world; I am not of this world. I said therefore unto you, that ye shall die in your sins: for if ye believe not that I am He, ye shall die in your sins." (FG 8:23-24)

The reason God has brought Israel to the mountain is to ramp up the process of mankind's redemption. The Ten Commandments, together with the rest of the edicts Moses will bring off the mountain, will make up God's Law. The purpose of this Law is to provide the ultimate yardstick by which to measure the depth of human transgression. This is not a point-scoring exercise between those who 'believe' and those who don't. *We're all in this together.* Welcome to the Earth Programme, the Predicament of Man. There is no 'holier-than-thou'; *all* have sinned and come short of the glory of God (Rom 3:23), and every mortal who ever lived must face the judgment seat of Christ after death to account for what they did on Earth (2 Cor 5:10). As they say in South Carolina: "Sayin' it ain't so don't make no nevermind!" All will be guilty. There is none righteous, no, not one (Rom 3:10). The gulf that exists between the purity of the universal, transcendent God of Creation and the utter filth and degradation of us lot on Earth cannot even begin to be comprehended by the degenerate mind. Our very best acts are but filthy rags in God's sight (Isa 64:6). The losing side of the Holy War is our default position. *In fact we're born losers.* If we have committed one sin – *just one,* we won't make it to Heaven Frank Sinatra's *My Way* and God knows it, which is why He went to such extremes to pay the penalty for our imperfections *Himself,* not only to satisfy His eternal justice and uncompromising perfection, but so He could dismiss the handwriting of ordinances pinned against us, and redeem us to become *joint heirs and friends* to rule a new Heaven and a new Earth with Him throughout eternity (Psa 82:6; FG 1:10-13; 10:34; Rom 8:14-17).

It's this very question of personal accountability that is at the heart of the Sinai experience – an accountability from which the flesh instinctively recoils. So we try the good works trip. We trundle through life on beatific autopilot, tossing the odd fiver into the poor box to feel good about ourselves, smiling at babes, sponsoring an African kid, being nice to gays and Muslims, joining Greenpeace, enjoying a good buzz. But on God's level of perfection *we're all finished*. God is a perfect God of universal justice and no-one gets away with anything – *ever*. Did you sin just once? Then you're done. During the Sermon on the Mount, Jesus summarises to His baffled disciples, **"Be ye therefore perfect, even as your Father which is in Heaven is perfect."** (Matt 5:48) Most believers take that as referring to the imputed righteousness of Christ after the covering of His blood after being 'born again', and it certainly does mean that in the post-crucifixion sense. But this statement was made by Jesus not only pre-crucifixion (obviously), but as part of the conclusion of His extraordinary Sermon on the Mount. Read Matthew 5 straight off, no interruptions, ending at verse 48 and prepare to be *freaked out*.

The Sermon on the Mount is taken by Christians to be the highest ethical teaching in the Bible, and it is; yet if you read it, it's horrifying. It's a complete, slow-motion car crash. The listener is left broken by condemnation before a perfect Creator's coming judgment *with zero visible means of reprieve*. The Sermon on the Mount is horrendous for man's eternal prospects. The Sermon on the Mount is certainly not anything man would *ever* have made up, Alain, then bounced off the sky to give it the *imprimatur* of some mythical bearded man in the clouds. The unsettling truth is that the Sermon on the Mount doesn't offer any of us a way out. Here we are, looking at the atrocities in the world around us, crying to God for justice when we should be begging for mercy. The Sermon on the Mount was not given to unbelievers *but to those Christ had already selected*. In effect, the Creator is stating that if you think living by the Ten Commandments is a tough one, try this: Even *thinking* of hurting or killing your enemy, even *imagining* ravishing your neighbour's wife, *even entertaining the notion of* lying, cheating, stealing paperclips from the office cupboard or saying a naughty word, *and you're finished.* With the commandments jacked to the metacosmic n'th degree, Yeshua is demonstrating just how you would have to live and die without

God's help to make it to Heaven *Your Way*. You won't understand the solution if you don't understand the problem. You're dealing with the Predicament of Man facing the uncompromising spiritual perfection and justice of an infinite Creator. According to the book that's never been wrong, God has decided that the entire world will be judged, condemned or redeemed purely on the basis of our attitude towards what happened to His Son on a wooden cross erected in Judaea 2,000 years ago. How astonishing is that if you really think about it? In other words, there is a judgment coming which will finish each of us utterly unless we claim the free pardon the Son purchased at great cost to give God the legal right to pronounce us 'not guilty' at our judgment bar and dismiss our case. You can even elect for the Judge to become your defence attorney. He's never lost a case! What does this 'Get out of Hell Free card' cost? Nothing. *Everything*. Just as the Israelites had to choose the blood to be protected from the Death Angel at Passover, so must we. Wild doesn't even cut it.

"But I don't even believe in Hell!"

There you go, believing again.

Sayin' it ain't so don't make no nevermind.

God wants you to make peace with Him *so He can move you to the next level* – the extraordinary destiny He's had in store for you from before the foundation of the world. And it won't be sitting on some cloud strumming Frank Sinatra's *My Way* on a harp either. How utterly unproductive.

"Come now and let us reason together," saith the LORD. "Though your sins be as scarlet, they shall be as white as snow. Though they be red like crimson, they shall be as wool. If ye be willing and obedient, ye shall eat the good of the land. But if ye refuse and rebel, ye shall be devoured with the sword, for the mouth of the LORD hath spoken." (Isa 1:18-20)

The fear of the LORD is the beginning of wisdom: and the knowledge of the holy is understanding. (Prov 9:10)

Some people have more prosaic questions about the Ten Commandments and those famous two tablets, upon which the Decalogue was inscribed. How big were those stones? Were they the size of gravestones as so often portrayed? If so, 80 year-old Moses would certainly have had problems negotiating the rocky trails juggling those two. We are told Moses cut the stones, after which God inscribed them with His finger (Exo 31:18; 34:1; Deut 9:17). Following ancient formats, they were likely not curved at the top but rectangular in shape with sharp edges. There was writing on both sides of each tablet, indicative of a contract/covenant document (Exo 19:5), and they appeared to be small enough for Moses to carry **in his hand/hands** (Exo 32:15). Were five commandments put on one tablet and the remainder on the other? Emeritus professor Dr Meshulam Margaliot, Department of Bible at Israel's Bar-Ilan University, takes a practical approach to that question:

"…we must take account of the historical context in which the Ten Commandments were given. According to Ex. 19, this was done in the course of establishing a covenant, a *berit,* between the Lord and Israel. Hence, we are dealing with the text of a covenant, a type of contract between two (or more) parties. For obvious reasons, it is customary for every written contract or agreement to be issued in duplicate, each party receiving a complete copy of the agreement, contract, or covenant….

"It would be reasonable for the pact made at Sinai to be issued in two copies, one for the Lord, and one for the Israelites. This practice explains why one tablet did not suffice, rather two were needed. It is self-evident that the Lord's tablet had to be placed where the Divine Presence (*shechina*, Biblical Hebrew *kavod*) was found (see Ex. 29:43 and 40:34), in the Holy Ark made specifically for this purpose: 'And deposit in the Ark the Pact which I will give you' (Ex. 25:16), 'He took the Pact and placed it in the ark' (Ex. 40:20). 'The Pact' [*edut*] is used as shorthand for the 'two Tablets of the Pact' (Ex. 31:18), also called *shnei luchot habberit*, the 'two Tablets of the Covenant' (Deut. 9:15).

"But what about the Israelites' copy, on the second Tablet, where was that copy placed? Here we note a common practice in the ancient Near East. When a treaty was made between parties of unequal status, the lesser partner, or vassal, would place his copy of the pact in the temple of his god, the reason being that the vassal had then to take an oath in the name of his god to 'the great king'. (See Ez. 17:11-19. The reference here is to the king of the Hittites, who made treaties with the rulers of smaller kingdoms in northern Syria during the first half of the first millennium B.C.E. This custom, however, undoubtedly dates much further back.)

"Depositing a copy in the temple of the vassal strengthened the vassal's obligation to the greater king. In addition, sanctity was ascribed to the treaty itself, because the gods of each side were witness to the agreement: Compare Laban's words to Jacob after striking a treaty: 'May the G-d of Abraham and the god of Nahor' – their ancestral deities – 'judge between us.' (Gen.31:53)

"Since the Israelites had the status of vassal vis-à-vis G-d and were the lesser partners to the Covenant, it was reasonable for them to file their copy of the Pact in the Holy Ark of the Lord their G-d. Thus we conclude that both Tablets were placed together in the Ark in the Tabernacle, and later in Solomon's Temple: 'There was nothing inside the Ark but the two tablets of stone which Moses placed there at Horeb, when the Lord made [a covenant] with the Israelites after their departure from the land of Egypt' (1 Kings 8:9)." [235]

Broken stones

Meanwhile, amid the searing bursts of crackling lightning, the electrical stench of the air, the crashing of thunder and deafening trumpet blasts, the children of Israel are quailing in horror on the plain before the mountain.

"Stricken with terror, the people beg Moses to excuse them from listening any further to God's voice and pledge to obey whatever Moses relays to them in God's name. Moses agrees, assuring them that this is what he and God had in mind all along. Moses re-enters the thick cloud covering the mountaintop while the people remain at a distance (Exodus 20:18-21), and the long-awaited giving of the law begins." [236]

Over the coming weeks, while the multitude camps before the mountain, the celestial strangeness of this unique meeting between man and his Creator unfolds.

And all the people saw the thunderings, and the lightnings, and the noise of the trumpet, and the mountain smoking: and when the people saw it, they removed, and stood afar off. And they said unto Moses, "Speak thou with us, and we will hear: but let not God speak with us, lest we die."

And Moses said unto the people, "Fear not: for God is come to prove you, and that His fear may be before your faces, that ye sin not."

And the people stood afar off, and Moses drew near unto the thick darkness where God was. And the LORD said unto Moses, "Thus thou shalt say unto the children of Israel, 'Ye have seen that I have talked with you from heaven. Ye shall not make with Me gods of silver, neither shall ye make unto you gods of gold. An altar of earth thou shalt make unto Me, and shalt sacrifice thereon thy burnt offerings, and thy peace offerings, thy sheep, and thine oxen:

---

[235] www.biu.ac.il/JH/Parasha/eng/kitisa/mar.html

[236] http://thetorah.com/what-happened-at-mount-sinai/

in all places where I record My name I will come unto thee, and I will bless thee. And if thou wilt make Me an altar of stone, thou shalt not build it of hewn stone: for if thou lift up thy tool upon it, thou hast polluted it. Neither shalt thou go up by steps unto Mine altar, that thy nakedness be not discovered thereon.' " (Exo 20:18-26)

Now God becomes insistent on altars being built, without hewn stone, just using natural rocks piled one upon another. Interesting. We'll find out the purpose of those in a minute. The weeks at Sinai are spent with Moses toing and froing between the children of Israel in the plain and God's presence on the mountain to report a blizzard of edicts which will make up the Mosaic Covenant, the foundation of Mosaic Judaism. God, having delivered His own from 'the world' (Egypt), now gets abruptly specific about what He wants from man. Moses is doubtless flabbergasted by the sheer volume and complexity of what is handed down, dealing with everything from laws concerning servants and animal control to feast days, ceremonial principles, justice, property rights, cleanliness, to the detailed blueprints for a mobile tabernacle with its special furniture, and that crown jewel: the Ark of the Covenant and Mercy Seat.

At one point, the LORD issues a 'time-out' and invites Moses, Aaron, and a small crowd of Israel's elders up to the mountain for a spectacular spot of R & R:

Then went up Moses, and Aaron, Nadab, and Abihu, and seventy of the elders of Israel: And they saw the God of Israel: and there was under His feet as it were a paved work of a sapphire stone, and as it were the body of heaven in His clearness. And upon the nobles of the children of Israel He laid not His hand: also they saw God, <u>and did eat and drink</u> (Exo 24:9-11).

How amazing is that? These fellows are eating and drinking in God's presence, and socialising at the same time! This reminds us of how Yeshua loved to eat, drink and fellowship with His friends, disciples, as well as the wider, sinful public during His human ministry. No impersonal Godforce He. We have a social, very personal Creator: One not averse to enjoying a bit of downtime with us; that is, if we don't have too much going on to clog up our schedule.

In fact, Moses receives not just the Ten Commandments but a total of 613 new edicts and laws in the weeks which follow. All are painstakingly recorded by God's prophet. Yet even while the patriarch is delayed on the mountain for weeks getting this lot on board, his rebellious Hebrews are down on the plain talking brother Aaron into a dangerous, alternative strategy:

And when the people saw that Moses delayed to come down out of the mount, the people gathered themselves together unto Aaron, and said unto him, "Up, make us gods which shall go before us. For as for this Moses [witness the ongoing contempt of their leader - amazing!]**, the man that brought us up out of the land of Egypt** [actually God brought you out of Egypt!]**, we wot not** [know not] **what is become of him** [yes, you do. He's up on the mountain interceding for you!]**."** (Exo 32:1)

Surrounded and intimidated, Aaron caves in. **"Break off the golden earrings, which are in the ears of your wives, of your sons, and of your daughters, and bring them unto me." And all the people brake off the golden earrings which were in their ears, and brought them unto Aaron. And he received them at their hand, and fashioned it with a graving tool, after he had made it a molten calf: and they said, "These be thy gods, O Israel, which brought thee up out of the land of Egypt."** (Exo 32:2-4)

Say what?? You've just made a calf out of earrings and ornaments *and now you're giving this bauble the credit for taking you out of Egypt, feeding you daily and destroying your enemies?* It seems incredible that a little while back in Exo 19:8, the people agreed to do whatever God told them, among which was the following:

"I am the LORD thy God, which have brought thee out of the land of Egypt, out of the house of bondage. Thou shalt have no other gods before Me. Thou shalt not make unto the any graven image, or any likeness of anything that is in Heaven above, or that is in the Earth beneath, or that is in the water under the Earth: Thou shalt not bow down thyself to them, nor serve them: for I the LORD thy God am a jealous God, visiting the iniquity of the fathers upon the children unto the third and fourth generation of them that hate Me; and shewing mercy unto thousands of them that love Me, and keep My commandments." (Exo 20:1-6)

These days we can't really identify with the picture of hundreds of idolaters cavorting around an idol in wild abandon, fires blazing, unless of course you are a regular club-rave fan. In fact, as the martyr Stephen proclaims in Acts 7:39, what the children of Israel are actually doing here is thrusting God from them (the Spirit) and turning back to Egypt (the world/flesh). Here we revisit the phenomenon of the astonishing beliefs people get into once they reject God. Even today, those who mock Moses, the Exodus, the Bible and God in general as fanciful, religious tommyrot are not long delayed in courting some fanciful, religious tommyrot of their own, be it monkey men, atheism or the demons of the Eastern religions. That they reject God is not in itself remarkable; a batch of uncomfortable scriptures reveals that God is calling some and He's not calling others.[237] God *has* given each of us the key, however, to make the first move (Jam 4:8). What is astonishing is what unbelievers get into once they reject God. In this particular case with Aaron and the rebelling Israelites, it's rejecting the majesty of God, which they have seen repeatedly demonstrated, and replacing His glory with a model of a four-legged bovine which drools, poos everywhere and eats grass, then giving this thing the credit for their deliverance from Egypt rather than giving their thanks to their Creator. Once again, the flesh is at enmity with the Spirit (Rom 8:7). Now, to their mind, it isn't God who has delivered them, but the work of their own hands. There is another lesson we learn here: Notice again that God will not violate the sovereignty He has given to us. If we persist in worshipping something or someone other than Him, He will give us over to the desires of our hearts (Acts 7:42; Rom 1:28).

There is another golden calf lesson we can take away with us for today: God wants us to learn how to overcome, not how to be overtaken. The experiences the Israelites endure during the Exodus are a lesson for each of us in how to hold the true course (1 Cor 10:6-12). How do we do this? Our Creator desires to see us living clean, simple and holy lives before Him, overcoming evil by doing good and serving others. Notice that doing good works (i.e. the work of our hands) can never earn us our salvation (deliverance from Egypt) – this can only be a free gift from God (Eph 2:8-10; Titus 3:5-7). What our changed behaviour *will* demonstrate is a) our love for Him (FG 14:14,23-24), b) that we truly know Him (Jer 22:15-16; Matt 7:21-23), and c) provides the proof to ourselves and others that we are trying, albeit imperfectly, to imitate God by practising how to live as Christ lives.[238] In short: we are to be fruit-bearers, not sin-bearers!

(God speaks to Cain) **"If you do well, will you not be accepted? And if you do not do well, sin lies at the door. And its desire is for you, but you shall rule over it** [God is telling Cain to overcome!]**."** (Gen 4:7, NKJV)

[237] Isa 49:1,5; Jer 1:5; Eph 1:4-5; FG 6:44; FG 6:64; Acts 13:48; Rom 1:7; 2 Tim 2:19; 2 Thess 2:13; Gal 1:15

[238] Eph 5:1; Matt 3:8; Luke 3:8; Acts 26:20; Eph 2:8-10

(John the Baptist speaks) **"Therefore bear fruits worthy of repentance, and do not think to say to yourselves, 'We have Abraham as our father.' For I say to you that God is able to raise up children to Abraham from these stones. And even now the axe is laid to the root of the trees. Therefore every tree which does not bear good fruit is cut down and thrown into the fire."** (Matt 3:8-10, NKJV)

(The Apostle Peter speaks) **"He who would love life and see good days, let him refrain his tongue from evil, and his lips from speaking deceit. Let him turn away from evil and do good** [i.e. works befitting repentance]**...."** (1 Pet 3:10-11, NKJV)

(The Apostle Paul speaks) **"Therefore King Agrippa, I was not disobedient to the heavenly vision, but declared first to those in Damascus and in Jerusalem, and throughout all the region of Judaea, and then to the Gentiles, that they should repent, turn to God, and do works befitting repentance."** (Acts 26:19-20, NKJV)

(Daniel addressing Nebuchadnezzar) **"Therefore, O King, let my advice be acceptable to you; break off your sins by being righteous** [i.e. works befitting repentance], **and your iniquities by showing mercy to the poor** [i.e. overcome evil by doing good!]. **Perhaps there may be a lengthening of your prosperity."** (Dan 4:27, NKJV)

Depart from evil and do good [Repent!]; **seek peace and pursue it.** (Psa 34:14, NKJV)

Depart from evil and do good [Repent!]; **and dwell forevermore** [have eternal life]. (Psa 37:27, NKJV)

Do not be overcome by evil, but overcome evil with good [Repent and do good]. (Rom 12:21, NKJV)

Let him turn away from evil and do good. (1 Peter 3:11, NKJV)

The LORD is not slack concerning His promises, as some count slackness, but is longsuffering towards us, unwilling that any should perish, but that all should come to repentance. (2 Pet 3:9, NKJV)

"And he who overcomes and keeps My works until the end, to him will I give power over the nations...." (Rev 2:26, NKJV)

And who is he who will harm you if you become followers of what is good? (1 Peter 3:13, NKJV)

"Therefore be imitators of God as dear children." (Eph 5:1, NKJV)

Aaron represents fallible man. Did we somehow expect more from him than ourselves? Do we cave in to peer pressure and do and say what we later regret? As the expression goes: "Whenever I went out among men, I always returned less of a man." Aaron makes the children of Israel a golden calf, yet these days a golden calf can be anything or anyone that replaces the primacy of God in our lives: a beautiful house, a Porsche, a wife or husband who leads us astray spiritually (1 John 5:21). Aaron even goes on to make an impromptu feast day to the LORD to celebrate! (Exo 32:5) It goes without saying that this is a monumentally foolish thing to do. Upon His mountain, God goes toxic:

And the LORD said unto Moses, "Go, get thee down; for thy people, which thou broughtest out of the land of Egypt, have corrupted themselves: They have turned aside quickly out of the way which I commanded them: they have made them a molten calf, and have worshipped it, and have sacrificed thereunto, and said, 'These be thy gods, O Israel, which have brought thee up out of the land of Egypt.' " And the LORD said unto Moses, "I have seen this people and, behold, it is a stiffnecked people. Now therefore let Me alone, that My wrath may wax hot against them, and that I may consume them. And I will make of thee a great nation." (Exo 32:7-10).

Notice how God disowns His people at this stage! ('**for thy people, which thou broughtest out of the land of Egypt, have corrupted themselves**') i.e. "They're YOURS, Moses. You know, the ones YOU brought out of Egypt..." Moses doubtless stares in disbelief as this news is broken to him, unsettled as to how he can possibly father a great nation now from a gaggle of crispy corpses once God is done with them. God declares His desire for maximum termination with extreme prejudice, yet one person stands in the way - Moses. In a scene reminiscent of Abraham's negotiation with God over the fate of Sodom and Gomorrah, Moses, in Christ's role as intercessor for the people, goes before God and tries to talk the Almighty out of it. Notice the first two things Moses does: he gives the people right back to the LORD! Then he reaffirms that it was not he, Moses, who brought them out of Egypt but the LORD:

And Moses besought the LORD his God, and said, "LORD, why doth Thy wrath wax hot against Thy people, which Thou hast brought forth out of the land of Egypt with great power, and with a mighty hand? Wherefore should the Egyptians speak and say, 'For mischief did he bring them out, to slay them in the mountains, and to consume them from the face of the Earth?' Turn from Thy fierce wrath and repent of this evil against Thy people.

Remember Abraham, Isaac, and Israel [Jacob]**, Thy servants, to whom Thou swarest by Thine own self and saidst unto them, 'I will**

multiply your seed as the stars of heaven, and all this land that I have spoken of will I give unto your seed, and they shall inherit it for ever.'" (Exo 32: 11-13)

Some extraordinary traits are revealed in God's nature here. Is God really on that short a fuse to desire a summary execution of His people? I don't believe so: certainly no more than He desires to kill you and I each day for the many ways in which we offend Him. Consider that God cannot learn, nor can He be surprised: these are attributes of His omniscient nature. Do you think God was *surprised* that Aaron and the Israelites did this? Of course not. God knows the end from the beginning, and has already seen everything we do before we do it! (Isa 46:9-10) So what is God up to?

- He is teaching Moses and the people that He takes sin extremely seriously
- That there is always a price that must be paid for wrongdoing
- That He will never change over this issue (Mal 3:6)
- That man often fails spectacularly right after a high point or victory
- That some will hold the course and be true (will overcome) while others won't (will be overtaken)
- That some believers are genuine (the wheat), and others, who look just like believers, have been faking belief and trust in Him all along (the tares) (Matt 13:24-30; 36-43)

Abraham took God to task over His desire to wreak vengeance on Sodom and Gomorrah. Abraham won a stay of execution, but the unrepentant wicked of Sodom condemned themselves anyway through their homosexual desire for God's angels (God gave them up to their hearts' desires). Now we have Moses, in Christ's intercessor role, attempting to forestall the Almighty's Hand in wiping out the Israelites for demonic calf worship, using, of all arguments, that God's Name will be sorely dented with the Egyptians if He slays those He has sworn to deliver. From this we infer the following:

- God can be reasoned with
- God actually cares what unbelievers might think of Him. In fact, part of the purpose God visits the plagues upon Egypt is to demonstrate His power to the Egyptians and world at large to force repentance. Word soon gets around (Josh 2:9-13)
- Moses reminds God of the promise He made to his forebears; quotes God's Word back to Him because God is bound by His Word, even to His own hurt (Rom 4:21)

- God shows remorse (Eze 18:23)
- After the Flood, God was sorry for what He had done (Gen 8:21)
- God wants everyone to repent (2 Pet 3:9)

Of course, we are struck by what a moany lot the Israelites are. Moses and Aaron have had trouble on their hands from the start. The Israelites constantly grumble at their plight despite the awesome judgments they have witnessed by God's hand upon Egypt, not to mention the incongruous escape from their oppressors, a not inconsiderable chunk of Egyptian booty in tow. It's easy to pour scorn on the Exodus Jews from our comfy chairs in modern housing, but what about us? Fat, fed and content, our every whim indulged, do we not moan whenever chance presents? Forget widescreen plasma TVs and the Internet, try living off quails and 'wassname' for a few weeks and see how you like it. Human nature versus God. The Holy War. We're fallen. The Predicament of Man is that we're born with a terminal nature in desperate need of a remedy. Those who believe mankind is spiritually evolving need to do their sums on the number of people killed by governments in the 20th century, the most deadly century by far. Is that the best we can do after 4,000 years of 'spiritual evolution'?

But the Israelites are going to get it from Moses. Incensed at their behaviour, the patriarch descends the mountain and returns to the camp with the holy tablets upon which God has carved the commandments. Seeing the golden calf and the Hebrews cavorting around it, he shatters the tablets in fury (the Law has been broken!) and confronts his elder brother.

"What did this people unto thee, that thou hast brought so great a sin upon them?"

And Aaron said, "Let not the anger of my lord wax hot: thou knowest the people, that they are set on mischief. For they said unto me, 'Make us gods, which shall go before us: for as for this Moses, the man that brought us up out of the land of Egypt, we wot not what is become of him.'

"And I said unto them, 'Whosoever hath any gold, let them break it off.' So they gave it me: then I cast it into the fire, and there came out this calf." (Exo 32:21-24)

Can you beat Aaron? "Don't blame me, Moses. You know what they're like. They gave me their gold, I tossed it in the fire, and out came this calf!" Brilliant. For some amazing reason Aaron gets off lightly, unlike the others.

Then Moses stood in the gate of the camp, and said, "Who is on the LORD'S side? Let him come unto me." And all the sons of Levi gathered themselves together unto him (Exo 32:26).

"Who is on the LORD's side?" is a question that should be asked among our nations today. The demon worship underway in our villages, towns and cities these days will shock you, and is a subject we will examine in *Origins VI - Parousia*. How about you? Are you on the LORD's side? And not just any generic Lord or god of any religion either. His name is YHWH; Yeshua; the LORD God of Israel; the Creator of the universe; the Name that is above every name; the One who gave His life in Judaea 2,000 years ago on a wooden cross so that the sins of many might be forgiven. That God.

Moses divides up the camp between those who are with God and those who are against Him. Then he instructs the Levites to go through the camp and execute the guilty. Three thousand are slaughtered (Exo 32:28).[239] Then Moses returns to the mountain to make amends with God, and receives two further stone tablets to replace those he recently broke in hot wrath.

"Oh, this people have sinned a great sin," Moses laments, **"and have made themselves gods of gold. Yet now, if Thou wilt forgive their sin; and if not, blot me, I pray Thee, out of Thy book which Thou hast written." And the LORD said unto Moses, "Whosoever hath sinned against Me, him will I blot out of My book."** (Exo 32:31-33)

From this we infer:

- Moses, incredibly, is willing to sacrifice his own salvation for the sake of his people (*cf.* Rom 9:2-3). Notice that God does not give that idea second thought. There is only One who will sacrifice Himself for the sins of His people, and His name is not Moses
- God has a book, wherein sinners are blotted out for unrepentant evil. We can reasonably infer that when you are made, your name goes in the book. This book crops up later in scripture under different but not dissimilar circumstances, and is known as the Book of Life (Phil 4:3; Rev 3:5; 20:12,15). We can infer more of God's character by the events in the desert:
- In the realm where God dwells, sin is a major deal

[239] It is interesting that while these 3,000 are lost, 3,000 will be saved on the Day of Pentecost (Acts 2:41).

- God reveals more of His nature, and perhaps even of Heaven, in the laws He enunciates, and the intricate artefacts He has Moses make. These include the Tabernacle (mobile sanctuary), the Ark of the Covenant (into which the tablets are placed), the bronze laver (washbasin), the altar of burnt offering, the seven-headed, golden lampstand (menorah), the table of showbread and the altar of incense

Moses had ordered boundary stones placed around the mountain to prevent the unclean coming into God's presence. He need not have worried.

And all the people saw the thunderings and the lightnings, and the noise of the trumpet and the mountain smoking. And when the people saw it, they removed and stood afar off. And they said unto Moses, "Speak thou with us and we will hear. But let not God speak with us, lest we die." And Moses said unto the people, "Fear not, <u>for God is come to prove you</u> [test you]**, and that His fear may be before your faces, that ye sin not."** (Exo 20:18-20)

The default human setting - wicked

God appoints the Israelites as a holy nation to Him (Exo 19:3-6). This is an unequivocal, unilateral charge, as the prophet Isaiah later reminds:

"Ye are My witnesses," saith the LORD, "and My servant whom I have chosen, that ye may know and believe Me and understand that I am He. <u>Before Me there was no God formed, neither shall there be after Me</u>. I, even I, am the LORD and <u>beside Me there is no saviour</u> [Yeshua Himself is speaking!]. **I have declared and have saved, and I have shewed, when there was no strange god among you: therefore ye are My witnesses," saith the LORD, "that I am God."** (Isa 43:10-12)

During the Exodus, God gives the tribes 613 directives to abide by. Rabbi Yacov Rambsel points out that the Hebrew phrase the 'Lord God of Israel' (Adonai Elohai Yisrael) has a gematrical value of 613. God personifies the Mosaic Law.

The purpose of these laws is to provide a yardstick for the measure of transgressions and increase awareness of sin. There are too many today who believe humans are basically good. What tosh. Look at all the laws they pass just to keep our murderous, violent, rebellious nature under control. I have a seven-year-old daughter and trust me, you don't have to teach her to be bad! I was just the same, and on occasions still am. The default setting for the human is sin, the curse of the Garden.

"The heart is deceitful above all things, and desperately wicked: who can know it? I the LORD search the heart, I try the reins, even to give every man according to his ways, and according to the fruit of his doings." (Jer 17:9-10)

These rosy-glow, apple-blossom, lip-quivering, left-wing social architects need to explain how, after millions of years of supposed human evolution, we are more wicked today than ever. Eisenhower insisted that ordinary Germans went to the concentration camps at WW2's conclusion to view the Nazi-slaughtered Jewish babies in piles outside the crematoria, along with hundreds of thousands of their relatives and ordinary citizens stacked like cord-wood across the camp concourses. Yet Hitler's Nazis were no one-off aberration. RJ Rummel, Professor Emeritus at the University of Hawaii and author of *Death by Government,* writes:

"I did a comprehensive overview of available estimates... and wrote a book, *Lethal Politics,* on Soviet democide to provide understanding and context for my figures. I calculate that the Communist regime, 1917-1987, murdered about 62,000,000 people, around 55,000,000 of them citizens.

"But these are all statistics and hard to grasp. Compare my total of 62,000,000 for the Soviet Union and 43,000,000 for Stalin to the death from slavery of 37,000,000 during the 16th to the 19th century; or to the death of from 25,000,000 to 75,000,000 in the Black Death (bubonic plague), 1347-1351, that depopulated Europe.

"Another way of looking at this is that the annual risk of a person under Soviet control being murdered by the regime was 1 out of 222. But compare. The annual risk of anyone in the world dying from war was 1 out of 5,556, from smoking a pack of cigarettes a day was 1 out of 278, from any cancer was 1 out of 357, or for an American to die in an auto accident was 1 out of 4,167.

"Now, I must ask, with perhaps an unconscious touch of outrage in my voice, why is this death by Marxism so incredible and significant in its magnitude, unknown or unappreciated compared to the importance given slavery, cancer deaths, auto accident deaths, and so on. Especially, especially I must add again, when unlike cancer, auto accidents, and smoking, those deaths under Marxism in the Soviet Union were murders?"[240]

So in Stalinist Russia, you had a 1 in 222 chance of being murdered. Think that's bad? Millions of babies, the most vulnerable, darling gifts to our society, can now be murdered by doctors in defence of 'a woman's right to choose....' Let's complete that sentence: 'A woman's right to choose whether to murder her baby for lifestyle reasons.' Today, governments and their abortion supporters rationalise that pregnancy is just evolution at work, so there's no judgment, it's just tissue, and it's apparently not human until 23 weeks old, so no remorse.

No remorse? Google the word 'Abortion' on the picture setting if you've the stomach for it, and get the visuals on what has been intellectualised as 'choice' by these godless fanatics. In the film, *The Silent Scream,* Dr Bernard Nathanson shows the true horror of abortion with the help of ultrasound technology. Dr Nathanson should know. He once headed the world's largest abortion clinic in the US:

> "Viewers are stunned to see a 12-week-old 'foetus' becoming desperate while attempting to escape the abortionist's suction curette. The tiny baby's heart rate doubles during the 'procedure' that ends its life." [241]

The abortion war continues between liberals and religious conservatives. The death toll so far in America is several abortionists and 44 million babies – more than the entire population of Canada. Reported global abortions, broken down by country, *are 945 million babies,* or 13% of the current world population killed. The true figure is far higher.[242] Forget Raqaa, Helmand, Mogadishu or Stalinist Russia, the most dangerous place to be on Earth today is in the womb of an American mother, *where you have a 1 in 4 chance of being murdered.*[243]

Baby/child slaughter is *ha-Satan's* favourite. It strikes at the heart of God's love and creative miracle and is *de rigeur* for all Satanic societies, whether ancient 'civilisations' or our enlightened modern

---

[240] www.distributedrepublic.net/archives/2006/05/01/how-many-did-stalin-really-murder/

[241] www.silentscream.org

[242] www.johnstonsarchive.net/policy/abortion/wrjp337sd.html

[243] **Missler, Chuck** *The Origin of Evil,* www.khouse.org

age. The Canaanites heated up bronze statues of the Satanic god Molech (*melech* – king) and placed babies into their glowing arms to appease his wrath. Pick a society today, see how it treats its young/elderly, and you'll have a reliable indicator of its hatred or love for God, and that goes for each of us personally too.

If this shocks, you have an inkling of how God views evil. Sin is a big deal to God and shown zero tolerance, but the sinner is taught that he can atone for his offence through the shedding of the innocent blood of another (the Lamb). This is not something easily comprehensible to the unregenerate mind. Cain had trouble getting it. Adam and Eve got it when God provided them animal skins with which to clothe their nakedness (awareness of sin). Theologians cite this as evidence for God's 'perfect' nature, of which sin has no part. God's perfect love is only made possible by God's perfect hatred of sin. Chuck Missler states that there are some intriguing things our boundless God cannot do:

1. He cannot condone sin
2. He cannot lie
3. He cannot be surprised
4. He cannot force you to love Him

So what is Mount Sinai all about? On the face of it, the Designer has a plan for man amid a storm of directives, to which mankind must adhere for his life or be punished. I'll save any newcomers the bother by telling you that you don't stand a hoot's chance of keeping all 613 commandments, collectively known as the Law. In fact, you won't keep just the Ten, and God knows that too, hence His insistence on the altars. Of course the Law is our guide, and just because if we are guilty in one we are guilty in all, this does not mean we can go around breaking the lot. The purpose of the Law is to condemn, to leave each of us guilty before a righteous God in desperate need of a Redeemer. To try to work our way to Heaven in spite of our sin is to blaspheme God's very nature. What God wants to know is, are you for Him or against Him? Will you surrender your human part in the Holy War against Him and form a relationship so He can deliver you, or are you just not interested? (Matt 7:21-23) This is not an intellectual exercise, this is between you and the One who divides each of your cells and sustains you at the sub-atomic level. God's not messing around, and neither are the Levites. Those who don't 'get it' will surely get it.

Consider the extraordinary experience of your own life in the context of this designed system – Project Earth. Nothing has happened to you by accident. You are taking part in a highly elaborate digital simulation, whether you like it or not, and you don't control the game for even a nano-second. Whether you die as a child of 3, a young man of 23 or an ancient of 98, there is a day in the future with your name on it. Yet we know that **all things work together for good to them that love God, to them who are the called according to His purpose** (Rom 8:28). Time itself is an artificial property of the Earth sub-realm rather than part of God's reality. God inhabits eternity (Isa 57:15), which is not 'lots of time', it's the absence of time. Even atheistic *Scientific American* admits that our existence is but a subset of a much larger reality.[244] These days, physicists talk in terms of one-dimensional superstrings vibrating in 10 dimensions, far beyond the four 'spacetime' dimensions we currently comprehend.

What's even more unnerving is that these additional dimensions, which quantum physics has confirmed, may be inferred but not directly known, render our world and everything in it completely transparent and visible to hyperdimensional beings, both good and bad. We are, as it were, beings perched on the skin of a bubble, able to be viewed from within and without, yet only ourselves aware of those perched with us on the skin. Here are some examples of hyperdimensional events mentioned in the Bible:

- Enoch raptured (Gen 5:24)
- Elijah raptured (2 Kings 2:11)
- Elisha showing his servant the armies of God (2 Kings 6:11-17)
- The angels Gabriel, Michael and the prophet Daniel (Dan 9:21; 10:4-21)
- The various appearances and disappearances of angels
- Yeshua taken by *ha-Satan* up to the pinnacle of the Temple (Matt 4:5; Luke 4:9)
- Philip's translation (Acts 8:39-40)
- Yeshua enters what we assume is a regular room without using the door and makes His exit the same way (FG 20:19-29). Jesus makes the point to His disciples that he is not a spirit but can eat (Luke 24:41-43). He can be handled as flesh and blood. He can and does disappear at will right in front of them, demonstrating His hyperdimensionality (Luke 24:31,36).
- The general Rapture (1 Thess 4:15-18; 1 Cor 15:51-55)

---

[244] *Scientific American*, June 2005

So we inhabit what amounts to a goldfish bowl. Everything we do and think is transparently viewable in the metacosm (full dimensionality). Detailed notes are being taken (Ecc 12:14; Matt 12:36-37; Rom 2:6; Rev 20:12). Our brief life on Earth is a job interview, on-the-job training and work experience under live-fire conditions with full free will in an intricately crafted environment to see if we are fit to rule with God and His Son for eternity. Each of us is being watched and assessed down to the sub-atomic level - every thought, word and deed. It's enough to turn you to religion.

In the desert, the Israelites are being taught all about what pleases God and what doesn't; the implications of free will - man's sovereignty, his choices, the nature of sin and its consequences; how a perfect Entity will resolve the extraordinary paradox of how to satisfy His eternal justice against sin, yet spend eternity with creatures who have heaped themselves in iniquity through the choices they have made. A God-like challenge, to be sure, and one in which God will star and eventually pay the ultimate price with His own life.

What's at stake here is a lot more serious than most might imagine. And immersed in Nimrod humanism for the hundreds of years they spent in Egypt, the twelve tribes of Jacob are understandably frightened now; hungry, exhausted and hopelessly out of their depth in comprehending the terrifying Entity confronting them on the mountain beyond, proclaimed by the thunderous blasts of that ethereal trumpet.

"I call Heaven and Earth to record this day against you, that I have set before you life and death, blessing and cursing. Therefore choose life, that both thou and thy seed may live. That thou mayest love the LORD thy God, and that thou mayest obey His voice, and that thou mayest cleave unto Him, for He is thy life and the length of thy days. That thou mayest dwell in the land which the LORD sware unto thy fathers, to Abraham, to Isaac, and to Jacob, to give them." (Deut 30:19-20)

The most dangerous and awesome gift God ever gave man was human sovereignty: the right to exercise full free will even in defiance of God, for only through free will can true love be born, and that is what God is all about. God does not want robots. He wants to see what each of us will do with the free will He has given us. It can sometimes take a lifetime before many of us realise that the best thing we can ever do with the sovereignty God gave us is to give it right back.

The blessings and cursings

The blessings that come upon those who obey God include the following:

Blessed shalt thou be in the city, and blessed shalt thou be in the field. Blessed shall be the fruit of thy body, and the fruit of thy ground, and the fruit of thy cattle, the increase of thy kine [cattle], **and the flocks of thy sheep. Blessed shall be thy basket and thy store. Blessed shalt thou be when thou comest in, and blessed shalt thou be when thou goest out. The LORD shall cause thine enemies that rise up against thee to be smitten before thy face: they shall come out against thee one way, and flee before thee seven ways. The LORD shall command the blessing upon thee in thy storehouses, and in all that thou settest thine hand unto; and He shall bless thee in the land which the LORD thy God giveth thee. The LORD shall establish thee an holy people unto Himself, as He hath sworn unto thee, if thou shalt keep the commandments of the LORD thy God, and walk in His ways. And all people of the Earth shall see that thou art called by the name of the LORD, and they shall be afraid of thee."** (Deut 28:3-10)

And for those who rebel, here are a selection of the curses:

But it shall come to pass, if thou wilt not hearken unto the voice of the LORD thy God, to observe to do all His commandments and His statutes which I command thee this day; that all these curses shall come upon thee, and overtake thee:

Cursed shalt thou be in the city, and cursed shalt thou be in the field.

Cursed shall be thy basket and thy store.

Cursed shall be the fruit of thy body, and the fruit of thy land, the increase of thy kine, and the flocks of thy sheep.

Cursed shalt thou be when thou comest in, and cursed shalt thou be when thou goest out.

The LORD shall send upon thee cursing, vexation and rebuke, in all that thou settest thine hand unto for to do, until thou be destroyed, and until thou perish quickly; because of the wickedness of thy doings, whereby thou hast forsaken Me...

The LORD shall cause thee to be smitten before thine enemies: thou shalt go out one way against them, and flee seven ways before them: and shalt be removed into all the kingdoms of the Earth...

The LORD will smite thee with the botch [boils] **of Egypt, and with the emerods** [haemorrhoids!] **and with the scab, and with the itch, whereof thou canst not be healed...**

Thou shalt betroth a wife and another man shall lie with her...

Thine ox shall be slain before thine eyes, and thou shalt not eat thereof...

The LORD shall bring a nation against thee from far, from the end of the Earth, as swift as the eagle flieth; a nation whose tongue thou shalt not understand. A nation of fierce countenance, which shall not regard the person of the old, nor shew favour to the young: And he shall eat the fruit of thy cattle, and the fruit of thy land, until thou be destroyed: which also shall not leave thee either corn, wine, or oil, or the increase of thy kine, or flocks of thy sheep, until he have destroyed thee. (Deut 28:15...)

The Tabernacle

During his time on the mountain, Moses is also given elaborate plans for the building of a mobile sanctuary, known as the Tabernacle, which God will use to dwell among His people (Exo 25:8 -29:46). The first noteworthy observation about this strange construction is that the Tabernacle is awarded more space as a single subject in the Bible than any other, excluding the LORD Himself. There are 13 chapters in Exodus on it; 18 in Leviticus, 13 in Numbers, 2 in Deuteronomy, and 4 in Hebrews. These cover the construction of the Tabernacle, the materials used, the priesthood to administer it, and the elaborate rituals that were to be performed for God to come and dwell among them. The Creation is only given two chapters, plus a smattering of mentions in the Psalms, Job and other books. If the measure of importance God attaches to a particular subject can be determined by the space devoted to it in the Bible, our antennae should be dancing the samba when it comes to the Tabernacle. As if to reinforce its importance to the Bible's central theme of redemption, there are *seven exhortations* in the scriptures for Moses to construct the Tabernacle according the pattern he was shown by YHWH on the mount. Apparently Moses was either given a vision or a model of the finished product to study.[245] Chuck Missler notices a telling detail about the way the Tabernacle is revealed to us in the Bible:

"In Exodus, Chapters 25-40 are all about the Tabernacle, except there is a parenthetical passage in the middle: Chapters 32 -33. From our study on Revelation, we know that those parenthetical passages are very important as they set the structure of the book. In these chapters we see

[245] Ex 25:9; 25:40; 26:30; 27:8; Num 8:4; Heb 8:5; Acts 7:44

that there is the showing of the plan to Moses, the Rebellion, and then the erection of the Tabernacle. The original plan for redemption was first ordained before the foundation of the world (1 Pet 1:19-20). So the pattern was to reveal the plan to Jesus, then the fall (fall of Adam, rebellion by people), and then the erection of the Tabernacle (or Jesus made flesh and tabernacling[246] among us)."[247]

So what did the Tabernacle look like, and what's the big deal about it? If you visit Timna Park, 17 miles north of Eilat in southern Israel, there is a full-scale replica of the Tabernacle set up in this extraordinary desert national park (see photo). The big deal with the Tabernacle is that it is a model of God's redemptive plan for you and I. It reveals how we are supposed to approach the Creator of the universe, and presents the way in which sinful man may dwell in His presence. In fact, once the Tabernacle construction is completed, God will come visibly to dwell in the Tabernacle's Holy of Holies from that point on in the form of the Shekinah Glory, a type of cloud emitting an all-embracing radiance that exalts, edifies, astonishes and terrifies those who witness it (Exo 40:34-35). When the cloud that fills the Holy of Holies rises up out of the Tabernacle and moves away, that is the signal for the children of Israel to strike their massive camp, the Levites to deconstruct the Tabernacle into its portable components, and set off after it, the Ark of the Covenant leading the way (Num 10:33-36).

The Tabernacle reflects Yeshua *Ha-Mashiach* at every turn, in every detail of the design. Jesus Christ's model of redemption is described right down to the types of materials used in the construction and the colours employed to embellish it (Psa 40:7; FG 5:39). The subject of the Tabernacle is avoided by almost all pastors, priests, ministers and Bible studies today as a dry and archaic subject not relevant for the modern age. Nothing could be further from the truth. Let's take a quick but privileged tour.

OVERVIEW OF THE COMPLEX

The Tabernacle is a portable sanctuary to be carried by the Israelites and set up whenever they make camp. It is the place where YHWH Himself will dwell with them, and the mobile temple the children of Israel will approach to sacrifice for their sins. When the

---

[246] FG 1:14: the Greek word used for 'dwelt' in this verse is literally 'tabernacled'

[247] Missler, Chuck, *Exodus notes*, op. cit., pp.115-116

multitudes which make up the Exodus camp, the twelve tribes of Israel are arrayed around the central site of the Tabernacle in a very specific pattern we will examine later. As you will see from the photo, the Tabernacle complex itself is simple enough to behold. It's rectangular in shape and comprises three spaces:

THE OUTER COURT: dimensions 150 x 75 feet.[248] The complex's perimeter wall is curtained off by A WHITE LINEN FENCE supported by pillars. Within the OUTER COURT are the following items: the BRONZE ALTAR, THE BRONZE LAVER, and SLAUGHTER TABLES. It is lit by daylight.

THE HOLY PLACE: The Tabernacle sanctuary itself, which is the building, takes up the western half of the complex and is divided into two enclosed spaces within: THE HOLY PLACE and THE HOLY OF HOLIES - space ratio 2:1. The HOLY PLACE (30 x 15 feet) has the following items within: THE GOLDEN LAMPSTAND, THE TABLE OF SHOWBREAD, and THE GOLDEN ALTAR OF INCENSE. THE HOLY PLACE is lit by the seven-stemmed 'Menorah' LAMPSTAND.

THE HOLY OF HOLIES: Separated from THE HOLY PLACE by THE VEIL, God's inner sanctuary measures just 15 x 15 feet. It contains the following: THE ARK OF THE COVENANT (remember *Raiders of the Lost Ark*?) with a separate piece on top: THE MERCY SEAT. There is no light within the HOLY OF HOLIES other than God's SHEKINAH GLORY, which illuminates this most sacred place.

How wild is all this? Our Designer is up to strange stuff again, which means we should dig to learn more (Prov 25:2). The Tabernacle is one big *remez,* so let's cautiously approach from the outside in our capacity as a Levite priest and unravel the mystery.

THE OUTER COURT (Exo 27:9-19)

Threading our way through the multitude of tents that make up the enormous desert camp of the children of Israel, we get to the centre and approach an enclosure almost twice the size of an American football field. The outer court enclosure (150 x 75 feet) is demarked by a white linen fence approximately 7.5 feet high (5 cubits) supported by 60 pillars (we assume made of acacia wood), which

---

[248] There is some dissention among scholars as to the precise dimensions of the Biblical cubit. The ancient Egyptian cubit was taken as the distance between the tip of the middle finger and the elbow, though this produces a variety of sizes (17-25 inches) depending on the forearm length. Cubit rods have been discovered, which standardised the measure in the ancient world.

have silver capitals (tops) and are set in bronze sockets. These pillars in turn are given strength and support by cords and bronze pegs.[249]

Silver, we shall learn, is a model for the blood of redemption, and bronze represents acquittal after judgment, since it is one of the metals that can withstand fire (judgment). The pegs are likened to bronze nails providing structure and strength for the enclosure. The white linen fence is a barrier to us and tall enough so we can't peek over. In fact, we can't see anything other than the white of God's righteousness - a terrifying prospect for sinful man (Isa 6:1-9; Luke 5:1-9). But notice that the righteousness is represented by fine-twined linen, celebrating Christ's redemptive death.[250] Notice also that there is only one gate/door/entrance at the eastern end of the complex; you can't just show up and enter the Tabernacle from any direction. This entrance/gate is 30 feet wide and demarked not by pure white, but by a screen comprising the startlingly bright colours of blue, scarlet, purple and white, the colours of righteous kingship. Standing in front of this sole gate, accessible only via the Camp of Judah, we are facing west, the opposite direction to the sun-worshipping pagans. This gate is Jesus Christ, who descended from the tribe of Judah, and He has a few things to tell us about the way in:

"I am the way, the truth, and the life: no man cometh unto the Father, but by Me." (FG 14:6) I.e. no other religious beliefs, no other path to Heaven!!

"I am the door: by Me if any man enter in, he shall be saved, and shall go in and out, and find pasture." (FG 10:9)

"And I say unto you, 'Ask, and it shall be given you; seek, and ye shall find; knock, and it shall be opened unto you.' " (Luke 11:9, NKJV)

"Enter by the narrow gate, for wide is the gate and broad is the way that leads to destruction, and there are many that go in by it. Because narrow is the gate and difficult is the way which leads to life, and there are few who find it." (Matt 7:13-14, NKJV)

"Not everyone who says to Me, 'LORD, LORD,' [i.e. Christians] **shall enter the kingdom of heaven, but he who does the will of My Father in Heaven. Many will say to Me in that day, 'LORD, LORD,**

---

[249] Exo 35:18; Ezra 9:8; Isa 22:23; 54:2

[250] Mark 15:46; Luke 24:12; Rev 15:6; 19:8,14. Christ's tomb coverings, made of linen, are left behind at the Resurrection. A search on 'linen' in the Bible is revealing. In *Origins IV – Tetelestai*, we will examine the identity of the man who fled the arresting mob in Gethsemane, apparently clad in nothing but a linen cloth. When the mob laid hold of him, he escaped naked, leaving the linen cloth behind him (Mark 14:51-52).

have we not prophesied in Your name, cast out many demons in Your name, and done many wonders in Your name?' And then I will declare to them, 'I never knew you; depart from Me, you who practise lawlessness." (Matt 7:21-23, NKJV)

Then one said to Him, "LORD, are there few who are saved?" And He said to them, "Strive to enter through the narrow gate, for many, I say to you, will seek to enter and will not be able." (Luke 13:23-24, NKJV)

"I said therefore unto you, that ye shall die in your sins: for if ye believe not that I am He, ye shall die in your sins." (FG 8:24)

Notice that it is down to *us* to make the choice to enter the Tabernacle and into God's presence. *God won't make us do it.* He will never violate the free will and sovereignty He gave man. There is just one problem if we decide to enter: our sin before a righteous Creator.

THE BRONZE ALTAR (EXO 27:1-8)

We step through the entrance into the outer court. Before us, towards the western end of the enclosure, is the Tabernacle building proper. Between us and the Tabernacle, however, is the BRONZE ALTAR and the BRONZE LAVER. In fact, everything outside the Tabernacle building is bronze, symbolising acquittal after judgment.

We cannot proceed further into God's presence without cleansing ourselves of sin in the only way God has decreed: by the shedding of innocent blood. We have brought a lamb with us, so we offer it to the priest presiding at the BRONZE ALTAR. Remember Abel bringing his bloodworthy sacrifice before God? Abel offered God the firstborn of his flock. Cain, on the other hand, brought the fruit of the ground (Gen 4:1-5). Cain's gift was rejected on the grounds that it came from the cursed ground and comprised the fruits of Cain's own labour, which can never atone (pay the penalty) for sin. The Cain and Abel message is this: man cannot *atone* for his own sin by works; it must be paid for by the shed blood of an innocent. And God will provide Himself the Lamb (Gen 22:8). Way back in Gen 4, God models the eventual sacrifice of Himself, the Lamb of God, on the *firstborn* of Abel's flock (*cf.* FG 1:29).

We take our animal sacrifice to the priest. We lay our hands on the poor animal and the priest kills it and offers the blood on the BRONZE ALTAR. The altar tools too are made of bronze, the symbol of God's method of judgment: the shovels, the small basins for the blood, the forks and the firepans. This is tough stuff for animal lovers, terrible for us to witness, but in a modern age where sinning is not only encouraged by law but avidly celebrated in our entertainment media, we should soberly reflect that God's view of wrongdoing has never changed (Mal 3:6). The LORD takes blood atonement extremely seriously. Without the shedding of blood there can be no forgiveness of sins (Lev 17:11; Heb 9:22). Not only are they His animals, Yeshua was His only Son, who freely gave His innocent blood in a once-and-for-all atonement for all mankind's sin (Lev 17:11; FG 10:18; 1 Cor 15:21-22). *Bible History* describes the scene in more detail:

"We are going to see blood all over the Old Testament. Since the beginning there were those who didn't agree and called it a 'slaughterhouse religion', but God's warning still stands just as he warned Cain. So throughout the Old Testament blood is everywhere. At certain times during the Passover celebration there were over 250,000 lambs slain with blood everywhere, all over the Temple, with so much blood flowing down the brook Kidron that it was called a 'horrifying sight'. Seeing the lamb which had become a household pet for four days, and then watching it kick and scream and be slaughtered in the presence of the family and the children was an object lesson that would forever make your skin crawl.

"Apart from the bronze altar there was no approach to God. In the blood covenant with Yahweh, the innocent animal represented the sinner and took his place on the altar. That is why there was the [collective] laying on of the hands upon the innocent sacrifice and then the violent slicing of the throat. A graphic imagery that would make your skin crawl which brought an incredible awareness of the awesomeness of sin, and the payment being death. Only then could you be accepted and declared clean. The blood of the animal would cover until God Himself (The Lamb of God) would come to take sin away once and for all." [251]

Not a sight a parent, or a child, would likely forget. God does not want us to forget it. He wants us to see sin the way He sees it: as the defining predicament of man. So, did God know we would mess up from the outset? Of course He did. Because God created us to share in His Creation (Gen 1:26) and to love Him, and love must be freely given, or it isn't love. And you can't have love without man being given the free will to grant that love *or withhold it*. God has a predicament too. In creating man's capacity to love Him, He is also giving man the free will to reject and hate Him. The most terrifying gift we have been given is our free will, the sovereignty of man; and

[251] www.bible-history.com/tabernacle/TAB4Blood_Atonement.htm

with that comes our right to mess up. And God has provided for that. He has the whole picture. We don't.

THE BRONZE LAVER (EXO 38:8)

Between where we are standing at the BRONZE ALTAR and the TABERNACLE proper is the BRONZE LAVER, a large washbasin on a stand. This was made from the bronze mirrors which the Israelite women brought out of Egypt. Interestingly, no measurements for it are given, speaking to some scholars of the LAVER'S limitless capacity for cleansing and spiritual regeneration. Any regular Israelite would not proceed further than the sacrifice at the altar. However, in our capacity as a Levite priest officiating in the Tabernacle, we must undergo ceremonial cleansing and purification before entering THE HOLY PLACE, and this will also be required upon departing.

Just as the Israelite women stared at themselves in the bronze mirrors, so we peer down now and ponder the reflection of our sinful selves in the water, perhaps flecked with the blood of the recent sacrifice. We wash our hands (our service, deeds) and feet (our spiritual walk), becoming ceremonially clean before the Creator. Failure to do this, and then making a burnt offering before the LORD in the Tabernacle, will result in immediate death at God's hand (Exo 30:19-21).

Water speaks of the Word and thus Yeshua, the ultimate sacrifice. In our worlds of bronze and judgment, we can partake of the divine and royal world we are about to enter (gold) not only through the once-and-for-all washing and consecration Aaron and his sons underwent (Exo 40:11-16), but through regular spiritual regeneration via God's Word. When an august member of the Sanhedrin, the supreme Jewish religious council, came to visit Jesus one evening, the exchange went as follows:

There was a man of the Pharisees, named Nicodemus, a ruler of the Jews. The same came to Jesus by night, and said unto Him, "Rabbi, we know that thou art a teacher come from God: for no man can do these miracles that thou doest, except God be with him."

Jesus answered and said unto him, "Verily, verily, I say unto thee, Except a man be born again, he cannot see the kingdom of God."

Nicodemus saith unto Him, "How can a man be b[illegible] is old? Can he enter the second time into his mothe[illegible] born?"

Jesus answered, "Verily, verily, I say unto thee, Except a man be born of water and of the Spirit, he cannot enter into the kingdom of God. That which is born of the flesh is flesh; and that which is of the Spirit is spirit. Marvel not that I said unto thee, 'Ye must be born again.' " (FG 3:1-7)

Sobering, isn't it, that Nicodemus is learning these truths from none other than the Creator of the universe Himself (FG 1:1-4,14), whom John the Baptist previously called **"The Lamb of God which taketh away the sin of the world"** (FG 1:29). God certainly has provided Himself a Lamb (Gen 22:8). The above exchange bothers Nicodemus, and yet as a Pharisee well trained in the Law, he would have been completely familiar with the BRONZE LAVER and the requirement regularly to wash himself clean before God. Nicodemus would later become convinced of Yeshua's true nature as the Word made flesh and the Lamb of God slain for the sin of the world when he brings a mixture of myrrh and aloes for Christ's burial anointing (FG 19:39)

The above passage is not the only occasion Yeshua speaks of water and the Word:

"Now ye are clean through the word which I have spoken unto you." (FG 15:3)

And He states the following on the last day of that great autumn harvest festival, the Feast of Tabernacles (*Sukkot* – 15th Tishrei): **"He that believeth on Me, as the scripture hath said, out of his belly shall flow rivers of living water."** (FG 7:38)

Bible History comments:

"When Jesus stood and cried, "If any man thirst let him come to Me and drink" [FG 7:37], it was on the great day of the feast of tabernacles when the Jewish leaders were pouring the water from the pool of Siloam onto the pavement of the temple, symbolizing that someday God will pour out the real water from heaven on His people as promised through the prophet Ezekiel." [252]

"For I will take you from among the heathen, and gather you out of all countries, and will bring you into your own land. Then will I sprinkle clean water upon you, and ye shall be clean: from all your filthiness, and from all your idols, will I cleanse you. A new heart also will I give you, and a new spirit will I put within you: and I will take away the stony heart out of your flesh, and I will

---

[252] www.bible-history.com/tabernacle/TAB4The_Bronze_Laver.htm

give you an heart of flesh. And I will put My Spirit within you, and cause you to walk in My statutes, and ye shall keep My judgments, and do them. And ye shall dwell in the land that I gave to your fathers; and ye shall be My people, and I will be your God." (Eze 36:24-28)

And to the woman at the well, Jesus says: **"Whosoever drinketh of this water shall thirst again: But whosoever drinketh of the water that I shall give him shall never thirst; but the water that I shall give him shall be in him a well of water springing up into everlasting life."** (FG 4:13-14)

THE HOLY PLACE

The Tabernacle building itself is the focus of the entire complex and measures 45 feet by 15 feet and 15 feet high. The building comprises two areas within: THE HOLY PLACE and THE HOLY OF HOLIES. THE HOLY PLACE is the first space encountered, and at 30 x 15 feet is twice the size of THE HOLY OF HOLIES (15 x 15 feet). The two spaces are separated by four pillars and a thick VEIL.

As we approach, we are struck by how drab, even ugly the outside badger-skin coverings of the building are.[253] Apart from the brightly coloured entrance screen before us, the Tabernacle from the outside has no form nor comeliness that we should desire it (*cf.* Isa 53:2). We push in through the purple, blue and scarlet woven screen (entering into the royal presence), which is supported by five (five = grace) pillars of acacia wood (wood = man/humanity) overlaid with gold (gold = royalty/the divine nature) anchored in five sockets of bronze (bronze/brass = judgment).

Acacia wood comes from the shittah tree, a native of the Sinai peninsula and Jordan valley. It is a thorny, 20–30 foot tree with a pale greenish or reddish bark, which is virtually indestructible to insects. At the base of the 1–4 inch feathery leaves there are two straight, light grey thorns, growing to 3 – 8 inches in length. The blossoms are displayed in round, bright yellow clusters approximately half an inch in diameter. Shittim wood was used by the Egyptians to make mummy caskets because of its hardy, long-lived and virtually indestructible nature.

God has chosen a thought-provoking material to provide the basic structure for his Tabernacle. Thorns are Levitically a type of sin (Gen 3:17-18). Yeshua spoke to Moses out of the burning *seneh* or

---

[253] Some scholars believe these to be porpoise skins.

thorn bush in Exo 3:2, which was not consumed by fire (judgment). Christ will wear a crown of thorns on the cross in the NT, symbolising His bearing the sins of the world, and those sins being judged. The non-perishable property of shittim wood reminds us of the incorruptibility of Christ, even as a man who went to the grave (Psa 16:10; Acts 2:31; 13:36-37; Gal 6:8). In the construction of the Tabernacle, acacia or thorn bush wood is taken and overlaid with gold, symbolising the God-man made sin for us, who nevertheless has God's divine nature.

Once inside the building, our eyes adjust to the very different light within, and we take stock of what is before us. Our first impression is of the royalty of gold everywhere and other astonishing colours above us. The solid inside walls of the Tabernacle are made of acacia wood frames overlaid with pure gold (wood/gold = the God-man) (Exo 26:26-28), rather than the plain, wooden appearance of the planks we saw on the outside. These frames are slotted together inside at the base using heavy, bifurcated silver sockets or 'tenons' (silver = the blood of redemption). Chuck Missler explains:

"These boards are the height of the Tabernacle [15 feet], they are side by side. Each board is sitting on silver blocks, (some estimate that the blocks weighed over 100 lbs each). 96 are here described. This foundation seems a bit excessive for a portable building. Silver (Ex 30:13; Lev 27:3) is redemption money (Lev 17:10-11; 1 Pet 1:18; 1 Cor 6:20; 3). Silver in the Old Testament is equivalent to blood, it is the blood money used for redemption (a ransom money paid to God). It was this silver that was brought together to make the foundation of the Tabernacle. Silver Levitically speaks of blood, Matt 27:3-4. Thus, everything in the entire Tabernacle sat on silver sockets; 1 Cor 3:11, the entire structure rests upon the blood of Jesus Christ. Every detail points to the cross." [254]

Since these 96 sockets, each comprising an estimated 100 lbs of pure silver (£15,279/US$23,808),[255] are sunk into the ground and not visible to the human eye, we cannot readily appreciate the price of God's redemption. The effect of the framed boards is to provide a highly solid structure on the three sides not occupying the entrance screen, which also provides for the hanging of the internal curtain-work that amazes us.

---

[254] Missler, Chuck, *Exodus notes*, p.124
[255] As of 20th July 2015

The Tabernacle has four layers of overhead covering. Starting with the fine-twined inner covering made of linen decorated with needlework, each subsequent covering is slightly larger than the previous layer, completely covering it. From the inside working outward:

LINEN: blue (the Heavenlies), purple (majesty) and scarlet (Earthly glory), decorated with artistic designs of the four-faced Cherubim, representing the holiness of God and the executors of His righteous will/government (Gen 3:22-24; Eze 1:4-14; Rev 4:6-8)

GOAT HAIR: Goats are Levitically a type of sin or sin offering (the scapegoat).[256]

RAM SKIN: The ram speaks of the substitutionary sacrifice, as with Isaac on Mount Moriah (Gen 22:13). In the Garden of Eden, God clothed Adam and Eve with skins as a symbolic covering for their sin (Gen 3:21).

BADGER/PORPOISE SKIN: The outer layer, visible from beyond. This type of skin is tough and durable, and was sometimes used in the ancient world for shoes, linking this material Levitically to a person's walk. The footwear of the Israelites did not wear out throughout the 40 years of the Exodus (Deut 8:4; 29:5). Since every original Israelite over 20, apart from Caleb and Joshua, perished in the desert during this period, the footwear God provided outlasted the owner!

THE GOLDEN LAMPSTAND ('MENORAH') (EXO 25:31-40)

The only light available in the HOLY PLACE is provided by a seven-stemmed LAMPSTAND on the left as we enter. Known by Jews as the menorah, this artefact is often erroneously referred to as a 'candlestand' in some translations. Significantly, the menorah burns oil, not wax. God gives very specific instructions to Moses for its construction:

- The menorah is to be hammered (beaten) out from one block of solid gold weighing a talent (75-100 lbs).[257] This equates to a value, in today's markets, of around £416,000 (US$660,000) *for this one artefact alone*
- The wick-trimmers and their trays are also to be fashioned of pure gold

[256] Num 7:16; 15:24; 28:22; 29:5; Lev 4:23-31; 16:20-22; 23:19

[257] Different talent weights were employed in the ancient world. A gold talent was believed to be approximately the same weight as a person.

- The lampstand is to comprise a central shaft with six branches coming off it, providing seven sources of light – the whole to be borne on a base
- Each branch is decorated with knobs, and ends in a small oil bowl the shape of an opened almond flower
- The oil used should be pure, beaten olive oil (Lev 24:2)
- God apparently shows Moses a detailed menorah model on the mountain (Exo 25:40)

The menorah is venerated by Jews the world over, and a five metre-high, bronze depiction of the famous lampstand stands in the Rose Garden in front of the Knesset (Israel's parliament) in Jerusalem.[258] The Jews view the menorah as symbolising the sevenfold Spirit of God,[259] and see the mission of Israel as helping to bring this light to the world (Isa 42:6-7; 49:6). Today, alas, most Israelis hold their religion in far less esteem than their tradition, and those who do adhere to the old ways are understandably unenamoured of the remarkable connections the golden lampstand of the Exodus Tabernacle has with New Testament scripture, especially concerning Yeshua *Ha-Mashiach*:

"Abide in me, and I in you. As the branch cannot bear fruit of itself, except it abide in the vine; no more can ye, except ye abide in Me. <u>I am the vine, ye are the branches</u>: He that abideth in Me, and I in him, the same bringeth forth much fruit: for without Me ye can do nothing." (FG 15:4-5)

Then spake Jesus again unto them, saying, "I am the light of the world: he that followeth Me shall not walk in darkness, but shall have the light of life." (FG 8:12)

"I must work the works of him that sent Me, while it is day: the night cometh, when no man can work. As long as I am in the world, I am the light of the world." (FG 9:4-5)

In the beginning was the Word, and the Word was with God, and the Word was God. The same was in the beginning with God. All things were made by Him; and without him was not anything made that was made. In Him was life; <u>and the life was the light of men</u>. <u>And the light shineth in darkness; and the darkness comprehended it not</u>. (FG 1:1-5)

The lampstand has seven stems (seven = God's number, completion). Notice the menorah has a central stem – Jesus – and the

---

[258] http://en.wikipedia.org/wiki/Knesset_Menorah

[259] Isa 11:1-2; *cf.* Rev 1:4; *cf.* 3:1; 4:5; 5:6

other six branches come off the central stem – they don't stand alone (six = number of man[260]). We are instructed by Jesus Himself to **"Let your light so shine before men, that they may see your good works, and glorify your Father which is in heaven."** (Matt 5:16). The menorah uses oil as a source of energy for the light. Oil Levitically speaks of the Holy Spirit, or that which anoints. The lampstand radiates the light but is not the source of the light, the oil is. The menorah is a parable for redemption itself:

If we say that we have fellowship with Him and walk in darkness, we lie, and do not the truth. But if we walk in the light, as He is in the light, we have fellowship one with another, and the blood of Jesus Christ His Son cleanseth us from all sin. (1 John 1:6-7)

The almond (*Heb:* 'awakening') is the first tree in Israel to bloom as a result of the light of spring. Thus the almond is the 'firstfruit' of Israel, reflective of the Feast of Firstfruits, which was being celebrated on the very day of Christ's resurrection in the spring (Passover). The apostle Paul writes:

But now is Christ risen from the dead, and become the firstfruits of them that slept. For since by man came death, by man came also the resurrection of the dead. For as in Adam all die, even so in Christ shall all be made alive. But every man in his own order: Christ the firstfruits; afterward they that are Christ's at his coming. (1 Cor 15:20-23)

Christ was beaten. The menorah is made of one beaten work. The oil powering the light is derived from pure, beaten olive oil (Spirit).

THE TABLE OF SHOWBREAD (EXO 25:23-30)

On the right as we enter into the HOLY PLACE, we see an elaborate golden table bearing twelve cakes of bread. The detailed instructions for the construction of this 'table of presence' are also given to Moses on the mountain. The table is 3 feet x 1.5 feet, and stands 2.25 feet tall. It is made of acacia wood overlaid with pure gold, speaking once again of the dual nature of God come in the flesh: wood (man) and gold (the divine). The implements used with the table are also fashioned of pure gold: its dishes, pans, pitchers and bowls. Rings are built into the legs so two poles can be passed through for bearing the table on journeys.

---

[260] The sevenfold 'heptadic' structure is evident throughout the Bible. 777 represents God's ultimate power/government. 666 is man's ultimate counterfeit in Rev 13:18.

The purpose of the table is always to display twelve cakes of showbread before the LORD in two rows of six. These loaves represent the twelve tribes of Israel and each is the same as the other, revealing no partiality. The bread is made of fine flour (derived from the earth like man - Gen 2:7), is baked (endures suffering), is unleavened (made sinless once borne on the acacia wood and gold table representing Christ), and sprinkled with frankincense (the prayers of the chosen). If you examine the Hebrew of Lev 24:5, these cakes are perforated or pierced (Strongs H2471 - *'challah'*). Every Sabbath, fresh loaves are provided by Aaron (representing the priesthood), and the priests are permitted to eat the old loaves, but only in the HOLY PLACE (Lev 24:5-9). The showbread is reflective of the manna the Israelites are eating in the desert, and the Table of Showbread is again a model of Jesus Christ:

And Jesus said unto them, "I am the bread of life: he that cometh to Me shall never hunger; and he that believeth on Me shall never thirst." (FG 6:35)

"I am the living bread which came down from heaven: if any man eat of this bread, he shall live for ever: and the bread that I will give is My flesh, which I will give for the life of the world.... This is that bread which came down from heaven: not as your fathers did eat manna, and are dead: he that eateth of this bread shall live forever." (FG 6:51,58)

Notice we are told that the priests' duties are to stand and minister continually before the LORD. This is not a fellowship table since there is no provision for seating. The writer of Hebrews picks up on this theme in the New Testament:

And every priest standeth daily ministering and offering oftentimes the same sacrifices, which can never take away sins. But this Man, after He had offered one sacrifice for sins for ever, sat down on the right hand of God; from henceforth expecting till his enemies be made His footstool. For by one offering He hath perfected forever them that are sanctified. (Heb 10:11-14)

Jesus breaks bread with sinners, declares that He is the bread of life, and institutes the LORD's Table at the Last Supper with the bread and wine. The ridge around the Table of Showbread is fashioned as a handbreadth, so we get the image of God's hands encompassing His chosen, providing perpetual protection. Jesus states:

"And I give unto them eternal life; and they shall never perish, neither shall any man pluck them out of My hand. My Father,

which gave them Me, is greater than all; and no man is able to pluck them out of My Father's hand." (FG 10:28-29)

THE GOLDEN ALTAR OF INCENSE (Exo 30:1-10)

We've entered the HOLY PLACE, studied the GOLDEN LAMPSTAND (menorah) on the left, the TABLE OF SHOWBREAD on the right, and directly before us is THE VEIL, which curtains off the inner sanctum, or HOLY OF HOLIES. Directly before THE VEIL is the third piece of furniture in the HOLY PLACE: THE GOLDEN ALTAR OF INCENSE.

Moses receives the instructions for making this artefact also. It is to be made of pure gold, stands 3 feet high, is 1.5 feet square, and has a crown around the top with a horn on each of the corners. Further down on two sides, two rings are located to accommodate the now familiar bearing poles. The rings are of pure gold, and the poles are to be fashioned of acacia wood overlaid with gold.

Unlike the BRAZEN ALTAR outside in the courtyard, God expressly forbids any sacrifice to be made upon the GOLDEN ALTAR. Instead, a coal is to be brought in a firepan from the BRAZEN ALTAR outside, and used as an energy source to burn a particular type of incense to the LORD twice a day - morning and evening:

And the LORD said unto Moses, "Take unto thee sweet spices, stacte, and onycha, and galbanum; these sweet spices with pure frankincense: of each shall there be a like weight: And thou shalt make it a perfume, a confection after the art of the apothecary, tempered together, pure and holy: And thou shalt beat some of it very small, and put of it before the testimony in the tabernacle of the congregation, where I will meet with thee: it shall be unto you most holy. And as for the perfume which thou shalt make, ye shall not make to yourselves according to the composition thereof: it shall be unto thee holy for the LORD. Whosoever shall make like unto that, to smell thereto, shall even be cut off from his people." (Exo 30:34-38)

The officiating priest would ensure that the incense was kept burning when he tended the oil and wicks of the menorah morning and evening. Frankincense we are familiar with; the identities of the other gums/spices - stacte, onycha and galbanum - appear to be lost to us. Sprinkling this unique combination of spices onto a heat source, however, would produce an amazing fragrance, if not from the frankincense alone, and it seems probable that some of the heady aroma would escape from the Tabernacle and waft away on the wind to be sniffed by a tantalised passer-by. Given the absolute restrictions as to its use, this unique spice concoction has a special importance to the LORD, as we shall see.

At certain times, blood from the sin offering would be sprinkled seven times on the four horns of the GOLDEN ALTAR (Lev 4:5-7). Elaborate procedures also accompanied the once-a-year Yom Kippur re-cleansing when the high priest (symbolised by Aaron) would offer incense in the Holy of Holies and sprinkle blood on the four horns of the GOLDEN ALTAR (Exo 30:10; Lev 16:18-19).

Amazing Discoveries writes:

"A lamb was burned upon the brazen altar in the court each morning and evening at the time the incense was renewed upon the altar (Exodus 29:38-40). The golden altar was an 'altar of continual intercession', representing the prayers of God's people coming up before Him continually; while the brazen altar was an 'altar of continual atonement', representing the putting away and destruction of sin, the only thing that separates us from God and prevents our prayers from being answered.

"The morning and evening lamb was offered as a whole burnt offering for the entire congregation, showing their desire to put away sin and consecrate themselves to the LORD, so that their prayers could ascend from off the altar with the fragrant incense." [261]

The four horns call to mind the four camps of the children of Israel, set up strategically around the Tabernacle. The connection between the burning of incense and the love and worship of the forgiven saints rising to God is a recurrent theme in scripture, as is the Tabernacle as an earthly model of those holy things seen in the Heavenlies:

Let my prayer be set forth before thee as incense; and the lifting up of my hands as the evening sacrifice. (Psa 141:2)

And when He had taken the book, the four beasts and four and twenty elders fell down before the Lamb, having every one of them harps, and golden vials full of odours, which are the prayers of saints. (Rev 5:8)

And another angel came and stood at the altar, having a golden censer; and there was given unto him much incense, that he should offer it with the prayers of all saints upon the golden altar which was before the throne. And the smoke of the incense, which came

[261] http://amazingdiscoveries.org/the-altar-of-incense

with the prayers of the saints, ascended up before God out of the angel's hand. (Rev 8:3-4)

The GOLDEN ALTAR is an antetype for Jesus Christ as our constant mediator with a perfect God in the matter of our sin and forgiveness. In the ancient days of Moses, blood was sprayed everywhere to atone for the sin of the Israelites. The Predicament of Man is hardly different today in an age where we celebrate debauchery on prime time TV, and hold the wholesale shedding of innocent blood of babies as a lifestyle choice. We need Christ's mediation and God's forgiveness more than ever. There is but one way:

"I am the way, the truth, and the life: no man cometh unto the Father, but by Me." (FG 14:6)

"For God so loved the world, that He gave His only begotten Son, that whosoever believeth in Him should not perish, but have everlasting life. For God sent not His Son into the world to condemn the world; but that the world through Him might be saved. He that believeth on Him is not condemned: but he that believeth not is condemned already, because he hath not believed in the name of the only begotten Son of God." (FG 3:16-18)

"Ye are from beneath; I am from above: ye are of this world; I am not of this world. I said therefore unto you, that ye shall die in your sins: for if ye believe not that I am He, ye shall die in your sins." (FG 8:23-24)

My little children, these things write I unto you, that ye sin not. And if any man sin, we have an advocate with the Father, Jesus Christ the righteous: And he is the propitiation for our sins: and not for ours only, but also for the sins of the whole world. (1 John 2:1-2)

For there is one God, and one mediator between God and men, the man Christ Jesus; Who gave himself a ransom for all, to be testified in due time. (1 Tim 2:5-6)

Seeing then that we have a great high priest, that is passed into the heavens, Jesus the Son of God, let us hold fast our profession. For we have not an high priest which cannot be touched with the feeling of our infirmities; but was in all points tempted like as we are, yet without sin. Let us therefore come boldly unto the throne of grace, that we may obtain mercy, and find grace to help in time of need. (Heb 4:14-16)

But Christ being come an high priest of good things to come, by a greater and more perfect tabernacle, not made with hands, that is to say, not of this building; Neither by the blood of goats and calves,

but by his own blood he entered in once into the holy place, having obtained eternal redemption for us. For if the blood of bulls and of goats, and the ashes of an heifer sprinkling the unclean, sanctifieth to the purifying of the flesh: How much more shall the blood of Christ, who through the eternal Spirit offered himself without spot to God, purge your conscience from dead works to serve the living God? (Heb 9:11-14)

J R Miller wrote in 1888:

"At the same time that the incense was burning on the golden altar within, the sacrifice of atonement was burning on the altar of burnt-offering in the court without. The fire was carried from the sacrificial altar to kindle the incense. No other fire was permitted. The incense odour would have been an abomination to God, had not the smoke of the burnt-offering mingled and ascended with it.

"The teaching is, that there will be no sweet savour in our prayers, no acceptableness before God, unless they are cleansed by the merits of Christ's atonement. We can approach God only in the precious name of Jesus Christ, and in dependence on his sacrifice for us." [262]

THE HOLY OF HOLIES – THE VEIL (Exo 26:31-33)

The only place left for us to inspect is the section of the HOLY PLACE that has been curtained off from our view by THE VEIL. No-one is permitted either to touch THE VEIL or enter the HOLY OF HOLIES but the high priest, and then only once a year on Yom Kippur, the Day of Atonement, and then only after great ceremonial preparation. Once again, God gives Moses intricate instructions on THE VEIL'S elaborate preparation:

And thou shalt make a vail of blue, and purple, and scarlet, and fine twined linen of cunning work: with cherubim shall it be made: And thou shalt hang it upon four pillars of shittim [acacia] **wood overlaid with gold: their hooks shall be of gold, upon the four sockets of silver. And thou shalt hang up the vail under the taches** [clasps], **that thou mayest bring in thither within the vail the ark of the testimony: and the vail shall divide unto you between the holy place and the most holy.** (Exo 26:31-33)

Notice that God ordains a barrier to be set up between the people and Himself. THE VEIL can only be traversed by the high priest, and then only once a year to make atonement for the sins of the nation.

---

[262] www.gracegems.org/Miller/sweet_fragrance_of_prayer.htm

THE VEIL again bears all the hallmarks of the dual 'Godman' nature of Yeshua *ha-Mashiach* in the acacia wood overlaid with gold, the whole supported on four sockets, or bases, of silver, emblematic of the blood of redemption. It will be this VEIL, dramatically thickened in Herod's embellishment of the second Temple, that will be supernaturally ripped from top to bottom when Yeshua dies on the cross for the sins of the world (Matt 27:51).[263]

Throughout Old Testament Judaism, this ritual of sin atonement, represented by all the accoutrements of the Tabernacle and subsequent temples, reflects the mission Yeshua Himself will fulfil on our behalf with His sacrifice:

Search the scriptures; for in them ye think ye have eternal life: and they are they which testify of Me (FG 5:39).

Then said I, "Lo, I come: in the volume of the book it is written of Me, I delight to do Thy will, O My God: yea, Thy law is within My heart." (Psa 40:7; *cf:* Heb 10:7-12)

In the OT, only the high priest can officiate this contact between man and God, and then only once a year on the Day of Atonement. In the NT, our new High Priest, Yeshua *Ha-Mashiach,* fulfils the Law and becomes our *only* Mediator through His once-and-for-all sacrifice on the cross; no more sacrifices of bulls, goats and lambs required (Heb 10:18). He is our VEIL, emblematic of the flesh, supported on sockets of silver representing His blood of redemption, only *now* through whom we can gain direct access to our Creator, washed clean of sin by the blood. Just as there was no other way into God's presence (the HOLY OF HOLIES) but by the high priest through the VEIL, our new High Priest becomes the only path now to the Father. Notice after the cross, THE VEIL is torn down (*viz:* flesh torn) and man is given direct access to God via Christ *alone* for atonement of sin, forgiveness, salvation and glorification (FG 8:24; 10:9; 14:6, etc.). The writer of Hebrews picks up on the significance of this torn VEIL/torn flesh model, as well as the joy of this removal of the hitherto legalistic and impenetrable barrier to God:

Having therefore, brethren, boldness to enter into the holiest by the blood of Jesus, by a new and living way, which He hath consecrated for us, through the veil, that is to say, His flesh; And having an high priest over the house of God; Let us draw near with

---

[263] Some researchers believe that the second Temple's veil was up to 18 inches thick, so tearing it from *top to bottom* (a non-trivial task), could only be accomplished by God Himself.

a true heart in full assurance of faith, having our hearts sprinkled from an evil conscience, and our bodies washed with pure water. (Heb 10:19-22)

And:

Looking unto Jesus the Author and Finisher of our faith; who for the joy that was set before Him endured the cross, despising the shame, and is set down at the right hand of the throne of God. (Heb 12:2)

HOLY OF HOLIES - THE ARK OF THE COVENANT AND MERCY SEAT (Ex 25:10-22)

Gaining access through THE VEIL, the first thing we notice about the Holy of Holies is how small it is: 15 x 15 x 15 feet. There is only one object within - in fact, to be technically accurate, two: the ARK OF THE COVENANT, and the MERCY SEAT, which sits on top of it. The only light within comes from God Himself - the very light of Creation known as the Shekinah Glory.

The purpose of the Tabernacle is to provide a place where man can meet God. The very heart of God's holy presence among men is the ARK OF THE COVENANT. God gives the now familiar, detailed instructions for the Ark's construction to Moses on the mount:

"And they shall make an ark of shittim [acacia] **wood: two cubits and a half shall be the length thereof, and a cubit and a half the breadth thereof, and a cubit and a half the height thereof. And thou shalt overlay it with pure gold, within and without shalt thou overlay it, and shalt make upon it a crown of gold round about.**

And thou shalt cast four rings of gold for it, and put them in the four corners thereof; and two rings shall be in the one side of it, and two rings in the other side of it. And thou shalt make staves of shittim [acacia] **wood, and overlay them with gold. And thou shalt put the staves into the rings by the sides of the ark, that the ark may be borne with them. The staves shall be in the rings of the ark: they shall not be taken from it.**

And thou shalt put into the ark the testimony which I shall give thee. And thou shalt make a mercy seat of pure gold: two cubits and a half shall be the length thereof, and a cubit and a half the breadth thereof. And thou shalt make two cherubim of gold, of beaten work shalt thou make them, in the two ends of the mercy seat. And make one cherub on the one end, and the other cherub on the other end: even of the mercy seat shall ye make the cherubim on the two ends thereof. And the cherubim shall stretch forth their wings on high,

covering the mercy seat with their wings, and their faces shall look one to another; toward the mercy seat shall the faces of the cherubim be.

And thou shalt put the mercy seat above upon the ark; and in the ark thou shalt put the testimony that I shall give thee. And there I will meet with thee, and I will commune with thee from above the mercy seat, from between the two cherubims which are upon the ark of the testimony, of all things which I will give thee in commandment unto the children of Israel." (Exo 25:10-22)

Some features to note:

- Once more, the Ark is a detailed model of Jesus Christ right down to the acacia wood overlaid with pure gold, symbolising the Messiah's dual 'Godman' nature: 100% human, 100% God
- The Ark of the Covenant is a rectangular wooden chest covered with pure gold, measuring 3.75 x 2.25 feet. The lid of the Ark is known as the Mercy Seat and is fashioned from pure gold (no wood). The Mercy Seat is referred to separately from the Ark a number of times in scripture, so is viewed as an individual artefact by scholars
- To open the Ark or even touch it, apart from using the carrying staves, is to invite instant death (Num 4:15). King David will get a nasty shock in connection with this property centuries later, as will an entire Jewish community who decide to have a peek inside (2 Sam 6:6)
- God will dwell between the Cherubim above the Mercy Seat, and a cloud will sit above the Tabernacle over the Holy of Holies as a symbol to all of His presence among them
- Contained in the Ark will be the two tablets of the Decalogue (Ten Commandments), symbolising the Law. A golden pot holding an omer of manna[264] will also be held within (*viz:* the Bread of Life) as a testimony to future generations. Later, Aaron's rod will be placed in the repository after it buds and blossoms in a single night, bearing ripe almonds, validating God's choice of Aaron and the Levites for the priesthood (Num 17:1-10; Heb 9:4). However, by the time the Ark is

[264] Under ancient Israel's dry measures system, an omer works out to today's 3.64 litres (6.4 pints). Since the Israelites were required to collect an omer of manna per person per day (Exo 16:16), this is taken to be the amount of manna an adult could consume on a daily basis.

placed in Solomon's temple centuries later, only the two tablets of stone will remain within (2 Chron 5:7-10)

- As the holiest artefacts in the Tabernacle, the Ark and Mercy Seat are where the high priest will come once a year on Yom Kippur to sprinkle the blood on the Mercy Seat to atone for the sins of the nation (Lev 16:14-15). God dwells between the Cherubim, so we have a picture of God looking down at the broken Law through the blood of sacrifice, and so stays the judgment of the Cherubim upon His people
- The Ark will be God dwelling among His people, even as Yeshua will do centuries later (FG 1:14; 10:4)
- The Ark will go before the children of Israel on their adventures. In fact, it will be carried about half a mile ahead of the column.
- Whenever the Ark is mobile, elaborate preparations are made to cover it from the eyes of the people, even the priests
- The Ark will terrify everyone, especially Israel's enemies, and will bring blessings and curses in the centuries to come (1 Sam 5)
- The Ark of the Covenant is last mentioned in 2 Chron 35:3 in the days of King Josiah. Thereafter it disappears from the Biblical record around the Babylonian conquest of Jerusalem in 587 BC. Various theories abound as to whether the Ark was destroyed, taken to safety, whether its current location is known, and even whether the Ark has a significant role to play in the future. We will examine these concepts as we go

Bible History summarises:

"The crown of gold around the top of the ark speaks of the Lord Jesus Christ as King of kings and LORD of lords. Jesus overcame the onslaught of opposition that was set against Him His whole life by the religious leaders, the wealthy Jewish aristocracy, Rome itself, and even all the power of the enemy. He overcame even death itself and rose triumphantly and was given a crown, and glory, and honor, because He is the King. According to John it was Jesus who Isaiah saw seated on the throne of glory with the angels crying 'holy, holy, holy'.

"The unbroken tables of stone set forth Jesus as the One who perfectly kept the Law and never broke God's Commandments. The Bible says that He 'committed no sin, nor was deceit found in His mouth.' Jesus felt the pressure of temptation at its full intensity yet He never sinned. Even the look in His eye and the tone of His voice reflected the very perfections of the holiness of God Himself. Aaron's rod that budded also speaks of Jesus. Something that had died and supernaturally came to life again. Jesus said, 'I am the resurrection and the life.' The golden pot of manna speaks of Jesus as the bread of life who came down from heaven to bring food, the Word of God, to a world in darkness and dying of hunger." [265]

God leads the Exodus generation

Exodus 40 covers God's detailed instructions for the construction of the Tabernacle, along with the installation of the artefacts. Once the tabernacle was completed, what followed next must have been awesome to behold:

Then a cloud covered the tent of the congregation, and the glory of the LORD filled the tabernacle. And Moses was not able to enter into the tent of the congregation, because the cloud abode thereon, and the glory of the LORD filled the tabernacle.

And when the cloud was taken up from over the tabernacle, the children of Israel went onward in all their journeys: But if the cloud were not taken up, then they journeyed not till the day that it was taken up. For the cloud of the LORD was upon the tabernacle by day, and fire was on it by night, in the sight of all the house of Israel, throughout all their journeys. (Exo 40:34-38)

Just as God has led the Israelites from Egypt to Sinai thus far in a pillar of cloud by day and a pillar of fire by night, so He will continue to lead them all the way to the Promised Land; a visible presence and comfort to any of the multitude who cast their eyes towards the Tabernacle and behold this astonishing sight.

The order of the camp

There are some fascinating details in the opening chapters of the Book of Numbers which most people miss. In the recently completed Tabernacle, God instructs Moses to take a census of the men of fighting age - twenty years old and above - for the purpose of putting together an army for the forthcoming invasion of Canaan. A reader of these opening two chapters of Numbers might yawn at all the detail of names and so many thousands of fighting men for each tribe, and may even be tempted to swish ahead a few pages to get to some action. If so, they will miss something remarkable. The results of the census are as follows:

---

[265] www.bible-history.com/tabernacle/TAB4The_Ark_of_the_Covenant.htm

Reuben - 46,500 fighting men
Simeon - 59,300
Gad - 45,650
Judah - 74,600
Issachar - 54,400
Zebulun - 57,400
Dan - 62,700
Asher - 41,500
Naphtali - 53,400
Ephraim - 40,500
Manasseh - 32,200
Benjamin - 35,400
Total fighting strength: 603,550.[266]

The Levites are excluded from the census, according to God's orders:

"Only thou shalt not number the tribe of Levi, neither take the sum of them among the children of Israel: But thou shalt appoint the Levites over the tabernacle of testimony, and over all the vessels thereof, and over all things that belong to it: they shall bear the tabernacle, and all the vessels thereof; and they shall minister unto it, and shall encamp round about the tabernacle. And when the tabernacle setteth forward, the Levites shall take it down: and when the tabernacle is to be pitched, the Levites shall set it up: and the stranger that cometh nigh shall be put to death. And the children of Israel shall pitch their tents, every man by his own camp, and every man by his own standard, throughout their hosts. But the Levites shall pitch round about the tabernacle of testimony, that there be no wrath upon the congregation of the children of Israel: and the Levites shall keep the charge of the tabernacle of testimony." (Num 1:49-53)

So the Levites are not counted, yet you will see that there are still twelve tribes listed above in the order of battle, even without Levi. Permit me to save you the trouble of working out what happened. The tribe of Joseph has been divided into its component membership of Manasseh and Ephraim, which are listed separately. The Levites have been set aside for the purposes of ministering to God and looking after all aspects of the Tabernacle, so they won't be fighting.

---

[266] 603,550 is some army. This is the figure from which scholars popularly estimate that the entire camp of Israel comprised upwards of 2 million souls, including the Levites (who are not counted here), the women, children, servants, and 'mixed multitude' that came with them.

"So what?" you say.

I'm getting there. The Levites are to camp protectively around the Tabernacle and literally slay anyone who ventures too close to God's holy residence to pollute it with their sinful person (Num 1:51). In Num 2, God further orders the fighting tribes to gather into four camps of three tribes each and array themselves at the cardinal points around the Tabernacle. They are instructed to camp as follows:

EAST - The Camp of Judah, comprising Judah, Issachar and Zebulun: Total 186,400

SOUTH - The Camp of Reuben, comprising Reuben, Simeon and Gad: Total 151,450

WEST - The Camp of Ephraim, comprising Ephraim, Manasseh, Benjamin: Total 108,100

NORTH - The Camp of Dan, comprising Dan, Asher, Naphtali: Total 157,600

Once the camp is deployed according to the above numbers, an aerial view of the camp reveals a perfect cross facing east. Notice the north and south military contingents are of similar strength, giving roughly equal arms to the cross. Coincidence? Or perhaps a further prefiguring of Christ's plan of redemption, played out in advance, hidden away in the holy text of the Jewish Torah.

The move to Kadesh

The Israelites spend almost a year at Sinai before decamping and heading north to Kadesh Barnea, stopping intermittently. (The full itinerary of the Exodus and wanderings can be studied in Numbers 33). The week following the departure from Sinai is characterised by complaints by the people about the shortcomings of their manna-exclusive diet, and Moses suffers an understandable meltdown from all the stress.

And when the people complained, it displeased the LORD: and the LORD heard it; and His anger was kindled; and the fire of the LORD burnt among them, and consumed them that were in the uttermost parts of the camp. And the people cried unto Moses; and when Moses prayed unto the LORD, the fire was quenched. And he called the name of the place Taberah: because the fire of the LORD burnt among them.

And the mixt multitude that was among them fell a lusting [craving]**: and the children of Israel also wept again, and said, "Who shall give us flesh to eat? We remember the fish, which we did eat in Egypt freely; the cucumbers, and the melons, and the leeks, and**

the onions, and the garlick: But now our soul is dried away: there is nothing at all, beside this manna, before our eyes." (Num 11:1-6)

Then Moses heard the people weep throughout their families, every man in the door of his tent: and the anger of the LORD was kindled greatly; Moses also was displeased. And Moses said unto the LORD, "Wherefore hast Thou afflicted Thy servant? And wherefore have I not found favour in Thy sight, that Thou layest the burden of all this people upon me? Have I conceived all this people? Have I begotten them, that Thou shouldest say unto me, 'Carry them in thy bosom, as a nursing father beareth the sucking child, unto the land which thou swarest unto their fathers?' "

"Whence should I have flesh to give unto all this people? For they weep unto me, saying, 'Give us flesh, that we may eat.' I am not able to bear all this people alone, because it is too heavy for me. And if Thou deal thus with me, kill me, I pray thee, out of hand, if I have found favour in Thy sight; and let me not see my wretchedness." (Num 11:10-15)

God instructs Moses to pick out seventy elders from the tribes and endues them with His Spirit so Moses can delegate future responsibilities and tasks. As for the moany congregation, God has something special in store:

"...Say thou unto the people, 'Sanctify yourselves against tomorrow, and ye shall eat flesh: for ye have wept in the ears of the LORD, saying, 'Who shall give us flesh to eat? For it was well with us in Egypt:' therefore the LORD will give you flesh, and ye shall eat.

"Ye shall not eat one day, nor two days, nor five days, neither ten days, nor twenty days; But even a whole month, until it come out at your nostrils, and it be loathsome unto you: because that ye have despised the LORD which is among you, and have wept before Him, saying, 'Why came we forth out of Egypt?' "

And Moses said, "The people, among whom I am, are six hundred thousand footmen; and thou hast said, 'I will give them flesh, that they may eat a whole month.' Shall the flocks and the herds be slain for them, to suffice them? Or shall all the fish of the sea be gathered together for them, to suffice them?"

And the LORD said unto Moses, "Is the LORD'S hand waxed short? Thou shalt see now whether My word shall come to pass unto thee or not."

And Moses went out, and told the people the words of the LORD, and gathered the seventy men of the elders of the people, and set them round about the tabernacle. (Num 11:18-24)

God duly endues the chosen Seventy with His Spirit. He's not slack in fulfilling his other promise either:

And there went forth a wind from the LORD, and brought quails from the sea, and let them fall by the camp, as it were a day's journey on this side, and as it were a day's journey on the other side, round about the camp, and as it were two cubits high upon the face of the earth.

And the people stood up all that day, and all that night, and all the next day, and they gathered the quails: he that gathered least gathered ten homers: and they spread them all abroad for themselves round about the camp. And while the flesh was yet between their teeth, ere [before] **it was chewed, the wrath of the LORD was kindled against the people, and the LORD smote the people with a very great plague. And He called the name of that place Kibroth Hattaavah: because there they buried the people that lusted.** (Num 11:31-34)

One gets the impression that God reaches the end of His tether on occasion. This won't be the last time. The next stop is Hazaroth, and here Aaron and Miriam take Moses to task over the Ethiopian woman he married - remember her? Fresh from quail overload, God is in no mood to be disrespected by these two either:

And the LORD spake suddenly unto Moses, and unto Aaron, and unto Miriam, "Come out ye three unto the tabernacle of the congregation!" And they three came out. And the LORD came down in the pillar of the cloud, and stood in the door of the tabernacle, and called Aaron and Miriam: and they both came forth.

And he said, "Hear now My words: If there be a prophet among you, I the LORD will make myself known unto him in a vision, and will speak unto him in a dream. My servant Moses is not so, who is faithful in all Mine house. With him will I speak mouth to mouth, even apparently, and not in dark speeches; and the similitude of the LORD shall he behold: wherefore then were ye not afraid to speak against my servant Moses?"

And the anger of the LORD was kindled against them; and He departed. And the cloud departed from off the tabernacle; and, behold, Miriam became leprous, white as snow: and Aaron looked upon Miriam, and, behold, she was leprous.

And Aaron said unto Moses, "Alas, my lord, I beseech thee, lay not the sin upon us, wherein we have done foolishly, and wherein we have sinned. Let her not be as one dead, of whom the flesh is half consumed when he cometh out of his mother's womb."

And Moses cried unto the LORD, saying, "Heal her now, O God, I beseech thee."

And the LORD said unto Moses, "If her father had but spit in her face, should she not be ashamed seven days? Let her be shut out from the camp seven days, and after that let her be received in again."

And Miriam was shut out from the camp seven days: and the people journeyed not till Miriam was brought in again. And afterward the people removed from Hazeroth, and pitched in the wilderness of Paran. (Num 12:4-16)

The twelve spies

Why did the Israelites wander for 40 years? It's a common and not unreasonable question. There is compelling evidence that they didn't actually 'wander' but may have stayed put at a particular location for the majority of this period. We'll examine this in a little while. Recall that four centuries before, Jacob and his family entered Egypt under Joseph's protection to last out the famine. Jacob's twelves sons multiplied exceedingly in the following years from a family to a nation, but went into oppression under an Assyrian Hyksos pharaoh (Isa 52:4). Centuries later, God raises up Moses to lead His people out of their Egyptian captivity back to the land of Canaan, which He had promised in perpetuity to Abraham, Isaac and Jacob. Miracles and dramas ensue as Pharaoh proves intransigent and God flexes celestial muscle in return. It's a classic tale and very readable, especially in the King James. The ten plagues are all aimed at humiliating the Egyptian pantheon, culminating in the blotting out of their sun god and slaughter of their firstborn, threatening Egypt's continued survival. The Israelites are finally released, taking great spoil of the Egyptians as they leave. Incensed, Pharaoh changes his mind and loses his northern army in the Red Sea disaster. Then we have the wonders at Mount Horeb and the giving of the Law on tablets of stone; the children of Israel reneging and worshipping a golden calf instead. Punishment, forgiveness, restitution. Throughout it all, God has shown that He will redeem and deliver His people, provide for them while in the wilderness, and slaughter all who come against them. The Israelites reward the Almighty by being vain, cowardly, duplicitous, slanderous, terminal lamenters and profane idol-worshipers. Moses and Aaron are threatened with violence by their own people on a regular basis. God has had enough.

Of course, it doesn't take forty years to walk from Egypt's Nile Delta back to Canaan (Israel). You can do it in nine days with a decent pair of shoes. God has His people take a more circuitous route in view of the Philistine mobilisation at that time **"...Lest peradventure the people repent when they see war and return to Egypt."** (Exo 13:17). This is too much for the Jews who lament that they should have remained in Egypt rather than die in the desert. In Deuteronomy 8:2-5, God declares that He kept them in the wilderness for so long to provide for them, test them, humble them, and earn their trust as their Father. What does God get in return? More moaning. We are those Israelites.

In Numbers 13, the Israelites arrive at the threshold of Canaan at a place called Kadesh Barnea eleven days after departing Mt Sinai (Deut 1:2). Here God instructs Moses to send a representative from each tribe into the Promised Land to carry out a reconnaissance mission before the invasion. 'Is the land good or bad?' 'Are the cities fenced or walled?' 'Are the indigenous people strong or weak?' 'Bring back the fruit of the land so we can learn of its bounty.' Off trek the spies, only to return 40 days later (40 days = time of proving, judgment, testing) with a supply of the local produce, including copious grapes, pomegranates and figs. Nevertheless, ten of the twelve spies nurse a most pessimistic report.

"We came unto the land whither thou sentest us, and surely it floweth with milk and honey, and this is the fruit of it. Nevertheless the people be strong that dwell in the land, and the cities are walled and very great: and moreover we saw the children of Anak there. The Amalekites dwell in the land of the south: and the Hittites, and the Jebusites, and the Amorites, dwell in the mountains: and the Canaanites dwell by the sea, and by the coast of Jordan."

And Caleb stilled the people before Moses, and said, "Let us go up at once and possess it, for we are well able to overcome it."

But the men that went up with him said, "We be not able to go up against the people, for they are stronger than we."

And they brought up an evil report of the land which they had searched unto the children of Israel, saying, "The land, through which we have gone to search it, is a land that eateth up the inhabitants thereof; and all the people that we saw in it are men of a great stature. And there we saw the giants [Heb: םיליפנה, *nephyl, Nephilim*]**, the sons of Anak, which come of the giants: and we were in our own sight as grasshoppers, and so we were in their sight."**

And all the congregation lifted up their voice and cried; and the people wept that night. (Num 13:27–14:1)

These Nephilim and mighty men are a throwback to Genesis 6, the reason God brought the Flood to erase *ha-Satan's* terminal gene pool venture. This demonic procreation between fallen angels and humans was to thwart the promise of the Seed of the woman (Yeshua) and, we are told, continued afterwards (Gen 6:4).[267] Now the Jews are facing the grim prospect of going up against these Titans[268] to lay claim to the land God has given them. One commentary confirms:

"The subject of the Nephilim is one of the great puzzles of the Bible. The same general theme is found throughout ancient writings of many peoples and is not confined exclusively to the Bible. The Nephilim were apparently a race of impressive physical stature compared to the smaller Hebrews, from Numbers 13:33. **"And there we saw the giants, the sons of Anak, which come of the giants: and we were in our own sight as grasshoppers, and so we were in their sight."** This particular reference is glossed by a statement which implies that the offspring of Anak in Canaan were descended from the renowned Rephaim or Nephilim."[269]

Steve Quayle writes:

"In the plural, Anakim means 'people of the necklace' or 'neck-piece', and so it is explained by the ancient rabbis. The name comes from *anaq*, the Hebrew word for 'necklace'. Moses, in Numbers 13:33, affirms that they descended from the Nephilim. Their uncommon height was, of course, enough to arouse in people of normal size some uneasiness. But the Anakim were also a fierce, half-wild people, given to deeds of great daring. Consequently, they loved war and regarded it as a normal way of life. So ingrained was their inclination to fight that when no common

---

[267] A full explanation of this is given in *Origins II – Holy War.*

[268] Ancient literature across the world is replete with legends of demi-gods derived from the progeny of sexual unions between gods and humans. These appear to have their origins in what is described in Genesis 6. The Titans, for instance, feature prominently in Greek literature, and so does Tartarus, the pit, abyss and hideous place of torment and suffering which, according to Homer's *Iliad*, is as far below Earth as the Earth is below Heaven. Tartarus is a geocentric location and far worse in its horror than Hades, the holding tank for the unrepentant dead. Tartarus is mentioned once in the Bible in 2 Peter 2:4 in direct connection to those angels who sinned prior to the Flood, who are now confined in chains in this terrible place awaiting their final judgment in the Lake of Fire. (cf. Jude 6-7)

[269] www.geocities.com/nephilimnot/nephilim.html

enemy could be found against whom they could exercise their natural belligerence, they fought among themselves. Such a hostile attitude, combined with their extraordinary stature, caused shivers in most people who came in contact with them." [270]

The scouts' report of the giants causes consternation among the children of Israel. Even with an army of 600,000 plus, motivation to get crushed like the grapes they see borne by the scouts is at an all-time low. Two of the spies, however - Caleb and the military commander Joshua - are enthusiastic about having a go, since God is with them. They are a minority. Amazingly, the people have no trust in God to deliver them, even after all they have been through. They turn on their leaders again:

And all the children of Israel murmured against Moses and against Aaron. And the whole congregation said unto them, "Would God that we had died in the land of Egypt! Or would God we had died in this wilderness!" (Num 14:2)

And God says, "Funny you should say that..."

YHWH is up for total Hebrew erasure at this point, but again a fascinating debate ensues. Moses revisits the argument he used on the Almighty at Mt Sinai and begs God to consider what the Egyptians will make of a God who takes His people out of bondage only to slaughter them in the desert because He could not deliver them to the land He promised. So, in a scene reminiscent of Abraham and God debating the fate of Sodom and Gomorrah, and also Moses's previous altercation with the Creator over the golden calf incident, Moses has at it again:

"And now, I beseech Thee, let the power of my LORD be great, according as Thou hast spoken, saying, 'The LORD is longsuffering and of great mercy, forgiving iniquity and transgression, and by no means clearing the guilty, visiting the iniquity of the fathers upon the children unto the third and fourth generation.' Pardon, I beseech Thee, the iniquity of this people according unto the greatness of Thy mercy, and as Thou hast forgiven this people, from Egypt even until now." (Num 14:17-19)

It's a career moment for Moses. God relents, proving once again that God hears entreaties. The judgment, however, will be harsh.

And the LORD spake unto Moses and unto Aaron, saying, "How long shall I bear with this evil congregation, which murmur against Me? I have heard the murmurings of the children of Israel,

[270] www.stevequayle.com/Giants/Mid.East/Giants.Mid.East3.html

which they murmur against Me. Say unto them, 'As truly as I live,' saith the LORD, 'as ye have spoken in Mine ears, so will I do to you: Your carcases shall fall in this wilderness; and all that were numbered of you, according to your whole number, from twenty years old and upward, which have murmured against Me, doubtless ye shall not come into the land, concerning which I sware to make you dwell therein, save Caleb the son of Jephunneh, and Joshua the son of Nun.

" 'But your little ones, which ye said should be a prey, them will I bring in, and they shall know the land which ye have despised. But as for you, your carcases, they shall fall in this wilderness. And your children shall wander in the wilderness forty years, and bear your whoredoms, until your carcases be wasted in the wilderness. After the number of the days in which ye searched the land, even forty days, each day for a year, shall ye bear your iniquities, even forty years, and ye shall know My breach of promise. I the LORD have said, I will surely do it unto all this evil congregation, that are gathered together against me: in this wilderness they shall be consumed, and there they shall die.' " (Num 14:26-35)

God kills the recalcitrant spies then and there with the plague (Num 14:36-37). The rest of the multitude will have to tough it out in the wilderness until the last carcass drops among the rocks (Num 14:29). God will make them pay a year for every day they scouted out the land, though the final tally will be 38 years, not 40 (Deut 2:14) - a sign of forbearance and mercy. Only two men over age 20 who came out of Egypt will be spared to enter the Promised Land – Joshua and Caleb – the two scouts who gave the favourable report. Incredibly, not even Moses, Aaron or Miriam will make it.

Kadesh Barnea

Scholars are divided at this point in the Exodus over three issues:

1) After God shuts them out of the Promised Land due to their refusal to go in and possess the Land, do the Israelites really wander aimlessly for the next 38 years before the successive generation finds itself on the plains of Moab in 1406 BC poised to invade Canaan?
2) Where exactly is Kadesh Barnea?
3) Could 2 million people really have survived in the desert for 40 years? I mean, come on! The logistics are impossible!

Regarding the first point, the Exodus itinerary laid out in Numbers 33 itemises a number of stops between Kadesh Barnea and the staging point for the invasion in the plains of Moab, east of the Jordan (Transjordan). The Exodus timeline becomes compressed after Israel refuses to enter the land at Kadesh, and only a selection of events are described during this period, a few of which we will examine. An extended stay appears to have occurred at Kadesh (Deut 1:46), after which scholars cite Deut 2:1-3, which describes how the Israelites circle Mt Seir **for many days**: evidence of their hapless loss of goals and direction. Yet God has the whole camp turn and head south into the wilderness, apparently down towards the northern tip of the Gulf of Aqaba, 'by the Way of the Red Sea', perhaps an allusion to taking the King's Highway (see **Chart H**).

Regarding Kadesh Barnea's location: at least fifteen candidates have been presented, including the proposal that there are two Kadesh's, which is unnecessary. The most popular view is that Kadesh is located at Ein el-Qudeirat, southwest of Canaan. Some reject this since this location is almost 30 km east of the Wadi Al-Arish, thought to have been the Biblical border between Egypt and Canaan at the time. Thus, it is reasoned, this Kadesh site lies within the Promised Land and may be discounted since the Israelites don't enter at this point. Another view is that Kadesh Barnea is located at or near Petra and forms the focus of the Israelites' existence for the next 38 years.

I think it is likely that Kadesh is located in or near the Arabah - that part of the Jordan Rift Valley that runs between the northern tip of the Gulf of Aqaba and the southern end of the Dead Sea. I believe this because Num 33:35-36 tells us that the Israelites encamp at Ezion Geber (modern-day Eilat), which is at the northern tip of the Gulf of Aqaba, from which they then journey into the Wilderness of Zin to pitch at Kadesh; after which, at some point, they move on to Mount Hor on the border of the kingdom of Edom, where Aaron dies and is buried. The famous King's Highway crosses the Jordan at Ezion Geber and turns north to run up the eastern part of the Arabah past Petra and into Moab and Syria, so it seems likely that the children of Israel would use this route. Later, when Moses petitions the king of Edom for Israel's passage through his kingdom, he does so from Kadesh Barnea which, if at or near Petra, would be just short of Edom's border. Moses makes mention that they will be taking the [King's] Highway in order not to inconvenience the king or beggar

Edom's resources without payment (Num 20:14-21).[271] Steve Rudd remarks:

"Kadesh Barnea, the Wilderness of Paran and Wilderness of Zin must be outside all boundaries of Israel, including the Negev. No Bible passage says that Kadesh Barnea, Paran or Zin were ever part of Israel or located in the Negev, or the western edge of the Arabah.

"From a careful study of the Exodus route, we can determine that the general order of places is as follows: Starting at the Dead Sea moving south, you first hit the Ascent of Scorpions and the Wilderness of Zin, then Kadesh, then Mt. Hor. Since Mt. Hor was located three miles south west of Petra, this places Kadesh at or just north of Petra, likely on the mountainous plateau, rather than in the Arabah valley below the cliffs.

"Kadesh Barnea was on the border of Edom: Num 20:16. Archeology has proved the fact that Edom was historically Transjordan (east of the Arabah) until [the Edomites] first moved into Judean territory after the Babylonian captivity.[272] This means that before 586 BC, Edom's territory was always Transjordan. Ein el-Qudeirat is nowhere near the border of Edom, which disqualifies it as Kadesh. Modern Bible maps make a grave error in locating Edom well into the Negev, not because of archeological evidence, but because they know the border of Edom was beside Kadesh. In a spectacular display of circular reasoning, these maps bring the border of Edom right beside Ein el-Qudeirat, where they wrongly believe Kadesh is located."[273]

And what about the question of whether the logistics to keep a population the size of Houston, Texas alive in the desert for 40 years are far-fetched to the point of lunacy, as some sceptics maintain? We're back to the classic argument over the word *eleph,* which is used in the Bible to denote sometimes 'clan', and sometimes 'thousand'. Some sceptics recalculate the 'thousand' figures used for the Exodus and other events in the Bible to be 'clans' instead of 'thousands', so there exists a view among scholars that variously no more than 7,000 - 20,000 people left Egypt in the Exodus, depending on the size of a clan. Steve Rudd refutes this, using scripture and context, citing the numbers of Hebrews killed in God's plagues in the desert, the sheer quantity of quails provided so the Israelites could stuff themselves (Num 11:31-34), and the redeeming of the firstborn and Levites

---

[271] https://3amthoughts.com/article/egypt-israel/kadesh-barnea-and-petra

[272] www.bible.ca/archeology/bible-archeology-edomite-territory-mt-seir.htm

[273] www.bible.ca/archeology/bible-archeology-exodus-kadesh-barnea.htm

males.[274] Also, look no further than Exo 1:8-10, in which we learn that the pharaoh **who knew Joseph not** was deeply concerned about the burgeoning number of **the people of the children of Israel** (the Hebrews and Hyksos Semitic peoples making up the majority of the slave-force), to the point where the Egyptian monarch considers them **"more and mightier than we"**. Egypt's population at this point has been estimated to be in excess of five million. Would Pharaoh really have concerned himself with 7,000 - 20,000 rebel slaves? I think not. The aforementioned calculation of 600,000-plus Israelites of fighting age would have a far more scary ring to it if I were the king of Egypt. Add to this number the Levites, women, children and mixed multitude who came out with the Israelites, and Amenhotep II certainly has a major problem when the majority of his slave-force departs Egypt. As we have seen, history records that Amenhotep II embarks on a hastily planned expedition into Canaan *in winter* to capture slaves and chariots, likely to replenish what was lost due to the Exodus and Red Sea disaster.

Secular historians are also bothered by how such a vast number of people could possibly have survived 40 years in one of the harshest environments on Earth. Calculators are whipped out. The Israelites would require in the order of 11 million gallons of water PER DAY, 2,000 tons of food PER DAY, 4,000 tons of firewood PER DAY, and a campsite two-thirds the size of Rhode Island every time they pitched.[275] The space requirements, however, need not be an issue. During World Youth Day in 2002, 850,000 people went to see Pope John Paul II at Downsview Park, Toronto and squeezed into 2.3 sq. km. Between 1 - 2 million people were reported present in the Mall, Washington DC, for Barack Obama's presidential inauguration. They squeezed into 2 sq. km. *Tekton Apologetics* writes:

"In terms of sustenance, the believer may obviously appeal to the miraculous provision of foodstuffs such as manna; but the Israelites also had their flocks and herds with them, and if needed, the ability to trade....

"In terms of providing water, we see of course the miraculous provision of springs at least twice in the accounts; one may justly argue, given that the Pentateuchal narratives have been clearly designed for the purpose of oral communication, that these incidents are representative of what happened during the whole trip. Certainly it is misguided for

---

[274] www.bible.ca/archeology/bible-archeology-exodus-route-population-of-jews-hebrews.htm

[275] www.ancient-hebrew.org/39_exodus.html

critics to argue using estimates of how many gallons of water, or how many trainloads of food or firewood, would be needed to support the Israelites and then remark that such provision would have been impossible in a desert setting (especially if, as some theorists suppose, the Exodus took place in a fertile part of Arabia, not the Sinai peninsula).

"Even without miraculous provision, we may add, how do they think other ancient nations survived? Were they all primitives that could not work out systems to provide for their needs? (The Scythians survived just fine without firewood; they used their own herd animals for such purposes; the bones made for firewood, and the carcasses made do as a stirring pot.)"[276]

And here's a summary point: Every feature of God getting the Hebrews out of Egypt has been deliberately designed to be miraculous so the world would not forget it, and it hasn't! The plagues, the looting of Egypt's substance, the crossing of the Red Sea, Marah, manna, Mount Sinai, the shoes not wearing out: you name it, God did it, and even atheists are still making films, TV programmes and writing books about Moses and the Exodus into our modern age. And I don't have the slightest problem believing any of the Old Testament's account of Moses's life, and not just because of the research I've done on the subject. Jesus Christ authenticated the Old Testament, the Torah, and especially the Law given on Mt Sinai,[277] so if you believe Yeshua is who He said He was, you'll have no problem reading the OT with His *imprimatur* and accepting all the nuggets therein. If you do not believe Jesus Christ is who He said he was, then it's possible you have more serious problems than how many Israelites came out of Egypt, and what they wore and ate.

Moses blows it

Shortly after the arrival of the Israelites at Kadesh Barnea (Kadesh = holy. Barnea = desert of wandering), perhaps even during the forty days the camp awaits the return of the scouts from Canaan, an event occurs which seems so unjust, so unfair, that scholars still debate the implications.

Then came the children of Israel, even the whole congregation, into the desert of Zin in the first month: and the people abode in Kadesh; and Miriam died there, and was buried there. And there

---

[276] www.tektonics.org/af/exoduslogistics.php

[277] Matt 5:17-19; Mark 7:10; 12:26-27; Luke 16:29-31; 24:27; FG 5:45-47; 7:19, etc.

was no water for the congregation: and they gathered themselves together against Moses and against Aaron. And the people chode [contended] **with Moses, and spake, saying, "Would God that we had died when our brethren died before the LORD! And why have ye brought up the congregation of the LORD into this wilderness, that we and our cattle should die there? And wherefore have ye made us to come up out of Egypt, to bring us in unto this evil place? it is no place of seed, or of figs, or of vines, or of pomegranates; neither is there any water to drink."** (Num 20:1-5)

Shortly after the Israelites arrive at Kadesh, Moses's sister Miriam dies and is buried there. Once again water is running short. Moses is frustrated to death with the Israelites who, as usual, are bemoaning their lot. The patriarch is understandably tetchier than normal since he has just lost his sister, who was buried in the wilderness of Zin.[278] As usual, the anger is about lack of water, and once again threats ring out against the two brothers.

And Moses and Aaron went from the presence of the assembly unto the door of the tabernacle of the congregation, and they fell upon their faces, and the glory of the LORD appeared unto them. And the LORD spake unto Moses, saying, "Take the rod, and gather thou the assembly together, thou, and Aaron thy brother, and speak ye unto the rock before their eyes. And it shall give forth his water, and thou shalt bring forth to them water out of the rock: so thou shalt give the congregation and their beasts drink."

And Moses took the rod from before the LORD, as he commanded him. And Moses and Aaron gathered the congregation together before the rock, and he said unto them, "Hear now, ye rebels; must we fetch you water out of this rock?"

And Moses lifted up his hand, and with his rod he smote the rock twice: and the water came out abundantly, and the congregation drank, and their beasts also.

And the LORD spake unto Moses and Aaron, "Because ye believed me not, to sanctify me in the eyes of the children of Israel, therefore ye shall not bring this congregation into the land which I have given them." (Num 20:6-12)

Just like that. Moses loses his own inheritance to the land of Israel over what seems a trite technicality. God's annoyance appears to be based around Moses' misrepresentation of the type or model God

---

[278] Miriam may well have been the same sister of Moses who oversaw her baby brother's trip down the Nile in his ark, to protect him from Pharaoh's extermination edict.

was attempting to convey. You say, 'Who cares?' God does. At the first rock-striking incident at Rephidim, the rock represents Yeshua who is smitten, and the living waters issue forth (1 Cor 10:1-6). This is a model of His first coming, when He was beaten and crucified. On the subsequent occasion at Kadesh, God wants Moses to *speak* to the rock so the waters come forth. This would have been a model of Christ's grace the second time around, but Moses not only does not obey, he insinuates his own works into the picture: **"Hear now, ye rebels; must we fetch you water out of this rock?"** God is upset enough for this to cost Moses his inheritance; though, as we shall see, YHWH may have a bewildering, future role in store for this unlucky prophet *in our own modern age* three and a half millennia after the latter's death.[279] It is certainly shocking that this should happen to Moses *at all* after all he has accomplished and been forced to endure over the past 120 years. It seems so unfair that a man who has been able to negotiate with the Creator of the universe and intercede on others' behalf on many occasions fails to prevent YHWH's condemnation of his own foolish *faux pas*. As some scholars opine, this should send chills into the regular believer, never mind the wicked. But God has His reasons.

The Exodus, then. An extraordinary, unique period, never to be repeated, during which the Designer chastises, tests, punishes, shapes and cajoles a people He has set apart for His purpose. A peculiar people who maintain disbelieving defiance even in the face of staggering demonstrations of heavenly power. Are we the same? Do we look at everything around us, even the wonders of our planet and own bodies, and attribute it all to the know-nothing-god of evolution? During their time in the desert, God has a royal sort-out, but something else happens as a result of the Jews' enforced adversity. They unify for the first time into a colossal army that will strike fear into the pagan Levant peoples, forewarned that God's new general, Joshua, intends taking the land God has given them.

Caleb and Joshua, the two spies who gave the optimistic report, will be the only two Hebrews from Egypt who make it into the land. And, as we shall see, so much the worse for those who get in their way.

---

[279] Jude 9; Rev 11:3-13

The brazen serpent

There is the following unsettling episode during the wilderness years:

And the people spake against God and against Moses, "Wherefore have ye brought us up out of Egypt to die in the wilderness? For there is no bread, neither is there any water; and our soul loatheth this light bread [manna]**." And the LORD sent fiery serpents among the people and they bit the people, and much people of Israel died.**

Therefore the people came to Moses and said, "We have sinned, for we have spoken against the LORD and against thee. Pray unto the LORD, that he take away the serpents from us."

And Moses prayed for the people. And the LORD said unto Moses, "Make thee a fiery serpent and set it upon a pole. And it shall come to pass that every one that is bitten, when he looketh upon it, shall live." (Num 21:5-8)

What a strange, strange command. Moses duly makes a serpent of brass and raises it on a pole. Sure enough, those who had been bitten by the fiery serpents survived if they gazed upon the fake serpent on the pole. Then the narrative moves on with no explanation for this bizarre episode throughout the rest of the Old Testament!

All right, you can understand God at the end of His tether with the ingratitude and constant moaning. You even go with Him on the fiery serpent thing to a lesser extent, believing the Israelites have it coming after so many unheeded examples of divine deliverance. But there is more. Serpents are a symbol of sin. As we've seen with the Tabernacle materials, brass/bronze/copper are symbols of judgment since they are metals associated with fire. The only time you get an explanation for this weird event *is in the New Testament* when Jesus has that late-evening visit from the Pharisee Nicodemus. Jesus states:

"And as Moses lifted up the serpent in the wilderness, even so must the Son of man be lifted up. That whosoever believeth in Him should not perish, but have eternal life. For God so loved the world that he gave His only begotten Son, that whosoever believeth in Him should not perish, but have everlasting life." (FG 3:14-16)

It's fascinating that perhaps the most famous quote of Christ's in the Bible is linked to this bizarre serpent deliverance during the Exodus. This is further proof that the OT and NT comprising the Bible are an integrated message system. The Apostle Paul comments: **For He hath made Him to be sin for us who knew no sin, that we might be made the righteousness of God in Him.** (2 Cor 5:21)

So in the wilderness, a pre-incarnate Yeshua is demonstrating to the Jews His chosen method of atonement. That God Himself will be made sin and raised high on a pole (cross) to be judged for all our sins, that we who look to that sacrifice will be saved for eternity. It's a stunning example of the theme of redemption running throughout the Bible, a sacrifice that will always be mocked and scorned by those who are perishing (1 Cor 1:18).

Even as today, the Israelites at the time did not understand it. They continued to bemoan their desert predicament, and indeed the very same brass serpent Moses raised up for their salvation would still be around hundreds of years later during the time of King Hezekiah (739-687 BC), when the Jews would actually be burning incense to it as an idol. Hezekiah has the serpent broken up, contemptuously referring to is as 'Nehushtan' - 'that brazen thing'. Ironically it will be Hezekiah's psychotic son, Manasseh, who will reintroduce paganism and devil worship upon ascending the throne, even murdering God's prophet, Isaiah, some say, by sawing him in half.[280]

Confronting Sihon the giant

The conquest of Canaan begins on the eastern side of the Jordan. The Bible states that Moses brings the Israelites up from Elath (Eilat/Aqaba) to the area of Transjordan prior to their invasion proper of central Canaan. Moses has evidently been told by God that a direct strike on the Ammonite stronghold of Jericho will begin the campaign across the river, but hitting the enemy now where they appear strongest - with the giants arrayed against them - will definitely make an impression on those further down God's hit-list.

www.bibliotecapleyades.net writes:

---

[280] Bible Q writes: "There is a tradition reported in the Martyrdom of Isaiah (a Christian text from around AD100, which expands on 2 Kings 21) that Isaiah was condemned to death by King Manasseh. Although he hid in a tree, he was found and the tree with Isaiah inside was sawn in half. A similar tradition is recorded in *Lives of the Prophets* (another Christian text from around AD100). The method of Isaiah's death (sawn in half) is also supported by the Jewish texts known as the Babylonian Talmud and the Jerusalem Talmud (both written after AD200). The only possible reference to this gruesome event is in Hebrews 11:37, which describes faithful people from the past: **"...they were stoned, they were sawn asunder, were tempted, were slain with the sword: they wandered about in sheepskins and goatskins; being destitute, afflicted, tormented..."** - http://bibleq.info/answer /3010/

"Their long march toward this well-known city of the giants took the Hebrew multitude through Edom, Moab, Gilead, and Bashan. Some four hundred years earlier, many Rephaim, Horim, Emim, and Zamzummim giants had possessed these lands. Then came Chedorlaomer and his Babylonian cohorts. On their punitive raids throughout Transjordan and Edom they slew many giants and wasted their cities. An unknown number managed to escape Chedorlaomer's sword, but their once-firm hold on those countries was forever broken. The 'land of the Rephaim', so-called because the giants had so completely dominated it, was no more. In later times, the Rephaim that still lived in Transjordan and Edom were defeated by the numerous descendants of Lot and Esau. This interesting bit of history appears only in Moses' journal. In his account of the Hebrews' wearying march toward Canaan's eastern border, the great lawgiver included several entries, written parenthetically, that tell us how the Gibborim mongrels that survived Chedorlaomer's onslaught were finally dispossessed."[281]

The centuries following the Nephilim proliferation post-Flood (Gen 6:4) have seen giant DNA sown among the Amorite peoples in Canaan as well as the tribes of Transjordan:

"They stood not quite as tall as the Rephaim, Horim, Emim, and Zamzummim [giants], but Biblical records and ancient monuments still represent them as a people of great size and strength. The prophet Amos, in a later reference to this campaign, describes them in these words: 'Thus says the LORD... "It was I who destroyed the Amorite before them, though his height was like the height of cedars and he was strong as the oaks." ' [Amos 2:9-10[282]]. The cedar, of course, denotes the Amorites' exceptional tallness. The oak symbolizes their great might. Some monuments discovered by archaeologists bear out Amos' description. On these, says historian Philip Hitti, the 'Amorite stature appears tall and martial. Their size and culture must have so impressed the primitive and short troglodytic inhabitants of southern Syria that legends grew that a

---

[281] www.bibliotecapleyades.net/gigantes/GiantsMidEast13.html#Anchor-Sihon's-54980

[282] [Thus saith the LORD:]**"Yet destroyed I the Amorite before them, whose height was like the height of the cedars, and he was strong as the oaks; yet I destroyed his fruit from above, and his roots from beneath. Also I brought you up from the land of Egypt, and led you forty years through the wilderness, to possess the land of the Amorite."** (Amos 2:9-10)

giant race came and intermarried the daughters of men, legends which were passed on to the Israelites.' "[283]

Presiding over the tribes of Transjordan are two Amorite kings, Sihon of Heshbon and Og of Bashan. It is believed Sihon is the Amorite referred to in the Amos passage, which would make him, if not a giant, then of an intimidating physical stature, descended from the giants. Og is definitely not of normal height. His bed was later found by scavenging Ammonites and squirreled away as a museum piece for centuries due to its impressive dimensions:

For only Og, king of Bashan, remained of the remnant of giants. Behold his bedstead was a bedstead of iron; is it not in Rabbath [modern-day Amman, Jordan] **of the children of Ammon? Nine cubits was the length thereof, and four cubits the breadth of it, after the cubit of a man.** (Deut 3:11) This makes King Og's bed 6 feet wide and 14 feet long. King Og's height is therefore estimated at over 12.5 feet.

That the giants were uppermost in the minds of Moses and the children of Israel is evident from the fascinating journal Moses keeps as they approach the entry to Canaan. It is clear that *ha-Satan's* pollution of the human gene pool is well underway with countless marriages between the Canaanite sub-groups. The LORD decides to have the heathen tribes fight among themselves, leaving the field relatively clear for the Hebrew army. Moses gives the children of Israel the following briefing on the politics of giants in the lands through which they will pass:

And when we passed by from our brethren the children of Esau, which dwelt in Seir, through the way of the plain from Elath, and from Ezion Geber, we turned and passed by the way of the wilderness of Moab.

And the LORD said unto me, "Distress not the Moabites, neither contend with them in battle, for I will not give thee of their land for a possession, because I have given Ar unto the children of Lot for a possession."

(The Emims dwelt therein in times past, a people great and many, and tall as the Anakims, which also were accounted giants as the Anakims; but the Moabites call them Emims. The Horims also dwelt in Seir beforetime, but the children of Esau succeeded them when they had destroyed them from before them and dwelt in their

---

[283] Ibid; **Hitti, Philip** *History of Syria,* New York, Macmillan, 1951, p.195

stead, as Israel did unto the land of his possession, which the LORD gave unto them).

"And when thou comest nigh over against the children of Ammon, distress them not, nor meddle with them, for I will not give thee of the land of the children of Ammon any possession because I have given it unto the children of Lot for a possession."

(That also was accounted a land of giants; giants dwelt therein in old time, and the Ammonites call them Zamzummims. A people great and many, and tall as the Anakims; but the LORD destroyed them before them; and they succeeded them and dwelt in their stead, just as he did to the children of Esau, which dwelt in Seir, when he destroyed the Horims from before them; and they succeeded them, and dwelt in their stead even unto this day. And the Avims which dwelt in Hazerim, even unto Azzah, the Caphtorims, which came forth out of Caphtor, destroyed them, and dwelt in their stead). (Deut 2: 8-12, 19-23)

Which leaves Moses and Joshua in a showdown with the two Amorite kings in Transjordan - Sihon and Og - to clear the way for Canaan. Rabbinical sources believe the two were actually brothers -

"...grandsons of Shamhazai, a fallen angel (Niddah 61a), who evidently was of the Nephilim. Sihon... resembled Og in stature and bravery (Midrash Agadah, Hukkat, ed. Buber, p. 130a). These old writings also identify him with Arad the Canaanite (Numbers 21:1), who was called 'Sihon' because he resembled the foals in the desert for swiftness....

"From what records we have, Sihon appears to have been the most powerful and probably posed the greatest threat to the advancing Hebrews' plan of attack. Having completed their long, hard march across Edom and Moab, Moses' legions now waded the Arnon, which formed the border between Moab and Sihon's kingdom. That night they pitched camp on the Bamoth plateau in the mountains of Abarim, not far from the famed peaks of Pisgah and Nebo. From this plateau the Israelites got their first view of the land promised to them. Only Sihon now stood between them and their resolve to enter and possess it. War with the giant king and his tall warriors thus seemed unavoidable. [284]

As a courtesy, Moses despatches messengers of peace to Sihon, as he had with Edom:

---

[284] www.bibliotecapleyades.net/gigantes/GiantsMidEast13.html#Anchor-Sihon's-54980 - "Until Sihon came and took it from them, this land east of the Jordan was possessed by the Moabites."

"Let me pass through thy land: I will go along by the [Kings?] **high way, I will neither turn unto the right-hand nor to the left. Thou shalt sell me meat for money, that I may eat; and give me water for money, that I may drink: only let me pass through on my feet (as the descendants of Esau which dwell in Seir, and the Moabites which dwell in Ar, did unto me), until I shall pass over** [the] **Jordan into the land which the LORD our God giveth us."** (Deut 2:27-29)

Moses's spies will have briefed the prophet and his ruling council on what they are up against. Sihon and Og are famous throughout the Middle East, not just for their maniacal stature, but for their martial skills and mighty rule. Their armies too are inbred with the Nephilic seed and evidently feature some disturbingly huge troops. These are professional killers whose every joy is to scare, fight, slaughter and conquer. Moses also learns that Sihon is faced with a dilemma. As ruler also of several lands west of the Jordan (*viz.* the five Amorite kings of Canaan), he will be obliged to come to the aid of his *sub-reguli* or lose face. Seeing the slight stature of the Hebrew ambassadors before him, Sihon is confident that he has the resources to intimidate the Jews into fleeing or else overcome them in battle. But Moses knows that Sihon is reckoning without the LORD, who is hardening Sihon's heart to offer himself up for slaughter.

Sihon predictably refuses safe passage for the Jews through his land and marshals his army for battle. God informs Moses that He has already delivered Sihon and his lands into his hands (Deut 2:31 – past tense!). The battle takes place on the plain outside the town of Jahaz in Moab (modern-day Jordan). Sihon is hugely outnumbered by the Israelite host and his warriors apparently take fright from some sort of divine intervention, perhaps the swarms of hornets later mentioned by Joshua in connection with this and other Israelite campaigns (Josh 24:11-13). One of the few other historical mentions of the battle comes from the 1st century AD Jewish chronicler Flavius Josephus, who adds detail to the Bible's brief rendition:

"As soon as the Hebrews saw them giving ground, they immediately pursued them close; and when they had broken their ranks, they greatly terrified them, and some of them broke off from the rest, and ran away to the cities. Now the Hebrews pursued them briskly, and obstinately persevered in the labors they had already undergone; and being very skillful in slinging, and very dexterous in throwing of darts, or anything else of that kind, and also having nothing but light armor, which made them quick in the pursuit, they overtook their enemies; and for those that were most remote, and could not be overtaken, they reached them by their slings and their bows, so that many were slain; and those that escaped the slaughter were sorely wounded, and these were more distressed with thirst than with any of those that fought against them, for it was the summer season; .and when the greatest number of them were brought down to the river out of a desire to drink, as also when others fled away by troops, the Hebrews came round them, and shot at them; so that, what with darts and what with arrows, they made a slaughter of them all.." [285]

In what will become standard operating procedure for Israel in the battles to come, the enemy is relentlessly pursued and cut down to the last man. Moses's journal relates: **And the LORD our God delivered him** [Sihon] **before us, and we smote him, and his sons, and all his people. And we took all his cities at that time and utterly destroyed the men and the women, and the little ones, of every city, we left none to remain. Only the cattle we took for a prey unto ourselves, and the spoil of the cities which we took.**

From Aroer, which is by the brink of the river of Arnon, and from the city that is by the river, even unto Gilead, there was not one city too strong for us; the LORD our God delivered all unto us. Only unto the land of the children of Ammon thou camest not, nor unto any place of the river Jabbok, nor unto the cities in the mountains, nor unto whatsoever the LORD our God forbad us. (Deut 2:33-37)

www.his-forever.com writes:

"In an ancient text of the Jews, we read an astonishing description of some of these gigantic Amorites whom the Israelites conquered. In Buber's *Tanhuma*, Devarim 7, the text tells us of a Rabbi Johnanan ben Zakkai's encounter with the Roman emperor Hadrian. This event occurred in about AD 135, soon after the Roman victory in the Bar Kochba war, when the Jews rebelled against the Romans. The text reads:

'The wicked emperor Hadrian, who conquered Jerusalem, boasted, "I have conquered Jerusalem with great power." Rabbi Johanan ben Zakkai said to him, "Do not boast. Had it not been the will of Heaven, you would not have conquered it." Rabbi Johanan then took Hadrian into a cave and showed him the bodies of Amorites who were buried there. One of them measured eighteen cubits [approximately 30 feet] in

[285] Josephus, *Antiquities*, op. cit., 4:5:2

height. He said, "When we were deserving, such men were defeated by us, but now, because of our sins, you have defeated us." '

"Thirty feet tall! The bones of these men were still in existence during the time of Josephus, the Jewish historian of the first century!" [286]

www.bibliotecapleyades.net writes:

"Following up their stunning victory over Sihon at Jahaz, the Hebrews seized Heshbon, his capital. It lay about twenty miles east of the Jordan River, on parallel with the northern end of the Salt Sea. After wandering forty years in the wilderness, these former slaves and sons of slaves now owned, by right of conquest, a piece of land. On that day they must have looked with exhilaration beyond the smoldering ruins of Heshbon to the surrounding countryside. Westward from where they stood on the crown of this low rocky hill, the Hebrews had the land of Canaan before them. Turning northward, they saw an elevated land crossed by well-wooded mountain ridges with broad fertile valleys intervening. Eastward they beheld a wide expanse of fruitful, rolling plains that extended unbroken to the desert. Beyond that distant wasteland rose a range of purple-fringed mountains. Greatly encouraged by their successes on the battlefield, they next besieged and captured the walled cities of Nophah, Medeba, and Dibon, putting all their lofty inhabitants to death. The rest of Sihon's towns and villages, being without protecting walls, soon afterward fell. The whole rich country situated between the Arnon to the south, the upper Jabbok to the north, and the Jordan to the west, along with its cities, crops, and cattle, thus came into the Hebrews' immediate possession."[287]

The end of Og

Sixty miles further north from the point where Joshua intends to cross the Jordan at the Jericho fords, the second Amorite king, Og of Bashan the giant, is roused at news of the Hebrews' pending attack on Sihon. Moses records:

Then we turned and went up the way to Bashan. And Og the king of Bashan came out against us, he and all his people, to battle at Edrei. And the LORD said unto me, "Fear him not, for I will deliver him, and all his people, and his land, into thy hand, and

---

[286] www.his-forever.com/giants_the_bible_and_enoch.htm; quoted in *Judaism*, edited by Arthur Hertzberg, pp.155-156, George Braziller, New York: 1962

[287] www.bibliotecapleyades.net/gigantes/GiantsMidEast13.html#Anchor-Sihon's-54980

thou shalt do unto him as thou didst unto Sihon king of the Amorites, which dwelt at Heshbon."

So the LORD our God delivered into our hands Og also, the king of Bashan, and all his people, and we smote him until none was left to him remaining. And we took all his cities at that time, there was not a city which we took not from them, threescore cities, all the region of Argob, the kingdom of Og in Bashan.

All these cities were fenced with high walls, gates, and bars, beside unwalled towns a great many. And we utterly destroyed them, as we did unto Sihon king of Heshbon, utterly destroying the men, women, and children of every city. But all the cattle, and the spoil of the cities, we took for a prey to ourselves. (Deut 3:1-7)

Josephus records:

"When matters were come to this state, Og, the king of Gilead and Gaulanitis, fell upon the Israelites. He brought an army with him, and in haste to the assistance of his friend Sihon: but though he found him already slain, yet did he resolve still to come and fight the Hebrews, supposing he should be too hard for them, and being desirous to try their valour; but failing of his hope, he was both himself slain in the battle, and all his army was destroyed. So Moses passed over the river Jabbok, and overran the kingdom of Og. He overthrew their cities and slew all their inhabitants, who yet exceeded in riches all the men in that part of the continent, on account of the goodness of the soil, and the great quantity of their wealth.

"Now Og had very few equals, either in the largeness of his body, or handsomeness of his appearance. He was also a man of great activity in the use of his hands, so that his actions were not unequal to the vast largeness and handsome appearance of his body. And men could easily guess at his strength and magnitude when they took his bed at Rabbath, the royal city of the Ammonites; its structure was of iron, its breadth four cubits, and its length a cubit more than double thereto. However, his fall did not only improve the circumstances of the Hebrews for the present, but by his death he was the occasion of further good success to them; for they presently took those sixty cities, which were encompassed with excellent walls, and had been subject to him, and all got both in general and in particular a great prey."[288]

The conquest has begun. The rich, arable and grazing land seized from the Amorites east of the Jordan, loosely referred to as part of

[288] Josephus, *Antiquities,* op. cit., 4:5:3

'Gilead', is given by Moses to the tribes of Reuben, Gad and half of Manasseh (Joseph) on the condition that they assist with the invasion alongside their brothers.

As promised, God makes the terror of the Israelites fill their enemies. Over the following years, ten Canaanite tribes will suffer God's controversial war of annihilation now their iniquity is full (Gen 15:16). The campaign continues with the destruction of Jericho and ends with the razing of Hazor in the north. During the campaign, the Nephilim too are despatched, cut off from the mountains and done to death in the cities which are burnt to the ground around them (Josh 11:21-22). The only giants left are in Gaza, Gath and Ashdod, the land of the Philistines.

And Moses? The flickerings of a trail. Mention is made by the Egyptian chronicler Manetho of a renegade priest from Heliopolis named Osarseph. The priest apparently helps the 'undesirables' escape from Egypt. Manetho tells us Osarseph later takes the name, Moses. Was Osarseph the original Hebrew birth name for Moses? We don't know at this time.

And Moses went up from the plains of Moab unto the mountain of Nebo, to the top of Pisgah, that is over against Jericho. And the LORD shewed him all the land of Gilead, unto Dan.... And the LORD said unto him, "This is the land which I sware unto Abraham, unto Isaac, and unto Jacob, saying, "I will give it unto thy seed: I have caused thee to see it with thine eyes, but thou shalt not go over thither."

So Moses, the servant of the LORD, died there in the land of Moab, according to the word of the LORD, and He buried him in a valley in the land of Moab, over against Bethpeor, but no man knoweth of his sepulchre unto this day. (Deut 34:1...6)

THE CANAAN HOLOCAUST

Yet it isn't over for Moses! Surprisingly, Yeshua's own brother in the New Testament records a dispute between *ha-Satan* and the archangel Michael over the old prophet's body in Jude 9. What's going on here? Later, during the ministry of Yeshua, Moses will appear with Elijah at Christ's transfiguration in what some expositors see as a staff meeting for the Second Coming.[289] Then we have the two witnesses in Revelation 11 who afflict the world in the last days during the frightening rule of Satan's global dictator, the Antichrist. As previously mentioned, the miracles these two perform are uniquely attributable to Elijah and Moses, leaving scholars to infer that these two Old Testament firebrands have been reserved for some special role in the months foreshadowing the return of Yeshua at the conclusion of the Great Tribulation. Jude is one of those fascinating but brief books in the Bible packed with strange insights. In just six verses we read:

I will therefore put you in remembrance, though ye once knew this, how that the LORD, having saved the people out of the land of Egypt, afterward destroyed them that believed not. And the angels, which kept not their first estate but left their own habitation, He hath reserved in everlasting chains under darkness unto the judgment of the great day.

Even as Sodom and Gomorrah, and the cities about them in like manner, giving themselves over to fornication, and going after strange flesh, are set forth for an example, suffering the vengeance of eternal fire. Likewise also these filthy dreamers defile the flesh, despise dominion and speak evil of dignities.

Yet Michael the archangel, when contending with the devil he disputed about the body of Moses, durst not bring against him a railing accusation but said, "The Lord rebuke thee".

But these speak evil of those things which they know not; but what they know naturally, as brute beasts, in those things they corrupt themselves. (Jude 5-10)

On the face of it, these verses cover the fact that God's forbearance lasts just so long before the hammer falls. The examples mentioned are:

---

[289] Matt 17:1-9; Mark 9:2-8; Luke 9:28-36

- The Israelites who fell in the desert during the Exodus because of their unbelief and lack of courage in taking the land God had given them
- The fiery end of the homosexuals of Sodom and Gomorrah, not only for their fleshly perversions, but for proposing the gang-rape of two of God's angels (**going after strange flesh**)[290]
- The wicked angels of Genesis 6 who kept not their first estate but discarded their *oiketerion* (heavenly bodies) to come down to Earth, steal those wives of humankind whom they found beautiful, and have sex with them. The resultant hybrids were giants, 'men of renown', 'Nephilim' before the Flood, and afterwards referred to as Nephilim ('fallen ones'), Rephaim ('the dead ones'), Emim ('the fearful ones') or the giants of Anak, or Anakim ('the long-necked ones'), who so terrified the spies Moses sent into Canaan prior to Israel's invasion.

It is in this context that Jude lets slip the struggle between Satan and Michael over Moses's body. This is the first and only mention of such an episode in the entire scriptures. One reasonably infers that Moses has a further role to play in the planet's destiny during our modern age, yet that's not the focus of Jude's point in bringing it up. One should not speak evil of dignities (dignitaries). Jude then goes on to cite what has to be the bizarrest example of a dignitary not to be dissed: Satan! Those who disrespect the devil have no idea what they are dealing with, as we shall see (Jude 10).

The new commander

But for now, Moses is dead and God buries him no-one knows where. The mantle falls to his most valorous commander, Joshua, son of Nun, to lead the Israelites in to possess the Land. We first met Joshua during the Exodus commanding the Israelite forces against the Amalekites at Rephidim (Exo 17:8-16). From a lineage which includes cattle thieves (1 Chron 7:20-28), Joshua evidently makes an early impression on God and Moses, for he is given progressive responsibility during the forty years of the Exodus. He accompanies

[290] God gives further reason for His anger at Sodom, which should cause modern societies a measure of disquiet: **"Behold, this was the iniquity of thy sister Sodom, pride, fulness of bread, and abundance of idleness was in her and in her daughters, neither did she strengthen the hand of the poor and needy. And they were haughty, and committed abomination before Me: therefore I took them away as I saw good."** (Eze 16:49-50)

Moses part way up Mount Horeb to receive the Ten Commandments (Exo 32:17). He is one of the twelve agents sent into Canaan by Moses to spy out the Land. Only he and Caleb give a good report of what they find, and encourage the Israelites to storm in and seize their inheritance. God is with us, they say, we are well able to overcome. For this they are almost stoned to death by their compatriots, who are terrified of reports of Nephilim/Anakim in the Land. For the Hebrews' fear, unbelief and general whingeing, God sentences the entire generation He brought out of Egypt to fall in the wilderness - hence the reason for remaining in the wilds for 38 years. Only the children of the Exodus generation, led by Joshua and Caleb, will survive to repopulate the land of their forefathers. Not even Moses makes it.

Joshua was born in Egypt, the firstborn of Nun, which means he would have had a particular interest in surviving the Passover of the Death Angel who slew the firstborn of those who did not have the lamb's blood on the lintel and door posts. Originally named Oshea, ('he saves' - Num 13:8), Moses promotes him by inserting God into his name. Oshea thus becomes Jehoshua ('YHWH is salvation' - Num 13:16). Wikipedia describes the etymology of the name thus:

> 'Jesus' is a transliteration, occurring in a number of languages and based on the Latin *Iesus*, of the Greek Ἰησοῦς (*Iēsoûs*), itself a hellenization of the Hebrew יְהוֹשֻׁעַ (*Yĕhōšuă'*, Joshua) or Hebrew-Aramaic יֵשׁוּעַ (*Yēšûă'*), both meaning 'Yahweh delivers' or 'Yahweh rescues'.[291]

So the first surprise is, we have a leading character in the OT with the same name as God's Son in the NT, and a book in the OT with Yeshua's name on it! As we will discover, the coincidences do not end there. No greater insight into the integrity/design characteristics of these 66 books which make up the Bible can be seen than in the parallels and types which will flow thick and fast in the forthcoming chapters. The unmistakable conclusion is that the Bible is a unified, codified intelligence system, wherein every detail maintains a relevance to the whole. Moses' successor exemplifies this in his parallels with the books of Ephesians and Revelation. For instance, Joshua is seen by many scholars as a type of Jesus in His military capacity as the Kinsman-Redeemer/Avenger of Blood at the Second Coming. This won't be the meek, cuddly Baby Jesus pushed at Sunday School, but terrifying Deity revisiting Earth with His legions

---

[291] http://en.wikipedia.org/wiki/Jesus

to set against the wicked with such ferocity, the blood will rise to the horses' bridles (Rev 14:19-20). In the OT, Joshua is poised to dispossess God's Land of the wicked Canaanites *and is expressly commanded by God to slaughter everyone* (Deut 7:2; 20:16-18; Num 31:17). This causes strictures with the good Christian ladies of the Church Flower Group. God sanctioning *genocide?* He has His reasons. And this is the same Jesus who will return at the end of this age to dispossess Earth of its usurpers, who won't fare much better in the terrifying Day of the LORD.

Yet for all the action approaching, God is slow to anger, unwilling that any should perish (Num 14:18; 2 Pet 3:9). The scriptures enable us to examine the character of our strange, all-consuming Creator in detail; observe how He reacts in a whole spectrum of predicaments; consider how He extends mercy and forgiveness for those who repent; metes out judgment and consternation for those who do not. It's not what one would expect from a provably transcendent message system. Never has the Earth been more 'spiritual' than today, but which spirit? We have extensive space research projects whose sole aim is to decode some extraterrestrial message and discover intelligent life on other planets, yet here we have the Creator of the universe making contact with us via His verifiable word in incredible, intimate detail, and what is our reaction? A fair chunk of the planet wants as little to do with Him as possible. Welcome to the Holy War, the Predicament of Man, of flesh versus spirit, the war going on inside each of us. *And we have to overcome.*

The real Holy War is dealing with our sinful nature with God's help and conforming to our Creator. Our enemy, *ha-Satan,* has been deliberately pitched against us to do all possible to thwart and destroy. In this spiritual warfare it is God's desire for each of us to know Him, and quick, for our eternal destiny hangs on this relationship or lack of it (Jer 22:15-16; Matt 7:13-23; FG 17:3).

What does God most wish to reveal about Himself? Moses asked to see God's glory on Mount Horeb.

And [the LORD] **said, "I will make all My goodness pass before thee, and I will proclaim the name of the LORD before thee, and will be gracious to whom I will be gracious, and will shew mercy on whom I will shew mercy."**

And He said, "Thou canst not see My face; for there shall no man see Me and live."

And the LORD said, "Behold, there is a place by Me and thou shalt stand upon a rock. And it shall come to pass, while My glory

passeth by, that I will put thee in a cleft of the rock and will cover thee with My hand while I pass by. And I will take away Mine hand and thou shalt see My back parts, but My face shall not be seen. (Exo 33:19-23)

And the LORD descended in the cloud and stood with him there and proclaimed the name of the LORD. And the LORD passed by before him [Moses] **and proclaimed, "The LORD, The LORD God, merciful and gracious, longsuffering, and abundant in goodness and truth, keeping mercy for thousands, forgiving iniquity and transgression and sin, and that** [He] **will by no means clear the guilty; visiting the iniquity of the fathers upon the children, and upon the children's children, unto the third and to the fourth generation."** (Exo 34:5-7)

Rather than God wishing us to know that He looks like Morgan Freeman, what most preoccupies Him is for us to know that He is **merciful and gracious, longsuffering, and abundant in goodness and truth, keeping mercy for thousands, forgiving iniquity and transgression and sin, and that will by no means clear the guilty.** People are drawn to God as to any parent, not through fear or judgment, but through the need to have their hearts right before Him. This is all there is. You're born, you live, you die. Just as with Cain, Abel, Noah, Shem, Abraham, Joseph, Moses and those before him, Joshua's Holy War will be all about crossing the Jordan to overcome the fleshly evil of Canaan and claim God's inheritance. And Joshua himself will fight his own personal battles along the way. Witness God's commission to Israel's new commander-in-chief.

"Moses, my servant, is dead. Now therefore arise, go over this Jordan, thou and all this people, unto the land which I do give to them, even to the children of Israel. Every place that the sole of your foot shall tread upon, that have I given unto you, as I said unto Moses. From the wilderness and this Lebanon even unto the great river, the river Euphrates, all the land of the Hittites, and unto the great sea toward the going down of the sun, shall be your coast.

"There shall not any man be able to stand before thee all the days of thy life. As I was with Moses, so I will be with thee. I will not fail thee nor forsake thee. Be strong and of a good courage, for unto this people shalt thou divide for an inheritance the land which I sware unto their fathers to give them.

"Only be thou strong and very courageous, that thou mayest observe to do according to all the law which Moses my servant

commanded thee. Turn not from it to the right hand or to the left, that thou mayest prosper whithersoever thou goest.

"This book of the law shall not depart out of thy mouth, but thou shalt meditate therein day and night, that thou mayest observe to do according to all that is written therein, for then thou shalt make thy way prosperous, and then thou shalt have good success. Have not I commanded thee? Be strong and of a good courage. Be not afraid, neither be thou dismayed, for the LORD thy God is with thee whithersoever thou goest." (Josh 1:2-9)

God's proclamation of support for Joshua is as simple as it is astonishing. In return for his *obedience,* God will not allow Joshua to be defeated or fail. God is setting a principle here and He does not change (Mal 3:6). Any faithful believer can avail themselves of this very same relationship.

The geographical description of the original land grant to Israel makes a mockery of today's boundaries; the inheritance is from the Mediterranean in the west to the River Euphrates in the east, and from the Negev in south to Lebanon in the north. Let us remind ourselves that God's gift of the Land to the Jews is *unconditional, unilateral and still in force today.* Unconditional, in that His people do nothing to merit the gift (and the Land is not even conditional on their obedience); unilateral, in that the Land is God's alone to gift to whom He pleases. Five times in the first chapter of Joshua, God repeats that the Land is *a gift* to His people (Josh 1:2,3,6,11,15). Five is the number of grace.[292] God's gift of the Land, as with salvation and any inheritance, is through grace; the Jews have done nothing to deserve it, *yet it has to be claimed.* The Land must be conquered. Our own flesh must be tamed. Canaan thus becomes a type of battlefield of the flesh which we must overcome with God's help. Notwithstanding the Jews will be set aside in God's plan several times in the coming centuries and even removed from the Land altogether on two occasions, God alone adjudicates the destiny of His Land and His people. Politicians in the 21st century dispute God's land charter and His hand on the Jews at their peril, as we shall see.

Genocide

Emerging from the wilderness, Joshua's army is huge and the total Israelite horde probably exceeds two million at this point. The land before them, Canaan, is a mish-mash of interwarring city-states,

---

[292] www.biblestudy.org/bibleref/meaning-of-numbers-in-bible/5.html

each ruled by an autocratic king. The most powerful of these is Jericho, or *Bet Yerah,* 'the House of the Moon God', as it still is today.[293] The name can mean 'fragrant'. Jericho is the lowest permanently inhabited city on Earth at 846 feet below sea-level. It is also one of the oldest. Joshua will take this city first and destroy every man, woman and child apart from one family.

Many become uncomfortable when they read of Joshua's genocidal Canaan war. There is no glossing over what God instructs his commander to do. None shall be spared. How can this decree of God's be reconciled with the loving Deity presented by Yeshua in the NT? In one word, *chērem.*

Chērem is Jewish Holy War specifically sanctioned by YHWH. Separation from, and complete extermination of the Canaanite races is decreed in Deuteronomy 7:1-5. Deuteronomy 20:16-18 reads:

"But of the cities of these people, which the LORD thy God doth give thee for an inheritance, thou shalt save alive nothing that breatheth. But thou shalt utterly destroy them; namely, the Hittites, and the Amorites, the Canaanites, and the Perizzites, the Hivites, and the Jebusites; as the LORD thy God hath commanded thee. That they teach you not to do after all their abominations, which they have done unto their gods; so should ye sin against the LORD your God.[294]

Walter Kaiser comments:

"[*Chērem*] means 'curse', 'that which stood under the ban' or 'that which was dedicated to destruction'. The root idea of this term was 'separation'; however, this situation was not the positive concept of sanctification in which someone or something was set aside for the service and glory of God. This was the opposite of the same side of the coin: to set aside or separate for destruction. God dedicated these things or persons to destruction because they violently and steadfastly impeded or opposed his work over a long period of time." [295]

Daniel Gard writes:

"In its purest form, the *chērem* in warfare refers to the devotion of all spoils to Yahweh and the destruction of all life (Josh 6:17-21; 7:11-15).

---

[293] Moon worship preceded Islam by 2,500 years (*cf.* Deut 4:19; 17:3; 2 Kings 21:3, 5; 23:5; Isa 3:16,18; Jer 8:2; 19:13; Zeph 1:5).

[294] Other relevant passages are Exo 23:20-33; 34:11-16; Num 21:2; Josh 6:17-21; 7:11-15 and 1 Sam 15.

[295] **Kaiser, Walter et al** *Hard Sayings of the Bible,* InterVarsity Press, 1996, p.206

Inflammable objects were to be burned (Deut 7:25-26) but noncombustible precious metals were to be taken to the sanctuary treasury (Josh 6:24). It was forbidden to spare any person that was under the *chērem*. In some cases, the *chērem* was partially eased by the exemption of women and children (Num 31:7-12; 17-18; Deut 20:13-14; 21:10-14) and, in particular, the young virgin women (Judg 21:11-21). A point of tension exists on the issue of cattle; according to Deuteronomy 2:34-35, they could be saved, but 1 Samuel 15:9, 21 demanded their destruction. In the matter of the people of the land, however, there was no equivocation: The Hittites, the Amorites, the Canaanites, the Perizzites, the Hivites and the Jebusites were to be utterly destroyed so that nothing that breathed should live (Deut. 20:16-18)." [296]

The command given utterly to destroy seven Canaanite peoples is very specific:

"When the LORD thy God shall bring thee into the land whither thou goest to possess it, and hath cast out many nations before thee: the Hittites and the Girgashites and the Amorites and the Canaanites and the Perizzites and the Hivites and the Jebusites, seven nations greater and mightier than thou; and when the LORD thy God shall deliver them before thee, thou shalt smite them and utterly destroy them. Thou shalt make no covenant with them, nor shew mercy unto them. Neither shalt thou make marriages with them. Thy daughter thou shalt not give unto his son, nor his daughter shalt thou take unto thy son. For they will turn away thy son from following Me, that they may serve other gods. So will the anger of the LORD be kindled against you and destroy thee suddenly." (Deut 7:1-4)

This is something new. The Israelite preparation for the Canaanite campaign is not something we have seen heretofore. The war will be conducted in sacred character almost as an act of worship. God decrees that the Jews be circumcised prior to commencement of hostilities. It's a surprise that the second generation after Egypt at this point have not been circumcised according to the Law. God will be intimately involved in the question of which campaigns will be sanctioned and which will not. Joshua is to seek His face in all things. Failure to do so will result in defeats and setbacks. Communication with God is carried out via 'the Angel of the Lord' (widely viewed as

[296] **Gard, Daniel** "The Case for Eschatological Continuity", in *Show Them No Mercy: 4 Views on God and Canaanite Genocide,* ed. Stanley Gundry, Zondervan, 2003, p.116

a pre-incarnate Jesus Christ since this angel receives worship), or seeking God's will (*cf.* 1 Sam 23:1-6). Adam Woods observes:

"Spiritual preparedness before battle is also evident in the way the second generation of Jewish males [from Egypt] was mass-circumcised prior to practising Canaanite *chērem* (Josh 5:2-9). This generation also observed Passover prior to battle (Josh 5:10-12). This sacral dimension prior to battle is also seen in the need for ritual purity in the war camp (Deut 23:9-14), which included abstention from sexual activity (2 Sam 11:11). Also, prior to battle the priest was to administer the appropriate animal sacrifice (1 Sam 7:9-10). The importance of this procedure is evidenced by the fact that Saul was told that his kingdom would not endure when he failed to comply with the procedure (1 Sam 13). Moreover, the placing of the Ark representing the presence of God at the head of the army also demonstrates Israel's spiritual preparedness prior to battle (Josh 6). It is probably for this reason that the Ark is mentioned seven times in Joshua 6."[297]

God does not need to answer for His actions because He is God, and He is certainly not looking for any input from us on how to run His universe. But the Bible teaches that the awful fate to befall the Canaanite nations is ordained by God and in the most part carried out by Joshua for the following reasons:

- To prevent Israel from practising idolatry (Deut 7:2-4).
- Since God has already threatened to destroy Israel if she practises idolatry (Deut 7:4), if the Canaanites remain in the land, Israel's established propensity for calf worship and worse will assure her destruction, and actually will do so centuries into the future. *Ha-Satan* will have done his work well.[298] The united monarchy under David and Solomon will break up due to Solomon's idolatry and adherence to Canaanite practices. The Northern Kingdom of Israel will be invaded by the Assyrians and their peoples suffer *diaspora* due to idolatry.[299] The Southern Kingdom of Judah will endure a 70-year servitude under the Babylonians for the same reason. God means what He says and says what He means.

---

[297] www.spiritandtruth.org/teaching/documents/articles/27/27.htm#_ftn10#_ftn10

[298] Divine threats against idolatry are repeated throughout Deuteronomy (8:19-20; 11:16-17; 30:17-18) and Joshua (11:20; 23:13, 15, 16; 24:20).

[299] Diaspora: dispersement of a population from its original homeland.

- To ensure the Messianic promises to Israel and the world will be fulfilled (Gen 12:3; 49:10). Frederic Bush writes:

"...the *chērem*.... must be viewed within the context of Israel's prophetic outlook. Yahweh acted for Israel and against Israel's enemies because of his covenant promises with the fathers. In fact, this makes the idea of total destruction an understandable item in Biblical religion, for the covenant's ultimate purpose is to provide for all the nations of the Earth the knowledge of Yahweh and the covenant blessings. Anything or any person that would prevent the working out of this redemptive purpose for all peoples must be removed as an enemy of Yahweh."[300]

- God's Land promise to the Jews will not be fulfilled if the Canaanites remain in the Land [301]
- God had already prophesied the destruction of the Canaanite races and His promises cannot be broken. Adam Woods explains:

"Not only did God predict that Israel would ultimately possess the land, but He also specified the timetable as to when this was to occur. Gen 15:16 says, "Then in the fourth generation they shall return here, for the iniquity of the Amorite is not yet complete." In other words, Israel was to return, take possession of the land and execute judgment upon the Canaanites after 400 years (Gen 15:13). Had this not happened, prophecy would have failed. God would not have allowed prophecy to fail since the Scripture cannot be broken (John 10:35)."[302]

- As with the miracles He performed in Egypt and during the Exodus, God will use His judgment on Canaan to teach all nations the fear of Him; His divine will; that He is God of all the Earth. The succession of 'judges'/leaders God will send to deliver Israel in the future will perform strange feats of bravery and daring, whose outcomes cannot be attributable to human agency alone. God will use His actions to testify of His power, glory and ultimate sovereignty
- And, of course, God will judge Canaan for its sin. Yet this is judgment of the permanent kind, as with the Flood which destroyed all mankind save eight, for committing unspeakable crimes against God and His Creation. YHWH is to punish the

---

[300] **LaSor W, Hubbard D and F Bush** *Old Testament Survey*, Eerdmans, 1996, p.154

[301] Gen 12:7; 13:14-15; 15:18-21; 17:8. These patriarchal Land promises are repeated throughout Deuteronomy: (1:6-8; 2:25-37; 3:1-22; 6:10-12; 7:1; 9:1-3; 11:23-25; 20:1-18; 29:6-8; 31:3-6).

[302] www.spiritandtruth.org/teaching/documents/articles/27/27.htm#_ftnref20

Canaanites in the manner of the final Great White Throne Judgment (Rev 20:11-15). It can be argued that the Canaanites receive a 38-year grace period to clean up their act and repent when the Jews fail to enter the land at Kadesh Barnea. Canaan was certainly aware of the Israelite hordes in the desert and the strange, terrifying happenings afflicting Egypt by the power of their Deity. They were not unmindful of the fate of Sodom and Gomorrah and the widely bruited, coming judgment on Canaan, yet interestingly no effort is made at repentance. Only one woman in Jericho will repent and believe, so she and her household will be the only ones spared.

Critics of God always cite the Canaanite genocide as triumphant proof of the dangers of 'God'. To Richard Dawkins, YHWH is a *"petty, unjust, unforgiving control freak; a vindictive, racist, infanticidal, genocidal, filicidal, malevolent bully,"*[303] so the Canaanites get off scot-free at Richard's values-relativist bar of liberal opinion, yet they are far from innocent victims. Their crimes are as bad as it gets, and when God's view is factored into the equation, Joshua's coming mission assumes a starkly different hue.

The sin of Canaan

You might recall from *Origins II - Holy War* that God cursed Ham's fourth son, Canaan, for some sexual shenanigans Ham had committed in Noah's tent shortly after the Flood:

And Noah began to be an husbandman [farmer] **and he planted a vineyard. And he drank of the wine and was drunken, and he was uncovered within his tent. And Ham, the father of Canaan, saw the nakedness of his father and told his two brethren without.** (Gen 9:20-22)

Wikipedia reports:

"The curse seems unusually severe for merely observing Noah unclothed. An explanation sometimes offered notes that the phrase 'expose father's nakedness' is used several times elsewhere in the Pentateuch as a euphemism for having sexual relations with one's mother, suggesting a different crime."[304]

It certainly does: **And the man that lieth with his father's wife hath uncovered his father's nakedness...** (Lev 20:11). And Leviticus

---

[303] **Dawkins, Richard** *The God Delusion,* Bantam, London, 2006, p.31

[304] http://en.wikipedia.org/wiki/Curse_of_Ham

18:7-8 states: **The nakedness of thy father, or the nakedness of thy mother, shalt thou not uncover: she is thy mother; thou shalt not uncover her nakedness. The nakedness of thy father's wife shalt thou not uncover: it is thy father's nakedness.**

Three suggestions for Ham's crime have been offered by scholars over the years:

1) Ham had sexual relations with his mother.
2) Ham sodomised his father.
3) Ham castrated his father, preventing him from having a fourth son. Thus Canaan, Ham's fourth son, is cursed in revenge.

In any case, Canaan receives God's curse and it all comes home to roost for his descendants when Joshua storms in. It's important to note that God orders the slaughter of the Canaanites not for being born to the wrong families, but because of the heinous nature of their crimes against humanity and thus God. In Genesis 15:16, we find God keeping score of these atrocities with the view to payback. Quartz Hill Theological School comments:

"Why were the Canaanites singled out for such severe treatment? They were cut off to prevent Israel and the rest of the world from being corrupted (Deut. 20:16-18). When a people starts to burn their children in honor of their gods (Lev. 18:21), practise sodomy, bestiality, and all sorts of loathsome vice (Lev. 18:23, 24, 20:3), the land itself begins to 'vomit' them out as the body heaves under the load of internal poisons (Lev. 18:25, 27-30). Thus, 'objection to the fate of these nations ... is really an objection to the highest manifestation of the grace of God'. [Some] liken this action on God's part, not to doing evil that good may come (though that does seem often to be God's methodology: the ends justify the means), but doing good in spite of certain evil consequences, just as a surgeon does not refrain from amputating a gangrenous leg even though in so doing he cannot help but cut off much healthy flesh."[305]

The Canaanites were deeply immersed in the Nimrod/ Semiramis sex and death cult and addicted to its lure. Back then the average citizen participated in grotesque temple orgies and sexually violent behaviour of the most depraved order as part of their religion. Today, our culture practises the same addiction via the Internet and Hollywood. Jerry Ropelato writes:

---

[305] www.theology.edu/canaan.htm

"The [pornography] statistics are truly staggering. According to compiled numbers from respected news and research organizations, every second $3,075.64 is being spent on pornography. Every second 28,258 internet users are viewing pornography. In that same second 372 internet users are typing adult search terms into search engines. Every 39 minutes a new pornographic video is being created in the U.S.

"It's big business. The pornography industry has larger revenues than Microsoft, Google, Amazon, eBay, Yahoo, Apple and Netflix combined. 2006 Worldwide Pornography Revenues ballooned to $97.06 billion. 2006 & 2005 U.S. Pornography Industry Revenue Statistics, 2006 Top Adult Search Requests, 2006 Search Engine Request Trends are some of the other statistics revealed."[306]

12% of the total Internet comprises 372 million pages of pornography. 8% of the Internet's total email traffic is pornographic. Worldwide visitors to pornographic websites: 72 million.[307] Tech Mission Safe Families website reports:

"Adults admitting to Internet sexual addiction: 10%; 28% of those are women. More than 70% of men from 18 to 34 visit a pornographic site in a typical month. More than 20,000 images of child pornography are posted online every week. Approximately 20% of all Internet pornography involves children.... At a 2003 meeting of the American Academy of Matrimonial Lawyers, two thirds of the 350 divorce lawyers who attended said the Internet played a significant role in the divorces in the past year, with excessive interest in online porn contributing to more than half such cases. Pornography had an almost non-existent role in divorce just seven or eight years ago." [308]

Then there's today's addiction to sex, horror and violence, rolled into one package by Hollywood. I won't waste your time going down the current top 50 horror films listed on iTunes - you get the picture. Back in Canaan, none of the sex, horror or violence was vicarious; you could participate to your heart's content. Susan Anthony writes:

"The book of Jasher is an ancient book mentioned in the Bible. It gives details about the evil in Sodom. For example, strangers and travelers who came into the city would be robbed, stripped, and held captive within the city. They would wander the streets slowly starving to

---

[306] http://internet-filter-review.toptenreviews.com/internet-pornography-statistics.html

[307] www.mykidsbrowser.com/pornography_stats.php

[308] www.safefamilies.org/sfStats.php

death to the great amusement of the citizenry. Another account relates that visitors to Sodom were offered a bed according to the Middle Eastern laws of hospitality, but it was a bed of torture. People too short were stretched. People too long had their legs cut off. If a traveler had no money, he would be offered bricks of gold and silver with his name on them! Only nobody would sell him bread and water, even for all that gold and silver. So the traveler slowly died of starvation. The Sodomites gathered around the corpse and took back the gold and silver. The people in Sodom were not only evil, they were proud of being evil….

"Archaeology gives hints of what the Canaanites did. On one of the high places, archaeologists found several stone pillars and great numbers of jars containing the remains of newborn babies. When a new house was built, a child would be sacrificed and its body built into the wall to bring good luck to the rest of the family. The firstborn were often sacrificed to Molech, a giant hollow bronze image in which a fire was built. Parents would place their children in its red hot hands and the babies would roll down into the fire. The sacrifice was invalid if the mother showed grief. She was supposed to dance and sing. The Israelites later copied this practice in a valley near Jerusalem called Gehenna. Hundreds of jars containing infant bones have been found there." [309]

We are learning that when God has had it with a people, get your tin hat on. The kings of the Canaanite tribes hide out in caves from Joshua's onslaught in much the same way the kings of the Earth will take cover during the Great Tribulation to escape the wrath of the Lamb (Jesus). **For the great day of His wrath is come; and who shall be able to stand?** (*cf:* Rev 6:15-17). This is one of many parallels we shall examine between the books of Joshua and Revelation. We'll see a similar trend occurring during the final 42 months leading up to Christ's Second Coming when millions are destroyed in the terrifying Tribulation which terminates the rule of Satan's Antichrist. God's final judgment of all mankind is in a similar, permanent vein resulting in eternal fellowship with God (Heaven) or eternal separation from Him (Hell).

Repent or perish

The model repeated throughout the OT and NT is consistent: God takes no pleasure in the death of the wicked. He is slow to judgment, giving each of us a chance to come to our senses, repent and get right

[309] http://susancanthony.com/Resources/Dennis/canaan.html

with Him.[310] If we don't, judgment comes. The pre-Flood population had, by some estimates, 120 years to repent but they refused so God destroyed the lot. God gave Amenhotep II every opportunity to see sense in releasing the Hebrews but he didn't, so God destroyed his civilization, firstborn and Egypt's northern army. God made it clear to Abraham that if just ten righteous were to be found in Sodom and Gomorrah, He would withhold judgment (Gen 18:32). In the end, Lot and his family were the only ones removed, and Sodom and Gomorrah got theirs. God sent Jonah to the king and people of Nineveh to get them to repent and they did, so God withheld His judgment. Throughout their history, God gives the Israelites every chance to turn from their idolatry and repent, and when they do He forgives and delivers them, but when they don't He destroys them. The Canaanites have had 400 years to repent, including a final 40 years to turn from their atrocities. They don't. Neither can they lay claim to ignorance. The Amorite harlot Rahab makes it very clear to Joshua's two spies that Jericho's population from the king down know what's coming, why it is coming, which God is bringing it to pass, and they are *terrified* (Josh 2:9-13):

"I know that the LORD hath given you the land, and that your terror is fallen upon us, and that all the inhabitants of the land faint because of you." (Josh 2:9)

Only Rahab repents and is saved, she and all her household. The rest perish. Susan Anthony summarises:

"Families who wished could have migrated out of the land and settled in nearby areas. God said repeatedly that he would drive out the inhabitants of the land before Israel. Those who wished to leave had time and opportunity. The point was to destroy the evil Canaanite *culture* rather than the individual Canaanite *people*. Only individuals who stubbornly refused to leave were destroyed with military force, along with their children, who could not have survived without parents. God gave no instructions to hunt down and kill Canaanites who left the land peacefully. Later in the Bible, Canaanite individuals like Uriah the Hittite show up as righteous characters. Rahab herself was a Canaanite harlot who repented before Jericho was destroyed. She is an ancestor of Jesus Himself. God's judgment was not based on racism or favoritism.

"God is never arbitrary or unjust, despite how some events appear at first glance. The same people who are angry because God doesn't do

---

[310] Exo 34:6; Psa 89:14; Eze 18:23; 33:11; 2 Pet 3:9

anything about all the evil in the world are the first to cry foul when He does. But those of us who know Him trust that His justice is perfect. His patience and forgiveness are immense. He waits for repentance. He gives everyone the opportunity to choose between salvation and judgment."[311]

Those who baulk at Yeshua bearing any resemblance to the OT's YHWH have never read the book of Revelation. The model is rolled out again. Repent or perish. Most of the world refuses to repent during the Great Tribulation and even curses God to His face. The slaughter of half the world's population which follows at the hand of Christ Himself makes the Canaan genocide look tame (Rev 6:8; 9:15), yet Jesus states that God desires mercy not sacrifice (Matt 9:13; 12:7). The whole purpose of God coming to Earth in human form is to call sinners to repentance to avoid just such an outcome.[312] With the way the Christian message is diluted these days, our LORD seems to hang on that cross for nothing. The next time He returns as terrifying Deity, it will be to destroy, but not before removing the repentant first ('the Rapture').[313]

The model remains consistent. God wants repentance, but in the end if you really won't repent, then you'd better get a spade and dig. If you don't want your Creator anywhere near your house, your family or your life, God will fix it so you are never bothered by Him again *for eternity* (Rev 14:10-11; 20:11-15). The real Holy War is not some Papist Crusader killing the Muslim infidel in the name of Jesus, or even *vice versa,* it's our own flesh, spirit and conscience warring against our Creator with *ha-Satan's* help. There is only one winner. The scriptures declare that the lost will be without excuse at the Great White Throne Judgment. Nobody will end up in Hell because of their sin. They will end up in Hell because they refused the provision God made for their sin. Which is His only Son.

The two spies go in

Before the invasion, Joshua sends two spies across the Jordan into Jericho, the capital of the Amorites - his first and hardest target. Initially the mission of these two agents appears to be plain, old-fashioned espionage - scouting out the city for strengths and

---

[311] http://susancanthony.com/Resources/Dennis/canaan.html

[312] See *Origins IV – Tetelestai.*

[313] The startling NT doctrine of the 'Rapture' (*harpazo*) is given a full airing in *Origins VI - Parousia.*

weaknesses, getting the feel of the target before Joshua sends in the cohorts. And what better place to start spying than at a tavern of ill-repute, located on the city wall in full flow of the city's mercantile traffic and gossip.[314]

The king of Jericho is tipped off immediately, which is a clue to the highly strung state of the city. The king's guard show up at the tavern and order Rahab, the harlot in charge, to hand over the Israelites. But she replies:

"There came men unto me but I wist not whence they were [i.e. "I have no idea where they came from"]**. And it came to pass about the time of shutting of the gate, when it was dark, that the men went out. Whither the men went I wot** [know] **not. Pursue after them quickly, for ye shall overtake them."**

But she had brought them up to the roof of the house and hid them with the stalks of flax, which she had laid in order upon the roof. (Josh 2:4-6)

Rahab tells a bald-faced lie – a harlot lying, imagine that. The first surprise is that the king's men take her word without apparent demur. Jack Heyford writes:

> "Perhaps the king's messengers were so easily convinced that Rahab was telling the truth because of her respected position in pagan society. Harlots (prostitutes) were often priestesses of the Canaanite religion and their profession was considered honourable."[315]

It's more likely that God has His hand on the situation, having led the men to Rahab in the first place. And in the king's eyes, what would Rahab, a dyed-in-the-wool Amorite, have to gain by hiding the spies of an invading army come to wipe them all out? What happens next further widens our eyes:

And she said unto the [men of Israel]**. "I know that the LORD hath given you the land, and that your terror is fallen upon us, and that all the inhabitants of the land faint because of you. For we have heard how the LORD dried up the water of the Red Sea for you when ye came out of Egypt; and what ye did unto the two kings of the Amorites that were on the other side of the Jordan, Sihon and Og, whom ye utterly destroyed. And as soon as we had heard these things, our hearts did melt, neither did there remain any more**

---

314 Archaeologists report that Jericho's walls were twelve feet thick in places, enabling dwellings to be built into them. Heyford, Jack, *Spirit-Filled Bible,* op. cit., p.309

315 Ibid., p.308

courage in any man because of you; for the LORD your God, He is God in Heaven above and in Earth beneath.

Now therefore, I pray you, swear unto me by the LORD, since I have shewed you kindness, that ye will also shew kindness unto my father's house and give me a true token: And that ye will save alive my father and my mother and my brethren and my sisters, and all that they have, and deliver our lives from death." (Josh 2:9-13)

Some interesting information here:

- The shoe's on the other foot now from the situation the Jews faced at Kadesh Barnea 38 years before. They were too terrified to go in, face the giants and conquer the land. All that has changed. All across Canaan, the city states are now in a state of terror – the roles reversed – Jericho in particular. Their fear? The Israelites and their God
- Even a tavern harlot knows enough about regional politics to realise Jericho is finished and will be utterly destroyed by what is coming
- It is common gossip on the street what the God of Israel did to the Egyptians and later to two Canaanite kings the other side of the Jordan
- Rahab's had her eyes opened by the LORD to know that the Hebrew Deity is not some tribal idol like those of Canaan but **God in Heaven above and in Earth beneath**
- She now wants to cut a deal with the Israelite agents to spare herself and her family

The Israelites agree and tell her to bind a scarlet cord in the window of her property on the city wall. The Jewish army will be instructed not to harm anyone in the house when it storms in, but if any of Rahab's family venture outside the house during the attack, all bets are off. The two parties agree, and the agents leave Jericho. They eventually return to Joshua on the other side of the Jordan after hiding out in the mountains for three days. They tell their commander: **"Truly the LORD hath delivered into our hands all the land, for even all the inhabitants of the country do faint because of us."** (Josh 2:24)

The story bears more than a passing resemblance to Passover night in Egypt, when the lamb's blood on the doorposts caused the Angel of Death to spare the occupants the death of their firstborn. The scarlet cord is also idiomatic of, not only the Messianic line, but the redemptive work of Yeshua on the cross, sparing those who look to it for salvation.

Some insights:

- Two spies go into a city to witness, reflective of the two witnesses of Rev 11
- You don't necessarily have to be a member of Rahab's household to be saved, you just have to be in the house (same as Passover)
- Rahab wants the oath sworn by the Hebrew God to bind the promise
- Rahab tells a blatant lie to the king's messengers, yet we find her listed in the New Testament 'Who's Who' as one of the faith greats, not because of her deeds but for her belief (Heb 11:31)
- God's overall redemptive plan is echoed here: On the way to the Jews receiving their inheritance (the Land), some Gentiles (the Church) are saved
- Rahab is not only spared from destruction, she becomes an ancestor to the Messiah Himself. Rahab is a sinner, but so is every other member of Yeshua's ancestry.

Crossing the Jordan

Joshua sends his commanders throughout the Israelite camp instructing the people to sanctify themselves in preparation. That the Jordan is in spring spate at this time, waters roiling over its banks, is sure to enhance the miracle God has in store. YHWH gives Joshua his orders: The Ark of the Covenant, borne by the Levites, will go first. The remainder of the Jews have been instructed not to come closer than 1,000 yards of the sacred icon for fear of… well, you saw *Raiders of the Lost Ark.* As soon as the feet of the Levites bearing the Ark touch the heaving waters, the Jordan will dry up. The priests will then remain in the midst of the river bed with the Ark while the Israelites cross over to the west bank.

This is a career-defining moment for Joshua. God tells him: **"This day will I begin to magnify thee in the sight of all Israel, that they may know that, as I was with Moses, so I will be with thee."** (Josh 3:7)

So the Levites bear up the Ark with the poles on their shoulders and head out towards the furious river ahead of the multitude. What must each priest be thinking? *Should we even be thinking? Take every thought captive lest we sink without a bubble!*

And as they that bare the Ark were come unto the Jordan, and the feet of the priests that bare the Ark were dipped in the brim of

the water, (for the Jordan overfloweth all his banks all the time of harvest,) that the waters which came down from above stood and rose up upon an heap very far from the city Adam, that is beside Zaretan: and those that came down toward the sea of the plain, even the salt sea [Dead Sea], **failed and were cut off, and the people passed over right against Jericho.**

And the priests that bare the Ark of the Covenant of the LORD stood firm on dry ground in the midst of Jordan and all the Israelites passed over on dry ground until all the people were passed clean over the Jordan. (Josh 3:15-17)

God instructs Joshua to nominate a man from each of the twelve tribes to pick up a stone (boulder) in the midst of the Jordan and remove it to the camp they will be setting that night at Gilgal. Joshua himself sets up twelve more stones in the midst of the Jordan where the priests are standing, then orders the Levites themselves to complete the Ark's crossing now the multitude has passed.

And it came to pass, when the priests that bare the Ark of the Covenant of the LORD were come up out of the midst of the Jordan, and the soles of the priests' feet were lifted up unto the dry land, that the waters of Jordan returned unto their place and flowed over all its banks, as they did before.

And the people came up out of the Jordan <u>on the tenth day of the first month</u> [= 10th Nisan] **and encamped in Gilgal in the east border of Jericho. And those twelve stones, which they took out of the Jordan, did Joshua pitch in Gilgal.**

And he spake unto the children of Israel, saying, "When your children shall ask their fathers in time to come, saying, 'What mean these stones?' Then ye shall let your children know, saying, "Israel came over this Jordan on dry land. For the LORD your God dried up the waters of the Jordan from before you until ye were passed over, as the LORD your God did to the Red Sea, which He dried up from before us, until we were gone over. That all the people of the Earth might know the hand of the LORD, that it is mighty; that ye might fear the LORD your God forever.'" (Josh 4:18-24)

Some types and observations:

- Those crossing include the warriors selected to raze Jericho. These include men from the tribes of Reuben, Gad and the half-tribe of Manasseh who, although they had already settled in lands east of the Jordan, had agreed with Moses to join the host of Israel in their fight for the Canaan inheritance

- It's spring time when the snows on Mount Hermon melt and send the waters into the Jordan
- The Ark must go ahead of the people alone as Yeshua went ahead for us, alone
- The priests must exercise major faith to step out on the current, Ark on shoulders, before the waters dry up. This prefigures the disciple Peter stepping out on the stormy waves of Lake Galilee in faith to reach Yeshua. Numerous other examples are given throughout the scriptures of stepping out in faith to trust God for deliverance. God is making the point that faith and trust in Him is what it takes to really know Him
- Once again, Israel walks on dry ground through adverse waters blocking her path
- To many scholars, crossing the Jordan symbolises a person's death on Earth and rebirth in Heaven (Canaan). If so, then Heaven's going to resemble the Battle of Stalingrad. In the ensuing invasion, Canaan will run red with blood and extreme violence as Israel settles in the land - not such a great analogy of Heavenly paradise. Much more fitting: crossing the Jordan signifies a person's moment of destiny/decision to trust God and change their lives to follow Him, hence the consecration ritual to separate themselves from sin unto God
- Notice that God Himself parts the waters for you because He chose you from the foundation of the world, you don't do it yourself.[316] Thereafter, you cross the Jordan, an act of volition (baptism and spiritual rebirth), whereupon you enter the fleshly land of Canaan and embark on the true Holy War of spiritual conquest of the flesh. This is the rocky road of sanctification in the spirit and the path to the rewards and inheritance God has in store for you. Sanctification is not a one-time event but a *process* leading to spiritual maturity
- The twelve stones taken from the Jordan and erected at Gilgal can signify those who were once dead raised to the newness of life. Notice the stones themselves do nothing to merit this salvation, they have to be carried. The stones left in the Jordan symbolise those yet to be resurrected or those who refuse to repent
- After forty years the manna ceases when they camp at Gilgal.

[316] Eph 1:4-5; FG 6:44; 6:64; 15:16; 2 Tim 2:19; 2 Thess 2:13; Rom 1:7; Acts 13:48; Isa 49:1,5; Jer 1:5; Gal 1:15

"It is interesting to watch the timing of the crossing of the Jordan," says Peter Wallace. "The spies spend one night with Rahab, when she tells them that the hearts of the people of Jericho have melted with fear. Then they spend three days in the hills before reporting to Joshua on the fourth day. The next day Joshua arises and brings Israel to the banks of the Jordan River. But they wait there for three days (fifth, sixth and seventh) before crossing on the eighth day."[317]

- Eight: the number of new beginnings
- The day they cross is 10th Nisan, which is the preparation day four days before Passover. This is the day when the lambs are selected and inspected prior to slaughter at Passover. Jesus also presents Himself as a Lamb and King to Jerusalem on 10th Nisan in the event known as the Triumphal Entry. Israel has just entered Canaan in time to celebrate Passing over the Jordan. They've made a spiritual commitment to God
- Centuries later, Jesus Himself will come to this very spot Himself to be baptised by John before embarking on His Holy War of the flesh. John the Baptist himself will make reference to the stones at Bethabara (Matt 3:7-10). Yeshua's own 'Canaan campaign' will include the famous temptations of *ha-Satan* in the wilderness and the constant badgering of the religious authorities. He moves through the time of His ministry to His destiny at the cross to claim His reward and inheritance as the Son: the redemption of all Creation. And us.
- Chuck Missler sees another type or model in this event:

"There are two seas, both fed by the same river, filled with the same source. One brings forth green fields, fruit bearing trees, and is surrounded by verdant beauty. The other is desert, surrounded by death. Nothing can grow in or near it. One is the Sea of Galilee. The other is the Dead Sea. Both are fed by the Jordan River .One passes its water on, and is synonymous with life itself. The other receives, but does not pass its water on further. It is contained in itself. It is synonymous with death. John the Baptist baptized Jesus in the Jordan at Beth Bara – the House of Passage – when He began His ministry."[318]

---

[317] www.peterwallace.org/sermons/Josh03-04.htm
[318] www.khouse.org, Joshua Notes, p.25

Forewarned and foreskinned

Once word of the Jordan miracle reaches them, one can only imagine the reactions of Jericho's Amorite king and the various city-state tyrants around Canaan. The Jews once again have done the impossible and spookily traversed a watery barrier with God's help without getting their sandals wet. Worse, they are now poised to sweep in and clean up, and if the spies' reports are to be believed, the Hebrew God wants every Canaanite man, woman and child utterly destroyed from the face of the Earth.

Canaan freaks out (*cf.* Exo 23:27). You would be forgiven for thinking that this is the moment when Joshua despatches his legions to storm in and set about the bloody business, but he doesn't. Instead, in what seems like an act of brazen foolishness, the son of Nun hamstrings his entire fighting force for a number of days by chopping off their foreskins.

The preparations for *chērem* - Jewish Holy War - are not yet completed. Since the second generation from Egypt has never been circumcised, the Israelites are out of the covenant relationship with YHWH, a matter requiring immediate redress before battle commences. The flint knives are honed keen. Row upon row of Jewish warriors grit their teeth as their manhood is trimmed, and while they heal in the camp, Passover is celebrated and for the first time they eat of the produce of Canaan. The hated manna, which sustained them six days a week for the previous forty years, ceases the following day. It's a landmark moment. The reproach of Egypt has been expunged (Josh 5:9); there will be no going back. If they are going to eat henceforth, it will be from the Land they have yet to conquer.

During this brief interlude before the assault on Jericho, Joshua has a strange, close encounter. It is assumed that he is carrying out reconnaissance near the city when he becomes aware of a man standing opposite with his sword drawn. Joshua challenges the stranger in the manner of a sentry.

"Art thou for us or for our adversaries?"

And [the man] **said, "Nay, but as Captain of the Host of the LORD am I now come."**

And Joshua fell on his face to the earth and did worship and said unto Him, "What saith my LORD unto His servant?"

And the Captain of the LORD's host said unto Joshua, "Loose thy shoe from off thy foot, for the place whereon thou standest is holy ground."

And Joshua did so. (Josh 5:13-15)

Scholars widely accept that these three brief verses describe a Christophany – a pre-incarnate appearance of Jesus Christ as commander of the LORD's army. Notice that:

- This angel receives Joshua's worship and does not rebuke him. This reveals the angel's identity. Rank-and-file angels must not be worshipped and the good angels rebuke men who do (Rev 22:8-9). On the other hand, *ha-Satan* and his minions encourage men's worship via the façade of a thousand pagan gods. Men also should not be worshipped (Acts 10:25-26)
- This heavenly Commander addresses Joshua in the same manner the voice of the burning bush addressed Moses decades before: **"Put off thy shoes from off thy feet, for the place whereon thou standest is holy ground."** (Exo 3:5) As Jesus identifies Himself as the voice of the burning bush in FG 8:58, scholars assume the Commander confronting Joshua is Yeshua Himself, the second person of the Godhead (*cf.* Psa 2:1-5). And indeed it will be Yeshua, as Commander of the Lord's host, who will reclaim the planet from the usurper (*ha-Satan*/Antichrist) as He opens the seven seals of the title deed of Earth in the Great Tribulation's war of annihilation prior to His Second Coming (*cf.* Rev 19:11) [319]
- The site where Joshua is standing is holy because a) the LORD is standing there and b) this is the LORD's Land
- The sword drawn signifies imminent judgment (*cf.* 1 Chron 21:16-17). Not only is the purpose of the invasion to reward the

---

[319] Luke tells of an early event in Christ's ministry when Jesus attends the synagogue at Nazareth, his home town, and brings His mission into the open. He is handed the book of Isaiah by the rabbi and reads from it to the whole assembly:

"The Spirit of the Lord is upon me, because he hath anointed me to preach the gospel to the poor. He hath sent me to heal the broken-hearted, to preach deliverance to the captives, and recovering of sight to the blind, to set at liberty them that are bruised, to preach the acceptable year of the Lord...."

And He closed the book, and gave it again to the minister and sat down. And the eyes of all them that were in the synagogue were fastened on Him. And He began to say unto them, "This day is this scripture fulfilled in your ears." (Luke 4:18-21)

Most reading this shrug and move on to the next verse, yet Yeshua didn't. His last statement above would have turned the assembled Pharisaic blood cold. Jesus is reading from Isaiah 61:1,2 and stops the reading at a comma, mid-sentence. The part He doesn't read is ...**and the day of vengeance of our God**. This scripture has yet to be fulfilled in this regard, and will herald Yeshua's Second Coming to the Earth, not as a meek peacemaker this time but as the Avenger of Blood to wreak havoc and judgment. Some have an uneasy feeling that if He hadn't stopped the reading where He did, that would have been it for Planet Earth.

Israelites with the Land God promised them, but also to dispossess and judge the unrepentant Canaanites. In a very real sense for us all it's 'repent or perish' (Luke 13:3-5). Not one of us knows the length of our days, standing as we do with our toes hanging over the edge of eternity. The LORD is slow to anger but when final judgment comes, it is total and irrevocable
- The Commander of the LORD's Army will fight the coming battle. In fact, the Jericho mission will be so weird, the whole world will come to know who really took the city. The LORD plays His part in all wars and these are recorded. All outcomes are His to determine (*cf.* Zech 14:3; Num 21:14)

The foolishness of God

God gives Joshua the battle-plan for Jericho. Whatever strategy Joshua was expecting to take down Canaan's finest, it won't have been this one. The LORD tells him to have his chosen men go once around the city with seven priests before the Ark bearing seven ram's horns, which they will continually blow. The host of Israel shall remain expressly silent as they walk (Josh 6:10). This procedure will be carried out for the first six days. On the seventh day, the Israelite army will go seven times around the city, and on the seventh turn, when the priests blow the trumpets, all the people shall give a great shout and Jericho's walls will fall down flat.

Can you imagine Joshua explaining this to his commanders at the staff meeting; the silence that follows? Yet Joshua is unabashed. A more preposterous plan cannot be imagined, but that's the whole point. Welcome to a concept known as *the foolishness of God*. What at first sight appears an oxymoron (*viz:* jumbo shrimp, honest politician, gamble responsibly, military intelligence, etc.) leads one into another remarkable revelation of God's character. Eschewing for a moment God's sense of humour concerning His earthlings, we get a unique insight into what is important to God and how He expresses it: His foolishness versus mankind's combined wisdom. On occasions when the LORD could so easily embark on a simple course of action to resolve an issue, He chooses instead the most bizarre demonstrations of His power:

- He saves eight people from the planet's extinction-level event in Noah's day by getting them to build *a big barge* which sits in Noah's driveway for up to 120 years while the latter tries (unsuccessfully) to turn the wicked around with his preaching

- God destroys Egypt's political and military infrastructure with the strangest of plagues, topped off by *the parting of the sea event* which consumes most of Egypt's northern army
- God feeds the Israelites for forty years in the wilderness *with manna*
- The walls of Jericho fall down flat, not through any enthusiastic use of C4, *but with a blast of trumpets and a great shout*
- Joshua requests that God *stills the sun in the sky* to give him some extra time to slaughter the Amorite coalition under Adonizedek (Josh 10:13-14).
- When Gideon faces a 135,000-strong force of Midianites, God whittles Gideon's volunteer force of 32,000 Jews down to 300 and gives them, not machine guns and mortars, *but trumpets, torches and pitchers.* Using these, Gideon puts the entire, colossal enemy army to rout, even causing the Midianites to slaughter each other in their panic (Judg 7:17–22)
- Samson slays 1,000 Philistines *with the jawbone of an ass*
- Jonah fails to obey God in the matter of going to Nineveh to preach repentance to the Hittites, so God has him *swallowed by a giant fish and spewed up on a beach* to get Jonah's attention. After this, Jonah is more co-operative, and Nineveh duly repents and is saved from God's destruction
- David, a slight shepherd boy, kills the most renowned professional warrior of the Philistines, the massive Goliath, *with a single slingshot*

God deliberately stretches the limits of credulity even for those who believe in Him. *Why?* The clue is in an 'ultimate foolishness' - namely that the whole world will be judged for their attitude towards a wooden cross erected in Judaea 2,000 years ago, upon which God Himself was crucified to settle the sins of mankind once and for all.

The NT apostle Paul knows a thing or two about God's weird stuff. He was raised Saul of Tarsus, a devout Pharisee taught by the legendary scholar, Gamaliel. Saul became an early persecutor of Jesus Christ's disciples. He held the coats for those who stoned Stephen. He embarked on a search-and-destroy mission to Damascus to root out the budding Christian Church. On the way, Saul was blinded by the Shekinah glory as the risen LORD revealed Himself to him. The Pharisee underwent a startling penance and conversion. Thereafter, now known as Paul ('small'), Saul became Christianity's most devastating apostle. Of all things celestially weird, Paul writes:

"For the preaching of the cross is to them that perish foolishness; but unto us which are saved it is the power of God. For it is written, 'I will destroy the wisdom of the wise, and will bring to nothing the understanding of the prudent'.

Where is the wise? Where is the scribe? Where is the disputer of this world? Hath not God made foolish the wisdom of this world? For after that in the wisdom of God the world by wisdom knew not God, it pleased God by the foolishness of preaching to save them that believe. For the Jews require a sign and the Greeks seek after wisdom, but we preach Christ crucified, unto the Jews a stumbling block and unto the Greeks foolishness, but unto them which are called, both Jews and Greeks, Christ the power of God and the wisdom of God.

Because the foolishness of God is wiser than men, and the weakness of God is stronger than men. For ye see your calling, brethren, how that not many wise men after the flesh, not many mighty, not many noble are called. But God hath chosen the foolish things of the world to confound the wise, and God hath chosen the weak things of the world to confound the things which are mighty; and the base things of the world, and things which are despised, hath God chosen, yea, and things which are not, to bring to nought things that are, <u>that no flesh should glory in His presence</u>. (1 Cor 1:18-29)

God goes to great lengths to testify of Himself in such a way that unbelievers will recognise His role in the affairs of men, **that no flesh should glory in His presence** and say "Hey, *we* did it!" Notice that to Paul there are only two groups of people on the planet: those who are perishing and those who are saved through faith in Christ to deliver them. Within the walls of Jericho there will be two groups of people. Those who will perish (almost everyone), and those in Rahab's house who will be saved through faith in Christ, the Commander of the LORD's army, to deliver them. It suits God to bring man's wisdom to nought by foolishness. **"For My thoughts are not your thoughts, neither are your ways My ways," saith the LORD. "For as the heavens are higher than the Earth, so are My ways higher than your ways, and My thoughts than your thoughts."** (Isa 55:8-9)

The stumbling block to those perishing is the foolishness of the cross. Many are called but few are chosen. The saved are always described as 'not many' (Matt 7:13-14; Matt 20:16; Luke 13:23-27; Rev 3:4, etc.). One commentator writes:

"You know the fairy tale about kissing a frog and it turns into a prince? Evolutionists believe that. 'A frog kissed with time bringeth forth a prince.' This is foolishness but people believe this based upon the same world, the same universe, the same creation, the same observations that you and I see. This must get the Lord angry.

"God sees this foolishness of man's wisdom and decides that by foolish preaching God will save those that believe! The foolishness of God is the aspect of preaching the cross. They think you're crazy and brain dead but the preaching of Christ crucified is wiser than man if you believe it. Why? It'll forgive your sin; man's wisdom cannot do that. You become a new creature; man's wisdom cannot do that. You now have peace with God; man's wisdom cannot do that. You have eternal life; man's wisdom cannot do that. Neither is there salvation in any other, for there is none other name under heaven given among men whereby ye must be saved. By Him, all that believe are justified from all things; man's wisdom cannot do that."[320]

Ground Zero Jericho

Joshua's mighty army moves on the first target. The firstfruits of the Canaan conquest - Jericho - must go to the LORD (Lev 23:10). Joshua warns his men:

"The city shall be accursed, even it and all that are therein, to the LORD. Only Rahab the harlot shall live, she and all that are with her in the house, because she hid the messengers that we sent. And ye, in any wise keep yourselves from the accursed thing lest ye make yourselves accursed, when ye take of the accursed thing and make the camp of Israel a curse and trouble it. But all the silver and gold and vessels of brass and iron are consecrated unto the LORD. They shall come into the treasury of the LORD." (Josh 6:17-19)

In other words, NO LOOTING! The city is accursed. Everything and everyone shall be utterly torched except the silver, gold, brass, and iron, which is the LORD's. So the army moves in, and so do the Levites with the Ark. Once a day for six days the priests encompass the city walls blowing their trumpets while the army escorts in silence (Josh 6:10). You can imagine the insults flying forth from what the

---

[320] www.studiesinthebook.com/studies/foolishness_and_weakness_of_god.pdf

Amorites consider impregnable walls. On the seventh day, it's seven times around the city and when the priests blow a long blast on their shofars, a mighty shout from the army of Israel thunders out... *and Jericho's walls fall down flat.* Every yard of wall topples except for the section upon which Rahab and her household dwell. Chuck Missler points out that the most dangerous place to be at that moment is on the walls of Jericho. And the safest place to be at that moment is in Rahab's house on the walls of Jericho! For God, nothing is too much trouble. Notice again the pattern. God protects the repentant through His judgments, He does not judge them.

Answers in Genesis fills in some topographical information:

"The mound of Jericho was surrounded by a great earthen rampart, or embankment, with a stone retaining wall at its base. The retaining wall was some four to five meters (12-15 feet) high. On top of that was a mudbrick wall two meters (six feet) thick and about six to eight meters (20-26 feet) high.[321] At the crest of the embankment was a similar mudbrick wall whose base was roughly 14 meters (46 feet) above the ground level outside the retaining wall. This is what loomed high above the Israelites as they marched around the city each day for seven days. Humanly speaking, it was impossible for the Israelites to penetrate the impregnable bastion of Jericho.

"Within the upper wall was an area of approximately six acres, while the total area of the upper city and fortification system was 50% larger, or about nine acres. Based on the archaeologist's rule of thumb of 200 persons per acre, the population of the upper city would have been about 1,200. However, from excavations carried out by a German team in the first decade of the 20th century, we know that people were also living on the embankment between the upper and lower city walls. In addition, those Canaanites living in surrounding villages would have fled into Jericho for safety. Thus, we can assume that there were several thousand people inside the walls when the Israelites came against the city."[322]

In between the inner and outer revetments and walls lived those 'on the wrong side of the tracks'. This was Rahab's twilight world of smoky alleys, dingy brothels, murky taverns and dodgy citizens. For her to display the protective scarlet from a window for the Israelites

---

[321] **Sellin, E and Carl Watzinger** *Jericho die Ergebnisse der Ausgrabungen,* Osnabrück, Otto Zeller Verlag, p. 58, 1973 (reprint of the 1913 edition)

[322] www.answersingenesis.org/articles/cm/v21/n2/the-walls-of-jericho#fnList_1_4

to behold, her property must have abutted the outer wall, reducing her treason's discovery.

There are those who still contend that no evidence exists that Jericho was sacked at all in the late Bronze Age, but the archaeology is settled. Old Jericho died a violent, flaming death in the correct period (*c.* 1406 BC), and no serious scientist without an agenda disputes this.[323] The Israelites swarm into the city and put the whole population to the sword and torch. Only Rahab and her household are spared. *Grace Through Truth* writes:

"The name Rahab means 'proud', but among the people of Jericho, all of whom knew of the God of Israel, only Rahab humbled herself before the two spies and confessed Him as 'God in Heaven above and Earth below.' And speaking of the spies, what about them? Except for reporting that all the people of Jericho were scared to death, did the spies bring Joshua any intelligence that helped develop the battleplan? No, the LORD had already determined the battleplan and they contributed nothing to it (Josh 6:2-5). So what was their true purpose in His plan? Seems like they were really two witnesses sent to hear Rahab's confession, save her from destruction, and give her a place among the LORD's people.

"From that time on, Rahab dwelt with the Israelites. She married a man from the tribe of Judah named Salmon and had a son whom they named Boaz. Boaz took a gentile bride from Moab named Ruth and they had a son named Obed, who had a son named Jesse who had a son named David who became King of Israel (Ruth 4:13-22). And 26 generations later, two distant cousins who were both descendants of King David (and therefore of Rahab and Salmon) married and became the earthly parents of our Lord Jesus. And so when you read the genealogy of Jesus in Matthew, you will find Rahab listed there (Matt 1:5)."[324]

Jericho is reduced to a smoking ruin. As a final condemnation, Joshua curses the city: **"Cursed be the man before the LORD that riseth up and buildeth this city Jericho. He shall lay the foundation thereof in his firstborn and in his youngest son shall he set up the gates of it."**

---

[323] www.biblearchaeology.org/post/2008/05/did-the-israelites-conquer-jericho-a-new-look-at-the-archaeological-evidence.aspx#Article

[324] http://gracethrufaith.com/childrens-stories-for-adults/the-gospel-in-joshua-the-story-of-rahab/

So the LORD was with Joshua, and his fame was noised throughout all the country. (Josh 6:26-27)

Lambert Dolphin points out some startling observations:

"It is interesting to notice the parallels in design between the Book of Joshua in the Old Testament and the Book of Revelation. Joshua's name is in Hebrew; in Greek it could be rendered 'Jesus'. Joshua's mission is to dispossess the usurpers from the Land on behalf of God's people; in Revelation, Jesus' mission is to dispossess the Planet Earth of the usurpers.

"Joshua initially sends ahead two witnesses. (We call them spies, but all they accomplished was getting a Gentile woman saved.) The two witnesses of Jesus in Revelation Chapter 11 are a prominent element.

"In the initial attack on the Amorite capital of Jericho, every rule of the Torah was violated: the Levites were exempt from military duties, yet they lead the procession. They were to do no work on Sabbath Day, yet here they march around Jericho once a day for six days, and then seven times on the seventh day! They are to keep silent until the final trumpet blast, etc. It is interesting that the Seven Trumpets in Revelation are introduced after a strange silence."[325]

Who is the commander of the LORD's army? Yeshua. Who is the LORD of the Sabbath? Yeshua. Notice that Rahab is removed before the city is destroyed in the same way that Lot is removed by the angels (another pattern of two witnesses) before Sodom's fiery end (Gen 19). End-time believers will also be removed in the *harpazo* prior to the LORD's Great Tribulation.[326]

The lesson of Ai

They say the best time to win a battle is straight after you've won a battle, but the word 'hubris' describes 'pride before a fall', and God hates pride. Something happens during the sack of Jericho and God is going to clean house.

With Jericho smouldering behind him, Joshua sends out agents to spy out the next target, a town called Ai ('ay-eye'). They report back to their commander: **"Let not all the people go up but let about two or three thousand men go up and smite Ai. Make not all the people to labour thither for they are but few."** (Josh 7:3). Joshua duly

[325] http://ldolphin.org/studynotes/rev.htm

[326] The controversial doctrine of the 'Rapture' (*harpazo*) will be examined in detail in *Origins VI - Parousia.*

despatches a small assault force but *does not consult the LORD*. When the Israelites arrive before the gates to the city, the men of Ai take the initiative, charge out in a sudden attack and slaughter thirty-six Israelites before the rest turn tail and flee. News of the rout hits Joshua hard. He falls on his face before God lamenting the defeat, but the LORD's reaction is not what Joshua expects:

"Get thee up! Wherefore liest thou thus upon thy face? Israel hath sinned and they have also transgressed My covenant which I commanded them, for they have even taken of the accursed thing and have also stolen, and dissembled also, and they have put it even among their own stuff. Therefore the children of Israel could not stand before their enemies but turned their backs before their enemies because they were accursed. Neither will I be with you any more except ye destroy the accursed from among you." (Josh 7:10-12)

God is sorely ticked off. The firstfruits of the Canaanite campaign should have been the LORD's, but someone's lifted some Jericho. Joshua realises that unless the miscreants are found, God won't stand with them, and the invasion will be doomed. The following morning, he rises early and heeds God's guidance. All Israel is brought before him by tribes, and the tribe of Judah is selected. Then the tribe of Judah is arrayed before him, and the clan of the Zahrites is taken. The Zahrites are arrayed before Joshua, and the family of Zabdi is taken. The family of Zabdi is arrayed before him, and Achan is taken. Joshua addresses the quivering warrior:

"My son, give, I pray thee, glory to the LORD God of Israel and make confession unto Him; and tell me now what thou hast done. Hide it not from me."

And Achan answered Joshua, and said, "Indeed I have sinned against the LORD God of Israel, and thus and thus have I done. When I saw among the spoils a goodly Babylonish garment and two hundred shekels of silver, and a wedge of gold of fifty shekels weight, then I coveted them and took them. And, behold, they are hid in the earth in the midst of my tent and the silver under it."

So Joshua sent messengers and they ran unto the tent; and, behold, it was hid in his tent and the silver under it.

What happens next has divided scholars and provided ready fuel for the 'God is a barbarian' brigade:

And they took [the treasures] **out of the midst of the tent and brought them unto Joshua, and unto all the children of Israel, and laid them out before the LORD. And Joshua, and all Israel with**

him, took Achan the son of Zerah, and the silver, and the garment, and the wedge of gold, and his sons, and his daughters, and his oxen, and his asses, and his sheep, and his tent, and all that he had, and they brought them unto the valley of Achor.

And Joshua said, "Why hast thou troubled us? The LORD shall trouble thee this day." And all Israel stoned them with stones and burned them with fire after they had stoned them with stones. And they raised over [the family] **a great heap of stones unto this day. So the LORD turned from the fierceness of His anger. Wherefore the name of that place was called 'The Valley of Achor' unto this day.** (Josh 7:19-26)

We are learning what upsets an omniscient, omnipotent, omnipresent universe-creating Being. God throws away the airbrush and not only depicts his humans, warts and all, but declares His own actions and will for all to know. In the messy business of life on Earth, God wants us to get it, or we shall surely get it. Some observations:

- It is not difficult to imagine the horror of what happened to Achan and his family. Why such harsh treatment? Because Achan had personally and deliberately violated the sanctity of God by robbing Him of the firstfruits. In the New Testament, who represents the firstfruit of them that slept? Yeshua, who rises from the dead on the Feast of Firstfruits. (Matt 27:52-53; 1 Cor 15:20-23; Rom 6:9). God therefore views Achan's sin as a direct desecration of His Son
- Joshua does not consult the LORD about Ai the way he sought His face about Jericho
- Ai has a population of 12,000 (Josh 8:25). Pride leads the Israelites to believe that they can overcome with a few
- Chuck Missler writes: *"36 Israelites died. 6 equals the number of man squared – failure!"*[327]
- The name Achan means 'trouble' and there is a Hebrew pun on the word 'Achor', the name of the valley where the incident occurs. **"Why hast thou troubled us? The LORD shall trouble thee this day."**
- J Hampton Keithley writes:

"We see that the LORD held the whole camp of Israel accountable for the act of one man and withheld His blessing until the matter was corrected. There was sin in the camp and God would not continue blessing the nation as long as this was so. This does not mean this was

[327] Missler, Chuck, *Joshua notes,* www.khouse.org

the only sin and the rest of the nation was sinless, but this sin was of such a nature (direct disobedience and rebellion) that God used it to teach Israel and us a couple of important lessons." [328]

- Occasionally God will single out a miscreant and act harshly to sharpen our attention (Gen 38:8-10; 2 Sam 6:1-7; Acts 5:1-11). It's more a mercy that He does not act this way *all the time,* or we would all be in trouble
- Be sure your sins will find you out (Num 32:23). Hide any wrongdoing from an omniscient God and expect trouble. Sin deliberately hidden before God is sin that will be judged. Sin persisted in shall be judged. This is why God encourages us to confess sin and separate ourselves from it (1 John 1:8-10). God sees and knows everything. If we confess and repent (separate ourselves from sin), we will find mercy (Psa 28:13)
- Sin destroys those we love and its tentacles reach far and wide. In Achan's case, 36 men died because of him at Ai. The family members of those casualties were also hurt. Achan's entire family was devastated and his immediate kin slain with him. Joshua and the people were mortified
- Though God instructed Moses that fathers should not be punished for the sins of their sons and vice versa (Deut 24:16), the implication is that Achan's family knew and was complicit in Achan's blasphemy
- Israel went through a detailed sanctification/purification procedure prior to launching *chērem* on Jericho. The consequences of Achan's blasphemy polluted this cleansing. God uses this incident as a severe object lesson for the rest of Achan's kind. A small piece of leaven leavens the whole lump (Gal 5:9; 1 Cor 5:6)

Depression sets in among the Israelites. God sees the dejection of His people and tells Joshua to go up against Ai a second time, now the sin is expunged. The plan this time is for Joshua to set a strike-force out of sight behind the city at night, while the main force approaches the city gates as on the previous occasion. When the king of Ai sees the hapless Israelites returning through the gloom for another drubbing, he rouses his men early. They pour out of the city gates as before and pursue the Israelites, who commence fleeing before them. When the city is empty of fighting men, Joshua's strike-

---

[328] http://bible.org/seriespage/defeat-ai-and-sin-achan-joshua-71-26

force behind Ai rises from its position, sweeps in and takes the city, putting it to the torch and slaughtering the inhabitants within.

And when the men of Ai looked behind them, they saw, and behold, the smoke of the city ascended up to Heaven, and they had no power to flee this way or that way, and the people that fled to the wilderness turned back upon their pursuers.

And when Joshua and all Israel saw the ambush had taken the city, and that the smoke of the city ascended, then they turned again and slew the men of Ai.

And the other [Israelite strike-force] **issued out of the city against them, so they were in the midst of Israel, some on this side, and some on that side: and they smote them so that they let none of them remain or escape. And the king of Ai they took alive and brought him to Joshua.** (Josh 8:20-23)

Joshua ensures that the slaughter is complete before he hangs the king of Ai from a tree. Come nightfall, the corpse is cut down, thrown into the gate of the smouldering city and covered with stones. Canaanite death-toll: 12,000. This time the spoils of the city - all the gold, silver, bronze, iron, livestock and miscellaneous knick-knacks - are shared out among the Israelites according to the will of the LORD.

The enemy gets wisdom

Real panic sets in across Canaan once the fate of Jericho and Ai becomes known. The Israelite version of the Death Star is coming and it can't be bargained with. Word spreads that the vengeful deity YHWH has decreed the total annihilation of the Canaanite peoples, and their land will be usurped by the Jews. *What can be done?*

The most obvious strategy is for the Canaanite kingdoms to form an alliance against Joshua, Israel and God (Josh 9:1-2). This reminds us of Psalms 2 and is also a type for the kingdoms of the Earth gathering together in the last days to make war against their Creator, depicted in the book of Revelation. A more ridiculous situation cannot be imagined than plotting against the omniscient, omnipotent, omnipresent One who made the universe. Does *ha-Satan* take note? God Himself expresses mirth:

Why do the heathen rage and the people imagine a vain thing? The kings of the Earth set themselves, and the rulers take counsel together against the LORD, and against His anointed, saying, "Let us break their bands asunder and cast away their cords from us."

He that sitteth in the heavens shall laugh. The LORD shall have them in derision.

Then shall He speak unto them in His wrath and vex them in His sore displeasure. (Psa 2:1-5)

How similar today when humanists blaspheme God or deny Him altogether while attributing the whole of Creation to evolution and chance, all the while the LORD patiently divides each of their cells, digests their burgers and sees to it that their children wake up every morning. The Hivites come up with a more pragmatic survival plan.

Their intelligence confirms that God has ordered the Canaanite peoples utterly destroyed, but Israel is permitted to make treaties with distant peoples. So the people of Gibeon, one of four Hivite cities marked for annihilation, choose ambassadors who don old and dirty clothes, grab torn and mended wineskins, patched and damaged sandals for their feet, and old and mouldy bread for provisions. They wend their way to Joshua at the chief Israelite base at Gilgal by the Jordan. Here they lie their pants off to save their skins:

"We be come from a far country. Now therefore make ye a league with us."

And the men of Israel said unto the Hivites, "Perhaps ye dwell among us, so how can we make a league with you?"

And they said unto Joshua, "We are thy servants."

And Joshua said unto them, "Who are ye and whence have you come?"

And they said unto him, **"From a very far country thy servants are come because of the name of the LORD thy God. For we have heard the fame of Him and all that he did in Egypt, and all that he did to the two kings of the Amorites, that were beyond Jordan, to Sihon king of Heshbon, and to Og king of Bashan, which was at Ashtaroth."** (Josh 9:6-10)

The men of Gibeon display their mouldy bread and patched-up wineskins as proof of their story. After incurring the initial suspicion of Israel, they are relieved that the ruse appears to be working. Joshua and his council of princes are duped into swearing a peace pact with them in the name of the LORD. Three days later, the cat's out of the bag when it's discovered who this lot really are. The children of Israel complain angrily to Joshua.[329] He and his war-council respond:

"This we will do to them; we will even let them live lest wrath be upon us because of the oath which we swore unto them."

---

[329] This is the only recorded murmuring that Israel levels against Joshua, in contrast to the constant whingeing Moses and Aaron had to tolerate.

And the princes said unto them, "Let them live but let them be hewers of wood and drawers of water unto all the congregation, as the princes had promised them." (Josh 9:20-21)

Joshua is understandably angry and embarrassed by the trick. He calls the Gibeonite ambassadors to him:

"Wherefore have ye beguiled us, saying, 'We are very far from you', when ye dwell among us? Now therefore ye are cursed, and there shall none of you be freed from being bondmen and hewers of wood and drawers of water for the house of my God."

And they answered Joshua and said, "Because it was certainly told thy servants how that the LORD thy God commanded his servant Moses to give you all the land and to destroy all the inhabitants of the land from before you. Therefore we were sore afraid of our lives because of you and have done this thing. And now, behold, we are in thine hand. As it seemeth good and right unto thee to do unto us, do."

And so did he unto them and delivered them out of the hand of the children of Israel, that they slew them not. And Joshua made them that day hewers of wood and drawers of water for the congregation and for the altar of the LORD, even unto this day, in the place which he should choose. (Josh 9:22-27)

www.christadelphianstudies.com writes:

"The town of Gibeon is identified with El-Jib about ten kilometres northwest of Jerusalem and about six miles southwest of Ai, in the hill-country in the centre of the land. Gibeon signifies *High Place* [idolatry]."[330]

In fact, the land rises to 777 metres on the southern edge of the modern village of Jib, where the remains of Gibeon can be seen. Which puts Gibeon a mere 20 miles from Gilgal. Doubtless many in the Israelite camp now believe God will punish them for disobeying the annihilation order and treating with the enemy. Scholars point out that the root of the word 'Hivite' means 'serpent', yet a surprising blessing derives from this incident.

From Gibeon's standpoint, to risk execution or perpetual slavery at the hand of Israel, they must be utterly convinced that this deceit is the only course open to them to safeguard their families and avoid destruction. It is evident that they are familiar with God's orders for Canaan's destruction in Deuteronomy 7. They therefore choose, in

---

[330] www.christadelphianstudies.com/sundayschool/Senior%20Stage%202%20 pdfs/Lesson%208%20Marking%20Notes.pdf

effect, to separate themselves from the rest of the Canaanite peoples and their evil ways. This saves their lives. As we will see, this desertion will be used by God to stage what is perhaps one of the most astonishing miracles in the OT. The key flaw in the Gibeonite strategy? *You can't deceive the LORD*. The Gibeonite punishment? Slavery. Their vindication? Faithful service in time brings forth redemption. This is an interesting model of our own redemption. Every human is up for utter destruction because of our sin before a perfect Creator, yet if we separate ourselves from evil and trust and serve the LORD with a pure heart, we will be redeemed from the penalty of the Law (1 John 1:5-7; *cf.* Matt 7:21-23).

From Israel's standpoint, the oath sworn to Gibeon is underpinned by the sanctity of God's holy name. God expects Israel to honour its protection of the Gibeonites in perpetuity. Chuck Missler remarks that the circumstances of Rahab and the Gibeonites are somewhat parallel. Both are of dubious character. Both hear and believe in the power of the Hebrew God to overcome. Both leave the kingdoms of God's enemies. Both are to prove their ultimate loyalty.

"Gibeon's service led to a place of religious privilege. Gibeon was one of the cities given to the line of Aaron. 400 years later, the Tabernacle would be there. One of David's mighty men, those who were closest to him in battle, was a Gibeonite. When Solomon ascended the throne, he made burnt offerings at Gibeon. Later still, about 500 years before Christ in the time of Zerubbabel, the returnees from Babylon included a list of the Gibeonites. In the days of Nehemiah, Gibeonites were among those who helped build the walls of Jerusalem.

"Even though their oath was made under deception, God expected them to keep it. If God will not tolerate the breaking of an oath made in His name, how much more will He never break His own oath and covenant made to us on the basis of the shed blood and infinite value of Jesus Christ?" (Heb 6:13-20)[331]

A few centuries later, when King Saul betrays this oath and slays some Gibeonites, God sends a three-year famine. The curse is only lifted when seven of Saul's relatives are given over by King David to the Gibeonites, who promptly hang them before the LORD at Gibeah (2 Sam 21:1-9; *cf.* Matt 5:33-37).

From God's standpoint, the Israelites have been punished because they did not seek His guidance! (Josh 9:14) You'd think this

---

[331] Missler, Chuck, *Joshua notes*, www.khouse.org

lesson would have been learned by now after 38 years of scorpions and heat-rash in the desert followed by that bad business at Ai. But aren't we the same? *Lamb of God* ministry writes:

"Is it because we are so like Israel, that when things seem to be going well, we take the credit and start to think we don't need any outside help? And it becomes, 'Thank you very much, God, but I will handle this one myself.' This lesson may be thousands of years old but we still haven't learned it. When it comes to a major step in our lives, do we turn to God and ask for His direction and guidance before we act?

"Secondly, this attempt at deceit was aimed in two directions. The first is the surface level of deceit aimed at Joshua and Israel. The direct and immediate consequences of that effort was to make the people of Gibeon and their descendants from that time forth slaves of the Israelites. But beneath the surface, the attempt was ultimately an effort to deceive God. And everyone who tries this will learn the painful truth that God cannot be deceived. And those who attempt such a foolish thing will learn there are subsequent consequences that are deep, wide and long-lasting."[332]

God is mollified by the attitude displayed by Israel over this embarrassing incident, but will watch to see they keep their oath. Gibeon thus becomes the servant of Israel and partially fulfils the slavery curse formerly placed upon Canaan, the fourth son of Ham, over another embarrassing incident which occurred in Noah's tent when the patriarch became drunk (Gen 9:20-27).

The sun stands still

The king of Jerusalem, the self-styled Adonizedek,[333] is hopping mad about the Hivite capitulation. The Gibeonites are a serious loss since their number comprises many hard warriors (Josh 10:2). Adonizedek realises Canaan is doomed to collapse and annihilation if such cowardice passes unpunished. He immediately sets about forming a coalition of five tribes to descend on Gibeon and make an example of the city. When the Gibeonites see the approaching forces, they urgently despatch messengers to Joshua at Gilgal:

---

332 www.log.org/media/pdf/wtm/42trans.pdf

333 A bizarre title, literally 'Lord of Righteousness'. *Ha-Satan's* counterfeit perhaps of the mysterious Melchizedek, the 'King of Righteousness', a former king and priest of Jerusalem, after whose eternal order the Messiah will spring (Heb 7).

"Slack not thy hand from thy servants! Come up to us quickly and save us and help us, for all the kings of the Amorites that dwell in the mountains are gathered together against us!" (Josh 10:6)

Chuck Missler jokes that if he were in Joshua's shoes he'd have retorted, "Seeing as you live *so far away*, I don't think we can make it in time." Joshua doesn't say that but immediately galvanises his army and sets off on a night yomp to Gibeon, not wishing to forgo the chance of nailing five city-states in one shot. A study of Joshua's military skills reveals his tactical use of speed, stealth, deception, feints and the lie of the land. The forced march involves 20 miles and climbing 4,000 feet. Adonizedek is taken by surprise the following morning when the Israelites strike.[334] The Amorite coalition panics and is put to flight with great slaughter. The cry goes up, "No prisoners!" and the pursuit begins.

The Canaanites are hunted down along the road to Beth-horon and southwest towards Azekah and Makkedah. On the way, huge hailstones rain down on the fleeing army, killing more of the enemy than the Israelites manage with their swords and spears (Josh 10:11). Encouraged by this show of heavenly support, Joshua proclaims in full hearing of his troops:

"Sun, stand thou still upon Gibeon! And thou, Moon, in the valley of Ajalon!" (Josh 10:12)

And guess what…?

Forget about the pagan multitudes; many believers have a major problem with this passage and wish to Heaven it had never been put in the Bible. But this is by no means the only occasion when God does strange antics with the sun and weird stuff in general, as we've seen. As for the hailstones, here we find more intriguing parallels with the end days of Revelation.

Huge hailstones first, then the sun and moon stay their positions for a full day to give Joshua time to complete his annihilation of the

---

[334] A similar strategy was used by King Harold II of England. When a Viking invasion led by Harald Hardrada of Norway struck the north of England in September 1066, Harold force-marched his army of *huscarls* 190 miles north from London to York and fell upon the enemy at Stamford Bridge, while the latter were lounging around awaiting hostages from a previous victory. Harold's exhausting strategy won him one of the most decisive victories in English history. Hardrada's Norse had left most of their heavy weapons and armour on their ships at Riccall due to the hot weather. Believing they had at least a week before having to confront another English challenge, the Norse found themselves completely unprepared for Harold's sudden onslaught.

Amorite coalition. Just so that the reader gets the message that these are *supernatural* events that occur literally, the hailstones only hit the bad guys. Regarding the celestial phenomenon, the scriptures state:

And the sun stood still, and the moon stayed until the people had avenged themselves upon their enemies. Is not this written in the book of Jasher? So the sun stood still in the midst of Heaven and hasted not to go down about a whole day. And there was no day like that before it or after it, that the LORD hearkened unto the voice of a man, for the LORD fought for Israel. (Josh 10:13-14)

I have to say, the miracles of the Battle of Beth-horon do not cause me the flutters others experience when reading this passage. Like the Flood, we have myths, legends and stories all over the world across dozens of cultures of a long day/night as well as other astronomic phenomena. T W Doane relates:

"We have, as an example, that which is related of Bacchus in the Orphic hymns, wherein it says that this god-man arrested the course of the sun and the moon. An Indian legend relates that the sun stood still to hear the pious ejaculations of Arjouan after the death of Crishna. A holy Buddhist by the name of Matanga prevented the sun, at his command, from rising and bisected the moon. . . . The Chinese also had a legend of the sun standing still, and a legend was found among the Ancient Mexicans to the effect that one of their holy persons commanded the sun to stand still, which command was obeyed." [335]

Harry Rimmer writes:

"In the ancient Chinese writings there is a legend of a long day. The Incas of Peru and the Aztecs of Mexico have a like record, and there is a Babylonian and Persian legend of a day that was miraculously extended. Another section of China contributes an account of the day that was miraculously prolonged in the reign of Emperor Yeo. Herodotus recounts that the priests of Egypt showed him their temple records, and that there he read a strange account of a day that was twice the natural length."[336]

Immanuel Velikovsky published his *Worlds in Collision* to controversial acclaim in 1950. In it he wrote:

---

[335] **Doane, TW** *Bible Myths and their Parallels in Other Religions,* Charles P. Somerby, 1882, p.91

[336] **Rimmer, H** *The Harmony of Science and Scripture* William B. Eerdmans Publishing Co., 1940, pp.269-270

"In the Mexican Annals of Cuauhtitlan – the history of the empire of Culhuacan and Mexico, written in Nahua-Indian in the sixteenth century – it is related that during a cosmic catastrophe that occurred in the remote past, the night did not end for a long time….

"Sahagun, the Spanish savant who came to America a generation after Columbus and gathered the traditions of the aborigines, wrote that at the time of one cosmic catastrophe the Sun rose only a little way over the horizon and remained there without moving; the moon also stood still."[337]

Richard Riss comments:

"Velikovsky's theory was that at some time in the middle of the second millennium B.C., either the Earth was interrupted in its regular rotation by a comet or the terrestrial axis was tilted <u>in the presence of a strong magnetic field</u> [emphasis mine], so that for several hours the sun appeared to lose its diurnal movement.

"Velikovsky's book brought about quite a bit of discussion on this topic. 'The Day The Sun Stood Still' by Eric Larabee was published in *Harper's* in January of 1950. It was reprinted in the *Minneapolis Sunday Tribune* on February 5 of that year with the comment that 'The article on this page – "The Day the Sun Stood Still" – will quite probably become the most discussed magazine piece of 1950. It was published in the current issue of *Harper's Magazine*, and the *Tribune* is the first newspaper to reprint it. The account is based on a book, *Worlds in Collision,* by Dr. Immanuel Velikovsky. The article has created such interest in publishing circles that the *Tribune* has learned, the editors of *Collier's* and of *The Reader's Digest* have other presentations of the same idea in preparation. *This Week* magazine, which is a section of the *Sunday Tribune* and twenty-five other Sunday newspapers, is preparing a pictorial presentation of some of Velikovsky's unusual theories which lace together elements of religious beliefs and scientific events and try to explain that once – within the recorded history of man – the sun stood still.' "[338]

Chuck Missler believes other legends hold a clue:

"Phaethon, in Greek mythology, was son of Helios, the sun-god and nymph Clymene (Greek phaethon = 'Shining', 'Radiant'). He persuaded his father to let him drive the chariot of the sun across the sky, but he lost control of the horses and, driving too near the Earth, scorched it. To

---

[337] **Velikovsky, I** *Worlds in Collision,* Macmillan, 1950, pp.45-46

[338] www.grmi.org/Richard_Riss/evidences/7longday.html, quoting **Sanden OE** *Does Science Support the Scriptures?* Grand Rapids, Zondervan, 1951, p.9

save the world from utter destruction, Zeus killed Phaethon with a thunderbolt. He fell to the Earth at the mouth of Eridanus, a river in northern Europe. In New Zealand, the Maori story of Maui is almost identical. Similar legends among American Indians, the Phoenix bird of Egypt, the dragon stories of China, Japanese lore, etc."[339]

The Amorites were sun- and moon-worshipers (Jericho = *Bet Yerah*, 'The House of the Moon God'), so there is no surprise that God would use His own power to overawe these venerated 'gods' just as He did in Egypt. I do not believe the Earth stopped rotating. This would present insurmountable geophysical problems, given what we know of orbital mechanics. The sun and moon *appeared* to stop - this is the language of appearance. With our modern knowledge, the most likely possibility is that something happened to Earth's axial tilt. Also, a long day in Israel would imply a long night in Mexico or New Zealand. Both the latter's ancient cultures have these legends.

Joshua's campaign is by no means the only place in scripture where such unsettling events unfold.

The sun and moon stood still in their habitation: at the light of thine arrows they went, and at the shining of thy glittering spear. Thou didst march through the land in indignation; Thou didst thresh the heathen in anger. (Hab 3:11-12)

...which commandeth the sun and it riseth not; and sealeth up the stars. (Job 9:7)

And this shall be a sign unto thee from the LORD, that the LORD will do this thing that he hath spoken: "Behold, I will bring again the shadow of the degrees, which is gone down in the sun dial of Ahaz, ten degrees backward." So the sun returned ten degrees, by which degrees it was gone down. (Isa 38:7-8)

So, no shortage of astronomical weirdom. And in what looks like a re-run of Joshua's campaign, John the Apostle records in the last days of the Antichrist New World Order in - you guessed it - Revelation:

And there fell upon men a great hail out of Heaven, every stone about the weight of a talent (100 lbs!)**. And men blasphemed God because of the plague of the hail, for the plague thereof was exceeding great.** (Rev 16:21)

Clearly quite a lot was happening before the generally accepted dawn of recorded history (*c.* Herodotus). On the spiritual level, God is the Creator for whom nothing is too hard. On the

[339] **Missler, Chuck** *The Long Day of Joshua,* www.khouse.org

physical/astronomic level, as we examined in *The Red God* chapter of *Origins II – Holy War*, some scientists conjecture that 'Joshua's Long Day' could have been one of those occasions every 54/108 years when the planet Mars carried out a near pass-by of Earth. A halting of the planet's rotation is not required to achieve the observational effect of the sun and moon 'standing still'. A pole-shift (Isa 24:19-20) or reversal (Isa 24:1) as a result of the intense gravitational/magnetic forces engendered by a pass-by will achieve the same precessional effect.[340]

Macro events are regularly reported in the Bible. Scientists Donald Patton, Ronald Hatch and Loren Steinhauer surmise that these catastrophes might relate to near pass-bys with Mars, appearing to occur every 108 years or multiple thereof.[341] Russell Grigg demurs:

> "One problem is that these authors postulate an ancient orbit for Mars different from its present one, and there is no proof that this ever happened. Other suggested causes have included impacts of asteroids on the Earth."[342]

Yet something is disrupting Earth in a major, periodic manner prior to 701 BC. Loren C Steinhauer, who taught orbital mechanics at Harvard and MIT, and Ronald R Hatch, who worked as a Navy navigational satellite systems senior engineer for Boeing's space division, are no scientific lightweights. They believe there is every proof Mars had a previous, eccentric orbit, perhaps after being struck by a tenth planet (named Astra) which left behind, not just the asteroids, but the catastrophic damage viewed on Mars today. And not just any old damage. The scale of devastation begs the question, *what the heck happened?*

As described in *Origins II – Holy War*, the Red Planet hosts the largest volcano and canyon in the Solar System as well as the most spectacular hit - the Hellas Crater. The Hellas Fragment produced a crater 990 miles in diameter, or 2.66 times the size of Texas. In European terms, the Hellas Crater is equal to the combined areas of Great Britain, Ireland, France, Belgium, Luxembourg, the Netherlands, Switzerland, Germany, Denmark, Austria, Italy,

---

[340] "Precession: the motion of the axis of rotation of a spinning body about a line that makes an angle with it, so as to describe a cone." (http://creation.com/joshuas-long-day#r8).

[341] **Patton D, Hatch R, Steinhauer LC** *The Long Day of Joshua and Six Other Catastrophies,* Baker Book House, Michigan, 1973

[342] http://creation.com/joshuas-long-day#f1

Monaco, San Marino, Liechtenstein and half of Hungary combined. Remember, this occurred on a planet only 28% the size of Earth. The Hellas Fragment was estimated to be 600 to 625 miles in diameter and struck Mars at 25,000 mph, or 7 miles per second. The devastation would have been unimaginable, but was by no means the only major impact on Mars that day.

The 'H' fragment was accompanied by a second rock, the Isidis asteroid, which produced a crater 684 miles in diameter. And yet a third projectile, which caused the Argyre Crater, 481 miles across. And yet a fourth, Cassini, 291 miles across. In all, 15 asteroids over 95 miles in diameter ploughed into the Clobbered Hemisphere, the larger smashing through the 20 miles of Mars crust, while the heaviest three penetrated deep into the 4,000 miles of molten magma, causing bulges to appear on the opposite side of the planet an hour later. These asteroids would have been *rotating* when they hit, adding considerable angular momentum to the impacts.

There is therefore considerable evidence that catastrophe played a big part in the lives of the planets as well as the ancient inhabitants on Earth. Patton, Hatch and Steinhauer start with the chief macro event, Noah's Flood, and move forward listing others, speculating on the period differences. This is not an effort to force the data, just to examine if there is a pattern:

Date BC	Period/Event	Period from last event
Oct 2146	Peleg ('the dividing')	
Oct 1930	Tower of Babel	2 x 108 = 216 years
Mar 1877	Sodom & Gomorrah	1 x 53 years
Mar 1663	Job	214 years
Mar 1447	Exodus Plagues	2 x 108 = 216 years
Oct 1404	Long Day, Joshua	43 years
Oct 1188	Deborah (Judges 5:20)	2 x 108 = 216 years
Oct 1080	Samuelic	80 years
Mar 1025	David (Lesser)	55 years
Oct 972	David (Greater)	53 years
Oct 864	Elijahic	108 years
Oct 756	Joel-Amos	108 years
Mar 701	Isaiahic	55 years [343]

[343] Patton D, Hatch R, Steinhauer LC, *The Long Day of Joshua and Six Other Catastrophies,* op. cit.

Chuck Missler cites other proofs relating to the changes in calendars:

"The Chaldeans, Egyptians, Hebrews, Greeks, Phoenicians, Chinese, Mayan, Hindus, Carthaginians, Etruscans and Teutons all had 360-day calendars, most with twelve 30-day months. However, all change in 701 B.C. The Romans add five days (like we use today). King Hezekiah added a month to the Jewish cycle every few years (3rd, 6th, 8th, 11th, 14th, 17th, and 19th year). Why did he have to change the calendar?"[344]

Many calibrations we use today are still on the same 60-base: 60 seconds to a minute, 60 minutes to an hour, 360 degrees to a circle. Missler points out that the ancients were consumed with the concept of 360: 360 icons in the gnostic genii; 360 gods in the theology of Greek Orpheus; 360 idols in the palace of Dairi in Japan; 360 statues surrounding Hobal in ancient Arabia. And then, of course, we have Mars itself, so feared by the ancients it was *worshipped.* Which is remarkable. No-one I know can even find Mars today in the night sky. Worshipping Mars makes no sense at all unless the planet intervened in people's lives in a real and terrifying manner.

There's also the matter of Jonathan Swift including some disturbingly accurate data about Mars's two moons, Phobos and Deimos, in his third book of *Gulliver's Travels.* This novel was published *151 years before* Professor Asaph Hall made astronomic history in August 1877 when he discovered, using the US Naval Observatory's latest state-of-the-art 66 cm telescope, that Mars had two moons. The revelation is all the more extraordinary given that these celestial bodies are tiny and among the least reflective in the solar system. The moons were named Phobos and Deimos ('fear' and 'panic') by the science master of Eton, Henry Madan, who thought the names appropriate considering Ares ('Mars', the god of war) summoned them in Homer's *Iliad*, book XV. Where on Earth did Swift get his information? The best two guesses are: either he was citing legends, or he was relating information recorded by ancient eye-witness accounts of a Mars pass-by.

That Mars could have passed so close that even its tiny moons could be glimpsed by the naked eye is terrifying but by no means the whole story. Any intervention by Mars would firstly cause hailstones (bolides) *and then* the apparent stilling of the sun and moon as the Earth rolled due to immense magnetic/gravitational stresses. This is

[344] Missler, Chuck, *The Long Day of Joshua*, op. cit.

the order reported in the book of Joshua. Patton's model puts the various pass-bys at 100,000 miles, even down to 70,000 miles, centre to centre. The catastrophic exchange of energy between Mars and Earth would have produced ample Biblical effects. Rising off the horizon an angry red, fifty times the size of the Moon, the god of war would have unleashed flux tubes of lightning and storms of bolides arcing in at terrific speeds to explode across Earth's landscape, in this case devastating the armies of Adonizedek's coalition. Immense gravitational forces could quite plausibly have created the type of pole-shift/reversal described later by Isaiah:

Behold, the LORD maketh the Earth empty and maketh it waste, and turneth it upside down and scattereth abroad the inhabitants thereof. (Isa 24:1)

And:

The Earth is utterly broken down, the Earth is clean dissolved, the Earth is moved exceedingly. The Earth shall reel to and fro like a drunkard and shall be removed like a cottage; and the transgression thereof shall be heavy upon it; and it shall fall and not rise again. (Isa 24:19-20)

The Angel of the LORD, the Commander of the LORD's army – a pre-incarnate theophany of Yeshua Himself – assists in the destruction of Adonizedek's coalition, much as He will do to the armies of the Earth which gather against Him at Armageddon. Thus Adonizedek becomes a type of Antichrist, a pseudo-Christ, a counterfeit 'Lord of Righteousness', a fake 'A to Z', a bankrupt 'Alpha and Omega' who hides out in a cave near Makkedah with four other kings. They have just witnessed the slaughter of their armies by both Heaven and Earth and their fear must be palpable. Joshua commands large stones to be rolled against the mouth of the cave and orders his men to pursue the remnants of the enemy until all have been slaughtered. Later, he orders the stones rolled away and the kings brought out before him. He gathers his captains together:

"Come near, put your feet upon the necks of these kings." And they came near, and put their feet upon the necks of them. And Joshua said unto them, "Fear not, nor be dismayed, be strong and of good courage, for thus shall the LORD do to all your enemies against whom ye fight."

And afterward Joshua smote them and slew them, and hanged them on five trees, and they were hanging upon the trees until the evening. (Josh 10:24-26)

Grim stuff, and no-one takes the Canaan campaign lightly. To understand why God acted in so grievous a fashion is to understand the extent to which the Canaanite races had grievously offended Him. The burning alive of babies was a commonplace religious ritual to the bloodthirsty god, Molech. The practice of worshipping demon gods on the high places and in the groves (avenues of phallic-shaped trees), followed by unbridled orgies and behaviour of the most depraved kind is not often discussed by either Richard Dawkins on the one hand or the ladies of the Church Flower Group on the other. God gives Canaan 400 years to clean up its act, even extending this grace by a further 38 years when the Israelites baulk at taking the land at Kadesh Barnea. But in the end, God will act and execute His unswerving judgment, and there you have it.

Today's world should take pause and tremble to imagine what God has in store for the 21st century after the public, doctors and politicians alike have carried out the slaughter of the equivalent of *13% of the global population* in unborn babies in abortion procedures since Roe versus Wade 1973. These killings continue today, not by placing these babies in the glowing arms of a Molech statue, but by murdering them in the holy of holies of their mother's womb, mostly because of lifestyle choice. Or how about this one:

RUSSIAN CITIES INTRODUCE BABY 'DROP BOXES' TO STOP UNWANTED CHILDREN BEING LEFT IN BINS

The Krasnodar Territory in south Russia bought five of the so-called baby drop boxes in the beginning of November so mothers could drop off unwanted children anonymously. The first three were installed in Sochi, Novorossiysk and Armavir, and by the end of the month one child had already been left. The move was aimed at providing sanitary conditions for unwanted children, instead of 'having them left in garbage containers', health officials told Ria Novosti.[345]

I am reminded of the words of American Founding Father, Thomas Jefferson:

"I tremble for my country when I reflect that God is just, and His justice cannot sleep forever."[346]

---

[345] *Daily Mail,* 28th January 2012

[346] Quoted on Panel 3 of the Jefferson Memorial, Washington DC.

The end of conquest

The conquest of Canaan takes seven years. Joshua divides the region in half and deals with the southland first. The son of Nun follows God's instructions to the letter. The enemy armies are engaged, God gives the Israelites the victory, the entire host is slaughtered and their kings brought forth and executed (Josh 10:28-43). The conquest also sees a continuation of God's judgment upon the giants, spawned by the evil angels of Genesis 6 (*cf:* Gen 6:4 - **and also afterward**), whose original sexual antics were punished by the Flood. Moses had already put paid to the creature kings Sihon and Og east of the Jordan. Joshua's invasion puts a significant dent in *ha-Satan's* Nephilim breeding programme, and David will finish the job generations later with the help of his own mighty men. Wikipedia records under 'Amorites':

"The term 'Amorites' is used in the Bible to refer to certain highland mountaineers who inhabited the land of Canaan, described in Genesis 10:16 as descendants of Canaan, son of Ham. They are described as a powerful people of great stature 'like the height of the cedars', who had occupied the land east and west of the Jordan; their king, Og, being described as the last 'of the remnant of the Rephaim' (Deut. 3:11). The terms Amorite and Canaanite seem to be used more or less interchangeably, Canaan being more general and Amorite a specific component among the Canaanites who inhabited the land.

"The Biblical Amorites seem to have originally occupied the region stretching from the heights west of the Dead Sea (Gen. 14:7) to Hebron (13:8; Deut. 3:8; 4:46-48), embracing 'all Gilead and all Bashan' (Deut. 3:10), with the Jordan valley on the east of the river (4:49), the land of the 'two kings of the Amorites', Sihon and Og (Deut. 31:4; Josh. 2:10; 9:10). Both Sihon and Og were independent kings. These Amorites seem to have been linked to the Jerusalem region, and the Jebusites may have been a subgroup of them. The southern slopes of the mountains of Judea are called the 'mount of the Amorites' (Deut. 1:7,19,20).[347]

The northern conquest follows a similar tack. The Canaanite monarchs set aside petty squabbles and unite against the Jewish invaders. All in vain. A colossal force of Canaanites arrays itself to face Joshua at Merom in the Plain of Esdraelon. Readers may be more familiar with 'Tel Megiddo' which overlooks this location - the mound of Megiddo or 'Armageddon', the scene of the famous end-

[347] http://en.wikipedia.org/wiki/Amorites

times showdown; yet another link with Revelation. The Jewish chronicler Flavius Josephus numbers the Canaanite army at Merom to be around 300,000 men, including 10,000 cavalry and thousands of chariots - …**as many people as the sand that is on the seashore in multitude, with very many horses and chariots'** (Josh 11:4). The enemy possesses the latest technology – iron chariots hauled by fleet warhorses, which have proved almost invincible on the plains. Even after all he's been through, the site of this enemy must have caused Joshua to gulp. The LORD encourages:

"Be not afraid because of them, for tomorrow about this time will I deliver them up all slain before Israel. Thou shalt hough [hamstring[348]] **their horses and burn their chariots with fire."**

So Joshua came, and all the people of war with him, against them by the waters of Merom suddenly, and they fell upon them. And the LORD delivered them into the hand of Israel, who smote them and chased them unto great Zidon, and unto Misrephothmaim, and unto the valley of Mizpeh eastward. And they smote them until they left them none remaining. And Joshua did unto them as the LORD bade him. He houghed their horses and burnt their chariots with fire. (Josh 11:6-9)

Horses are used in the Bible literally and as a type. Dean Van Druff explains:

"Horses are used in the main to represent a carnal strength, a trusting in flesh; relied on by the enemies of God to their peril. Along this line:

Deut 17:16a (NIV) **The king, moreover, must not acquire great numbers of horses for himself.**

Psa 20:7 (NIV) **Some trust in chariots and some in horses, but we trust in the name of the LORD our God.**

Psa 33:17 (NIV) **A horse is a vain hope for deliverance; despite all its great strength it cannot save.**

Isa 31:1 (NIV) **Woe to those who go down to Egypt for help, who rely on horses, who trust in the multitude of their chariots and in the great strength of their horsemen, but do not look to the Holy One of Israel, or seek help from the LORD.**

Isa 30:16 (NIV) **"You said, 'No, we will flee on horses.' Therefore you will flee! You said, 'We will ride off on swift horses.' Therefore your pursuers will be swift!"**

---

[348] Scholars are generally in agreement that 'houghing' is hamstringing a horse, permanently crippling the animal by slicing the tendon at the back of the legs.

"In the modern sense, a good equivalent for horses would be money. It is that in which we place our confidence, our hope... outside of (or in competition with) the LORD.

"Beyond 'horses' in plural, a real, individual horse is used as a negative image of the spiritually dull person - along with the mule and donkey - as one who does not (or cannot) understand the will of the LORD.

Ps 32:9 (NIV) **Do not be like the horse or the mule, which have no understanding but must be controlled by bit and bridle or they will not come to you.**

Pr 26:3 (NIV) **A whip for the horse, a halter for the donkey, and a rod for the backs of fools!**

Jer 8:6 (NIV) **I have listened attentively, but they do not say what is right. No one repents of his wickedness, saying, "What have I done?" Each pursues his own course like a horse charging into battle.**

"Spiritual or heavenly horses represent judgment, and usually dramatic judgment for the sake of violent purification. The movie *Fellowship of the Rings* from *The Lord of the Rings* trilogy visually conveys this sense of dreadful horses rather well with the wraith-riders. They are a portent of bad things to come. In scripture, the symbolic horse generally represents a particular aspect or agent of punishment or plague. In Rev 6, we get a taste of things to come in terms of horses riding out with the first 'seals' [four horsemen of the apocalypse]." [349]

The LORD Himself, Yeshua, will come to do war with the nations at His Second Coming, riding a white horse. The counterfeit to Yeshua – the Antichrist – also appears on a white horse (Rev 6). Horses are one of dozens of types used in the Bible consistently across 40 authors, providing further proof of the Message System's epistemological integrity.

At Merom, an astonishing victory is won by the LORD for Joshua and the Israelites, breaking the back of the remaining resistance. In researching this period, I am struck by the fact that no archaeological find to date appears to controvert a Biblical reference. No better summary of the Canaan campaign is found than the following:

And Joshua at that time turned back and took Hazor, and smote the king thereof with the sword, for Hazor beforetime was the head of all those kingdoms. And they smote all the souls that were

---

[349] www.acts17-11.com/dialogs_horses.html.

therein with the edge of the sword, utterly destroying them. There was not any left to breathe. And he burnt Hazor with fire.

And all the cities of those kings and all the kings of them did Joshua take, and smote them with the edge of the sword and he utterly destroyed them, as Moses the servant of the LORD commanded. But as for the cities that stood still in their strength, Israel burned none of them save Hazor only; that did Joshua burn.

And all the spoil of these cities, and the cattle, the children of Israel took for a prey unto themselves, but every man they smote with the edge of the sword until they had destroyed them. Neither left they any to breathe.

As the LORD commanded Moses his servant, so did Moses command Joshua, and so did Joshua. He left nothing undone of all that the LORD commanded Moses.

So Joshua took all that land, the hills, and all the south country, and all the land of Goshen, and the valley, and the plain, and the mountain of Israel, and the valley of the same. Even from the mount Halak that goeth up to Seir, even unto Baalgad in the valley of Lebanon under Mount Hermon. And all their kings he took, and smote them, and slew them.

Joshua made war a long time with all those kings. There was not a city that made peace with the children of Israel save the Hivites, the inhabitants of Gibeon; all other they took in battle. For it was of the LORD to harden their hearts, that they should come against Israel in battle, that he might destroy them utterly, and that they might have no favour, but that he might destroy them, as the LORD commanded Moses.

And at that time came Joshua and cut off the Anakim [aka. Nephilim, giants] **from the mountains, from Hebron, from Debir, from Anab, and from all the mountains of Judah, and from all the mountains of Israel. Joshua destroyed them utterly with their cities. There was none of the Anakim left in the land of the children of Israel: only in Gaza, in Gath, and in Ashdod, there remained.**[350]

So Joshua took the whole land, according to all that the LORD said unto Moses; and Joshua gave it for an inheritance unto Israel according to their divisions by their tribes. <u>And the land rested from war</u>. (Josh 11:10-23)

Inheritance, refuge and warning

[350] The only surviving Anakim fled to the land of the Philistines and will later be dealt with by that most famous of kings – David.

In the lull which follows, Joshua apportions the land to each of the twelve tribes for an inheritance. Whilst well aware that there is yet more land to be vanquished, the hardships, battles and years have etched their marks upon the son of Nun. Joshua is now too old and fatigued to continue. The tribes will have to clear their own districts before extending their reach into the furthest lands God has set aside for them.

From the outset, God has set his own personal stamp on Israel. Out of the entire Creation, God has selected this patch of real estate for Himself. The gift of it to His people is unconditional (Gen 15), but their occupation of it will be contingent upon their obedience. If they obey God's ways, they will be blessed and victorious; if they blaspheme His name through disobedience and turning to false gods, God will sharpen His sword for them. On several occasions in the centuries to come, the Jews will be removed from the land for apostasy, idol worship and disobedience to the Torah. It's a surprise to many that the Creator of the entire universe would actually select a land on Earth just for Himself, but He chose Israel, and He chose the Earth. Contesting the ownership of Israel, Palestine, Canaan, the Levant - call it what you will - is as futile as an atheist denying the One who made him. The universe is God's. The solar system is God's. The planets are God's. And one particular piece of turf on one particular planet has eternal significance for the LORD. It's not very long and not very wide at present, and it curls the toes to watch generations of politicians, zealots and terrorists picking over its dust, deciding who owns what in the Middle East. Knowing what I know now, I would not do that if I were them.

The distribution of the land to each of the tribes is covered in detail in Joshua chapters 13-21. Among the blizzard of information given, God instructs Joshua to set up six cities of refuge (Josh 20:1-6). Here we have six verses tucked away that have abiding significance for our own futures. If you commit manslaughter, the next of kin of the slain will come after you and be legally entitled to kill you as 'the avenger of blood'. Your only recourse lies in reaching one of those six cities of refuge, three east and three west of the Jordan river (*cf:* Exo 21:13; Num 35:11-24). Once inside, if the elders of the city find you guilty of murder, you are handed over to the avenger to be killed. If they find you innocent of murder but guilty of manslaughter, you can remain in safety inside the city and the avenger cannot touch you on pain of his own death. Stray outside the city and you're fair game.

When the high priest eventually dies, you are free to go your way with impunity and the avenger can no longer touch you. These six cities of refuge are Kadesh, Shechem and Hebron west of the Jordan and Bezer, Ramoth and Golan east of the river. Jerry Bouey writes:

"From what we read in Numbers 35, Deuteronomy 19 and Joshua 20, we can distinguish a number of characteristics of the cities of refuge:

- They were established by God before they were needed.
- They were available to all as well as accessible to all.
- Their gates were always open.
- They were widely advertised.
- All the cities of refuge were prominently located at high elevations so they could be seen from great distances.
- Everyone was within a day's journey from at least one of them.
- Whosoever needed to flee to one of the cities was free to do so, whether or not he was an Israelite." [351]

The cities of refuge are a perfect foreshadowing of Jesus/Yeshua, our own city of refuge and High Priest. In God's perfect realm, all mankind is guilty under the Adamic curse, even of murder if we have harboured just one bad thought about someone.[352] The avenger of blood is now after us. Who is that? God Himself. So we need a city of refuge, which is Yeshua, provided by God. In Him we are safe from the slayer until the high priest (also Yeshua) dies (on the cross). Now we are free and the slayer (God's judgment) has no power over us. Ralph Matthews summarises:

"The [slayer's] situation changed when the high priest died (Num 35:25). When that happened, the refugee was free again. He was absolved from all blame. The death of the high priest was a form of substitution for the death that had been caused. The debt was paid in full when the high priest died. We see in this the substitutionary death of Jesus Christ. He died in the sinner's place. **For He hath made Him to be sin for us, Who knew no sin; that we might be made the righteousness of God in Him** (2 Cor 5:21)." [353]

Realising his own time is short, Joshua summons the elders of the twelve tribes. To the leaders he declares:

---

[351] www.earnestlycontending.com/ewministries/jerry/citiesofrefuge.html

[352] *cf.* Matt 5:21-32; Rom 3:19,23; FG 3:18,36

[353] **Matthews, R** "Cities Of Refuge", *Foundation* magazine, May-June 2003

"I am old and stricken in age. And ye have seen all that the LORD your God hath done unto all these nations because of you, for the LORD your God is He that hath fought for you.

"Behold, I have divided unto you by lot these nations that remain, to be an inheritance for your tribes, from Jordan, with all the nations that I have cut off, even unto the great sea westward [Mediterranean]. **And the LORD your God, He shall expel them from before you, and drive them from out of your sight; and ye shall possess their land, as the LORD your God hath promised unto you.**

"Be ye therefore very courageous to keep and to do all that is written in the book of the law of Moses, that ye turn not aside therefrom to the right hand or to the left. That ye come not among these nations, these that remain among you; neither make mention of the name of their gods, nor cause to swear by them, neither serve them, nor bow yourselves unto them. But cleave unto the LORD your God as ye have done unto this day. For the LORD hath driven out from before you great nations and strong: but as for you, no man hath been able to stand before you unto this day.

"One man of you shall chase a thousand, for the LORD your God, He it is that fighteth for you, as He hath promised you. Else if ye do in any wise go back and cleave unto the remnant of these nations, even these that remain among you, and shall make marriages with them, and go in unto them, and they to you, know for a certainty that the LORD your God will no more drive out any of these nations from before you. But they shall be snares and traps unto you, and scourges in your sides, and thorns in your eyes, until ye perish from off this good land which the LORD your God hath given you." (Josh 23:2-13)

Sound advice indeed. After all they have been through and all the miracles witnessed, do the children of Israel take heed and hold their God before them? The adventures which follow are an astonishing revelation of their own, and hold valuable insights into the human condition, the Predicament of Man, that there is nothing new of human nature in our own modern age. The snares of old ensnare us still. The cycle of nations continues to turn. History repeats. God acts.

A LOVE STORY

It's been an unremitting slog through the Canaan campaign, but there is a remarkable four-chapter book in the Bible which will give pause to all the slaughter. The book of Ruth turns out not only to be one of the greatest love stories in literature, it's an astonishing, prophetic window into our own age and future, revealing some startling attributes of the Creator.

Affliction brings opportunity

The story begins back in the years following Joshua's conquest of Canaan, when the Land has been settled by the Israelites. A man of Bethlehem named Elimelech ('My God is King') decides to emigrate with his family because of a famine. He takes with him his wife, Naomi ('pleasant'), and their two sons, disconcertingly named Mahlon ('weak', 'sickly') and Chilion ('failing', 'pining'). The implication is that in leaving Judah, Elimelech forfeits his own land either through choice or indebtedness. Elimelech moves to Moab with his family, a pagan nation to the east across the Jordan. After this, Elimelech dies. Naomi marries her Jewish sons off to two pagan Moabite girls, one named Orpah ('fawn'), the other Ruth ('beauty', 'desirable'). In time, both sickly sons also die, leaving Naomi in a foreign land with two gentile daughters-in-law and no means of support.

Some time later, word comes that the famine in Judah is lifting and conditions are improving. Naomi decides to return to her homeland of Bethlehem. She tells her daughters-in-law they are free to go back to their families in Moab and find new husbands. The girls put up stout resistance, not wanting to leave her, which tells us something about the character of Naomi. Not only is she beloved, even while burdened by her own straitened circumstances, she's deciding what's best for others. She takes them to task like a good Jewish mother:

"Turn again, my daughters. Why will ye go with me? Are there yet any more sons in my womb, that they may be your husbands? Turn again, my daughters, go your way, for I am too old to have a husband. If I should say, 'I have hope, if I should have a husband also tonight, and should also bear sons', would ye tarry for them till they were grown? Would ye stay for them from having husbands?

Nay, my daughters; for it grieveth me much for your sakes that the hand of the LORD is gone out against me." (Ruth 1:11-13)

Orpah is finally persuaded to leave but Ruth grimly clings to her mother-in-law. Her plea to remain at Naomi's side is one of the most moving in scripture:

"Intreat me not to leave thee or to return from following after thee, for whither thou goest, I will go, and where thou lodgest, I will lodge. Thy people shall be my people, and thy God my God. Where thou diest, will I die, and there will I be buried. The LORD do so to me and more also if ought but death part thee and me." (Ruth 1:16-17)

Ruth is prepared to turn her back on her own family, land and culture forever and embrace the strange new civilisation of the Israelites and their God. No mean feat, cedes Robin Weber:

> " '*Where you die, I will die, And there will I be buried.*' There is more than symbolism; there is reality in this. Even with her young husband dead and the chance to go home, Ruth is abandoning her past. She is fully clinging to this new family of Naomi and saying, 'I will be buried with your family. I'm giving up on Moab. I'm giving up on my own father (who the scriptures indicate was still alive.) I'm giving up on the old world, the old ways. Life hasn't been fair but I'm going to step out with you. I'm going to step out in faith.'
>
> "In fact, the commentaries say that, in this poem, this song, she does not use the term *Elohim*, but she uses the other term of *Yahweh,* of a personal God, not the great God, not the *Elohim*, not the term that foreigners used, but the term of *Yahweh,* and personalized it, that she was going to walk a new way of life." [354]

As for Naomi, Jack Heyford comments that the matriarch's perspective is understandable (**'the hand of the LORD is gone out against me'**), given the limited revelation of God's true nature at this time (1 Sam 3:1). She's lost her homeland, then her husband, and now her two sons. Naomi knows there is a God but does not fully comprehend the reason for her plight. As with all grief, while we remain baffled and desolate as to the reason, we need to understand that there are subsequent chapters to a disaster, especially for believers, which provide that meaning.[355] The apostle Paul, no stranger to adversities and setbacks himself, writes:

---

[354] www.ucg.org/sermon/lessons-book-ruth/

[355] Heyford, Jack, *The Spirit-Filled Bible,* op. cit., p.389

And we know that all things work together for good to them that love God, to them who are the called according to His purpose. For whom He did foreknow, He also did predestinate to be conformed to the image of His Son, that He might be the firstborn among many brethren. (Rom 8:28-29)

In Ruth and Naomi's case, God allows a disaster/evil in His free system on Project Earth to bring about His will for a greater good in the two women's future. Notice that even as Naomi laments her predicament, she is acting as a beacon for Ruth who will follow her. And so it can be with us toward others.

"Ruth is insistent, **'Entreat me not to leave you'**. Her oft-quoted poem of commitment is not mere emotion. She is reaching beyond friendship to faith. **'The Lord do so...'** indicates that Ruth understands the nature of Yahweh. She invokes His name with an oath. Her commitment is rooted in the understanding of the living God, of whom she has learned from Naomi." [356]

So the two return to Bethlehem ('the House of Bread'). The whole township is stirred at their arrival, which suggests that Elimelech and Naomi were originally citizens of substance in the region, perhaps even of old and established nobility, and therefore landowners. Ruth too attracts Bethlehem's attention as a pagan maiden accompanying the Jewish matriarch. Naomi is bitter at the public's reaction to her return:

So they two went until they came to Bethlehem. And it came to pass, when they were come to Bethlehem, that all the city was moved about them, and they said, "Is this Naomi?"

And she said unto them, "Call me not Naomi ['Delightful', 'pleasant', 'lovely'], **call me Mara** ['bitter'], **for the Almighty hath dealt very bitterly with me. I went out full, and the LORD hath brought me home again empty. Why then call ye me Naomi, seeing the LORD hath testified against me, and the Almighty hath afflicted me?"**

So Naomi returned, and Ruth the Moabitess, her daughter-in-law, with her, which returned out of the country of Moab. And they came to Bethlehem in the beginning of the barley harvest. (Ruth 1:19-22)

So Naomi's back but she's broke. The narrative then introduces a plot development.

---

[356] Ibid.

And Naomi had a kinsman of her husband's, a mighty man of wealth, of the family of Elimelech; and his name was Boaz. And Ruth the Moabitess said unto Naomi, "Let me now go to the field and glean ears of corn after him in whose sight I shall find grace." And [Naomi] **said unto her, "Go, my daughter."**

And she went, and came, and gleaned in the field after the reapers, and her hap [i.e. it just so happened] **was to light on a part of the field belonging unto Boaz, who was of the kindred of Elimelech.** (Ruth 2:1-3)

What are the chances?

Our initial suspicions are correct. We are introduced to one of Elimelech's relatives: Boaz ('swiftness'). **A mighty man of wealth** in the Hebrew suggests that Boaz is more than just loaded, he wields power, influence and standing in the community and was probably a warrior earlier in his career.

Ruth begs permission of Naomi to go and glean in the fields nearby. Gleaning was a form of welfare employed by the Jews at that time to assist the poor. If you were a landowner, your reapers were allowed to pass through the fields once but were not to harvest the corners fully, after which anything left could be gleaned (gathered) by the poor or strangers for their own use.[357] Farmers did not cultivate complete fields as is customary today, rather there were large tracts of land divided up among owners and demarked by stones. Notice Ruth's attitude. Unlike today's layabouts who wallow in a culture of entitlement, Ruth is up at dawn and ready to rumble. Workshy she ain't.

And then we have this little word 'hap' tossed into the text, upon which hangs one of the great philosophical debates of our existence. Ruth just 'happens', 'by chance', 'coincidentally' to come upon the part of the field owned by Boaz. When you just 'happen' to come upon a new acquaintance, is it luck? When it just happens to be raining on the day of your wedding, is it chance? Should you read anything into the extraordinary, seemingly haphazard occurrences of your daily life? Your options are limited if you believe in God. He's either the God of everything or He isn't. Your God is either working minutely every second to bring about His will for you, or He's not big

---

[357] **And when ye reap the harvest of your land, thou shalt not wholly reap the corners of thy field, neither shalt thou gather the gleanings of thy harvest.** (Lev 19:9; *cf.* Lev 23:22)

enough to matter, in which case, don't waste your time. An honest scientist will admit that there is no such thing as true randomness in the universe, just a lack of information. So what about 'chance' encounters? Gary McFlurry comments:

"I just happened to bump into so-and-so. Just by chance I called into the butchers. Coincidences, random happenings, chance encounters. What is it you think of when these things happen to you? You might imagine it's the randomness of a random universe. Nothing special or amazing. We find such an event in Ruth chapter 2. Ruth and her mother-in-law Naomi are both widows with no means of support. So Ruth decides to go and glean, to pick up the leavings of the harvest, to survive....

"To quote a famous line from the movie *Casablanca*: 'Of all the bars in all the world, she had to walk into mine.' Or perhaps as Boaz would have said, 'Of all the fields around Bethlehem, she had to glean in mine.' The purpose of these words is clear. This was not just a random chance. Rather, God was in sovereign control to order these events so that Ruth finds herself in her worthy relative's field." [358]

But Gary is a priest, so he would say that. I find it intriguing that like death, God appears to have left our interpretation of 'chance' up to us. Dr Sean Pitman explains:

"While the appearance of randomness may be all around us, there is no such thing as true randomness in the Christian perspective. We are told that **all things work together for good to them that love God** (Rom 8:28). We are also told that God sees **the end from the beginning** (Isa 46:10) and answers all prayers asked with a sincere and earnest heart in accordance with His will; that He gives in answer to prayer that which He would not otherwise give or be able to bless had we not asked (**'Ask, and it shall be given you; seek, and ye shall find; knock, and it shall be opened unto you:'** (Matt 7:7)). Yet, in answering our prayers, He often re-interprets our requests according to what we ourselves would really want if we knew as He knows. **'Would any father give his son a stone when asked for bread?'** Sometimes we think we ask for bread when, if our prayers were answered as asked, we would get a stone in the long run. That is why it is best to close our requests to God as Jesus did, 'Not as I will, but as You will...Your will be done.' "[359]

---

[358] http://garymcmurray.blogspot.fr/2009/01/happenstance.html
[359] www.detectingdesign.com

Remember Dr Stuart Crane's analysis of Truth?[360] Anything I wish to know about, if I wish to know the Truth about it, I need to know about its relationship *with all other things in the universe.* Truth will never have an exception in the past, will never have one ongoing in the present, and can never have an exception in the future. It will always stand alone as the Truth. All else is error.

Truth with a capital 'T' is impossible to the finite mind, says Dr Crane. Truth is only possible to an infinite mind, one without limitations. The only way Truth could exist in the universe is if there were an Infinite Mind. And even if there were an Infinite Mind in the universe, then Truth would only be possible to humankind if that Infinite Mind chose to reveal it to us. Has this occurred? We cannot get Truth on our own by discovery, by work or by diligence. Truth is only possible through revelation by the Infinite Mind if the Infinite Mind so chooses to tell us. The only way we can keep from error *is to steal ourselves to follow the Infinite Mind.* This trust is known as *faith.* Faith is a belief which taps into the Truth of the Infinite Mind.

Not as I will but as You will.

Now notice Naomi's worldview: while she ascribes her predicament to God's disfavour (not chance), she does not make that extra leap to conclude that God, rather than mindlessly having it in for her, could just be arranging circumstances for her future if she responds in faith. Thus, what appears to be happenstance in the secular realm (or even tragedy or victimisation) is the outworking of the Infinite Mind in the metacosm.[361] While God does not violate the sovereignty of human free will, the peculiar nature of His hyperdimensionality enables Him to 'set things up' to punish or reward, or to just see how we do. Are you willing to glean to see what you'll get? Gleaning is a step out in faith, expecting the Landowner to provide. Life on Earth is our on-the-job training and selection programme for eternity under live-fire conditions. Once we get our heads around that one, a whole vista of understanding opens up and our great purpose is revealed. Get busy. Get out and glean. Trust in God to provide and steer us. Overcome the flesh. Obey and follow the

---

[360] *Origins II – Holy War,* 'The definition of truth'

[361] A corroboration of God's mechanism with cause and effect is echoed in the unfathomable complication of the human body. Cells, hormones, vitamins, minerals, substrates, fats and micro-organisms all operate synergistically. Every effect has a cause and every cause an effect. Only the Infinite Mind can keep track; man has no clue how it all works; don't let anyone fool you otherwise!

LORD in all things. *Finish well.* The scriptures are replete with examples, yet in *Origins V – Sons of Thunder,* once we move outside the Biblical timeline (*c.* 135 AD), we will see this is ever the case in human history right down to our own modern age.

Back to young Ruth gleaning in the fields. The landowner Boaz shows up a little later and greets his farmworkers. Boaz is probably aged 55 - 65 and, since he is the son of the harlot Rahab (who saved the lives of the Israelite spies in Jericho), the Ruth and Boaz story is popularly dated about 70 years after Jericho's destruction. How Boaz greets his farmworkers tells us something about the man.

And, behold, Boaz came from Bethlehem and said unto the reapers, "The LORD be with you." And they answered him, "The LORD bless thee!" (Ruth 2:4)

Not, "WORK HARDER, you gizzard-gobbling scum, or there'll be HELL TO PAY!" Boaz blesses his workers in the LORD's name and they return the favour. Boaz is positive, cheerful, knows the region is coming out of famine, and that life is good. He also knows how to treat people with respect. Ruth doubtless witnesses this scene and forms her initial impression of her new benefactor.

After perusing the scene, Boaz takes his foreman aside and enquires after the young woman gleaning in his field. The foreman replies that it is the Moabitess damsel who accompanied Naomi out of Moab; that she asked permission to glean after the reapers among the sheaves, and has been working even from the morning until now, though she's taken a break in the shelter once in a while (Ruth 2:4-7). Intrigued, Boaz summons the girl:

"Hearest thou not, my daughter? Go not to glean in another field, neither go from hence but abide here fast by my maidens. Let thine eyes be on the field that they do reap and go thou after them. Have I not charged the young men that they shall not touch thee? And when thou art athirst, go unto the vessels and drink of that which the young men have drawn."

Then she fell on her face, bowed herself to the ground, and said unto him, "Why have I found grace in thine eyes, that thou shouldest take knowledge of me, seeing I am a stranger?"

And Boaz answered and said unto her, "It hath fully been shewed me all that thou hast done unto thy mother-in-law since the death of thine husband; and how thou hast left thy father and thy mother, and the land of thy nativity, and art come unto a people which thou knewest not heretofore. May the LORD recompense thy

work, and a full reward be given thee of the LORD God of Israel, under whose wings thou art come to trust."(Ruth 2:8-12)

An immediate bond

Ruth is astonished at Boaz's empathy and kindness. The beneficence extended is not only because of the loyalty shown by Ruth to Naomi in her trials, but also her faith in making her future with the LORD God of Israel and His people, whom she knew not. We also suspect the two are personally attracted to one another. There's a snapshot of the times: Boaz finds it necessary to warn his young men not to interfere with Ruth, inferring that she is attractive and that such behaviour is common towards foreigners at that time. Then again, as Ruth's name suggests, she's also pretty with a demure character, so perhaps Boaz is looking after his own interests. He's certainly a hands-on boss, and finds reasons to remain in the field until lunch-break:

And Boaz said unto her at mealtime, "Come thou hither and eat of the bread, and dip thy morsel in the vinegar." And she sat beside the reapers and he passed her parched corn, and she did eat and was sufficed, and kept some back.

And when she was risen up to glean, Boaz commanded his young men, saying, "Let her glean even among the sheaves and reproach her not. And let fall also some of the handfuls on purpose for her, and leave them, that she may glean them, and rebuke her not."

So she gleaned in the field until evening, and beat out that she had gleaned, and it was about an ephah of barley. And she took it up and went into the city [Bethlehem]**, and her mother-in-law saw what she had gleaned. And** [Ruth] **brought forth and gave to** [Naomi] **what she had reserved after she was sufficed.** (Ruth 2:14-18)

Naomi is not a stupid woman. When she lays eyes upon the extent of Ruth's haul, she knows something is up. Upon quizzing the girl, she learns that Boaz, a near kinsman, is the benefactor, the implications of which are initially lost on Ruth, who tells her mother-in-law:

"He [Boaz] **said unto me also, 'Thou shalt keep fast by my young men, until they have ended all my harvest.' "**

And Naomi said unto Ruth her daughter-in-law, "It is good, my daughter, that thou go out with his maidens, that they meet thee not in any other field."

So [Ruth] **kept fast by the maidens of Boaz to glean unto the end of barley harvest and of wheat harvest, and dwelt with her mother-in-law.** (Ruth 2:21-23)

Often missed by commentators is the all-important period between Ruth's initial encounter with Boaz and the end of the barley and wheat harvest, during which the two can get to know and observe one another while the crops are brought in. Naomi, meanwhile, sees a way out of her own and Ruth's impoverished predicament. She also recognises the LORD's hand in what's happening, finally (Ruth 2:20). Tucked away in the obscure details of the Torah is the role of the kinsman-redeemer or *'goel'* (Lev 25:25, 47-55). A benevolently disposed near kinsman can assist in redeeming lost status and/or property to an unfortunate relative. Naomi's mind begins working furiously:

"My daughter, shall I not seek rest for thee, that it may be well with thee? And now is not Boaz of our kindred, with whose maidens thou wast? Behold, he winnoweth barley tonight on the threshing-floor.

Wash thyself, therefore, and anoint thee, and put thy raiment upon thee, and get thee down to the floor. But make not thyself known unto the man until he shall have done eating and drinking. And it shall be, when he lieth down, that thou shalt mark the place where he shall lie, and thou shalt go in and uncover his feet and lay thee down, and he will tell thee what thou shalt do."

And [Ruth] **said unto her, "All that thou sayest unto me I will do."** (Ruth 3:1-5)

Wait, what did I just read? That Naomi is putting Ruth up to propositioning Boaz? It's worse than that.

Firstly, some quick background on the agricultural practices of the day. Wheat or barley is harvested by cutting the stalks in the field and binding them together into sheaves. The sheaves are then brought into the threshing area, unpacked and scattered across the floor. The wheat or barley grains the farmer wants are housed in a group of 'ears' or 'husks' located on the end of the long stalk. To separate the grain from the husks, the crop is 'winnowed'. This means variously whacked, beaten, thrashed, threshed, trampled by animals/children (really), then the mixture scooped up on shallow, flat trays and tossed into the air. Ideally you want your threshing floor on a hilltop or saddleback (two high-points separated by a slight dip) to provide a constant supply of light wind, so the air carries away the lighter husk/ fibres/junk/chaff while the heavier grain (the bit you want) drops back onto the tray. Some farmers harvesting a major crop dispense with the trays and use large scoops to toss up the mix. If they do it correctly, they end up with three piles: the lightest chaff furthest downwind; the heavier husk fibres nearer, and the grain at their feet. Google up 'winnowing' and click on the images setting to see what's going on in various non-industrialised cultures today.

The harvest was naturally a time of great celebration in Biblical times. When God blessed the communities with food for the continuance of life, there were parties, and in Boaz's case, eating and drinking before getting your head down beside your crop so no-one stole it. Naomi is asking Ruth to approach Boaz when the time is right to commence the kinsman-redeemer process. What at first sight seems a highly dubious proposition turns out to be a process loaded with significance *for each of us into eternity.*

Ruth is to go in and uncover Boaz's feet as he sleeps. This will have the effect of waking him to discover the girl at his feet. Let's see what happens.

And [Ruth] **went down unto the floor and did according to all that her mother-in-law bade her. And when Boaz had eaten and drunk and his heart was merry, he went to lie down at the end of the heap of corn. And she came softly and uncovered his feet and laid her down.**

And it came to pass at midnight that the man was afraid [a mistranslation: should be 'shivered with cold'] **and turned himself: and, behold, a woman lay at his feet. And he said, "Who art thou?" And she answered, "I am Ruth, thine handmaid. Spread therefore thy skirt over thine handmaid, for thou art a near kinsman."**

And he said, "Blessed be thou of the LORD, my daughter, for thou hast shewed more kindness in the latter end than at the beginning, inasmuch as thou followedst not young men, whether poor or rich. And now, my daughter, fear not; I will do to thee all that thou requirest, for all the city of my people doth know that thou art a virtuous woman. And now it is true that I am thy near kinsman, howbeit there is a kinsman nearer than I. Tarry this night, and it shall be in the morning, that if he will perform unto thee the part of a kinsman, well, let him do the kinsman's part. But if he will not do the part of a kinsman to thee, then will I do the part of a kinsman to thee, as the LORD liveth. Lie down until the morning."

And she lay at his feet until the morning, and arose before one could know another [i.e. while it was still dark]**. And he** [Boaz] **said**

[to his smirking gangmen], **"Let it not be known that a woman came into the threshing floor."** (Ruth 3:6-14)

A few points here:

- Naomi's suspicions are correct. Boaz is not only attracted to the young girl, he reacts as expected and agrees to play the part of the kinsman-redeemer (*goel*). But the story introduces a further plot-twist. There is a kinsman closer to Ruth than Boaz who must be given first refusal. *Sheesh!*
- Boaz is flattered that she is propositioning him and not going after younger men. One implies from this that she's quite a catch, and Boaz is aware that many of his young men are eying her up
- Boaz may have been shy in approaching a much younger woman and is gratified that she has made the first move. The fact that he has allowed her to make the first move is significant, as we will shortly see
- **Spread therefore thy skirt over thine handmaid** in OT Jewish culture means, 'take me as your wife/take me under your authority' (Eze 16:8). Ruth's actions are sometimes misinterpreted as licentious when this story is studied today. Even at the time, Boaz was keen that no-one should know of the midnight visit in case witnesses misconstrued the motive
- This scene also introduces another facet of Jewish culture: the law of levirate marriage. If a woman's husband dies, a near kinsman (usually the brother) may take her to wife to raise up seed to continue the dead husband's line.[362] Boaz knows enough about Ruth's widowhood to realise he is also assuming this role
- Hems, skirts and fringes in this culture are a symbol of rank/authority. In the New Testament (NT), a woman with a chronic haemorrhage (issue of blood) will seek to touch the hem of Yeshua's garment to be healed (Matt 9:20. *cf.* 14:36). David will covertly slice the fringe off King Saul's cloak while the latter is relieving himself in a cave, not only to show Saul that he could have taken his life, but also that Saul's authority has been impugned and even taken by David (1 Sam 24:1-7). David later regrets this imprudent act against the LORD's anointed (v.5).

Before Ruth leaves Boaz for Bethlehem in the morning, Boaz does a puzzling thing:

---

[362] Levirate marriage is found in cultures throughout history where clan structure and law dictated that marriages should not be made outside the culture.

Also he said, "Bring the vail [veil] **that thou hast upon thee and hold it." And when** [Ruth] **held it, he measured six measures of barley and laid it on her; and she went into the city.**

And when she came to her mother-in-law, [Naomi] **said, "Who art thou, my daughter?" And she told her all that the man had done to her.**

And [Ruth] **said, "These six measures of barley gave he me, for he said to me, 'Go not empty unto thy mother-in-law.' "**

Then [Naomi] **said, "Sit still, my daughter, until thou know how the matter will fall, for the man will not be in rest until he has finished the thing this day."** (Ruth 3:15-18)

Before Ruth departs, Boaz asks for her shawl, into which he pours six ephahs of barley (a fair amount). When Ruth returns to Bethlehem, Naomi is briefed on all Boaz has done for her, including the barley bit at the end. Expositors argue that in his generosity, Boaz was merely giving Ruth a token that he would abundantly provide for her in the future. Other scholars believe Boaz was giving her a reason for being at the threshing floor so early (to fetch grain before the heat of the day). It might be both of these, yet Chuck Missler sees a different interpretation:

"The six measures of barley are a code. Boaz gave it for Naomi, not Ruth (note v. 17). How long did it take God to create the Earth? Six days (Gen 1 and Ex 20:11). And on the seventh day He rested. When Boaz gives six measures to Naomi, she understands that he is saying that he won't rest until the matter is resolved." [363]

Shoes in the gate

Boaz is fired up, motivated, in love, and on the case. He goes to sit in Bethlehem's gate, convening ten elders as witnesses,[364] plus the near-kinsman of which he spoke, and gets down to the matter. The gate is effectively Town or City Hall in this culture (Later, the strongman Samson will make off with Gaza's gate!). All who come and go can be inspected by the city elders, and strangers scrutinised and questioned 'in the gate'. It's an obvious form of municipal security, and we will see it crop up again as we proceed through the era of the monarchy. Boaz could even have been Bethlehem's 'mayor'. We gather from Ruth 4:10 that Elimelech was originally a member of Bethlehem town council.

---

[363] Missler, Chuck, *Judges notes*, p.175

[364] Ten is regarded as the number of the Law, witness and testimony.

And [Boaz] **said unto the** [near-] **kinsman, "Naomi, that is come again out of the country of Moab, selleth a parcel of land, which was our brother Elimelech's. And I thought to advertise thee, saying, 'Buy it before the inhabitants and elders of my people. If thou wilt redeem it, redeem it, but if thou wilt not redeem it, then tell me, that I may know, for there is none to redeem it beside thee, and I am after thee.' "**

And he said, "I will redeem it."

Then said Boaz, "What day thou buyest the field of the hand of Naomi, thou must buy it also of Ruth the Moabitess, the wife of the dead, to raise up the name of the dead upon his inheritance [i.e. levirate marriage, raising up seed with Ruth for her dead husband]**."**

And the kinsman said, "I cannot redeem it for myself, lest I mar mine own inheritance. Redeem thou my right to thyself, for I cannot redeem it." (Ruth 4:3-6)

Jack Heyford comments:

> "Since the property would belong to any son born of Ruth, the relative refers to issues of commitment already within his own family. These would be confused by any obligations potentially altering procedures already in place. It is also possible that he simply could not afford the financial impact of securing the field and taking a bride at the same time. Also conceivable is the fact that his response infers racial prejudice, Ruth being a Moabitess."[365]

Why am I getting into all this? Because what at first sight seems an obscure point of Jewish law in an ancient story *has supreme global significance,* as we shall see. While the Earth and everything therein is the LORD's,[366] the land of Israel is, to state again, a particular piece of real estate God has picked out for Himself. Israel is the Jews' inheritance and God has allowed them to dwell in His Land and maintain it under conditions of obedience. Thus, land apportioned to the tribes and families remains with the family. When we read of Jewish land being 'sold', it is *the use* of the land being transferred, akin to a lease; the family never loses title. Though Elimelech left with his family for Moab under straitened circumstances, his family (and thus kinsmen - Naomi/Ruth) still hold title to the land.

Anyway, Naomi, Ruth and Boaz all get the outcome they desire. The near-kinsman apparently has no trouble redeeming the land, but

---

[365] Heyford, Jack, *Spirit-Filled Bible,* op. cit., p.392

[366] Deut 10:14; Psa 24:1, 1 Cor 10:26, etc.

marrying Ruth to raise up seed for Mahlon is apparently a deal-breaker. Then he does a strange thing:

Now this was the manner in former time in Israel concerning redeeming and concerning changing, for to confirm all things, a man plucked off his shoe and gave it to his neighbour, and this was a testimony in Israel. Therefore the kinsman said unto Boaz, "Buy it for thee." So he drew off his shoe. (Ruth 4:7-8)

'Shoes' are another surprising type throughout the Bible. They seem to represent a man's personal authority or 'walk'. In this case, the near-kinsman is surrendering his personal right/authority to Boaz to do the decent thing by Ruth and thus Elimelech's seed. Here follows some other shoe stuff:

1. YHWH instructs Moses to remove his shoes at the burning bush, for the place where the patriarch is standing is holy ground. Human authority must withdraw before God's own (Exo 3:5).

2. In like manner, Joshua has an enigmatic encounter with the captain of the LORD's army (Yeshua) prior to the destruction of Jericho. (One Yeshua meeting another!) Joshua is instructed to remove his shoes (renounce his authority) because he is standing on holy ground (in the LORD's presence) (Josh 5:15).

3. Believers are encouraged to be kitted out and ready to leave at a moment's notice (shoes on!) while partaking of the first Passover meal in Egypt (Exo 12:11).

4. God preserves the Israelites' shoes during the Exodus, allowing them to maintain their personal authority and dignity while under His care and provision (Deut 29:5).

5. The shaken/thrown shoe represents the believer's absolute victory over the enemy (Psa 108:9). George W Bush had shoes thrown at him by a Muslim journalist during a visit to Iraq in December 2008.[367]

6. John the Baptist declares that he is not worthy to loosen the shoe of the One coming after him (Yeshua). Our authority must decrease so that Yeshua's may increase in our lives (Matt 3:11; *cf.* Mark 1:7, Luke 3:16, John 1:27, Acts 13:25).

7. In the Prodigal Son parable, the doting father orders shoes to be put on his wastrel son's feet, restoring the young man's personal authority and position in the family (Luke 15.22). This is analogous to a worthless sinner, upon repentance, being restored (justified) and accepted into God's forever family.

---

[367] *BBC News*, 15th December 2008, http://news.bbc.co.uk/2/hi/7782422.stm

8. Yeshua orders His twelve disciples to take nothing with them on their travels but rudimentary attire, including sandals. God will work through the personal authority of the original twelve disciples provided they have total trust in Him (Mark 6:9). Then he sends out seventy more evangelists, this time with no shoes! (Luke 10:4; *cf,* Luke 22:35)

9. The apostle Peter is broken out of jail by an angel who commands him to put on his shoes (Acts 12.8).

10. The apostle Paul warns believers to have their shoes on as our preparation of the Gospel of peace (Eph 6:15). In other words, if we walk the walk, our authority becomes that of the LORD's as His representatives.

And Boaz said unto the elders and unto all the people, "Ye are witnesses this day that I have bought all that was Elimelech's, and all that was Chilion's and Mahlon's, of the hand of Naomi. Moreover, Ruth the Moabitess, the wife of Mahlon, have I purchased to be my wife, to raise up the name of the dead upon his inheritance, that the name of the dead be not cut off from among his brethren, and from the gate of his place. Ye are witnesses this day." (Ruth 4:9-10)

Ruth - the surprising summary

The whole town blesses Ruth and Boaz's future and Naomi is obviously nearby with the wide smile of a proud Jewish mother. She is now able to cast her mind over the previous years of hardship and see the LORD's footsteps in her life. What she is not aware of at this stage is just how significant will be her lineage. The town elders unwittingly give a prophecy in their jubilation, and this is how the story of Ruth ends... or does it?

And all the people that were in the gate, and the elders, said, "We are witnesses. The LORD make the woman that is come into thine house like Rachel and like Leah, which two did build the house of Israel [Jacob's two wives], **and do thou worthily in Ephratah** [Bethlehem's region], **and be famous in Bethlehem! And let thy house be like the house of Pharez, whom Tamar bare unto Judah, of the seed which the LORD shall give thee of this young woman."**

So Boaz took Ruth, and she was his wife, and when he went in unto her, the LORD gave her conception and she bare a son. And the women said unto Naomi, "Blessed be the LORD, which hath not left thee this day without a kinsman, that his name may be

famous in Israel. And he shall be unto thee a restorer of thy life, and a nourisher of thine old age, for thy daughter-in-law, which loveth thee, which is better to thee than seven sons, hath born him."

And Naomi took the child and laid it in her bosom and became nurse unto it. And the women, her neighbours, gave it a name, saying, "There is a son born to Naomi!" And they called his name Obed ['servant', 'worshiper']. **He is the father of Jesse, the father of David.** (Ruth 4:11-17)

So Ruth the Gentile Moabitess, a descendant of Lot, Abraham's nephew, makes it into the genealogy of none other than the great King David, and through him Yeshua, the Messiah, the Creator of the universe Himself! (Matt 1:5-17) The **'may your house be like Pharez'** prophecy is noteworthy: Pharez was a bastard son of Judah by his daughter-in-law, Tamar. According to Deut 23:2, the lineage of a bastard cannot inherit until the tenth generation. The tenth patriarch listed from Pharez is David, of the tribe of Judah, fulfilling Jacob's Messianic prophecy in Gen 49:10 that the Messiah would come through the line of Judah.

There are four women in the lineage of Jesus Christ, three of whom have dodgy reputations:

1. Tamar - who pretended to be a prostitute to sleep with her father-in-law, Judah, to raise up seed for her dead husband
2. Rahab (Boaz's mother) - a Canaanite brothel-keeper from Jericho
3. Ruth - the chaste Moabitess
4. Bathsheba - the wife of Uriah the Hittite who committed adultery with King David.

God is prepared to forgive and forget the sin of those with a contrite heart. He works with broken vessels by extending His grace. Which is a relief to all who love God.

The Bride prefigured - that's you...

There's a startling model presented in the Ruth/Boaz story if you assign roles to the main characters:

Naomi - a Jewish matriarch, representing national Israel

Ruth - a pagan Moabitess, representing the Gentiles

Boaz - the Jewish kinsman-redeemer, representing YHWH/Yeshua

The unnamed foreman - representing the Holy Spirit, the Unnamed Servant who testifies not of Himself (FG 16:13) but always introduces characters relevant to the lineage of the Messiah, who smooths the path to redemption.

Chuck Missler comments:

"Ruth is introduced to Boaz by an unnamed servant (Gen 24; John 16:13). In order to bring Ruth to Boaz, it was necessary for Naomi to be exiled from her land (Isa 6:9-13; Rom 11:11, 12)."[368]

i.e. The Gentiles (Ruth) are introduced to Christ (Boaz) via the Holy Spirit (unnamed servant/foreman). In order to bring the Gentiles (Ruth) to Christ (Boaz), it is necessary for the Jews (Naomi) to be exiled from their Land (Israel).

"Ruth, a Gentile, is brought in through the exile of Naomi. Law legally forbade intermarriage (Deut 7:2, 3; esp. Moabite: Deut 23:3). Law shut her out; grace took her in (Rom 8:3,4). Ruth does not 'replace' Naomi. Until Ruth is ready to become the bride of Boaz, Naomi remains in exile!" [369]

i.e. The Gentile Church is grafted in during the spiritual and physical exile of Israel (**'until the fullness of the Gentiles be come in...'** - Rom 11:25). Torah Law shuts the Gentiles out, God's grace takes them in. *The Church does not replace Israel,* they are joint heirs (Rom 11:25-26). Until the Church is ready to become the bride of Christ at the Rapture (*'harpazo'*), Israel remains in spiritual and physical exile! We see a fascinating depiction of God's grace modelled in Ruth 2:10:

Then she [Ruth/the Gentiles/Church] **fell on her face, and bowed herself to the ground, and said unto him** [Boaz/Kinsman-Redeemer/Yeshua], **"Why have I found grace in thine eyes, that thou shouldest take knowledge of me, seeing I am a stranger?"**

And [Boaz/kinsman-redeemer/Yeshua] **answered and said unto her, "It hath fully been shewed me all that thou hast done unto thy mother-in-law** [Naomi/Israel/the Jews] **since the death of thine husband, and how thou hast left thy father and thy mother and the land of thy nativity** [i.e. turned your back on your pagan culture], **and art come unto a people which thou knewest not heretofore. The LORD recompense thy work, <u>and a full reward be given thee of the</u>**

---

[368] Missler, Chuck, *Ruth notes,* www.khouse.org

[369] Ibid.

LORD God of Israel [i.e. Ruth/the Gentiles/Church will become joint heirs with Christ – full reward - Eph 3:5-6], **under whose wings thou art come to trust."** (Ruth 2:10-12)

In the New Testament, the redemption of the Gentiles by Yeshua is modelled on the Jewish wedding; the Gentiles become the Bride of Christ and are washed (baptised), anointed (by the Holy Spirit) and given a pure white raiment to be presented to the Bridegroom (Yeshua/Boaz). This is modelled in Ruth 3:1-3 when Ruth washes and anoints herself and puts on her best garment prior to going to Boaz. Notice the Jews are spiritually blinded and bitter at God while this process occurs in the New Testament (**'Crucify Him!' 'We have no king but Caesar!'**), in the same way Naomi cannot fathom why the LORD has afflicted her and is bitter (Ruth 1:20-21). There's more. How deep do you want to go?!

"No matter how much Boaz loved Ruth, he had to await her move...!" [370]

No matter how much God/Yeshua loves the Gentiles, He has to await their move to come to Him (James 4:8). It's also fascinating that the book of Ruth is usually read by the Jews at Shavuot, the Feast of Pentecost, *the birthday of the Christian Church!* The book of Ruth is viewed by expositors as a code for the 'Mystery of the Church', veiled in the Old Testament, but given by God to the apostle Paul to reveal in the NT.[371] Chuck Missler again:

"Naomi = "pleasant" (Land). She is driven out of the promised land into the land of the Gentiles. Only 25% survive (Deut 4:27; 28:62,64-67). During the exile of Israel, the land lay waste and famine-ridden... Israel's widowhood as the "wife of Jehovah": Isa 54:4-8, 10; Hos 1:3-9; 2:1, 2, 5, 14, 16; 3:4, 5. In exile until Bride is ready: Rom 11:25, 26; Lev 26:42, 44; Ezek 36:24, 28; 37:25; Acts 15:13-16.

"Boaz & Naomi 'never meet' (John 1:11). Naomi only learns of Boaz *through Ruth!* Ruth learns of Boaz's ways through Naomi. Naomi is complaining of being 'empty'. 'A son is born to Naomi!' She is the profound recipient." [372]

All this happens around Bethlehem, the 'House of Bread', echoing Yeshua's **"I am the Bread of life"** (FG 6:35). Throughout the

---

[370] Ibid.

[371] Rom 16:25; Eph 3:3-5; 8-10; *cf.* Matt 13:11,13-15; FG 12:36-41

[372] Ibid.

story, Ruth is always emphasised as 'the Moabitess', so the reader gets the message that God is moving in the lives of foreigners and Gentiles too (Isa 42:6-7). It's a foreshadowing of the Church and will not be a popular message among the Pharisees in the NT when we get to *Origins IV – Tetelestai* (*cf.* Luke 4:21-30). The fact that Boaz is the son of none other than Rahab, the Gentile harlot from Jericho, may explain why Boaz has no problem marrying a Gentile foreigner to raise up levirate seed for Elimelech/Mahlon, in contrast to the near-kinsman's rejection of Ruth for undisclosed reasons.

Kinsman-Redeemer for the Creation

And so, a four-chapter snapshot of a love story in ancient Israel introduces us to the profound, universal role God Himself will play as our Kinsman-Redeemer of Creation in our near future (Rev 5). It's an area fraught with ignorance for both Jews and Christians, yet unnervingly timely these days for those who cast a chary eye on where the world is headed.

So far as Israel is concerned, the Jews haven't yet accepted their Messiah, whose entry into Jerusalem 2,000 years ago was predicted *to the day* by the archangel Gabriel.[373] As we'll come to discover in the next chapter and also *Origins IV,* many denominational Christians have no idea of the period into which the world is currently being plunged, nor that the Jesus they worship will be returning to Earth *in a physical manner,* not only to prevent the world from destroying itself at Armageddon, but to take up the throne of David prophesied throughout the OT and announced to Mary, the mother of Jesus, by Gabriel himself in the NT. Many of today's Christians have been sold Augustine's amillennial perspective to their eschatology,[374] which runs something like, "Jesus is not *really* coming back *physically,* silly! He's returning spiritually to rule in our hearts!"

The truth is, all Jewish persecutions up to now will pale into insignificance next to what will happen to God's chosen in the forthcoming years. The infamous Great Tribulation, so beloved of doomsayers and conspiracy buffs, looms large on today's horizon with its depictions of one-world government and religion, a cashless society, nuclear weapons, aliens, human-animal hybrids, mass beheadings, ecological catastrophes, and the rise of *ha-Satan's* counterfeit to Christ, the coming charismatic world leader, known as

---

[373] See Daniel 9:24-27; a full exposition is given in *Origins IV – Tetelestai*

[374] The study of the end of things/end times.

the Antichrist, complete with his religious supremo, known as 'the False Prophet'.

Most Christians, who have even delved into the OT, ignore the fact that 'Daniel's Seventieth Week', elaborated in frightening detail in Revelation ch. 6–19, is a period specifically designated by God *for the Jews* (not the Church) to force them to repentance and to petition the return of their Messiah (Hos 5:15; Matt 23:39; Luke 13:34-35). In more extreme cases, Christians have been taught the lies promulgated by the early medieval (Catholic) Church that Israel forfeited its privileged status for crucifying Christ, and that God's blessings have now devolved to the Church. This 'replacement theology' had its roots in the anti-Semitism of early church fathers such as Origen, Turtullian, Justin Martyr and Augustine. Adherents to this doctrine have carried out some of the worst acts of barbarism against the Jews throughout the centuries in the belief that they were doing God a favour (prophesied by Yeshua in FG 16:2). Today's anti-Semitic Christians have no clue that praying "Thy Kingdom come, Thy Will be done on Earth as it is in Heaven…." is petitioning Yeshua Himself to return, destroy the Antichrist and False Prophet at the end of the Great Tribulation, sort out which believers looked after His Jews in the dark times and who didn't, chain *ha-Satan* for a thousand years, then set up His Millennial Kingdom on Earth as a *Jewish King* to rule the world from Jerusalem![375] Chuck Missler points out that in most Christian seminaries today, there is one branch of the scriptures studiously ignored and *not* taught to ministers, which constitutes 80% of the Bible: Israel's role and destiny in God's plan. Dr Missler writes:

> "The return of Christ to rule [is given in] 1,845 references in the Old Testament (17 books give prominence to the event), and 318 references in the New Testament (216 chapters and 23 of 27 books give prominence to the event). For every prophecy of Christ's 1st coming, there are 8 of His Second Coming!"[376]

---

[375] *Ha-Satan's* human world leader (the 'Antichrist' – literally 'pseudo-Christ') will attempt to sell himself to the world as the Messiah, and may well have a Christian/Jewish/Islamic heritage or connection, which provides his universal appeal.

[376] Missler, Chuck, *Israel and the Church* notes, p.13, www.khouse.org: "**Promised to David:** 2 Sam 7:12-17; 23:5; under oath: Ps 89:34-37. **Predicted in the Psalms and the Prophets:** Ps 2; 45; 110; Isa 2:1-5; 4:1-6; 11:1-9; 12:1-6; 30:18-26; 35:1-10; 60, 61:3-62; 66; Jer 23:3-8; 32:37-44; Ezek 40-48; Dan 2:44-45; 7:13-14; 12:2-3; Mic 4:1-8; Zech 12:10-14:21. **Promised to Mary:** Luke 1:32; Micah 5:2; Isa 9:6, 7; Dan 2:44; **Reaffirmed to**

By denying Israel's unique inheritance, identity and destiny, separate from the Church, anti-Semitic Christians are calling God a liar. The Abrahamic Covenant (Gen 12), the unconditional Land Covenant (Gen 15), the Davidic Covenant (2 Sam 7), the Everlasting Covenant (Jer 31:31) and the New Covenant ('the New Testament') all attest that God has made *unconditional* promises to the Jews which He has no intention of betraying. In His role as our Kinsman-Redeemer, Yeshua will redeem not only believing mankind and the entire Creation (a right purchased as the Passover Lamb with His sinless life and shed blood on the cross), but also fulfil all the promises God made to the Jews down through the ages.

And as the clock ticks on, Ruth and Boaz have a little boy called Obed in Bethlehem. And Obed has Jesse, and Jesse has eight sons, the youngest of whom is a comely shepherd lad by the name of David.

Apostles: Luke 22:29-30. **Lord's Prayer:** "Thy Kingdom come": Matt 6:10, 13; Acts 1:6; Ps 45, 46, 47, 48. **Rule:** Psalm 2; 110. "Rod of Iron" (Rev 12:5; 19:15); "Every knee should bow" (Phil 2:6-11). **Note:** The Millennial Temple will only be open on *Shabbat* and the new moons!"(Ezek 46:1)

THE JUDGES

"Surely the LORD GOD will do nothing but He revealeth His secret unto His servants the prophets." (Amos 3:7)

"For whatsoever things were written aforetime were written for our learning, that we through patience and comfort of the scriptures might have hope." (Rom 15:4)

"All scripture is given by inspiration of God, and is profitable for doctrine, for reproof, for correction, for instruction in righteousness..." (2 Tim 3:16)

The period after the Canaan Conquest is sometimes referred to as 'the time of the Judges', and takes us up to the inauguration of the Israelite monarchy under the prophet Samuel and King Saul. The Judges era is the mindboggling story of a new, landed nation which almost fails at the starting gate. I say 'mindboggling' until one looks at our nations today and sees the same traits. There's a saying that goes, "If you learn from every one of your mistakes, you'll still be a fool. There's no shortage of other people's mistakes you could have learned from instead." And so it is with all of us, and with Israel under the Judges.

Joshua passes away with the Conquest incomplete. He has appointed no successor. Each tribe has been apportioned its share of the land and must clear what remains of God's enemies before the job is done. Four statements characterise the disasters and violence which follow:

- There was no king in Israel
- Everyone was doing what was right in their own eyes
- God's Word was marginalised, then forgotten
- The children of Israel repeatedly did evil in the sight of the LORD

Needless to say, having inherited the Land, most of Israel's tribes do not conquer their portions properly. The tribe of Dan seems disinterested in taking on the enemy, so is confined by the Amorites to the hill country (Judg 1:34). How about this strange verse: **And the LORD was with Judah; and he** [the tribe of Judah] **drove out the inhabitants of the mountain but could not drive out the inhabitants of the valley, because they had chariots of iron.** (Judg 1:19) Come again? They fail even though God is with them?

There is a major spiritual reason why Judah falls short. It all starts optimistically enough. The Israelites initially enquire of the LORD concerning which tribe should go up first against the Canaanites to clear the Land. Seeking the LORD's face in any matter is a good move. Judah and Simeon - blood-brother tribes born of the same mother, Leah – agree to help clear each other's regions (Judg 1:3). God has declared that He is with Judah, so why does Judah need the additional numbers of Simeon? Together they defeat the Canaanites and Perizzites, slaughtering 10,000 of their number at Bezek. They capture the enemy king, Adonibezek, but instead of executing him, they cut off his thumbs and toes. This is apparent retribution for what the pagan king previously did to seventy other kings. This style of mutilation is to prevent the victim ever again drawing a bow, throwing a spear or leading men into battle. Or ruling. Cripples were traditionally passed over for command or kingship, not only in the Canaanite cultures but also the Hebrew peoples.

Judah captures Jerusalem but does not drive out the Jebusites, an act that will not be accomplished until the time of Israel's greatest OT king, David. Hebron is captured and three descendants of Anak (giants/Nephilim), are destroyed - Sheshai, Ahiman and Talmai, but Hebron is not occupied. The surviving inhabitants are spared and allowed to remain. Disobedience is already seeping in. God has declared that He will rule Israel and be their King (Ex 19:1-8; *cf:* Judg 8:23), but Israel resists obedience and acts in the flesh.

Instead of experiencing a surge in spiritual and patriotic fervour as a result of the Exodus and Conquest with God at the helm, Israel degenerates into apostasy and defeat. Instead of experiencing peace and safety in a new land devoid of enemies, they spare their foes instead of destroying them, treat with them, marry into them, have children by them, imitate them, and eventually worship their gods. Moses ordered the book of Deuteronomy to be read to all the children of Israel every Sabbatical year (seventh year) on the Feast of Tabernacles to educate the people on the fear of God and His requirements (Deut 31:10-13). If this had been done, the people would have heard Deuteronomy 7, which called for the defeat and *complete annihilation* of those pagan races which offended God. By what follows, we know that these readings were never carried out. Within two generations, the Exodus, Wilderness and Conquest miracles are forgotten, and Israel is whoring after the Nimrod/Semiramis sex and death cults, worshipping Ashtoreth, Ishtar, Baal and Molech. Instead of heeding the LORD's express order to submit to Him and destroy these Canaanite peoples, the Jews permit them not only to survive and thrive among them, they take pagan wives for themselves and sacrifice their children in the burning arms of the bronze demon god, Molech. Three guesses what happens next.

And when Joshua had let the people go, the children of Israel went every man unto his inheritance to possess the land. And the people served the LORD all the days of Joshua, and all the days of the elders that outlived Joshua, who had seen all the great works of the LORD, that he did for Israel.

And Joshua the son of Nun, the servant of the LORD, died, being an hundred and ten years old. And they buried him in the border of his inheritance in Timnathheres in the mount of Ephraim, on the north side of the hill Gaash.

And also all that generation were gathered unto their fathers. And there arose another generation after them, which knew not the LORD, nor yet the works which he had done for Israel. And the children of Israel did evil in the sight of the LORD and served Baalim.

And they forsook the LORD God of their fathers, which brought them out of the land of Egypt, and followed other gods, of the gods of the people that were round about them, and bowed themselves unto them, and provoked the LORD to anger. And they forsook the LORD and served Baal and Ashtaroth. (Judg 2:6-13)

The cycle of sin

It's a human trait that we squander our victories and inheritance. World War 2 is a classic example. Britain limped home to victory in 1945, but by the swinging '60s, the sacrifice of the fallen in both world wars was being openly mocked on TV and radio.[377]

The cycle of sin into which Israel falls is symptomatic of human nature in general and the cycle of nations in particular. Most won't repent, turn from sin and come to God unless we are put into a position of utter, dire peril. God is compelled to bring judgment upon post-Conquest Israel since His people not only spare the enemy, they begin imitating the indigenous peoples, worshipping their gods, and eventually are conquered, ruled and slaughtered by them.

---

[377] **Day, Phillip** *Ten Minutes to Midnight,* Credence, 2003

The time of the Judges teaches us of the absolute spiritual and moral bankruptcy of the human condition. Man's inherently sinful nature cannot be fixed by man, no matter how many times John Lennon sings *Imagine*. Most of the time, man chooses to ignore his fallen predicament. God is perpetually at war with sin, so to avoid God destroying man along with his nature, man must separate himself from his sin, which is an act of volition. God will do the rest. Man will only repent under extreme duress. God's redemption can only be accomplished from without; by external input; by a divine

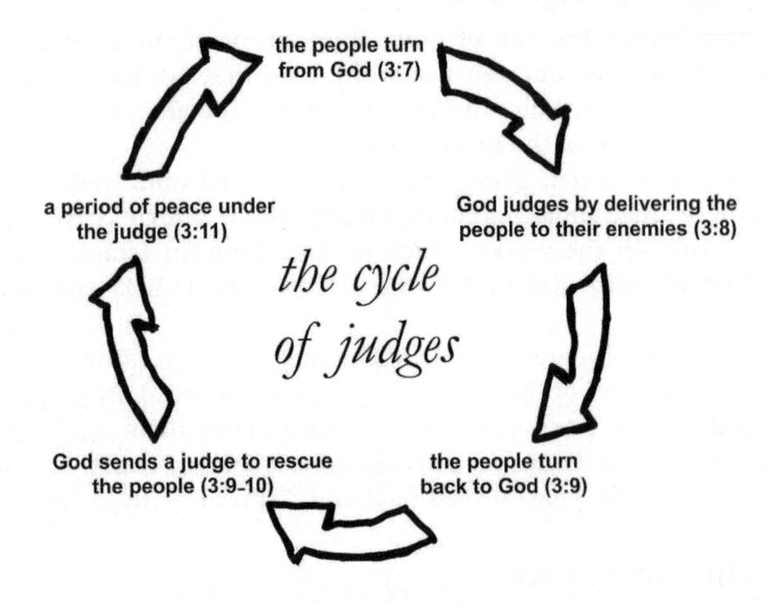

Deliverer. In the Judges era, God will raise up ordinary people (misnamed 'judges') to carry out extraordinary tasks to deliver Israel from their carnal predicaments; yet the nation's spiritual bankruptcy remains, and so too the cycle of its sin. God reserves a handful of Canaanite tribes, including the five lords of the Philistines, to test Israel. The oft-quoted Hegel adage, "History teaches that man learns nothing from history" describes this bankruptcy. The way out of the cycle, as the time of the Judges teaches us, is through submission and complete obedience to God, and to seek His face in all things. If this pattern has not become clear already, witness the following carnage.

Othniel

And the children of Israel did evil in the sight of the LORD, and forgat the LORD their God, and served Baalim [i.e. multiple

Baals (plural), demon gods, *ha*-Satan, etc.] **and the groves. Therefore the anger of the LORD was hot against Israel, and He sold them into the hand of Chushanrishathaim king of Mesopotamia: and the children of Israel served Chushanrishathaim eight years.** (Judg 3:7-8)

We are reminded of the constant disobedience the children of Israel engaged in during the wilderness wanderings. Commentators scratch their heads, wondering how on Earth a people could have experienced those miracles first-hand, manifesting God's obvious involvement, yet troll after false idols. The point is not so much that they did, *it's why we're doing the same thing today*. The miracles that have characterised, for example, British, Australian and American history are all too soon forgotten by subsequent generations. For example, England's enemies have been delivered into her hand numerous times in miraculous fashion: Agincourt, Crécy, the Spanish Armada, Waterloo, World War 1, The Battle of Britain, World War 2, and so on. Incredibly, within a generation of Britain emerging from WW2 bruised, broke, battered but victorious, the Sixties Revolution superintend a full-on attack against the old institutions and Church in particular, ushering in a new era of militant atheism. Within that generation, the miraculous was replaced by the comfortable yawn of the self-indulgent liberal apologist. H W Prentis's famous 'Fatal Sequence' (often misattributed to Sir Alexander Fraser Tytler as 'The Tytler Cycle'), describes the cycle of a nation's fate as follows. Ask yourself where your nation is in the cycle:

From bondage to spiritual faith;
From spiritual faith to great courage;
From courage to liberty;
From liberty to abundance;
From abundance to selfishness;
From selfishness to complacency;
From complacency to apathy;
From apathy to dependence;
From dependence back to bondage.

In the war between the Spirit and flesh for the new Israel, the flesh wins. The Semiramis/Nimrod sex and death cults across Canaan prove too alluring. The children of Israel once more succumb. Such practices include the usual drunken orgies from which babies are produced, who would then be roasted alive in the bronze arms of *ha-Satan's* statue-god, Molech. Known as 'passing their children through the fire', these atrocities were an abomination to God and were expressing forbidden by Him in the Torah:

And thou shalt not let any of thy seed pass through the fire to Molech, neither shalt thou profane the name of thy God: I am the LORD. (Lev 18:21)

Again, thou shalt say to the children of Israel, Whosoever he be of the children of Israel, or of the strangers that sojourn in Israel, that giveth any of his seed unto Molech, he shall surely be put to death. The people of the land shall stone him with stones. And I will set My face against that man, and will cut him off from among his people, because he hath given of his seed unto Molech to defile My sanctuary and to profane My holy name.

And if the people of the land do any ways hide their eyes from the man, when he giveth of his seed unto Molech, and kill him not, then I will set my face against that man and against his family, and will cut him off, and all that go a whoring after him, to commit whoredom with Molech, from among their people. (Lev 20:2-5)

These abominations were usually carried out on 'the high places'. For 'groves', read copses of specially shaped, phallic trees. Later in Jerusalem, such sacrifices would occur in the Hinnom Valley (2 Kings 23:10; 2 Chr. 28:3, 33:6; Jer 7:31; 19:2-6; 32:35), giving rise to 'Gehenna', an idiom Yeshua uses for Hell (Mark 9:44; 9:46; 9:48). Older Christian tradition ascribes Gehenna to a perpetually burning rubbish tip in Jerusalem's Hinnom Valley, upon which the dead bodies of criminals and animals were thrown and consumed. The practice of sacrificing babies to Baal, Molech and other Canaanite demon-gods continued into the later Judaean monarchy. *Ha-Satan's* footprints can always be discerned in the killing of babies, as ever in our own modern age where millions permit the murder of their unborn children to rid themselves of an inconvenient child produced through sexual gratification. To punish contumacious Israel, God delivers his people into bondage at the hand of a Mesopotamian warlord for eight years.

And when the children of Israel cried unto the LORD, the LORD raised up a deliverer ['judge'] **to the children of Israel, who delivered them, even Othniel the son of Kenaz, Caleb's younger brother.** (Judg 3:9)

This is the same Caleb who, along with Joshua, alone remained of the original generation of Hebrews who left Egypt in the Exodus. All we are told is that with God's Spirit, Caleb's nephew, Othniel, delivers his people from the hand of Chushanrishathaim by war and the land has respite for forty years until Othniel dies.

Ehud

Then the cycle repeats. The children of Israel do evil again in the sight of the LORD, whereupon God puts them under bondage to Eglon, king of Moab (east of the Jordan), who invades the land and sets up his base of operations west of the Jordan at Jericho, 'the City of Palm Trees', *Bet Yerah,* 'the City of the Moon God'. The tribute, corruption and bondage Eglon compels upon the twelve tribes are tolerated for a surprising eighteen years. After that, the children of Israel cry out to the LORD to deliver them and God raises up an activist ('judge') named Ehud.

Ehud is from the tribe of Benjamin, noted for their fierce warrior ethic. Benjamites are trained in the ambidextrous use of weapons - indeed 'Benjamin' means 'Son of the Right Hand', provoking parallels with Yeshua, who sits at the right hand of the Father. The Bible tells us Ehud has some sort of physical handicap, probably with his right arm or hand, necessitating an unusual (for the time) use of his left hand. His disability would have been widely known to his compatriots and even to King Eglon himself, since Ehud is used by the children of Israel to convey their annual tribute payment to the king at Jericho.

Jericho must have rankled with Ehud, since it had been the scene of the startling victory Yeshua had given Israel years before. Ehud must have wondered in a moment of realisation, "What the heck are we doing serving Moab in our own land with the God of the universe to lead us?" Like Othniel before him, Ehud is the man of the moment upon whose heart God places the burden of His people.

Ehud's first stop? Like any self-respecting alpha male, Ehud heads straight for the garden shed/workshop. He fashions a dagger eighteen inches long with a double edge. This is no ordinary weapon, for King Eglon is no ordinary target. The king is extraordinarily fat, necessitating a longer blade than usual for maximum penetration. Ehud hones the dagger's blade, then straps the weapon to his *right* thigh to avoid the customary search of the king's guards.

Then Ehud summons his servants to accompany him to Jericho bearing the annual tribute chests. It is after the harvest in high summer and, in addition to the usual gold and silver, the tribute likely contains a host of foods and sweetmeats designed to appeal to the king's gluttonous palate. When the delegation arrives at Eglon's summer palace, the guards recognise Ehud, submit him to the customary search, miss the dagger on his right thigh, frisk his servants, then admit the party into the king's presence. The venue is a rooftop atrium or rest-chamber in Eglon's palace, designed to take advantage of the cool evening breeze. One can almost picture the bloated Eglon's reptilian tongue flicking across wet ruby lips in contemplation of the Israelite gold, silver and feastly things laid at his stubby feet. Eglon is a picture of fleshly desire with the safeties off. With the king distracted, Ehud dismisses his own servants and closes for the kill.

"I have a secret errand unto thee, O king."

The king said, "Keep silence!" [i.e. "Don't tell everybody!"] **And all that stood by him went out from him.**

And Ehud came unto him, and [Eglon] **was sitting in a summer parlour, which he had for himself alone. And Ehud said, "I have a message from God unto thee."**

And he arose out of his seat. And Ehud put forth his left hand and took the dagger from his right thigh, and thrust it into [the king's] **belly. And the haft also went in after the blade; and the fat closed upon the blade so that he could not draw the dagger out of his belly; and the dirt came out."** (Judg 3:19-22)

The King James leaves little to the imagination. It seems from the narrative that Ehud's assault produces a gaping wound which severs the intestines, from which faeces gush forth. Either way, the dagger is locked in the king's belly from all the flab, so Ehud abandons it and makes good his escape.

Then Ehud went forth through the porch and shut the doors of the parlour upon him and locked them. When he was gone out, [the king's] **servants came. And when they saw that, behold, the doors of the parlour were locked, they said, "Surely he covereth his feet in his summer chamber."** [i.e. "Surely he's going to the toilet."]

And they tarried till they were ashamed: and, behold, he [the king] **opened not the doors of the parlour. Therefore they took a key and opened them: and, behold, their LORD was fallen down dead on the earth.**

And Ehud escaped while they tarried, and passed beyond the quarries, and escaped unto Seirath. (Judg 3:23-26)

The end of the matter? No, for Ehud it's the start. Just because the fat king is dead doesn't mean Israel's servitude under Moab is over. Ehud summons the rest of the tribes in the traditional manner, with blasts of a shofar in the mountains of Ephraim, and in the quick campaign that follows, Ehud's strategy is simple. He orders his men to block all the fords across the Jordan by which Eglon's troops can receive reinforcements from Moab, then slaughters the entire Moabite contingent west of the river in the ensuing battle, most of which comprise the staunch warriors of Eglon's own Praetorian Guard. **So Moab was subdued that day under the hand of Israel. And the land had rest fourscore years.** (Judg 3:30)

Shamgar

It seems that not long after this episode, Israel has further problems in the west of the country, this time with the Philistines who govern what is now the coastal strip of Gaza. The Philistines feature prominently in Israel's trials for the next few centuries, polarising their control across five cities governed by the five Philistine lords. The cities of Gath, Ashkelon, Ashdod, Ekron and Gaza are the last remaining enclaves supporting giants/Nephilim/six-fingered ones, of which Goliath and his family are examples (*cf.* Gen 6).

We infer from the narrative order that the 'judge' Shamgar, whom God raises up to deal with the Philistine incursions, is contemporary to Ehud, though scholars dispute this. Yet he is mentioned in the Song of Deborah as preceding her in a time so unsettled, that travellers avoided the highways in favour of by-roads, for fear of getting robbed or killed (Judg 5:6-7). In any case, Shamgar is a *mensch.* We don't know much about him other than that he slaughters *six hundred Philistines* with an ox goad. Now that's something you don't see every day. We are not told whether this carnage happened at one go. Most probably Shamgar was what we would term today a 'martial artist': a champion from the tribe of Naphtali perhaps, judging by his 'Anath' heritage (Judg 1:33).[378] This warrior appears to have become proficient in the deadly use of an eight-foot-long farm implement, featuring an iron spike at one end (to prod lazy beasts and stab Philistines), and another implement on the other, usually a plough-scraper (to whack Philistines after stabbing them). Shamgar was evidently the Bruce Lee of his generation, for we are told that the Philistines left Israel alone for a while thereafter.

Deborah

The next hero is actually a heroine. Two heroines, to be precise. The cast of Deborah's drama features the following characters and,

[378] A town in the Naphtali region.

like everything else in this period, is brought to you with a conspiracy and violence rating 'X'. The cast comprises:

Deborah - an Israelite mother, councillor, warrior, prophetess and deliverer ('judge') of Israel. Her name means 'honeybee'.

Barak - Israelite commander. His name means 'lightning'.

Jabin - The pagan king of Hazor/Canaan who has oppressed Israel for 20 years. Hazor was a fortified city eight miles north of Lake Galilee. Today it is the largest ruin in Israel and a designated UNESCO World Heritage Site. 'Jabin' is thought to be a title rather than a proper name. As 'King of Canaan', it seems likely that Jabin is a powerful leader of a coalition of Canaanite city states.

Sisera - The commander of Jabin's army. He possesses 900 iron chariots and a formidable army, rendering the Canaanite oppression of Israel inviolable. Sisera's base is at Harosheth Hagoyim, thought to be near modern-day Haifa on the coast.

Heber - A Kenite (distant relatives of Moses) and collaborator with Jabin and Sisera. He betrays Deborah and Israel to the Canaanites.

Jael - The wife of Heber.

We're familiar with the preamble by now:

And the children of Israel again did evil in the sight of the LORD, when Ehud was dead. And the LORD sold them into the hand of Jabin, king of Canaan, that reigned in Hazor, the captain of whose host was Sisera, which dwelt in Harosheth of the Gentiles. (Judg 4:1-3)

Dr Peter Pett writes:

"Hazor was an important city state in northern Canaan which had great influence over its neighbours (Joshua 11.1-2, 10). Archaeology tells us that it had been there since the third millennium BC and in the second millennium was extended by the building of a lower city. At this stage it would have about forty thousand inhabitants, a large city indeed. The lower city contained a Canaanite temple and a small shrine. It was referred to regularly throughout the centuries, by Egypt, Mari and Babylon, as an important political centre, and its ruler was given the title 'Great King' (sarrum), a status above that usually conferred on rulers of city states." [379]

---

[379] www.angelfire.com/ok/bibleteaching/judges2.html

And the children of Israel cried unto the LORD: for he [Sisera] **had nine hundred chariots of iron, and twenty years he mightily oppressed the children of Israel.**

And Deborah, a prophetess, the wife of Lapidoth, she judged Israel at that time. And she dwelt under the palm tree of Deborah between Ramah and Bethel in mount Ephraim, and the children of Israel came up to her for judgment. (Judg 4:3-5)

We can be blasé, sitting in our centrally-heated living-rooms sipping coffee, opining, "Oh, those wicked Israelites, here they go again…" but a nation's attitude to YHWH even today unsettlingly impacts its fate at every level. God does not change (Mal 3:6), but is prepared to forgive and heal a land if the people called by His name humble themselves, pray, seek His face and turn from their wickedness (2 Chron 7:14). Note that only those who have accepted YHWH can do this; the Great Unwashed have no say because God does not hear the prayers of the wicked before repentance.[380] It's noteworthy that while Israel cries out to the LORD for deliverance in each sin cycle, the nation fails to repent and does not turn from its sin for long, so the cycle repeats itself and Israel's predicament progressively worsens.

Hazor was previously razed by Joshua after defeating a coalition of pagan city-states under a former King Jabin who possessed iron chariots (Josh 11:1-15). That the current Jabin (probably a descendant) **mightily oppressed the children of Israel** was no doubt revenge for what the Jews had done to his predecessor and city. Judges 5 tells us that Jabin and Sisera's rule was so harsh in Shamgar and Deborah's day that the highways were deserted, village life all but came to an end due to depredations, and people travelled along the byways and stayed out of sight to avoid trouble. As before, things got to the point where something had to be done. That Israel's predicament was down to her pursuit of strange gods and desertion of YHWH was known but not readily confessed.

And [Deborah] **sent and called Barak the son of Abinoam out of Kedesh Naphtali and said unto him, "Hath not the LORD God of Israel commanded, saying, 'Go and draw toward Mount Tabor, and take with thee ten thousand men of the children of Naphtali and of the children of Zebulun. And I will draw unto thee to the river Kishon Sisera, the captain of Jabin's army, with his chariots and multitude, and I will deliver him into thine hand'."**

---

[380] FG 9:31; Prov 28:9; Prov 15:29; Psa 66:18; Psa 73:1; Jam 5:16; Isa 59:2; 1 Pet 3:12, etc.

And Barak said unto her, "If thou wilt go with me, then I will go. But if thou wilt not go with me, then I will not go." (Judg 4:6-8)

Some interesting dynamics here. Deborah is one of ten prophetesses featured in the Bible.[381] A male-dominant Hebrew society would be ambivalent about such a seer, especially one ordering a subservient Israel into what appears to be a suicidal rebellion against a superior, occupying power. But Deborah is God's prophet and Barak knows it. Scholars argue over whether Barak's response indicates a lack of faith, or whether he wishes Deborah to accompany the army to receive further words from the LORD to guide him. It's clear from the text (Judg 4:9) that Deborah thinks the former, yet Barak is listed as one of the faith greats in the book of Hebrews' 'Hall of Faith', so there is obviously something more going on here (Heb 11:32).

Put yourself in Barak's position. A woman (albeit a prophetess) is ordering a rebellion against an organised, professional army, which has brutally oppressed Israel for twenty years. Almost certainly Sisera, in charge of law and order, has seen to it that the Israelites were disarmed from the outset, given their past penchant for trouble. **Mightily oppressed** suggests persecution and violence against the Jews seldom seen in the past. Any weapons that might be available to Barak's 10,000 volunteers will be the few squirreled away by rebellious souls (Judg 5:2,8-9). The rest will have to be taken from the occupying power – no mean feat.

Another point is that since there is no king to rule over Israel, the twelve tribes have no centralised command structure. This works to their detriment and permits each tribe to do as it pleases, which causes trouble later. Yet each 'judge' God raises up unifies command over portions of Israel for a while, but when they die the old ways return. God intends to be Israel's King, but the nation is not willing (*cf.* 1 Sam 8:7).[382] In this particular episode with Deborah and Barak,

---

[381] The others are Miriam (Mic 6:4), Huldah (2 Kings 22:14), Noadiah (Neh 6:14), Isaiah's wife (Isa 8:3), Anna (Luke 2:36), and the four daughters of Philip (Acts 21:8-9).

[382] Israel's rejection of God's sovereignty is a major theme throughout the scriptures. The nation rejects God as their King persistently (1 Sam 8), and even when He comes to Earth, the Jews cry, **"We have no king but Caesar!"** (FG 19:15). The nation, fathered by the patriarch Jacob, is well named. You may recall from *Origins II – Holy War,* that Jacob is given the new name, 'Israel', by God after a bizarre fight. The name is curiously ambiguous as to meaning. Expositors have variously rendered it: 'He

the tribes of Zebulun and Naphtali are the principal warriors, but we learn that cohorts from Issachar, Benjamin, Manasseh and Reuben are present, though Reuben dithers, true to his nature (Gen 49:3-4). Asher and Dan don't bother showing up, preferring to continue their activities on the coast. The picture is of a fragmented Israel with most elements serving their own interests.

The focal point for the action is Mount Tabor, an impressive, isolated monadnock outcrop rising to 1,886 ft over the eastern end of the Jezreel Valley. The landmark offered strategic control over the confluence of the major north-south and east-west roads in the region, so unsurprisingly Tabor has been the site of battles throughout history, and is not far from Tel Megiddo itself ('Armageddon'). The mount overlooks the Kishon River in Lower Galilee and is believed by Church tradition to have been the site of Yeshua's Transfiguration incident in the NT.[383]

The Kishon River, which plays a significant role in Deborah's career, is today highly polluted with mercury and other heavy metal contaminants from nearby chemical plants - an ongoing source of outrage for environmental groups. It is claimed that washing your hands in its waters induces chemical burns. A BBC report states:

> "Put your hand into the river for long enough and, scientists say, the acid will begin to burn it. Yellow froth clings to the river's surface as pipes from the nearby factories and the local sewage plant spew a vile cocktail of biological waste, chemicals, mercury and even arsenic into its waters. The mixture is so potent, according to environmental campaign group Greenpeace, that chemical reactions are taking place under the surface, spawning new toxic substances. Nowadays nothing can survive in this water, not even bacteria. Tests show that fish put in the water die in less than three minutes. Their whitened undersides litter the river banks as evidence."[384]

As we'll find out, the Kishon won't be good news for Sisera either.

Probably to Barak's surprise, Deborah agrees to go with him to participate in Israel's deliverance: **And** [Deborah] **said, "I will surely**

---

who struggles with God', 'One who has prevailed with God', 'One who struggled with the divine angel', 'Persevere with God', and so on.

[383] Matthew 17:1-9, Mark 9:2-8, Luke 9:28-36. See also 2 Peter 1:16-18. Interestingly the site of the Transfiguration is not named in the Synoptics, presumably to prevent the location becoming a source of worship. Another candidate location is Mount Hermon on the Syrian/Lebanon border.

[384] http://news.bbc.co.uk/1/hi/world/middle_east/941317.stm

go with thee, notwithstanding the journey that thou takest shall not be for thine honour, for the LORD shall sell Sisera into the hand of a woman." And Deborah arose and went with Barak to Kedesh. And Barak called [the tribes of] **Zebulun and Naphtali to Kedesh. And he went up with ten thousand men at his feet, and Deborah went up with him.** (Judg 4:9-10)

Most readers assume that Deborah will be the woman into whose hand the LORD delivers Sisera, but the plot has a surprising twist. As the Israelites tramp up Mount Tabor to form their defence, they know they and their families will be brutally punished if they fail. As if to nix the rebellion before it starts, a Kenite neighbour of Barak's named Heber decides to betray the Jewish plot to Sisera. This is all the more reprehensible since Heber is descended from Moses' father-in-law and therefore a distant relative of Barak and Deborah (Num 10:29).

Forewarned of the treachery of his vassals, Sisera masses his 900 chariots and a hefty army and leads off to sort out the Hebrew rebels. He's confident of victory since it is the dry season and his chariots work well in the plain around Tabor.

And Deborah said unto Barak, "Up! For this is the day in which the LORD hath delivered Sisera into thine hand! [Note past tense] **Is not the LORD gone out before thee?" So Barak went down from Mount Tabor, and ten thousand men after him. And the LORD discomfited Sisera and all his chariots and all his host with the edge of the sword before Barak, so that Sisera lighted down off his chariot and fled away on his feet.** (Judg 4:14-15)

How on Earth can Sisera lose? Deborah, Barak and the Israelites descend the mountain and engage a vastly superior force, trusting in God to deliver them, and He does. The Judges 4 narrative is brief at this point, merely declaring victory to the Jews, but chapter 5 fleshes out what actually happened using the device of 'The Song of Deborah', a battle poem of celebration. Once again, God is given the glory for the impressive victory. Dr Peter Pett again:

"Barak was a warleader, not a prophet. He considered the ten units he would have with him on Mount Tabor and he considered the nine units of chariots, and the further large army of fighting men, a standing army trained for war, and he did not like the odds. So, yes, he was willing to trust Yahweh's plan, but only if Deborah confirmed her faith in it by going with him. Furthermore he felt that this would aid the fulfilment of the plan, for he had every confidence that Yahweh would fight for Deborah. And the men of Naphtali (with Issachar) and Zebulun would be far more likely to come if she was among them, so great was the common belief that Yahweh was with her. He had faith but he also wanted some kind of confirmation and guarantee." [385]

Which is not long in coming. The LORD has gone out before them and does not disappoint. As battle is joined, YHWH causes a massive storm to sweep down the valley, raining torrents of water onto the plain. Deborah implies in her song that the earthquake and violent thunderstorm accompanying were similar to those experienced at Mount Sinai at the LORD's appearance during the Exodus. There's wordplay too in the midst of battle. Barak, whose name means 'lightning', becomes God's thunderbolt against the impotent Baal (*ha-Satan*), the Canaanite god of storms. God knows how to strike an enemy where it hurts, just as He did with the Egyptians when he blotted out their sun-god.

The kings came and fought, then fought the kings of Canaan in Taanach by the waters of Megiddo; they took no gain of money. They fought from heaven; the stars in their courses fought against Sisera. The river of Kishon swept them away, that ancient river, the river Kishon. O my soul, thou hast trodden down strength. (Judg 5:19-21)

Science commentators such as Patton, Hatch and Steinhauer believe the above allusion to **the stars in their courses fought against Sisera** could be more than poetic hyperbole. Was this another of those Mars near pass-bys producing meteors, bolides, flux lightning and catastrophic events? The Kishon River bursts its banks and floods the plain, turning the earth to goo. Guess what happens to Sisera's 900 heavy iron chariots? Most intriguingly, something spooks Sisera to such an extent that he leaps from his bogged-down chariot and legs it. What on earth would account for a seasoned commander behaving in such a manner – and before his own men? This tips us off that the supernatural hand of the LORD is very much in evidence, and that this is no ordinary battle.

Barak and the proud warriors of Naphtali and Zebulun pursue the fleeing Canaanites all the way up the Kishon valley towards Sisera's base at Harosheth Hagoyim on the coast. Contingents of other Jewish tribes pitch in on the rout. Any Canaanite found is overtaken and slaughtered, yet Sisera cannot be found. Deborah and

[385] www.angelfire.com/ok/bibleteaching/judges2.html

Barak know the battle is not won until the cruel commander has been taken, but the LORD plays His hand.

Sisera makes it as far as the tent dwelling of his Kenite ally, Heber, who shopped the Israelites to him in the first place. Heber is apparently not at home but his wife Jael is. She recognises King Jabin's right-hand man in an instant:

And Jael went out to meet Sisera and said unto him, "Turn in, my lord, turn in to me; fear not." And when he had turned in unto her into the tent, she covered him with a mantle.

And he said unto her, "Give me, I pray thee, a little water to drink, for I am thirsty." And she opened a bottle of milk and gave him drink, and covered him. (Judg 4:18-19)

Of course, Jael knows about the Jewish rebellion and subsequent battle – her husband was the informant. Sisera showing up alone at her place in such a muddied state with no armed guard tips Jael off that the Canaanite hold over Israel has been broken. She allows a surprising breach of protocol to take place. In Jael's culture it is death for a stranger to enter the tent of a man's wife, yet Sisera doesn't give it a second thought, knowing this is the last place a Jewish death squad would think of looking for him.

He said unto her, "Stand in the door of the tent, and it shall be, when any man doth come and enquire of thee and say, 'Is there any man here?' that thou shalt say, 'No'." (Judg 4:20)

This is Sisera's final mistake and Jael's confirmation. Jael has fed Sisera milk not water. This has a soporific effect on the exhausted warrior and he nods off.

Then Jael Heber's wife took a nail of the tent, and took an hammer in her hand, and went softly unto him, and smote the nail into his temples, and fastened it into the ground: for he was fast asleep and weary. So he died.

And, behold, as Barak pursued Sisera, Jael came out to meet him and said unto him, "Come, and I will shew thee the man whom thou seekest." And when he came into her tent, behold, Sisera lay dead, and the nail was in his temples.

So God subdued on that day Jabin the king of Canaan before the children of Israel. And the hand of the children of Israel prospered and prevailed against Jabin the king of Canaan, until they had destroyed Jabin king of Canaan. (Judg 4:21-24)

Jael knows she must mitigate the damage done by her husband's betrayal of Israel. God gives her this opportunity by having the enemy commander delivered into her hand, fulfilling Deborah's prophecy that a woman would finish Sisera. Was Jael wrong to have acted in this way? She breached the cardinal rule of hospitality by harming a guest under her own roof. She lied by telling Sisera not to fear. She betrayed the peace treaty between her people and Jabin. She was guilty of a major cultural infraction by inviting a man other than her husband into her tent. And she committed murder. Yet she is lauded in the Song of Deborah by the LORD's prophetess herself, who recounts Jael's part in the drama with victorious glee:

Blessed above women shall Jael the wife of Heber the Kenite be, blessed shall she be above women in the tent. He asked water and she gave him milk; she brought forth butter in a lordly dish. She put her hand to the nail and her right hand to the workmen's hammer, and with the hammer she smote Sisera, she smote off his head, when she had pierced and stricken him through his temples. At her feet he bowed, he fell, he lay down: at her feet he bowed, he fell: where he bowed, there he fell down dead. (Judg 5:24-27)

I summarise the whole Deborah/Barak/Jael drama in my own mind as 'women thinking clearly'. In all fairness, for twenty years Israel had suffered harsh oppression under Jabin and Sisera, which would have included summary rapes, murders, beatings, robberies and executions for minor infractions. The rebellion was necessary and had to succeed to free Israel from her predicament. The reprisals for failure would have been terrifying. The victory was the LORD's.

Lessons for nations

What does the Designer wish us to learn of His motives and character?

- He is not short on forgiveness and restitution, but we have to make the first move
- God always steers the action to accomplish His will
- What pleases God most is for believers to get their hearts right before Him, then step out in faith and trust Him to deliver them
- God abhors sin and once again brings a pagan power to judge Israel for her apostasy. This is an aspect of God's character we can take to the bank. If a nation sins against Him, Deuteronomy 28 cuts in on time, every time. Not happy with the state of your country? The believers in the LORD are on the hook to carry out 2 Chron 7:14, for the

wicked don't know how to be anything other than wicked.

"If My people, which are called by My name, shall humble themselves, and pray, and seek My face, and turn from their wicked ways; then will I hear from Heaven, and will forgive their sin, and will heal their land."

The lesson is timely today. Britain, formerly a world power, is now a province in a European superstate. As covered in my book, *Ten Minutes to Midnight,* my nation's political decline began soon after her social and spiritual degradation. On HW Prentis' Cycle of Nations, the reign of Edward VII began Britain's complacency period when a liberalised society took root and old conventions were swept away with the last of Victoriana. Belief in God took a serious hit after World War 1 - how could a righteous Deity allow such carnage? Yet man was given free will and Earth is on-the-job training for eternity under live-fire conditions. God did not fire those artillery shells, load up the Vickers and Maxim machine-gun belts or fix bayonets. Man did these things of his own free will. God did not send clouds of toxic phosgene wafting into the enemy trenches, man did this of his own free will. In the two decades following the Great War, the rot continued. We had the Great Depression, mass unemployment, crime, rebellion against God, and the rise of the new atheist intelligentsia of which Orwell spoke.[386]

Then came World War 2, which broke Britain as an imperial power. The 1950s saw more hardship and depression, along with the launch of the fledgling EU. The purpose of a United Europe was to prevent any possibility of a future European war. The counterculture revolution hit in the 1960s to '80s, after which the new prophets were popstars blaspheming God at every turn with *Imagine, Sympathy for the Devil* and *Material Girl.* The Nimrod/Semiramis sex and death

---

[386] In *The Lion and the Unicorn,* George Orwell wrote in 1941: "In intention, at any rate, the English intelligentsia are Europeanised. They take their cookery from Paris and their opinions from Moscow. In the general patriotism of the country, they form a sort of island of dissident thought. England is perhaps the only great country whose intellectuals are ashamed of their own nationality. In left-wing circles it is always felt that there is something slightly disgraceful in being an Englishman, and that it is a duty to snigger at every English institution, from horse racing to suet puddings. It is a strange fact, but it is unquestionably true, that almost any English intellectual would feel more ashamed of standing to attention during 'God Save the King' than of stealing from a poor box."

cults of the Canaanites were back with a vengeance, this time resurrected by *Hair,* Woodstock and the Haight-Ashbury hippies. There is nothing new about the New Age; it's old paganism revived, sporting the promiscuity practised by the Canaanites and Israel of old. And no-one wants these modern babies either. A generation wept buckets for the carpet-bombed Vietcong, disenfranchised Palestinians, Mediterranean migrants and starving African children, yet few of the same eyes shed any tears over the wholesale slaughter of millions of unwanted babies inside the holy of holies of a mother's womb.

Today Britain has moved to the apathy period. These days we are completely answerable to a foreign power, a state of affairs that would have had our forebears recoiling in horror. Today our overlords are the European Union, a foreign, unelected, unanswerable, criminal cabal of committees which embezzles ten percent of the annual budget provided by European taxpayers. In return we are reliant on this corrupt club for 100 percent of our laws – and boy, don't they provide them. From how bendy a banana should be to a legal ban on declaring that water can cure dehydration or that prunes are laxatives, Britons and other European countries are stitched up and buried under a yearly avalanche of asinine legislation. And what are we doing about it? Nothing. What should be doing about it? 2 Chronicles 7:14:

"If My people, which are called by My name, shall humble themselves and pray and seek my face and turn from their wicked ways, then will I hear from Heaven, will forgive their sin, and heal their land."

Hyperspaces and the 'metacosm'

Let's pause the narrative at this point to set Joshua, Ehud, Deborah, Barak and the other judges into a more startling context – the one in which God views them. Throughout the *Origins* series so far we've examined the peculiar nature of what we term 'reality'. We've looked at the current scientific wisdom which suggests that in addition to the four 'physical' dimensions which humans experience (x, y, z and time – collectively known as 'spacetime', or what I term 'The Earth Program'), physicists believe there are at least six further dimensions curled into 10^{-33} cm (below the sub-atomic/quantum/Planck limit) which can be inferred; we just can't get at them. Sometimes known as the 'spiritual' dimensions or metacosm, they impart bizarre and truly remarkable properties to the physical realm which are relevant to understanding the Message System. A number of disturbing inconsistencies slot into place once we achieve a 'God's eye view' of our physical existence. I believe that the purpose of the Message System is to give us this 'God's eye view'.

One of the great discoveries of the 20th century is that what we term 'time' is a physical dimension/property which varies according to mass, acceleration and gravity. In fact, time is a rather slippery concept, reckons *Discover* magazine:

"Time… is not something that exists apart from the universe. There is no clock ticking outside the cosmos. Most of us tend to think of time the way Newton did: 'Absolute, true and mathematical time, of itself, and from its own nature, flows equably, without regard to anything external.' But as Einstein proved, time is part of the fabric of the universe. Contrary to what Newton believed, our ordinary clocks don't measure something that's independent of the universe. In fact, says Lloyd, clocks don't really measure time at all.

"'I recently went to the National Institute of Standards and Technology in Boulder,' says Lloyd. (NIST is the government lab that houses the atomic clock that standardizes time for the nation.) 'I said something like, "Your clocks measure time very accurately." They told me, "Our clocks do not measure time." I thought, "Wow, that's very humble of these guys." But they said, "No, time is defined to be what our clocks measure." Which is true. They define the time standards for the globe: Time is defined by the number of clicks of their clocks.' " [387]

Strewth, *clocks don't measure time?*

In school we were taught to depict the life of a person or the birth and death of an empire with a two-dimensional timeline on paper that runs from left to right, upon which we place the labels 'birth' 'life', 'death', after which the person or empire 'runs out of time' or dies. Eternity, on the other hand, is not lots of time, it's the absence of time. Take a quantum physicist out to lunch and he'll wax lyrical on the Wheeler-DeWitt Equation, Einsteinian Relativity, hyperspaces, one-dimensional superstrings vibrating in ten dimensions, and so on. But to normal mortals like me, it boils down to this: Humans are part software and part hardware. While our hardware (bodies, houses, cars, iPhones, etc.) dwell in the four, physical Earth dimensions (x, y, z and 'time'), our software (thoughts, feelings, life-force, soul, spirit,

---

[387] http://discovermagazine.com/2007/jun/in-no-time/article_view?b_start: int=1

ethereal concepts, etc.) are thought to reside in the six spiritual dimensions, collectively known as the metacosm. Your software is not part of the physical 'Earth' dimensions since it has zero mass/weight (if mass = 0, t = eternal). So when we sleep, dream, think, believe, hate, love and despair, some scientists posit that we are doing these things in the spiritual realm wherein God, *ha-Satan,* demons, angels and miscellaneous spiritual entities dwell (though the latter have access to all Earth dimensions).

The Bible is replete with transcendent incidents showing what happens when the spacetime veil is temporarily manipulated by God to permit us a peek into the Great Beyond. We see examples of this with every hyperdimensional visitation from angels and even the Angel of the LORD (Yeshua). During the Exodus, God repeatedly breaks through spacetime to provide some amazing hyperdimensional offerings: the burning bush; His visitation to the summit of Mt Sinai, and Moses' glimpse of God's back (Exo 33:18 ff.) as examples so far. We shall be sensitive to further incidents as we proceed; in fact, there is an excellent one with Gideon, the very next judge we will study.

Currently, spacetime (Earth) dimensions are subject to the Edenic curse of entropy and death, while the metacosmic dimensions appear not to be affected. When we die, our hardware dies in the physical plane (x, y, z and time) but our software survives intact in the metacosm. Our software is *eternal* whether we like it or not. Whether we have ended our Holy War against God or not. Whether we are 'saved' or not.

God's full dimensionality is the real reality and is summarised by one word - light. **Let there be light.** Earth and the current universe are but a shadow of this - a temporary digital projection due to be replaced with an infinitely more stunning **new heavens and a new Earth.** The New Jerusalem has the Lamb (Yeshua) as its light (Rev 21 & 22). This will be a universe resplendent in its full dimensionality and no longer subject to time or the entropy which has dogged Creation since the Fall, when, some commentators believe, the four Earth dimensions were fractured from the other six. We know next to nothing about the conditions which prevailed pre-Curse. It's speculated that Adam and Eve enjoyed a similar dimensionality to God but this is not expressly stated in scripture. Adam and Eve did notice they were naked after their sin, and God was heard walking in the Garden (Gen 3:7-9), so there is some congruence there. Some speculate that Adam and Eve were clothed in light prior to the Fall; a covering (dimensionality) they subsequently lost. This is not stated in scripture either, but it's provocative that some angels in scripture appear as humans, while others present themselves clothed in light (Dan 10:5-10; 2 Cor 11:14). The wicked angels of Genesis 6 apparently shucked off their heavenly bodies (*oiketerion*) prior to indulging in those sexual activities with the daughters of men, for which they and all the peoples of the Earth were severely punished (Gen 6 and the Flood).[388] Yeshua is clothed in light at the Transfiguration. The redeemed will be able to see God as He really is in eternity since we shall be like Him (1 John 3:2: 1 Cor 15:35-58). It is noteworthy that God has been educating us on eternal concepts without most of us having the slightest clue what they really represent. The Law, the Ark of the Covenant, the brazen serpent on the pole; the Jerusalem Temple; baptism; the sacrificial lamb; forgiveness, etc. We've been picking up on these 'types' or 'prefigurements' as we go. How about prayer? When you humble yourself before your Creator, ask forgiveness and pray, you are communicating directly into God's throne room. Did you know that you can *change God's mind?* Moses did (Exo 32:11-14).

True prophets of God receive revelations from the Infinite Mind, *where the event has already happened*. In fact, the extensive prophetic record of the Bible is absolutely unique and proves beyond measure its origin outside spacetime. There's another fascinating aspect to the time dimension, posited by Einstein. An observer outside of time has the ability to view all events on the Earth Programme simultaneously in what amounts to a constant, *interrelational* 'now'. In God's realm, Hannibal is preparing for the battle of Cannae *right now*. Cain is slaying Abel *right now*. Oppenheimer is preparing the atomic bomb, *right now*. God's Son still hangs on the Cross, *right now*. Does the sin we commit today have the ability in God's realm to increase Christ's suffering on the cross, *right now?* Yeshua's execution took six hours, yet in that time he paid for all sins, past and future.[389] *How,* if not hyperdimensionally?

When God tells Deborah to announce to Barak and Israel their deliverance from Jabin and Sisera, notice the news is given in the past tense. To God, it's already done:

---

[388] See former chapter, *The Doomed Earth*. Also Genesis 6; Jude 6-7; 2 Pet 2:4-5

[389] Col 2:13-15; Heb. 9:11-12; 10:10-14; FG 1:29; 2 Cor. 5:21; 1 Jn. 3:5; Rom. 4:25; 1 Pet. 2:22, 24

And Deborah said unto Barak, "Up! For this is the day in which the LORD hath delivered Sisera into thine hand! Is not the LORD gone out before thee?" So Barak went down from Mount Tabor, and ten thousand men after him. And the LORD discomfited Sisera and all his chariots and all his host with the edge of the sword before Barak, so that Sisera lighted down off his chariot and fled away on his feet. (Judg 4:14-15)

Blink and you'll miss it. Once you get used to this intriguing way the Designer deals with man, a whole new vista opens up. Einstein was fond of stating that "Reality is merely an illusion, albeit a very persistent one." In regard to a recently departed colleague, he said:

> "Now he has departed from this strange world a little ahead of me. That means nothing. People like us who believe in physics know that the distinction between past, present, and future is only a stubbornly persistent illusion." [390]

In other words, what we term 'past, present and future' on Earth are seen *simultaneously* in God's realm. To God the entire Earth Programme *has already been completed* because He sees the end from the beginning. No clearer examples of God's transcendence can be seen than in the following passages:

"Present your case," says the LORD. "Set forth your arguments," says Jacob's King. "Bring in your idols to tell us what is going to happen. Tell us what the former things were, so that we may consider them and know their final outcome. Or declare to us the things to come, tell us what the future holds so we may know you are gods. Yes, do good or do evil, that we may be dismayed and see it together. Indeed you are nothing, and your work is nothing. He who chooses you is an abomination." (Isa 41:21-24, NIV)

"I am God, and there is none like Me, declaring the end from the beginning, and from ancient times the things that are not yet done, saying, "My counsel shall stand and I will do all My pleasure.'" (Isa 46:9-10)

"I have declared the former things from the beginning. They went forth from My mouth and I caused them to hear it. Suddenly I did them and they came to pass.... Even from the beginning I have declared it to you. Before it came to pass I proclaimed it to you, lest you should say, 'My idol has done them, and my carved image and my moulded image have commanded them'." (Isa 48:3,5, NKJV)

---

[390] http://rescomp.stanford.edu/~cheshire/EinsteinQuotes.html

The Flats

'The Flats' are an example of the beauty of dimensions. Take a sheet of paper and draw two stick figures. Let's name them Mr and Mrs Flat. Draw them holding hands and gazing lovingly into each other's eyes if you want; it will add drama to what's coming in a minute.

Now examine your handiwork. You've just drawn a couple of two-dimensional figures. In other words, Mr and Mrs Flat have a length and width but no depth. They're flat! Now take the tip of your finger and hover it over Mrs Flat and see how close you can get to the paper without actually touching it. Notice that you enjoy an extra dimension denied to the Flats - depth – but if you don't touch that paper, they will never be aware of your presence. You can enjoy a closeness and intimacy with Mrs Flat that even her husband cannot experience, yet she won't be aware of your presence until you choose to touch the paper and enter her realm with the tip of your finger. When you do touch the paper, Mr and Mrs F will only see you as a dot quickly expanding to a small circle as you press the tip of your finger onto the paper. In other words, they will only be aware of the two-dimensional cross-section of your finger.

Mrs Flat turns to her husband, exclaiming: "I've just seen Phillip!"

Mr Flat: "Coots, what did he look like?"

Mrs Flat, triumphant: "He's a circle!"

Do either of them have the slightest idea what I really look like? No, because they don't have my dimensionality. As with the skit where a group of blind men feel different parts of an elephant and conclude that the beast looks like the bodypart they are holding, none have a total picture of what the elephant looks like. Notice, in the case of the Flats, I can be all around their realm – above them, below them, to one side or the other – witnessing everything they do and say, and they'll never have the slightest idea I'm right with them until I choose to reveal myself to them by touching their dimensionality.

Now cut out a circular section of the paper above their heads, hold the paper up horizontally and drop a marble through the hole. All Mr and Mrs Flat will fleetingly glimpse is a dot expanding to a circle, going back to a dot before disappearing. Remember this example as it has a surprising relevance in *Origins IV - Tetelestai.*

So, to summarise: We have millions of people today who are atheists because it suits them not to believe in an extradimensional God but to remain in spacetime to escape an ultimate accountability and judgment which is coming upon them anyway. An atheist is like a bacterium inside a lion which says to his companions. "You deluded saps, there's no such thing as a lion! Who knows why we are here? Do what you want!" Atheists reject God with their toes hanging over the edge of eternity. God continues to divide their cells and water their eyes while providing ample opportunity to seek Him while He yet may be found.[391]

The coming of the desert scourge

The destruction of Sisera and Jabin's power buys Israel forty years of peace and freedom. But in this cycle of sin, Israel slips back into idolatry after the death of the judge who delivered her. This tells us something about Israel's need for a strong, central leader, which is supposed to be YHWH. Having the Creator of the universe as your personal King is the central theme of the Message System and certainly provides many major advantages, not least of which is not having to suffer the vagaries of a human successor when your human king dies. This particular problem curses Israel to this day, and will certainly be a thorn in her side throughout the centuries following the period we are currently studying.

After Deborah and Barak die ...**the children of Israel did evil in the sight of the LORD. And the LORD delivered them into the hand of Midian seven years. And the hand of Midian prevailed against Israel. And because of the Midianites, the children of Israel made themselves the dens which are in the mountains, and caves and strongholds.**

And so it was, when Israel had sown, that the Midianites came up, and the Amalekites, and the children of the east, even they came up against them, and they encamped against them and destroyed the increase of the earth, till thou come unto Gaza, and left no sustenance for Israel, neither sheep, nor ox, nor ass.

For they came up with their cattle and their tents, and they came as grasshoppers for multitude; for both they and their camels were without number: and they entered into the land to destroy it.

And Israel was greatly impoverished because of the Midianites; and the children of Israel cried unto the LORD. (Judg 6:1-6)

Once again it's back to the worship of *ha-Satan,* who has lurked behind every false god and promise since the Garden. *Ha-Satan's* aim is to **be like the Most High** (Isa 14:11-17), which includes total

---

[391] 1 Chron 28:9; Psa 34:8, 18; Jer 29:12-14; Joel 2:32; Isa 55:6-7; Jam 4:8; FG 3:19-21, etc.

domination over the death, sex and procreation processes brazenly mocked in the rituals of the Canaanites. But the scriptures don't say *ha-Satan* 'wants to be the Most High', only **like the Most High.** It's a puzzle to figure out the devil's end-game. What does he expect to gain from his rebellion? He was already the most powerful being in the cosmos next to God, he must surely know what an incomprehensible gulf exists between his own faculties as a created being and those of his limitless, ubiquitous, omniscient Creator. The answer: pride, which caused *ha-Satan* to fall in the first place. Yeshua's sentence of eternal death, pronounced upon his once most beloved shining one, has already been carried out in the eternal realm. In the Earth realm on spacetime, we are witnessing the last, desperate acts of a condemned super-being attempting to thwart his fate by foiling the coming of God in human form to Earth to triumph over him. In this respect, the more damage *ha-Satan* can do to the Creation in general and God's Jews in particular, the better, for it will be through the descendants of Abraham, Isaac and Jacob that man's Redeemer and Satan's Executioner will be born. Nothing less than the total destruction of the Israelites is called for, and what better way than to have that destruction come at the hand of the very God who purports to love them? Lure Israel into flagrant idolatry. God's perfect righteousness will not tolerate it for long. But as with all things devilish, there is tactical cunning but little strategic foresight.

The Midianites and Amalekites are old enemies of Israel.[392] Midian was one of the sons of Abraham through his wife Keturah (Gen 25:1-2), and gave his name to a region which is reliably placed in modern-day, northwestern Arabia. Even today it's a desolate, desert place. Moses fled to Midian after killing the Egyptian taskmaster. The Midianites now plaguing the Israelites are nomadic warriors and farmers often allied to Moab (Jordan). They worship Baal-Peor (*ha-Satan*), indulge in all the usual profanities (avidly promoted by *ha-Satan*), and also venerate Ashtoreth, the 'Queen of Heaven' (*ha-Satan*).

And the Amalekites are back; on-off allies to the Midianites since both inhabit the desert and mountain wastes. Amalek was a grandson

[392] Joseph, son of Jacob, was sold by his brothers to Midianite traders. Midian was also the region where Moses entered self-appointed exile after murdering the Egyptian. While in Midian, Moses marries Zipporah, one of seven daughters of Jethro, the priest of Midian. The Hebrews and Midianites were a constant source of worry to each other during the wilderness wanderings (Num 22:4; 25:16-18). In Numbers 31, God instructs Moses to put an army together to destroy them.

of Esau and fathered a nomadic tribe which became a byword for violence, ruthlessness and cunning. They too have scores to settle with the Israelites. We last encountered them picking off Israelite stragglers during the wilderness wanderings in the Sinai peninsula.

Gideon - a farmer is called

During the forty years of respite after Deborah and Barak's memorable episode, Israel has a chance to prosper and thrive. Now for the past seven years, the nomadic oppressors have been onto a good thing. Striking Israel just after harvest-time, their marauding cohorts arrive in hordes to rob valuable crops, steal livestock, destroy property and rape and kill their old enemy at will. The depredations become so severe that the Jews have taken to living in caves, clefts and dens in the mountains to protect their families. It's a far cry from the victorious, invading army Joshua led across the Jordan 200 years before to conquer the land God had given them.

And so it was, when Israel had sown, that the Midianites came up, and the Amalekites, and the children of the east, even they came up against them, and they encamped against them and destroyed the increase of the earth, till thou come unto Gaza, and left no sustenance for Israel, neither sheep, nor ox, nor ass. For they came up with their cattle and their tents, and they came as grasshoppers for multitude; for both they and their camels were without number: and they entered into the land to destroy it. And Israel was greatly impoverished because of the Midianites; and the children of Israel cried unto the LORD. (Judg 6:3-6)

Once more, God upbraids Israel for not obeying His voice, and once more He takes pity. The Angel of the LORD visits a young farmer from the tribe of Manasseh named Gideon, whom He finds threshing what wheat he possesses behind a winepress to hide it from the invaders. This desperate, frightened act to avoid his family's starvation is rendered all the more ridiculous when the Angel greets Gideon thus: **"The LORD is with you, you mighty man of valour!"** (Judg 6:12)

So far as Gideon is concerned, he's being addressed rather impudently by a dusty stranger sat under a terebinth tree. Gideon's under no illusions about his own cowardice and remonstrates with the man that if the LORD were with them, why would all this have happened? **"Did not the LORD bring us up from Egypt? But now the LORD hath forsaken us and delivered us into the hands of the Midianites!"** (Judg 6:13)

Gideon has suffered personal loss from these marauders. His step-brothers were slaughtered at Tabor, probably during a raid when they tried to do something about the attack (Judg 8:18-19). Gideon's fear and sense of impotence is understandable and keenly felt in his plea.

And the LORD looked upon him and said, "Go in this thy might, and thou shalt save Israel from the hand of the Midianites. Have not I sent thee?" (Judg 6:13-14)

Notice the past tense! Gideon hasn't gone anywhere yet. These surprising, wonderful words bring Gideon up short; hint that this stranger is something more. The Angel of the LORD always speaks as God in the first person, this time enduing Gideon with qualities he will possess in the future as if he already has them (In God's realm he already does). At this point, Gideon has his Eureka moment and realises he's talking with the LORD. His knee-jerk reaction from the shock is to indulge in a humble-pie, excuse-making exercise similar to Moses at the burning bush:

And [Gideon] **said unto Him, "Oh my LORD, wherewith shall I save Israel? Behold, my family is poor in Manasseh and I am the least in my father's house."**

And the LORD said unto him, "Surely I will be with thee and thou shalt smite the Midianites as one man."

And [Gideon] **said unto Him, "If now I have found grace in Thy sight, then shew me a sign that Thou talkest with me. Depart not hence, I pray Thee, until I come unto Thee and bring forth my present and set it before Thee."**

And He said, "I will tarry until thou come again." (Judg 6:15-18)

Gideon's having a hard time getting his head around the fact that he is conversing with the Creator of the universe. Not unreasonably he wants proof. If a dusty stranger showed up at your farm one day and started talking this way, what would you do? Gideon pops indoors to prepare an offering comprised of meat and soup made out of a young goat and what amounts to an irresponsibly large amount of unleavened bread made into cakes. He then brings the lot out to the terebinth tree and presents it to the stranger.

And the Angel of God said unto [Gideon]**, "Take the flesh and the unleavened cakes and lay them upon this rock and pour out the broth."**

And he did so. Then the angel of the LORD put forth the end of the staff that was in His hand and touched the flesh and the unleavened cakes. And there rose up fire out of the rock and

consumed the flesh and the unleavened cakes. Then the Angel of the LORD departed out of his sight.

And when Gideon perceived that He was an angel of the LORD, he said, "Alas, O LORD GOD, because I have seen an angel of the LORD face to face!"

And the LORD said unto him, "Peace be unto thee, fear not. Thou shalt not die."

Then Gideon built an altar there unto the LORD and called it Jehovah Shalom ['The LORD is peace']**. Unto this day it is yet in Ophrah of the Abiezrites.** (Judg 6:20-24)

Gideon is given a profound demonstration of hyperspace manipulation. It's noteworthy that God indulges Gideon's desire for proof and waits patiently beneath the terebinth tree while the farmer fusses about preparing the offering. The acceptance of the sacrifice with holy fire, followed by the translation of the Angel (Yeshua) from Gideon's spacetime domain must have made a tremendous impression, so much so that Gideon now believes that, true to the Torah, he will perish for having seen God directly (Exo 33:20). In fact, God has not revealed His true form to Gideon but a human simulation with which Gideon will be comfortable (*cf.* Mr and Mrs Flat).

Gideon is given further instructions by God later that evening that definitely make the farmer gulp.

"Take thy father's young bullock, even the second bullock of seven years old, and throw down the altar of Baal that thy father hath, and cut down the grove that is by it. And build an altar unto the LORD thy God upon the top of this rock in the proper arrangement, and take the second bullock and offer a burnt sacrifice with the wood of the grove, which thou shalt cut down."

Then Gideon took ten men of his servants and did as the LORD had said unto him. And so it was, because he feared his father's household and the men of the city that he could not do it by day, so he did it by night. (Judg 6:25-27)

This is no small request God asks of Gideon. Gideon is scared, and God wants Gideon to do it scared. Those Baal stone altars are pretty elaborate affairs and so are the wooden phalli (pruned tree grove) standing beside it. It will be a good night's work for Gideon and his crew to tear them down and build an altar to the LORD in their place from stone uncut by human hands (which won't be the

Baal stones).[393] Moreover, destroying the town's pagan altar will guarantee Gideon, and also the frightened servants dragooned into colluding in this enterprise, a gruesome death.

There are three important insights from the text: Firstly, Gideon is a believer in the LORD but his father and family are apostates. This demonstrates that God calls some but not others within a family, though in this case, Gideon's kin do repent. Secondly, while Gideon may have cause to fear death from the Baal-worshipping Jews for his actions, the fact that the whole Israelite town has been worshipping *ha-Satan* in defiance of YHWH guarantees the lot the chop under Mosaic Law. So who should be scared? Thirdly, you can't build an altar in your heart to the LORD until you first tear down the false ones. You can't shine a light for the LORD until first you are broken and of a contrite spirit (Psa 51:15-17). God comes to those who have come to the end of themselves. God values broken things because broken vessels shine with the most light. He doesn't go a bundle on folk selectively choosing which parts of His Word to believe in (syncretism). Gideon is compelled by God to show where his true allegiance lies, but God is not worried. What He intends is for Gideon and the town's benefit. Gideon's advantage is his brokenness and fearful availability. Can you imagine the reaction the following morning when the townsfolk wipe the sleep from their eyes to find the mess of Baal's altar and grove, and the LORD's altar in their place?

And they said one to another, "Who hath done this thing?" And when they enquired and asked, they said, "Gideon the son of Joash hath done this thing."

Then the men of the city said unto Joash, "Bring out thy son that he may die, because he hath cast down the altar of Baal and because he hath cut down the grove that was by it."

And Joash said unto all that stood against him, "Will ye plead for Baal? Will ye save him? He that will plead for him, let him be put to death whilst it is yet morning. If [Baal] **be a god, let him plead for himself because one hath cast down his altar."**

---

[393] Martin G Selbrede writes: "Altars to God could not be made of stones that were worked by human hand, implying that man has something to offer to the worship of God: **'And if thou wilt make me an altar of stone, thou shalt not build it of hewn stone: for if thou lift up thy tool upon it, thou hast polluted it'** (Ex. 20:25). Only stones that God made are fit for the altars for God. Such stones don't need man's workmanship to 'improve' them. Man can only pollute such elements of worship." - http://chalcedon.edu/research/articles/without-human-hand/

Therefore on that day he called [Gideon] **Jerubbaal, saying, "Let Baal plead against him because he hath thrown down his altar."** (Judg 6:29-32)

Joash is not much of a pagan. It seems he slipped into idolatry since that suited the rest of the town. Gideon's courageous action snaps Joash back to reality. He now champions his son's cause before the whole town and shames the people into backing down. After all, what good is worshipping Baal if such a god can't even defend his own altar?

News of Gideon's defiance soon spreads through the souks and bazaars and earns Gideon his word-fame. And just as well, for word comes of a huge army of Midianites and Amalekites which has just crossed the Jordan and encamped in the Valley of Jezreel in preparation for their customary robbing and killing bonanza. This invading force almost certainly includes freebooting Edomites, Ammonites and other **people of the East** with a grudge against Israel and an eye for plunder.

Israel awakens to her predicament. The Spirit of the LORD falls upon Gideon. Jack Heyford points out that the Hebrew phrase literally translates: "The Spirit of the LORD clothed Himself with Gideon" - a much more apposite description. The shofar is blown and messengers despatched throughout Manasseh, Asher, Zebulun and Naphtali to rally support against the enemy. A volunteer force of 32,000 gathers and presents itself to Gideon, who abruptly realises he's not a farmer anymore. He hasn't had a day's military training in his life and he's facing 135,000 tough, experienced warriors who have invaded Israel from the desert seven times before and know what they're doing (Judg 8:10). Not unsurprisingly, Gideon is assailed by a further crisis of courage. He is the 'judge' given the most column-inches in the Bible, and also the one of whom we are given special insights into his doubts and misgivings:

And Gideon said unto God, "If thou wilt save Israel by mine hand, as Thou hast said, behold, I will put a fleece of wool in the floor; and if the dew be on the fleece only, and it be dry upon all the earth beside, then shall I know that Thou wilt save Israel by mine hand, as Thou hast said."

And it was so: for he rose up early on the morrow and thrust the fleece together, and wringed the dew out of the fleece, a bowl full of water.

And Gideon said unto God, "Let not Thine anger be hot against me, and I will speak but this once. Let me prove, I pray Thee, but

this once with the fleece; let it now be dry only upon the fleece, and upon all the ground let there be dew."

And God did so that night, for it was dry upon the fleece only, and there was dew on all the ground. (Judg 6:36-40)

Put yourself in Gideon's position. You are outnumbered four to one. Is God really going to come through for you because He said so? Gideon seeks God's confirmation by putting out the fleece, an idiom used by believers today seeking God's support for an enterprise by setting the Designer a test. Deuteronomy specifically states, **"Ye shall not tempt the LORD your God...."** It appears that asking God for a sign because of your lack of faith is forbidden, but asking God for a sign to clarify an action is permitted, as in Gideon's case (*cf.* Matt 4:5-7). Notice God's forbearance in playing along, which tells us something about Him. He puts Himself in our shoes and knows our predicament better than us. Gideon receives his confirmation two different ways and takes his army out to the well of Harod ('trembling' - which, let's face it, we would be too), and encamps opposite the Midianite horde in the valley.

But if Gideon thinks he can go out and fight the heathen with odds of 4 to 1 against him, he's in for a shock. God tells him his Israelite force *is too big* for the Midianites to be given into his hand. What concerns God is that the Jews might claim victory through their own prowess rather than God's. The whole purpose of the exercise is to bring the nation back to Him. So God tells Gideon:

"Now therefore go and proclaim in the ears of the people, saying, "Whosoever is fearful and afraid, let him return and depart early from mount Gilead." And here returned of the people twenty and two thousand, and there remained ten thousand. (Judg 7:3)

Now the odds are 13.5 to 1 - still too many for God.

And the LORD said unto Gideon, "The people are yet too many. Bring them down unto the water and I will try them for thee there. And it shall be that of whom I say unto thee, 'This shall go with thee', the same shall go with thee; and of whomsoever I say unto thee, 'This shall not go with thee', the same shall not go.

So he brought down the people unto the water, and the LORD said unto Gideon, "Every one that lappeth of the water with his tongue, as a dog lappeth, him shalt thou set by himself; likewise every one that boweth down upon his knees to drink."

And the number of them that lapped, putting their hand to their mouth, were three hundred men, but all the rest of the people bowed down upon their knees to drink water.

And the LORD said unto Gideon, "By the three hundred men that lapped will I save you and deliver the Midianites into thine hand. And let all the other people go every man unto his place."

So the people took victuals in their hand and their trumpets, and he sent all the rest of Israel, every man unto his tent, and retained those three hundred men, and the host of Midian was beneath him in the valley. (Judg 7:4-8)

Three hundred up against 135,000? Now you're talking. The odds stand at 450 to 1 – much more to God's liking. There is no way Israel can now claim glory for the victory; it will be the LORD's alone. This selection process for the three hundred is usually interpreted to mean that God chose the three hundred who were alert and not burying their faces in the water when an enemy could strike. The Jewish chronicler Josephus, however, begs to differ, believing that God chose the real losers to sharpen the lesson.[394] Either way, God has just selected Gideon's strike-force *based on how they drink water!*

The strangest battle ever

Of all of the conflicts throughout human history, Gideon's battle with the Midianite rates as one of the most unequal and, frankly, bizarre. YHWH pronounces Gideon's victory in past tense again the night before to encourage him (**"Arise, get thee down unto the host, for I have delivered it into thine hand."** (Judg 7:9). Yet God senses that his new general is still nervous. He recommends Gideon take his servant and sneak down to the enemy camp under cover of darkness to hear the talk and gauge the mood. Gideon obeys and he and Purah come upon an enemy warrior chatting to a colleague.

"Behold, I dreamed a dream, and, lo, a cake of barley bread tumbled into the host of Midian, and came unto a tent, and smote it that it fell and overturned it, that the tent lay along."

And his fellow answered and said, "This is nothing else save the sword of Gideon the son of Joash, a man of Israel, for into his hand hath God delivered Midian, and all the host."

And it was so, when Gideon heard the telling of the dream and the interpretation thereof, that he worshipped, and returned into the host of Israel and said, "Arise, for the LORD hath delivered [past tense] **into your hand the host of Midian."** (Judg 7:13-15)

The incident is just what Gideon needs. The Midianites know all about the God of the Hebrews, how He fought for them in the past.

---

[394] Josephus, *Antiquities,* op. cit., 5:6:3

From the dramas of the Egyptian plagues to the Exodus, through the Canaanite invasion two hundred years before to the destruction of Adonizedek's coalition by flaming bolides and Sisera's army from a flash flood, all God's exploits have made for superstitious gossip around ten thousand camp fires. Even superior enemies have cause to tremble. Who can fight against such a God? What hope triumph? We are not told whether the friend's response to his compadre's barley-cake dream is heartfelt or ironic. The Midianites are not unmindful of their human superiority, and many are itching to get stuck in as in previous years, yet this time there's a new champion of the Hebrew God: Gideon, son of Joash. The mood in the Jezreel Valley is confident with a broad streak of caution.

The barley bread is symbolic of poor-grade peasant food representing a besieged Israel's agricultural lifestyle. Notice the dream incident is purely for Gideon's benefit to stiffen his resolve for what lies ahead. Which means that God cares about our nerves before our challenges, and no conversation we engage in, witness or overhear is *ever* without significance. The metacosm is taking notes.[395]

Gideon prepares his 300 for battle, which isn't to say that those Israelites not picked for Gideon's initial action are dismissed; they will be needed for the mop-up operation which will be considerable. Some commentators like to draw parallels between Gideon's battle and Leonidas I's stand with his 300 Spartans against the Persians at Thermopylae (August 480 BC), yet Leonidas and his men, however brave, were slaughtered to the man without mercy - an opposite outcome to Gideon's battle. Perhaps if Leonidas had beseeched the God of Israel to his cause...? Gideon's instructions to his 300 definitely raise more eyebrows.

And he divided the three hundred men into three companies, and he put a trumpet in every man's hand, with empty pitchers, and lamps within the pitchers. And he said unto them, "Look on me and do likewise: and, behold, when I come to the outside of the camp, it shall be that, as I do, so shall ye do. When I blow with a trumpet, I and all that are with me, then blow ye the trumpets also on every side of all the camp, and cry, 'The sword of the LORD and of Gideon!'" (Judg 7:16-18)

---

[395] Yeshua says: **"But I say unto you that every idle word that men shall speak, they shall give account thereof in the day of judgment. For by thy words thou shalt be justified, and by thy words thou shalt be condemned."** (Matt 12:36-37)

The reaction of the 300 to their battle-plan goes unrecorded. Off they troop and surround the Midianites in the dark, one trumpet and pitcher per man. They execute their strategy just as the middle watch commences (around 10 pm), a time when warriors are growing weary.

So Gideon and the hundred men that were with him came unto the outside of the camp in the beginning of the middle watch; and they had but newly set the watch. And they blew the trumpets and brake the pitchers that were in their hands. And the three companies blew the trumpets and brake the pitchers and held the lamps [torches] **in their left hands and the trumpets in their right hands to blow withal. And they cried, "The sword of the LORD and of Gideon!"** [396]

And they stood every man in his place round about the camp, and all the host ran, and cried, and fled. And the three hundred blew the trumpets, and the LORD set every man's sword against his fellow, even throughout all the host. And the host fled to Bethshittah in Zererath, and to the border of Abelmeholah, unto Tabbath. (Judg 7:19-22)

No-one wore uniforms back then. With the sudden trumpet cacophony, the signal for imminent attack, God strikes terror into the superstitious Midianites and all hell breaks loose. How do you know the man over there is your brother or enemy? You don't. Kill him anyway. It's dark and you can't see anything. It's him or you. The constant, deafening trumpet blasts signifying a huge army descending. Your worst fears are realised, the terrifying battle-cry turning your heart to water: **"The sword of the LORD and of Gideon!"**

And the men of Israel gathered themselves together out of Naphtali, and out of Asher, and out of all Manasseh, and pursued after the Midianites. And Gideon sent messengers throughout all Mount Ephraim, saying, "Come down against the Midianites, and seize from them the watering places as far as Beth Barah and the Jordan." Then all the men of Ephraim gathered themselves together and seized from them the watering places as far as Beth Barah and the Jordan.

And they took two princes of the Midianites, Oreb and Zeeb. And they slew Oreb upon the rock Oreb, and Zeeb they slew at the

---

[396] God makes use of broken vessels so that His light shines forth! (*cf.* 2 Cor 4:6-12).

winepress of Zeeb, and pursued Midian, and brought the heads of Oreb and Zeeb to Gideon on the other side of the Jordan. (Judg 7:23-25)

There is an incident when the men of Ephraim get funny with Gideon for not including their tribe in the '300' initial deception action. The tribe of Ephraim, as we'll find out later, will earn a reputation for being glory-riders, troublemakers and crackbrains, even if they haven't already. Gideon flatters them for their subsequent prowess in capturing the Midianite princes. Ephraim's anger is assuaged for now.

But the pursuit of the fleeing enemy is on; there are the two Midianite kings to be captured - Zebah and Zalmunna. Exhausted but determined to wipe out the enemy down to the last nomad, Gideon and his valiant 300 swing by the Gad town of Succoth for provisions. The elders of the town prove less than enthusiastic. They doubt Gideon's ability to bring the two kings to book and know that if the fleeing kings successfully escape, a subsequent Midianite invasion will punish their town for having given aid to Gideon. Gideon blows his top:

"Therefore when the LORD hath delivered Zebah and Zalmunna into mine hand, then I will tear your flesh with the thorns of the wilderness and with briers!"

And he went up thence to Penuel, and spake unto them likewise, and the men of Penuel answered him as the men of Succoth had answered him. And he spake also unto the men of Penuel, saying, "When I come again in peace, I will break down this tower." (Judg 8:7-9)

Zebah and Zalmunna end up getting cornered by the Israelites along with 15,000 enemy survivors. Gideon takes the two kings captive and butchers the rest without mercy. On his return, he interrogates a young man from Succoth and records the names of the seventy-seven city elders in the town. He then returns to Succoth, dragging the two captive monarchs before the townspeople and elders:

"Behold Zebah and Zalmunna, with whom ye did upbraid me, saying, 'Are the hands of Zebah and Zalmunna now in thine hand, that we should give bread unto thy men that are weary?'"

And he took the elders of the city, and thorns of the wilderness and briers, and with them he taught the men of Succoth. And he beat down the tower of Penuel and slew the men of the city. (Judg 8:15-17)

Not a man to mess around with, Gideon. Expositors are divided over how Gideon 'taught' the men of Succoth with briars and thorns. Did he give them a good thrashing or beat them to death? I fear the latter, given what he did to the recalcitrants of Penuel.

And now the reckoning for the two Midianite kings, Zebah and Zalmunna, who face their fate with equanimity. Which ticks off Gideon:

Then said [Gideon] **unto Zebah and Zalmunna, "What manner of men were they whom ye slew at Tabor?" And they answered, "As thou art, so were they; each one resembled the son of a king."**

And he said, "They were my brethren, <u>even the sons of my mother</u>. As the LORD liveth, if ye had saved them alive I would not slay you."

And he said unto Jether his firstborn, "Up, and slay them." But the youth drew not his sword, for he feared because he was yet a youth.

Then Zebah and Zalmunna said, "Rise thou, and fall upon us. For as the man is, so is his strength." And Gideon arose and slew Zebah and Zalmunna, <u>and took away the crescent ornaments</u> that were on their camels' necks. (Judg 8:18-21)

The Midianite kings, worshipers of the moon god (later Al-Ilah),[397] were responsible for the wilful murder of Gideon's brothers at Tabor. Mostly likely, from the Hebrew used, these victims were Gideon's stepbrothers. Gideon invites his firstborn, Jether, to execute the kings who murdered his uncles. The manner of death was important for a warrior's word-fame, for a king even more so. Having a downy-cheeked kid do the deed would be heaping unbearable humiliation on these murderers. Naturally also, Zebah and Zalmunna wish the death-blow to be quick and accurate. Put a sword in a boy's hands and what's the worst that can happen? In the end, Jether baulks and won't draw his weapon. The kings sarcastically tell Gideon to get on with it. Doubtless piqued that his boy could not rise to such an

---

[397] Chuck Missler writes: "When Abraham was called out of the Ur of the Chaldees, the prevalent worship throughout the region was the worship of the moon god. In Assyria, he was called Sin (*cf.* Sin-echerib, et al.). In Arabia he was called Al-Ilah, later contracted to Allah (long before Mohammed, who then repackaged this occultic religion into a monotheistic form). The worship of Al-Ilah, the moon god, was the predecessor to Islam; the crescent moon still adorns every mosque throughout the Muslim world. These Ishmaelites (v.24) are so called as a term for nomads, not limited to traceable descendants of Ishmael. Ishmaelites believed it was Ishmael, not Isaac, whom Abraham offered on Mt. Moriah." – www.khouse.org, *Judges notes*

important occasion before his peers, Gideon draws his sword and executes them.

In summary: an outstanding victory, with which Israel effectively *refuses to credit the LORD*. How do we know? An attempt is immediately made to persuade Gideon to become Israel's king and father a dynasty, uniting the twelve tribes against future external attacks and preventing infighting. Yet it beggars belief that God is passed over for the desire for a human ruler. And this is still the case today. How many nations these days have made the Creator of the universe their king? Not even Israel.

Then the men of Israel said unto Gideon, "Rule thou over us, both thou and thy son, and thy son's son also, for thou hast delivered us from the hand of Midian."

And Gideon said unto them, "I will not rule over you, neither shall my son rule over you. The LORD shall rule over you." (Judg 8:22-23)

But Gideon does set himself up with a nice little retirement plan. He requests all the golden earrings plundered from the Ishmaelites be handed to him, and the children of Israel agree. The total amounts to 73 pounds weight of gold (33 kg). Gideon takes the treasure and creates an ephod from it – a religious artefact - which he sets up in the city of Ophrah. What could possibly go wrong? Before long Israel starts playing the harlot with this 'relic', a fact which doubtless troubles Gideon who, before he dies, perhaps senses the nation slipping once more back into idolatry. Small wonder.

The LORD's farmer-commander survives 40 years after his famous battle, riding high on his popularity as civic leader or 'judge' over the people. By the time he is laid to rest, Gideon has managed another noteworthy feat. He has fathered 70 sons and goodness knows how many daughters from an army of wives and concubines.[398] During his lifetime Israel remains at peace, no more troubled by Midian, Amalek or any other peripatetic, murderous

---

[398] A concubine is a female slave, mistress or lower social-order wife who cannot join the first division for political, class or religious reasons. While concubines often enjoyed the same privileges and recognition as a lord or chief's wife, they generally did not have dowries and did not inherit. In ancient cultures where children were considered a major blessing, leading figures often took concubines when a wife appeared to be barren. Abraham, Jacob, Gideon and Solomon are examples of leading biblical figures who had concubines. Later we will see pretenders to Israel's throne 'going into' the current king's concubines to send the message that they are now in control.

power. Yet trouble is already a-brewing for an unrepentant, idol-prone Israel. The cycle of sin is refreshed anon, and this time the problem will not come from without, but from the heart of Israel herself.

Trouble called Abimelech

Gideon has no ambition to be Israel's king, so he goes to his Maker in old age content that his 70 sons will ensure the survival and prosperity of his seed. But the mighty Jerubbaal has reckoned without one troublemaker whom he fathered by a pagan concubine from Shechem, and this son is very bad news indeed.

Abimelech's name means 'my father is king'. Some expositors make large of a purportedly backhanded reference to Gideon failing to take Israel's crown. In fact, as Jack Heyford points out, the first part of his name *ab*, 'My Father', refers to the LORD, and the second part, *'melech'* - (מלך) to the LORD's position as King in Israel.[399] It was Gideon's wish that Israel accepted God as King as well as LORD, yet not only did they fail to do so, but Abimelech, the one whose name celebrates God's patriarchy of Israel, is driven by an insatiable desire from the outset to be top dog himself in defiance of the LORD.

Though born to a Gentile concubine and thus a second-division son of Gideon, Abimelech realises he has an advantage over his fully Jewish siblings. As part-Jew part-Canaanite he will appeal to both constituencies. He wastes little time, and heads for Shechem to make contact with his mother's family, in order to gain support and press his case:

"Speak, I pray you, in the ears of all the men of Shechem, Whether it is better for you, either that all the sons of Jerubbaal [Gideon], **which are threescore and ten persons, reign over you, or that one reign over you? Remember also that I am your bone and your flesh."**

And his mother's brethren spake of him in the ears of all the men of Shechem all these words, and their hearts inclined to follow Abimelech, for they said, "He is our brother."

And they gave him threescore and ten pieces of silver out of the house of Baal Berith, wherewith Abimelech hired worthless and reckless persons which followed him. (Judg 9:2-4)

Shechem is a key city in central/northern Israel at this time due to its location on chief trade routes. Jacob's sons, Simeon and Levi, led

---

[399] Heyford, Jack, *Spirit-Filled Bible,* op. cit. p.360

the slaughter of the pagan male inhabitants centuries before after Dinah's defiling (Gen 34). Shechem has played an important role in Canaan's history thus far as an administrative centre, and is recorded in several archaeological discoveries, not least the Amarna Letters. Abimelech plays on his heritage and connection with this important political hub. Everyone is aware Israel needs a centralising figure like Gideon to unite the people against future marauders. What better than a son of the great Jerubbaal himself who appeals to both Jew and Canaanite? The men of Shechem agree and front Abimelech some starting cash from Satan's temple of Baal Berith. He uses this to hire a gang of likely boys. His next move is decisive and grisly:

And [Abimelech] **went unto his father's house at Ophrah and slew his brethren, the sons of Jerubbaal, being threescore and ten persons, upon one stone, notwithstanding yet Jotham the youngest son of Jerubbaal was left, for he hid himself.**

And all the men of Shechem gathered together, and all the house of Millo, and went and made Abimelech king by the plain of the pillar that was in Shechem. (Judg 9:5-6)

Consider where your heart would have to be to go back to your father's community, invade it with hired thugs, then take each of your step-brothers, one after the other, and execute them on a single stone. How often do we see a great generation immediately followed by a worthless one? How soon the miracle of Midian's defeat is forgotten, and it's business as usual with the petty squabbling, idolatry and behaviour which so offends the LORD.

Gideon's surviving son, Jotham ('God is perfect'), flees the area after prophesying Abimelech's downfall to the men of Shechem from Mount Gerizim. He warns them of the tyranny to come in what amounts to the first parable in the Bible given to the crowd below from a pulpit-type ledge on the side of the mountain (Judg 9:7-21). After that, Jotham heads for the hills in a hurry before Abimelech can nail him.

Abimelech's reign lasts three years, but soon wears thin for the region, and the men of Shechem in particular. Grumbles turn to active opposition. Abimelech attempts to quell the rebellion in the only way he knows how. He slaughters Shechem's inhabitants, demolishes the city and ploughs the ground with salt to ensure nothing grows there in the future. That'll do it. If you can't get your subjects to obey you, kill the lot. A thousand survivors flee to the pagan temple of Baal Berith and take refuge in the tower. Abimelech has his goons set fire to the structure and burns the remainder to death, fulfilling Jotham's prophecy.

God won't be pleased. Shechem was where Abraham built an altar to the LORD after YHWH appeared to him and confirmed the Land would belong to Abraham's descendants (Genesis 12:6-8) Abimelech's destruction of Shechem has been established by archaeologists at around 1100 BC.

Next stop for Abimelech: Therez, a neighbouring town which has also rebelled. The inhabitants all flee into a mighty tower too at that location and Abimelech sets about repeating the success of Shechem. He approaches the door to the tower to lay fire to immolate the occupants. It's his final mistake:

But a certain woman cast a piece of a millstone upon Abimelech's head, and all to brake his skull. Then he called hastily unto the young man, his armour-bearer, and said unto him, "Draw thy sword and slay me, that men say not of me, 'A woman slew him'." And his young man thrust him through and he died.

And when the men of Israel saw that Abimelech was dead, they departed every man unto his place. Thus God rendered the wickedness of Abimelech, which he did unto his father, in slaying his seventy brethren. And all the evil of the men of Shechem did God render upon their heads, and upon them came the curse of Jotham, the son of Jerubbaal. (Judg 9:53-57)

Abimelech's worthless life is often used as a warning to others over unbridled ambition, pointless materialism, might over right, and what happens when a man accedes to power without a godly sense of right and wrong. In Abimelech we see a parallel with *ha-Satan's* wish to **'be like the most High'.** Satan drives Abimelech to destroy his father's legacy and replace it with his own in the most destructive way possible, *and God lets him do it.* What better illustration of Abimelech's spiritual bankruptcy than his final, hopeless act? After receiving a mortal bash by the millstone, the most pressing thing on Abimelech's mind (apart from the stone) is the crime that posterity might remember him as the one killed by (gasp) *a woman.* In other words, Abimelech couldn't give a hoot about his coming judgment before the Father of Creation; the Earth Programme is all that matters.

God abhors murderers, especially killers of their own kin. In Abimelech's case, the only purpose of his life is to serve as a warning to others. Abimelech's lesson goes out to all dictators and ne'er-do-wells throughout history. You're all on God's clock, not your own. And when you are dead, you'll wish you were deader than you find yourself before the Great White Throne of YHWH Himself in the judgment. And this judgment is in the metacosm – *it is eternal.* "Vengeance is mine," saith the LORD. "I will repay." (Deut 32:35; Rom 12:19; Rev 20:11-15)

Note again the statements which characterise this most turbulent period in Israel's early history, the Time of the Judges:

1) There was no king in Israel
2) Everyone did what was right in his own eyes
3) God's Word was ignored
4) Judgment and bondage came from the LORD as a result of disobedience.

Israel finds herself staggering from one crisis to another, and all because she does not do what God commanded her to do in the first place. Instead of wiping out God's enemies as the LORD commanded, the children of Israel spared many to enslave them, treat with them, make peace with them, marry into them, have children with them, and adopt their gods and worship them. And even with all this, the Creator of the universe grieves at their predicament and forgives their sin over and over and over again. God wants repentance for His forgiveness.[400] He is the God of the second chance. And the third. And fourth. But if there is no repentance, judgment follows.

A good case of worms

There's an enigmatic two verses which follow Abimelech's disgraceful life:

And after Abimelech there arose to defend Israel Tola the son of Puah, the son of Dodo, a man of Issachar; and he dwelt in Shamir in Mount Ephraim. And he judged Israel twenty and three years, and died, and was buried in Shamir. (Judg 10:1-2)

That's all you get on Tola. Most who are even in this part of the OT these days perhaps just shrug and shuffle off to put the kettle on. Tola gets the page turned on him once more, and that's that. But we're learning by now that nothing is in the Message System by accident. Let's do a little digging.

The 'judge' Tola comes after Abimelech, so he's got a mess to clear up. Tola is the son of Puah ('Splendid'), who's the son of Dodo(!) ('Beloved one'). Tola's of the tribe of Issachar, yet he's put his roots down in Ephraim, a tribe characterized by hotheaded and oft-violent

[400] 2 Chron 7:14; Matt 18:21-22; Luke 13:3,5; 1 John 1:8-9, etc.

pride. Tola's name derives from *tola'ath,* which means 'worm'. Not too encouraging. Eschewing for a moment the flak Tola must have caught as a youngster (what parents would name their child 'worm'?), *tola'ath* is also used in the Bible to denote 'scarlet', which is much more interesting. Alfred Day (no relation) writes:

"*Tola'ath shani,* 'scarlet', is the scarlet-worm, *Cermes vermilio,* a scale-insect which feeds upon the oak, and which is used for producing a red dye. It is called by the Arabs *dudeh,* 'a worm', a word also used for various insect larvae. It is also called *qirmiz,* whence 'crimson' and the generic name *Cermes.* This scarlet-worm or scale-insect is one of the family *Coccidae* of the order *Rhynchota* or *Hemiptera.* The female is wingless and adheres to its favourite plant by its long, sucking beak, by which it extracts the sap on which it lives. After once attaching itself it remains motionless, and when dead its body shelters the eggs which have been deposited beneath it. The males, which are smaller than the females, pass through a complete metamorphosis and develop wings. The dye is made from the dried bodies of the females."[401]

All well and good, but so what? In the original OT Hebrew, *tola'ath* (worm) also implies crimson or scarlet due to its connection with the dye the worm produces when crushed. All this wormery takes on surreal significance when you discover that God refers to Himself as 'a worm' in Psalms 22, one of the most astonishing, prophetic passages in the Bible. The psalm is written by King David a thousand years before Christ, yet reads as if Jesus Christ Himself is dictating it from the cross. The psalm begins with the first words Yeshua utters on the cross, **"My God, My God, why hast thou forsaken Me?"** and ends with His final words before dying, **"That He has done this"**, or **"it is finished."** The beginning of Psalms 22 reads:

<<To the chief Musician upon Aijeleth Shahar, A Psalm of David.>>

My God, My God, why hast Thou forsaken Me? Why art Thou so far from helping Me and from the words of My roaring?

O my God, I cry in the daytime but Thou hearest not; and in the night season, and am not silent. But Thou art holy, O Thou that inhabitest the praises of Israel.

---

[401] www.bibletools.org/index.cfm/fuseaction/Def.show/RTD/isbe/ID/9237/ Worm-Scarlet-worm.htm#ixzz1uNwy5AFs

Our fathers trusted in Thee: they trusted, and Thou didst deliver them. They cried unto Thee and were delivered. They trusted in thee and were not confounded.

But I am a worm and no man; a reproach of men, and despised of the people.

All they that see me laugh Me to scorn: they shoot out the lip, they shake the head, saying, "He trusted on the LORD that He would deliver Him. Let Him deliver Him, seeing He delighted in Him." (Psa 22:1-8)

What better example of hyperspace distortion/prophecy than this? God provides David with time-warp intelligence of His own forthcoming crucifixion a thousand years hence, and goes on to reveal intimate details of His death a full five hundred years before crucifixion *was even invented* (by the Persians) as a method of execution. The phrase "**My God, My God, why hast Thou forsaken Me?"** is the only occasion in Yeshua's life when He does not call Him 'Father', but 'God'. Why? Because He is in our shoes as the Lamb's sacrifice for our sins. The two colours implied here are red (the blood) and white (the lamb's wool). The psalm even describes the mocking of the religious authorities watching Christ's execution close by: **"He trusted on the LORD that He would deliver Him. Let Him deliver Him, seeing He delighted in Him!"** Not a bad rendition of the gospel's actual recording of the event:

Likewise also the chief priests mocking him, with the scribes and elders, said, "He saved others, himself he cannot save. If he be the King of Israel, let him now come down from the cross and we will believe him. He trusted in God. Let Him deliver him now, if he will have him: for he said, 'I am the Son of God.' " (Matt 27:41-43)

In summary, in just one word - 'Tola' - we have Yeshua's redemptive mission summarised with an amazing metaphor *of a worm* over eleven hundred years before Christ is born! Jesus refers to Himself in Psa 22 as a *tola'ath,* a worm, brought to dust and reproach by the sins of the world. The worm is attached to the tree ('cross' – *cf:* Deut 21:23; Gal 3:13; Rom 8:3) and is used as a living sacrifice by its children, who partake of its body to survive (*cf.* the bread and wine. **"Take, eat, this is My body...."** (Matt 26:26). The crimson dye was even used to make priests' garments. How fitting that believers will be both kings and priests in the heavenly kingdom to come (**'Thy kingdom come...'** - *cf.* Rev 1:5-6). Jerry Ogles elaborates:

"The crimson worm is common to the region of old Israel and was used in the dyeing of garments to scarlet. The natural characteristics and life-cycle of this worm are noteworthy. When the crimson worm is prepared to reproduce offspring (and she does so only once in her life), she rigidly attaches herself to a tree or a wooden fencepost in such a way that she can never be removed without tearing her body completely apart. And when her young ones arrive, they feed upon the living body of the mother - a decidedly painful sacrifice. Then, when the young are able to survive apart from the mother, she dies. And as she dies, she exudes a scarlet dye which not only stains the tree but her young ones as well. Thus they are colored by the mother's scarlet dye and remain so for the remainder of their lives."[402]

In other words, they are 'covered by the blood' and live. The Designer summarises His timeless approach to the sin of His loved ones and their redemption thus:

"Come now and let us reason together," saith the LORD. "Though your sins be as scarlet, they shall be as white as snow. Though they be red like crimson, they shall be as wool." (Isa 1:18)

Jon Courson gives us some final wormy details:

"The female tola, when it reproduces, climbs to a branch of a tree and bears its eggs on it. When the eggs hatch and become larvae, they eat the body of the mother worm. The worm dies in the process, and a crimson spot is left in the branch of the tree. The scarlet/crimson spot then, after 3 or 4 days, dries out and changes color to a snow white color - and falls off/flakes away…."[403]

Only a Designer existing outside of time could include such detail. The blood on the cross is followed three days later by the white of redemption/resurrection/forgiveness, but the children have to make the first move. If the baby worms don't partake of their mother's sacrifice, they die. God goes on to summarise the plight of mankind in general and Israel in particular:

"If ye be willing and obedient, ye shall eat the good of the land. But if ye refuse and rebel, ye shall be devoured with the sword, for the mouth of the LORD hath spoken it." (Isa 1:19-20)

Isn't it also remarkable that Tola's Dad was 'Splendid', his grandfather was 'The beloved one', and Jesus, who referred to Himself as a worm ('tola'), is also called 'Wonderful' in Isaiah 9:6.

---

402 www.antioch.com.sg/cgi-bin/Agora-Pub/get/messageboard/148/4.html

403 www.joncourson.com

Yeshua also shows up as the Angel of the LORD in Judges 13:17-19 and gives His name as 'Wonderful' and does a 'wondrous thing' in taking up the sacrifice of Samson's father! [404]

Jephthah - hard man with a heart

After Tola comes the judge Jair, of which not much is known other than he was wealthy. And then, you guessed it, the sin cycle repeats:

And the children of Israel did evil again in the sight of the LORD, and served Baalim, and Ashtaroth, and the gods of Syria, and the gods of Zidon, and the gods of Moab, and the gods of the children of Ammon, and the gods of the Philistines, and forsook the LORD, and served not Him. (Judg 10:6)

This time God sells Israel into the hands of the Philistines to the west and Ammonites to the east. The oppression lasts 18 years. Ammon loosely correlates to areas of modern-day Jordan. The capital of the Ammonites was Rabbath Ammon, known today as Amman, the capital of Jordan. The Philistines are a people whose origins are shrouded in mystery. Some scholars maintain that they originated from the Aegean isles or even Crete or Cyprus as part of a confederation of 'Sea Peoples' who afflicted Egypt during the 19th and 20th dynasties; others that they were a warlike people who hailed from early Mizraic Egypt. Dr Bryant Wood contends that Israel's most implacable Iron Age enemy may have been the Cretan Minoans under a different name, which is noteworthy since Philistine pottery finds appear similar.[405]

The Philistines are mentioned in the Bible as early as Abraham's era, so are already in their territory by the time of the Exodus (Gen 21:32; 26:1) Dr Chuck Missler agrees with an early Levant settlement for the Philistines:

"The Philistines were originally from Mizraim (Egypt); (Deut 2:23; Gen 10:13, 14, from Caphtor, originally the northern delta of the Nile, from which the Phoenicians emigrated to Asia). Crete was an intermediate resting place and gave rise to the legends as their source. Tacitus (Hist., 5:2) says 'the inhabitants of Palestine came from Crete.' The time of migration must have been very early as the Philistines were

---

[404] NKJV and NIV translations. KJV uses the word 'secret' instead of 'wonderful'.

[405] http://christiancadre.blogspot.co.uk/2006/03/philistines-minoans-and-patriarchs.html

settled in Palestine in Abraham's time (Gen. 21:32,34). Their immigration to the neighborhood of Gerar in the south country was before Abraham's time, for he deals with them as a pastoral tribe there (Gen 21:32,84; 26:1,8).

"*Philistiym* means immigrants, from the Ethiopic *fallasa*. Philistia is derived from the Ethiopic *falasa* 'to emigrate', Hebrew *palash*, 'wander'. (In the W. of Abyssinia are the Falashas, i.e., emigrants, probably Israelites from Palestine.) The Romans later deliberately named the region Palestina (Latin for Philistines) after the enemies of the Jews, in an attempt to erase their memory. Thanks to the British, they almost succeeded.

"By the time of the Exodus, the Philistines had become formidable (Ex 13:17; 15:14). At Israel's invasion of Canaan they had advanced north and fully possessed the seacoast plain from the river of Egypt (el Arish) to Ekron in the N. (Josh 15:4,47), a confederacy of the five cities (originally Canaanite) Gaza (the leading one), Ashdod, Ashkelon, Gath, and Ekron (always put last).

"The Shephelah plain was famed for its fertility in grain, vines and olives (Judg 15:5), so that it was the refuge from times of famine (2 Kgs 8:2; compare Gen 26:12). It suited war chariots, while the low hills of the Shephelah afforded sites for fortresses.

"[Philistia] was the commercial thoroughfare between Phoenicia and Syria to the north and Egypt and Arabia in the south. Ashdod and Gaza were the keys of Egypt, and the latter was the depot of Arabian produce. The term 'Canaan' (merchant) applied to the Philistine land (Zeph 2:5) and proves its commercial character. They sold Israelites as slaves to Edom and Greece, for which God threatens retribution in kind, and destruction (Amos 1:6-8; Joel 3:3-8). They were proficient in smelting iron; they had so subjugated Israel as to outlaw all smiths and indigenous iron workers (1 Sam 13:19). They sometimes burned their prisoners alive (Judg 15:6; Psa 78:63). Their speech differed from the Jews' language (Neh 13:23,24)." [406]

The Ammonites and Philistines then: a formidable enemy for Israel. One can only imagine the grisly goings-on for those who dared oppose these professional hard-men. Israel would need someone special to deliver them. Of course, that will be their Creator, to whom they eventually cry out. But this time it looks like God is not interested.

---

[406] www.khouse.org, *Judges notes*, p.104

And the children of Israel cried unto the LORD, saying, "We have sinned against Thee, both because we have forsaken our God and also served Baal<u>**im**</u>**!** [plural - multiple Baals/Satans]"

And the LORD said unto the children of Israel, "Did not I deliver you from the Egyptians, and from the Amorites, from the children of Ammon, and from the Philistines? The Zidonians also and the Amalekites and the Maonites did oppress you, and ye cried to Me and I delivered you out of their hand. Yet ye have forsaken Me and served other gods. <u>**Wherefore I will deliver you no more**</u>**. Go and cry unto the gods ye have chosen! Let them deliver you in the time of your tribulation!"** (Judg 10:10-14)

Even to a people as jaded as Israel, God's declaration that He's finished and won't come to their aid must have pulled them up short. There's an intriguing insight into the Creator's character here. Like any father at the end of his tether with a perpetually misbehaving child, God says, "That's it! I'm not going to help you any more! Suffer what you must suffer!" Though fathers don't usually mean it, it's a way of snapping the miscreants back to sense. I particularly like YHWH telling them to run to the gods they have chosen to see if they will help them (*cf.* Isa 8:19; 41:22-24). Echoes of Gideon's Dad, Joash, defending his son's destruction of the Baal altar against the townsfolk:

"Will ye plead for Baal? Will ye save him? He that will plead for him, let him be put to death whilst it is yet morning. If [Baal] **be a god,** <u>**let him plead for himself because one hath cast down his altar**</u>**."**

Therefore on that day he called [Gideon] **Jerubbaal, saying, "Let Baal plead against him because he hath thrown down his altar."** (Judg 6:31-32)

Eventually, like any father who loves his child, the constant bleating for forgiveness softens God's heart, but He is TICKED OFF.

And the children of Israel said unto the LORD, "We have sinned. Do Thou unto us whatsoever seemeth good unto Thee. Deliver us only, we pray thee, this day!"

And they put away the strange gods from among them and served the LORD. <u>**And His soul was grieved for the misery of Israel**</u>**.** (Judg 10:15-16)

Did you know God grieves? Jack Heyford comments that the Hebrew of the last phrase can equally be translated **"The plight of Israel became intolerable to Him"**, giving the added dimension of God's intransigence with sin.

Anyway, a champion is needed, but who?

Then the children of Ammon were gathered together and encamped in Gilead. And the children of Israel assembled themselves together and encamped in Mizpeh. And the people and princes of Gilead said one to another, "What man is he that will begin to fight against the children of Ammon? He shall be head over all the inhabitants of Gilead." (Judg 10:17-18)

Gilead is a Biblical term often used in the OT to describe the land east of the Jordan river, wherein the tribes of Reuben, Gad and half of Manasseh settled following the wilderness wanderings and destruction of the Amorite giants Sihon and Og. The Israelites have no leader, at least no-one of Gideon or Barak's stature. What can be done?

As before, God raises up the unlikeliest of heroes, this time one Jephthah, son of a man also known as Gilead. Unlike his brothers and sisters, Jephthah is born on the wrong side of the tracks, the result of a liaison between Dad and a prostitute. As a result, Jephthah catches a great deal of stick from his siblings, is no doubt constantly picked on and beaten up, and eventually told he shall have no inheritance in his father's house because he's a whore's whelp. Nice.

Jephthah's domestic situation becomes so intolerable that he flees home and hearth. The townsfolk want him gone in any case, indicating that Jephthah's parentage has become a religious/legal/tribal issue (Judg 11:7). Apparently not even his father stops his departure. Put yourself in Jephthah's shoes. Angry, upset, rejected, worthless, *up for a fight,* Jephthah heads out to the land of Tob,[407] where his evident aptitude for leadership and punch-ups attracts a gang of reckless adventurers, who go out under his command and raid the surrounding pagans. If you've not been given, you learn to take, and Jephthah and his merry men help themselves at the point of a sword. Jephthah manifestly makes a name for himself as a roughneck leader for, in no short order…

…when the children of Ammon made war against Israel, the elders of Gilead went to fetch Jephthah out of the land of Tob. And they said unto Jephthah, "Come, be our captain, that we may fight with the children of Ammon."

And Jephthah said unto the elders of Gilead, "Did not ye hate me and expel me out of my father's house?" And why are ye come unto me now when ye are in distress?"

---

[407] Identified with the mountainous region of north-west Jordan, south-east of the Sea of Galilee.

And the elders of Gilead said unto Jephthah, "Therefore we turn again to thee now, that thou mayest go with us and fight against the children of Ammon, and be our head over all the inhabitants of Gilead."

And Jephthah said unto the elders of Gilead, "If ye bring me home again to fight against the children of Ammon, and the LORD deliver them before me, shall I be your head?"

And the elders of Gilead said unto Jephthah, "The LORD be witness between us, if we do not so according to thy words." (Judg 11:5-10)

Which tells us something about Jephthah. He is willing to forgive and return to defend his people, but ensures he'll be given control of the region if successful. We also learn that Jephthah, though a roughrider with attitude, is remarkably a man of the LORD. He makes clear to the sheep on the city council *that YHWH will be the one who delivers them*. The reaction of Jephthah's own family to the return of the black sheep as commander of the entire army and potential saviour of Gilead, alas, goes unrecorded, but it is not unprecedented. Remember Joseph's rejection by his family, whose kin sold him into slavery, only for Joseph to ascend to the dizzying heights of Egyptian statehood years later by the LORD's hand. Or Yeshua Himself, rejected by his own people, even by some in His family (Psa 69).

Jephthah soon turns in another surprise. While getting a huge army tooled up and ready for the Ammonites, he remarkably sends messengers to the king of Ammon *to see if hostilities can be settled peaceably* (Judg 11:12). Not only is this a Torah requirement in dealing with peoples 'afar off' (Deut 20:10-18), as a fighting man Jephthah recognises the true tragedy of war, unlike armchair generals who rush in where angels fear to tread and count not the cost of war.

His messengers respectfully ask the King of Ammon what they have against Jephthah and why they want to fight against him in his own land.

The king replies: "Because Israel took away my land when they came up out of Egypt, from Arnon even unto Jabbok, and unto Jordan. Now therefore restore those lands again peaceably."

In return, Jephthah gives the king of Ammon a lesson in real history. Israel did not take away the land of Moab, nor the land of the people of Ammon. When the children of Israel came out of Egypt, Moses repeatedly requested permission for his huge following to pass through the lands of the various tribes they encountered. The king of Edom would not consent, nor the king of Moab. Nevertheless Moses respected their territories and did not violate their sovereignty. He requested passage through the land of Sihon, king of the Amorites - *land which Sihon had originally taken from Moab.* The giant Sihon not only refused passage to the children of Israel but called up his army and fought against them. God delivered Sihon and his Amorites into Israel's hand, so now this Amorite territory, which once belonged to Moab, belongs to Israel. Jephthah points out that even over the past 300 years, no-one has contested Israel's right to Gilead, not even Balak and the other kings of Moab, until now. The fact is, the LORD gave Israel the land in victory, so in fighting against Israel, the king of Ammon is, in effect, fighting against the Creator of the universe. Case closed. (Judg 11:14-27)

All of which falls on deaf ears in royal Rabbath Ammon. So Jephthah prepares his army for battle and makes a battlefield vow, which he probably should not have done.

Jephthah's daughter

Battlefield vows were common enough in the old days and were a way of soliciting God's help to your cause. We will encounter some astonishing ones as the *Origins* series proceeds. Vows are voluntary oaths you take, but the LORD expects you to keep them - even today. In a marriage ceremony, or when taking a civic position, the Bible (Message System) is used for the applicants to swear their oath upon. As time progresses and our godless society takes firmer hold, God and the Bible are outlawed in favour of swearing your vow... before a human (registrar, company board, etc.), but on what? A battered copy of *Moby Dick?* Back in Jephthah's day, these vows were taken in deadly earnest. Jephthah swears to God as follows:

"If Thou shalt without fail deliver the children of Ammon into mine hands, then it shall be that whatsoever cometh forth of the doors of my house to meet me, when I return in peace from the children of Ammon, shall surely be the LORD'S, and I will offer it up for a burnt offering." (Judg 11:30-31)

That having been done, Jephthah leads his army to war and hours later, the king of Ammon is routed. Later, twenty Ammonite cities are taken and the enemy's army slaughtered in the subsequent flight and clean-up. And then comes the heartbreak:

And Jephthah came to Mizpeh unto his house, and, behold, his daughter came out to meet him with timbrels and with dances. And she was his only child; beside her he had neither son nor daughter.

And it came to pass, when he saw her, that he rent his clothes and said, "Alas, my daughter! Thou hast brought me very low, and thou art one of them that trouble me, for I have opened my mouth unto the LORD and I cannot go back." (Judg 11:34-35)

It's a plot-crash moment. No violence of battle, no rejection by his own family could have struck Jephthah harder than that moment. Scholars have debated this scene for centuries, wondering whether Jephthah really sacrificed his daughter to God as a burnt offering. Many expositors today maintain that he did. Let's look further. Jack Heyford writes:

"Jephthah's home may have been planned to accommodate both families and livestock. A two-floor home from this period has been excavated. Archaeologists have suggested that one ground-floor room served as an entrance vestibule and another as a stairwell, while the other ground-floor rooms were probably used for storage and animals. If Jephthah's home had been constructed in this manner, it would have been possible for an animal, rather than his daughter, to come out first."[408]

Now let's see the daughter's reaction:

"And she said unto him, "My father, if thou hast opened thy mouth unto the LORD, do to me according to that which hath proceeded out of thy mouth, for the LORD hath taken vengeance for thee of thine enemies, even of the children of Ammon."

And she said unto her father, "Let this thing be done for me. Let me alone two months, that I may go up and down upon the mountains <u>and bewail my virginity</u>, I and my fellows."

And he said, "Go." And he sent her away for two months, and she went with her companions and <u>bewailed her virginity upon the mountains</u>.

And it came to pass at the end of two months that she returned unto her father, who did with her according to his vow which he had vowed, <u>and she knew no man....</u> (Judg 11:36-39)

Some intriguing questions:

1. Was God to blame for Jephthah's oath?
2. Was Jephthah daft enough to make his vow knowing a human might be the first to greet him?
3. What if a pig or other unclean animal came out first? Would he sacrifice that to the LORD?

---

[408] Heyford, Jack, *Spirit-Filled Bible,* op. cit. p.367

4. What right would Jephthah have to sacrifice the life of, say, a neighbour's child or visiting stranger who was in his house and came out upon his return?
5. Did he *actually* sacrifice his daughter?

In the verse before he makes his vow, the scriptures state that **the Spirit of the LORD came upon Jephthah** (Judg 11:29). Does God bear the blame for what Jephthah subsequently swears, as some scholars insist? The God-hating brigade often use this passage as an example of a misogynistic Deity having it in for women. Poor virgin, strapped to a blazing pyre, imaginations run riot; but hold your horses for a moment. God would have known Jephthah was going to make this vow from the foundation of the world, there's no getting out from under God's omniscience, yet mankind has free will. James Patrick Holding states that if you study other passages in the Bible where the Spirit of the LORD influences a human to do something, the details of the influenced action are mentioned *immediately after*. Holding cites the following examples:

But when they cried out to the LORD, he raised up for them a deliverer, Othniel son of Kenaz, Caleb's younger brother, who saved them. THE SPIRIT OF THE LORD CAME UPON HIM, so that he became Israel's judge and went to war. The LORD gave Cushan-Rishathaim, king of Aram, into the hands of Othniel, who overpowered him. (Judg 3:9-10, NIV)

THEN THE SPIRIT OF THE LORD CAME UPON GIDEON, and he blew a trumpet, summoning the Abiezrites to follow him. (Judg 6:34, NIV)

THE SPIRIT OF THE LORD CAME UPON HIM IN POWER, so that he tore the lion apart with his bare hands as he might have torn a young goat. But he told neither his father nor his mother what he had done. (Judg 14:6, NIV)

THEN THE SPIRIT OF THE LORD CAME UPON HIM IN POWER. He went down to Ashkelon, struck down thirty of their men, stripped them of their belongings and gave their clothes to those who had explained the riddle. Burning with anger, he went up to his father's house. (Judg 14:19, NIV)

As he approached Lehi, the Philistines came toward him shouting. THE SPIRIT OF THE LORD CAME UPON HIM IN POWER. The ropes on his arms became like charred flax, and the bindings dropped from his hands. (Judg 15:14, NIV)

Now let's examine Jephthah's anointing:

THEN THE SPIRIT OF THE LORD CAME UPON JEPHTHAH, and he passed over Gilead, and Manasseh, and passed over Mizpeh of Gilead, and from Mizpeh of Gilead he passed over unto the children of Ammon. (Judg 11:29)

Holding comments:

"If the Spirit of the Lord inspired Jephthah to do anything at all, it was to go travelling around recruiting his army to go to war with the Ammonites. The fact that the vow is reported separately indicates that it was not something done under the Spirit of the Lord at all."[409]

Those who aver that Jephthah committed some ghastly human sacrifice have no grasp of Judaism or basic text comprehension. Firstly, human sacrifice and the shedding of innocent blood are an abomination to the LORD. In the strongest possible terms, God hates and condemns those who 'put their children through the fire' in sacrifice to Molech (Lev 18:21; 20:1-5; Deut 12:31; 18:10). We know Jephthah has a sound grasp of Jewish history since he has just got through lecturing the Ammonite king on that very subject. We therefore assume Jephthah knows Mosaic Law and would certainly not wish to incur God's wrath prior to a battle, for which he has entreated the LORD's favour. Chuck Missler gives other reasons:

"It's doubtful that Jephthah's friends and neighbors would have permitted him to slay his own (and only) daughter in order to fulfil a foolish vow. (King Saul's soldiers didn't let him kill his son Jonathan, who had violated his father's foolish vow (1 Samuel 14:24-46).) Where would Jephthah offer his daughter as a sacrifice? The LORD only accepted sacrifices at the Tabernacle altar (Lev 17:1-9), and they had to be offered by the Levitical priests. He would have to travel to Shiloh to fulfil his vow (Deut 16:2, 6, 11, 16). It's doubtful that even the most unspiritual priest would offer a human sacrifice on the sanctified altar. Furthermore, it is unlikely that Jephthah would have gone to Shiloh, since it lies in the territory of the Ephraimites, with whom there was a deadly feud (Judg 12:1-6). Such a trip would certainly have yielded some comment in the text. And even if a priest did offer Jephthah's daughter as a burnt offering, the sacrifice would not be acceptable: a burnt offering had to be a male (Lev 13:10).

"When Jephthah would have arrived at Shiloh, he would have learned from any priest that *paying the proper amount of money could have redeemed his daughter* (Lev 27:1-8). As a successful soldier just returning

---

[409] www.tektonics.org/gk/jepthah.html

from looting the enemy, Jephthah could easily have paid the redemption price. Jephthah was a pious man (v.11); none of this is consistent with the presentation of him in the text." [410]

In fact, the problem is cleared up by one conjunction in the text - a *waw* ('vav'), which can mean either 'and' or 'or'. Jephthah's vow to God should be translated:

"If Thou shalt without fail deliver the children of Ammon into mine hands, then it shall be that whatsoever cometh forth of the doors of my house to meet me, when I return in peace from the children of Ammon, shall surely be the LORD'S, <u>or</u> I will offer it up for a burnt offering." (Judg 11:30-31)

Other inconsistencies slot into place. If Jephthah's daughter really thought she was going to be carved and kindled as a sacrificial offering, I'm certain her virginity would be the last thing on her mind to bewail. All this business of her bewailing her virginity points to her being 'set aside' for future service to the LORD according to Lev 27:2-8. In fact, under these conditions, rabbis generally understood 'setting aside' to mean just that - the person or animal becomes holy and is no longer put to human/animal work.[411] As a woman's work includes child-bearing, this effectively sentences Jephthah's daughter to a life of celibacy and spinsterhood which, by implication, means Jephthah has unwisely condemned his own line to extinction, her being his only daughter. We see exactly this being expressed in the summary of her fate, **<u>and she knew no man....</u>** (Judg 11:39)

In fact, there's an even more disturbing aspect to this story few commentators remark upon. Jephthah's daughter cannot have been unmindful of the very public vow her father swore prior to carving up the Ammonites. *Does she purposely ensure that she will be first out of the door,* barging all animals aside, upon her father's victorious return? She certainly sees to it that everyone in the neighbourhood knows she's there with her public show of timbrels and dances. News of her father's victory would have swept the region days prior to his return, so she would be ready. James Holding concurs:

"Since Jephthah's daughter knew of the vow and knew what it meant, her coming from the house first was no tragic accident, but something done intentionally. Why? [Pamela] Reis hypothesizes - I think correctly - that Jephthah's daughter was a 'spoiled child' who saw the

---

[410] www.khouse.org, *Judges notes*

[411] www.tektonics.org/gk/jepthah.html

vow as a way for her not to be given away in marriage to some other household, remain the sole object of her father's affections, and - I would add - also become sole inheritor of her father's property. Signs of Jephthah's deference in this regard are not difficult to discern. Of course, many are familiar with the motif of an only daughter as a spoiled princess; strong signs of this do appear in the text.

"In contrast to his questioning of adult rivals with 'why' challenges (11:7, 11:26, 12:3), Jephthah does not ask his daughter why she did what she did. Additionally, note again her words in Judges 11:36, where several times she emphasizes that it was Jephthah's own words, and his own vow, that lay behind what happened. In essence, this says, 'If something has gone wrong here, it's your fault for making the vow.' "[412]

Deep waters indeed. What does God intend us to learn from this incident? That God takes all vows and commitments seriously, and we choose not to honour these at our peril. To both Jephthah and his daughter's credit, they both acquiesce to the vow in a peaceable, mature manner. We can have little understanding of what Jephthah must have gone through emotionally, yet isn't it remarkable that YHWH sets the stage for Jephthah to blow off steam almost immediately after this heartbreak over what has to be one of the most foolish things an Israelite tribe has done thus far.

War with Ephraim

Jephthah abruptly finds himself confronted by the notorious, angry tribe of Ephraim at Zaphon: [413] "You went across the Jordan to fight the Ammonites and did not call us? We will burn your house down with you inside it!"

Nice. The Ephraimites are pulling an old stunt, hankering after Ammonite booty without risking their necks to earn it. Ephraim are the bullyboys on the block, but they've met their match. You may recall the occasion when the men of Ephraim got funny with Gideon for not including their tribe in the initial '300' deception action. Gideon flattered them for their subsequent prowess in capturing the Midianite princes Oreb and Zeeb. Ephraim's anger was thus assuaged. Notice that Jephthah attempted a diplomatic settlement

[412] Ibid.

[413] The original tribe of Joseph is divided into two sub-tribes: Manasseh and Ephraim. 'Ephraim' becomes a collective, catch-all phrase referring to the 'northern tribes', which come to be known as 'the House of Israel', as distinct from Judah and Benjamin to the south, which come to be known as 'the House of Judah'.

with the Ammonites but doesn't bother with Ephraim. There's no point reasoning with unreasonable people. There has been a longstanding antagonism between the tribes west of the Jordan and those of Gilead (Transjordan, comprising Reuben, Gad and half of Manasseh), since the western tribes feel that those east of the Jordan have not been pulling their full weight in setting up Israel proper. This is alluded to in Ephraim's comment in Judg 12:4. But the bullyboys are reckoning without the hand of God, and they certainly fail to measure the man they are up against. Jephthah's eyes turn into slits:

"I and my people were at great strife with the children of Ammon, and when I called you, ye delivered me not out of their hands. And when I saw that ye delivered me not, I put my life in my hands and passed over against the children of Ammon, <u>and the LORD delivered them into my hand</u>. Why then are ye come up unto me this day to fight against me?" (Judg 12:2-3)

Jephthah again gives God the credit for the Ammonite victory, in effect implying that Ephraim was not required. Ephraim had not responded to Gilead's plight *throughout the previous 18 years,* why now? Jephthah knows what they're after and gives them scant time to contemplate their folly before gathering his Gilead forces and falling upon them. Ticked off over the matter of his beloved daughter, Jephthah's in a mood to crack heads. The slaughter is great and the surviving Ephraimites flee to the Jordan in an attempt to re-cross the river to their homeland. The problem is, every ford they reach is now in the possession of Jephthah's granite-faced hardmen. They're trapped.

As each Ephraimite arrives and approaches the blockade, they cry, "Let me cross over!"

Jephthah's guards close in. "Are you an Ephraimite?"

"No!" they lie.

"Good, then you won't mind saying the password 'Shibboleth' ['stream', 'river', 'Ear of grain']."

"All right. 'Sibboleth'."

An Ephraimite cannot pronounce the 'sh' syllable due to his tribal accent. It's a dead giveaway. As soon as the fugitive is unmasked, he's dragged into the river and killed. The lesson? If people don't know who you are when you're silent, they certainly will when you open your mouth.[414] Forty-two thousand Ephraimites are slaughtered during this action; a further indication, if one were necessary, of how far Israel has fallen from God's ideal, and how disparate the tribes have become.

It's the last we hear of Jephthah. He judges Israel a further six years before passing away. He does crop up in the Hebrews Hall of Faith, though, in the NT alongside Deborah, Barak, Gideon and Samson (Heb 11:32). Another mark of his legacy survives to this day. The word 'shibboleth' in the English language refers to a codeword or distinguishing trait of a particular group.

The coming of the wild Nazirite

Three minor judges follow Jephthah over the next 25 years - Ibzan, Elon and Abdon - yet the Philistines grow as a major threat in the west during these years. No pork beans for guessing the reason:

And the children of Israel did evil again in the sight of the LORD; and the LORD delivered them into the hand of the Philistines forty years. (Judg 13:1)

The sin cycle repeats, but it's a little different this time. We are told that the Philistines dominate Israel for forty years, yet not once during this period does Israel cry out to be delivered. The truth is, Israel's enduring a contented compromise and apostasy under her overlords, and everyone's mucking along just fine. This doesn't stop YHWH from casting around for a deliverer to get His nation back onside. This time, He picks one from the womb.[415] Everyone's heard of this wild man, but Samson's life has come to symbolise blown opportunities and a betrayal of God - a lesson many of us feel uncomfortable in heeding today in our own contented apostasy. Dr Peter Pett writes:

"The Philistine aristocracy were established in many towns and were so hated that they had themselves constantly to be on guard, and as a result they would react violently to any attempt to undermine them. Because of this it was indeed difficult to see how they could be attacked

---

[414] Yeshua says: **"For by thy words thou shalt be justified, and by thy words thou shalt be condemned."** (Matt 12:37). Simon Peter had the same problem with his accent when he denied Yeshua (Matt 26:73-74).

[415] Other servants of God chosen before birth include Isaac, Samuel, Jeremiah, John the Baptist, the Apostle Paul and Yeshua Himself, indicating God's intimate involvement with a baby's fortunes prior to birth. (*cf:* 1 Sam 1; Jer 1:4-5; Gal 1:15; Luke 1). How then to reconcile with today's pagan ritual of abortion?

in any way, for they held all in iron control under a kind of martial law and reacted violently. Any disobedience would have been stamped on, and any reaction or retaliation severely dealt with. The country that they controlled was held in thrall. But God raised up a kind of one-man army by the name of Samson, an Israelite aristocrat (a judge of Israel) who mingled with the Philistine aristocracy, probably welcomed by them because of his status and phenomenal strength. And he developed his own way of attacking the Philistines, and did so in such a way that no repercussions were brought upon his own people. Indeed by the time of his death, the Philistines had been severely weakened as a result of [Samson's] activities." [416]

Samson starts promisingly enough.

And there was a certain man of Zorah, of the family of the Danites, whose name was Manoah; and his wife was barren and bare not. And the Angel of the LORD [Yeshua] **appeared unto the woman and said unto her, "Behold now, thou art barren and bearest not, but thou shalt conceive and bear a son. Now therefore beware, I pray thee, and drink not wine nor strong drink, and eat not any unclean thing, for, lo, thou shalt conceive and bear a son. And no razor shall come on his head, <u>for the child shall be a Nazarite unto God from the womb</u>, and he shall begin to deliver Israel out of the hand of the Philistines."** (Judg 13:2-5)

The woman wastes no time in telling her husband of the heavenly visitation. Manoah goes on his knees before the LORD, requesting the Angel appear to them again with instructions on what they should do for the child. *www.gotquestions.org* explains:

"The Nazirite/Nazarite vow is taken by individuals who have voluntarily dedicated themselves to God. The vow is a decision, action, and desire on the part of people whose desire is to yield themselves to God completely. By definition, the Hebrew word *nazir*, simply means 'to be separated or consecrated'. The Nazirite vow, which appears in Numbers 6:1-21; has five features. It is voluntary, can be done by either men or women, has a specific time frame, has specific requirements and restrictions, and at its conclusion a sacrifice is offered." [417]

Only three people are mentioned in scripture who can be described as life-long Nazirites - Samson, Samuel, and John the Baptist. Interestingly, all are born to women who were barren

---

[416] www.angelfire.com/ok/bibleteaching/judges5.html
[417] www.gotquestions.org/Nazirite-vow.html

(Manoah's wife, Hannah and Elizabeth). Later the Angel of the LORD (Yeshua) re-appears to the woman, this time in the fields. Her husband is absent, so the wife fetches him. Manoah inspects the visitor and has no idea who He is:

"Art thou the man that spakest unto the woman?" And He said, "I am." (Judg 13:11).

It's a trademark response from Yeshua to Abraham (Gen 15:1) and to Moses at the burning bush incident. God's name is YAHWEH, YHWH, "I AM THAT I AM" (Exo 3:14). In fact, a study of the 'I AM' statements of God/Christ is very instructive. In the Psalms, widely viewed as prophetic of Jesus, there are seven 'I AM' statements which, on a *sod* interpretive level, describe the *Mashiach* (Messiah) as a suffering servant, and speak of His humanity and mission 'in our shoes':

"I am a worm and no man." (Psa 22:6)
"I am poor and needy." (Psa 40:17)
"I am... a stranger unto my brethren." (Psa 69:8)
"I am full of heaviness." (Psa 69:20)
"I am poor and sorrowful." (Psa 69:29)
"I... am as a sparrow alone on the rooftop." (Psa 102:7)
"I am withered like grass." (Psa 102:11)

Conversely, there are seven I AM statements made by Yeshua in the fourth gospel in the NT which speak of His godly nature and mission:

"I am the bread of life." (FG 6:35)
"I am the light of the world." (FG 8:12)
"I am the door." (FG 10:7)
"I am the good shepherd." (FG 10:11,14)
"I am the resurrection and the life." (FG 11:25)
"I am the way, the truth and the life." (FG 14:6)
"I am the true vine." (FG 15:1,5)

You start to notice God responding "I AM" to questions posed to Him throughout the Message System, including this incident with Samson's father. Each is a fascinating *remez,* a hint of something deeper. Remember that famous exchange between the Jewish leaders and Jesus in the NT? Note the tense in Yeshua's response, indicating His eternal nature.

Then said the Jews unto Him, "Thou art not yet fifty years old, and hast thou seen Abraham?"

Jesus said unto them, "Verily, verily, I say unto you, Before Abraham was, I AM." (FG 8:57-58)

The Jews in this incident are under no illusions that Yeshua is claiming to be the God of the burning bush, and they take up stones to murder Him. Jesus Christ, the human manifestation of the Creator, inhabits the entire Old Testament (Luke 24:44; FG 5:39; Heb 10:7). Here's another example in the Samson story, in which Manoah still thinks he's dealing with a human prophet of some sort:

And Manoah said unto the Angel of the LORD, "I pray thee, let us detain thee until we shall have made ready a kid for thee."

And the Angel of the LORD said unto Manoah, "Though thou detain Me, I will not eat of thy bread. And if thou wilt offer a burnt offering, thou must offer it unto the LORD." For Manoah knew not that he was an Angel of the LORD.

And Manoah said unto the Angel of the LORD, "What is thy name, that <u>when</u> [not if!] **thy sayings come to pass we may do thee honour?"**

And the Angel of the LORD said unto him, "Why askest thou thus after My name, seeing it is <u>secret</u>?" (Judg 13:15-18)

It's an extraordinary reply. The Hebrew word *phlai* from the root *pala* (Strongs #6381) means 'wonderful', 'marvellous', 'secret', 'unfathomable', 'beyond understanding'. The King James translates the word as 'secret', while other translations, including the New King James, use the more appropriate (in my view) 'wonderful'. The word root is used in the context of identifying the coming *Mashiach* in Isaiah 9:6-7:

For unto us a child is born, unto us a son is given: <u>and the government shall be upon His shoulder</u>, <u>and his name shall be called Wonderful</u>, Counsellor, The mighty God, The everlasting Father, The Prince of Peace. Of the increase of His government and peace there shall be no end, upon the throne of David, and upon his kingdom, to order it, and to establish it with judgment and with justice from henceforth even forever. The zeal of the LORD of hosts will perform this. (Isa 9:6-7)

When has Earth's government ever been on Yeshua's shoulder? The answer is, it hasn't yet. When we pray "Thy Kingdom come…" we are praying for the coming thousand-year ('Millennial') world order when God Himself sets up His physical rule on Earth on David's throne after the mess of the Great Tribulation. *Ha-Satan* will attempt to thwart and counterfeit this rule with the coming of his Antichrist and False Prophet, but to no avail. Notice Hitler also attempted to inaugurate a thousand-year Reich, leading many to believe at the time that he was the Antichrist.

For unto us a child is born [human], **unto us a son is given** [God's Son, divine]. We get a fascinating glimpse of the fully divine, fully human nature of Yeshua through Isaiah centuries before He is born. The King James translates the above passage as: **And the Angel of the LORD said unto him, "Why askest thou thus after My name, seeing it is secret?"** (Judg 13:15-18), which raises the question of the secret name of God alluded to in the book of Revelation (Rev 3:12; 19:12). These are some of the fascinating enigmas we will study in *Origins VI – Parousia.* Let's get back to Samson:

So Manoah took a kid with a meat offering and offered it upon a rock unto the LORD, and the Angel did wondrously, and Manoah and his wife looked on.

For it came to pass, when the flame went up toward Heaven from off the altar, that the Angel of the LORD ascended in the flame of the altar. And Manoah and his wife looked on it and fell on their faces to the ground. (Judg 13:19-20)

Here's another hyperdimensional event which must have been quite a sight. Notice this Angel receives the burnt offering, ascending with it. Regular angels don't do that. The scene has a stupefying effect on the couple, as Yeshua intends. Expositors see this event as anticipatory of the resurrection of Jesus Christ.

But the Angel of the LORD did no more appear to Manoah and to his wife. Then Manoah knew that he was an Angel of the LORD. And Manoah said unto his wife, "We shall surely die because we have seen God."

But his wife said unto him, "If the LORD were pleased to kill us, He would not have received a burnt offering and a meat offering at our hands, neither would He have shewed us all these things, nor would as at this time have told us such things as these." (Judg 13:21-23)

Manoah is being scriptural in fearing God might destroy them (Exo 33:20; Deut 18:16), but his wife steps in and once again we have a woman thinking clearly. She sensibly grounds him by pointing out that having a son and raising him will be quite tricky if they're *struck dead* by the One who just blessed them.

And the woman bare a son and called his name Samson. And the child grew and the LORD blessed him. (Judg 13:24)

Samson's name ***shimshown*** **שמשון** is derived from *shemesh,* sunshine. The LORD makes a special point of blessing Samson alone out of all the Judges. Though Sunshine's career starts out in light, it will end in darkness. A hint comes when the Angel tells Manoah and his wife that Samson won't deliver Israel from the Philistines, he will only *begin to* - a key point (Judg 13:5). In fact, the bellicose, iron-hogging Philistines will remain a major impediment to Israel right up until David and his mighty men punch their ticket during the zenith of Israel's monarchy. Allan McGregor comments:

"Unfortunately, Hollywood must take its share of the blame for the misrepresentation of the Philistines because, while many envisage Samson as Victor Mature and Delilah as Hedy Lamarr, too many people's impressions of the Philistines have been coloured by the suave and sophisticated cinema performance of the urbane George Sanders. If fiction were to be believed, the Philistines were basically a debauched bunch of pagan hedonists, who worshiped Dagon and partied a lot.

"In fact, they were a rapacious military nation who lived by the conquest and enslavement of others. And, as for their religion, even the Romans were repulsed by their brutality because the Phoenicians were practitioners of child sacrifice - the burning of infants on a brazen altar to their pagan deities. We know this from the archaeological remains of the graves of sacrificed children discovered in the ruins of the Phoenicians' chief African enclave of Carthage, which the Romans razed in their indignation at the Phoenician appetite for infanticide. And I'm talking about the same Romans who viewed gladiatorial killings as public entertainment, and crucified criminals.

"The Carthaginians were Phoenicians. The Philistines were Phoenicians. They got about, and they weren't nice people. So don't wonder that God wanted his Chosen People to rid them from his Promised Land. That was God's purpose, and Samson was one of those installed to carry it out." [418]

The first time we're introduced to Sunshine as a young adult, he's making his first error. Samson sees a woman at Timnah and wants to marry her, which is a problem because she's a Philistine and the Torah condemns Jews marrying pagans, especially Canaanites (*cf.* Exo 34:16; Deut 7:3) Samson's parents have to be involved with getting Samson a wife, but they object to this match in the strongest possible terms:

"Is there never a woman among the daughters of thy brethren, or among all my people, that thou goest to take a wife of the uncircumcised Philistines?"

---

[418] http://allanmcgregor.hubpages.com/hub/Lessons-from-the-life-of-Samson

And Samson said unto his father, "Get her for me, for she pleaseth me well." (Judg 14:3)

Allan McGregor again:

"As a Nazarite, [Samson] was brought up quite differently from his peers; and being *different* can be a hurtful experience for any child. His long *womanly* hair, strict diet and separation from the dead and unclean marked Samson out in a community where vineyards were commonplace and idol worship the norm.

"Secondly, as the cherished son of formerly childless parents, he may have been unduly indulged, as appears to be corroborated by the brusque manner with which he addressed them."[419]

Samson's reply can be equally translated, "Get her for me, for she is right in my eyes", which echoes the curt manner of the spoilt – indeed the cardinal moniker of Israel herself throughout the Judges era: **Everyone was doing what was right in their own eyes**. But the scriptures state that it is the LORD's doing to have Samson commence His judgment against the Philistines in the way that He does (Judg 14:4). God usually uses nations to bring judgment upon other nations. In the case of the Philistines, He's going to open the attrition proceedings with Samson, a wild man from the backslidden, pagan-worshipping Jewish tribe of Dan. Had Samson's character been completely different, God would surely have modified His plans and used the Danite to achieve His will by more peaceful means. God never violates our free will. Sometimes people mewl as if He should. God can choose the wildest, most misguided wretch to accomplish His will. As the saying goes, "It may be that the only purpose of your life is to serve as a warning to others". With Samson, the lessons are extraordinary. Buckle up for the ride.

Samson and his parents travel down to Timnah to get the marriage business underway with the Philistine woman, and apparently set a date (Judg 14:7). Manoah is unhappy, need it be said, and more so his wife, who received Samson's holy commission from the Angel of the LORD personally. As a devout Hebrew, she would view any marriage between her lovely Nazirite son (blessed by the LORD) and a Dagon-(*ha-Satan*)-worshipping Philistine wench as decidedly off-mission. Samson is spoilt and couldn't care less: we can tell by his actions. While on his own in the vineyards of Timnah,

[419] Ibid.

doubtless perusing what the wedlock might bring him, a young lion abruptly appears and attempts to attack him.

<u>And the Spirit of the LORD came mightily upon</u> [Samson]**, and he rent** [the lion] **as he would have rent a kid** [young goat]**, and he had nothing in his hand** [no weapons]**. But he told not his father or his mother what he had done.**

And he went down and talked with the woman, and she pleased Samson well. And after a time he returned to take her, and he turned aside to see the carcase of the lion. And, behold, there was a swarm of bees and honey in the carcase of the lion. And he took thereof in his hands and went on eating, and came to his father and mother, and he gave them, and they did eat: but he told not them that he had taken the honey out of the carcase of the lion. (Judg 14:6-9)

Firstly, imagine tearing a lion apart with your bare hands. How would that feel? All those snarling, snapping fangs and the final yelp as the sinews are rent asunder. We experience the Danite's crazy courage and astonishing strength, though he has the Spirit of the LORD upon him, which means the lion slaying is condoned by YHWH, though not perhaps all else which derives from this incident.

It's a hallmark of Samson's career that nothing gets in Samson's way. What Samson wants, Samson gets, including the Philistine woman and a much bigger pickle that's coming up. Later, when the Danite returns to Timnah with his parents to marry the woman, he does a fly-by of the lion carcass on his own, presumably to admire his handiwork. At this point he finds the bees and honey therein. The questions start. What's Samson the Nazirite doing in a vineyard for starters(!), then messing about with a dead body(!!), let alone eating the produce found in one(!!!), then causing his parents to slurp on same unawares(!!!!) Samson couldn't care less. *Jesusalive.cc* explains the strict nature of the Nazirite commitment outlined in the Torah (Num 6:1-21):

"1. A man or woman could make this (voluntary) vow to dedicate themselves to the LORD.

"2. During the vow, they could not drink wine, vinegar, grape juice or similar drink, nor could they eat vine products such as grapes or raisins.

"3. They could not cut their hair.

"4. They could not touch, or even go near, a dead body, not even a grave or building containing a dead body. This included mother, father, sister, or brother.

"5. When the vow was completed, 4 different offerings were to be made at the Tabernacle: burnt, peace, sin, drink/meal. He (or she) were also to shave the head, and the hair was to be burned (as part of the peace offering).

"Afterwards, the person was released from their vow.

"The Bible does not say how long these vows were to be. According to Jewish tradition, they were generally 30 days, but could run to 100 days. However, it appears that several men in the Bible were dedicated to be Nazirites for their whole lives before they were even born: Samuel (1 Sam 1:9-11), Samson (Judg 1:7-14) and John The Baptist (Luke 1:13-17)(Matt 11:18-19)." [420]

Party animal

To celebrate his nuptials, Samson throws a party in Timnah and the local Philistines bring their mates, as is the custom, and the feasting continues seven days with these thirty men toasting Samson's future as his groomsmen. This detail illustrates the ease with which the Israelites in general have come to accept Philistine domination. But no mention is made of Israelite friends attending the nuptials. In fact, throughout the Samson narrative, no mention is made of any Israelite involvement or assistance given to Samson, or requested by him, in harassing the Philistines. Israel would have been loathed to participate in any case; Judah's readiness to arrest and hand Samson over to the five lords a little later is ample proof that no-one desires any confrontation with their masters.

There's another reason why there are no Israelites at the marriage feast. Samson's going to make his move and doesn't want his countrymen in the firing line. Both cultures, Israelite and Philistine, have rubbed along up to now; economically things are working well, and this in itself speaks to our own rich but godless society, which daily erodes and corrupts an individual's attempt at a life of God-led spirituality. God is going to use an apostate Nazirite to get the Jews back on track.

It's fair to assume neither Samson nor his Philistine companions are drinking Dr Pepper or Diet Cokes at this bacchanalia, so Samson's violating another of his Nazirite vows to abstain from strong hooch.

---

[420] http://jesusalive.cc/ques193.htm

Apparently Samson becomes particularly friendly with one of the Philistines who is chosen as an *ad hoc* best man. During the festivities, Samson turns to his companions:

"I will now put forth a riddle unto you. If ye can certainly declare it me within the seven days of the feast and find it out, I will give you thirty sheets and thirty change of garments. But if ye cannot declare it me, then shall ye give me thirty sheets and thirty change of garments."

And they said unto him, "Put forth thy riddle, that we may hear it."

And he said unto them, "Out of the eater came forth meat, and out of the strong came forth sweetness."

And they could not in three days expound the riddle. (Judg 14:12-14)

It's a Goodfellas moment, though Samson is bigger than Joe Pesci. On the seventh day, the Philistines still have no clue to the riddle's answer. The mood turns ugly. They are being rousted by an Israelite and don't like it. They confront Samson's wife:

"Entice thy husband, that he may declare unto us the riddle, lest we burn thee and thy father's house with fire. Have ye called us [i.e. invited us] **to take what is ours? Is it so?"** (Judg 14:15)

Samson's wife panics. These crackbrains are capable of anything. She takes the only course of action she can think of:

And [she] **wept before** [Samson]**, and said, "Thou dost but hate me and lovest me not. Thou hast put forth a riddle unto the children of my people and hast not told it me."**

And he said unto her, "Behold, I have not told it my father nor my mother, and shall I tell it thee?"

And she wept before him the seven days while their feast lasted. And it came to pass on the seventh day that he told her because she lay sore upon him [nag, nag, nag]**. And she told the riddle to the children of her people.** (Judg 14:16-17)

It's likely, but not mentioned, that she blabs the riddle's answer to the best man. In any case, on the last day of the feast before the sun sets, the Philistine men gleefully confront Samson with the riddle's answer:

"What is sweeter than honey? And what is stronger than a lion?"

And [Samson] **said unto them, "If ye had not plowed with my heifer** [er, wife]**, ye had not found out my riddle."** (Judg 14:18)

Samson is angry, and you wouldn't like Samson when he's angry. The Spirit of the LORD comes upon him mightily. He gets up, leaves his father-in-law's house, goes down to Ashkelon - one of the five cities of the Philistine lords - and there slaughters thirty Philistine men, steals their clothing, and returns to give the spoils to the victors. As this is all done under the Spirit, Samson's murderous actions against the Philistines *are God's will.* It's worth pointing out that Samson does not slaughter his wedding guests, so there's a modicum of restraint. After paying off the bet, Samson departs and goes back to his father's house at Zorah. Such is the mood in which he leaves his father-in-law's house that the latter assumes the nuptials are off and gives Samson's wife to the Philistine who acted as best man. The father is doubtless relieved that his daughter will now marry one of her own kind, and not that wild, terrifying, unpredictable, shaggy-haired, bushy-bearded, Israelite lunatic (Judg 14:20). Samson doesn't know about this latest development yet, but he will.

Outfoxed

The following May during the wheat harvest, Samson decides to pay his wife a visit at Timnah – which is very considerate of him. The overbearing, male-dominant society really comes out during the Judges era. Women are bartered like chattels and abandoned when it suits the men, though Samson does seem to harbour genuine affection for this particular lass. The terror on the father-in-law's face can only be imagined as he spies that familiar, frightening form loping down the road towards him, goat in tow. News of what happened to the thirty men in Ashkelon has doubtless done the rounds, and all Timnah have an uncomfortable feeling they know where the thirty changes of clothing came from to redeem Samson's bet.

Samson and father-in-law meet outside the house:

[And Samson said]**: "I will go in to my wife into the chamber." But her father would not suffer him to go in.**

And her father said, "I verily thought that thou hadst utterly hated her. Therefore I gave her to thy companion. Is not her younger sister fairer than she? Take her, I pray thee, instead of her."

And Samson said concerning them, "This time I shall be more blameless than the Philistines, though I do them a displeasure." (Judg 15:1-3)

Which is clumsy King James for, "Right, that's it. The Philistines are getting theirs."

What Samson wants, Samson gets, and if Samson doesn't get, then everyone within a 10-mile radius would do well to grab a spade and start digging. God uses Samson's overweaning pride to wreak havoc on the Philistines in a unique manner. The Danite sets about trapping 300 jackals.[421] He ties their tails together, sticks a lighted firebrand in the knot, then sets the screaming, frenzied creatures loose among the Philistines' wheat fields. Being the start of the dry season, the blaze not only ravages the wheat in the fields but also the harvested sheaves. The fire spreads to the vineyards and olive groves – anywhere the crazed animals drag one another with their shrieks. It's a sight you don't see every day, and for the Philistines to be appalled says something. It doesn't take long for them to discover the culprit.

Witnesses cry: "It was Samson, the son-in-law of the Timnite! The father-in-law took Samson's wife and gave it to the Danite's companion!"

Philistine revenge is summary and swift. A death squad descends on the hapless father-in-law's house and burns the property to the ground with both father and daughter inside. It's justice Philistine-style, but they reckon without Samson, by now in full Hulk mode, who falls upon the assassination party and slaughters the lot without mercy.

After the heinous carnage (derived from a drunken bet!), Samson now officially tops the Five Lords of the Philistines' Most Wanted List. Samson hides out in the cleft of the rock of Etam. The Philistines mobilise an army and head for Judah, deploying themselves against the Israelites outside the border town of Lehi ('jawbone'). The men of Judah emerge and hail their Philistine overlords:

"Why are ye come up against us?"

And they answered, "To bind Samson are we come up, to do to him as he hath done to us."

Then three thousand men of Judah went to the top of the rock Etam and said to Samson, "Knowest thou not that the Philistines are rulers over us? What is this that thou hast done unto us?"

And he said unto them, "As they did unto me, so have I done unto them." (Judg 15:10-11)

---

[421] The word is translated 'foxes', but is more likely to be the jackals indigenous to the area, which roamed in packs for food, making them relatively straightforward to trap.

It is certainly an indictment of the times that 3,000 men of Judah go up against one solitary member of their own people (albeit Samson) to arrest and hand him over to Israel's sworn enemy to maintain the peace! This is the only time Israel manages to mobilise an army during the Philistine oppression. No sense of irony, the men of Judah:

"We are come down to bind thee, that we may deliver thee into the hand of the Philistines."

And Samson said unto them, "Swear unto me that ye will not fall upon me yourselves."

And they spake unto him, saying, "No, but we will bind thee fast and deliver thee into their hand, but surely we will not kill thee." And they bound him with two new cords and brought him up from the rock.

And when he came unto Lehi, the Philistines shouted against him. And the Spirit of the LORD came mightily upon [Samson]**, and the cords that were upon his arms became as flax that was burnt with fire, and his bands loosed from off his hands. And he found a new jawbone of an ass and put forth his hand and took it, and slew a thousand men therewith.** (Judg 15:12-15)

Some expositors react with disbelief that one man could have slaughtered a thousand professional warriors, but they go along with it anyway: "Well, it's in the Bible so God expects us to believe it." My question is, why is anyone so sure Samson *didn't* kill a thousand men with God's help? We are not told how long it took to kill a thousand men, whether it was one event or several, or whether the Hebrew word *'eleph'* translated 'thousand' actually means 'a military unit', as it does elsewhere in the scriptures. Proficient warriors racking up large body-counts are not uncommon either in history or the Bible. In 2 Samuel 23, we are given a review of King David's mighty men, and some of these are true skullcrackers with hundreds of kills to their credit. Yet scholars have for years been unsettled by the unusually large numbers of soldiers quoted in the Bible. Is this poetic licence or is there a more prosaic explanation? Boyd Seevers PhD elaborates:

"One may also understand the numbers literally, but differently than as usually translated. This distinction hinges on the understanding of the term 'eleph' (אָ לֶ ף). Though 'eleph' usually meant 'thousand(s)', the word could also mean a part of a tribe (perhaps best translated 'clan') that was smaller than the tribe but larger than an extended family ('father's house' אָב יתֵב - Josh. 22:14). For example, Gideon protested to the divine messenger who had called him to leadership, saying "my clan ('eleph') is the weakest in [the tribe of] Manasseh, and I am the least in my family" (Judg. 6:15). In a later event, Saul sought the fugitive David among all the 'clans' (1 Sam. 23:23 - אַלְפֵי יְהוּדָה) of Judah. Given that 'eleph' can mean 'clan', and Israelite soldiers may well have mustered and fought by clans, then 'eleph' might stand for the soldiers who mustered from a particular clan. If correct, this suggests that the Bible may often refer to numbers of tribal units rather than total numbers of troops.

"Understanding 'eleph' as a unit rather than 'thousand' seems to solve many of the problems of large numbers associated with the Israelite military. Most of the large numbers that appear too large shrink down to a more believable but still indefinite size if 'eleph' means the unit of troops drawn from a clan. It is perhaps more likely that Saul mustered 330 units of soldiers to rescue Jabesh Gilead rather than 330,000 soldiers. If the Hebrew writers also used the same term to describe enemy troops, then Samson may have killed an entire Philistine unit with an animal's jawbone rather than one thousand men."[422]

Dr Seevers goes on to stipulate that this doesn't solve all translational concerns of large numbers in the Bible (as we saw with the numbers of Israelites in the Exodus), but it pays to understand what the writer intended to convey to his readership. This takes us back to the concept of ethnocentricity: gaining an understanding of an ancient culture through the latter's frame of reference, not our own.

Clearly, Samson's very name would have loosened Philistine bowels. No-one would have wished to take on this crazy man first-hand. The men of Judah only feel safe mobilising 3,000 men (3 military clans/units?) to arrest him. Interestingly, Samson seems to seek assurance from the men of Judah that he will not be attacked by *them*, not for his own safety, but *so they do not force him to defend himself and kill his own people.* We know Judah's fear is justified by the havoc Samson subsequently wreaks on the Philistines.

And we know by now that it suits the LORD to fight with the strangest of weapons, so no flesh may glory in His presence. God wants the credit. It's His planet and universe, we are His creations, so God should get the credit. Thus Shamgar and his ox goad did not kill 600 men, the Commander of the LORD's Army (Yeshua) did. Gideon with his 300 torches and pitchers did not put the entire Midianite

---

[422] www.nwc.edu/c/document_library/get_file?uuid=209dd793-8165-4652-b25e-3b2754820504 &groupId=12124

army to flight, Yeshua did. Samson did not singlehandedly kill a thousand men (or a Philistine army unit, at any rate) with the recently dead, moist jawbone of a jackass, Yeshua did that too (Judg 15:14-15). What's fascinating is that God overlooks Samson once more violating his Nazirite oath not to touch any dead thing. When YHWH works through broken people, He examines their hearts and motives, as He does for each of us today. We'll get a clear lesson on this when we study King David. Israel's most famous OT king will commit adultery and murder, yet God will describe him as **'a man after My own heart'** (1 Sam 13:13-14; Acts 13:22). God abhors adultery and murder, but works through damaged people who have a contrite heart and are headed in the right direction. Samson makes it into the Hebrews Hall of Faith in Heb 11, and if God can justify Samson, He can justify you and me.

The Great Jawbone Massacre is one of the most famous of Samson's exploits. The place where the Nazirite tops a whole contingent of Philistines is named Ramath Lehi or 'Jawbone Heights' in his honour, but Samson's troubles are only just beginning. His eye for Philistine women starts all the trouble again, and this time leads him into a trap of pride and betrayal, from which not even Samson will be able to extricate himself.

Gates away

A while later, Samson is visiting a whore in Gaza. The Philistines are told of his presence and lie in wait at the city gate. By now, Samson's word-fame has built him into a hero to Israel and a demon to the five lords. The Philistine chieftains are uncomfortably aware that all the while the Danite comes and goes across Philistia wreaking havoc with impunity, rank-and-file Philistines know the five lords don't rule.

Samson realises there will be an ambush when he emerges from doing his business. He failed to arrive at the harlot's house surreptitiously - doubtless on purpose. At midnight he emerges into the night air. What happens next becomes the stuff of legends:

And Samson lay till midnight, and arose at midnight and took the doors of the gate of the city, and the two posts, and went away with them, bar and all, and put them upon his shoulders, and carried them up to the top of an hill that is before Hebron. (Judg 16:3)

The only explanation is that the people of Gaza shrank before Samson as he strode down the street like some avenging angel. Samson likes to kill Philistines for sport, and here he is now, falling upon them. They flee and the Danite sets about ripping down the doors of Gaza's entry gate.

In the Canaanite and Hebrew cultures of the day, the city gate represents the seat of municipal power. The king and worthies sit 'in the gate' to adjudicate city business (remember Boaz?). We'll come across Kings Saul and David doing the same, as also a host of other monarchs and princes as we proceed. By uprooting and carting away the city's doors and posts, Samson is hijacking the city's symbol of governance, calculated once again to emasculate the five lords in the eyes of their people. The strength required to execute this prank is only made possible by God's Spirit. Samson's immense physical prowess enables him to harass and embarrass the Philistines, but he does not free Israel from their domination, and his pride and moral weakness for the ladies will lead to his downfall. Scholars are divided as to whether Samson actually hauled Gaza's gates 38 miles to a hill overlooking Hebron, or whether he carted the lot up a closer hill which faced, or was on the way to Judah's capital. Either way, the feat knocks modern Olympic efforts into a cocked hat, and only adds to Samson's terrifying reputation with Israel's oppressors.

Betrayed by beauty

A while later, Samson falls in love with another woman named Delilah. This one lives in the Valley of Sorek,[423] so it's unclear whether our famous seductress is a Philistine or apostate Hebrew. Some expositors even suggest that she could have come from Samson's own tribe of Dan. She certainly has no trouble mixing with the Philistines. Intriguingly, the Hebrew etymology of her name suggests 'delicate, languishing, amorous, seductive', and is a play on לילה *laylah*, Strong's #3915 (pronounced 'lie-lah'), the Hebrew for 'night'. The beginning root *dal* means 'weak, poor'. So Sunshine meets Nightime, Light meets Dark, and as soon as the five lords get to hear of it, they sense a *coup* and waylay the lass to make her an offer she can't refuse:

---

[423] The Valley of Sorek is a drainage basin in the Judaean Hills running south-east to north-west towards Haifa, bordering the lands of Philistia and the tribe of Dan. Sorek means 'fruitless/empty/worthless', a timely reference to Samson's dealings with Delilah.

And the lords of the Philistines came up unto her, and said unto her, "Entice him and see wherein his great strength lieth, and by what means we may prevail against him, that we may bind him to afflict him. And we will give thee, every one of us, eleven hundred pieces of silver." (Judg 16:5)

That's a total of 5,500 pieces of silver across the five lords, a monstrous amount of money, equivalent to 700 lbs of silver. If Scorsese were doing the screenplay, he'd have the five lords top Delilah to save on the payoff once Samson is in their hands, yet the scriptures don't record Delilah's fate. The very fact the offer is made illustrates the desperation of the Philistine élite to have Samson done and dusted for good.

Delilah's nothing if not a game girl for that kind of cash. She and Samson are at ease in each other's company and evidently have a taste for intimate game-playing. Everyone knows the five lords are after Samson (he even teases her about it), so she pretends to dare him. It's clear to the reader, though not to love-struck Samson, that Delilah's only in it for the money and has no regard for the Danite. After 20 years of embarrassing the Philistines with God's help, Samson has deluded himself into invincibility. I have the seductress in my mind's eye running her fingers down Samson's biceps, purring:

"Tell me, I pray thee, wherein thy great strength lieth, and wherewith thou mightest be bound to afflict thee."

And Samson said unto her, "If they bind me with seven green bowstrings that were never dried, then shall I be weak and be as another man." (Judg 16:6-7)

When Delilah reports this piece of intelligence to her string-pullers, the five lords provide the seven bindings. In their next intimate session, Delilah ties Samson up with them to see if he can escape. Some researchers see these bowstrings derived from vines, others from the viscera of animals. In any event, they are immensely strong to be bowstrings. Unknown to the Danite, the five lords have also secreted men in Delilah's chamber to seize him when the time comes. It's hard not to smile at the picture this paints. Samson nods off. Delilah retreats a safe distance, then shrieks with alarm:

"The Philistines be upon thee, Samson!"

But he broke the bowstrings as a thread of yarn is broken when it toucheth the fire. So the secret to his strength was not known.

The hidden men obviously shrink down and remain hidden to save their lives. Delilah rounds on her lover angrily.

"Thou hast mocked me and told me lies! Now tell me, I pray thee, wherewith thou mightest be bound."

And he said unto her, "If they bind me fast with new ropes that never were occupied, then shall I be weak and be as another man." (Judg 16:10-11)

One can imagine the smirk on the Nazirite's face as he teases her anew. Yet we know how the tale ends. The Philistines come up with the new ropes and next session, Delilah's up to her old tricks again. She trusses the Danite as tight as a turkey and later, after Samson dozes off, she retreats once more, crying:

"The Philistines be upon thee, Samson!"

But he breaks the bonds once more as if they are thread. The men in the room stay hidden. Delilah's hungry for her loot and no closer to payday. She rounds on Samson anew:

"Hitherto thou hast mocked me and told me lies! Tell me wherewith thou mightest be bound!" And he said unto her, "If thou weavest the seven locks of my head into the web of the loom."

Even by Samson's standards, it's a weird one. He invites her to weave seven plats of his hair into the fabric already on Delilah's loom. So she does.

And she fastened it with the pin and said unto him, "The Philistines be upon thee, Samson!" And he awoke out of his sleep and went away with the pin of the beam and with the web. (Judg 16:13-14)

By now the game is wearing thin. The ones I feel sorry for are the Philistine warriors secreted in the room, crippled with cramp; bowels bloated from their corn diets; dying to relieve themselves; in danger of imminent discovery and dismemberment by Samson. I am certain the Danite knows they are there!

And she said unto him, "How canst thou say, 'I love thee', when thine heart is not with me? Thou hast mocked me these three times and hast not told me wherein thy great strength lieth!"

And it came to pass, she pressed him daily with her words and urged him, so his soul was vexed unto death [nag, nag, nag], **that he told her all his heart, and said unto her, "There hath not come a razor upon mine head, for I have been a Nazirite unto God from my mother's womb. If I be shaven, then my strength will go from me and I shall become weak and be like any other man."** (Judg 16:15-17)

It is ironic that Samson is physically invincible with the LORD's Spirit, yet *twice* is nagged by women into giving up a secret. If people know nothing else about Samson, they know the strange tale of Delilah giving him a haircut so he loses his strength. In fact, God has had enough. Did you know that there comes a time when our persistent sin grieves the Spirit to the point when God backs off?[424] God uses our sinful predicament to chastise and bring us back. He hands over persistent offenders to their own devices and appetites (Rom 1:24,26). Notice that God does not desert Samson in the end, but uses the baleful circumstances of the Danite's fate to accomplish His judgment on the Philistines.

And when Delilah saw that he had told her all his heart, she sent and called for the lords of the Philistines, saying, "Come up this once, for he hath shewed me all his heart." Then the lords of the Philistines came up unto her, and brought money in their hand.

And she made [Samson] **sleep upon her knees and she called for a man, and she caused him to shave off the seven locks of his head. And began to afflict him and his strength went from him.**

And she said, "The Philistines be upon thee, Samson!" And he awoke out of his sleep, and said, "I will go out as at other times before and shake myself." And he wist not that the LORD was departed from him. (Judg 16:18-20)

Roger Ellsworth writes:

> "Does this story seem too far-fetched to be believed? Why, after it was obvious what Delilah was up to, did Samson continue even to see her, let alone talk to her about the source of his strength? Why would he take such a terrible risk? Here we see the dreadful weakness of human nature. This was not just true of Samson, it is true of all of us. We flirt with things that we know will destroy us. Tell me how many times you have been burned by sin and gone right back to it, and I will tell you why Samson kept going back to Delilah."[425]

Samson finally betrays his Nazirite covenant to a pagan seductress. God bails. The secret to Samson's strength is not in his hair but his sacred relationship with YHWH. The shearing of Samson's locks symbolises the final breaking of his Nazirite covenant, in effect counting his sacred bond with YHWH a common thing by sharing it with an apostate who collaborates with Israel's enemies.

---

[424] *cf:* 1 Sam 16:14; Eze 10:4,19; 11:23; 1 Thess 5:19; Eph 4:30. Though the Spirit of God left King Saul through his persistent disobedience, the prophet Samuel remarks in the witch of En Dor scene (1 Sam 28:19) that tomorrow Saul and his sons *will be with him* (i.e. dead and with Samuel), implying that Saul will be saved.

[425] **Ellsworth, Roger,** www.founders.org/journal/fj31/article2.html

Notice that long hair is a dishonour to a man (1 Cor 11:14) and symbolises submission. The theme of 'hair length' in the scriptures is consistent and intriguing. The woman (long-haired) submits to the man (short-haired) who submits to Christ (1 Cor 11:3-16). Yeshua Himself was a Nazarene (from Nazareth) not a Nazirite, so would have had short hair (1 Cor 11:14).[426] The very requirement for a Nazirite to go unshorn is a badge of his total submission to, and dependence on God while separated from the world/mankind. Notice that God has used an unusual weapon once more - Samson's superhuman strength - to accomplish feats impossible for a normal man, so no flesh may glory in His presence, and all may see the LORD's hand. But Samson has never come to terms with his Nazirite separation to God in the way Samuel and John the Baptist will.

When the Philistines come for the Danite the final time, Samson realises the LORD has taken his strength and he's finished. The fact that Delilah herself doesn't do the shearing in no way absolves her of the blame of her betrayal. The Philistines drag Samson away, dig out his eyes (the very organs that led him astray in the first place), take him to Gaza in fetters of brass, and put him to work grinding flour in prison.

The wildest party

Hubris prevents the Philistines from killing Samson, since death would rob the five lords of every chance to mock the one who humiliated them. They also need to restore their supremacy and political dignity. But in victory's gloating, no-one seems to notice that Samson's hair is growing back, and with it his relationship with YHWH, and with those two, Samson's primal desire for revenge. His chance soon comes:

Then the lords of the Philistines gathered them together for to offer a great sacrifice unto Dagon their god, and to rejoice, for they said, "Our god hath delivered Samson our enemy into our hand."

And when the people saw him, they praised their god, for they said, "Our god hath delivered into our hands our enemy, and the destroyer of our country, which slew many of us."

---

[426] The apostle Paul addresses male grooming in this verse, declaring that long hair is a dishonour to a man. The converted Pharisee dwelt with those who had known Jesus personally, such as Peter and James (Gal 1:18), as well as having been taught by the ascended LORD Himself. He is unlikely to have castigated long hair if Jesus had looked like Andrew Lloyd Webber's hippie superstar.

And it came to pass, when their hearts were merry, that they said, "Call for Samson, that he may make us sport. And they called for Samson out of the prison house and he made them sport; and they set him between the pillars. (Judg 16:23-25)

A temple similar to the one depicted in the story has been uncovered in Philistia, its roof supported by two pillars in the centre. Seismologists believe this particular temple was destroyed by an earthquake M=8.0 Richter or greater, powerful enough to flatten the robust structure (perhaps even the famous quake mentioned in Isaiah and Amos). The discovered Dagon's temple may have met its end at the hands of one of the Mars fly-bys, even the final one around 701 BC, which would be contemporary to both prophets. *The Jerusalem Post* reports:

"Archaeologists have uncovered a Philistine temple and evidence of a major earthquake in biblical times, during digs carried out at the Tel Tzafit National Park near Kiryat Gat. The site is home to the Philistine city of Gath, the home of the ancient warrior Goliath.

"Prof. Aren Maeir, of Bar-Ilan University's Martin (Szusz) Department of Land of Israel Studies and Archaeology, said on Wednesday that the temple may shed light on the architecture in Philistia at the time when Jewish hero Samson purportedly brought the temple of Dagon down upon himself. Maier said the architecture of the Philistine temple, the first ever found at Gath, sheds light on what the temple of Dagon would have looked like, in particular the two pillars that anchored the centre of the structure."[427]

Picture the scene. The huge temple is packed with humanity. Torchlight dances off the walls to the music and raucous laughter, the air pungent with sweat, incense and pagan expectation. As a highlight to the five lords' elaborate celebrations, Samson is dragged in and chained between the pillars of Gaza's temple of Dagon so the Philistines can make sport of him. The champion has become a comedian. Dagon (*ha-Satan*) is the chief deity of the Philistines, originally a Babylonian deity spawned out of the Nimrod/Semiramis heresy. Chuck Missler gives us some background:

"Worshipped from before the 20th century BC, Dagon was regarded as the father of Baal and variously seen as a storm god, a sea god, or of grain or fertility. The Philistines, from a seafaring heritage, usually represented him as having the head and upper parts human, while the

---

[427] *Jerusalem Post*, 29th July 2010

rest of the body resembled a fish. In the 14th century BC and earlier, Dagon had a temple at Ugarit in North Phoenicia, identified by two *stelae* in it dedicated to his name. This temple had a forecourt, an antechamber and probably a tower. At Bethshan, one temple discovered may be that of the desecration of Saul's body (1 Chr 10:10).[428]

On Earth, the Philistines believe their fish god Dagon has triumphed over the God of Israel. Big mistake. In the metacosm, God now moves to protect His holy name. It will be the Danite's defining moment. As he was in life, so he will be in death. Samson's going out with a bang.

And Samson said unto the lad that held him by the hand, "Suffer me that I may feel the pillars whereupon the house standeth, that I may lean upon them."

Now the house was full of men and women, and all the lords of the Philistines were there. And there were upon the roof about three thousand men and women that beheld while Samson made sport.

And Samson called unto the LORD and said, "O Lord GOD, remember me, I pray thee, and strengthen me, I pray thee, only this once, O God, that I may be at once avenged of the Philistines for my two eyes."

And Samson took hold of the two middle pillars upon which the house stood, and on which it was borne up, of the one with his right hand, and of the other with his left. And Samson said, "Let me die with the Philistines." And he bowed himself with all his might, and the house fell upon the lords, and upon all the people that were therein. So the dead which he slew at his death were more than they which he slew in his life. (Judg 16:26-30)

Samson in summary

Wikipedia reports:

"Samson is believed to have been buried in Tel Tzora in Israel overlooking the Sorek valley. There reside two large gravestones of Samson and his father Manoah. Nearby stands Manoah's altar (Judges 13:19-24). It is located between the cities of Zorah and Eshtaol."[429]

Samson's story is often mythologised, yet there is no reason to suppose Samson was not a proper historical figure and 'judge' of

---

[428] Missler, Chuck, *Judges notes*, p.121, www.khouse.org

[429] http://en.wikipedia.org/wiki/Samson

Israel as presented in the Message System. Did Samson inspire the Greek myth of Hercules? There are intriguing parallels. Chuck Missler cites the supernatural strength of each; that both were in slavery to women; both tore apart a lion; both suffered a violent death through the machinations of a woman, part voluntary, part forced; and both forced two pillars apart, in the case of the mythological Hercules, the 'two pillars' spanning the Straits of Gibraltar, Mount Abila and Mount Calpe.[430] We are used to this confluence of reality and myth with Adam and Eve, the Flood, Noah, Nimrod, Semiramis and other historical figures morphed into legends. There is no smoke without fire, and legends do not eschew an historical foundation. Stories are retold across different cultures, changed and embellished. In his pulpit commentary in *Judges* (vol 3, p.175), A C Hervey writes:

"Herodotus describes the Temple of Hercules at Tyre: Two pillars - gold, and smaragdus (an emerald-like green stone). On his visit to Egypt: 'The Greeks say that when Hercules went down to Egypt, the Egyptians surrounded him and led him in a procession to sacrifice him to Jupiter; that he kept quite still for a time, but that when they were commencing the sacrifice at the altar' (the first act of which was cutting off the hair), 'he turned in self-defense and by his prowess slew them all.' On which Herodotus remarks, 'How was it possible for him, being but one, and being only a man, to slay many myriads?'

"The prevalence of the worship of Hercules among the Phoenicians, as at Tyre and Thasos, a Phoenician colony, and the close connection of Egypt with Gaza, where the prowess of Samson was so well known, are points not to be omitted in considering the probability of some of the legends of Hercules being drawn from the history of Samson."

Samson's name means 'sunshine', but he ends up in darkness at the hands of a woman whose name is a play on 'night'. Samson failed to deliver Israel from the carnal Philistines because he could not deliver himself from his own carnal nature. He lost sight of God and the big picture, and in the end lost his own sight. As a blind man in prison, Samson had ample time to contemplate the cost of his mistakes without the diversion of human vision. Whenever Samson visited Philistia, he went *down* to Philistia, a preposition speaking as much to his moral degradation as physical destination. Samson commenced service as a Nazirite - consecrated, separate unto God - but from the outset his eyes were lured by the flesh and ways of the

---

[430] Missler, Chuck, *Judges notes,* www.khouse.org

world. Samson wanted to be like everyone else, yet lust makes fools of men. Once again, as the saying goes, "Whenever I went out among men, I always returned less of a man." Samson defeated a lion and countless enemy strongmen, but could not defeat his own flesh. It's a lesson all believers feel uncomfortable with today. Samson's story is of that most basic, insidious of conflicts between the flesh and the Spirit, a defining aspect of the Predicament of Man. Christians are set apart by Yeshua, yet how many of us mix it with the world and its appetites? Are we like Samson, double-minded men and women, unstable in all our ways? (Jam 1:8). We are human, yet God wants to transform us for eternity. He can only do this with our permission. Have we yet asked Him to?

At his wedding, Samson partied with the very Philistines he should have been delivering Israel from. One minute his wife captivated Samson completely, the next she was his 'heifer'. The real predicament for each of us is not against our Philistines, but our inherent sinful nature, and what it leads us to do. Samson teaches that we are nothing without the One who divides our cells and gives, sustains and takes life. Roger Ellsworth summarises:

"The picture of Samson is as pathetic as any could be, but there is also great hope and consolation to be found in his story. In the final analysis, the Philistines did not overpower Samson because they were stronger but because he was faithless. Christians sometimes fall into the trap of thinking that the godless culture which surrounds them is their greatest enemy. Godless culture is, of course, an enemy, but only in a secondary sense. Our greatest enemy is ourselves. If we are oppressed today, it is not because the baby boomer beliefs and lifestyle are stronger than we, but because we have been faithless to the God who makes us strong.

"How we need to take this home to our hearts! Our calling is to be faithful to God! But what about that child of God who has already been unfaithful? What about that Christian who has been seduced by mistaken dogmas of a godless culture? Thank God, there is another consolation from the life of Samson for such a case! Spiritual hair grows back! The child of God may be seduced by his pagan culture, but he will ultimately come back to the LORD and be renewed. And, as Samson was finally vindicated, so each child of God is going to be ultimately vindicated. There is coming a blessed day when we will be taken out of the culture that despises the things of God, and we will shine as the stars of the firmament forever, and the whole universe will know that we were right to walk with God."[431]

Scott Carson adds:

"A painter named William Blake once painted a beautiful but strong and vicious tiger. Then he wrote some lines in which he asked, "Did He who made the lamb make thee?" We have to admit that sometimes it seems as if there are two Gods, one who makes lambs and one who makes tigers. But there isn't. The same God who loves the world and gave His Son on Calvary is holy and just, and will judge the world for sin. Friend, if you do not come to Him as Savior, you will face Him as your Judge." [432]

---

[431] Ellsworth, Roger, http://www.founders.org/journal/fj31/article2.html
[432] www.gracechurchwi.org/pastors_pen/PP2002/082502.html

SAMUEL, LAST OF THE JUDGES

There was a certain man of the tribe of Levi named Elkanah, who dwelt in Ramah of Ephraim in the hill country north of Jerusalem.[433] This Elkanah has two wives: Peninnah ('pearl', precious stone') and Hannah ('beauty', 'grace'). Penninah has children but Hannah has none. Every year, when Elkanah journeys to worship and sacrifice to the LORD at Shiloh, his wives go with him. When the time comes to make the offering, Elkanah gives many portions of the sacrificial meat to Peninnah and her sons and daughters, but to Hannah he gives a double portion, for he loves Hannah, though the LORD has closed her womb.[434]

On these occasions, Peninnah is not above making sport of Hannah over her infertility - a cursed affliction to a woman in Jewish culture. So what should have been a joyous annual outing for all is a painful ordeal for Hannah. On one particular pilgrimage, Elkanah finds his favourite wife off her food and weeping outside the festivities:

"Hannah, why weepest thou? And why eatest thou not? And why is thy heart grieved? Am I not better to thee than ten sons?" (1 Sam 1:8)

Elkanah is indeed a generous husband who genuinely loves Hannah. She wipes her eyes and goes back into the feast to eat, wishing to please her husband, and doubtless avert her gaze from Peninnah's smirks. After the festivities, Hannah finds herself wandering down to Shiloh's famous Tabernacle, intent on spending some time alone with the LORD.

Now Eli the priest sat upon a seat by a post of the temple of the LORD. And [Hannah] **was in bitterness of soul and prayed unto the LORD, and wept sore. And she vowed a vow and said, "O LORD of hosts, if thou wilt indeed look on the affliction of thine handmaid and remember me, and not forget thine handmaid, but wilt give unto thine handmaid a man child, then I will give him unto the**

---

[433] 1 Sam 1:1-5. Caution must be exercised as to tribal affiliations, since the tribal names often denote geographical regions where the tribes settled. Thus Elkanah is a Levite living in Ephraim (*cf.* 1 Chron 6: 3-15, 18-22).

[434] We can assume Hannah is Elkanah's first wife, and when she proves barren, Peninnah is picked to continue Elkanah's line.

LORD all the days of his life, and there shall no razor come upon his head."

And it came to pass, as she continued praying before the LORD, that Eli marked her mouth. Now Hannah, she spake in her heart, only her lips moved, but her voice was not heard, therefore Eli thought she was drunken. And Eli said unto her, "How long wilt thou be drunken? Put away thy wine from thee!"

And Hannah answered and said, "No, my lord, I am a woman of a sorrowful spirit. I have drunk neither wine nor strong drink, but have poured out my soul before the LORD. Count not thine handmaid for a daughter of Belial [i.e. a good-for-nothing[435]]**, for out of the abundance of my complaint and grief have I spoken hitherto."**

Then Eli answered and said, "Go in peace, and the God of Israel grant thee thy petition that thou hast asked of Him."

And she said, "Let thine handmaid find grace in thy sight." So the woman went her way and did eat, and her countenance was no longer sad. (1 Sam 1:9-18)

Warren Wiersbe comments:

"The original tabernacle was a tent surrounded by a linen fence, but from the description in the text we learn that God's sanctuary now included some sort of wooden structure with posts (1 Sam 1:9) and doors (1 Sam 3:2,15), and in which people could sleep (1 Sam 3:1-3). This structure and the tabernacle together were called 'the house of the LORD' (1 Sam 1:7), 'the temple', 'the tabernacle of the congregation', and God's 'habitation' (1 Sam 2:32). It was here that aged Eli, the high priest, sat on his priestly throne to oversee the ministry, and it was there that Hannah went to pray. She wanted to ask the LORD for a son and to promise the LORD her son would serve Him all the days of his life."[436]

One is immediately struck by Hannah's dignity and depth of character both in beseeching the LORD for a son as well as her response to Eli. All this is in marked contrast to Peninnah the 'Pearl', who comes across less like a treasure than a trinket. Eli too will not be above reproach. Here he is reproving Hannah for supposed intemperance, when his own two sons, Hophni and Phinehas, both priests to the LORD, are themselves 'sons of Belial' and professional

---

[435] In ancient Jewish/Christian culture, Belial is a demon associated with worthlessness, pointlessness and self-destruction.

[436] Wiersbe, Warren, *Old Testament Commentary,* op. cit. p.495

charlatans. Everyone sees what these two are doing, and that the LORD is being openly blasphemed. Gien Karssen writes:

"The priest who hadn't dared deal harshly with his own sons felt no reservation in dealing with Hannah. The old man revealed a lack of insight and poor self-control. His words also revealed that in those days drunk people and immoral women were not an unusual sight in the house of God. Even Eli's own sons slept with the women who gathered at the door of the tabernacle" [437]

Once again we are given another example of how the Holy Spirit deals with its Biblical characters, warts and all, ever to expose for us all the bankruptcy of the human condition, even in God's own heroes.

The birth of Israel's last Judge

And so in time, Elkanah and Hannah have a child at Ramah and Hannah names him Samuel (שְׁמוּאֵל, Strongs: *Shemuwel,* 'heard/asked of God') **"Because I have asked for him from the LORD."** (1 Sam 1:20) Samuel is destined to be the last of the Judges, the first of the prophets, the link between the Judges and the monarchy, and one of the most significant characters in the Bible. Once again, as with Isaac, Samson, John the Baptist and Yeshua, we have a child chosen by God from the womb. And as with Samson's mother, God is placing a special emphasis on the child's birth and holy calling through the mother's previous infertility. Because only God can.

Hannah raises young Samuel until he is weaned (around age 3), and then she and her husband make the journey to Shiloh to hand him over to Eli. I write that glibly, yet as a father can I even imagine the distress of such an act? But Elkanah and Hannah's circumstances are different. They have a child from God under extraordinary circumstances, and Hannah made a vow that any male child would serve the LORD as a Nazirite. And it seems Elkanah is a man who understands God, and like Jephthah before him treats his wife's vow as sacred. How about us? Would we keep our word under such circumstances?

And when [Hannah] **had weaned him, she took him up with her with three bullocks, one ephah of flour** [around half a bushel]**, and a bottle of wine, and brought him unto the house of the LORD in Shiloh. And the child was young. And they slew a bullock and brought the child to Eli.**

---

[437] **Karssen, G** *Her Name is Woman,* Navpress, 1998

And [Hannah] **said, "Oh my lord, as thy soul liveth, my lord, I am the woman that stood by thee here, praying unto the LORD. For this child I prayed; and the LORD hath given me my petition which I asked of Him. Therefore also I have lent him to the LORD. As long as he liveth he shall be lent to the LORD."**[438]

And [they] **worshipped the LORD there.** (1 Sam 1:24-28)

No rivers of tears here but an extraordinary, joyous outpouring from Hannah to the LORD. Hannah exemplifies the godly mother. Her prayer-warrior words contain an exquisite snapshot of her own theology, as well as prophecy which could only have been revealed to her by the Creator. We have her in the Hebrew entreating the LORD as YHWH (Yahweh) in her intensely personal supplication (1 Sam 2:1-10; *cf.* Luke 1:46-55; 2 Tim 1:5). She recognises the Resurrection and the eternal inheritance even of the righteous poor to be joint heirs with Him for eternity (Psa 82:6; FG 10:34). She mentions the final judgment; she even mentions the *Mashiach* (Messiah), who shall be God's Anointed and King! Here is the second half of Hannah's prayer:

"[YHWH] **killeth and maketh alive. He bringeth down to the grave and bringeth up.** [YHWH] **maketh poor and maketh rich. He bringeth low and lifteth up. He raiseth up the poor out of the dust, and lifteth up the beggar from the dunghill, to set them among princes, and to make them inherit the throne of glory; for the pillars of the earth are** [YHWH's], **and He hath set the world upon them.**

The adversaries of [YHWH] **shall be broken to pieces; out of heaven shall He thunder upon them.** [YHWH] **shall judge the ends of the Earth, and He shall give strength unto His King, and exalt the horn of His Anointed."** (1 Sam 2:6-10)

Robbing God and the consequences

Elkanah and Hannah are knowingly leaving their precious child in the care of a man who cannot even control his own dysfunctional sons. How must that have felt? Danielle Ayers Jones writes:

"But [Hannah] knew God heard her prayers. This had already been proven. And as she dedicated Samuel to the LORD's service, she prays one of the most beautiful prayers in all of scripture, foreshadowing Mary's Magnificat. And no doubt in the years to come, as she sewed Samuel his new little robe each year to give to him when they went to the

[438] Lent means given. Samuel will serve the LORD his whole life.

tabernacle, that prayer echoed in her heart. With each stitch a prayer for him would be on her lips.

"And God's blessings did not end with Samuel. Hannah would go on to bear three more sons and two daughters. She would no longer be the childless subject of Peninnah's insults." [439]

It turns out, God is not only aware of the wickedness in Eli's household, He is going to act using His new protégé, Samuel. Imagine what it must have been like for the young Samuel, growing up in the austere environment of Shiloh's Tabernacle surrounds, taught by the kindly but weak Eli; wearing the linen ephod (apron) and ministering before the LORD; witnessing the carnal depredations of the wicked Hophni and Phinehas; knowing he had a singular calling but knowing not what it was. And each year his mother would make Samuel a little coat and bring it with her when she and Elkanah made the journey to Shiloh for the yearly sacrifice. Eli would bless Elkanah and his wife and say, "The LORD give thee seed of this woman for the loan which is lent to the LORD". They would visit their beloved Samuel for a little while, then take the road home. In time, the LORD indeed blessed the couple with three further sons and two daughters. Meanwhile to the north, Samuel grew before the LORD in the Tabernacle and ministered unto Him daily. (1 Sam 2:18-21)

Around Samuel's twelfth year, God decides to act.

Now Eli was very old, and heard all that his sons did unto all Israel; and how they lay with the women that assembled at the door of the tabernacle of the congregation. And he said unto them, "Why do ye such things? For I hear of your evil dealings by all this people. Nay, my sons, for it is no good report that I hear. Ye make the LORD's people to transgress. If one man sin against another, the judge shall judge him, but if a man sin against the LORD, who shall entreat for him?"

Notwithstanding they hearkened not unto the voice of their father <u>because the LORD would</u> <u>[desired to]</u> **<u>slay them</u>.** (1 Sam 2:22-25)

After this, Eli receives a visit from an unnamed man of God. This prophet delivers a devastating message from God to Eli, couched in the strongest possible terms:

"Thus saith the LORD, 'Did I plainly appear unto the house of thy father, when they were in Egypt in Pharaoh's house? And did I choose him out of all the tribes of Israel to be My priest, to offer

[439] http://dancingbythelight.com/2010/04/01/hannah-a-woman-of-prayer/

upon Mine altar, to burn incense, to wear an ephod before Me? And did I give unto the house of thy father all the offerings made by fire of the children of Israel?

"'Wherefore kick ye at My sacrifice and at Mine offering, which I have commanded in My habitation, and honourest thy sons above Me, to make yourselves fat with the chiefest of all the offerings of Israel, My people?'

"Wherefore the LORD God of Israel saith, 'I said indeed that thy house, and the house of thy father, should walk before Me forever,' but now the LORD saith, 'Be it far from Me, for them that honour Me I will honour, and they that despise Me shall be lightly esteemed.

"'Behold, the days come, that I will cut off thine arm, and the arm of thy father's house, that there shall not be an old man in thine house. And thou shalt see an enemy in My habitation, in all the wealth which God shall give Israel, and there shall not be an old man in thine house forever.

"'And the man of thine, whom I shall not cut off from Mine altar, shall be to consume thine eyes and to grieve thine heart, and all the increase of thine house shall die in the flower of their age.

"'And this shall be a sign unto thee, that shall come upon thy two sons, on Hophni and Phinehas; in one day they shall die, both of them.

"'And I will raise Me up a faithful priest that shall do according to that which is in Mine heart and in My mind, and I will build him a sure house, and he shall walk before Mine Anointed forever.

"'And it shall come to pass, that every one that is left in thine house shall come and crouch to him for a piece of silver and a morsel of bread, and shall say, "Put me, I pray thee, into one of the priests' offices, that I may eat a piece of bread." ' " (1 Sam 2:27-36)

Eli, whose ancestors go back to Aaron, the original priestly patriarch of Levi, has just been sacked. In fact, the dismissal will take place in the future in the most devastating fashion. We don't know who this man of God is, but it's fair to assume that Eli is shaken and keeps the prophecy to himself. Usually, a prescient utterance such as this requires confirmation from two or more witnesses.[440] Such validation of his fate shall come to Eli in an unnerving form, as we shall see.

---

[440] Deut 17:6; 19:15; Matt 18:16; 2 Cor 13:1. This is actually the case with all true doctrine covered in the Message System.

Samuel grows and waxes strong in the LORD before Eli. He's probably around 12 or 13 at this stage. On four occasions, the text highlights Samuel's faithfulness to God in implied contrast to Eli's sons (1 Sam 2:11,21,26; 3:1). One night, as Eli lays in his bed and young Samuel dozes in his, the lad hears a voice:

"Samuel! Samuel!"

Samuel jerks awake. "Here I am!"

He runs to Eli's bed but the old priest tells him he did not call.

Samuel returns to his bunk non-plussed, and lies down once more.

"Samuel!" says the voice.

Samuel dutifully trots back to Eli's bunk. "Here I am, for you called me!"

Eli tuts, "I did not call, my son! Lie down again!"

Back Samuel goes, only to be summoned a third time: "Samuel! Samuel!"

On this occasion, when Samuel reports to Eli, the old man realises the LORD is calling the lad. He says, "Go and lie down. And it shall be if He calls you, that you must say, 'Speak, LORD, for your servant heareth.' "

Samuel returns to his bunk and sure enough, the small voice is heard again:

"Samuel! Samuel!"

"Speak, LORD, for thy servant heareth."

And the LORD said to Samuel, "Behold, I will do a thing in Israel, at which both the ears of every one that heareth it shall tingle. In that day I will perform against Eli all things which I have spoken concerning his house. When I begin, I will also make an end. For I have told him that I will judge his house forever for the iniquity which he knoweth; because his sons made themselves vile and he restrained them not. And therefore I have sworn unto the house of Eli that the iniquity of Eli's house shall not be purged with sacrifice nor offering forever." (1 Sam 3:11-14)

Strewth. Laying that lot on a twelve-year-old is something, especially since Samuel has been an unwilling witness to the nefarious goings-on around the Tabernacle compound for years. Notice God is judging Eli's house, not only based on the fact that Hophni and Phinehas have been running riot as priests, but also because Eli has done nothing. Eli is not intrinsically wicked, he's a weak and ineffective father. He's had a whine and a moan at his reprobate seed, but hasn't even removed them from the priesthood.

This is what offends God. These two have been robbing the Almighty of the sacrificial meat and carrying on in a vile manner in the house of the LORD, blaspheming God's name and reputation, in effect, so Eli's punishment will be for his seed to lose the Aaronic priesthood forever. And Samuel's job will be to tell Eli what's coming.

And Samuel lay until the morning, and opened the doors of the house of the LORD. And Samuel feared to show Eli the vision.

Then Eli called Samuel, and said, "Samuel, my son."

And he answered, "Here am I."

And he said, "What is the thing that the LORD hath said unto thee? I pray thee hide it not from me: God do so to thee and more also if thou hide anything from me of all the things that He said unto thee."

And Samuel told him everything and hid nothing from him.

And [Eli] **said, "It is the LORD. Let him do what seemeth Him good."**

And Samuel grew and the LORD was with him, and did let none of his words fall to the ground. And all Israel, from Dan even to Beersheba,[441] **knew that Samuel was established to be a prophet of the LORD.** (1 Sam 3:15-20)

Eli doesn't fight it. In the mouths of two or more witnesses let a thing be established. It's confirmation of the prophecy given to Eli earlier by the unnamed man of God, which Samuel could not possibly have known. It is to Eli's credit that he accepts God's judgment without demur, though he knows not how severe or total the punishment will be. God strengthens Samuel's gift of prophecy as time passes, and the young lad becomes a prodigy throughout the land as the first national prophet since Moses.

Trouble with the Ark

Meanwhile, the Philistines are back and mobilise against Israel. The five lords put themselves into battle array at Aphek, 20 miles to the west of Shiloh, and Israel comes out to meet them at Ebenezer. The Philistines are doubtless still smarting from the drubbing Samson gave them during his judgeship, yet this age-old confrontation between Israel and Philistia is about to be taken to a whole new level.

---

[441] This becomes an iconic phrase to describe the length and breadth of Israel, analogous to America's 'from Maine to California' or Britain's 'from Land's End to John O'Groats'.

Battle is joined and the Israelites are routed, with four thousand slain. The elders of Israel are really upset:

"Wherefore hath the LORD smitten us today before the Philistines? Let us fetch the Ark of the Covenant of the LORD out of Shiloh unto us, that, when it cometh among us, it may save us out of the hand of our enemies." (1 Sam 4:3)

The chieftains among Israel are too far gone spiritually to realise the significance of what has just happened. Four thousand slain should have been a solid signal of God's displeasure; instead, it's God's fault so they call for the Ark. Notice they believe 'it' will save them rather than the LORD. Using the Ark as a military gee-gaw is hardly likely to endear Israel to the LORD, but it gives us an insight into their current state of spiritual apostasy. For hundreds of years since the Conquest, Israel has whored after Canaanite idols. Reducing the Ark to an idol to carry into battle is not going to sit well with the Creator.

So the people sent to Shiloh, that they might bring from thence the Ark of the Covenant of the LORD of hosts, who dwelleth between the cherubims: and the two sons of Eli, Hophni and Phinehas, were there with the Ark of the Covenant of God. (1 Sam 4:4)

The LORD is often referred to in scripture as 'dwelling between the cherubim'.[442] You may recall that the Ark is a chest made of shittim (acacia) wood overlaid with gold, which contains the two tablets of the Law God gave Moses at Mount Horeb (Sinai): a representation of Israel's covenant relationship with God. The lid of the Ark is the Mercy Seat, a separate piece of furniture comprising two cherubim of solid gold with their wings folded forward almost meeting each other, in effect forming a seat. God dwells between them (Num 7:89). It is likely that the Mercy Seat, always referred to separately from the Ark,[443] may have a prophetic role to play after Christ's Second Coming. Some scholars surmise the Seat may become the throne from which Yeshua rules Earth in His physical Millennium reign after the Great Tribulation and Armageddon. For some

---

[442] 'Cherubim' is already plural in the Hebrew. The King James translators are in error in adding an 's'. Cherub - singular. Cherubim – plural.

[443] Exo 25:10-22; 30:6; 31:7; 35:12; 39:35, etc.

scholars, this seems to fit the details given in Revelation concerning how God's throne is configured in Heaven.[444]

Anyway, guess who brings the Ark from Shiloh down to battle at Aphek, much to Eli's chagrin? His two sons, Hophni and Phinehas.

And when the Ark of the Covenant of the LORD came into the camp, all Israel shouted with a great shout, so that the Earth rang again.

And when the Philistines heard the noise of the shout, they said, "What meaneth the noise of this great shout in the camp of the Hebrews?" And they understood that the Ark of the LORD was come into the camp.

And the Philistines were afraid, for they said, "God is come into the camp." And they said, "Woe unto us! For there hath not been such a thing heretofore. Woe unto us! Who shall deliver us out of the hand of these mighty Gods? These are the Gods that smote the Egyptians with all the plagues in the wilderness. Be strong, and quit yourselves like men, O ye Philistines, that ye be not servants unto the Hebrews, as they have been to you. Quit yourselves like men and fight!" (1 Sam 4:5-9)

You've got to hand it to the Philistines. Deceived though they may be, they're still up for a scrap in spite of the terror inculcated into them over the years concerning the God of the Hebrews. Notice how potent God's reputation remains among the heathen for what He did for Israel centuries before in Egypt. The Philistines won't be unmindful either of what YHWH did for the Jews in Deborah and Barak's time, nor with Gideon against the Midianites; also during their own uncomfortable twenty years at the sharp end of Samson's one-man Phili-Fest, culminating in the destruction of Dagon's temple along with all five lords in one shot and three thousand Philistine nobles and miscellaneous citizens to boot. In fact, the Philistines are demonstrating more respect and fear for the God of Israel than Israel!

But the men of Gaza know how to fight, so they come out to face Israel once more, this time against the Ark in the enemy camp. The Philistines win a resounding victory, killing twenty thousand

---

[444] God's throne in Heaven is surrounded by four living creatures, represented by the lion, the ox, the man and the eagle (Rev 4:6-7). To some, this is analogous to the wilderness wanderings Tabernacle being surrounded by the four camps of Israel, whose standards are, by tradition, represented by the lion (Judah), the ox/calf (Ephraim), the eagle (Dan) and the man (Reuben).
For more, see http://njkproject.blogspot.co.uk/2011/01/four-living-creatures-throughout-bible.html

Hebrews, among whom are Hophni and Phinehas, slain in one day according to God's word given by the unnamed prophet to Eli (1 Sam 2:34). *And the Philistines capture the Ark.*

This strikes terror into the fleeing Israelites. God has deserted them. The first Eli and the rest of Shiloh know of the catastrophe is when a Benjamite runner arrives in the town half-dead with fatigue, clothes rent and dirt on his head.

And when he came, lo, Eli sat upon a seat by the wayside watching, for his heart trembled for the ark of God. And when the man came into the city and told it, all the city cried out. And when Eli heard the noise of the crying, he said, "What meaneth the noise of this tumult?" And the man came in hastily and told Eli.

Now Eli was ninety and eight years old, and his eyes were dim, that he could not see.

And the man said unto Eli, "I am he that came out of the army, and I fled today out of the army."

And [Eli] **said, "What is there done, my son?"**

And the messenger answered and said, "Israel is fled before the Philistines, and there hath been also a great slaughter among the people, and thy two sons also, Hophni and Phinehas, are dead, and the Ark of God is taken."

And it came to pass, when he made mention of the Ark of God, that [Eli] **fell from off the seat backward by the side of the gate, and his neck broke, and he died, for he was an old man and heavy. And he had judged Israel forty years.** (1 Sam 4:13-18)

It doesn't say much for Eli's standing as high priest in the community that the Benjamite runner tears right past the old man and tells the townsfolk first about the defeat and the Ark's fate. There is no better picture of a priesthood discredited either than the order of importance in which the runner finally reports the news to Eli:

1) Israel is defeated
2) There's been a great slaughter of the people
3) Your sons, Hophni and Phinehas, are dead
4) The Philistines have taken the Ark.

It's a tragic end for Eli, who is presented to us as weak but not evil. Chuck Missler wonders at the dynamics which lead righteous parents sometimes to having wayward offspring. Is it because:

1) Busy parents don't give enough time to their children?
2) Godliness in parents is not attractive to children?
3) Godly parents expect too much of their children and turn them away?

4) Godly parents are a good influence but influence cannot determine what a person will become?

5) Children, like parents, have to make their own spiritual commitments? [445]

Samuel will have a similar problem when he appoints his own sons, Joel and Abiah, judges in Beersheba. In the end, children become adults who exercise the gift of free will and become responsible for their own lives and spiritual condition, for which God holds them accountable. The Bible teaches that parents should nurture and raise their children in the LORD's ways (Prov 22:6; Eph 6:4). Eli's mistake was in not disciplining his sons by removing them from the priesthood. Failure to do this resulted in their acts blaspheming YHWH's holy name before Israel. Hophni and Phineas were, in effect, 'taking the LORD's name in vain'. They accepted the office to represent the LORD as priests, then brought shame upon His name by their actions.

In society, when a person transgresses, repentance and forgiveness are all very well, but under the Biblical model there should always be a penalty to pay under the Law. A stiff but balanced punishment programme is a much needed component to a successful society *in addition to contrition*. Likewise with children, there should always be a suitable punishment, even after repentance and forgiveness, so the child learns that there are consequences to their wrongdoing which will *always* find them out. Britain yet refuses to heed the lesson in what goes wrong when we go long on forgiveness and short on punishment. The carnal, criminal mind merely takes it as society's weakness and promptly re-offends. We have a police force which spends all day form-filling, calling the public 'civilians', or arresting shop-owners who put golliwogs in their windows, rather than confronting serious crime. When the British police do actually catch someone, liberal judges fail to punish, sometimes even awarding huge payouts to the criminals for their distress, hardship and 'right to a family life', as laid out in the UK's Human Rights Act. Little surprise, therefore, that Britain has become the judicial soft-touch and laughing stock of the world; a place every criminal in the world dreams of gate-crashing to wreak havoc while claiming benefits. Murder gets you eight years, out in five. For the duration, you are incarcerated in a comfy lock-up with colour TV, video games and all the porn and drugs you can manage, which mysteriously seem

---

[445] Missler, Chuck, *1 & 2 Samuel notes*, www.khouse.org

to find their way into these institutions while the warders' backs are turned. There are actually sections of British society who think this approach is a triumph. The figures, however, paint a different picture. Our forebears would find it hard to recognise 21st century Britain, languishing in thrall to skyrocketing murder, rape, violent gang crime, atrocities and perversions against children, and just about every other offence you can name and a few you dare not. Criminals laugh out loud at their treatment by the courts while the victims retreat behind bolted doors, weeping, disdained, forgotten. In crackbrained Britain, don't look for justice. If you want to survive, avoid getting noticed.

Yet we have a holy God who cannot co-exist with evil; who never forgets transgressions against the righteous - ever; who *will* repay. There is a war going on, and remaining neutral is an option you have not been given. You are either for God or you are His enemy (Exo 32:26); you are either the redeemed or an 'Earth-dweller'.[446] God gives us the leaders we deserve (Rom 13:1-2; *cf.* Acts 5:29), which means that many nations are now under judgment for deserting the Creator in favour of secular humanism (*ha-Satan*). Since most are not getting the message even now, God will use future events to turn the screws on the Earth-dwellers to screaming pitch.

In Samuel's day, with the Ark taken, both the Philistines and Israel are about to get a serious tutorial in God's justice and ineffable holiness. When Israel finally gets a national monarchy (in lieu of God), the reigns of Saul, David and Solomon will provide further object lessons in problem-parenting, hopeless government, treason, adultery and contract murder. Hegel observed that history's greatest lesson is that man learns nothing from history: The Judges sin cycle; the disinclination to follow God to a better future; the Philistines believing they have finally got one over on the Creator of the universe. I wouldn't believe that if I were them.

A painful lesson in hubris

So God 'hands Himself over' to the pagan enemy. The Philistines take the Ark from the battlefield at Ebenezer and triumphantly install it in the temple of Dagon (*ha-Satan*) at Ashdod alongside the pagan god himself.

---

[446] See Rev 6:10; 13:14; 14:6; 17:8. The apostle Paul succinctly defines only two types of people on Earth: those who are perishing, and those who are saved (1 Cor 1:18).

And when they of Ashdod arose early on the morrow, behold, Dagon was fallen upon his face to the earth before the Ark of the LORD. And they took Dagon, and set him in his place again.

And when they arose early on the morrow morning, behold, Dagon was fallen upon his face to the ground before the Ark of the LORD, and the head of Dagon and both the palms of his hands were cut off upon the threshold. Only the stump of Dagon was left to him.

Therefore neither the priests of Dagon, nor any that come into Dagon's house, tread on the threshold of Dagon in Ashdod unto this day. (1 Sam 5:3-5)

It's a bad day when you have to pick up the pieces of the god you worship and set him on his plinth again. Jack Heyford comments:

"Dagon was the primary god of the Philistine people with the torso, arms and head of a man and the lower body of a fish. He was worshiped as the father of Baal. The statue of Dagon fell prostrate on the ground as though worshiping before the Ark…. The idol had not simply fallen and broken [the second time] but had been dismembered. So profound was this catastrophe in the eyes of these Philistines that they would not even step on the threshold where the limbs and head of their god had lain in utter defeat." [447]

But a busted Dagon is just the start of the five lords' problems. Joe Kovacs explains:

"God was not pleased that these worshipers of… Dagon possessed the Ark, so he put the heat on them with a flaring case of hemorrhoids: **But the hand of the LORD was heavy upon them of Ashdod, and he destroyed them, and smote them with emerods, even Ashdod and the coasts thereof.** (1 Sam 5:6)…. The Bible does not casually mention this affliction in one verse and leave it alone. It goes out of its way to point out that the Philistines had a big problem in their pants: **And it was so that… the hand of the LORD was against the city with a very great destruction: and he smote the men of the city with a very great destruction: and he smote the men of the city, both small and great, and they had emerods in their secret parts.**" (1 Sam 5:9) [448]

The Hebrew word translated 'emerods' is *t'chor*. The Gesenius Lexicon describes these as *"tumours of the anus, haemorrhoidal mariscoe,*

---

[447] Heyford, Jack, *Spirit-Filled Bible,* op. cit., p.403

[448] Kovacs, J, *Shocked by the Bible,* op. cit., p.90

protruding from the anus". Not a nice thing on a Tuesday. It's not long before Ashdod has had a rear-endful of this abuse and convenes an urgent tactical meeting:

And when the men of Ashdod saw that it was so, they said, "The Ark of the God of Israel shall not abide with us, for his hand is sore upon us, and upon Dagon our god."

They sent therefore and gathered all the lords of the Philistines unto them, and said, "What shall we do with the Ark of the God of Israel?" And they answered, "Let the Ark of the God of Israel be carried about unto Gath." And they carried the Ark of the God of Israel about thither. (1 Sam 5:7-8)

That's the answer! Send it downrange for someone else to deal with. The Gathites fare little better, with deadly tumours and a plague of rats breaking out among the population, leading some scholars to surmise that this could have been a lymphatic issue such as *yersinia pestis* (bubonic plague). When the Ark is passed on to Ekron, the people of that city are in uproar: "They have brought Ark of the God of Israel to us to kill us and our people!" The five lords are at their wits' end. They had understood the Ark to be a talisman of martial invincibility before whom all foes would be vanquished. What they've got is a terrifying disaster that threatens to wipe out their race. There's only thing for it:

So they sent and gathered together all the lords of the Philistines, and said, "Send away the Ark of the God of Israel, and let it go again to his own place, that it slay us not, and our people." For there was a deadly destruction throughout all the city; the hand of God was very heavy there.

And the men that died not were smitten with the emerods: and the cry of the city went up to Heaven. And the Ark of the LORD was in the country of the Philistines seven months. (1 Sam 5:11-12, 6:1)

The five lords convene their priests and diviners to determine the appropriate method of returning the Ark to Israel with the minimum fallout to Philistia. The diviners give their verdict:

"If ye send away the Ark of the God of Israel, send it not empty, but in any wise return Him [YHWH] **a trespass offering. Then ye shall be healed, and it shall be known to you why His hand is not removed from you."**

Then [the five lords] **said, "What shall be the trespass offering which we shall return to Him?"**

They answered, "Five golden emerods, and five golden mice, according to the number of the lords of the Philistines: for one plague was on you all and on your lords. Wherefore ye shall make images of your emerods, and images of your mice that mar the land, and ye shall give glory unto the God of Israel, peradventure He will lighten His hand from off you, and from off your gods, and from off your land.

"Wherefore then do ye harden your hearts, as the Egyptians and Pharaoh hardened their hearts? When He [YHWH] **had wrought wonderfully among them, did they not let the people go, and they departed?**

"Now therefore make a new cart, and take two milch kine [cows], **on which there hath come no yoke, and tie the kine to the cart, and bring their calves home from them. And take the Ark of the LORD and lay it upon the cart; and put the jewels of gold, which ye return Him for a trespass offering, in a coffer by the side thereof; and send it away, that it may go.**

"And see, if it goeth up by the way of His own coast to Beth Shemesh, then He hath done us this great evil. But if not, then we shall know that it is not His hand that smote us, it was a chance that happened to us." (1 Sam 6:3-9)

Some points:

- Chuck Missler wants to know who they picked to model the golden haemorrhoids
- One gets a further snapshot of how the fear and reputation of YHWH have spread throughout the Canaanite peoples and wider Levant since the Egyptian Exodus
- The Philistines culturally know all about rendering a trespass offering to appease an offended god. This would typically take the form of a representation of the plague suffered – in this case, rats and haemorrhoids
- The Philistines are also smart enough to put their trespass offerings into a small chest and set it beside the Ark, not open the Ark itself. You saw what happened to the Nazis in *Raiders of the Lost Ark*
- The five lords engineer an ingenious type of 'fleece' to determine whether their woes have been specifically suffered at the hand of YHWH, or by chance. Unbroken (unyoked) cows deprived of their calves are going to be stroppy. If the cart they are lashed to is taken straight up

the road to Beth Shemesh (unlikely, given that their calves are behind them), then they know God has had a hand in their punishment and divinely ordained the course of the cows. If the cows go sideways, it was chance

- From this we may determine that the Philistines don't believe in the concept of an all-powerful God, who would steer every event in His Creation anyway
- God is watching and wants to send a clear message to the Philistines that He is in charge.

And the men did so, and took two milch kine and tied them to the cart, and shut up their calves at home. And they laid the Ark of the LORD upon the cart, and the coffer with the mice of gold and the images of their emerods. And the kine took the straight way to the way of Beth Shemesh, and went along the highway, lowing as they went, and turned not aside to the right hand or to the left. And the lords of the Philistines went after them unto the border of Beth Shemesh. (1 Sam 6:10-12)

Israel punished

The people of Beth Shemesh are in the fields harvesting their wheat when lo, they hear a mooing. They look up and blink in disbelief. Two cows pulling a cart are plodding into a certain Joshua's field, where they stop near a large stone. Atop the cart is the most holy relic of Israel, the fabled Ark of the Covenant. None but the high priest would ever have seen the Ark in person before the Battle of Ebenezer, since it was kept in the Holy of Holies in the Tabernacle enclosure at Shiloh. All the fighting men of that part of Israel saw the Ark on the day of Israel's ignominious defeat, however. Now here it is in their field! A terrific shout of rejoicing goes up.

From afar, the five lords look on bemused as the distant figures mill around the vehicle, wondering what to do. The Israelites remove the Ark from the cart, break up the cart for the wood, slaughter the two cows, and offer a sacrifice to the LORD upon the stone. Beth Shemesh is around 12 miles from the Philistine city of Ekron, whence came cart and kine. These cows have gone the twelve miles, straight as an arrow. The five lords have their answer. Defeated by a God greater than their own, they return to Ekron in despondency the same day.

What they don't witness is a few of the men of Beth Shemesh lifting the lid of the Ark for a peek. Oh dear. The Hebrew of the verse of 1 Samuel 6:19 contains an unusual construction which has led many scholars to surmise that the numbers of dead quoted are wrong. Most translations read:

And He smote the men of Beth Shemesh because they had looked into the Ark of the LORD, even He smote of the people fifty thousand and threescore and ten men: and the people lamented because the LORD had smitten many of the people with a great slaughter. (1 Sam 6:19)

The Hebrew text separately confirms a great slaughter took place, which could be just the seventy out of the village, or perhaps comprising the Israelites in the field that day who touched the Ark, none of whom were apparently Levites. Jack Heyford points out that the common understanding is that 70 in Beth Shemesh were killed, followed by 50 *eleph* (units/clans), or perhaps 50,000 in the surrounding country.[449] Other scholars have a problem with such a large number and detect some corruption of the text by copyists, maintaining the 50,000 figure was added later. First century Jewish chronicler, Flavius Josephus, who had access to ancient sources no longer extant, confirms the belief that only the 70 were killed for infringing God's holiness:

"Now there was a certain village of the tribe of Judah, the name of which was Beth Shemesh, and to that village did the kine go; and though there was a great and good plain before them to proceed in, they went no farther but stopped the cart there. This was a sight to those of that village, and they were very glad; for it being then summertime, and all the inhabitants being then in the fields gathering in their fruits, they left off the labours of their hands for joy, as soon as they saw the ark, and ran to the cart, and taking the ark down, and the vessel that had the images in it, and the mice, they set them upon a certain rock which was in the plain; and when they had offered a splendid sacrifice to God and feasted, they offered the cart and the kine as a burnt offering: and when the lords of the Philistines saw this, they returned back.

"But now it was that the wrath of God overtook them, and struck seventy persons of the village of Beth Shemesh dead who, not being priests, and so not worthy to touch the Ark, had approached to it. Those of that village wept for these that had thus suffered, and made such a lamentation as was naturally to be expected on so great a misfortune that was sent from God; and every one mourned for his own relation.

---

[449] Heyford, Jack, *The Spirit-Filled Bible,* op. cit., p.404

"And since they acknowledged themselves unworthy of the Ark's abode with them, they sent to the public senate of the Israelites, and informed them that the Ark was restored by the Philistines; which when they knew, they brought it away to Kirjath Jearim, a city in the neighbourhood of Beth Shemesh." [450]

The Ark is moved to Kirjath Jearim, and for the next 20 years resides at the house of Abinadab, cared for by his consecrated son, Eleazar, which is an interesting name that crops us more than once in scripture. One of its meanings is 'Comforter', a reference to the Holy Spirit.

"Make us a king!"

It seems likely that Samuel commences his judgeship in his thirtieth year, which is the age at which Levites usually begin serving in the Tabernacle/Temple to assist the priests (1 Chron 23:3-5; Num 4:1-3; 21-23; 29-30).[451] It is interesting that Yeshua is baptised and begins His ministry around His thirtieth year (Luke 3:23), though He does not represent a Levitical High Priest after the order of Aaron, but God's High Priest after the exalted order of Melchizadek (Heb 7:11).

Samuel, by now an accepted prophet throughout the length and breadth of Israel, begins the task of bringing the nation back to God. There is evidence that the children of Israel are already moving in that direction as a result of circumstances (1 Sam 7:2). The first task is repentance, or a turning away from the behaviour that so offends God:

And Samuel spake unto all the house of Israel, saying, "If ye do return unto the LORD with all your hearts, then put away the strange gods and Ashtaroth from among you and prepare your hearts unto the LORD and serve Him only. And He will deliver you out of the hand of the Philistines."

Then the children of Israel did put away Baalim and Ashtaroth, and served the LORD only.

And Samuel said, "Gather all Israel to Mizpeh and I will pray for you unto the LORD."

And they gathered together to Mizpeh, and drew water, and poured it out before the LORD, and fasted on that day, and said

---

[450] Josephus, *Antiquities,* op. cit., 6:1:3-4

[451] God sometimes changes the age of commencement, such as in Num 8:23-26, 1 Chron 23:24-32 and Ezra 3:8.

there, "We have sinned against the LORD." And Samuel judged the children of Israel in Mizpeh. (1 Sam 7:3-6)

Over and over again the lesson is taught. A perfect God is not surprised at our sin, but He expects us to separate ourselves from it and follow the means He has provided for atonement. In the OT this process comprises repentance (acknowledging wrongdoing with no 'ifs' or 'buts'), turning from sin, and having the sin atoned for by blood sacrifice, a model of Yeshua Himself. There are no shortcuts. *Notice that even doing this does not abrogate the punishment we may receive as a result of the Law.* In the NT, the New Covenant process for repentance and atonement is summarised as follows:

This then is the message which we have heard of Him and declare unto you, that God is light, and in Him is no darkness at all. If we say that we have fellowship with Him and walk in darkness, we lie and do not the truth, but if we walk in the light, as He is in the light, we have fellowship one with another, and the blood of Jesus Christ his Son cleanseth us from all sin [a conditional].

If we say that we have no sin, we deceive ourselves and the truth is not in us. If we confess our sins, He is faithful and just to forgive us our sins and to cleanse us from all unrighteousness [a conditional].

If we say that we have not sinned, we make Him a liar, and His Word is not in us.

My little children, these things write I unto you, that ye sin not. And if any man sin, we have an advocate with the Father, Jesus Christ the righteous [the Creator]. **And He is the propitiation for our sins, and not for ours only, but also for the sins of the whole world.** (1 John 1:5 - 2:2)

What atheists, agnostics and subscribers to all manner of religions fail to understand is that there is but one Creator who has made Himself and His laws unequivocally known to mankind. This is not 'my religion is better than your religion', it's about globally-declared Truth. All else is error. Mankind has a terminal sin predicament, and the only path to redemption the Creator has laid down for Planet Earth is through His Son, a pardon available to everyone for the asking. Most won't. Pride, not intellect, keeps the atheist from acknowledging their Creator. John Ritenbaugh writes:

"God's children may look no different on the outside, but they have been given something inside, something spiritual, that makes them different from others and special to God. They are different only because of something God has done, which also makes them His personal, treasured possession.

"John 1:12-13 declares, 'But as many as received Him, to them He gave the right to become children of God, even to those who believe in His name: who were born not of blood, nor of the will of the flesh, nor of the will of man, but of God.' That 'something' is the right or *power* (KJV) to believe the Word of God, which opens our minds and imparts to us the knowledge of God and His purpose, faith, the fear of God, the love of God, and so much more."[452]

The reality of God's OT dispensation for His chosen people is slowly dawning on the Jews. It's a sombre and deeply moving time for Israel at Mizpeh. Alas, God Himself is not the only one looking on.

And when the Philistines heard that the children of Israel were gathered together to Mizpeh, the lords of the Philistines went up against Israel. And when the children of Israel heard it, they were afraid of the Philistines.

And the children of Israel said to Samuel, "Cease not to cry unto the LORD our God for us, that He will save us out of the hand of the Philistines."

And Samuel took a sucking lamb and offered it for a burnt offering wholly unto the LORD. And Samuel cried unto the LORD for Israel, and the LORD heard him.

And as Samuel was offering up the burnt offering, the Philistines drew near to battle against Israel; but the LORD thundered with a great thunder on that day upon the Philistines, and discomfited them, and they were smitten before Israel.

And the men of Israel went out of Mizpeh and pursued the Philistines, and smote them, until they came under Bethcar. (1 Sam 7:7-11)

God keeps His end of the bargain. Israel's decisive victory over the Philistines occurs at the same place - Ebenezer - where the Jews were previously routed and the Ark seized. In addition, God restores all lands to Israel previously taken by Philistia, and sets His hand against the Philistines continually during Samuel's lifetime. Even the Amorites, the most powerful of the pagan Levant coalitions, make peace with Israel (1 Sam 7:14).

Samuel himself leads a peripatetic life on a judge's circuit, taking him on the road to Bethel, Gilgal, Mizpeh and back home to Ramah.

---

[452] **Ritenbaugh, JW** "A Priceless Gift", www.cgg.org

It's a chance to put his face around the nation. As the years pass, Israel increases in prosperity and stability. As Samuel ages and becomes less mobile, he appoints his two sons, Joel and Abijah, judges down in Beersheba to save him taking the long haul south. Unfortunately, like Eli's Hophni and Phinehas before them, Samuel's boys provoke contempt and distrust by gaining reputations for taking bribes and perverting the course of justice. This, of course, *never* occurs among the professional classes of our own modern age.

Then all the elders of Israel gathered themselves together and came to Samuel unto Ramah, and said unto him, "Behold, thou art old, and thy sons walk not in thy ways. Now make us a king to judge us like all the nations."

But the thing displeased Samuel, when they said, "Give us a king to judge us." And Samuel prayed unto the LORD.

And the LORD said unto Samuel, "Hearken unto the voice of the people in all that they say unto thee, for they have not rejected thee, but they have rejected Me that I should not reign over them. According to all the works which they have done since the day that I brought them up out of Egypt even unto this day, wherewith they have forsaken Me and served other gods, so do they also unto thee.

Now therefore hearken unto their voice, howbeit yet protest solemnly unto them, and shew them the manner of the king that shall reign over them." (1 Sam 8:4-9)

God equates Samuel's mission with His own, an indication of how close God and His prophet have become. God sometimes judges our intransigence and pride by giving us over to ourselves and our sin (Rom 1). On one level, Israel's request for a king is understandable, given the unifying effect and further stability this might engender. The downside will be the quality of the king. God intended all along for Israel to have a king, just not yet. In fact, Genesis 49:10 specifies the chosen dynasty as the tribe of Judah, through which the Messiah will come. *Ha-Satan* has monitored this lineage ever since, knowing it will be the line through which the Seed of the Woman will be birthed, and his own downfall assured. Moses predicted in Deut 17:14 that Israel would clamour for a king 'to be like the other nations' – the very notion which angers the LORD. Israel is not like other nations, it is a people set apart for God's purpose. The qualities of any king of Israel were laid out in Deut 17:14-20 long before the Hebrews possessed the Land.

So Samuel goes before the elders of Israel, obeys God and gives it to them straight. The following would not have come as a surprise to many, who probably had in their own minds the liberties traditionally enjoyed by monarchs. Samuel, though, is effectively telling Israel that things are about to change, and not necessarily for the better.

"This will be the manner of the king that shall reign over you: He will take your sons and appoint them for himself, for his chariots, and to be his horsemen; and some shall run before his chariots. And he will appoint him captains over thousands, and captains over fifties; and will set them to ear [plough] **his ground and to reap his harvest, and to make his instruments of war and instruments of his chariots.**

And he will take your daughters to be confectionaries, and to be cooks, and to be bakers. And he will take your fields and your vineyards and your oliveyards, even the best of them, and give them to his servants. And he will take the tenth of your seed, and of your vineyards, and give to his officers and to his servants.

And he will take your menservants and your maidservants and your goodliest young men, and your asses, and put them to his work.

He will take the tenth of your sheep: and ye shall be his servants.

And ye shall cry out in that day because of your king which ye shall have chosen you; and the LORD will not hear you in that day." (1 Sam 8:11-18)

In other words, on your head be it. Listen to Israel's response:

Nevertheless the people refused to obey the voice of Samuel; and they said, "Nay, but we will have a king over us, <u>that we also may be like all the nations</u>; and that our king may judge us, and go out before us and fight our battles." (1 Sam 8: 19-20)

In other words, they want a human king to do everything the LORD has been doing for them all along. God sighs at Israel's continued rejection, even sharing the experience with his prophet, then tells Samuel to get it done. This is an example of God's permissive will. The king, which God will instruct Samuel to appoint, will not be God's first choice, but He will surely use the astonishing experience that follows to shape Israel into a mighty nation which will change the world (Rom 8:28-29).

SAUL AND THE BIRTH OF THE MONARCHY

The king's heart is in the hand of the LORD, as the rivers of water: He turneth it whithersoever He will. (Prov 21:1)

Let every soul be subject unto the higher powers. For there is no power but of God: the powers that be are ordained of God. Whosoever therefore resisteth the power, resisteth the ordinance of God: and they that resist shall receive to themselves damnation. (Rom 13:1-2)

A father summons his son. "We've lost the donkeys. Please take a servant and see what has become of them."

The father is Kish, a well-heeled noble of the tribe of Benjamin and major powerbroker in the region. His son is Saul, a young, married man with a son named Jonathan. Saul is strikingly good-looking, towers head and shoulders above the rest, and is strong and athletic. He's also obedient. He takes a servant and sets off from his home town of Gibeah in good humour, passing through the mountains of Ephraim and down through the land of Benjamin, searching everywhere.

No donkeys.

Arriving at Ramah, hot, dusty and frustrated by their lack of success, Saul tells his servant that they had better head home before his father starts worrying.

The servant considers. "We're in Ramah, the home of Samuel, an honourable man. All he prophesies comes to pass. Perhaps he can tell us where the donkeys are."

Saul hesitates. "We've got nothing to offer him. Even our bread's finished."

"I've got a quarter shekel. Think that'll work?"

Saul claps him on the back. "Let's go." (1 Sam 9:6…10)

Some locals point out the old prophet to the two young men. They approach Samuel coming out of the town on his way to conduct a sacrifice at the high place. What happens next astonishes Saul.

Now the LORD had told Samuel in his ear a day before Saul came, saying, "Tomorrow about this time I will send thee a man out of the land of Benjamin, and thou shalt anoint him to be captain [king/leader] **over my people Israel, that he may save My people**

out of the hand of the Philistines. For I have looked upon My people because their cry is come unto Me." [After the entire Judges period, God is still compassionate!]

And when Samuel saw Saul, the LORD said unto him, "Behold, the man whom I spake to thee of! This same shall reign over My people."

Then Saul drew near to Samuel in the gate, and said, "Tell me, I pray thee, where the seer's house is."

And Samuel answered Saul and said, "I am the seer. Go up before me unto the high place, for ye shall eat with me today, and tomorrow I will let thee go and will tell thee all that is in thine heart. And as for thine asses that were lost three days ago, set not thy mind on them, for they are found. And on whom is all the desire of Israel? Is it not on thee and on all thy father's house?"

And Saul answered and said, "Am not I a Benjamite, of the smallest of the tribes of Israel? And my family the least of all the families of the tribe of Benjamin? Wherefore then speakest thou so to me?" (1 Sam 9:15-21)

Saul will be well acquainted with Samuel's holy reputation, making the prophet's proclamation all the more astonishing. He knows about the asses! *I am the hope of Israel?!!* Note Saul's humility at this point. Even more amazing is when Samuel later leads Saul and his servant into the hall where a sacrificial feast has been prepared with thirty distinguished guests in attendance. Better still, Samuel serves Saul the choicest part of the sacrifice, the thigh with its upper part, usually the portion set aside for the priests (Exo 29:27; Lev 7:32). This must have boggled the young man.

Saul is thinking 'crazy old man', 'mistaken identity', but the strange hospitality does not end there. Later that evening, Samuel and Saul chat in the cool breeze on the flat roof of Samuel's house, and it's a fair bet Samuel uses this occasion to explain to the son of Kish his royal destiny. There's just a catch. Samuel is very well versed in the scriptures and knows that God's chosen royal line will be coming down the line of Judah. What's a Benjamite doing appointed as Israel's king, especially in view of Benjamin's chequered past as a tribe, and Saul's home town of Gibeah in particular?

During the period of the Judges, a sordid incident occurred, in which a visiting Levite's concubine had been sexually abused and murdered by the townsfolk of Gibeah (Judg 19 & 20). The subsequent outrage across Israel resulted in a brief civil war against Benjamin after the latter's elders refused to surrender the miscreants. Only 600

Benjamites survived the subsequent battles around Gibeah. Israel finally relented, distraught that one of her tribes had been so nearly annihilated. Dark times indeed. Samuel doubtless takes this history to God and prays it out. Why Saul, LORD? God's answer will be that He has a certain king in mind who is not ready yet. In the meantime, Saul will serve God's purposes well enough.

The following morning, Samuel escorts Saul to the edge of Ramah to pack the young man and his servant on their way. He has some parting words:

And as they were going down to the end of the city, Samuel said to Saul, "Bid the servant pass on before us... but stand thou still a while, that I may shew thee the word of God."

Then Samuel took a vial of oil and poured it upon his head, and kissed him, and said, "Is it not because the LORD hath anointed thee to be captain over His inheritance? When thou art departed from me today, then thou shalt find two men by Rachel's sepulchre in the border of Benjamin at Zelzah; and they will say unto thee, 'The asses which thou wentest to seek are found: and, lo, thy father hath left the care of the asses, and sorroweth for you, saying, "What shall I do for my son?" ' Then shalt thou go on forward from thence, and thou shalt come to the plain of Tabor, and there shall meet thee three men going up to God to Bethel, one carrying three kids, and another carrying three loaves of bread, and another carrying a bottle of wine. And they will salute thee and give thee two loaves of bread, which thou shalt receive of their hands.

"After that, thou shalt come to the hill of God, where is the garrison of the Philistines. And it shall come to pass, when thou art come thither to the city, that thou shalt meet a company of prophets coming down from the high place with a psaltery, and a tabret, and a pipe, and a harp, before them; and they shall prophesy. And the Spirit of the LORD will come upon thee and thou shalt prophesy with them, and shalt be turned into another man.

"And let it be, when these signs are come unto thee, that thou do as occasion serve thee, for God is with thee. And thou shalt go down before me to Gilgal and, behold, I will come down unto thee, to offer burnt offerings, and to give sacrifices of peace offerings: seven days shalt thou tarry till I come to thee, and shew thee what thou shalt do." (1 Sam 9:27 - 10:7)

It all happens as Samuel prophesies. When Saul arrives back in Gibeah, the Holy Spirit falls upon him, God 'gives him another heart', and the son of Kish falls in with the prophets. Those looking on are astonished:

And when they came thither to the hill, behold, a company of prophets met [Saul]**, and the Spirit of God came upon him, and he prophesied among them. And it came to pass, when all that knew him beforetime saw that, behold,** [Saul] **prophesied among the prophets, then the people said one to another, "What is this that is come unto the son of Kish? Is Saul also among the prophets?"... Therefore it became a proverb, 'Is Saul also among the prophets?'** (1 Sam 10:10…12)

Jack Heyford comments:

"Gibeah, meaning 'hill of God', was Saul's home. Samuel was the first prophet around whom a colony of young men gathered for the purpose of learning to dedicate themselves to the service of God. Such a group of prophets formed in Ramah, Samuel's hometown. Music was a significant part of their expressions of praise, and was often written under the spirit of prophecy, which came upon them from the LORD." [453]

King David will later re-organise the priesthood into 24 'courses', which will have their reflection in the 24 elders redeemed and found in Heaven following the *harpazo* (Rapture) in Revelation 4. It's also fascinating that God's Message System contains a sizeable chunk of prophecy in the form of 150 Psalms, many of them written by David himself, resonating with the times of testing he undergoes during his tumultuous life. Many of these have a prophetic interpretation, and more than a few reveal stunning information about the forthcoming Messiah. We'll examine these as we move forward into the monarchy.

For now, Saul, son of Kish, returns home at the conclusion of these mind-blowing few days and is greeted by his uncle.

And Saul's uncle said unto him and to his servant, "Whither went ye?"

And [Saul] **said, "To seek the asses. And when we saw that they were nowhere to be found, we came to Samuel."**

And Saul's uncle said, "Tell me, I pray thee, what Samuel said unto you."

And Saul said unto his uncle, "He told us plainly that the asses were found."

But of the matter of the kingdom, whereof Samuel spake, he told him not. (1 Sam 10:14-16)

---

[453] Heyford, Jack, *Spirit-Filled Bible,* op. cit., p.409

And the servant kept his mouth shut too.

Saul proclaimed king

Samuel sends messengers far and wide across Israel and gathers the people together to Mizpeh. He wastes no time and addresses the multitude as the voice of the LORD:

Thus saith the LORD God of Israel, "I brought up Israel out of Egypt, and delivered you out of the hand of the Egyptians, and out of the hand of all kingdoms, and of them that oppressed you. And ye have this day rejected your God, who Himself saved you out of all your adversities and your tribulations; and ye have said unto Him, 'Nay, but set a king over us!' Now therefore present yourselves before the LORD by your tribes, and by your thousands." (1 Sam 10:18-19)

The method used to whittle down the throng to determine the king is not specifically given, but is probably determined by casting lots. There are other occasions where this method is used in scripture. The Holy Land is divided up by casting lots in Josh 18:6. Jonah is exposed by his shipmates the same way and thrown overboard to calm the tempest. Matthias is chosen by the casting of lots to replace Judas as the twelfth disciple (Acts 1:26). Proverbs 16:33 states: **The lot is cast into the lap, but its every decision is from the LORD.** (NKJV)

That having been said, Kevin de Young argues that lots should not be cast, either to determine today's ecclesiastical matters, nor even financial or social affairs, not only because believers are indwelt with the Spirit these days and should be guided thus, but because God has laid out a precedent in the NT for believers *appointing* church elders and taking decisions by seeking God's face, not resorting to what they think is chance.

"God is sovereign over all things. He superintends the rolling of the Scattergories dice, the shake of the Magic 8-Ball, and the falling of sparrows and hairs. **But this does not mean He intends for us to employ these means in making decisions**, especially on the other side of Pentecost and with the completion of sacred scripture.

"If these foregoing reasons are not convincing, consider this last one: **you don't really believe in the casting of lots.** Sometimes we talk like it's especially spiritual to make decisions by providentially-random draws. But would you choose your pastor this way? If God wants us to cast lots to determine His will, why not throw darts at a list of pastoral candidates? Why don't you narrow down your choice of a spouse to a couple of good choices, then when you propose, explain, 'I flipped a coin and you came up heads. Congratulations, want to get married?' We don't really trust lots to make wise decisions for us in other areas, so why would we use it for one of the most crucial decisions in the life of your church?"[454]

And there is no such thing as randomness, in any case! He's either the God of everything or He isn't. Samuel is obviously told by God to use this method of selection to reveal His permissive will of choice for king for the benefit of both Saul and all Israel present at Mizpeh. The measure should quell any doubt that the LORD Himself is behind Saul's selection. Unfortunately, it doesn't.

And when Samuel had caused all the tribes of Israel to come near, the tribe of Benjamin was taken. When he had caused the tribe of Benjamin to come near by their families, the family of Matri was taken, and Saul the son of Kish was taken. And when they sought him, he could not be found.

Therefore they enquired of the LORD further, if the man should yet come thither. And the LORD answered, "Behold, he hath hid himself among the stuff [Love that King James! – 'stuff'= baggage]**."**

And they ran and fetched [Saul] **thence: and when he stood among the people, he was higher than any of the people from his shoulders and upward.**

And Samuel said to all the people, "See ye him whom the LORD hath chosen, that there is none like him among all the people?" And all the people shouted, and said, "God save the king."

Then Samuel told the people the manner of the kingdom, and wrote it in a book, and laid it up before the LORD. And Samuel sent all the people away, every man to his house.

And Saul also went home to Gibeah; and there went with him a band of men, whose hearts God had touched. But the children of Belial said, "How shall this man save us?" And they despised him and brought him no presents. But he [Saul] **held his peace.** (1 Sam 10:20-27)

Some points here:

- Commentators state that Saul hid himself among the stuff (baggage) out of modesty. Certainly, our early

[454] http://thegospelcoalition.org/blogs/kevindeyoung/2011/02/11/should-churches-select-elders-by-casting-lots/

impressions of Israel's first king are of striking directness, as well as modesty

- It is significant to note that Saul does start out well
- According to the above passage, Samuel also wrote some kind of constitution for the new Israelite monarchy, which has not survived
- Early on, Saul gains a core of supporters strengthened by the LORD. He also incurs the usual political opposition, which will almost come unstuck in a minute after a timely victory

The siege of Jabesh

It's not long before God puts Saul's resolve to the test. Though he has been appointed king in the eyes of Israel, Saul has not yet been crowned when the Ammonites make a serious incursion across the Jordan against the northern Israelite town of Jabesh Gilead. The inhabitants of Jabesh come out to treat with Nahash, the pagan king, to avoid a massacre.

"Make a covenant with us and we will serve you."

Nahash is unimpressed: "Very well, on one condition. That I might gouge out the right eye of all the inhabitants as a reproach to Israel."

You can imagine the reaction of the Jabesh elders. "Hold off for seven days, that we may send messengers to all the territories of Israel. And then, if there is no-one who will save us, we will come out to you."

When the messengers arrive at Gibeah, Saul's home town, the grisly news is given in full hearing of the people, which sets off a lamentation.

And, behold, Saul came after the herd out of the field; and Saul said, "What aileth the people that they weep?" And they told him the tidings of the men of Jabesh.

And the Spirit of God came upon Saul when he heard those tidings, and his anger was kindled greatly. And he took a yoke of oxen and hewed them in pieces, and sent them throughout all the coasts of Israel by the hands of messengers, saying, "Whosoever cometh not forth after Saul and after Samuel, so shall it be done unto his oxen." And the fear of the LORD fell on the people, and they came out with one consent.

And when [Saul] **numbered them in Bezek, the children of Israel were three hundred thousand, and the men of Judah thirty thousand.** (1 Sam 11:5-8)

Saul doesn't mess around. Gruesome though his methods are, the son of Kish does what it takes to secure a unanimous muster among the tribes to confront the Ammonite threat and relieve Jabesh Gilead. He sends messengers to the besieged city with the message: "Tomorrow, by the time the sun is hot, you shall have help."

One can only imagine the relief that washes over the sweating inhabitants upon learning this welcome news. Unbeknownst to both Jew and Ammonite, however, Saul takes his huge force, divides it into three, and commences his attack on the Ammonite encampment at 3 am on the morning in question. The slaughter is total and the Israelites continue killing Ammonites well beyond noon. In fact, the victory is so total and euphoria so widespread, Saul's supporters round on some closer adversaries: namely those who opposed Saul's appointment as monarch in the first place.

And the people said unto Samuel, "Who is he that said, 'Shall Saul reign over us?' Bring the men, that we may put them to death."

And Saul said, "There shall not a man be put to death this day, for today the LORD hath wrought salvation in Israel."

Then said Samuel to the people, "Come, and let us go to Gilgal and renew the kingdom there."

And all the people went to Gilgal; and there they made Saul king before the LORD in Gilgal; and there they sacrificed sacrifices of peace offerings before the LORD; and there Saul and all the men of Israel rejoiced greatly. (1 Sam 11:12-15)

The end of the Judges

Before all Israel at Gilgal, Samuel signs off on his own career, marking the end of the Judges era and transition to the monarchy. Now all political power will be aggregated to the king; even the prophets will be subservient. Samuel declares himself blameless before the people. Notice he does not absolve his bribe-taking sons:

"Behold, I have hearkened unto your voice in all that ye said unto me, and have made a king over you. And now, behold, the king walketh before you: and I am old and gray-headed; and, behold, my sons are with you: and I have walked before you from my childhood unto this day.

Behold, here I am: witness against me before the LORD, and before His anointed: Whose ox have I taken? Or whose ass have I

taken? Or whom have I defrauded? Whom have I oppressed? Or of whose hand have I received any bribe to blind mine eyes therewith? And I will restore it you."

And they said, "Thou hast not defrauded us, nor oppressed us, neither hast thou taken ought of any man's hand." (1 Sam 12:1-4)

Samuel then takes his huge audience through the various events of the Judges period and shows them how disobedience against God was at the heart of the Israel's tribulations. And now they have sought a human king, and in so doing have rejected the LORD Himself as monarch over them (1 Sam 12:12). So be it, Samuel tells them darkly:

"Now therefore behold the king whom ye have chosen, and whom ye have desired! And, behold, the LORD hath set a king over you. If ye will fear the LORD and serve Him, and obey His voice, and not rebel against the commandment of the LORD, then shall both ye and also the king that reigneth over you continue following the LORD your God. But if ye will not obey the voice of the LORD, but rebel against the commandment of the LORD, then shall the hand of the LORD be against you, as it was against your fathers.

Now therefore stand and see this great thing, which the LORD will do before your eyes." (1 Sam 12:13-16)

It is the time of the wheat harvest when bad weather is rare. God brings down thunder and rain upon the assembly all that day and the people fear greatly. They acknowledge their sin and Samuel calms them, repeating his message of obedience to the LORD as before.

"Fear not. Ye have done all this wickedness, yet turn not aside from following the LORD, but serve the LORD with all your heart. And turn ye not aside: for then should ye go after vain things, which cannot profit nor deliver, for they are vain. For the LORD will not forsake His people for His great name's sake, because it hath pleased the LORD to make you His people.

Moreover as for me, God forbid that I should sin against the LORD in ceasing to pray for you, but I will teach you the good and the right way. Only fear the LORD and serve Him in truth with all your heart, for consider how great things He hath done for you. But if ye shall still do wickedly, ye shall be consumed, both ye and your king." (1 Sam 12:20-25)

It's a timely summary and caution, especially for us today. God does not change (Mal 3:6), and expects the same obedience from His people today. But this new king of Israel will barely leave the starting gate before disaster strikes.

Saul blows it

Around two years into Saul's reign, the new king of Israel decides to provoke the Philistines into conflict, signalling the start of a war of independence to throw off the occupation of Philistia. Saul decides on a pincer movement to attack the Philistine garrison at Geba, north of Jerusalem. He marshals his own force of 3,000 at Michmash[455] and in the Bethel mountains north of Geba, while his son Jonathan brings a force of 1,000 up from Gibeah to the south. The subsequent successful assault on Geba by Jonathan and slaughter of the enemy force is broadcast by messengers throughout Israel. Needless to say, the news is not well received by the five lords, who mobilise an overwhelming army of infantry, chariots and horsemen and move it up to Michmash to crush Israel.

Saul decamps his troops east to Gilgal to await Samuel before moving into battle. But Samuel doesn't show up. During the seven days of waiting, Saul's army starts to desert in the face of overwhelming and intimidating opposition. The king senses the ebb of his leadership. Rumours do the rounds of the camp. Word comes that some men have fled across the Jordan to Gilead. Finally, unwilling to delay further, Saul makes a rash decision that will change everything:

And Saul said, "Bring hither a burnt offering to me, and peace offerings." And he offered the burnt offering.

And it came to pass, that as soon as he had made an end of offering the burnt offering, behold, Samuel came; and Saul went out to meet him, that he might salute him.

And Samuel said, "What hast thou done?"

And Saul said, "Because I saw that the people were scattered from me, and that thou camest not within the days appointed, and

---

[455] Michmash is identified with modern-day Mikhmas: Google Earth: 31°52'22.14"N 35°16'36.69"E. Wikipedia records: "During World War 1, British forces under the command of General Allenby were to face the Turks at the same location. Major Vivian Gilbert of the British army relates the story of an unnamed brigade major who was reading his Bible while contemplating the situation against the Ottoman forces. The brigade major remembered a town by the name of Michmash mentioned somewhere in the Bible. He found the verses, and discovered that there was a secret path around the town. He woke the brigadier general, and they found that the path still existed and was very lightly guarded. The British forces used this path to outmanoeuver the Ottomans, and so took the town." https://en.wikipedia.org/wiki/Michmash. *cf.* **Gilbert, Vivian** *The Romance of the Last Crusade*, Appleton, 1923, pp.183-186

that the Philistines gathered themselves together at Michmash; Therefore said I, 'The Philistines will come down now upon me to Gilgal, and I have not made supplication unto the LORD': I forced myself therefore, and offered a burnt offering."

And Samuel said to Saul, "Thou hast done foolishly: thou hast not kept the commandment of the LORD thy God, which He commanded thee: for now would the LORD have established thy kingdom upon Israel forever. But now thy kingdom shall not continue: the LORD hath sought Him a man after His own heart, and the LORD hath commanded him to be captain over His people, because thou hast not kept that which the LORD commanded thee." (1 Sam 13:9-14)

Heavy stuff. What is Saul's sin here? Firstly, the king and priesthood are separate. Saul should never have usurped Samuel's role as high priest in offering the sacrifice. Can you imagine how Saul feels? So recently installed as Israel's saviour king, *he has just been sacked*. Not only that, God has someone better in mind - a man after the LORD's own heart. In that unnerving way of announcing future events in the past tense, God tells Saul through Samuel that his royal dynasty has just been pinched out. John McTernan writes:

"Under the law of Moses, the king and high priest could never be united under one person. Both being a king or high priest depended on genealogy. The kings were [to be] from the tribe of Judah and the line of David while the high priests were from the tribe of Levi and the line of Aaron. Thus, it was impossible for the same person to be both king and priest.

"The penalty was death for anyone but the high priest to enter into the most holy place of the [tabernacle/temple] and minister. It was impossible for any king of Israel to enter into the holy place and minister as a priest.... Neither King David nor Solomon ever went into the most holy place of the temple. For anyone other than the descendants of Aaron entering, it meant certain death. This is shown in the following verses:

"Numbers 4:15 'And when Aaron and his sons have made an end of covering the sanctuary, and all the vessels of the sanctuary, as the camp is to set forward; after that, the sons of Kohath shall come to bear it: **but they shall not touch any holy thing, lest they die**....

"(19) 'But thus do unto them, that they may live, **and not die**, when they approach unto the most holy things: Aaron and his sons shall go in, and appoint them every one to his service and to his burden: (20) But they shall not go in to see when the holy things are covered, **lest they die**.'

"Thus, under the law, it was impossible for one person to be both the king of Israel and the high priest at the same time. The throne of David will be in the holy place of the temple. For King Messiah to sit on the throne in the holy of holies, He also has to be a priest. He cannot be just a priest, but He has to be the high priest to enter into the most holy place."[456]

Later in Israel's history, King Uzziah breaks this rule, goes into the sanctuary and burns incense against the priests' vehement protestations. As they are arguing at the altar, the LORD strikes Uzziah with leprosy on his forehead (2 Chron 26:16-21).

What might seem an overlaboured technicality with this king and priest business is viewed very differently by God in the metacosm because it reflects on His Son. Samuel is Levitically pure, Saul most certainly is not. Notice in the entire Message System, there are only three people described as both kings and priests: Melchizedek (prior to Mosaic Law - Gen 14:18; Heb 7:2-3,6), Yeshua Himself (Heb 6:19-20; 7:26-28), and, a surprising one, the redeemed Christian Church (the 'Bride/the Body of Christ' – Rev 5:9-10).

Saul's sin of presumption has just doomed his kingship and royal lineage. Some say that, as a child of Benjamin and not Judah, Saul was set up by God to fail in the first place anyway. On the one hand, perhaps; yet Saul has exercised free will throughout; no-one forced him to conduct the sacrifice. What YHWH desires more than sacrifice is obedience, and this point will be made by Samuel to Saul as the latter digs himself deeper into trouble as his reign progresses (1 Sam 15:22-23). Lack of obedience to the Creator has been the problem all along with Israel (Isa 1:1-11), even as with nations and individuals today in our own modern age.

Jonathan's two-man army

The Philistine army still needs to be dealt with. Saul moves his army from Gilgal to Gibeah to link up with his son Jonathan's force. Weapons are in short supply since the Philistines banned smiths among those under their occupation (1 Sam 13:19). Warren Wiersbe comments:

---

[456] www.defendproclaimthefaith.org/MessiahKingPriest.html

"It was bad enough that Saul lacked men, but it was even worse that his men were not properly equipped. When the Philistines moved in and subjected the land of Israel to their rule, they deported all the ironworkers so that the Jews couldn't make weapons or even repair their farm implements. They had to pay exorbitant prices to have their implements sharpened… So the Jewish army was small in number and had small supplies of weapons, but they had a great God, if only they would trust Him." [457]

So no-one's relishing the coming battle, not least because the Philistines have that disconcerting habit of burning prisoners alive *pour encourager les autres.* Saul sets up court under a pomegranate tree outside Gibeah, giving us a picture of how raw his administration is at the start. While the waiting continues, Jonathan loses patience and draws his armour-bearer aside:

"Come, and let us go over unto the garrison of these uncircumcised. It may be that the LORD will work for us, <u>for there is no restraint to the LORD to save by many or by few</u>."

And his armour-bearer said unto him, "Do all that is in thine heart: turn thee [i.e. 'Fine, let's go.']; **behold, I am with thee according to thy heart."**

Then said Jonathan, "Behold, we will pass over unto these men, and we will discover ourselves unto them. If they say thus unto us, 'Tarry until we come to you', then we will stand still in our place and will not go up unto them. But if they say, 'Come up unto us', then we will go up, for the LORD hath delivered them into our hand, and this shall be a sign unto us. (1 Sam 14:6-10)

Needless to say, all this is planned without Saul's knowledge. This is the first we see of Jonathan, Israel's new prince and heir, who makes an immediate impression which will not dissipate. Remarkable, isn't it, that we've had several examples of righteous parents producing wayward children (Eli and Samuel, for starters). Here we have a wayward parent producing a righteous son. Jonathan puts his trust in God's limitless resources, but sets up a 'fleece' (remember Gideon?) to determine the LORD's will to deliver the enemy. While the rest are quailing in the camp from fear of the Philistines, Jonathan itches to tug the tiger's tail and wants God in on the action. Talk about guts. And the armour-bearer's up for it too!

The two slip away unnoticed and negotiate the wilderness landscape before climbing up a steep rocky outcrop to come upon the

---

[457] Wiersbe, W, *Bible Commentary,* op. cit., p.514

Philistines unawares. When they are ready, they reveal themselves to a group of enemy guards who are startled at the direction of the incursion.

"Look, the Hebrews are coming out of the holes where they have hidden!"

The guard hails Jonathan and his seneschal. "Come up to us and we'll show you a thing or two!"

Jonathan turns to his companion, "Follow me. The LORD has delivered them into the hand of Israel."

The two Hebrews finish their climb and dust themselves down, noting that the twenty Philistines are effectively isolated in an area of around half an acre. Perhaps the Philistines view the two Hebrews as deserters coming over to their cause. This has happened already (1 Sam 14:21). Without warning, Jonathan and his companion draw their weapons and fall upon the startled guard with such ferocity and skill, the Philistines are caught unawares and hewn down. At precisely that moment, a strong earthquake rattles the rocky hills, sending up great clouds of dust. A cry of alarm goes up in the Philistine camp.

Afar off down the pass toward Gibeah, Saul's scouts cannot believe their eyes. In the distance, the Philistine multitude is decamping in a hurry and withdrawing. In places there appears to be fighting. King Saul is immediately suspicious.

"Carry out a roll-call and see who's missing."

Then, unwilling to delay further, Saul calls his army into battle order and advances, binding his men under an oath to abstain from food for the rest of the day until he is revenged on his enemies.

As the Israelites approach, they stare astonished at the bizarre spectacle of Philistine fighting Philistine in the swirling clouds of dust shaken up by the violent temblor. A contingent of Hebrew mercenaries, who had been aiding the five lords, defects to Saul. As word spreads that the Philistines are turning tail and fleeing, determination seizes the Israelites. They fall upon the heathen and the slaughter begins. Somewhere in the midst of the turmoil, Jonathan and his armour-bearer are whooping praises to the LORD as their blades eat flesh and they wash their feet in the blood of their enemies. The rout continues to Beth Aven where the fighting enters the forest. Josephus records God's intervention in the battle as follows, drawing on some sources no longer extant:

"God disturbed their enemies with an earthquake, and moved the ground under them to such a degree that he caused it to tremble, and made them to shake, insomuch that by its trembling, He made some unable to keep their feet, and made them fall down, and by opening its chasms, He caused that others should be hurried down into them; after which He caused such a noise of thunder to come among them, and made fiery lightning shine so terribly round about them, that it was ready to burn their faces; and He so suddenly shook their weapons out of their hands, that He made them fly and return home naked. So Samuel with the multitude pursued them to Bethcar, a place so called; and there he set up a stone as a boundary of their victory and their enemies' flight, and called it the *Stone of Power,* as a signal of that power God had given them against their enemies."[458]

It's worth wondering why Jonathan did not share his daring idea with his father. Perhaps because the king already has a track record of disdaining the LORD's hand (1 Sam 14:2,18-19) and placing his trust in flesh, while Jonathan can effortlessly step out in faith. So Saul watches while Jonathan gains a second victory. Wiersbe writes:

"Saul is a tragic example of the popular man of the world who tries to appear religious and do God's work, but who lacks a living faith in God and a heart to honour Him. Unfortunately, church history records the lives of too many gifted people who 'used God' to achieve their own purposes, but in the end abandoned Him and ended life in disgrace."[459]

We see a poignant divergence in spiritual destinies between father and son in what happens next. When Jonathan reaches the wood, he is fêted as a hero. Seeing some honey by the woodside and realising he's famished, the popular prince dips his staff in the unguent liquid, gets a serious sugar hit and refreshes himself.

Then answered one of the people, and said, "Thy father straitly charged the people with an oath, saying, 'Cursed be the man that eateth any food this day'." And the people were faint.

Then said Jonathan, "My father hath troubled the land. See, I pray you, how mine eyes have been enlightened, because I tasted a little of this honey. How much more, if haply the people had eaten freely today of the spoil of their enemies which they found? For had there not been now a much greater slaughter among the Philistines?" (1 Sam 14:28-30)

---

[458] Josephus, *Antiquities*, 6:2:2

[459] Wiersbe, W, *Bible Commentary,* op. cit., p.515

Saul forcing such an oath onto an army about to do battle is nothing short of lunacy, and highlights the deterioration of his judgment. By day's end the army is famished to such an extent that when the troops come upon the Philistine baggage that evening after Saul's edict has been lifted, they attack the spoil, helping themselves to the livestock, slaughtering sheep, oxen and calves, and eating them with the blood - an act expressly forbidden under Levitical law (Lev 3:17; 17:10-14;19:26, etc; *cf:* Gen 9:4). This infuriates Saul, who is still trying to mend bridges with God. He instructs that proper butchering procedures be undertaken. He enquires of the LORD whether he should pursue the Philistines, but the LORD does not answer. Instead of imputing God's reticence to his own sin, Saul finds a new scapegoat after learning that Jonathan flouted the food ban.

And Saul said, "Draw ye near hither, all the chief of the people, and know and see wherein this sin hath been this day. For, as the LORD liveth, which saveth Israel, though it be in Jonathan my son, he shall surely die." But there was not a man among all the people that answered him.

Then said he unto all Israel, "Be ye on one side, and I and Jonathan my son will be on the other side." And the people said unto Saul, "Do what seemeth good unto thee."

Therefore Saul said unto the LORD God of Israel, "Give a perfect lot." And Saul and Jonathan were taken but the people escaped.

And Saul said, "Cast lots between me and Jonathan my son." And Jonathan was taken.

Then Saul said to Jonathan, "Tell me what thou hast done." And Jonathan told him, and said, "I did but taste a little honey with the end of the rod that was in mine hand, and, lo, I must die."

And Saul answered, "God do so and more also, for thou shalt surely die, Jonathan."

And the people said unto Saul, "Shall Jonathan die, who hath wrought this great salvation in Israel? God forbid! As the LORD liveth, there shall not one hair of his head fall to the ground, for he hath wrought with God this day." So the people rescued Jonathan, that he died not. (1 Sam 14:38-45)

God deliberately vexes Saul, not by words but by outcomes. Could Saul redeem his place at the head of the kingdom even now? Certainly not by acting like a lunatic. The elders of Israel correctly identify Jonathan as the instrument God has chosen to bring about so great a victory; a victory that could have been greater had Saul not compromised the fighting ability of his men with his food curse. Saul pursues his own personal affront even to the mortal threat of his own son. Once again, terrible judgment is displayed and publicly witnessed. While we do not enjoy watching Saul commit dynastic suicide, Saul's fate will have a surprising outcome, which most expositors miss.

Further kingly disobedience

Saul is destined to rule Israel for 40 years, or a further 38 after Samuel tells the king he has lost the kingdom due to his disobedience in carrying out the pre-battle sacrifice. In a similar fashion to how God extended grace to the high priest Eli – in other words, judgment does not come immediately – Saul's grace period will be used by the LORD to toughen up His true candidate for kingship. God does not change. Is He using adverse circumstances and enemies to toughen us up too? In dark times God comes with an invitation for intimacy. We are experiencing the Earth boot-camp training programme under live-fire conditions, so we can be of use to Him as joint heirs with Christ in the Eternal Kingdom, which will rule the universe. **We will be like Him: for we shall see Him as He really is**. (1 John 3:2) How about that for an inheritance?[460] What are you prepared to do to receive such a gift? *Do as you're told?*

In the years following the Philistine victory, God permits Saul to extend his kingship over all Israel, binding the disparate Hebrew tribes into some form of nation. But it is not given to Saul to conquer the Philistine nation; that will be David's privilege. Saul carries out further campaigns against Moab, Edom, Ammon and the five lords to secure his borders. Particularly hated are the Amalekites, those old desert bandits to the south who harassed Israel as she emerged from the Egyptian captivity centuries before. One day Samuel approaches Saul:

"The LORD sent me to anoint thee to be king over His people, over Israel. Now therefore hearken thou unto the voice of the words of the LORD.

Thus saith the LORD of hosts, 'I remember that which Amalek did to Israel, how he laid wait for him in the way, when he came up from Egypt. Now go and smite Amalek and utterly destroy all that they have, and spare them not; but slay both man and woman, infant and suckling, ox and sheep, camel and ass.'" (1 Sam 15:1-3)

---

[460] Psa 17:15; FG 10:31-36; 2 Tim 2:12; 2 Pet 1:4; Rom 8:14-19; 1 John 3:1-2; Phil 3:20-21

Presented with what he sees as an opportunity to vindicate himself before God, Saul wastes little time assembling a colossal force at Telaim in the Negev before heading south. Coming against a city of the Amalekites, the king warns the indigenous Kenites to flee.[461] This is to be *chērem,* holy war, against the personal enemies of God. Total annihilation has been ordered by the King of the Universe. All spoil is to be set aside for God under 'the ban' - remember what happened to Achan and his family who disobeyed and helped themselves at Jericho?

And Saul smote the Amalekites from Havilah until thou comest to Shur, that is over against Egypt. And he took Agag the king of the Amalekites alive, and utterly destroyed all the people with the edge of the sword.

But Saul and the people spared Agag, and the best of the sheep, and of the oxen, and of the fatlings, and the lambs, and all that was good, and would not utterly destroy them: but everything that was vile and refuse, that they destroyed utterly. (1 Sam 15:7-9)

Whoops. Samuel is not tardy in seeking out Israel's king, even being told beforehand the son of Kish has arrogantly erected a monument to himself at Carmel in honour of the victory. It is hard to imagine Saul so blinded to God's ways at this point, but the subsequent meeting between king and prophet at the Israelite base at Gilgal seals the monarch's doom:

King Saul greets Samuel: "Blessed are you of the LORD! I have performed the commandment of the LORD!"

Samuel: "Really? Then what's this bleating of sheep in my ears, and the lowing of oxen which I hear?"

King Saul: "My men brought them from the Amalekites. They spared the best of the sheep and the oxen to sacrifice to the LORD your God. The rest we utterly destroyed."

Samuel: "Be quiet! Let me tell you what the LORD said to me last night."

King Saul, warily: "Go on."

Samuel: "When you were humble in your own eyes, were you not made head of the tribes of Israel, and the LORD anointed you king over Israel? Now the LORD sends you on a journey and says, 'Go and

---

[461] The Kenites have been traditional allies of Israel since Moses, whose father-in-law Jethro was of this tribe (Judg 1:16). Jael, the wife of Heber the Kenite, was instrumental in killing Sisera, the Canaanite commander and oppressor of Israel, in the days of Deborah and Barak.

utterly destroy the sinners the Amalekites, and fight against them until they be consumed.' Why have you disobeyed the voice of the LORD and swooped on the spoil to do evil in the sight of the LORD?"

King Saul: "You are mistaken. I have obeyed the voice of the LORD, have gone the way which the LORD sent me, and brought back Agag, the king of Amalek, and utterly destroyed the Amalekites. It was the people who took the spoil, sheep and oxen, the chief of the things which should have been utterly destroyed, to sacrifice to the LORD your God in Gilgal."

Samuel: "Has the LORD as great a delight in burnt offerings and sacrifices as in obeying the voice of the LORD? Behold, to obey is better than sacrifice, and to hearken than the fat of rams. For rebellion is as the sin of witchcraft, and stubbornness is as iniquity and idolatry. Because you have rejected the word of the LORD, He has also rejected you from being king."

King Saul (heavy sigh): "I have sinned, for I have transgressed the commandment of the LORD, and your words, because I feared the people and obeyed their voice. Now therefore, I pray you, pardon my sin, and turn again with me, that I may worship the LORD."

Samuel: "I will not return with you. You have rejected the word of the LORD, and the LORD has rejected you from being king over Israel."

As Samuel turns to leave, Saul seizes the prophet's mantle, which rips. It's a dark moment.

Samuel: "The LORD has rent the kingdom of Israel from you this day and given it to a neighbour of yours who is better than you. The Strength of Israel will not lie nor repent, for He is not a man that He should repent."

King Saul: "I have sinned, yet honour me now, I pray, before the elders of my people and before Israel, and turn again with me, that I may worship the LORD your God."

Samuel relents and they worship together.

Samuel, arising: "Now Bring Agag the king of the Amalekites to me."

The captive king is brought before the prophet with some misgiving.

Agag: "Surely the time for death is now past!"

Samuel: "As your sword hath made women childless, so shall your mother be childless among women."

With that, Samuel takes a sword and hacks King Agag into pieces before the LORD at Gilgal. Not someone to mess with, Samuel. (1 Sam 15:13-33)

Then Samuel went to Ramah, and Saul went up to his house to Gibeah of Saul. And Samuel came no more to see Saul until the day of his death. Nevertheless Samuel mourned for Saul, and the LORD repented that He had made Saul king over Israel. (1 Sam 15:34-35)

The above exchange yields some interesting points:

- Saul initially tries to blame his underlings like any good bureaucrat
- I like the part where Saul protests that he has done right, and Samuel asks the meaning of the bleating of sheep in his ears!
- Saul is, in fact, worthy of death for transgressing the *chērem* ban on the spoil (*cf.* Achan), but God spares him
- This is now Saul's second confirmation that he and his descendants will forfeit the royal house
- God places obedience to Him above any earthly sacrifice. Conversely, rebellion (disobedience) against Him is viewed in the same light as devil worship which, if you think about it, is what rebellion against God actually is
- Saul finally repents, but asks Samuel for his continued support. Samuel refuses and says it's over. As the prophet turns to leave, Saul grabs the fringe of Samuel's mantle, the mark of his priestly authority, and it rips, symbolising the breaking of Saul with God, the significance of which would have devastated the king
- Saul is still concerned with keeping up appearances, and entreats Samuel to accompany him before the elders. After worshipping the LORD, Samuel summons Agag, who supposes he will be spared, since he was not immediately executed like his generals. More fool Agag. The Hebrew implies that he comes before Samuel 'delicately'
- Samuel hacks the pagan king to pieces - perhaps even with Saul's own sword - restoring Israel's obedience to YHWH
- Samuel returns to his hometown of Ramah and Saul to his at Gibeah. Though only a short distance apart, the two are not destined to meet again in this life
- Samuel mourns for Saul, which tells us something about Samuel. Though we are not told of the prophet's personal feelings for the king whom he raised, the two must have been close

- The LORD regrets making Saul king. Such regret does not imply bad judgment on God's part, but reveals another example of the Creator's *permissive* will: Making Saul king was not the best course of action but one God permitted after the people's petition. God uses any circumstances to bring about His will (Rom 8:28-29). Contrariwise, how many times do we consider the blessing of the prayers of ours *which God did not answer?*

Warren Wiersbe writes:

"Saul's sin at Gilgal cost him the dynasty, and his sin involving the Amalekites cost him the kingdom. He eventually lost his crown and his life. God wanted a king with a heart that was right toward God, a man with a shepherd's heart." [462]

---

[462] Wiersbe, W, *Bible Commentary,* op. cit. p.513

DAVID, THE SHEPHERD BOY

God instructs Samuel to seek out Jesse the Bethlehemite to anoint one of his sons king. So as not to incur King Saul's wrath on a potentially treasonous mission, Samuel enters Bethlehem with the view to conducting a sacrifice to the LORD, and Jesse and his sons are invited. During the proceedings, Samuel meets Jesse's eldest son, but God is not impressed.

"Look not on his countenance or on the height of his stature, because I have refused him: for the LORD seeth not as man seeth; for man looketh on the outward appearance, but the LORD looketh on the heart." (1 Sam 16:7)

The other six sons invited to the sacrifice are discarded by God in like fashion.

Samuel to Jesse: "Are these all your children?"

Jesse nods: "All but the youngest who is keeping the sheep."

Samuel: "Fetch him to me please. We won't sit down for the feast until he is here."

The youngest boy, David, is duly summoned.[463]

Now he was ruddy and withal of a beautiful countenance, and goodly to look to. And the LORD said, "Arise, anoint him, for this is he."

Then Samuel took the horn of oil and anointed him in the midst of his brethren. And the Spirit of the LORD came upon David from that day forward. So Samuel rose up and went to Ramah. (1 Sam 16:12-13)

David is around 15 years old at the time and has no idea what just happened to him. At the same time the anointing brings God's Spirit upon David, It departs from Saul to be replaced by a 'distressing spirit'. Saul descends into a depression which alarms his servants. They suggest finding a skilled harpist to soothe the king's troubled temperament. Saul agrees and is told Jesse the Bethlehemite has a son

---

[463] It is noteworthy that David is given as the eighth son (eight = new beginnings) in 1 Sam 16:10-11, but the seventh (seven = completion) in 1 Chron 2:15. Atheists use this apparent discrepancy as evidence for Biblical errancy and non-inspiration of the text. Yet it is entirely possible that one of David's brothers died between David's anointing and later events, thus amending the count to include just the living. This practice was common then, even as now.

who has a way with the instrument. Saul duly sends word to Jesse to supply his youngest, David, for musical duty.

And David came to Saul and stood before him. And Saul loved him greatly; and [David] **became his armour-bearer. And Saul sent to Jesse, saying, "Let David, I pray thee, stand before me, for he hath found favour in my sight."**

And it came to pass, when the evil spirit from God was upon Saul, that David took an harp and played with his hand, so Saul was refreshed and was well, and the evil spirit departed from him. (1 Sam 16:21-23)

David and Goliath

Some time later, David's teenage stint as a court musician to soothe Saul becomes part-time (presumably because of an improvement in Saul's mental state), so David periodically goes home to Bethlehem to tend his father's sheep (1 Sam 17:15). Around this time, the Philistines mobilise against Israel once more and muster their army in the Valley of Elah between Azekah and Sochoh, 14 miles west of Bethlehem. Here there is a valley, either side of which the opposing armies occupy the high ground.[464] This time, though, there is a difference in the heathen challenge.

And there went out a champion out of the camp of the Philistines, named Goliath of Gath, whose height was six cubits and a span [9 feet 9 inches]**. And he had an helmet of brass upon his head, and he was armed with a coat of mail; and the weight of the coat was five thousand shekels of brass** [126 lbs/57.3 kg]**. And he had greaves of brass upon his legs, and a target of brass between his shoulders.**

And the staff of his spear was like a weaver's beam; and his spear's head weighed six hundred shekels of iron [16 lbs/7.2 kg]**: and one bearing a shield went before him.**

And he stood and cried unto the armies of Israel, and said unto them, "Why are ye come out to set your battle in array? Am not I a Philistine, and ye servants to Saul? Choose you a man for you and let him come down to me. If he be able to fight with me and to kill me, then will we be your servants. But if I prevail against him and kill him, then shall ye be our servants and serve us."

And the Philistine said, "I defy the armies of Israel this day! Give me a man, that we may fight together." (1 Sam 17:4-10)

---

[464] Google Earth: 31°41'25.10"N 34°57'07.70"E

This monster is terrifying. Go outside your house and measure 9 feet 9 inches up your outside wall to gain perspective of what the Israelite army is up against. No-one wants to fight the giant from Gath, neither do the commanders on either side wish to commit to full battle due to casualties. So there's an impasse, and it goes on for forty days and nights (the period of God's testing).

David's three elder brothers are in the Israelite army, victims of this stalemate. Jesse decides to send David with some victuals to perk them up and learn the latest on the confrontation:

And David rose up early in the morning and left the sheep with a keeper, and took, and went, as Jesse had commanded him; and he came to the trench as the host was going forth to the fight, and shouted for the battle. For Israel and the Philistines had put the battle in array, army against army.

And David [left his supplies in the hand of the quartermaster], **and ran into the army, and came and saluted his brethren. And as he talked with them, behold, there came up the champion, the Philistine of Gath, Goliath by name, out of the armies of the Philistines, and spake according to the same words. And David heard them. And all the men of Israel, when they saw the man, fled from him and were sore afraid.**

And the men of Israel said, "Have ye seen this man that is come up? Surely to defy Israel is he come up. And it shall be, that the man who killeth him, the king will enrich him with great riches, and will give him his daughter, and make his father's house free in Israel." (1 Sam 17:20-25)

David considers Israel's predicament, then looks around him. No-one seems up for the challenge: "Tell me again what shall be done to the man that kills this Philistine, and takes away the reproach from all Israel?" The troops around him shrug. Untold riches. The king's daughter for wife. Tax-exemption for life. David marvels. "Who is this uncircumcised Philistine, that he should defy the armies of the living God?"

David's eldest brother has had enough and reacts angrily to David's implicit disrespect of the troops. Soon Saul gets to hear of the ruckus and summons the lad. He recognises David as one of his court musicians.

David: "O King, let no-one's heart quail because of this fellow! Your servant will go out and deal with this Philistine!"

Saul: "You're going nowhere. You're just a boy, and this fellow has been trained as a professional warrior from his youth."

David (unfazed): "Sire, your servant used to keep sheep. On several occasions, they were attacked by lions and bears, so I went out and dealt with these creatures the same as I will do to this uncircumcised Philistine who defies the armies of the living God. The LORD, who delivered me from the paw of lion and bear, will surely deliver me from the hand of this Philistine!"

Perhaps Saul is fed up with the impasse and needs a sacrificial victim to provoke his army to battle. Perhaps he sees something in David's eyes that startles him. Before he can stop himself, the words are out of his mouth and into the ears of those around him: "Go, and the LORD be with you."

After that, time passes in a blur of activity for David. Saul has him garbed in his own armour with bronze helmet and mailcoat, but such is the weight of the war-gear, David can scarcely stand, let alone walk. He shucks off the lot, announcing that he'll be fighting light instead. To those around, these are the words of a madman going to his doom. As David heads out into the valley for battle, the baffled Saul turns to Abner, his commander:

Saul: "Remind me whose son is this one."

Abner: "Haven't the faintest idea, lord."

Saul: "Find out."

Meanwhile, David… **took his staff in his hand, and chose him five smooth stones out of the brook, and put them in a shepherd's bag which he had, even in a scrip; and his sling was in his hand: and he drew near to the Philistine.**

And the Philistine came on and drew near unto David; and the man that bare the shield went before him. And when the Philistine looked about and saw David, he disdained him, for he was but a youth and ruddy, and of a fair countenance.

And the Philistine said unto David, "Am I a dog, that thou comest to me with staves?" And the Philistine cursed David by his gods. And the Philistine said to David, "Come to me, and I will give thy flesh unto the fowls of the air, and to the beasts of the field." (1 Sam 17:40-44)

Amazing drama. Goliath is completely insulted that this is the best Israel can come up with. Goliath of Gath is used to men fainting in his presence. He can only be further provoked by David's refusal to be intimidated, not least by his unequivocal riposte:

"Thou comest to me with a sword and with a spear and with a shield, but I come to thee in the name of the LORD of hosts, the God of the armies of Israel, whom thou hast defied! This day will

the LORD deliver thee into mine hand, and I will smite thee, and take thine head from thee, and I will give the carcases of the host of the Philistines this day unto the fowls of the air, and to the wild beasts of the Earth, that all the Earth may know that there is a God in Israel. And all this assembly shall know that the LORD saveth not with sword and spear, for the battle is the LORD's, and He will give you into our hands." (1 Sam 17:45-47)

That little speech must have loosened the bowels of David's brothers and everyone else within earshot. What *chutzpah!* What brass neck! There's nothing for it now but to fight. As Goliath closes for the kill, David actually starts *running* towards the Philistine,[465] thrusting his hand into his bag for a stone, then whirling the slingshot about his head before letting the missile fly - straight into the Philistine's forehead. The scriptures state that the stone sinks into the giant's skull and he drops down dead.

An awestruck hush falls across the valley as every eye plays witness. David grabs Goliath's sword and wields it with some effort to decapitate the giant. As soon as the Philistines see their giant down, they panic and flee, hotly pursued by the Israelite army, now galvanised by bloodlust and well up for the fight. Abner wastes no time rescuing David and bringing him before Saul, Goliath's head still in the youth's firm grasp, dripping blood on the grass.

King Saul: "Whose son are you, young man?"

David: "I am the son of your servant, Jesse the Bethlehemite."

Jack Heyford reminds us that Saul is not discovering David for the first time, but since the king's intention is to bring David into his military leadership, make him a permanent member of his élite bodyguard, grant his father's house tax exemption for life, and marry David off to his daughter, a thorough background check is in order.[466]Also attending this meeting is the king's son, Jonathan, prince of Israel and Saul's heir. After Saul has finished with David, David and Jonathan become firm friends. This relationship is often misrepresented among liberals as homosexual in nature. It isn't. They hit it off like bosom buddies from the outset, their relationship described thus:

---

[465] Some scholars speculate that in running towards his enemy, David could have been taking advantage of poor eyesight common to those with gigantism. I prefer the view that David was merely demonstrating his utter conviction of victory. It certainly invigorated the slackers in Saul's army!

[466] Heyford, Jack, *Spirit-Filled Bible,* op. cit. p.421

And it came to pass, when he had made an end of speaking unto Saul, that the soul of Jonathan was knit with the soul of David, and Jonathan loved him as his own soul. And Saul took [David] **that day and would let him go no more home to his father's house. Then Jonathan and David made a covenant, because he loved him as his own soul. And Jonathan stripped himself of the robe that was upon him and gave it to David, and his garments, even to his sword, and to his bow, and to his girdle.** (1 Sam 18:1-4)

We've all heard of the encounter between David and Goliath. Here are some insights:

- Was Goliath one of the Nephilim? The scriptures state that Goliath was one of five sons of the giant in Gath, of the six-fingered variety, so yes (2 Sam 21:16-22). These giants are the result of Satan's attempt to pollute the human gene pool (Gen 6), and the reason God destroyed the Earth with the Flood. According to Gen 6:4, this problem persisted after the Inundation, and we have periodically come across these giants in the OT. God's instructions to Joshua utterly to destroy certain tribes in the Canaan invasion must be viewed in this light. The Nephilim and offspring thereof have all been marked for destruction
- If David thought God was with him, why did he pick five stones from the brook prior to his encounter with Goliath, son of the giant? Did he think he would miss? Perhaps he chose five stones because Goliath had four brothers. David was ready for all five. David's mighty men will eventually slay the rest of the giant's seed and stamp out the Nephilic gene pool in Philistia over the next few decades [467]
- David's skill with a slingshot doubtless derives from his upbringing among the Benjamites, renowned not only for their ambidextrous ability, but also their unrivalled skill with this weapon

---

[467] Some commentators state that the notion Goliath had four brothers is without scriptural merit. They are wrong. There was a giant in Gath - some scholars name him Rapha - who fathered Goliath and at least four others. Three of Goliath's brothers are named in scripture as sons of the giant, and one goes unnamed. Those named are: Ishbi-benob, slain by Abishai (2 Sam 21:16-17). Saph, slain by Sibbechai the Hushathite (2 Sam 21:18, 1 Chron 20:4). Lahmi, slain by Elhanan (2 Sam 21:19, 1 Chron 20:5). The unnamed son was killed by Jonathan, son of Shimea (2 Sam 21:20-21, 1 Chron 20:6-7).

- With David's improbable victory over the giant, God begins overtly to steer the action. Henceforth, Saul will find himself a victim of events, not the architect
- Jonathan knows of Samuel's rejection of Saul and his line as the royal house, so intuitively recognises that David is the king chosen by God. Notice how, from the outset, Jonathan acquiesces to God's will and does not contest David's destiny, unlike his father. In handing over his royal robe (with fringe) and sword to David, Jonathan acknowledges David as the heir to Israel in his stead. This tells us something of Jonathan's calibre, in marked contrast to his father. Jonathan's love for David will drive a wedge between king and son. It all starts innocently enough:

And David went out whithersoever Saul sent him, and behaved himself wisely: and Saul set him over the men of war, and he was accepted in the sight of all the people, and also in the sight of Saul's servants.

And it came to pass as they came, when David was returned from the slaughter of the Philistine, that the women came out of all cities of Israel, singing and dancing, to meet King Saul, with tabrets, with joy, and with instruments of musick.

And the women answered one another as they played, and said, "Saul hath slain his thousands, and David his ten thousands!"

And Saul was very wroth, and the saying displeased him; and he said, "They have ascribed unto David ten thousands, and to me they have ascribed but thousands: and what can he have more but the kingdom?"

And Saul eyed David from that day forward. (1 Sam 18:5-9)

Saul's pride comes to the fore, indicating the return of the evil spirit. David is now squarely in *ha-Satan's* crosshairs. Saul falls into a mania the following day. Seizing the javelin, the symbol of his kingship, he hurls it at David in an attempt to pin him to the wall. David escapes on this occasion, but apparently Saul attempts this strategy more than once in an effort to murder the son of Jesse.

Of course Saul fears David. He senses the diminishing of his own authority while David's grows. David's caution in 'behaving himself wisely' and acting righteously endears him to a population sick to death of corruption and unrighteous behaviour in its past rulers and priests. David is the new breeze blowing through Judaism. People welcome him. They sense a corner in the nation's fortunes has at last been turned.

David at court

But now commences the troubling period of David's life at Saul's court. Imagine your attendance being mandatory, yet living in constant fear of your life, as experienced by those unfortunates who made up Herod the Great's court or Nero's, or Henry VIII's, or a hundred other despots' company throughout the ages. Let's take a look at Saul's family:

Leading wife: Ahinoam, daughter of Ahimaaz
Sons: Jonathan, Abinadab, Malchishua and Ishbosheth.
Daughters: Merab and Michal

Concubine: Rizpah, daughter of Aiah
Sons: Armoni and Mephibosheth. (2 Sam 21:8) [468]

Saul must make good his pledge of a daughter as wife for David, so he hands over Merab, his elder daughter, then gives her away to another, believing that a betrothal extended by way of fulfilling a debt is contrary to Jewish law.[469] David is unfazed and is heard about court praising the king as usual and conveying in humble fashion that it is no light thing to be a king's son-in-law, seeing that he is poor and lightly esteemed. For his part, Saul's strategy is to have David slain by the Philistines (1 Sam 18:17-19), as if that stands any chance of thwarting the plan of God. He instructs his servants to tell David that the dowry for Michal, his other daughter, will be no less than one hundred foreskins of the Philistines, bagged and tagged.

And when his servants told David these words, it pleased David well to be the king's son-in-law, and the days were not expired.

Wherefore David arose and went, he and his men, and slew of the Philistines two hundred men; and David brought their foreskins, and they gave them in full tale to the king, that he might

---

[468] This is not the same Mephibosheth as the son of Jonathan, whom David later protects.

[469] *Jewish Women's Archive,* http://jwa.org/encyclopedia/article/merab-daughter-of-saul-midrash-and-aggadah

be the king's son-in-law. And Saul gave him Michal his daughter to wife.

And Saul saw and knew that the LORD was with David, and that Michal, Saul's daughter, loved him. And Saul was yet the more afraid of David. And Saul became David's enemy continually.

Then the princes of the Philistines went forth: and it came to pass, after they went forth, that David behaved himself more wisely than all the servants of Saul; so that his name was much set by. (1 Sam 18:26-30)

David reckons Saul deserves a double portion. In the end, because of Saul's pride and animosity, two hundred Philistines are now dead and mutilated. Michal and Israel love David all the more, and the fighting men of Israel respect him for hitting the five lords where it hurts.

And Saul spake to Jonathan his son, and to all his servants, that they should kill David. But Jonathan, Saul's son, delighted much in David, and Jonathan told David, saying, "Saul my father seeketh to kill thee. Now therefore, I pray thee, take heed to thyself until the morning, and abide in a secret place and hide thyself. And I will go out and stand beside my father in the field where thou art, and I will commune with my father of thee; and what I see, that I will tell thee."

And Jonathan spake good of David unto Saul his father, and said unto him, "Let not the king sin against his servant, against David, because he hath not sinned against thee, and because his works have been to thee very good. For he did put his life in his hand and slew the Philistine, and the LORD wrought a great salvation for all Israel. Thou sawest it and didst rejoice. Wherefore then wilt thou sin against innocent blood, to slay David without a cause?"

And Saul hearkened unto the voice of Jonathan. And Saul sware, "As the LORD liveth, he shall not be slain."

And Jonathan called David, and Jonathan shewed him all those things. And Jonathan brought David to Saul, and he was in his presence, as in times past. (1 Sam 19:1-7)

So David is now back at court, shoulder-blades twitching at the prospect of further incoming javelins. The Philistines mobilise once more, and David leads the army out and gives them such a trouncing with God's help, that the five lords flee the field in disarray. More good news of David's military prowess depresses Saul further:

And the evil spirit from the LORD was upon Saul, as he sat in his house with his javelin in his hand: and David played [the harp] **with his hand. And Saul sought to smite David even to the wall with the javelin, but** [David] **slipped away out of Saul's presence, and he smote the javelin into the wall; and David fled and escaped that night.**

Saul also sent messengers unto David's house, to watch him, and to slay him in the morning. And Michal, David's wife, told him, saying, "If thou save not thy life tonight, tomorrow thou shalt be slain."

So Michal let David down through a window: and he went and fled, and escaped. (1 Sam 19:9-12)

When Saul learns of David's escape, he views Michal's participation as a personal betrayal. His daughter's excuse is: "David said to me, 'Let me go! Why should I kill you?' What was he to do, Father? You threatened to kill him!"

David takes refuge with Samuel at the latter's school of prophets at Ramah. Once Samuel has been briefed on Saul's homicidal predilections, both he and David feel it wise to retire to the countryside and seek refuge. For his part, Saul despatches three missions to bring David in, all of which fail when the Spirit of God falls upon the arresting soldiers who begin prophesying in the manner of the prophets around them. This must have been a spooky experience. Exasperated, Saul finally heads up to Ramah himself and falls prey to the same unearthly experience:

Then went [Saul] **also to Ramah, and came to a great well that is in Sechu. And he asked, "Where are Samuel and David?" And one said, "Behold, they be at Naioth in Ramah."**

And [Saul] **went thither to Naioth in Ramah, and the Spirit of God was upon him also, and he went on and prophesied, until he came to Naioth in Ramah. And he stripped off his clothes also, and prophesied before Samuel in like manner, and lay down naked all that day and all that night. Wherefore they say, "Is Saul also among the prophets?"** (1 Sam 19-22-24)

By this time, Saul is too blinded by jealousy, depression and hatred to recognise that the LORD is steering circumstances. Often we too forget who's really in charge when calamity strikes, or our plans don't turn out as intended. Have each of us made that fundamental decision that stands before all others: that either He is the God of everything or He isn't?

David steals a clandestine encounter with his friend Jonathan to sound out the king's current mood. They reaffirm their friendship and Jonathan agrees to see how things stand with his father. In return, Jonathan has David pledge that he will not destroy Jonathan's descendants once the LORD has granted the kingdom to the son of Jesse. They arrange a code between them so Jonathan can convey the king's true intentions regarding David. Jonathan will take a young lad into a meadow on a prearranged day for some archery practice. If he instructs the boy to retrieve the arrows beyond where he is standing, David, hidden close by, will know that he must flee because Saul seeks his life.

On the occasion of the feast of the new moon, David's place remains empty. On the second day, when David still has not appeared, Saul asks Jonathan of his whereabouts. Jonathan replies that David requested leave to attend the sacrifice at Bethlehem with his family. Saul blows his top:

"Thou son of the perverse rebellious woman! Do not I know that thou hast chosen the son of Jesse to thine own confusion, and unto the confusion of thy mother's nakedness? For as long as the son of Jesse liveth upon the ground, thou shalt not be established, nor thy kingdom. Wherefore now send and fetch him unto me, for he shall surely die!"

And Jonathan answered Saul his father, and said unto him, "Wherefore shall he be slain? What hath he done?"

And Saul cast a javelin at him to smite him, whereby Jonathan knew that it was determined of his father to slay David. So Jonathan arose from the table in fierce anger, and did eat no meat the second day of the month, for he was grieved for David, because his father had done him shame. (1 Sam 20:30-34)

Never be around Saul when he has a javelin in his hand. At the appointed time, Jonathan goes out to the meadow with a lad and shoots some arrows over the boy's head. When the lad runs to the place where the arrows land, Jonathan cries out, "Is not the arrow beyond you?"

The lad retrieves the arrows. Jonathan instructs him to take them back to the city. When the boy has left, David arises from his place of concealment, and the two friends embrace with tears.

And Jonathan said to David, "Go in peace, forasmuch as we have sworn both of us in the name of the LORD, saying, 'The LORD be between me and thee, and between my seed and thy seed

forever'." And [David] **arose and departed, and Jonathan went into the city.** (1 Sam 20:42)

A bloody showdown

David is now a fugitive. He flees to Nob with a small group of loyalists and seeks help from the high priest, Ahimelech, the great-grandson of the prophet Samuel's own mentor, Eli. David takes care to disguise the reason for his presence. He tells the high priest a bald-faced lie: that he and his men are on a secret mission on the king's business, and no-one must know. In fact, the lie is given to protect Ahimelech from Saul in the matter of any complicity in harbouring a fugitive, but the ploy will tragically backfire.

Ahimelech tells David that there is nothing to eat but the showbread of the Tabernacle, to which he is welcome if his men have kept themselves from women. David replies that they have, for three days at least. Jack Heyford comments:

"When the showbread was replaced, it could be eaten, but usually only by the priests. The showbread comprised 12 loaves made of pure wheat flour, which were set in the sanctuary before Yahweh [YHWH], fresh each Sabbath day. Jesus referred to this event in teaching that He was Lord of the Sabbath, and that human need must be considered before ritual (Matt 12:3-4; Lev 24:5-9)."[470]

David has another request of the priest:

"And is there not here under thine hand spear or sword? For I have neither brought my sword nor my weapons with me, because the king's business required haste."

And the priest said, "The sword of Goliath the Philistine, whom thou slewest in the valley of Elah, behold, it is here wrapped in a cloth behind the ephod. If thou wilt take that, take it: for there is no other save that here."

And David said, "There is none like that. Give it me." (1 Sam 21:8-9)

Refreshed with the LORD's bread, and armed with what must be the mightiest piece of ordnance in the land, David departs Nob with his men and heads east. There's just one problem. The whole exchange between David and Ahimelech at Nob has been witnessed by one of Saul's spies, the wretched Doeg the Edomite, who departs immediately for Gibeah to spill the beans to the king.

---

[470] Heyford, Jack, *Spirit-Filled Bible,* op. cit. p.425

David's next move is unusual. He knows Saul will hunt him down to protect his kingship, so the son of Jesse decides to go where Saul won't look - into Philistine country, to the city of Gath, the hometown of Goliath, armed with Goliath's sword! Any hope of David remaining *incognito* is blown almost immediately when he is recognised by the men of one of the five lords, the king of Gath, Achish.

David's next tactic is nothing short of bizarre. In Philistine culture, the mad are regarded as an evil sign and exempt from harm lest the gods grow angry. So, David **changed his behaviour before them, and feigned himself mad in their hands, and scrabbled on the doors of the gate, and let his spittle fall down upon his beard. Then said Achish unto his servants, "Lo, ye see the man is mad! Wherefore then have ye brought him to me? Have I need of madmen, that ye have brought this fellow to play the madman in my presence? Shall this fellow come into my house?"** (1 Sam 21:13-15)

The ruse works and David is set free, but this has to be the low-point of David's career thus far. It must have felt as though God was far from him and things could only get worse. In fact, things start to look up almost immediately. David and his gang flee to the cave of Adullam, 20 miles southwest of Jerusalem on the border of Philistine territory, and only a few miles from his stunning victory at Elah against Goliath. David's family receives word that he's close by, so they leave Bethlehem and the danger of Saul's retribution behind them, and travel out to join David. At the same time, the grapevine across Judah is a-buzz. Every ne'er-do-well, cut-throat, debt-ridden and disaffected citizen for miles around learns that David is recruiting. Many hoof it out to join the gang at the cave. Before David knows it, he is the *de facto* chieftain of four-hundred heavily armed desperados who have nothing to lose. This is the beginning of the legend of David's 'mighty men', whose exploits will become famous throughout the Levant.

Before Saul hears of it, David takes his small army out to Mizpeh of Moab, and finds favour there with the king and people of his beloved ancestor Ruth. Some scholars believe that David makes use of the unassailable stronghold of Masada by the Dead Sea as his base of operations.

Meanwhile: **When Saul heard that David was discovered, and the men that were with him, (now Saul abode in Gibeah under a tree in Ramah, having his spear in his hand** [naturally]**, and all his**

servants were standing about him [warily]**), then Saul said unto his servants that stood about him, "Hear now, ye Benjamites. Will the son of Jesse give every one of you fields and vineyards, and make you all captains of thousands, and captains of hundreds? All of you have conspired against me, and there is none that sheweth me that my son** [Jonathan] **hath made a league with the son of Jesse, and there is none of you that is sorry for me, or sheweth unto me that my son hath stirred up my servant against me, to lie in wait, as at this day?"**

Then answered Doeg the Edomite, which was set over the servants of Saul, and said, "I saw the son of Jesse coming to Nob, to Ahimelech the son of Ahitub. And he enquired of the LORD for him, and gave him victuals, and gave him the sword of Goliath the Philistine." (1 Sam 22:6-10)

Note that Saul's power appears to have shrunk to the extent that his entourage comprises just his own tribe of Benjamin. In no small part, this accounts for his unreasoning jealousy, vindictiveness and rage against David, which finds no target until Doeg spills the beans about David's visit to Ahimelech at Nob. Suddenly it's all God's fault. Ahimelech and his entire priest caste are summoned to answer to the king at Gibeah.

Saul (furious): "Why have you conspired against me with David? You gave him food, *that* sword, and enquired of the LORD for him, that he should rebel against me even now!"

Ahimelech: "And who is so faithful among all your servants as David, your own son-in-law? He has always done as he was bidden and behaved honourably in your house at all times. As for me, I have done nothing wrong. Neither I nor any in my father's house know anything of this!"

Saul: "You shall surely die, Ahimelech, you and all your father's house!"

The death sentence pronounced, the king spins to face his footmen, ordering them to take arms and kill Ahimelech and his priests forthwith. The troops refuse, incensing Saul further. But Doeg is a different matter. As an Edomite, he has nothing but contempt for Israel in general and Jews in particular. He gleefully rips out his sword and sets to work on the loathed priests of Israel, hewing down the lot with impunity – eighty-five priests in total.

And Nob, the city of the priests, smote [Saul] **with the edge of the sword, both men and women, children and sucklings, and oxen, and asses, and sheep, with the edge of the sword. And one of the**

sons of Ahimelech the son of Ahitub, named Abiathar, escaped, and fled after David. And Abiathar shewed David that Saul had slain the LORD'S priests.

And David said unto Abiathar, "I knew it that day, when Doeg the Edomite was there, that he would surely tell Saul. I have occasioned the death of all the persons of thy father's house. Abide thou with me, fear not, for he that seeketh my life seeketh thy life, but with me thou shalt be in safeguard." (1 Sam 22:19-23)

David blames himself for the death of Ahimelech's house and priesthood, yet while he may have been the unwitting cause for the slaughter, this tragic scene is the fulfilment of the prophecy God gave Samuel, that he would remove Eli and his descendants from the priesthood forever for Eli's failure to discipline his wayward sons, Hophni and Phineas (1 Sam 3:11-14).

Saul now realises that he has burnt all his bridges with God. How far the son of Kish has fallen. From the young man full of promise all those years ago, who stood head and shoulders above the rest; Saul's downfall has been a process: a downward spiral of disobedience, presumption, arrogance, ignorance and jealousy, which eventually delivers him to the point where he could steal God's spoil and spare the Amalekite king (whom God expressly ordered destroyed), yet has no problem overseeing the brutal murder of all God's priests on a whim.

In fact, not all: one priest alone survives the carnage - Abiathar - who flees with the linen ephod and priestly regalia to David, to serve the son of Jesse for the future. Yet even Abiathar must be expunged from the priesthood at some point, and this eventually comes to pass later in David's reign according to prophecy.[471]

Hounded from pillar to post

The fugitive priest finds David near the city of Keilah, currently under attack by the Philistines, whose favoured strategy is to rob the

---

[471] Abiathar serves David faithfully during the latter's monarchy as co-high priest with Zadok, but backs Adonijah instead of Solomon as David's successor. For this he is banished to his estates at Anathoth by Solomon. Thereafter the priesthood passes to Zadok, and Eli's priestly line is expunged forever, according to the prophecy. The *Jewish Encyclopedia* asserts that David's male line receives divine retribution for David's culpable role in bringing Saul's wrath onto the house of Eli. Every cause has an effect, and every effect a cause. Deep waters indeed. There is always a penalty under the Law.

threshing floors of grain at harvest-time to feed their own armies, in turn starving their enemies. The matter is brought before David, who promptly does what each of us should do with our dilemmas: he takes it before the LORD. Via Abiathar, God tells David twice to go up to fight the Philistines and He will deliver them into David's hand.

By now, David's force numbers six hundred. They fall upon the raiding Philistine force and wreak havoc, taking back the stolen livestock and other booty, and putting the invader to the sword. You would think the people of Keilah would be delighted with such an eleventh-hour deliverance, but you would be wrong. Saul hears of David's deliverance of Keilah and believes he has him trapped in the town. David's worst suspicions are confirmed by God via Abiathar. The citizens of Keilah fear they might end up like the poor folk of Nob for treating with David. God warns David that the citizens of Keilah will have no compunction in handing him over to save their own necks. David and his force saddle up and head for the wilderness of Ziph to escape Saul and his vengeance.

The next months are spent moving from one mountain stronghold to another, food and resources a constant battle for an outlaw force so large. It is during this period, while Saul manically searches for his nemesis, that Jonathan risks his life to seek out his old friend once more. Quite what system Jonathan and David devise to find one another is not explained, but Jonathan successfully tracks him down in a forest. The meeting is an emotional one:

And [Jonathan] **said unto him, "Fear not, for the hand of Saul my father shall not find thee, and thou shalt be king over Israel, and I shall be next unto thee; and that also Saul my father knoweth."**

And they two made a covenant before the LORD: and David abode in the wood, and Jonathan went to his house. (1 Sam 23:17-18)

Saul is apparently quite clear that David will rule, and that his own son has renounced the dynasty in obedience to God to permit this to happen. In fighting this, Saul has set himself against God. It is probable that in this final meeting between the two friends, part of the covenant struck will entail David's protection of Jonathan's lineage upon David becoming Israel's king. Once more, Jonathan's willingness to obey God and forsake his own claim as Saul's heir endears him to the reader. This remarkable situation is almost unique in history. All too often, an heir or pretender is happy to carve and slay his way to the top to secure the throne - or in Saul's case, the fêted javelin. The depth of David and Jonathan's patience and obedience to God is humbling.

Saul is tipped off by the perfidious men of Ziph that David and his men are hiding out in the forests near the town. However, by the time Saul, his commander Abner, and a sizeable hit squad arrive at the spot four miles south-east of Hebron, David and his force have moved into the wilderness of Maon. Even then, there are more spies willing to betray David's whereabouts to the king. Saul and his men head into the mountains of Arabah on a tip-off, and at one point, unknowingly, have David's force surrounded. Just then, a messenger pushes into the king's presence with urgent news that the Philistines have invaded. Not knowing how close he has come to finishing David, Saul breaks off the hunt and heads north to deal with this new threat. God saves David's skin once more. Hugely relieved, the son of Jesse takes his mighty men and heads the force out east to the Dead Sea to take refuge at the oasis of Ein Gedi and in the mountain strongholds south around Masada.

Weeks later, Saul resumes his vendetta after chasing off the Philistines. Receiving word that David and his men have been spotted in the wilderness of Ein Gedi, the king and Abner order the troops to commence the search on the Rocks of the Wild Goats and in the caves along the road.[472] Unbeknownst to them, David and a few of his men are taking refuge in the very cave Saul chooses, in which to relieve himself.

And the men of David said unto [David], **"Behold the day of which the LORD said unto thee, 'Behold, I will deliver thine enemy into thine hand, that thou mayest do to him as it shall seem good unto thee.'"**

Then David arose, and cut off the hem of Saul's robe privily [clandestinely]. **And it came to pass afterward, that David's heart smote him, because he had cut off Saul's hem. And he said unto his men, "The LORD forbid that I should do this thing unto my master, the LORD'S anointed, to stretch forth mine hand against him, seeing he is the anointed of the LORD."**

So David stayed his servants with these words and suffered them not to rise against Saul. But Saul rose up out of the cave and went on his way. (1 Sam 24:4-7)

The hem of a robe – as we saw with Boaz, Jesus and other examples – represents a person's authority. David is, in effect,

[472] The wild goats of the region are still around today, visited by tourists.

removing the badge of Saul's authority: an action of which he repents almost immediately. God granted Saul's authority to rule; far be it from David to raise his hand against the LORD's anointed, though the king seeks his life. It's another unique moment in history. As David's story unfolds, several individuals will misread David's allegiance to Saul to their own catastrophe.

But Saul won't be let off the hook completely. After the king leaves the cave, David himself arises and goes out after him, crying, "My Lord, the King!" When Saul looks back, David stoops with his face to the earth and bows himself.

And David said to Saul, "Wherefore hearest thou men's words, saying, 'Behold, David seeketh thy hurt'? Behold, this day thine eyes have seen how that the LORD had delivered thee to day into mine hand in the cave: and some bade me kill thee: but mine eye spared thee, and I said, 'I will not put forth mine hand against my lord, <u>for he is the LORD'S anointed</u>'.

"Moreover, my father, see, yea, see the skirt of thy robe in my hand, for in that I cut off the skirt of thy robe and killed thee not, know thou and see that there is neither evil nor transgression in mine hand, and I have not sinned against thee, yet thou huntest my soul to take it!

"The LORD judge between me and thee, and the LORD avenge me of thee, but mine hand shall not be upon thee. As saith the proverb of the ancients, Wickedness proceedeth from the wicked, but mine hand shall not be upon thee.

"After whom is the king of Israel come out? After whom dost thou pursue? After a dead dog, after a flea. The LORD therefore be judge, and judge between me and thee, and see, and plead my cause, and deliver me out of thine hand." (1 Sam 24:8-15)

David's words cut Saul to the heart. **"Is this thy voice, my son David?"** the king sobs. **"Thou art more righteous than I, for thou hast rewarded me good whereas I have rewarded thee evil. And thou hast shewed this day how that thou hast dealt well with me, forasmuch as when the LORD had delivered me into thine hand, thou killedst me not. For if a man find his enemy, will he let him go well away? Wherefore the LORD reward thee good for that thou hast done unto me this day.**

"And now, behold, I know well that thou shalt surely be king, and that the kingdom of Israel shall be established in thine hand. Swear now therefore unto me by the LORD that thou wilt not cut

off my seed after me, and that thou wilt not destroy my name out of my father's house." (1 Sam 24: 16-21

David swears by the LORD. Saul, Abner and their troops depart. Yet David and his men collect their stuff and head back to the others at the stronghold, their leader not taken in for an instant with Saul's public show of repentance. The king's mania has become an all-too-familiar pattern. One minute you're playing the harp and admiring the view out of the window, the next there's a javelin quivering in the wall by your head, and only if you're lucky. These days, Saul is despatching armies after David. The constant desire to kill his son-in-law is not endearing the king to his nation, and Jonathan is beside himself with anger, embarrassment and despair over what his father has become.

The fool and the prize

A fatal resignation sets in with David and his band at this point. The effort of foraging for food, water and supplies in the blasted wilderness around the Dead Sea is taking its toll. David's roving force has resorted to fighting other people's wars when chance arises, or running protection rackets in return for food and clothing. The temptation to have killed Saul in the cave when he had the chance must still be playing on David's mind, yet the son of Jesse knows God is strengthening his resolve with each new day. David has been toughened from his youth through trials. The LORD tested him as a shepherd boy with a lion and Syrian bear before his ordeal with Goliath. In David's exile, the God of Israel is teaching him the kingly virtues of leadership, patience, mercy and wisdom. David is a fast learner, content for God to deal with Saul when He is ready. In the meantime, he must live in daily trust that God will provide for them in the wilderness in the same way the LORD did for Israel during the Exodus.

David's fortunes turn the corner in a strange way. Word comes that beloved Samuel has died and been buried at his home in Ramah. The prophet's passing marks the end of the ancient, troubled era of the Judges. Samuel has overseen Israel's transition from a disparate band of squabbling tribes into a nation united under one monarch, albeit one beset with manic depression and surrounded on all sides by enemies. While grieving for his old friend and mentor, David knows that Samuel's death will badly weaken Saul. Will that be enough to end his own ordeal? What will God do next?

Meanwhile the force must eat. David's new shakedown target is a wealthy merchant-farmer named Nabal (*lit:* 'fool'), whose business interests are in Kurmul, on the edge of the Paran wilderness way down south.

And David sent out ten young men, and David said unto the young men, "Get you up to Kurmul and go to Nabal, and greet him in my name. And thus shall ye say to him that liveth in prosperity, "Peace be both to thee, and peace be to thine house, and peace be unto all that thou hast. And now I have heard that thou hast shearers. Now thy shepherds which were with us, we hurt them not, neither was there ought missing unto them, all the while they were in Kurmul. Ask thy young men and they will shew thee. Wherefore let the young men find favour in thine eyes, for we come in a good day. Give, I pray thee, whatsoever cometh to thine hand unto thy servants, and to thy son David."

And when David's young men came, they spake to Nabal according to all those words in the name of David, then ceased.

And Nabal answered David's servants and said, "Who is David? And who is the son of Jesse? There be many servants nowadays that break away every man from his master. Shall I then take my bread, and my water, and my flesh that I have killed for my shearers, and give it unto men whom I know not whence they be?"

So David's young men turned their way and went again, and came and told [David] **all those sayings.** (1 Sam 25:5-12)

There's a saying that goes, "'Tis better to say nothing than something, for if men think you a fool and you speak, they could have it confirmed in short order." Nabal doesn't heed this, and he certainly has no idea of the mettle of person with whom he is dealing. As for David, the son of Jesse is not pleased at being referred to as a wayward servant deserting his master. From what we learn of his demeanour at this point, David is stressed. He's angry at having been forced to live the life of an outcast for ten years for doing nothing wrong. He hates sleeping with the scorpions; compelled to be constantly on the move, wondering where the next attack will come from. He loathes the disrespect and flat-out ingratitude levelled by fools like Nabal, when David and his men actually *did* protect Nabal's work-force from genuine marauders while they were in their company. Besides, if it hadn't been for David, the whole country would be speaking Philistine by now. From general of the Israelite army to a backwoods bandit: David is at the end of his tether. He orders four hundred men to tool up and two hundred to remain behind with the stuff. They're going to hit Nabal, wipe out the fool and his family, clean him out of everything they need to survive, and shut the ingrate down.

What David doesn't know is that one of Nabal's shearers even at that moment is hastily seeking an audience with Abigail, Nabal's unsuspecting, long-suffering wife, to explain with some urgency the danger they are in.

But one of the young men told Abigail, Nabal's wife, saying, "Behold, David sent messengers out of the wilderness to salute our master, and he railed on them. But [David's] **men were very good unto us and we were not hurt, neither missed we anything as long as we were conversant with them, when we were in the fields. They were a wall unto us both by night and day, all the while we were with them keeping the sheep. Now therefore know and consider what thou wilt do, for evil is determined against our master and against all his household, for he is such a son of Belial** [worthless wretch, crackbrain] **that a man cannot speak to him."** (1 Sam 25:14-17)

The workforce, it seems, has the full measure of its boss, and of Abigail too, for the worker to feel comfortable in speaking his mind so to the boss's wife. Abigail doesn't miss a beat. Without delay she sets about rounding up two hundred loaves and two bottles of wine, five sheep readily dressed, five measures of parched corn, a hundred clusters of raisins and two hundred cakes of figs, and sets the lot on donkeys for a speedy departure. Wisely she tells her husband nothing to avoid further damage. She is out of the residence and Kurmul before Nabal even knows she has gone.

Abigail and her donkey train meet up with David and his force. We are told Abigail is a woman of good understanding and beautiful appearance, but this cuts little ice with the furious David, who launches into her as soon as she makes herself known:

"Surely in vain have I protected all that this fellow hath in the wilderness, so that nothing was missed of all that pertained unto him! And he hath requited me evil for good! So and more also do God unto the enemies of David, if I leave of all that pertain to him by the morning light *any* that pisseth against the wall!" (1 Sam 25:21-22)

David is stressed for sure, but Abigail knows how to deal with stressed, belligerent men. Though the King James translation may be earthy, we can admire the skill with which she entreats David to spare her family, even her fool husband, and turn the situation to everyone's benefit:

And when Abigail saw David, she hasted and lighted off the ass, and fell before David on her face, and bowed herself to the ground and said, "Upon me, my lord, upon me let this iniquity be: and let thine handmaid, I pray thee, speak in thine audience, and hear the words of thine handmaid.

"Let not my lord, I pray thee, regard this man of Belial, even Nabal, for as his name is, so is he. Nabal is his name, and folly is with him, but I, thine handmaid, saw not the young men of my lord, whom thou didst send.

"Now therefore, my lord, as the LORD liveth, and as thy soul liveth, seeing the LORD hath withholden thee from coming to shed blood, and from avenging thyself with thine own hand, now let thine enemies, and they that seek evil to my lord, be as Nabal.

"And now this blessing, which thine handmaid hath brought unto my lord, let it even be given unto the young men that follow my lord.

"I pray thee, forgive the trespass of thine handmaid, for the LORD will certainly make my lord a sure house; because my lord fighteth the battles of the LORD and evil hath not been found in thee all thy days.

"Yet a man is risen to pursue thee and to seek thy soul, but the soul of my lord shall be bound in the bundle of life with the LORD thy God, and the souls of thine enemies, them shall He sling out, as out of the middle of a sling.

"And it shall come to pass, when the LORD shall have done to my lord according to all the good that He hath spoken concerning thee, and shall have appointed thee ruler over Israel, that this shall be no grief unto thee, nor offence of heart unto my lord, either that thou hast shed blood causeless, or that my lord hath avenged himself. But when the LORD shall have dealt well with my lord, then remember thine handmaid." (1 Sam 25:23-31)

Wow! Just WOW!

"You, David, are blameless before the LORD and the nation! You don't have to stain your hands and wordfame with the blood of a fool like Nabal!" I can picture David's hardened veterans sniggering behind their lord's back at such eloquence. Perhaps this is one of the few times in his life that David is left speechless, not only on account of Abigail's humility and passion, but also her beauty. What man does not care for beauty beholden? When David pulls himself together, one can hear the teenage bluster in his riposte:

"Blessed be the LORD God of Israel, which sent thee this day to meet me. And blessed be thy advice, and blessed be thou, which hast kept me this day from coming to shed blood, and from avenging myself with mine own hand. For in very deed, as the LORD God of Israel liveth, which hath kept me back from hurting thee, except that thou hadst hasted and come to meet me, surely there had not been left unto Nabal by the morning light any that pisseth against the wall!" (1 Sam 25:32-34)

"Good job you came, Abigail, or I would have cleaned house!"

The confrontation over, David relieves Abigail of her gifts of provisions and despatches her back to her husband at Kurmul: "Go in peace to your house. See, I have heeded your voice and respected your person."

When Abigail arrives home, her husband is enjoying a feast fit for a king with his cronies. In fact, he's so drunk, Abigail resolves not to tell him of their reprieve until the following morning. When day breaks and she does, we infer from the text that Nabal blows his top and works himself up into such a lather, he has a stroke! Ten days later, having lain insensate on his bed, Nabal is smitten by the LORD, and he dies.

And when David heard that Nabal was dead, he said, "Blessed be the LORD, that hath pleaded the cause of my reproach from the hand of Nabal, and hath kept his servant from evil, for the LORD hath returned the wickedness of Nabal upon his own head." And David sent and communed with Abigail, to take her to him to wife.

And when the servants of David were come to Abigail to Kurmul, they spake unto her, saying, "David sent us unto thee, to take thee to him to wife."

And she arose and bowed herself on her face to the earth, and said, "Behold, let thine handmaid be a servant to wash the feet of the servants of my lord."

And Abigail hasted and arose, and rode upon an ass, with five damsels of hers that went after her; and she went after the messengers of David, and became his wife. (1 Sam 25:39-42)

It tells us something of Abigail's calibre that David immediately marries her. No period of mourning for Nabal! We are told in 1 Sam 25:43 that David also marries a lady called Ahinoam of Jezreel, and it seems reasonable to assume that he married her before Abigail, as Ahinoam always comes first in the wives' list; and her firstborn,

Amnon, becomes David's heir. You may recall that David was already married to Michal, the king's daughter, whom Saul gave to David as a prize for slaying Goliath. After David's exile, however, Saul gives Michal away to Paltiel, son of Laish, probably as punishment for her having assisted David's escape from her father's assassins.

Saul and David – the end game

The Ziphites pay Saul another visit, tattling that David and his force have now been spotted in the hill of Hachilah, opposite Jeshimon. His previous public repentance forgotten, Saul mobilises three thousand chosen men under his first cousin and trusty commander Abner, and they head down to the wilderness. David's scouts, however, give the son of Jesse ample warning of Saul's treachery. David discovers where his enemies are camping for the night and asks among his own veterans: "Who will go down with me to Saul in the camp?"

It is here that we are first introduced to the indomitable Abishai, one of three sons of Zeruiah who will figure prominently in David's future. Zeruiah is an enigma to scholars. She is named in scripture as a sister to David (1 Chron 2:16), but we glean another piece of intelligence in 2 Samuel 17:25, wherein Zeruiah is given as the daughter of Nahash. Scholars speculate several explanations, one of the more plausible being that Jesse, David's father, may have married Zeruiah's mother, who was previously married to Nahash, king of Ammon, by whom she had Zeruiah and the three boys. Whatever the truth, Zeruiah is David's sister or half-sister, and the three skullcracking sons, Joab, Abishai and Asahel, are David's nephews, who probably joined him at the time Jesse and David's kin quit Bethlehem for their own safety after David was forced into exile. Scholars have wondered why the three brothers are constantly referred to as the sons of Zeruiah, their mother, and not by the expected patronymic. The conclusion is that Zeruiah's husband must have died before the events in question, so her three sons are given as the 'sons of Zeruiah'.[473]

In any case, we are going to discover that none of these three mighty men shy away from trouble. They are fiercely loyal to David even to their own hurt, as we shall see. Abishai, the eldest, steps

---

[473] The use of the matronymic could also imply a particular strength of character of the mother.

forward without hesitation to accompany David in his 'special forces' mission down to Saul's camp. Sneaking past guards after dark without detection is what Abishai lives for, and they work their way through the encampment to where the king himself is sleeping. Abishai whispers to David:

"God has delivered your enemy into your hand. Let me smite him with my spear to the earth, and I won't need to smite him a second time!"

David: **"Destroy him not: for who can stretch forth his hand against the LORD'S anointed and be guiltless? As the LORD liveth, the LORD shall smite him; or his day shall come to die; or he shall descend into battle and perish. The LORD forbid that I should stretch forth mine hand against the LORD'S anointed. But, I pray thee, take thou now the spear that is at his bolster, and the cruse of water, and let us go."** (1 Sam 26:9-11)

They steal Saul's famous javelin and water canteen, and successfully steal away from the scene, **for they were all asleep because a deep sleep from the LORD was fallen upon them** (v.12). The following morning, David hails Abner, the king's commander, from the top of a nearby hill:

David: "Have you nothing to say for yourself, Abner?"

Abner: "Who are you, calling out to the king?"

David: "Abner, they say you are a valiant man and there is none like you in all Israel! That being the case, why have you failed to protect your lord, the king? One of his enemies came into the camp last night to destroy him! Not good, Abner. In fact, failing to protect your lord the king is worthy of death. Where is the king's spear and his water bottle, which were by his pillow?"

Abner begins to sweat. Saul raises his eyes to the hill.

"Is that your voice, my son, David?"

"It is my voice, my king. Why does my lord pursue his servant so? What evil have I done? Hear the words of your servant, I pray you. If God has stirred you up against me, then let Him accept an offering, but if my accusers be the children of men, then cursed be they before the LORD, for they have driven me out this day from abiding in the inheritance of the LORD, saying, 'Go, serve other gods'.

Now therefore, let not my blood fall to the earth before the face of the LORD, for the king of Israel comes out to seek a flea, as when one hunts a partridge in the mountains!"

Then said Saul, "I have sinned. Return, my son David, for I will no more do thee harm because my soul was precious in thine eyes

this day. Behold, I have played the fool and have erred exceedingly."

And David answered and said, "Behold the king's spear! And let one of the young men come over and fetch it. The LORD render to every man his righteousness and his faithfulness, for the LORD delivered thee into my hand today, but I would not stretch forth mine hand against the LORD'S anointed.

"And, behold, as thy life was much set by this day in mine eyes, so let my life be much set by in the eyes of the LORD, and let him deliver me out of all tribulation."

Then Saul said to David, "Blessed be thou, my son David. Thou shalt both do great things and also shalt still prevail."

So David went on his way, and Saul returned to his place. (1 Sam 26:21-25)

But to David it's Groundhog Day. The same cycle of Saul's vengeance will run and run. So David makes an unusual decision and takes the force east across the country and crosses over into Philistine territory to look up an old enemy contact. This time, Achish, king of Gath, is more predisposing towards Goliath's slaughterer. News of David's famous exploits with Saul has traversed the Levant. Instead of playing the madman, David makes an effort to put the Philistine monarch at ease and become his friend. Achish warily welcomes him to court and David minds his own business, behaves impeccably, and is allowed to dwell peacefully - he, his men, and all their households - around Gath. It is clear to Achish that Saul and David are mortal enemies, which could be played to the five lords' advantage. For his part, when Saul is told that David has taken refuge in Philistia, the fight goes out of the king and He seeks David no more. Saul cannot overcome the Philistines without God's help, and he knows he won't get that if David and his force have allied themselves with the enemy. Truly now, Saul feels alone. Samuel is gone. He can't talk to David. And because he killed every priest of Eli's house bar Abiathar, he can't talk to God either. Perhaps in the final days of the son of Kish, Jonathan is Saul's one solace, though even Jonathan must now be worn out with all the hatred and fear his father has harboured for the one they both love.

David petitions Achish at the royal court at Gath: "If I have found grace in your eyes, grant me a place in some town in the country, that I and my men may dwell there. I don't wish to make things difficult for either of us by crowding you out in the royal city."

In fact, David wants some space to relax, put down roots, honour and worship the LORD free of pagan contamination, give his hard-pressed warriors and friends time to decompress with some sorely needed R & R, and wait out Saul's fate at the hand of God. Achish accedes to his request, and David is given the town of Ziklag on the border of Judah as a possession.[474] David agrees to govern Ziklag in the capacity of a feudal lord to protect Philistia's southern frontier. It's a display of trust by Achish which David will not betray. In fact, David proves invaluable to the Philistines during his sixteen-month sojourn in their land, conducting raids against mutual enemies to the south, building his wealth and reputation with the livestock and other spoils garnered thereby. David is not above lying to Achish on occasion concerning these forays, however, especially in the matter of raids allegedly against his own tribe, Judah. But the king is utterly convinced, telling those around him that "David has made his people Israel utterly abhor him, therefore he shall be my servant forever."

But David sees a problem developing. When the Philistines prepare to go to war with Israel anew in the spring, Achish is most enthusiastic that David's force should take its rightful place in the Philistine vanguard:

"Of course, you know I expect you to ride out with me to battle, you and all your men."

David replies cautiously, "Surely you know what your servant can do."

Achish smiles. "I might make you a personal bodyguard forever."

I imagine David raising his goblet to drink, exchanging glances with his own Jewish bodyguard with some misgivings - his trusted new commander, Joab, son of Zeruiah, especially.

Meanwhile, Saul is coming to the end of himself. Denied further pursuit of David, cut off from the LORD after killing Ahimelech and the priesthood, Saul feels the deep loss of his old mentor, Samuel. The Philistines have mobilised anew and encamped at Shunem, and this time it looks like a major invasion. Saul and Abner call up the armies of the tribes and marshal them at Gilboa, but Saul has no way now to receive any direction from God. What happens next is contained in one of the most controversial passages of the scriptures, the import of

[474] Ziklag is identified with Haluza in the Negev along the old Nabatean Incense Route: Google Earth 31.097°N 34.652°E

which has divided scholars for centuries. Bereft of guidance, Saul decides to consult a witch – an act he himself has outlawed on pain of execution.

Then said Saul unto his servants, "Seek me a woman that hath a familiar spirit, that I may go and enquire of her."

And his servants said to him, "Behold, there is a woman that hath a familiar spirit at En Dor."[475]

And Saul disguised himself, and put on other raiment, and he went, and two men with him, and they came to the woman by night. And he said, "I pray thee, divine unto me by the familiar spirit, and bring me him up, whom I shall name unto thee."

And the woman said unto him, "Behold, thou knowest what Saul hath done, how he hath cut off those that have familiar spirits, and the wizards, out of the land. Wherefore, then, layest thou a snare for my life, to cause me to die?"

And Saul sware to her by the LORD, saying, "As the LORD liveth, there shall no punishment happen to thee for this thing." (1 Sam 28:7-10)

From the circumstances of the visit, the strength of the stranger's oath, and the assurance that no harm will come to her, the witch must suspect that she's dealing with someone unusual. Jack Heyford draws our attention to the degree to which Saul has deceived himself:

> "Saul swears to an outlaw necromancer by the LORD!"[476]

The witch proceeds cautiously: "Whom shall I bring up?"

"Bring me up Samuel."

And when the woman saw Samuel, <u>she cried with a loud voice</u>. And the woman spake to Saul, saying, "Why hast thou deceived me? For thou art Saul!"

And the king said unto her, "Be not afraid. What sawest thou?"

And the woman said unto Saul, "I saw gods ascending out of the earth."

And he said unto her, "<u>What form is he of?</u>" [Note that Saul can't see Samuel]

And she said, "An old man cometh up; and he is covered with a mantle."

---

[475] En Dor lies around six miles north of Saul's position at Gilboa.

[476] Heyford, Jack, *Spirit-Filled Bible,* op. cit., p.435

And Saul perceived that it was Samuel, and he stooped with his face to the ground and bowed himself.[477]

And Samuel said to Saul, "Why hast thou disquieted me, to bring me up?" And Saul answered, "I am sore distressed; for the Philistines make war against me, and God is departed from me, and answereth me no more, neither by prophets, nor by dreams: therefore I have called thee, that thou mayest make known unto me what I shall do."

Then said Samuel, "Wherefore then dost thou ask of me, seeing the LORD is departed from thee, and is become thine enemy? For the LORD hath done to him, as He spake by me: for the LORD hath rent the kingdom out of thine hand, and given it to thy neighbour, even to David. Because thou obeyedst not the voice of the LORD, nor executedst His fierce wrath upon Amalek, therefore hath the LORD done this thing unto thee this day. Moreover the LORD will also deliver Israel with thee into the hand of the Philistines, <u>and tomorrow shalt thou and thy sons be with me</u>. The LORD also shall deliver the host of Israel into the hand of the Philistines." (1 Sam 28:12-19)

It's an incredible scene, which historically provokes all manner of raised eyebrows from Jews and Christians, and whoops of glee from New Agers that God's infallibility is in tatters. For surely here is the Almighty Himself, permitting one of His top prophets to be brought up from the dead by a medium! And this, after all the fierce admonitions in the Torah against divination and necromancy!

Actually, the witch is utterly shaken when Samuel appears to her, indicating that the prophet's raising has not been occasioned by her but by God Himself. The witch knows that she is in over her head; that this is no normal session. There is further proof of God's participation in this event with Samuel's prophecy of Saul's defeat and death along with his sons, which comes true. A quick study of secular prophets reveals that they are invariably wrong. There is also a detail tie-up worth noting. The scriptures state in 1 Sam 15:35 that after cutting ties with the king, Samuel comes no more to see Saul until the day of his (Samuel's) death. Atheists point out that the integrity of the scriptures is broken, since Samuel in fact appears to Saul the day before Saul's death in this apparent séance at En Dor. But

---

[477] This is doubtless the same mantle Saul tore when he grabbed Samuel at their final meeting.

Saul never actually *sees* Samuel, he only hears his voice (1 Sam 28:14,20). It's a small point of detail, but God has it covered.

The witch is scared to death that she will be executed for subjecting the king to such a terrifying ordeal, but Saul remains true to his word, and he and his servants depart after the witch feeds them. Haunted, dejected, Saul makes his way back to his lines at Gilboa for tomorrow's date with destiny. How do you fight a battle you already know you will lose; one which will cost you your life?

A nasty surprise

At the same time, David finds himself in an awkward situation with the Philistine host at Aphek. Obliged by Achish, king of Gath, to bring his men up from Ziklag for the forthcoming confrontation with Israel at Gilboa, David does not relish the idea of fighting his own people. He even tried communicating this to Achish at a previous meeting in a way that would not engender disrespect, but Achish ignored him (1 Sam 28:1-2). The four other Philistine lords inadvertently come to David's rescue.

"What are these Hebrews doing here?" Hostility streams from Philistine nostrils. Murmurings in the heathen ranks.

Achish is unfazed. "David defected from Saul and has been with me for a while. I find no fault in him."

Snorts from the nobility. "No way! Send him and his men away and do not go down to battle with them! What better way for him to seek Saul's forgiveness than to hand our heads on a plate by turning against us in battle?"

It's no use. Achish draws David aside. "No good deed goes unpunished, my friend. I have found no fault with you or your men for all the months you have served me, but these other lords do not favour you. Best you leave and return home to Ziklag now, rather than make further trouble."

David makes a show of displeasure before the other lords for Achish's honour, but once again God has delivered the son of Jesse from an unrighteous battle. David rounds up his force and sets off back to Ziklag. On the third day, a smudge of smoke in the distance provokes a murmur from those around David. The column quickens its pace, and soon an awful realisation sets in.

The Amalekites had invaded the south and smitten Ziklag, and burned it with fire. And had taken the women captive that were therein. They slew not any, either great or small, but carried them

away and went on their way. So David and his men came to the city and, behold, it was burned with fire, and their wives, and their sons, and their daughters, were taken captive.

Then David and the people that were with him lifted up their voice and wept until they had no more power to weep. And David's two wives were taken captive, Ahinoam the Jezreelitess, and Abigail the wife of Nabal the Carmelite. And David was greatly distressed, for the people spake of stoning him because the soul of all the people was grieved, every man for his sons and for his daughters. But David encouraged himself in the LORD his God. (1 Sam 30:1-6)

We can glibly read the account, not really getting the trauma. But when we pause and consider everything these men have been through over the past ten years, it starts to soak in. The Amalekites are ancient enemies of the Jews: cowards who skulk in the wadis and mountains in the southern deserts to shirk a fair fight. They strike at dawn with no warning, somehow knowing no force will oppose them. Your beloved wife, your infant son and daughter are rounded up like cattle, terrorised, jewellery torn from their fingers and necks; then they are beaten, chained and hauled off to God knows where. As they are dragged off, your house is torched before their eyes, your herds and flocks stolen, Ziklag abandoned in ruins behind them. When faced with such a catastrophe, what is the first thing David does? He encourages himself in the LORD his God. Do we do the same when disaster strikes us?

David has a different perspective. God is the God of everything, so this raid has been permitted. For what purpose David has no clue, but he soon will (Rom 8:28-29). He summons Abiathar, the sole remaining priest of the linen ephod, and enquires of the LORD through him.

"Shall I pursue after this troop? Shall I overtake them?"

Abiathar answers him, "Pursue, for you shall surely overtake them and without fail recover all."

David doesn't need telling twice. He immediately mobilises his exhausted force and heads out to the brook Besor, deciding that the Amalekite raiders are heading north across the desert to find water at the wadi. Six miles later at the brook, however, a third of his men are ready to drop. He leaves two hundred by the river and crosses over with the remaining four hundred in pursuit of the enemy.

And they found an Egyptian in the field and brought him to David, and gave him bread, and he did eat; and they made him

drink water. And they gave him a piece of a cake of figs and two clusters of raisins. And when he had eaten, his spirit came again to him, for he had eaten no bread, nor drunk any water, three days and three nights.

And David said unto him, "To whom belongest thou? And whence art thou?"

And he said, "I am a young man of Egypt, servant to an Amalekite. And my master left me because three days agone I fell sick. We made an invasion upon the south of the Cherethites, and upon the coast which belongeth to Judah, and upon the south of Caleb; and we burned Ziklag with fire."

And David said to him, "Canst thou bring me down to this company?"

And he said, "Swear unto me by God, that thou wilt neither kill me nor deliver me into the hands of my master, and I will bring thee down to this company." (1 Sam 30:11-15)

David swears by the LORD, and the Egyptian does his part. Hours later at twilight, David and his *comitatus* are surveying thousands of the enemy spread out before them across the desert plain, eating and drinking and dancing in celebration of the spoil they have taken from the Philistines and land of Judah. Defences are down, guards desultory. David orders an immediate attack just as darkness descends.

The Amalekites are not expecting trouble, must less an attack launched at night with the ferocity of personal anger. Unaware in the dark that the attack force comprises a mere four hundred of the enemy, the men of Amalek echo the confusion of the Midianite hordes before Gideon, and flee for their lives. David's mighty men pursue them throughout the night and the next day until evening. The scriptures unassumingly declare that of the thousands of the enemy force, only four hundred Amalekites escape: equal in number to David's assault force! When the son of Jesse takes stock of all they have recovered, astonishingly all loved ones are accounted for, including his two wives, Ahinoam and Abigail. All Ziklag herds and belongings are intact. In addition, there is all that Philistine booty the Amalekites lifted from their recent raiding adventure.

David's warriors must have stared at each other, amazed that utter disaster had been converted to stunning triumph in short order. God's hand is starkly in evidence. Yet the grins turn to scowls and dark murmuring among some when they return to the brook Besor, and David orders the spoil to be shared out with the two hundred fighters they left behind:

Then answered all the wicked men and men of Belial, of those that went with David, and said, "Because they went not with us, we will not give them ought of the spoil that we have recovered, save to every man his wife and his children, that they may lead them away and depart."

Then said David, "Ye shall not do so, my brethren, with that which the LORD hath given us, who hath preserved us, and delivered the company that came against us into our hand. For who will hearken unto you in this matter? But as his part is that goeth down to the battle, so shall his part be that tarrieth by the stuff. They shall part alike." (1 Sam 30:22-24)

In fact, David makes it law among his men from that day that this will be so in the future. When the force returns triumphant to Ziklag, David sets aside part of the spoil and sends it to the elders of Judah: to those who have sustained and supported him all these years in exile. With the gifts he sends a message: "Behold a present for you of the spoil of the enemies of the LORD."

The Battle of Gilboa and aftermath

Samuel's prophecy of Saul's defeat and death at the hand of his enemies tragically comes to pass at the Battle of Mount Gilboa:

Now the Philistines fought against Israel. And the men of Israel fled from before the Philistines and fell down slain in Mount Gilboa. And the Philistines followed hard upon Saul and upon his sons. And the Philistines slew Jonathan and Abinadab and Malchishua, Saul's sons. And the battle went sore against Saul, and the archers hit him; and he was sore wounded of the archers.

Then said Saul unto his armour-bearer, "Draw thy sword and thrust me through therewith, lest these uncircumcised come and thrust me through and abuse me."

But his armour-bearer would not, for he was sore afraid. Therefore Saul took a sword and fell upon it. And when his armour-bearer saw that Saul was dead, he fell likewise upon his sword and died with him.

So Saul died, and his three sons, and his armour-bearer, and all his men, that same day together. And when the men of Israel that were on the other side of the valley, and they that were on the other side of the Jordan, saw that the men of Israel fled, and that Saul and

his sons were dead, they forsook the cities and fled. And the Philistines came and dwelt in them. (1 Sam 31:1-7)

The armourer-bearer's job is to keep his king alive under any circumstances. That the king asked this servant to run him through would have been unthinkable. Saul's is one of only seven suicides described in the Bible,[478] a tragic end to a king who began with such promise. The son of Kish walked head and shoulders above other men; was popular, humble and attentive to the LORD in his early days; yet his impatience, disobedience and wilful pride against God would bring him low and cost him the LORD's favour, the crown of Israel and eventually his life and the lives of his sons. Especially traumatic to David will be the loss of his good friend, Jonathan.

The day following the battle, the Philistines recover Saul's body and those of his sons. They cut off Saul's head, strip his body of armour, and hang it as a trophy in the temple of the Ashtoreths. The Philistines view this as a victory of their gods over YHWH; perhaps also a revenge of sorts for David decapitating Goliath's corpse and dedicating the giant's monstrous sword to the LORD's Tabernacle at Nob. Saul's body and those of his sons are hung from the city walls at Beth Shan. When the valiant men of Jabesh Gilead hear this, they travel the twelve miles by night and risk their lives to recover the corpses, returning them to Jabesh, where they are cremated to prevent further abuse. The remains are buried under a tamarisk tree. The town fasts for seven days. The men of Jabesh have much to thank Saul for. We may recall that, forty years before, as the newly anointed 20-year-old king of Israel (though not yet crowned), Saul had saved the city from the Ammonites, whose king, Nahash ('serpent'), had threatened to gouge out the right eye of every inhabitant as a reproach

---

[478] Actually, seven suicides plus one attempted suicide. The wicked Abimelech is struck on the head by a millstone during a siege, and orders his armour-bearer to slay him (Judg 9:54). Samson brings Gaza's temple of Dagon down upon himself and 3,000 Philistines (Judg 16:26-31). Ahithophel, grandfather of Bathsheba and one of David's councillors, takes part in a plot to overthrow David. When his counsel is ignored by David's rebellious son, Absalom, he sets his affairs in order and hangs himself (2 Sam 17:1,23). Zimri attempts to usurp the throne of Israel in 1 Kings 16. When he fails, he goes into the royal palace and burns it to the ground around him (1 Kings 16:18). Judas Iscariot hangs himself after betraying Yeshua (Matt 27:4-5). The attempted suicide: A jailer at Philippi believes all his prisoners have escaped during an earthquake, thus ending his career and life, so he prepares to fall on his sword. The apostle Paul, one of the prisoners, prevents him from taking his life, and brings the jailer and his household to the LORD (Acts 16:26-29).

to Israel. Saul had raised an army and slaughtered the Ammonites and their king, before being crowned himself at Gilgal.

David gets the news

Three days after David and his force return to Ziklag with their recovered loved ones, a stranger staggers into the town, clothes rent, dirt on his head. The mystery man is brought before David:

David: "Where have you come from?"

Stranger: "I have escaped from the camp of Israel."

David: "How did the battle go?"

Stranger: "The people have fled from the battle. Many soldiers are fallen. Saul and Jonathan his son are dead also."

David: "How do you know Saul and Jonathan are dead?"

Stranger: "I happened by chance to be on Mount Gilboa, and there was Saul, leaning on his spear with the enemy's chariots and horsemen hard-pressed after him. He looked behind, saw me and called me over. 'Who are you?' he asked me. 'I am an Amalekite,' I replied. He said to me, 'Please, stand over me and slay me, for anguish has come upon me, but I yet live.' So I stood over him and killed him, because I was certain he could not live from his wounds. I took the crown from his head and the bracelet off his arm and have brought them directly here to you, my lord."

It's a different story from the previous account. No mention is made of Saul's armour-bearer. That the Amalekite is bearing Saul's crown and bracelet is evidence enough that the king is dead, and probably therefore Jonathan, who would have fallen along with the king's *comitatus* defending his father. But why would an Amalekite - foe to both Philistine and Israelite - be on Mount Gilboa in the first place, the scene of a battle that had been anticipated for days?

Then David took hold on his clothes and rent them; and likewise all the men that were with him. And they mourned and wept and fasted until evening, for Saul, and for Jonathan his son, and for the people of the LORD, and for the house of Israel; because they were fallen by the sword. (2 Sam 1:11-12)

At nightfall, the Amalekite is brought before David again.

David: "How was it that you were not afraid to put forth your hand to destroy the LORD's anointed?"

Whoops. The Amalekite blenches, having anticipated a handsome recompense for bringing tangible proof of the death of David's adversary. He is not expecting the dangerous look he sees now in David's eyes. In fact, David and his council have worked out that the Amalekite is either an opportunistic looter hanging out by a battlefield to see what he can steal (a trademark Amalekite occupation), or he really did kill Saul, in which case, he had the temerity to carry out what David had refused to do himself on two occasions, namely the murder of the LORD's anointed. The Amalekite has completely misread David's reaction, and he won't be the last. He also appears completely ignorant of his tribe's recent attack on Ziklag and the abduction of David's loved ones; even that the children of Amalek are an extinction-level project for God and any able-bodied Jew in any event.

David turns to one of his young warriors. "Fall upon this one and slay him."

The warrior obliges, steps forth and slaughters the Amalekite on the spot.

David looks down at the corpse: "Your blood is upon your own head, for your own mouth has testified against you, saying, 'I have slain the LORD's anointed'."

Saul eternal

Which gives rise to an interesting question. Was Saul ultimately saved? Most expositors argue that he behaved in such an abhorrent fashion that God would not have redeemed him. But hold your horses for a moment. We are told, **For whatsoever things were written aforetime were written for our learning, that we through patience and comfort of the scriptures might have hope** (Rom 15:4). In other words, we have a huge amount to learn about our Creator by studying His motives and interactions with characters of old. Let's look a little further.

Saul starts well. As a young man he is fresh, tall, strong and humble. His salvation experience is recorded in 1 Sam 10:1-12, where Saul is anointed by Samuel to be captain over the LORD's inheritance. Saul later encounters a group of prophets and prophesies with them, being turned into 'a new man' - OT-speak for the new birth or 'born again'. It appears Saul is given the gospel of Jesus Christ at this point, for we learn from Acts 10:43 that all the OT prophets have taught that salvation is through Jesus Christ and by faith alone.[479] In other words, salvation is an eternal gift of God, which man's works cannot taint.

---

[479] Gal 3:8-9; Eph 2:8-10; Titus 3:5-6; Rom 3:26-28

Which does not mean a naughty believer cannot lose his inheritance and rewards in the next world (2 John 8; 1 Cor 3:15), or even be chastised, corrected or taken out of this world early (Acts 5:1-11; 1 Cor 5:1-5).

Israel and Saul fit into this category. The Promised Land (Canaan) was granted by God to Israel as an inheritance, yet out of approximately one and a half million souls over age 20, only Joshua and Caleb gain the Promised Land; the rest drop in the desert due to disobedience and lack of faith. Even Moses fails to enter (Deut 4:21-22). Does this mean God that did not grant eternal salvation to Moses and the failed Israelites? Of course not. How about Reuben, who was disinherited because of adultery (1 Chron 5:1-2)? Did God damn him too, or did Reuben just forfeit his inheritance? And if Reuben lost his salvation through adultery, why won't King David go to Hell the same way because of the adultery he will commit with Bathsheba in the future? Those who are confused about God's gift of salvation are usually confusing God granting salvation *through a believer's faith alone* with God granting inheritance and rewards in the afterlife *for a believer's performance during the Earth training programme.* Yeshua Himself confirms that of those God has chosen, none can be lost (FG 6:37,39; 10:28-29). *Do we believe this?* Notice that this is very different from those who *think* God has chosen them![480] A full treatment of this subject is given in *Origins IV – Tetelestai.*

For now, witness another spectacular pattern. Have you noticed how often God chooses the second over the first for His purposes? Chuck Missler lists:

> "Not Cain but Abel (and Seth). Not Japheth but Shem. Not Ishmael but Isaac. Not Esau but Jacob. Not Manasseh but Ephraim. Not Aaron but Moses. Not Eliab but David. Not the Old Covenant but the New. Not the first Adam but the Last Adam [Yeshua]." [481]

Not the first Israelite king but the second. Not Saul but David. Notice 'the second before the first' is also the gist of Stephen's fervent plea before the Sanhedrin in Acts 7. This on-fire Christian convert, full of the Holy Spirit, is hauled before the Jewish authorities allegedly for blaspheming God and Moses. The real reason is perhaps because no-one is able to resist the wisdom by which he speaks concerning Christ. The gist of Stephen's impassioned defence is that the Jews always

---

[480] Matt 7:21; 13:24-30; 1 John 1:6-7; 3:10, etc.

[481] Missler, Chuck *Inheritance and Rewards notes*, www.khouse.org

blow it on the first occasion, only to come through on the second. And so it will be with their Messiah, whom they first rejected but will later receive.

Back to Saul. 1 Sam 16:14 tells us that as Saul's wilful presumption and disobedience take over, **the Spirit of the Lord departed from Saul.** Saul had free will to act as he wished, but chose to persecute David, kill the priests of God, and behave in a downright disreputable fashion. Yet there is a detail in the story of the son of Kish, which may shed a surprising light on Saul's eternal fate.

In his spooky encounter with Saul and the witch at En Dor, Samuel tells the king, "...**tomorrow shalt thou and thy sons be with me**." Samuel is speaking as an OT saint, so the afterlife scenario he is describing will be the same expounded by Jesus in Luke 16. Remember the story of the rich man and the beggar Lazarus? Most take this as a parable, yet parables do not use real names. I believe that Jesus is giving an actual, hyperdimensional account of a real event occurring in the metacosm. We will be studying Heaven and Hell in some detail in *Origins IV – Tetelestai,* but here follows a summary of the Luke story as told by Yeshua Himself:

"There was a certain rich man, who was clothed in purple and fine linen, and fared sumptuously every day. And there was a certain beggar named Lazarus, who was laid at his gate full of sores and desiring to be fed with the crumbs which fell from the rich man's table. Moreover the dogs came and licked his sores.

"And it came to pass that the beggar died and was carried by the angels into Abraham's bosom. The rich man also died and was buried. And in Hades he lifted up his eyes, being in torments, and seeth Abraham afar off and Lazarus in his bosom.

"And he cried and said, 'Father Abraham, have mercy on me and send Lazarus, that he may dip the tip of his finger into water and cool my tongue, for I am tormented in this flame.'

"But Abraham said, 'Son, remember that thou in thy lifetime received thy good things, and likewise Lazarus evil things. But now he is comforted and thou art tormented. And beside all this, between us and you there is a great gulf fixed, so that they which would pass from hence to you cannot, neither can they pass to us, that would come from thence.'

"Then he said, 'I pray thee therefore, father, that thou would send him [Lazarus] **to my father's house, for I have five brethren. That he may testify unto them lest they also come into this place of torment.'**

"Abraham saith unto him, 'They have Moses and the prophets, let them hear them.'

"And he said, 'Nay, father Abraham, but if one went unto them from the dead, they will repent.' And he said unto him, 'If they hear not Moses and the prophets, neither will they be persuaded, though one rose from the dead.' " (Luke 16:19-31)

Let us unpack the rich man and Lazarus story enough to see what is being said about the afterlife. We can deduce the following from these passages:

- If Jesus and His Word are true, then these events and sayings must be a truthful representation of what occurs in the afterlife
- Jesus Himself told leading Pharisee Nicodemus in the NT that no man had ascended to Heaven up to the time He spoke those words (FG 3:13. *cf:* Prov 30:4; Acts 2:34-35). This will include OT characters such as Moses, Samuel, Saul, David and Jonathan
- The rich man/Lazarus story does not appear to be a parable, since Lazarus is named.[482] Parables do not contain names. Some scholars believe Yeshua was either citing an actual example from outside spacetime, or drawing from a popular Jewish folk tale, which had its roots in Egypt [483]
- Lazarus is not in Heaven yet, but in a comforting part of the temporary realm of the dead - Sheol (*Gr.* Hades) - known as 'the bosom of Abraham'. This infers, therefore, that *the spirits of all dead* prior to the death and Resurrection of Christ, including Abraham himself, David, Moses and all the prophets, *including Samuel,* are likewise NOT in Heaven in their glorified state yet, but in Sheol (the good part) awaiting the resurrection of their physical bodies at the conclusion of 'Jacob's Trouble' (the Great Tribulation) at the end of the age (Dan. 12:1-2; Isa. 26:19; Eze. 37:13-14). Some dead saints appear to have been resurrected early immediately after Yeshua's death on the cross (Matt 27:50-53)
- The rich man is not in Hell yet, but in Hades/Sheol, the temporary abode of the dead, which apparently has two

[482] This is not the same Lazarus whom Yeshua raises from the dead, but there are intriguing parallels which will be covered in *Origins IV – Tetelestai.*
[483] **Jeremias, Joachim** *The Parables of Jesus,* Scribners, 1972, p.183

compartments prior to Christ's own resurrection: one in which the wicked experience torment, and the other for the redeemed (the aforementioned 'Abraham's Bosom')

- These two abodes are separated by an immense, impassable gulf
- Contact appears to be possible between those in the two abodes of Sheol, at least in the case of the rich man and Lazarus

Now let us review Samuel's final words to Saul in the witch's house at En Dor: "...**tomorrow shalt thou and thy sons be with me**": in other words, in 'Abraham's Bosom', along with Jonathan and Saul's other two sons, Abinadab and Malchishua - all killed in the Battle of Gilboa. Does this mean that Saul was saved? It seems so. Does it mean that Saul lost his inheritance and rewards in the afterlife? Only the LORD Himself can answer that question.

KING DAVID, THE LORD'S ANOINTED

Saul's death must come as an all-enveloping relief to David. His time playing the fugitive is over. The slow-motion train-wreck of Saul's life becalms itself to eternity. The leaderless Israel facing David now is defeated, broken, hurt, divided; shamed by its recent Philistine rout, during which most of its vaunted cohorts threw down their weapons and fled the field in terror. Warren Wiersbe writes:

"For ten years David was an exile with a price on his head, fleeing from Saul and waiting for the time when God would put him on the throne of Israel. During these difficult years David grew in faith and godly character, and God equipped him for the work He had chosen for him to do. When the day of victory did arrive, David was careful not to force himself on the people, many of whom were still loyal to the house of Saul."[484]

Far from gloating over the inglorious end of his tormentor - perhaps the inclination of a lesser man - the son of Jesse is genuinely moved to lead the nation in a heartfelt lamentation over the loss of Saul and Jonathan in the Song of the Bow:

The beauty of Israel is slain upon thy high places: how are the mighty fallen!

Tell it not in Gath, publish it not in the streets of Ashkelon, lest the daughters of the Philistines rejoice, lest the daughters of the uncircumcised triumph.

Ye mountains of Gilboa, let there be no dew, neither let there be rain upon you, nor fields of offerings, for there the shield of the mighty is vilely cast away, the shield of Saul, as though he had not been anointed with oil.

From the blood of the slain, from the fat of the mighty, the bow of Jonathan turned not back, and the sword of Saul returned not empty.

Saul and Jonathan were lovely and pleasant in their lives, and in their death they were not divided: they were swifter than eagles, they were stronger than lions.

Ye daughters of Israel, weep over Saul, who clothed you in scarlet, with other delights, who put on ornaments of gold upon your apparel.

---

[484] Wiersbe, W, *The Wiersbe Bible Commentary*, op. cit. p.552

How are the mighty fallen in the midst of the battle! O Jonathan, thou wast slain in thine high places.

I am distressed for thee, my brother Jonathan: very pleasant hast thou been unto me: thy love to me was wonderful, passing the love of women.

How are the mighty fallen, and the weapons of war perished! (2 Sam 1:19-27)

A deep, despondent lament for beloved Jonathan, who is no more. Not a single word of censure against Saul. With the death of the LORD's anointed, the glory of Heaven has been dimmed. David is set apart from others as the man with no grievance; the one who committed all his woes to God, knowing that no matter the circumstances or outcome, all will be well for those who put their trust in God (Rom 8:28-29). We should learn from that.

David enquires of the LORD, and is instructed to make his way to Hebron ('brotherhood') with his two wives, Ahinoam and Abigail, and the force and its families. In Hebron and surrounding cities, he is proclaimed king of Judah by the elders, most of whom have covertly supported David throughout his exile, knowing that the son of Jesse has been chosen by God (1 Sam 16:1,12). Though the remainder of the country is now mostly under Philistine control following their victory at Gilboa, it's the end of a long road to a crown of sorts for David. The nation's land will be reclaimed in time, but the newly fêted King David of Judah is nothing if not magnanimous in his treatment of other sections of Israel at this point.

He singles out the men of Jabesh Gilead for their heroic rescue of Saul's and Jonathan's bodies, nailed to wall of Beth Shan, which they returned to Jabesh to be burnt and buried there. He exhorts them in their struggle against the Philistines (**'be valiant'** - 2 Sam 2:5-7) Cynics point out that David might be executing a shrewd ploy to gain wider political support among the northern tribes for the full crown over Israel once Philistia is driven back to the coastlands. Perhaps, but this is consistent with David's sense of humility, fair play and inclusive governance. It will set him apart for centuries to come as Israel's most famous king.

A problem called Abner

Five years after Gilboa there's more trouble. David receives word that Abner, Saul's commander, has declared one of Saul's sons,

Ishbosheth,[485] king of Israel. Not often discussed among scholars is one awkward question: What is Abner still doing alive after the Battle of Gilboa? As head of the army, should he not have perished along with his king? Abner, as we'll discover, is a wily old fox not fogged in the arts of survival. Chuck Missler writes:

"Abner was a first cousin of Saul, commander of the forces, and held in high respect throughout the country. Loyalty to the house of his late master was mixed up with opposition to David and views of personal ambition in his originating this factious movement. He, too, was sensitive to the importance of securing the eastern tribes; so, taking Ishbosheth across the Jordan [for safety against the Philistine threat], he proclaimed him king at Mahanaim, a town on the north bank of the Jabbok, hallowed in patriarchal times by the divine presence (Gen 32:2). There he rallied the tribes around the standard of the unfortunate son of Saul." [486]

The weak Ishbosheth has no choice but to rely on Abner's military prowess in securing Israel's Gilead tribes (Transjordan), and reclaim the north from Philistia. To the south, David is furious at what he suspects is a power-grab by Abner against the LORD's own word, which declared the crown for David (1 Sam 13:14; 15:28; 16:1). The son of Jesse is in no mood for compromise, and instructs his own military chief, Joab, to contact Abner and set up a contest:

And Abner the son of Ner, and the servants of Ishbosheth the son of Saul, went out from Mahanaim to Gibeon. And Joab the son of Zeruiah, and the servants of David, went out, and met together by the pool of Gibeon. And they sat down, the one on the one side of the pool, and the other on the other side of the pool.

And Abner said to Joab, "Let the young men now arise and play before us."

And Joab said, "Let them arise."

Then there arose and went over by number twelve of Benjamin, which pertained to Ishbosheth the son of Saul, and twelve of the servants of David. And they caught every one his fellow by the

[485] Ishbosheth, also Esh-Ba'al (1 Chron 8:33; 9:39). The name has some ambiguity in Hebrew. Ish is 'great man' and bosheth 'given to shame, humility'. Put together, they seem to suggest a man destined for great things brought low by shame or humility. Since Ishbosheth was named as a baby before his immature nature came to light, the name is prophetic. Other scholars claim that names ending in Ba'al (Lord) soon became *déclassé*, due to their connection with pagan worship, and were changed to -bosheth, as in Jonathan's son, Mephibosheth (Meri-Ba'al).

[486] **Missler, Chuck** 1 & 2 Samuel commentary notes, www.khouse.org

head, and thrust his sword in his fellow's side, so they fell down together, wherefore that place was called Helkathhazzurim, which is in Gibeon. (2 Sam 2: 12-16)

It suits Abner to settle the question of sovereignty via a combat match, since his forces were all but annihilated at Gilboa. The result of the bloody contest, however, displeases everyone and a fierce and unforgiving battle breaks out between the two factions. Outmatched and outnumbered, Abner's force is slaughtered to such an extent that Abner himself is forced to flee from the battlefield on foot. He is hotly pursued by Joab and Abishai's younger brother, Judah's Usain Bolt of the day, the fleet-footed warrior Asahel:

And there were three sons of Zeruiah there, Joab, and Abishai and Asahel: and Asahel was as light of foot as a wild roe. And Asahel pursued after Abner, and in going he turned not to the right hand nor to the left from following Abner.

Then Abner looked behind him, and said, "Art thou Asahel?" And he answered, "I am."

And Abner said to him, "Turn thee aside to thy right hand or to thy left, and lay thee hold on one of the young men, and take thee his armour." But Asahel would not turn aside from following of him.

And Abner said again to Asahel, "Turn thee aside from following me, wherefore should I smite thee to the ground? How then should I hold up my face to Joab, thy brother?"

Howbeit he refused to turn aside. Wherefore Abner, with the hinder end of the spear, smote him under the fifth rib, that the spear came out behind him, and he fell down there and died in the same place. (2 Sam 2:18-23)

The sons of Zeruiah - Joab, Abishai and Asahel - lead the *comitatus* of David's mighty men. The loss of Asahel is a terrible blow. The fact that his brother has been slain by the hand of his opposite number will not be forgiven by Joab, yet David's commander treads a fine line between employing his own earthy methods to get what he wants, and accommodating the more altruistic demands of his sworn lord and king. Joab and Abishai finally track Abner to the crest of a hill at Ammah, where the puffed-out commander receives some recently arrived reinforcements from Benjamin.

"Shall the sword devour forever?" Abner yells at Joab. "This is going to end in tears unless you call off your lot from pursuing their brethren." (2 Sam 2:24-28)

Outnumbered for now, Joab has no choice but to cancel the pursuit and head back to Gibeon with his men. When they count up the fallen, Judah has 20 dead and Abner's Israel 360. We should not be surprised at the result. David's tough fighting force has had a decade to hone its skills as outlaw roughneck raiders, while Abner's troop was doubtless drawn from the same men who fled the field at Gilboa. But there's another more subtle nuance coming to light: namely the first real breach of the fault-line that has quietly developed between the southern and northern tribes of the Jews. Initially it will manifest as a struggle between the house of David (Judah) and the house of Saul (Benjamin). Seventy years hence it will split the nation in fatal civil war.

Bloodfeud

Abner returns to his puppet king, Ishbosheth, son of Saul, for whom he has an abiding contempt. Ishbosheth is in his early 40s, weak, given to having a snooze during the day, and ideally suited for the wily Abner to manipulate in his plot to seize Israel's throne. But whatever play Abner has in mind, his hand is curiously forced when he is accused by Ishbosheth of running high with one of Saul's concubines, Rizpah. Concubines are considered kingly property, passed from father to son, and messing with the royal harem is serious business. In so doing, the perpetrator is assuming the rights of a king in defiance of the reigning monarch, thereby committing treason. Ishbosheth may be weak and fearful of his 'uncle', but the evidence against Abner is apparently compelling enough for Ishbosheth to say something, so he does. Abner goes toxic.

And Saul had a concubine whose name was Rizpah, the daughter of Aiah. And Ishbosheth said to Abner, "Wherefore hast thou gone in unto my father's concubine?"

Then was Abner very wroth [angry] **at the words of Ishbosheth and said, "Am I a dog's head, which against Judah do shew kindness this day unto the house of Saul thy father, to his brethren, and to his friends, and have not delivered thee into the hand of David, that thou chargest me to day with a fault concerning this woman? So do God to Abner and more also except, as the LORD hath sworn to David, even so I do to him. To translate the kingdom from the house of Saul, and to set up the throne of David over Israel and over Judah, from Dan even to Beersheba."**

And Ishbosheth could not answer Abner a word again because he feared him. (2 Sam 3:7-11)

Abner's immature petulance breaks up the alliance, so we suspect the accusation is neither trivial nor wide of the mark.[487] Abner resolves to move the allegiance of Israel to David to spite Ishbosheth, so we see God employing Abner's sin of pride to David's advantage. Abner is suffering a crisis of confidence at this point. Not only do we assume he ignominiously fled the field at Gilboa, abandoning his king and princes, Abner was dished a trouncing by Joab at the pool of Gibeon. So now to have this royal coxcomb question him about his sex life is beyond the pale for Abner. He wastes little time in sending messengers to David pledging Israel's support for his complete kingship of Israel in return for a deal. David replies that he is willing to talk so long as Abner brings David's first betrothed, Michal, whom Saul pledged in return for a hundred foreskins of the Philistines.

You may recall that Saul set up this ridiculous challenge in the hope that David would perish in his special forces action into Philistia with a pair of scissors and a sharp knife. In fact, to Saul's fury, David returns with no less than two hundred of the crinkly trophies in return for Michal, the king's daughter (1 Sam 18:27; 19:11,12). And while there was evidently genuine affection between David and Michal at the outset (1 Sam 18:28), Michal was given away by her father to another noble, Paltiel, as soon as David fled into exile.[488] In requesting Michal's return now, it's more likely that David intends all Israel to know that he has no quarrel with the house of Saul. In other words, he'll not be relying on Abner to consolidate his position. Smart.

Ishbosheth is compelled to order Michal taken from her husband and sent to Judah. Paltiel weeps along behind her as far as the border. Meanwhile Abner encourages the rest of the tribes to throw in their lot with David, paying special attention to Benjamin, Saul's tribe: the least likely to agree to the shift of power.

And Abner went also to speak in the ears of David in Hebron all that seemed good to Israel, and that seemed good to the whole house of Benjamin. So Abner came to David to Hebron, and twenty men with him. And David made Abner and the men that were with him a feast.

---

[487] David's son Adonijah will attempt to undermine Solomon's rule by requesting one of David's concubines, Abishag the Shunammite, in marriage. The treason leads to Adonijah's execution (1 Kings 2:17-25).

[488] Critics state that Michal could not legally be returned to David after her marriage to Paltiel, citing Deut 24:1-4. Jewish scholars argue that David was forced to flee Saul on the very night of his marriage, therefore did not consummate the union.

And Abner said unto David, "I will arise and go, and will gather all Israel unto my lord the king, that they may make a league with thee, and that thou mayest reign over all that thine heart desireth."

And David sent Abner away, and he went in peace. (2 Sam 3:19-21)

All's well that ends well? Unfortunately not. Joab returns with his men from a raid, only to learn of Abner's visit to David. Furious, Joab confronts the king.

"What hast thou done? Behold, Abner came unto thee; why is it that thou hast sent him away, and he is quite gone? Thou knowest Abner the son of Ner, that he came to deceive thee, and to know thy going out and thy coming in, and to know all that thou doest!" (2 Sam 3:24-25).

The dynamics are straightforward to Joab. Firstly, Abner is the murderer of his brother, Asahel, so there's to be a reckoning. Secondly, as commander of Israel's army, Abner is clearly seeking to oust Joab as head of David's military, and further his own career under the new state. Abner felt safe coming to David at Hebron, not only because he had what David wanted - the allegiance of the other tribes - but also because Hebron is a city of refuge, and no vengeance can be taken by Joab or Abishai for the death of their brother. Asahel's death was caused in the heat of war, so Joab has no right to assume the role of *goel* (avenger of blood). All cleverly thought through by Abner, but for one flaw. He has completely misread Joab.

David gives Joab short shrift, doubtless claiming the greater good as his aim in uniting Israel. Seething, Joab sends messengers after Abner as if to recall him to David. When Abner comes in through the gate of Hebron, Joab takes him quietly aside as if for a chat, and stabs him under the fifth rib, the same method Abner used to kill Asahel. Abishai is also implicated in this act of vengeance. (2 Sam 3:27)

For David, the hit on Abner is a potential, political catastrophe. He publicly excoriates Joab and Abishai for the murder, and makes a point of publicly mourning for Abner and following the coffin for burial.

And they buried Abner in Hebron: and the king [David] **lifted up his voice and wept at the grave of Abner, and all the people wept. And the king lamented over Abner and said, "Died Abner as a fool dieth? Thy hands were not bound, nor thy feet put into fetters. As a man falleth before wicked men, so fellest thou."**

And all the people wept again over him.

And when all the people came to cause David to eat meat while it was yet day, David swore, saying, "So do God to me and more also if I taste bread, or ought else, till the sun be down."

And all the people took notice of it and it pleased them, as whatsoever the king did pleased all the people. For all the people and all Israel understood that day that it was not of the king to slay Abner the son of Ner.

And the king said unto his servants, "Know ye not that there is a prince and a great man fallen this day in Israel? And I am this day weak, though anointed king; and these men, the sons of Zeruiah, be too hard for me. The LORD shall reward the doer of evil according to his wickedness. (2 Sam 3:32-39)

This event redefines the relationship between Joab and David. While David has never been tardy in executing judgment upon others, he curiously takes no action over Joab, but rather commits his judgment to God (2 Sam 3:39). Both have been roughshod comrades-in-arms throughout the thick and thin of the ten-year exile. On key occasions to come, Joab will carry out murders and executions, most notably for David's benefit, yet in other matters acting arguably for the good of the state and not least himself, though thoroughly against David's own mores and righteous will. Joab thus becomes David's enforcer, a Dirty Harry who gets his hands bloody for the good of Israel, so that David doesn't have to. The relationship, which David often laments, is destined to end badly.

King over all Israel

Bad news travels quickly. When Ishbosheth learns of Abner's fate, his heart fails him, and the rest of Israel is troubled. Worse, those holding out for a promotion by throwing their lot in with Abner realise their stock has spectacularly crashed. A grand gesture is needed to impress the new king.

Two Benjamites, Rechab and Baanah, enter Ishbosheth's residence in the heat of the day when the king is on his bed. Feigning a wheat collection chore, they seize the hapless monarch, stab him to death, cut off his head, escape into the plain and head south to Hebron all night with their grisly booty.

And they brought the head of Ishbosheth unto David to Hebron, and said to the king, "Behold the head of Ishbosheth, the son of Saul thine enemy, which sought thy life. And the LORD hath avenged my lord the king this day of Saul, and of his seed."

And David answered Rechab and Baanah his brother, the sons of Rimmon the Beerothite, and said unto them, "As the LORD liveth, who hath redeemed my soul out of all adversity, when one told me, saying, 'Behold, Saul is dead!' thinking to have brought good tidings, I took hold of him and slew him in Ziklag, who thought that I would have given him a reward for his tidings. How much more, when wicked men have slain a righteous person in his own house upon his bed? Shall I not therefore now require his blood of your hand and take you away from the Earth?"

And David commanded his young men, and they slew them, and cut off their hands and their feet, and hanged them up over the pool in Hebron. But they took the head of Ishbosheth, and buried it in the sepulchre of Abner in Hebron. (2 Sam 4:8-12)

Chuck Missler comments:

"Hands and feet are the instruments in perpetrating their crime. The exposure of the mutilated remains was intended as not only a punishment of their crime, but also the attestation of David's abhorrence."[489]

Once again, ambitious ne-er-do-wells misjudge the son of Jesse. And once more, David is given the chance to show all Israel that he bears no grudge against the house of Saul. The violent but shrewd act stops any further civil war in its tracks. The twelve tribes go to counsel and agree that David should be anointed King of Israel to rule over them:

Then came all the tribes of Israel to David unto Hebron, and spake, saying, "Behold, we are thy bone and thy flesh. Also in time past, when Saul was king over us, thou wast he that leddest out and broughtest in Israel. And the LORD said to thee, 'Thou shalt feed My people Israel, and thou shalt be a captain over Israel.'" (2 Sam 5:1-2)

Thus David is crowned king over all Israel, fulfilling the prophecy that David is God's chosen man to pull Israel together and launch the nation on its parabolic rise to greatness. He originally proved himself in the famous confrontation with Goliath, though God had previously tested him in the fields with wild beasts. In the following decade of battles, plots and skirmishes, David proves himself superior to every wile of the enemy due to his obedience and the LORD's favour. David commences his kingly role in Judah at the all-important 30 years of age, the same age as the commencement of

---

[489] Missler, Chuck, *1 & 2 Samuel notes*, op. cit., p.155

the ministry of priests, and that of Jesus Christ Himself. David rules Judah for seven and a half years before being crowned king of Israel. He will become Israel's most famous Old Testament monarch of a united Israel for a further 33 years, but he will not be without his mistakes or flaws in kingship, which makes him a worthy case-study for each of us. In spite of all, God will describe David as a man after His own heart. (1 Sam 13:4; Acts 13:22)

Yerushalayim - capital seat of holiness

Shortly after his coronation (*c.* 1002 BC), the Philistines mobilise their forces to attack David twice in the Valley of the Rephaim (Nephilim).[490] The intent seems to be to destroy David before he establishes a permanent power-base. Both times the five lords are roundly trounced by David's reliance on the LORD's tactics. These two victories mark the beginning of the end for Philistia as a credible threat to Israel for the remainder of the united monarchy, fulfilling the promise God gave in the days of Samson (Judg 13:5; *cf:* 2 Sam 8:1).[491]

Next, David moves his army against the Jebusites in Jerusalem, a curiously neutral city on the border of Judah and Benjamin. Though

---

[490] The name *Rephaim* is another allusion to the giant offspring harking back to the demonic Nephilim of Genesis 6 (see 6:4). The word is variously interpreted 'the dead ones', 'the spiritually dead', 'the walking dead'. I am intrigued that the atheist-leaning Wikipedia gives the word an unusually clear explanation: "In the Hebrew Bible, 'Rephaim' can describe an ancient race of giants in Iron Age Israel, or the places where these individuals were thought to have lived: see Gen. 14:5, 15:20; Deut. 2:10-1,20, 3:11,13; Josh. 12:4, 13:12, 15:8, 17:15, 18:16; 2 Sam. 5:11, 22, 23:13; 1 Chr. 11:15, 14:9, 20:4. In the Biblical narrative, the Israelites are instructed to exterminate the previous inhabitants of the 'promised land', i.e. 'Canaan', which include various named peoples, including some unusually tall/large individuals. See the passages listed above in the book of Joshua, and also Deut. 3:11, which implies that Og, the King of Bashan, was one of the last survivors of the Rephaim, and that his bed was 9 cubits long in ordinary cubit. (An ordinary cubit is the length of a man's forearm according to the New American Standard Bible, or approx. 18 inches, which differs from a royal cubit. This makes the bed over 13 feet long.). *cf.* the reference to Nephilim and the 'sons of God' in Gen. 6:1-3. Anak was a Rephaite (Deuteronomy 2:11).
The area of Moab at Ar, (the region East of the Jordan) before the time of Moses, was also considered the land of the Rephaites. Deuteronomy 2:18-21 refers to the fact that Ammonites called them 'Zamzummim', which is related to the Hebrew word זמזום, which literally translates into 'Buzzers', or 'the people whose speech sounds like buzzing'. In Arabic the word زمزم (zamzama) translates as 'to rumble, roll (thunder); murmur'. As per Deut 2:11, the Moabites referred to them as the Emim." - http://en.wikipedia.org/wiki/Rephaim

[491] David and his mighty men will later put paid to the remaining giants in 2 Sam 23.

believed to be impregnable by the Canaanite inhabitants (who taunt David's efforts from the walls - 2 Sam 5:6), the city is overcome and David establishes Israel's new national capital as the 'City of David', a fortress on the southern end of the Mount Moriah saddleback. Israel has a focal point of governance for the first time. Building and repair works are immediately set in motion, securing the city from attack. After this, David receives some welcoming emissaries from up north:

And Hiram king of Tyre sent messengers to David, and cedar trees, and carpenters, and masons, and they built David a house. And David perceived that the LORD had established him king over Israel, and that He had exalted His kingdom for His people Israel's sake.

And David took him more concubines and wives out of Jerusalem, after he was come from Hebron, and there were yet sons and daughters born to David. (2 Sam 5:11-13)

Hiram I of Tyre will become a close friend of David's, providing magnificent cedarwood and the expertise necessary to build David a royal home. It's a sea change for the son of Jesse, who lived rough for ten years during his campaigning and exile, then settled to a degree of permanence in Hebron. Hiram's generosity will become known throughout the region, win the Sidonian king access to the trade routes of Egypt and Arabia, and cement David into the international psyche as a national monarch with whom enemies must contend. How odd it must seem finally for David to know beyond doubt that the uncertainty is over, and to call a place home.

During the seven and a half years as Judah's king in Hebron, David had not been idle in the bedroom either. A firstborn son and heir, Amnon, was provided by Ahinoam the Jezreelitess. A second son, Daniel/Chileab,[492] was born to Abigail, the widow of Nabal the Carmelite. A third, Absalom, was born to Maacah, the gentile daughter of King Talmai of Geshur.[493] And yet a fourth son, Adonijah,

---

[492] With the deaths of heirs and general turmoil to engulf David's house, Chileab, curiously, will be passed over for succession, even as second-born. He is given a different name in 1 Chron 3:1 – that of Daniel. Chileab/Daniel receives no further mention in scripture beyond 1 Chron 3:1 and 2 Sam 3:3. Some scholars believe Abigail may have been made pregnant by her first husband Nabal immediately prior to meeting David, thus sowing some doubt as to Chileab's legitimacy as heir.

[493] Geshur is in Syria, north of Israel. David's marriage to Maacah is doubtless a political match to provide David with an ally to box in the northern Israelite tribes. Maacah is also doubtless stunning, since her son Absalom becomes famous for his physical beauty throughout the kingdom (2 Sam 14:25), as does his sister Tamar, who drives her half-brother Amnon mad with lust (2 Sam 13:1-2).

to David's wife, Haggith. And a fifth, Shephatiah to Abital, and a sixth, Ithream, to David's wife, Eglah.

Now settled in Jerusalem, David takes on more wives and concubines, resulting in a veritable army of sons and daughters. The first observation is that David is starting a wifely collection, a move expressly forbidden in the Torah (Deut 17:17), along with the accumulation of gold, silver and horses. God wants the king of Israel's eyes on Him only. Unfortunately, the custom of pagan kings to be multiply wenched, and even to possess a harem of concubines, had been adopted by Saul, Ishbosheth, and now David, and will be taken to new heights by David's profligate successor, Solomon. If one in a thousand schoolchildren know nothing else about King Solomon of Israel, it is that he possessed some mines, an astonishing 700 wives and some 300 porcupines.[494] Can you imagine the prickly arguments among that lot? God's warning in Deut 17:17 that multiple wives will 'turn the heart away' will come home to roost in David's household in heartbreaking fashion. It will also become the chief reason why God will tear the united kingdom from Solomon eventually upon the latter's death in 931 BC.[495]

But for now, God is blessing Israel, all is well, and the City of David is home. Jerusalem is one of the oldest, continuously inhabited cities on Earth. It has been destroyed twice, besieged 23 times, attacked 52 times, and captured and recaptured 44 times.[496] It was first settled after the Flood, traditionally by Shem and Eber, in the area around the Gihon Spring known as the 'Old City'. 'Salem' crops up in Abraham's day when the patriarch visits the mysterious Melchizedek, king and priest of the town, to offer tithes (Gen 14:18-20). Abraham also brings his son Isaac to Mount Moriah to offer him for sacrifice in obedience to God's command. At the last moment, God provides a substitute (Gen 22).

Jerusalem is mentioned in Egyptian correspondence down through the centuries as the pharaohs' control across the region ebbs and flows. After Israel enters the Land in Joshua's conquest, the area of Jerusalem is allocated to the tribe of Benjamin, though they never

---

[494] Due to the atheist agenda practised in most British schools today, few children even get to find out about the Bible, much less study fascinating characters such as David and Solomon, and learn the important lessons from them.

[495] See *Origins IV – Tetelestai.*

[496] http://en.wikipedia.org/wiki/Jerusalem, *Moment Magazine*

possess it, and the city remains under independent Jebusite control until David takes it in 1003 BC.

Jerusalem itself remains an enigma. It has nothing physical going for it apart from a reasonable defensive position on three sides, betrayed by the north.[497] It's neither a major port nor confluence of any important trade routes, yet has maintained a surreal importance and historic relevance down through the ages against all odds into the modern era. As the religious nexus of the world's three leading montheistic religions - Judaism, Christianity and Islam – Jerusalem's history has been drenched in blood, yet its future role as the focal point of the Tribulation era and Millennial Kingdom is incredibly destined to eclipse all previous dramas.

This, then, is the city David establishes as Israel's capital, yet even in this the son of Jesse exhibits his characteristic political acumen. Located three miles south of Benjamite Saul's stronghold at Gibeon, Jerusalem is effectively 'neutral territory' between Judah and the rest of Israel, paying heed both to disaffected Benjamin and the other alienated tribes. In time, David's charisma will begin to heal the rift between Israel and Judah, and as befitting the chief city of the nation God has chosen and blessed from Abraham, a most vital presence needs to be installed without delay for the spiritual 'homecoming' to be truly complete.

The Ark comes to Jerusalem

You may recall that around 70 years before, the Philistines had captured the Ark in battle at Ebenezer and triumphantly installed it next to their pagan god Dagon in the temple at Ashdod. Over the following months the holy artefact wrought havoc across Philistia, raining plagues of rats and haemorrhoids upon the hapless five cities. In desperation, the five lords commanded the Ark to be put on a cart towed by kine and trundled back to Israel. The Ark came to rest in fields just over Judah's border at Beth Shemesh. Overjoyed to have their Ark back, some of the locals could not help themselves and peeped inside the artefact, resulting in seventy Jews being slain by God on the spot for violating His holiness. Terrified, Beth Shemesh beseeched the town of Kirjath Jearim to make haste to collect the Ark. It was finally installed in the house of Abinadab in Kirjath Jearim, where it remained attended to by this consecrated family for 70 - 100

[497] This will be the route Rome will use in 70 AD to conquer the city.

years until David's accession to Israel's throne and his capture of Jerusalem.

The lesson of Beth Shemesh is that God expects His holiness to be taken seriously and respected at all times, and God does not change. During the following century, this lesson is not only forgotten, the protocol for moving the Ark is botched by the house of Abinadab when David commands the Ark to be brought in processional triumph to Jerusalem.

Again, David gathered together all the chosen men of Israel, thirty thousand, and David arose and went with all the people that were with him from Baale of Judah [Kirjath-jearim], **to bring up from thence the Ark of God, whose name is called by the name of the LORD of hosts that dwelleth between the cherubim.**

And they set the Ark of God upon a new cart and brought it out of the house of Abinadab that was in Gibeah, and Uzzah and Ahio, the sons of Abinadab, drove the new cart. And they brought it out of the house of Abinadab which was at Gibeah, accompanying the Ark of God, and Ahio went before the Ark.

And David and all the house of Israel played before the LORD on all manner of instruments made of fir wood, even on harps, and on psalteries, and on timbrels, and on cornets and on cymbals. (2 Sam 6:1-5)

All well and good until the cart hits a rut by Nachon's threshing-floor. Uzzah thrusts forth his hand to prevent the Ark from toppling. Big mistake. For this breach of God's holiness, Uzzah is struck dead on the spot, and his lifeless body drops by the wayside.

David is furious, not only for Uzzah and his family, but also for himself. After all he's been through, after all the trials and tribulations the son of Jesse has endured to bring about the LORD's will for Israel, this is how God repays him? And what about Uzzah, whose family protected and served the Ark for a century after that last God-punishing incident at Beth Shemesh? Is this how the LORD repays the faithful?

Later, David calms down and thinks it all through. The lessons of Beth Shemesh are re-learned. God is not some tavern drinking-buddy, He is THE CREATOR OF THE UNIVERSE. His holiness is a hyperdimensional phenomenon of its own. The LORD fully explains in the Torah how He and the Ark should be handled. These instructions were not laid down for God's benefit, but to protect man from the destructive effects of Earthly sin coming into contact with the Creator's perfection. We can have absolutely no idea what this truly entails. Jack Heyford writes:

"Not even the priests were allowed to touch the ark or look into it because of its sacredness. Because the ark was not being handled according to God's directions, when the difficulties arose, there was no way of dealing with them. Had the ark been carried on the shoulders of the priests, as the Law directed, this would not have happened." [498]

A fire in the living room is cosy, familiar and comforting, but it's still fire which burns if you abuse it. God is a consuming fire (Heb 12:29). One purpose of the *Origins* series is to gain a broader understanding of the Creator's character and Nature in the light of His actions and Word, what He would have of us, and what our destinies have in store for us in the days, years and eternity ahead.

Which similar notions must have been occupying David and his men as they beheld Uzzah's body placed on a slatter and hauled off for burial.

And David was afraid of the LORD that day, and said, "How shall the Ark of the LORD come to me?"

So David would not remove the Ark of the LORD unto him into the city of David, but David carried it aside into the house of Obed-Edom the Gittite [a Philistine from Gath, Goliath's home town!]. **And the Ark of the LORD continued in the house of Obed-Edom the Gittite three months. And the LORD blessed Obed-Edom and all his household.** (2 Sam 6:9-11)

Can you imagine Obed-Edom's reaction when the Ark is borne into his living room? And after that, when he, a Philistine, and his household are blessed by YHWH for their hospitality? There is a detail to note here. Sources indicate that David's army comprises a number of disaffected Philistines by this stage who sensed a change in the political wind and defected. The reasons may have been practical, prosaic, financial, political and even religious. The LORD has demonstrated both His love for Israel and anger against her enemies throughout Philistine history. Some Gentiles have had their eyes opened, such as Rahab and Obed-Edom. God loves to bless a Gentile, given half a chance. That's most of us.

In *Origins IV - Tetelestai,* which continues the Creator's story, we'll come across the Cherethites and Pelethites – two ethnic groups which serve as part of David's personal bodyguard and the general army.

---

[498] Heyford, Jack, *The Spirit-Filled Bible,* op. cit., p.449

Scholars are divided as to their origin, but the evidence indicates that these were Philistine clans David befriended during his exile. One commentary enlightens:

"[These are] foreign mercenaries who formed David's bodyguard. The Cherethites are first mentioned in I Samuel 30:14 which records the Amalekites' raid on Ziklag and the 'south (Negeb, in Hebrew) of the Cherethites', an area also named the land of the Philistines (1 Sam 30:16) implying that the Cherethites' territory constituted the southern part of Philistia. The Cherethite region may be identical with the Hazerim of Gaza (Deut 2:23), a territory of the Caphtorim of Caphtor.

"After David's accession to the throne, he established a military unit consisting of Cherethites and Pelethites under the command of Benaiah the son of Jehoiada (II Sam 8:18). The unit remained loyal to the king when Absalom revolted (II Sam 15:14, 18); it participated in the war against Sheba the son of Bichri (II Sam 20:7), and was present at Solomon's enthronement (I Kgs 1:38, 44). The Cherethites were still mentioned in the 6th century B.C. in Zephaniah's prophecy on the Philistines (Zeph 2:4-5), possibly indicating that the Philistines and the Cherethites were identical and that the Cherethites were named after Crete, their island of origin. It has also been suggested that the Cretans arrived before the Philistine invasion of the 12th century B.C., and that the two peoples merged. However, as the Cretan origin of the Cherethites is uncertain, the meaning of the name Cherethites and Pelethites still requires further research." [499]

It became common practice in ancient times for a powerful king or emperor to have his personal bodyguard comprise foreign mercenaries. This prevented palace plots against the ruler, in contradistinction to Rome, where the Praetorian Guard was traditionally home-grown, and regularly bumped off unpopular emperors.[500] The Byzantine emperors ('Rome East') learned this lesson, and from 988 AD employed the notorious Varangian Guard for security. The Varangians comprised some of the most legendary Norse (Viking) mercenaries, whose thirst for loot secured their loyalty, fêted as they were with fabulous pay, perks, lifestyle and a share of the plunder.

---

[499] www.answers.com/topic/cherethites-and-pelethites

[500] Fifteen Roman emperors were murdered by the Praetorian Guard. http://en.wikipedia.org/wiki/Category:Roman_emperors_murdered_by_the_Praetorian_Guard

And it was told King David, saying, "The LORD hath blessed the house of Obed-Edom, and all that pertaineth unto him, because of the Ark of God."

So David went and brought up the Ark of God from the house of Obed-Edom into the city of David with gladness. And so it was that when they that bare the Ark of the LORD had gone six paces, he sacrificed oxen and fatlings. And David danced before the LORD with all his might, and David was girded with a linen ephod.

So David and all the house of Israel brought up the Ark of the LORD with shouting, and with the sound of the trumpet. And as the Ark of the LORD came into the city of David, Michal, Saul's daughter, looked through a window and saw King David leaping and dancing before the LORD, and she despised him in her heart.

And they brought in the Ark of the LORD and set it in his place, in the midst of the tabernacle that David had pitched for it. And David offered burnt offerings and peace offerings before the LORD.

And as soon as David had made an end of offering burnt offerings and peace offerings, he blessed the people in the name of the LORD of hosts. And he dealt among all the people, even among the whole multitude of Israel, as well to the women as men, to every one a cake of bread, and a good piece of flesh, and a flagon of wine. So all the people departed, every one to his house. (2 Sam 6:12-19)

Sadly, upon returning to his house, Michal makes the mistake of confronting her king over his 'errant' behaviour.

Then David returned to bless his household. And Michal the daughter of Saul came out to meet David, and said, "How glorious was the King of Israel today, who uncovered himself in the eyes of the handmaids of his servants, as one of the vain fellows shamelessly uncovereth himself!"

And David said unto Michal, "It was before the LORD, who chose me before thy father, and before all his house, to appoint me ruler over the people of the LORD, over Israel. Therefore will I play before the LORD. And I will yet be more vile than thus, and will be base in mine own sight, and of the maidservants which thou hast spoken of, of them shall I be had in honour."

Therefore Michal the daughter of Saul had no child unto the day of her death. (2 Sam 6:20-23)

It's a troubling episode in Michal's life, based on jealousy aroused with anger at seeing her husband act so before the maidens of the kingdom, misreading David's intentions entirely. Michal doubtless believes she has been snatched from her husband Paltiel (with whom there is evidence of genuine affection – 2 Sam 3:16), to be used as a pawn by David to secure the favour of Benjamin and the other tribes to establish national unity. Her love for David has grown cold, curtailed not least by the current army of wives, concubines and step-children with whom she must contend. It's a far cry from her exalted position ten years earlier, when she stood by the side of her father, Israel's first king, before Saul brought the kingdom to ruin.

The everlasting house

One day, during a visit to his house by Nathan the prophet, David remarks:

"Look how I live in a house of cedar, but the Ark of the LORD dwells inside tent curtains."

Nathan replies, "Then go and do all that is in your heart, for the LORD is with you."

But the LORD straightens Nathan out that night with a vision, during which another vital covenant is laid out by the Creator for the future of Israel and Planet Earth. It's worth quoting this new covenant in its entirety for the astonishing declaration God reveals for the future:

"Go and tell my servant David, 'Thus saith the LORD, Shalt thou build me an house for me to dwell in? Whereas I have not dwelt in any house since the time that I brought up the children of Israel out of Egypt, even to this day, but have walked in a tent and in a tabernacle.

" 'In all the places wherein I have walked with all the children of Israel, spake I a word with any of the tribes of Israel, whom I commanded to feed my people Israel, saying, "Why build ye not Me an house of cedar?'

"Now therefore, so shalt thou say unto my servant David, 'Thus saith the LORD of hosts, I took thee from the sheepcote, from following the sheep, to be ruler over My people, over Israel. And I was with thee whithersoever thou went, and have cut off all thine enemies out of thy sight, and have made thee a great name, like unto the name of the great men that are in the Earth.

" 'Moreover I will appoint a place for My people Israel, and will plant them, that they may dwell in a place of their own and move no more; neither shall the children of wickedness afflict them any more as beforetime. And as since the time that I commanded judges to be over My people Israel, and have caused thee to rest from all

thine enemies. Also the LORD telleth thee that he will make thee a house.

" 'And when thy days be fulfilled, and thou shalt sleep with thy fathers, I will set up thy seed after thee, which shall proceed out of thy bowels, and I will establish His kingdom. He shall build a house for My name, and I will establish the throne of His kingdom forever.' " (2 Sam 7:5-13)

In a few short verses, God confirms his previous commitments to His people,[501] declaring that He will settle them into a place of their own, and that David's line will endure and rule, not just for a long time, but *forever*. **I will establish his kingdom** refers not only to David's lineage, but the Messiah who will derive from it. A thousand years in the future, the angel will announce Mary's coming conception thus:

"Fear not, Mary, for thou hast found favour with God. And, behold, thou shalt conceive in thy womb and bring forth a son, and shalt call his name Jesus. He shall be great and shall be called the Son of the Highest; and the Lord God shall give unto Him the throne of His father David. And He shall reign over the house of Jacob forever, and of His kingdom there shall be no end." (Luke 1:31-33)

But God has a caution and a blessing for David's successor(s).

I will be his Father and he shall be My son. If he commit iniquity, I will chasten him with the rod of men, and with the stripes of the children of men, but My mercy shall not depart from him, as I took it from Saul, whom I put away before thee. And thine house and thy kingdom shall be established forever before thee: thy throne shall be established forever. (2 Sam 7:14-16)

God repeats the eternal nature of David's kingdom and house in the last section, declaring that wrongdoing in David's line will be punished *by human agency*. Notice once again that the overall bequest by God to David - that his line, throne and kingdom will be established forever - is *unconditional*. It is not contingent on Israel's compliance or behaviour, *nor even on their acceptance or otherwise of Jesus Christ as their Mashiach*. And the land of Israel doesn't belong to the UN, Hamas, Iran, the PLO, ISIS, Sean Penn or Angelina Jolie either.

---

[501] Gen 13:15; 15:18; 17:8; Deut 34:4. God has given the Land to His people *forever. Unconditionally*. These promises and covenants made by God are being directly challenged by governments and the Palestinians in the Middle East today. I wouldn't do that if I were them.

Genesis 38 codes

That the LORD has had His eternal eye on David is intriguingly corroborated in the Torah itself. Way back in Genesis, there's the strange Chapter 38 inserted into the epic story of Joseph being sold into slavery by his jealous siblings. Chapter 38 seems utterly out of place, and not even chronological to the Joseph narrative, since the contents cover three generations. Some researchers believe that the purpose of Chapter 38 is to hit the pause button on the Joseph tale to build suspense, and indeed it does. In Robert Alter's *Art of Biblical Narrative,* the author argues that the narrative function of the Judah/Tamar tale is to enhance the larger storyline of Joseph. There's actually an even more spooky reason for Chapter 38 being where it is, but before we can appreciate its miracle, let's quickly review what Chapter 38 actually says. If the Holy Spirit put it there, there's a good reason.

Centuries before, in the years prior to the Egyptian captivity of Joseph's descendants, you will recall that Joseph's father, the patriarch Jacob, had twelve sons who went on to father the twelve tribes of Israel. Son number four is Judah who, we are told in the parenthetical Chapter 38, marries a gentile Canaanite woman named Shua. He has three sons by her named Er, Onan and Shelah.

Judah provides a wife for Er, his firstborn - a girl named Tamar. Unfortunately Er does wickedly (we're not told what), so God kills him. Under the Jewish levirate law of marriage, if an heir dies childless, it is the duty of the next son in line - Onan in this case - to go in to the widow (Tamar) to raise up seed for his dead brother. The problem is, Onan knows that any heir born via Tamar will not be his, so he obeys his father by going in to Tamar, but spills his seed on the ground to frustrate the project. Sordid, I know. And God doesn't like it either, so He kills Onan.

Judah is now two sons down in this developing nightmare of his lineage. Under 'normal' circumstances, Judah would order his third son Shelah in to Tamar, but Shelah is too young, so Judah puts Tamar in a holding pattern, requesting that she remain a widow in her father's house until Shelah is of sufficient age to perform. Then, third time lucky, they can all have another go at the business of giving Judah an heir to preserve his lineage, and all will live happily ever after.

Except that tragedy strikes anew with the death of Judah's Canaanite wife, Shua. By this time Shelah is grown, but has not been offered to Tamar. Feeling isolated, forgotten and sensing Judah will bail on his obligations to provide for her future and lineage, the widow Tamar hatches a plan. She's heard that Judah is heading up to Timnah to shear his sheep, so she removes her mourning apparel, kits herself out as a pagan temple prostitute (complete with veil), and finds a spot by the roadside to advertise her charms.

Who should trip along but the recently widowed Judah. Liking what he sees, he propositions his disguised daughter-in-law. Before the act, Tamar requests that he leaves her some surety that he will pay her a goat for her services. She requests his signet, bracelets and staff, which he gives her. Negotiations settled, they do the deed, which for Judah is not only an act of fornication, but Canaanite cult-idolatry (with what he thinks is a pagan temple prostitute). Judah proceeds on to Timnah, where he instructs a friend to drop the young goat back to the prostitute as payment, reclaiming his signet, bracelets and staff. The friend, however, finds no trace of the temple prostitute when he goes to the indicated spot by the roadside.

Then he asked the men of that place, saying, "Where is the harlot who was openly by the wayside?" And they said, "There was no harlot in this place."

And he returned to Judah and said, "I cannot find her; and also the men of the place said that there was no harlot in this place."

And Judah said, "Let her take it to her lest we be shamed. Behold, I sent this kid [goat] **and thou hast not found her."** (Gen 38:21-23)

A grimy matter, to be sure, illustrating how casually depraved the society had become, into which Judah married. Three months go by, then the bombshell drops:

And it came to pass about three months after, that it was told Judah, saying, "Tamar thy daughter-in-law hath played the harlot; and also, behold, she is with child by whoredom."

And Judah said, "Bring her forth, and let her be burnt."

When she was brought forth, she sent to her father-in-law, saying, "By the man whose these are, am I with child." And she said, "Discern, I pray thee, whose are these, the signet, and bracelets and staff."

And Judah acknowledged them, and said, "She hath been more righteous than I; because that I gave her not to Shelah my son." And he knew her [had sex with her] **again no more.**

And it came to pass in the time of her travail that, behold, twins were in her womb. And it came to pass, when she travailed, that the

one put out his hand, and the midwife took and bound upon his hand a scarlet thread, saying, "This came out first." And it came to pass, as he drew back his hand, that, behold, his brother came out. And she said, "How hast thou broken forth? This breach be upon thee!" Therefore his name was called Perez.

And afterward came out his brother, who had the scarlet thread upon his hand: and his name was called Zarah. (Gen 38:24-30)

You might ask, what does all this have to do with David? Fret not, we're getting there, and it's worth the trip. Perez is technically Judah's heir, but neither son is considered part of the Jewish congregation as they are born illegitimate. Deuteronomy 23:2 states that **a bastard shall not enter into the congregation of the LORD; even to his tenth generation shall he not enter into the congregation of the LORD.**

Fast forward to the charming story of Ruth and Boaz six generations later. At their wedding feast, you may recall that the guests propose a toast to the bride and groom: **"Let thy house be like the house of Perez, whom Tamar bare unto Judah, of the seed which the LORD shall give thee of this young woman!"** (Ruth 4:12) In other words, God's clock is ever ticking on its way to the redemptive, tenth generation from Perez, which turns out to be David! In fact, to underscore this interpretation, the book of Ruth ends with the following triumphant postscript on lineage:

Now these are the generations of Perez: Perez begat Hezron, And Hezron begat Ram, and Ram begat Amminadab, And Amminadab begat Nahshon, and Nahshon begat Salmon, And Salmon begat Boaz, and Boaz begat Obed, And Obed begat Jesse, and Jesse begat David. (Ruth 4:18-22)

Chuck Missler comments:

"One of the reasons that the sordid tale of Judah and Tamar has been included in the Scriptures is because this incident is included in the family tree of the Messiah! [502] It is interesting that hidden within the text of Genesis 38, at 49-letter intervals, are the names of Boaz, Ruth, Obed, Jesse, and David - in chronological order! Note that Hebrew goes from right to left, and the names are coded backwards. [503]

"These names anticipate, five generations in advance, the next five generations climaxing in David, a total of ten generations. Here in the Torah we find the names of the principals of the Book of Ruth, and a delineation of their descendants leading up to the royal line. How did

---

[502] *cf:* Matt 1:1-11 (vv.5, 6)

[503] See video at www.youtube.com/watch?v=BQUwqKDgqn8

Moses know all this centuries before the fact? We know that Moses himself wrote the Torah: Jesus verified that very fact numerous times.[504]

"The presence of such features of the Biblical text is a profound demonstration of its supernatural origin. There is absolutely no way that these details could have been anticipated in advance except by Divine guidance, and the control of the most subtle aspects of the recorded text – far outstripping any insights of the authors themselves."[505]

David's mighty men

Much is made in the scriptures of David's mighty men and their accomplishments. There are detailed lists of these warriors given 1 Chron 11 & 12, and also in 2 Sam 23, most of whom mean nothing to us now. But isn't it interesting that God keeps detailed records of those who are faithful to Him and who fight on His behalf, even if man does not. And so it can be with us if our deeds are selfless and worthy of His favour.

A *Jewish* or *Christian* soldier is not an oxymoron. YHWH is a God of battles, and it will be ever so until the end of evil on Earth. Jesus Christ Himself is the Commander of the LORD's host. What about **Thou shalt not murder**? Is it OK under certain circumstances to kill? Can you slaughter, yet remain under Grace? Evil has certainly been carried out in the LORD's name, as we've already seen. In *Origins V* and *VI,* we will study the dynamics of the whole gamut of atrocities carried out, not just by Jews and Christians, but also by Muslims and atheists. No faith has its hands untarnished, *especially those of no faith.*

Disbelief has been expressed in certain quarters over the numbers of warriors slain at one time by some of the following champions. It's worth pointing out that such Old Testament engagements were quite different from the pitched battles of the medieval era. OT battles are sometimes conflicts of annihilation, where deciding the outcome of a quarrel (the medieval model) is secondary to killing as many of the enemy as possible. Consequently, once the losing side flees the field, they are relentlessly pursued, sometimes for days, until all are accounted for. Your enemy cannot attack you again if they have no army. OT armies are also generally far larger in manpower than their medieval or even modern counterparts.

---

[504] Matt 8:4; 19:7,8; 23:2; Mark 1:44; 7:10; 10:3–5; 12:26; Luke 5:14; 16:19, 29–31; 20:37; 24:27, 44; FG 3:14; 5:39,45-47; 6:32; 7:19, 22,23

[505] www.khouse.org/articles/2004/522/#notes#notes

The other point is that such OT warriors each had a 'name' or 'word-fame' which carried before them, provoking dread in the enemy (*viz:* Goliath). It's certainly not beyond credulity that poorly trained cohorts of the enemy could fall piecemeal to such professionals. The Bible is unabashed. The following men, singled out for special mention among David's *comitatus*, were as hard as nails and veritable killing machines.

The Three

Jashobeam, the son of a Hachmonite: Chief of the captains, Jashobeam slaughtered 300 men in one battle with a spear. (1 Chron 11:11)

Eleazar, son of Dodo the Ahohite: After most of the Israelite army fled from the Philistines at Ephesdammim (1 Sam 17:1), Eleazar was one of the three mighty men who remained with David to defend a lentil field. Eleazar slew so many of the enemy that the muscles in his hand seized, his sword stuck ('clave') to his hand, and he was unable to open it. A tremendous victory was had that day, and the rest of the Israelite army who fled slunk back to partake of the spoil (2 Sam 23:9-10)

Shammah, son of Agee, a Hararite: Another of the lentil-patch warriors. Hundreds killed, provoking such terror among the enemy that they eventually fled. Shammah is sometimes identified with Shamgar, who slew 600 Philistines with an ox-goad in Judges 3:31. Some scholars believe the two could be the same warrior, and Shamgar's deeds might be an anachronistic reference to the lentil-field incident.

The Thirty

After the above Three, there's a further group of Thirty singled out for special mention, Actually more than thirty. Among these are:

Adino the Eznite: Slew 800 of the enemy in one battle. (2 Sam 23:8).

Abishai, son of Zeruiah, brother of Joab: Racked up a death-toll of 300 enemy (1 Chron 11:20).

Benaiah, son of Jehoiada: Killed countless numbers of the enemy. Put paid to two mighty champions of Moab. Slew a lion in a pit on a snowy day. Killed a seven-foot-six Egyptian when he approached him with his staff, wrenched the Egyptian's spear from him, then slew him with it. Will later head up Solomon's Praetorian in *Origins IV* (1 Chron 11:22-25).

Asahel ben Zeruiah, brother of Joab and Abishai, nephew of David: Was slain by Abner, whom he pursued after the skirmish at the pool of Gibeon.

Elhanan, son of Dodo: Slew Goliath's brother.

Uriah the Hittite: Later famously murdered by Joab on David's orders so David could steal his wife, Bathsheba. Uriah fought for David over the years, and the two became more than friends, as evidenced by how close to David's palace Uriah and Bathsheba lived.

David establishes his empire

Over and above the Thirty, dozens more warriors are listed by name as part of David's burgeoning Israelite army, including the accomplished Benjamite warriors of Saul, lethal with the sling and bow. Some join David's ranks during the exile as Israel's faith in Saul begins to wane. Some of the warriors of Benjamin and Judah come to David at his stronghold at Hebron. David goes out to meet them:

"If you have come in good faith to help me, my heart will be united with yours. But if you have a mind to betray me to my enemies, since there is no wrong in my hands, may the God of our fathers look thereon and bring judgment."

Amasai, chief of the captains, is filled with the Spirit, "We are yours, David, and on your side, son of Jesse. Peace be upon you and yours, for God lends His hand to you this day."

David welcomes them in and promotes the most skilled according to their experience. A sizeable contingent of officers from Manasseh defect to David at his stronghold at Ziklag: Adnah, Jozabad, Jediael, Michael, Jozabad, Elihu and Zilthai - all captains of the thousands of the half-tribe of Manasseh. These lend assistance to David when he goes after the Amalekites following the sack of Ziklag and kidnap of the force's families (1 Chron 12:16-22).

Tens of thousands more defect from Saul's service to David at Hebron, vowing to make him king over all Israel. They are numbered as follows:

Warriors of Judah: 6,800
Warriors of Simeon: 7,100
Warriors of Levi: 4,600
Warriors of the Aaronites: 3,700

Warriors of Benjamin: 3,000
Warriors of Ephraim: 20,800
Warriors of Manasseh: 18,000
Warriors of Issachar: 200 officers (Men uncounted)
Warriors of Zebulun: 50,000
Warriors of Naphtali: 1,000 officers and 37,000 infantry
Warriors of the Danites: 28,600
Warriors of Asher: 40,000
Warriors of the Gilead region
(Reubenites, Gadites and Manasseh from east of Jordan): 120,000
(1 Chron 12)

All these men of war that could keep rank, came with a perfect heart to Hebron, to make David king over all Israel. And all the rest also of Israel were of one heart to make David king.

And there they were with David three days, eating and drinking, for their brethren had prepared for them. Moreover they that were near to them, even unto Issachar and Zebulun and Naphtali, brought bread on asses, and on camels, and on mules, and on oxen, and meat, meal, cakes of figs and bunches of raisins, and wine, and oil, and oxen, and sheep abundantly: for there was joy in Israel. (1 Chron 12:38-40)

Notice that last phrase. The winds of change are blowing across God's Holy Land, and all Jews sense the dawning of a new era. Months later, David establishes himself in Jerusalem after overcoming the Jebusites, most of whom he spares. The Ark of the Covenant is brought into the captured city and set up in its Tabernacle. The Philistines, beaten twice in quick succession, are given little rest to re-group. David leads out a huge army of determined warriors and obliterates Philistia's remaining resistance, capturing Gath and its towns, securing the surrender of the five lords, and payment of tribute henceforth.

David's next target, Moab, is controversial and unexpected. His treatment of the desert kingdom is unusually harsh, resulting in the execution of two-thirds of the surrendering army. David orders every enemy combatant to lie on the ground. They are then measured off with a cord. Every first two to be measured are executed, the third spared (2 Sam 8:2). Since David himself has Moabite blood in his veins via his great-grandmother, Ruth, and even committed the safety of his family to the king of Moab when Saul turned against him (1 Sam 22:3-4), his violent treatment of the desert kingdom now is troubling.

The most likely explanation, some scholars maintain, is that Moab mistreated or even murdered David's parents and family. In fact, there exists a Jewish tradition to this effect.[506] Independent verification of the fate of David's parental family has not come down to us, other than the explanation that Moab capitulated and thereafter paid Israel tribute.

The next high-value target on David's list is Hadadezer king of Zobah, a city-state in Syria, north of Damascus. Zobah is a kingpin city-state in the rising Aramean empire, and is allied to Syria-Damascus and Ammon (modern-day Jordan). As Hadadezer is heading out from Zobah to secure his territory by the River Euphrates, David strikes. Josephus records that in the subsequent rout as far as Hamah, David destroys twenty thousand of Hadadezer's infantry, around seven thousand of his horsemen, and takes a thousand of his chariots, destroying the greatest part of them.[507]

Hadad, king of Syria-Damascus, is incensed at the attack on his Zoban ally, and mobilises his own forces to engage David's army. The result is a disaster for the Syrians, who lose 22,000 infantry, with the rest put to flight. David garrisons both Zobah and Damascus on his return, and exacts tribute from these populations as new client-states to Israel. The famed golden shields of Zobah are seized, along with huge quantities of bronze, looted from the cities of Tibhath and Chun. The booty is returned to Jerusalem and dedicated to the LORD. The bronze will later be used by Solomon to make the huge laver, pillars and artefacts of the First Temple (1 Chron 18:3-8).

Now when Tou, king of Hamah, heard how David had smitten all the host of Hadadezer king of Zobah, he sent Hadoram his son to King David to enquire of his welfare, and to congratulate him because he had fought against Hadadezer and smitten him (for Hadadezer had war with Tou), and with him all manner of vessels of gold and silver and brass were brought. Them also king David dedicated unto the LORD, with the silver and the gold that he brought from all these nations; from Edom, and from Moab, and from the children of Ammon, and from the Philistines, and from Amalek. (1 Chron 18:9-11)

We're talking *major* treasure here. Meanwhile the force of the dauntless Abishai, Joab's brother, slaughters 18,000 Edomites in the

---

[506] *Midrash Tanhuma*, Wayera, 25

[507] Josephus, *Antiquities*, op. cit., 7:5

Valley of Salt, south of the Dead Sea, and loots and garrisons cities in Edom, the lords of which bend the knee to David, swear allegiance and thereafter pay tribute.

Not long after this, King Nahash of Ammon dies. David has spared the Ammonites Israel's wrath up to now, since Nahash (*lit.* 'serpent') apparently showed some kindness to David in the past. It's all a bit of a mystery since this appears to be the same pitiless Nahash, who came against Jabesh Gilead in the early days of Saul, and threatened to gouge out the right eye of every inhabitant as the price for peace. Saul's first test as prospective king was to deal with this menace, which he did with the LORD's help in uncompromising fashion (1 Sam 11:5-15).

So scholars wonder how David and Nahash could possibly be on good terms *now*, mere decades after Saul's decisive slaughter of the Ammonites; unless, as Jerome suggests, David and Nahash became allies, as they were both enemies of Saul (i.e. 'the enemy of my enemy is my friend').[508] Interestingly, the aforementioned rabbinical tradition that David entrusted his family to the King of Moab for safety during his flight from Saul, and that his loved ones were subsequently killed, also has a brother of David escaping the family slaughter in Moab to seek sanctuary with Nahash at Rabbah (modern-day Amman). Whatever the reason, upon Nahash's death, David now feels compelled to extend kindness to the dead king's son, Hanun, and despatches ambassadors to Rabbah to comfort the heir concerning his father's passing. A nice gesture, we might suppose.

Hanun is weak and vulnerable to bad advice from his royal council. The princes of Ammon are understandably unsettled by the region's bellicose new Jewish conqueror extending them a diplomatic mission of empathy. They harangue their impressionable new king:

"Do you honestly think David honours your father, and that he has sent men to comfort you? These men are spies sent to scout out the city before David assaults us!"

So what does Hanun do? He has the Hebrew ambassadors seized and reverses his father's pro-Israel stance in imaginative fashion. He has half their beards shaved off (a complete insult to a Jew), and their long, flowing robes cut off at the back above the waist. Hebrews wear

---

[508] **Jerome** *Hebrew Questions.* Scholars generally recognise that Nahash (lit. 'serpent') is a royal title, so this recently deceased individual need not necessarily be the same person who afflicted Jabesh in Saul's early days.

no pants under such vestments, so Israel's diplomats are despatched back to David with bare buttocks amid great heathen hilarity.

David's anger is kindled when he is told. He sends word for the diplomats to remain at Jericho until their beards are re-grown. Presumably new uniforms are also provided. The jubilation at the court of Ammon mellows upon learning of David's fury and imminent reprisal. Without delay, Hanun courts the support of his traditional Syrian allies close by and throws together a coalition, which includes Hadadezer, the disenfranchised king of Zobah, who, you might recall, was securing his territory east of the Euphrates when David previously struck.

And when David heard of it, he sent Joab and all the host of the mighty men. And the children of Ammon came out and put the battle in array at the entering in of the gate. And the Syrians of Zoba, and of Rehob, and Ishtob, and Maacah were by themselves in the field.

When Joab saw that the front of the battle was against him before and behind, he chose of all the choice men of Israel and put them in array against the Syrians. And the rest of the people he delivered into the hand of Abishai his brother, that he might put them in array against the children of Ammon.

And he said, "If the Syrians be too strong for me, then thou shalt help me. But if the children of Ammon be too strong for thee, then I will come and help thee. Be of good courage and let us play the men for our people, and for the cities of our God, and the LORD do that which seemeth him good."

And Joab drew nigh and the people that were with him, unto the battle against the Syrians, and they fled before him. And when the children of Ammon saw that the Syrians were fled, then fled they also before Abishai and entered into the city. So Joab returned from the children of Ammon, and came to Jerusalem. (2 Sam 10:7-14)

The Syrians prove stubborn in defeat. Hadadezer sends for more troops beyond the Euphrates, and sets his most experienced general, Shobach, as captain of the host. David's spies report the renewed activity, and David orders Joab to get the army together. The two forces meet east of the Jordan at Helam.

And the Syrians fled before Israel; and David slew the men of seven hundred chariots of the Syrians, and forty thousand horsemen, and smote Shobach the captain of their host, who died there.

And when all the kings that were servants to Hadarezer saw that they were smitten before Israel, they made peace with Israel, and served them. So the Syrians feared to help the children of Ammon any more. (2 Sam 10:18-19)

That last sentence sums up the incredible transference of power across the Levant due to the onward march of David's legions. There is a temptation to gloss over the extent of such casualties in ancient wars, but it's worth getting some perspective on the size of these armies and their military engagements. David's army has gone from 600 roughnecks during the ten-year period of his exile to over *one million* by the time his conquests are finished. The most deadly battle ever fought on English soil was the Battle of Towton between the Houses of York and Lancaster during the War of the Roses in 1461. A total of 50,000 soldiers participated in the action, and 28,000 were killed.

Militarily, it's all over bar the shouting. With martial skill born of years of hard campaigning, David and his generals have extended Israel's influence from the shores of the Mediterranean east to the River Euphrates, and from Syria in the north to the Gulf of Aqaba in the south. And this is where we must leave the story of David for now, at the zenith of his glory before both God and men. With such a dramatic rise to power across the Levant – that vital land-bridge between Africa, Asia and Europe – a tremendous national confidence grips Israel. This results in a renewed faith in the LORD, who fights their battles for them; international political influence; untold riches; foreign powers despatching impressive ambassadors and priceless gifts to Israel; a boom in trade with states near and far;[509] and David in the centre of it all, born for such a time as this; Israel's greatest Earthly king, with God's promise that the house of David shall endure forever as the line of the Messiah to come.

The chronicler finishes a chapter with the following words: **So David reigned over all Israel, and executed judgment and justice among all his people. And Joab the son of Zeruiah was over the host, and Jehoshaphat the son of Ahilud, recorder. And Zadok the son of Ahitub, and Abimelech the son of Abiathar, were the priests; and Shavsha was scribe. And Benaiah the son of Jehoiada was over the Cherethites and the Pelethites** [David's bodyguard]**; and the**

[509] David's recent conquests cause the two major trade routes of the Levant – The Way of the Sea and The King's Highway – to fall under Israelite control.

sons of David were chief ministers by the side of their king. (1 Chron 18:14-17)

Once again, notice the meticulous recording of names and positions. And how precious the sentence: **So David reigned over all Israel, and executed judgment and justice among all his people.** Would that we could have some of that across our nations today. But most countries have outlawed God from their schools, governments and public psyche, so God in turn is turning His back on them in preparation for judgment. We should study Romans 1 and Deuteronomy 28:15ff. for the judgments God levels upon a nation, which denies its Creator and charges after the hot and ready alternative. The lessons David learned, alas, will be those the world will be forced to re-learn in the coming years, as nations once more rise up against Israel, missiles are readied, tanks mobilised, the safety catches slide to fire, and an unreasoning hatred is yet again levelled against God's ancient people by an unregenerate Earth.

POSTSCRIPT

We leave David for now at the zenith of his career in his newly established capital of a unified Israel. Throughout the dramas of Exodus, Judges and the monarchy, we have witnessed the struggle of Israel coming to terms with its unique relationship with the Creator. Indeed, the very name 'Israel' is indicative of this struggle: 'He who contends with God'. It is a conflict all of us must face at some point in our lives, if we wish to have any answers to those four extraordinary questions:

Who am I?

Where did I come from?

What am I doing here?

And what will happen to me when this life is over?

David is, without doubt, one of the great heroes of the Bible, yet the son of Jesse will paradoxically face disaster, betrayal, grief, treason and tragedy for the rest of his life as Israel's most famous king. How can such a thing be allowed to happen to a favourite, whom the Creator Himself described as a man after His own heart? The answer is as simple as it is chilling: disobedience. Moses was barred from entering the Promised Land because he struck the rock at Meribah instead of speaking to it. Countless times during the Exodus, wilderness wanderings, the time of the Judges and the monarchy, disobedience brings judgment even upon God's elect, resulting in a loss of inheritance and rewards.

How about the question Moses thundered at the thousands of idolaters prancing around the golden calf after he descended from Mt Horeb? It's a question that has underpinned the many adventures described throughout *Origins III,* and is equally a cry that should ring out across neighbourhoods, villages, towns and cities around the world today: **"Who is on the LORD's side?"** (Exo 32:26)

Running amok

What a laughable misconception it is among many today that we are somehow doing God a favour by believing in Him; in sending up the odd prayer, or finding time to pop into a church or synagogue on those special occasions of births, marriages and deaths. Nothing could be further from the truth. God abhors 'religion', which is man's futile attempt to cover himself before a perfect Creator.[510] What God desires is a relationship with us through obedience and fellowship. It is a process, not the casual flick of a switch.

"Huh, I tried God and it didn't work."

What was the problem? Did the shoe not fit? Jesus Himself will declare during His ministry in the NT:

"Not every one that saith unto me, 'Lord, Lord,' shall enter into the kingdom of Heaven; but he that doeth the will of My Father which is in Heaven. Many will say to me in that day, 'Lord, Lord, have we not prophesied in Thy name? And in Thy name have cast out devils? And in Thy name done many wonderful works?' And then will I profess unto them, 'I never knew you: depart from Me, ye that work iniquity.' " (Matt 7:21-23)

I mentioned in *Origins III's* introduction that our Creator could quite simply sky-write His existence to us every morning, when we draw back the curtains and yawn at the coming day. That He does not tells us a lot. There is a selection process underway. God wants us to exercise the free will He gave us in order to learn how to make choices which accord with His will. God's will, which Jesus refers to in the above passage, is for us to do God's ways, by which we come to know Him (Jer 22:15-16). It is a learning process; a moment-by-moment step; taking every thought into captivity; conforming ourselves to His image, not maintaining our own. God guides us along the way, leaving just enough breadcrumbs at the corner for believers to make the turn. We deliberately seek His face, just as David did during the trials of his exile. This is not an intellectual exercise. God is calling some and He is not calling others.[511]

We have also learned what happens to a nation which disparages a great heritage and deliverance from evil, then turns its back on God: The Israelites in the Exodus and wilderness; Israel during the Judges period; Saul and his nation's defeat at the Battle of Mount Gilboa. God does not change (Mal 3:6). Britain too enjoyed a great heritage founded upon a strong faith, which ended the scourge of slavery; built the nation's empire into the greatest the world has ever seen; exported its culture, legal system and civilisation to developing nations the world over. Britain was delivered from two world wars, which had threatened to obliterate her way of life, but the spiritual

---

[510] Matt 23:13-29; Mark 7:6; Luke 12:56

[511] Isa 49:1,5; Jer 1:5; FG 6:44; 6:64; Acts 13:48; Rom 1:7; Eph 1:4-5; 2 Tim 2:19; 2 Thess 2:13; Gal 1:15

rot set in with a vengeance during the counter culture revolution, which followed in the 1960s. After a great victory often comes a test and failure. Remember Jericho and Ai? Remember Samson?

For Britain, religion, morality, patriotism and literature took a complete beating. The Sixties revolution caricatured and poured scorn on the Church, the state, monogamy and chastity, as well as the classics. The new pop culture wrote countless songs damning existing civilisation as warmongering, sexually repressed and a danger to everyone. Targets considered sacrosanct - especially Jesus and the Christian faith - made particularly juicy targets, since the socialists were now firing at the very icons they believed judged their way of life.

This Was the Week that Was (TW3), Benny Hill and a thousand other programs from the 1960s to the present day hacked mercilessly at the institutions, politics and mores that had upheld the Old Order. The atheist liberal-socialist revolution was all about changing human behaviour, and the only way to engender a national change of values was for the voice of the majority not to be heard. If the Old Ways were shown on prime time at all, they were ridiculed and mocked all the way to bedtime.

Cynicism and satire suffocated everything, even the sanctity of the lives sacrificed during the war years. No doubt shame was felt at the mocking of areas hitherto regarded as hallowed ground, yet many indulged in it anyway. The new television personalities, such as Jonathan Miller, Peter Cook, Michael Palin, John Cleese and Alan Bennett, were astonishingly different from anything the public had seen before; far cleverer, funnier and more incisive than those watching them could ever be.

Education and entertainment were gradually reduced to the lowest common denominator. The working class was given the first forbidden taste of saying, doing, swearing and feeling whatever it wanted, free of guilt. After all, God was dead, according to Nietzsche, and a world without God was a world in which sin, Hell and judgment no longer existed. The Anglican Church was gradually taken over by bishops and vicars who didn't believe the Bible was the Word of God, nor even that Jesus was His Son.

Stripped of the need for deference, forelock-tugging and subservience, working Britain began to prefer the better-looking socialist version it now saw of itself. Wronged by the ruling class; strong; able to flex its industrial muscle and negotiate on its own behalf; working-class warriors were now able to fight for their own lot rather than die in the dirt for others. The liberal-socialist media fed them a steady, putrid diet of sex, beer, cars, sex, working-class heroes, rock and roll, swearing, sex, drugs, robbery, adultery, murder, cigarettes and more sex. The television, still a recent enough reminder of the Old Way to carry the *imprimatur* of authority, now seemed to be saying that inflaming the animal within was cool; that it was OK; that it was not *that* bad.

The British middle-class was given a consistent, abrasive and hypocritical version of itself to contemplate on TV. Suburban dwellers to be pitied. Hen-pecked husbands washing their Ford Capris on Sunday morning, the symbol of fading virility. Wives attempting a genteel snobbery, only to invite the laughter of the upper class. Five hundred completely silent souls on the 8:10 am train to Charing Cross. Those garden boundary wars.

Ben Elton napalmed the Surrey set; Harry Enfield, the local pompous Conservative MP. Middle-class British squirrels all busy hoarding their nuts. Through the cynical lens of the camera, the middle class truly became the class caught in the middle: Ridiculous, unfaithful, rudderless on an ocean of banality. Eventually destined to die without ever having really lived.

But it was the upper class, with its tweed and grouse-shooting, that received both barrels of the satire Purdy; so sent up and savaged that it soon lost the moral bottle to remain in charge. Laughter was one of the chief weapons used because there was no known defence against it. The *Spitting Image* puppets effortlessly achieved what the Messerschmitts couldn't: the destruction of any respect the British still cherished for their leaders. What peculiar power could be harnessed in the presence of comedy! Where was the harm in laughter and fun? After the shock and dreadfulness of the previous fifty years, Britain started guffawing again; and to the many, for whom the previous decades had harboured precious little to laugh about, it was a wonderful, alien sensation.

The new Baby-Boomers - too young to remember the Doodlebugs, bomb shelters and rationing bacon to one ounce - found themselves increasingly isolated from, and suspicious of their parents. They didn't understand the quaint moral reserve and sense of duty; were insulted by the disapproval of the freedom espoused by the new sexual revolution. They harboured contempt for the faith that had sustained the country through unimaginable times they had never witnessed. Peter Hitchens writes:

"As the war generation grew old, they found themselves living on an alien landscape where their traditional morals and values were increasingly mocked and derided by each generation which followed.... The society they now lived in, where the word of television was law, suddenly allowed only one point of view to be expressed openly, and it was not theirs...." [512]

In 2003, Alastair Campbell, the UK government's Director of Communications, famously interrupted Tony Blair to prevent him from blurting out his faith before the world's press. Campbell growled, "We don't do God".[513] Campbell's public rejection of the LORD was enthusiastically endorsed by the by-now legions of God-haters around the country. As usual, good men did nothing: a pattern we have come to recognise on our *Origins* quest thus far. **"This people honoureth Me with their lips, but their heart is far from Me"**, Jesus laments in Mark 7:6.

Who is on the LORD's side?

It goes without saying that most British classrooms don't do God today, let alone show the kids a Bible and let them make up their own minds. So today, God no longer 'does' Britain, and has given the nation over to its own desires (Acts 7:42; Rom 1:24,26,28). The resultant disasters speak for themselves. Values relativism: you have your truth, I have mine. People would sooner believe a reassuring lie than an inconvenient truth. Murders, robberies and violent crime are at an all-time high, though many now go unreported in the press. Massed illegal immigration threatens Britain's borders. Uncontrolled welfare imperils our economy. The slaughter of babies via abortion has shifted into top gear – after all, "a woman has the right to choose". Today, Britain is proud of its right-on, inclusive approach to the legalisation of same-sex marriage, gay priests and gay pride. We have scandals today that were unthinkable even fifty years ago: paedophilia in high places, a former prime minister currently under investigation by seven police authorities for alleged child sex

---

[512] Hitchens, Peter, *The Abolition of Britain*, Quartet Books, 1999

[513] "Campbell interrupted Blair as he spoke of his faith: 'We don't do God' ", *Daily Telegraph*, 4th May 2003

offences.[514] At the time *Origins III* goes to press for the first time, the following article has just hit the news wires:

DEPUTY SPEAKER OF HOUSE OF LORDS RESIGNS AFTER 'BEING FILMED SNORTING COCAINE WITH TWO PROSTITUTES'

"A British deputy speaker in charge of upholding standards in the House of Lords has resigned after allegedly being filmed snorting cocaine with two sex workers. Video obtained by the *Sun on Sunday* allegedly shows Baron John Sewel, 69, naked and snorting white powder from a woman's breasts at his rent-protected London apartment. The married father of four, who is involved in legislating on sexual offences acts, prostitution and brothel-keeping laws, now faces a police investigation."[515]

The bra-wearing Lord Sewel reluctantly resigns his position a few days later amid salacious media gossip. The response by an unhealthily large cross-section of the public? "Good on yer, mate!" Mirth follows, with the inevitable Internet memes.

Not to be outdone by its leaders, the British public is happy to drink, snort and cuss its way through the neon-lit, felt-lined corridors of its modern-day bacchanalia. *Ha-Satan* plays his part in our Earth training programme, stirring up lust, anger, violence, hate and animosity further to dishonour God. If you have made it through the *Origins* series thus far, and the notion of a devil still strikes you as comical and cartoonish, consider that the 'god of this world', who was behind the abhorrent Canaanite religions of idol worship, child sacrifice and depraved sexual practices, is especially active today in the lead-up to national judgment. Modern idol worship runs the gamut from toe-curling materialism in the coveting of cars, iPhones, watches, designer labels and 'recreational drugs'; across the spectrum of New Age, pagan beliefs involving tarot, Ouija, crystals, horoscopes and Stonehenge sun-worship; to our favourite TV millionaire evangelist with his hand held out. The child sacrifice of old is today's genocide of babies aborted in the womb by the million: The total murdered currently exceeds 15% of the world's population.[516] As for

---

[514] "A vanished file and troubling claims about Heath and young musicians", *Daily Mail*, 8th August 2015

[515] www.news.com.au/world/europe/deputy-speaker-of-house-of-lords-resigns-after-being-filmed-snorting-cocaine-with-two-prostitutes/story-fnh81p7g-1227457965932

[516] www.johnstonsarchive.net/policy/abortion/wrjp336al.html

depraved sexual practices, you need look no further than the British Parliament and House of Lords, your daily newspaper or favourite Internet porn site.

No learning takes place. The cycle of nations repeats.

The remedy

As bad as things have become, however, God has established a principle to break the cycle, and we have seen this pattern play out too. What has the Creator taught us of His motives, character and promises thus far?

- After a great success, there often comes a test and a failure
- God cares, and is all about forgiveness and restitution. He wants to give each of us a future and a hope, but we have to repent
- God always steers the action to accomplish His will
- What pleases God most is for believers to get their hearts right before Him, then step out in faith and trust Him to deliver them
- God abhors sin, whether we call it sin or not, and will always judge a nation for unrepentant apostasy. This usually takes the form of the target nation being taken over by a pagan people, raised up for just such a purpose
- Judgment is an aspect of God's character we can take to the bank. Deuteronomy 28:15ff cuts in on time, every time. God's perfect justice must be vindicated by God's perfect judgment of sin
- Not happy with the state of your family, village, town, city or country? God does grace and mercy too. Notice that *believers in the LORD* are required to carry out the remedy offered in 2 Chron 7:14; the wicked are not invited to participate (2 Pet 2:12; Jude 10).

"<u>If My people, which are called by My name</u>, shall humble themselves, and pray, and seek My face, <u>and turn from their wicked ways</u>; then will I hear from Heaven, and will forgive their sin, and will heal their land."

The question is, will we?

THE END

Books in the *Origins* series

Origins 1 – The Greatest Scientific Discovery (2009)
Origins II – Holy War (2014)
Origins III – The Predicament of Man (2015)
Origins IV – Tetelestai (2016)
Origins V – Sons of Thunder (2018)
Origins VI – Parousia (2019)

INDEX

1

12th Dynasty, 33, 157
15th Dynasty, 34, 36, 39
17th Dynasty, 38, 52
18th Dynasty, 33, 39, 40, 43, 50, 145

A

Aakheperure, 58, 144
Aaron, 49, 53, 54, 61, 62, 71, 81, 87, 93, 101, 103, 104, 105, 109, 110, 112, 113, 114, 116, 117, 118, 120, 121, 122, 124, 126, 128, 130, 131, 132, 136, 148, 155, 165, 184, 186, 187, 188, 189, 191, 195, 196, 198, 199, 200, 201, 202, 205, 207, 220, 221, 222, 223, 225, 226, 241, 248, 250, 255, 257, 261, 262, 265, 266, 267, 271, 318, 320, 446, 459, 474, 521
Abdon (judge), 416
Abel, 140, 239, 287, 380, 521
Abiathar (high priest), 499, 500, 510, 515, 554
Abigail, 505, 506, 507, 515, 516, 526, 535
Abijah (son of Samuel), 462
Abimelech, 397, 398, 399, 400, 518, 554
Abinadab, 459, 492, 517, 524, 537, 538
Abishag, 530
Abishai, 490, 508, 528, 531, 548, 549, 551, 553
Abital, 536
Abner, 488, 489, 501, 503, 508, 509, 511, 526, 527, 528, 529, 530, 531, 532, 533, 549
Abortion, 230, 330, 416, 561
Abraham (patriarch), 33, 36, 83, 85, 90, 91, 92, 93, 96, 112, 113, 140, 176, 177, 183, 204, 205, 218, 223, 224, 225, 233, 262, 265, 282, 287, 297, 353, 384, 395, 396, 399, 404, 405, 418, 522, 523, 524, 536, 537
Abraham's Bosom, 524
Absalom, 518, 535, 540
Acacia wood, 89, 237, 243, 244, 247, 249, 252, 253, 254, 255
Achan, 314, 315, 316, 481, 483
Achish, King, 497, 510, 511, 514
Adam and Eve, 140, 180, 231, 245, 379, 438
Adonijah, 499, 530, 535
Adonizedek, 308, 321, 322, 329
Adullam, Cave of, 497
Agag, King, 481, 482, 483
Ahab, King, 172
Ahimelech (high priest), 496, 498, 499, 511
Ahinoam, 492, 507, 515, 516, 526, 535
Ahithophel, 518
Ahmose I, Pharaoh, 32, 39, 43, 51, 60, 66
Ahmose, Queen, 51, 53
Ai, 313, 315, 316, 317, 319, 321
Ain Musa, 182
Allenby, Edmund (general), 473
Altar of Incense (Tabernacle), 237, 249
Amalekites, 195, 196, 263, 284, 383, 384, 385, 389, 406, 480, 481, 482, 484, 514, 515, 516, 540, 549
Amenemhat I, Pharaoh, 30
Amenemhat, Crown Prince, 30, 58, 105, 144
Amenemopet, 58, 144
Amenhotep I, Pharaoh, 51, 52, 53, 60, 66, 105
Amenhotep II, Pharaoh, 40, 41, 44, 45, 57, 58, 69, 78, 85, 95, 103, 105, 106, 107, 108, 109, 110, 114, 117, 121, 124, 125, 129, 142, 143, 144, 145, 146, 147, 148, 155, 171, 172, 173, 174, 175, 176, 177, 269, 297
Amenmose, Crown Prince, 53, 60, 66
Ammonites, 276, 277, 281, 389, 404, 405, 408, 412, 413, 414, 415, 470, 471, 518, 534, 552
Amorites, 88, 90, 150, 263, 275, 279, 281, 289, 290, 298, 299, 311, 318, 322, 325, 331, 359, 406, 409, 461
Amram, 24, 54, 71, 81
Amun-Ra, 65, 135
Anakim, 264, 284, 285, 334
Angels and Demons (film), 23
Anthrax, 127
Antichrist, 49, 114, 116, 117, 119, 151, 283, 296, 306, 325, 329, 333, 357, 419
Apepi, Pharaoh, 36, 37
Aphek, 448, 450, 514
Arabah, The, 183, 267, 268, 501
Aristotle, 157
Ark of the Covenant, 155, 191, 193, 218, 219, 220, 228, 236, 237, 254, 255, 256, 257, 291, 301, 302, 303, 307, 310, 380, 448, 449, 450, 451, 453, 454, 455, 456, 457, 458, 459, 461, 537, 538, 539, 541, 542, 550
Armageddon, 69, 133, 329, 331, 356, 371, 449
Armoni, 492
Asahel, 508, 528, 531, 549
Ashdod, 282, 334, 367, 405, 453, 454, 455, 537
Asher, 46, 258, 259, 371, 389, 393, 550
Ashkelon, 367, 405, 411, 426, 525
Assyria, 61, 64, 172, 395
Assyrians, 172, 291
Astra (planet), 326
Atheism, 18

Attenborough, David, 10
Augustine, 356, 357
Avaris, 31, 37, 39, 81
Azekah, 322, 486
Aztecs, 323

B

Baal Zephon, 160, 165, 166, 167
Baanah, 532, 533
Babel, 159, 327
Babylon, 33
Babylonians, 33, 291
Bale, Christian, 24, 154, 164
Barak, 368, 369, 370, 371, 372, 373, 374, 375, 377, 380, 381, 383, 385, 407, 416, 450, 481
Bashan, 88, 275, 276, 280, 281, 318, 331, 534
Bathsheba, 353, 518, 521, 549
Benaiah, 540, 548, 554
Benjamin, 46, 258, 259, 365, 371, 414, 464, 465, 466, 469, 475, 498, 527, 528, 529, 530, 534, 536, 537, 542, 549, 550
Beth Aven, 477
Beth Shemesh, 155, 456, 457, 458, 459, 537, 538
Bethabara, 205, 304
Bethel, 369, 461, 466, 473
Beth-horon, 322, 323
Bethlehem, 338, 340, 342, 344, 345, 348, 349, 352, 355, 358, 485, 486, 495, 497, 508
Bezek, 360, 471
Birket Misallat, 160, 167, 184
Bithiah, 57, 155
Boaz, 83, 312, 341, 342, 344, 345, 346, 347, 348, 349, 350, 351, 352, 353, 354, 355, 356, 358, 431, 501, 546
Bolides, 139, 328, 329, 373, 392
Book of Life, 227
British Museum, 29, 30, 31, 32
Bronze Altar (Tabernacle), 237, 239, 241
Bronze Laver (Tabernacle), 237, 239, 241, 242
Brooklyn Museum, 34
Brunner, Yul, 110
Burning Bush, The, 86, 89, 92, 93, 95, 101, 116, 136, 184, 202, 204, 306, 351, 379, 386, 418, 419
Bush, George W (president), 351

C

Cain, 140, 222, 231, 239, 240, 287, 380, 521
Caleb, 196, 245, 263, 265, 266, 272, 285, 364, 411, 516, 521
Campbell, Alastair, 560
Canal of the Pharaohs, 157, 166, 184
Cancer, 573
Carchemish, Syria, 52
Carmel, 481
Cayce, Edgar, 14
Charterhouse, 573
Cherethites, 516, 539, 540, 554
Chileab, 535
Chilion, 338, 352
China, 323, 325
Church of Satan, 19
Circumcision, 84, 96, 97, 98, 99, 100, 101
Cleese, John, 558
Cleopatra, Pharaoh, 67, 75
Cleopatra's Needle, 75
Conservative Party, 559
Constantine, Emperor, 86, 200
Contact (film), 12
Cook, Peter, 558
Cornuke, Robert, 160, 164, 200
Crane, Stuart, 11, 343
Crowley, Aleister, 20
Crucifixion, The, 136, 139, 194, 216, 402

D

Da Vinci Code, The (film), 23
Dagon, 421, 422, 435, 436, 437, 450, 453, 454, 455, 518, 537
Damascus, 183, 223, 308, 551
Dan, 46, 55, 64, 88, 116, 129, 170, 190, 194, 203, 232, 258, 259, 282, 357, 359, 371, 380, 422, 431, 448, 523, 529
Darius I, 157
David, King, 353
Dawkins, Richard, 11, 293, 330
de Botton, Alain, 212, 213, 214
Dead Sea, 201, 267, 268, 302, 304, 331, 497, 501, 503, 552
Death Angel, 107, 143, 148, 217, 285
Deborah (judge), 327, 367, 368, 369, 370, 371, 372, 373, 374, 375, 377, 380, 381, 383, 385, 416, 450, 481
Deir el-Bahri, 29, 67, 68, 76
Delilah, 421, 431, 432, 433, 434, 435
DeMille, Cecil B, 24
Demons, 93, 222, 239
Devil, The, 19, 20
Djehutymes. *See* Tuthmosis I
Djeser-Djeseru, 76, 77
Documentary Hypothesis, 25
Doeg (Edomite), 496, 498, 499
Dream Stele, 146, 147

E

Earthquakes, 139
Ebenezer, 448, 453, 457, 461, 537
Edgerton, Joel, 110
Edom, 41, 163, 267, 268, 275, 277, 405, 408, 480, 539, 541, 551, 552
Edomites, 268, 389, 551
Edward VII, King, 376
Eglah, 536
Eglon, King, 365, 366, 367
Egypt, 28, 33, 34, 35, 36, 38, 39, 47, 50, 57, 58, 59, 78, 79, 80, 154, 155, 156, 158, 169, 170, 282
Ehud (judge), 365, 366, 367, 368, 377
Eilat, 95, 102, 160, 163, 183, 184, 198, 199, 201, 236, 267
Ein el-Qudeirat, 267, 268
Ein Gedi, 501
Ekron, 367, 405, 455, 457
Elah, Valley of, 486, 496, 497
Eleazar (one of the Three), 548
Eleazar (priest), 459
Eleph, 110, 155, 268, 428, 429, 458
Elhanan, 490, 549
Eli (high priest), 441, 442, 443, 445, 446, 447, 448, 449, 450, 451, 452, 462, 476, 480, 496, 499, 510
Eliab, 521
Eliezer, 62, 83, 84, 95
Elijah (prophet), 49, 81, 116, 202, 232, 283
Elimelech, 338, 340, 341, 349, 350, 351, 352, 356
Elkanah, 441, 443, 444, 445
Elon (judge), 416
Elton, Ben, 559
En Dor, 512, 513, 522, 524
Encyclopaedia Britannica, 52, 61, 63, 67
Enfield, Harry, 559
Enoch, 232
Enterprise Passage, 164, 165
Ephraim, 88, 258, 259, 361, 366, 369, 393, 394, 400, 414, 415, 441, 464, 521, 550
Er, 544
Ermutet, 132
Esau, 195, 275, 276, 277, 278, 385, 521
Esdraelon, 331
Etham, 154, 157, 158, 161, 162, 179, 184
Ethiopia, 39, 63
Euphrates, River, 41, 52, 55, 69, 75, 183, 287, 288, 551, 553, 554
European Union, 377
Exodus - God and Kings (film), 24
Exodus, The, 154
Ezion Geber, 102, 163, 267, 276

F

False Prophet, 49, 114, 116, 151, 357, 419
Feast of Firstfruits, 54, 139, 247, 315
First Intermediate Period, 29
Franz, Gordon, 87, 159, 160, 163, 165, 166, 171, 201

G

Gabriel (archangel), 232, 356
Gad, 46, 258, 259, 282, 302, 394, 407, 415
Galilee, 7, 303, 368, 371
Gath, 282, 334, 367, 405, 436, 455, 486, 487, 488, 490, 497, 510, 514, 525, 539, 550
Gaza, 156, 161, 282, 334, 349, 367, 383, 385, 405, 430, 431, 435, 436, 438, 450, 518, 540
Gehenna, 296, 364
Gershom, 62, 82, 83, 95, 96, 99, 100, 101, 103
Gethsemane, 180, 238
Giants, 11, 17, 263, 264, 265, 274, 275, 276, 277, 280, 282, 284, 300, 331, 334, 360, 367, 407, 490, 534
Gibeah, 320, 464, 465, 466, 467, 469, 470, 473, 475, 476, 477, 483, 496, 497, 498, 538
Gibeon, 318, 319, 320, 321, 322, 334, 527, 528, 529, 530, 537, 549
Gideon (judge), 308, 379, 385, 386, 387, 388, 389, 390, 391, 392, 393, 394, 395, 396, 397, 398, 406, 407, 414, 416, 428, 429, 450, 476, 516
Gilead, 275, 279, 281, 282, 331, 390, 407, 408, 409, 412, 415, 429, 471, 473, 527, 550, 552
Gilgal, 302, 303, 318, 319, 321, 461, 466, 471, 473, 474, 475, 481, 482, 483, 484, 519
Gilmore, Peter, 19
Giza, 106, 143, 146
Golden calf, 222, 224, 226, 262, 265
Golden Lampstand (Tabernacle), 237, 245, 249
Goliath, 308, 367, 436, 486, 487, 488, 489, 490, 496, 497, 498, 503, 508, 510, 518, 533, 539, 548, 549
Gomorrah, 159, 224, 225, 265, 283, 284, 293, 297, 327
Goshen, 48, 50, 81, 104, 109, 122, 124, 126, 128, 130, 135, 154, 158, 159, 161, 198, 200, 201, 202, 203, 334
Grafton Passage, 164
Great Bitter Lake, 157, 161, 163, 184
Great Tribulation, The, 283, 296, 298, 306, 313, 356, 357, 419, 523
Groves, 330, 363, 364, 427
Gulf of Aqaba, 87, 95, 102, 162, 163, 179,

183, 184, 198, 199, 201, 202, 267, 274, 554
Gulf of Suez, 125, 157, 160, 161, 162, 163, 165, 166, 167, 171, 184, 202
Gulliver's Travels, 328

H

Hadad, King, 551
Hadadezer. King, 551, 553
Hades, 523, *See* Sheol
Hadrian, Emperor, 279
Haggith, 536
Hall, Asaph, 328
Hannah, 418, 441, 442, 443, 444, 445
Hanun, King, 552, 553
Har Karkom, 201
Harald 'Hardrada', King, 322
Haran, 205
Harold II, King, 322
Harvard University, 10
Ha-Satan, 26, 48, 94, 111, 114, 115, 116, 124, 135, 148, 151, 170, 190, 191, 230, 232, 264, 276, 283, 284, 286, 291, 296, 298, 304, 306, 317, 321, 331, 356, 357, 363, 364, 373, 379, 383, 384, 388, 398, 399, 419, 422, 436, 453, 462, 490, 491
Hathor, 125
Hatshepsut, Pharaoh, 51, 53, 56, 57, 58, 60, 61, 62, 63, 64, 65, 66, 67, 68, 69, 70, 71, 72, 73, 74, 75, 76, 77, 78, 80, 81, 84, 94, 105, 111, 143, 155, 175, 176
Hazaroth, 261
Hazor, 282, 333, 334, 368, 369
Heaven, 223, 238, 523
Heber, 368, 372, 374, 375, 481
Hebron, 331, 334, 336, 360, 430, 431, 526, 530, 531, 532, 533, 535, 549, 550
Helena, 86, 200
Heliopolis, Egypt, 37, 159, 183, 282
Helios, 324
Hell, 217
Herakleopolis, 29
Herod the Great, King, 63, 172, 492
Herodotus, 87, 121, 166, 323, 325, 438
Heston, Charlton, 24, 154
Heyford, Jack, 299, 339, 350, 389, 397, 406, 410, 454, 458, 467, 489, 496, 512, 539
Hezekiah, King, 274, 328
Hikau khasut. *See* Hyksos
Hill, Benny, 558
Hinnom Valley, 364
Hiram I, King, 535
Hitchens, Peter, 560
Hittites, 41, 90, 150, 218, 263, 287, 289, 290, 308
Hivites, 90, 150, 289, 290, 318, 334
Hobab, 82
Holy of Holies (Tabernacle), 236, 250, 254, 255, 457
Holy Place (Tabernacle), 237, 241, 243, 245, 247, 248, 249, 252
Hophni, 28, 442, 445, 446, 447, 449, 450, 451, 452, 462, 499
Horn, Thomas, 11
Horus Road, 161, 176
Hyksos, 31, 32, 33, 34, 35, 36, 37, 38, 39, 41, 42, 43, 46, 47, 50, 51, 52, 55, 56, 60, 64, 66, 78, 94, 111, 158, 175, 262, 269

I

Iaret, 58, 144, 155
Ibzan (judge), 416
Incas, 323
Isaac (patriarch), 33, 83, 85, 90, 91, 93, 96, 112, 113, 140, 152, 204, 224, 233, 245, 262, 282, 384, 395, 416, 443, 521, 536
Ishbosheth, King, 172, 492, 527, 529, 530, 532, 533, 536
Ishmael, 152, 395, 521
Ishmeelites, 35
Islam, 14
Israel, 14
Israelites, 50, 93, 157, 159
Issachar, 46, 258, 259, 371, 372, 400, 550
Ithream, 536
Itjtawy, 30

J

Jabesh Gilead, 470, 518, 526
Jabin, King, 368, 369, 374, 375, 380, 383
Jacob (patriarch), 28, 33, 36, 46, 83, 85, 90, 91, 93, 99, 112, 113, 155, 177, 195, 203, 204, 218, 224, 233, 262, 282, 352, 353, 381, 384, 396, 397, 521, 523, 543, 544
Jael, 368, 374, 375, 481
Jair (judge), 404
Jambres, 114, 116
Jannes, 114, 116
Jashobeam (one of the Three), 548
Jebel al-Lawz, 87, 200, 201
Jebel al-Madhbah, 201
Jebel Ataqa, 166, 167
Jebel Khashm el-Tarif, 201
Jebel Musa, 86, 96, 199, 200
Jebel Um Adaami, 201
Jebusites, 90, 150, 263, 289, 290, 331, 360, 534, 537, 550
Jephthah (judge), 404, 407, 408, 409, 410, 411, 412, 413, 414, 415, 416, 443

Jericho, 83, 274, 280, 282, 289, 293, 297, 298, 299, 300, 302, 304, 305, 307, 308, 309, 310, 311, 312, 313, 314, 315, 316, 317, 325, 344, 351, 353, 356, 365, 553
Jerusalem, 107, 116, 136, 139, 152, 153, 181, 210, 223, 246, 256, 274, 279, 296, 304, 319, 320, 321, 331, 356, 357, 360, 364, 379, 436, 441, 473, 497, 534, 535, 536, 537, 538, 550, 551, 553
Jesse, 312, 353, 358, 485, 486, 487, 489, 491, 495, 497, 498, 499, 501, 503, 504, 508, 514, 516, 525, 527, 533, 535, 537, 538, 546, 549
Jethro, 62, 82, 83, 84, 86, 87, 88, 90, 95, 101, 102, 104, 126, 198, 200, 202, 384, 481
Jews, 154, 155, 156, 159, 169
Jezebel, Queen, 172
Jezreel Valley, 371, 392
Joab, 508, 511, 527, 528, 529, 530, 531, 532, 548, 549, 551, 553, 554
Joash, 388, 389, 391, 392, 406
Jochebed, 26, 54, 55, 56, 57, 71, 81
Joel (son of Samuel), 110, 136, 153, 327, 383, 405, 452, 462
John Paul II, Pope, 269
John the Baptist, 140, 223, 242, 304, 351, 416, 417, 424, 435, 443
John Zebedee (apostle), 133, 180, 325
Jonah (prophet), 297, 308, 468
Jonathan (son of King Saul), 328, 412, 464, 473, 475, 476, 477, 478, 479, 489, 490, 491, 492, 493, 495, 496, 498, 500, 501, 503, 510, 517, 518, 519, 523, 524, 525, 526, 527
Joseph (patriarch), 27, 28, 33, 34, 35, 36, 37, 38, 39, 40, 41, 42, 43, 46, 47, 50, 83, 88, 152, 154, 161, 170, 209, 258, 262, 269, 282, 335, 384, 408, 414, 544
Josephus, Flavius, 34, 58, 61, 278, 332, 458
Joshua, 59, 88, 195, 196, 245, 265, 266, 272, 277, 278, 280, 284, 285, 287, 288, 289, 290, 291, 293, 294, 296, 297, 298, 300, 301, 302, 304, 305, 306, 307, 308, 310, 312, 313, 314, 315, 316, 317, 318, 319, 320, 321, 322, 325, 326, 327, 328, 329, 331, 332, 333, 334, 335, 336, 338, 351, 359, 361, 364, 368, 369, 377, 385, 457, 490, 521, 534, 536
Josiah, King, 256
Judah, 46, 97, 155, 172, 238, 258, 259, 291, 312, 314, 334, 338, 352, 353, 359, 360, 414, 424, 427, 428, 429, 431, 458, 462, 465, 471, 474, 475, 497, 511, 516, 517, 526, 528, 529, 530, 533, 534, 535, 537, 538, 544, 545, 546, 549
Judas Iscariot, 152, 468, 518
Justin Martyr, 357

K

Kadesh Barnea, 41, 195, 199, 200, 201, 202, 259, 263, 266, 267, 268, 270, 271, 272, 293, 300, 330, 336
Kamose, Pharaoh, 39
Karnak, 32, 51, 53, 75, 77, 143
Keilah, 499, 500
Kenites, 62, 368, 372, 374, 375, 481
Keturah, 384
Khaemwaset, 58, 144
Khendjer, Pharaoh, 31
Khenti-hen-nefer, 39
Kidron Valley, Jerusalem, 240
King's Highway, 95, 100, 101, 102, 104, 105, 183, 198, 199, 201, 202, 204, 267
Kirjath Jearim, 459, 537
Kish, 464, 465, 467, 469, 471, 481, 499, 510, 518, 522
Kishon River, 371, 373
Kovacs, Joe, 159, 454
Kurmul, 504, 505, 507

L

Lake Balah, 160
Lake Bardawil, 161
Lake Menzaleh, 160
Lake Timsah, 157, 160, 161, 184
Last Supper, 140, 248
LaVey, Anton, 19, 20
Lazarus, 523
Lehi, 411, 427, 428, 430
Leonidas, King, 392
Levant, 31, 68, 105, 106, 157, 173, 174, 177, 272, 335, 404, 456, 461, 510, 554
Levites, 28, 46, 54, 99, 227, 231, 236, 255, 258, 259, 268, 301, 302, 310, 313, 397, 441, 446, 458, 459, 474, 549
Lewontin, Richard, 10
Linen, 237, 245
Locusts, 130, 131, 132, 133, 134, 147, 163
London, 36, 38, 55
Lower Egypt, 31, 33, 34, 37, 38, 42, 43, 47, 49, 51, 65, 144, 198
Lucifer. *See Ha-Satan*
Luxor, 32, 105, 173

M

Maacah, 535, 553
Magnusson, Magnus, 54, 55
Mahanaim, 527
Mahlon, 338, 351, 352, 356

Malchishua, 492, 517, 524
Mamre, 204
Manasseh, 88, 258, 259, 274, 282, 302, 371, 385, 386, 389, 393, 407, 412, 414, 415, 429, 521, 549, 550
Manasseh, King, 274
Manetho, 31, 34, 39, 42, 282
Manna, 26, 188, 189, 190, 191, 192, 193, 248, 255, 257, 259, 260, 269, 270, 273, 303, 305, 308
Manoah, 417, 418, 419, 420, 422, 437
Maon, Wilderness of, 501
Marah, 177, 178, 179, 180, 181, 182, 183, 184, 185, 190, 270
Mari (Tell Harriri), 33
Mark of the Beast, 151
Mars (planet), 326, 327, 328, 329, 373, 436
Masada, 497, 501
Maspero, Gaston, 60, 61, 64
Matrix, The (film), 22
Matthias (apostle), 468
Megiddo (Armageddon), 40, 41, 69, 156, 331, 371, 373
Melchizadek, 459
Memphis, Egypt, 30, 41, 48, 49, 53, 80, 94, 106, 145, 158, 166, 167, 173, 174, 176
Menorah (Tabernacle), 228, 245, 246, 247, 249
Mentuhotep II, Pharaoh, 29, 30
Mephibosheth, 492, 527
Merab, 492
Mercy Seat (Tabernacle), 220, 237, 254, 255, 256, 449
Mered, 57, 155
Merom, 331, 332, 333
Mesopotamia, 33, 54, 55, 205
Messiah, 72, 94, 152, 194, 255, 301, 321, 353, 354, 356, 357, 418, 444, 462, 467, 475, 522, 543, 546, 554
Metacosm, 94, 138, 233, 343, 377, 378, 379, 392, 437, 475, 522
Mexico, 323, 324, 325
Michael (archangel), 284
Michal, 50, 492, 493, 494, 508, 530, 541
Michmash, 473, 474
Middle Kingdom, 30, 31, 33
Midian, 44, 45, 50, 59, 62, 80, 81, 82, 83, 84, 85, 87, 88, 90, 93, 94, 95, 99, 101, 102, 104, 105, 117, 164, 183, 184, 198, 199, 200, 201, 202, 383, 384, 391, 394, 396, 398
Midianites, 308, 383, 384, 385, 386, 389, 390, 391, 393, 450
Migdol, 165, 166
Miller, Jonathan, 558
Miriam, 54, 56, 61, 62, 71, 81, 170, 261, 262, 266, 270, 271, 370
Missler, Chuck, 47, 81, 89, 90, 122, 147, 148, 152, 182, 191, 211, 230, 231, 235, 236, 244, 304, 311, 315, 320, 324, 325, 328, 349, 354, 355, 357, 395, 404, 412, 436, 437, 438, 451, 452, 456, 521, 527, 533, 546
Mitanni, 40, 105, 109, 173, 174
Mizpeh, 332, 407, 409, 412, 459, 461, 468, 469, 497
Moab, 83, 183, 266, 267, 275, 276, 277, 278, 282, 312, 338, 339, 340, 344, 350, 365, 366, 384, 404, 408, 480, 497, 534, 548, 550, 551, 552
Molech, 231, 296, 330, 360, 363, 364, 412
Moringa oleifera, 178
Moses (prophet), 18, 27, 28, 55, 56, 57, 59, 64, 73, 79, 80, 89, 156, 158, 204, 205, 271, 282, 523
Mount Catherine, 200
Mount Gilboa, 511, 512, 514, 517, 519, 524, 525, 526, 527, 528, 529, 530
Mount Hermon, 303, 334, 371
Mount Moriah, 140, 245, 535, 536
Mount Seir, 199, 202, 267, 276, 277, 278, 334
Mount Tabor, 369, 371, 372, 381, 395
Mount Yerhoram, 201
Mutnofret, 51, 53, 72

N

Nabal, 504, 505, 506, 507, 515, 535
Nahash, King, 470, 508, 518, 552
Naomi, 338, 339, 340, 341, 342, 343, 344, 345, 346, 347, 348, 349, 350, 352, 353, 354, 355
Naphtali, 46, 258, 259, 367, 369, 371, 372, 373, 389, 393, 550
Napoleon Bonaparte, 73, 74, 75, 157, 173
Nathanson, Bernard, 230
Nazirite, 416, 417, 422, 423, 424, 430, 433, 434, 435, 438, 443
Nazis, 229, 456
Nebuchadnezzar, King, 203, 223
Necho II, Pharaoh, 157
Nedjem, 58, 144
Neferure, Princess, 58, 64, 67, 72, 73
Nefrubity, Princess, 51, 53, 60, 66
Nehemiah, 320
Nephilim, 20, 263, 264, 275, 277, 282, 284, 285, 331, 334, 360, 367, 490, 534
Nepri, 132
New Kingdom, 32, 36, 43, 51, 175, 176
New Zealand, 325
Nicodemus, 241, 242, 273, 523
Nietzsche, Friedrich, 558
Nile, River, 34, 53, 55, 56, 271
Nimrod, 233, 294, 360, 363, 376, 436, 438
Nineveh, 297, 308

Noah (patriarch), 54, 159, 287, 293, 307, 321, 327, 438
Noah's Ark, 54, 159
Nob, 496, 498, 500, 518
Nostradame, Michel de, 14
Nubia, 30, 31, 32, 39, 52, 60, 61, 66, 67, 75, 85, 105
Nuweiba, 159, 160, 163

O

Obama, President Barack, 269
Obed, 312, 353, 358, 539, 541, 546
Og, King, 276, 278, 280
Onan, 97, 544
Ophrah, 387, 396, 398
Oreb, 393, 414
Origen, 357
Origins I - The Greatest Scientific Discovery, 7, 133, 210
Origins II – Holy War, 25, 34, 36, 99, 187, 264, 293, 326, 343, 370
Origins IV - Tetelestai, 238, 298, 356, 382, 521, 522, 523, 536, 539, 547, 549
Origins V - Sons of Thunder, 344
Origins VI - Parousia, 227
Orpah, 338, 339
Osarseph, 282
Othniel (judge), 362, 364, 365, 411
Ottomans, 473
Outer Court (Tabernacle), 237

P

Palin, Michael, 558
Palm Sunday, 139, 152
Paltiel, 508, 530, 541
Panspermia, 9
Paris, 376
Passover, 26, 54, 107, 139, 140, 149, 151, 153, 186, 217, 240, 247, 285, 291, 300, 301, 304, 305, 351, 358
Paul/Saul (apostle), 47, 81, 149, 191, 194, 223, 247, 308, 339, 352, 355, 435, 518
Peleg, 327
Pelethites, 539, 540, 554
Penninah, 441
Pentecost, 195, 227, 355, 468
Penuel, 394, 395
Pepy II, Pharaoh, 29
Peter (apostle), 223, 352
Petra, Jordan, 183, 201, 267, 268
Petrovich, Doug, 40, 41, 51, 76, 77, 106, 109, 144, 145, 172, 174, 176, 177
Phaethon, 324
Pharez, 352, 353
Philistia, 161, 174, 405, 430, 431, 436, 438, 448, 455, 461, 473, 490, 510, 511, 526, 527, 530, 534, 537, 540, 550
Philistines, 156
Phillips, Graham, 33, 34, 35, 36, 38, 47
Phinehas, 442, 445, 446, 447, 449, 450, 451, 462
Pi-Hahiroth, 165, 166, 167
Pink, Arthur W, 124, 181
Pi-Ramesses, 104, 154, 156, 158, 161
Pithom, 38, 45, 46
Pliny the Elder, 157
Pornography, 295
Potiphar, 35
Praetorian Guard, 367, 540
Pritchard, James B, 173
Prodigal Son, 351
Prophecy, 14
Ptolemy II, Pharaoh, 157
Putnam, Cris, 11

R

Raamses, 38, 45, 46
Rabbath Ammon (Amman), 404, 409
Rahab, 83, 297, 299, 300, 301, 304, 309, 310, 311, 312, 313, 320, 344, 353, 356, 539
Ramah, 369, 441, 443, 461, 462, 464, 466, 467, 483, 485, 494, 497, 503
Ramesses II, Pharaoh, 44, 45
Rapture, 151, 232, 298, 313, 354, 467
Ras el-Adabiya, 160, 167
Rawlinson, George, 36, 37
Re (god), 35
Rechab, 532, 533
Redford, Donald B, 145, 146, 175, 176
Remez, 35, 205
Rephidim, 183, 193, 195, 196, 203, 272, 284
Reuben, 46, 258, 259, 282, 302, 371, 407, 415, 521
Reuel, 82
Revelation (Book of), 20
Rizpah, 492, 529
Rodeheaver, Steve, 185
Romans, 48, 63, 115, 279, 328, 405, 421, 555
Ruth (Moabitess), 83, 178, 312, 338, 339, 340, 341, 342, 344, 345, 346, 347, 348, 349, 350, 351, 352, 353, 354, 355, 356, 358, 497, 546, 550

S

Sagan, Carl, 10
Salmon, 312, 546

Samson (judge), 308, 349, 404, 416, 417, 418, 419, 420, 421, 422, 423, 424, 425, 426, 427, 428, 429, 430, 431, 432, 433, 434, 435, 436, 437, 438, 439, 443, 448, 450, 518, 534
Samuel (prophet), 210, 290, 359, 412, 416, 417, 424, 428, 434, 435, 443, 444, 445, 447, 448, 452, 453, 458, 459, 460, 461, 462, 463, 464, 465, 466, 467, 468, 469, 470, 471, 472, 473, 474, 475, 476, 478, 480, 481, 482, 483, 485, 491, 494, 496, 499, 503, 508, 510, 511, 512,513, 514, 517, 518, 520, 522, 523, 524, 527, 533, 540
Sanhedrin, 38, 59, 89, 191, 241, 521
Sanskrit, 13
Santorini. *See* Thera eruption
Sarai, 92
Sargon, King (of Assyria), 54, 55, 56
Satanism, 19, 20
Satiah, 105
Saul, King, 44, 172, 196, 291, 308, 320, 348, 359, 412, 429, 431, 434, 437, 453, 464, 465, 466, 467, 468, 469, 470, 471, 473, 474, 475, 476, 477, 478, 479, 480, 481, 482, 483, 484, 485, 486, 487, 488, 489, 490, 491, 492, 493, 494, 495, 496, 497, 498, 499, 500, 501, 502, 503, 508, 509, 510, 511, 512, 513, 514, 517, 518, 519, 520, 521, 522, 524, 525, 526, 527, 529, 530, 532, 533, 536, 537, 541, 543, 549, 550, 552
Scallion, Gordon M, 14
Scientific American, 232
Scott, Ridley, 24, 44, 164
Sea of Galilee, 108, 174, 304, 407
Second Intermediate Period, 31, 32, 33, 42
Semiramis, 294, 360, 363, 376, 436, 438
Senenmut, 67, 68, 74, 81
Sennacherib, King, 172
Seqenenre II, Pharaoh, 38
Serbonian Bog, 161, 162
Sermon on the Mount, 216
Serpent, 26, 48, 89, 93, 103, 113, 114, 117, 273, 274, 319, 380, 518, 552
Sesostris, Pharaoh, 40, 157
SETI, 12
Sewel, John, 561
Shamgar (judge), 367, 369, 429, 548
Shammah (one of the Three), 548
Sharm el-Sheikh, 87
Shechem, 99, 336, 397, 398, 399
Shekinah Glory, 236, 254
Shelah, 544, 545
Shem (patriarch), 287, 521, 536
Sheol, 523, 524
Shephatiah, 536
Shiloh, 412, 441, 443, 445, 448, 449, 450, 451, 457
Shittim. *See* Acacia wood
Shobach, 553
Shua, 544
Sibbechai, 490
Sihon, King, 274, 275, 276, 277, 278, 279, 280, 281, 299, 318, 331, 407, 409
Silver, 238, 244
Simeon, 46, 99, 258, 259, 360, 397, 549
Sin, Wilderness of, 26, 182, 187
Sisera, 368, 369, 370, 371, 372, 373, 374, 375, 380, 381, 383, 392, 481
Sobekhoteb III, Pharaoh, 34
Sochoh, 486
Sodom, 159, 224, 225, 265, 283, 284, 293, 295, 297, 313, 327
Solomon, King, 43, 44, 72, 107, 150, 163, 219, 256, 291, 320, 396, 453, 474, 499, 530, 536, 540, 549, 551
Sphinx, 146
St Catherine's Monastery, 199
Stamford Bridge, 322
Stephen (evangelist), 308
Strabo, 87, 157
Succoth, 154, 156, 157, 158, 161, 394, 395
Suez Canal, 157, 166, 167
Suez City, 160, 166, 167, 184
Swift, Jonathan, 328

T

Tabernacle, 26, 89, 152, 219, 228, 235, 236, 237, 239, 241, 243, 244, 245, 246, 249, 250, 253, 254, 255, 256, 257, 258, 259, 273, 320, 412, 424, 441, 445, 447, 457, 459, 496, 550
Table of Showbread (Tabernacle), 237, 247, 249
Tamar, 352, 353, 535, 544, 545, 546
Tartarus, 264
Telaim, 481
Tell el-Maskhuta, 156
Tell Hariri, Syria, 33
Ten Commandments, 24, 27, 86, 110, 159, 191, 207, 208, 211, 212, 215, 216, 217, 218, 220, 255, 285
Tetragrammaton, 90
Thebes, 29, 30, 31, 32, 33, 34, 37, 38, 46, 48, 51, 67, 68, 94, 105, 106, 146
Thera eruption, 119, 157, 158
Thoth, 127
Tiaa, Queen, 57, 107, 124, 142, 144, 146, 173
Timna Park, Israel, 236
Timnah, 421, 422, 423, 424, 426, 545
Timsah, Lake, 157, 163, 184
Tiran, Straits, 87, 160, 163, 164, 165, 179, 198, 200
Titus, Roman general, 190
Tola (judge), 400, 401, 402, 403, 404

Towton, Battle of, 554
Transfiguration, The, 371, 380
Trans-Sinai Highway, 95, 184, 202, *See* King's Highway
Turtullian, 357
Tuthmosis I, Pharaoh, 48, 50, 51, 52, 53, 56, 57, 58, 59, 60, 66, 71, 72, 85, 94
Tuthmosis II, Pharaoh, 53, 59, 60, 61, 62, 63, 64, 65, 66, 68, 72, 73
Tuthmosis III, Pharaoh, 45, 64, 65, 66, 67, 68, 69, 73, 74, 75, 76, 77, 78, 80, 84, 85, 93, 94, 95, 105, 106, 108, 110, 117, 142, 143, 145, 156, 173, 175, 177
Tuthmosis IV, Pharaoh, 57, 144, 146, 147

U

Uriah the Hittite, 297, 353, 549
Uzzah, 538, 539
Uzziah, King, 475

V

Valley of the Kings, 70, 105
Vandersleyen, Claude, 174
Varangian Guard, 540
Vatican, The, 11
Veil, The (Tabernacle), 237, 243, 249, 252, 253, 254
Velikovsky, Immanuel, 323, 324
Vikings, 76, 322, 540

W

Wadi Tumilat, 157
Wadjmose, Prince, 53, 60, 66
Washington DC, USA, 269, 330
Way of the Sea. *See* Horus Road
Webensenu, 58, 144
Wembley Stadium, 169
Wiersbe, Warren, 24, 25, 48, 442, 475, 476, 478, 484, 525
World War 1, 363, 376
World War 2, 361, 363, 376
Wyatt, Ron, 159, 160, 200

Y

Yakob-aam, Pharaoh, 36, 47
Yam Suph, 163
YHWH, 17, 89, 158, 204
Yom Kippur, 250, 252, 256

Z

Zalmunna, King, 394, 395
Zebah, King, 394, 395
Zebulun, 46, 258, 259, 369, 371, 372, 373, 389, 550
Zeeb, 393, 414
Zelzah, 466
Zerubbabel, 320
Zeruiah, 508, 511, 527, 528, 532, 548, 549, 554
Zeus, 160, 325
Ziklag, 511, 514, 515, 516, 517, 519, 520, 533, 540, 549
Ziph, 500, 501
Zipporah, 62, 82, 83, 84, 95, 96, 97, 98, 99, 100, 101, 102, 103, 104, 384
Zobah, 551, 553

ABOUT THE AUTHOR

Phillip Day was born in England in 1960. He was educated at the leading British education establishments Selwyn and Charterhouse, and throughout his 20s had a successful entrepreneurial career founding businesses in sales and marketing. With a firm grounding in business and the ways of the media, Phillip's research career began after he became interested in wars going on in the realms of health and politics over issues that were being deliberately withheld or misreported to the public.

His research into AIDS and cancer, as two examples of the establishment's entrenched scientific error and brazen profiteering to society's cost, culminated in two books that have captured the public's imagination: *Cancer: Why We're Still Dying To Know The Truth* and *The Truth About HIV*. Phillip Day has written twelve further books on health, and today his speaking schedule takes him all over the world, lecturing on the subject of entrenched scientific error.

Phillip Day heads the publishing and research organisation Credence and lives in Kent, England. He is married to Samantha and they have a daughter, Anna.